The

Routledge Guide to

Broadway

The
Routledge Guide to
Broadway

Ken Bloom

Routledge
Taylor & Francis Group
New York   London

Routledge is an imprint of the
Taylor & Francis Group, an informa business

Routledge
Taylor & Francis Group
270 Madison Avenue
New York, NY 10016

Routledge
Taylor & Francis Group
2 Park Square
Milton Park, Abingdon
Oxon OX14 4RN

© 2007 by Ken Bloom
Routledge is an imprint of Taylor & Francis Group, an Informa business

Printed in the United States of America on acid-free paper
10 9 8 7 6 5 4 3 2 1

International Standard Book Number-10: 0-415-97380-5 (Softcover) 0-415-97379-1 (Hardcover)
International Standard Book Number-13: 978-0-415-97380-9 (Softcover) 978-0-415-97379-3 (Hardcover)

Library of Congress Cataloging-in-Publication Data

Bloom, Ken, 1949-
   The Routledge guide to Broadway / Ken Bloom.
      p. cm.
    ISBN 0-415-97379-1 -- ISBN 0-415-97380-5
      1. Theater--New York (State)--New York--Dictionaries. I. Title.

PN2277.N5B43 2006
792.09747'1--dc22   2006031344

**Visit the Taylor & Francis Web site at
http://www.taylorandfrancis.com**

**and the Routledge Web site at
http://www.routledge-ny.com**

Contents

Introduction

"Broadway may only be a street to some people, but to some of the rest of us it's a religion." So claimed Eddie Foy Sr. on stage at the Palace Theater, and thousands of people have proved his statement true.

Times Square is the only spot where the hundreds of different worlds that comprise New York City meet face to face. The result has been funny, dramatic, and sometimes deadly. Times Square mixes hookers, Broadway stars, gangsters, newspapermen, schnorrers and bon vivants, rubber neckers and passersby. These worlds all coexist in ten blocks of Broadway.

The history of Times Square goes back to before the founding of the United States. In 1776, the English general William Howe attacked Manhattan from the East River, near what is today 37th Street. This later became the subject of Robert E. Sherwood's play *Small War on Murray Hill* and the Rodgers and Hart musical *Dearest Enemy*. When news of Howe's landing reached General George Washington, he immediately brought his troops down from Harlem, where they were headquartered. From downtown came the American General Israel Putnam (who later had a Times Square building named after him). Putnam's guide was Aaron Burr.

Washington and Putnam occupied sites on what are now Bryant Park, behind the New York Public Library on 42nd Street between Fifth and Sixth Avenues, and the area near the present-day Broadway between 43rd and 44th Streets. Years later, Washington would enjoy taking his wife, Martha, on a carriage ride through the area.

During the early 1800s, this area was the home of squatters who settled along the creek known as Great Kill. The stream was later filled in and became 42nd Street. The area was known for its goat farms and as the site of manure dumping, a big business given the importance of the horse in the nineteenth century. Dutch farmers began settling the area and erecting farms.

John Jacob Astor and William Cutting purchased a seventy-acre plot of land between Broadway and the Hudson River, bounded by 42nd Street to the south and 46th Street to the north, for $25,000 and built Medreef Eden farm. Astor had arrived in the country in 1784 from Waldorf, Germany. He began a fur trade called the American Fur Company (the Astor Place subway station features a beaver in tile decoration as a tribute to Astor). Astor built a series of forts in Oregon to protect his fur business and began trading with China from the Pacific Coast. He also dealt in English pianofortes.

John J. Norton owned a large farm on the west side of 42nd Street. On September 28, 1825, he ceded a part of his farm, the Hermitage, to the city so that it could construct 42nd Street. The city paid Norton $10 for the rights of passage.

In 1829, a local paper carried an advertisement that read in part: "To let-large and commodious house and garden spot situated on Forty-second and Forty-third Streets, and 100 feet from Eighth Avenue. Well calculated for boarding school, summer retreat or private family-being pleasantly situated on high ground with view of North River. House has 25 rooms, good well and pump in cellar. Garden is laid out and at present planted for spring vegetables."

The streetcar line finally reached the summer homes around East 42nd Street in 1839.

The 42nd Street thoroughfare was used to drive cattle from the docks to slaughter houses on the East Side. The cattle arrived at 42nd Street on the Weehawken Ferry from New Jersey. Horsecar lines from the ferry also took passengers downtown.

Houses, stores, schools, and churches were built in the area. Bloomingdale's Baptist Church (1841), the Forty-second Street Presbyterian Church (1868) and the Methodist-Episcopal Asylum for the Aged and Infirm (c. 1855) all opened on 42nd Street. The Bloomingdale's Baptist Church became the Central Baptist Church in 1868, the Forty-second Street Presbyterian Church became St. Luke's Evangelical Lutheran Church in 1875, and the Asylum closed its doors in 1883 and was converted into the Clinton Apartment House. In 1878, St. Louis College "for Catholic boys of refined families" occupied 224 West 58th Street. The Church of St. Mary the Virgin at 228 West 45th Street was an Episcopal church with 600 members. In 1866, the Sisterhood of St. John the Baptist opened the Midnight Mission "for the reclamation of fallen women, who are here given homes, and, if found worthy, aided in obtaining permanent homes or employment." The mission was at 208 West 46th Street. The George Bruce Memorial Circulating Library was situated at 226 West 42nd Street beginning in 1883.

The area, named after London's Long Acre, became the center of the carriage industry. Where the Winter Garden theater now stands was Tattersall's American Horse Exchange. Harness shops and stables made up the majority of the businesses on Longacre Square. As the theater industry moved into the area, the carriage shops moved northward and were transformed into garages and automobile showrooms when the horse became passé.

Slowly but surely, the New York theater industry came uptown from the City Hall area to 14th Street and Union Square to 23rd Street and Madison Square to 34th Street and Herald Square. The theaters followed the diagonal swath that Broadway cut through the city.

Little by little, new theaters began nearing Longacre Square. Among the first theaters built in the Longacre Square area was the Metropolitan Concert Hall at 41st and Broadway. Built in May 1880, the concert hall was never a success. It became the Metropolitan Casino, Alcazar, Cosmopolitan Theatre, a roller-skating rink, and an exhibition hall. It was demolished in 1887 to make way for the Broadway Theatre, a very successful venture.

T. Henry French and two partners built the Broadway, which opened on March 3, 1888, with a production of *La Tosca* starring Fanny Davenport. French was the son of Samuel French whose name graces the still popular play-publishing business he founded. The new Romanesque building seated 1,776 patrons with a 75-foot-wide stage. Like many theaters of the time, the Broadway was home to acting companies, in this case led by De Wolf Hopper and Francis Wilson. Both companies specialized in comic operas. The Broadway Theatre left the legitimate field in 1908 when vaudeville and movies took over its stage. The theater was torn down in 1929 and replaced with a garment-center building.

The Casino Theatre, built in 1882 at the corner of 39th Street and Broadway, was a favorite of audiences and performers. In 1900, the same year that Macy's moved from the "Ladies Mile" to Herald Square, the Casino had a roof garden built over its auditorium, the first of a popular breed of theaters around the turn of the century.

One year after the construction of the Casino, the Metropolitan Opera House opened on Broadway between 39th and 40th Streets. The arrival of the distinguished opera company gave the area a new cachet, and soon society began to look at the West Side as an attractive area. The Opera House suffered a major fire in 1892, but was rebuilt and lasted until 1966 when a new (and inferior) Metropolitan Opera House was constructed in Lincoln Center.

By 1893, New Yorkers were spending $6 million a year on entertainment. That same year (the year of the World's Columbian Exposition and Grover Cleveland's inauguration as president), land owner Robert Goelet built a theater on his plot of land on 38th Street and Broadway and called it Abbey's Theatre after producer Henry Abbey. *King's Handbook of New York* (1893) predicted that the Abbey would occupy "a prominent and worthy place among the most notable theatres of New York and the world." But this was not to be. Abbey left the theater in 1896, and the name was changed to the Knickerbocker Theatre under the auspices of Al Hayman. The Knickerbocker was torn down in 1930.

The first theater on 42nd Street was the American Theatre built in 1893, the year of a great stock market panic. The parcel of land included property on 41st Street, 42nd Street, and Eighth Avenue and was purchased for producer T. Henry French by theatrical real estate agent Hartie I. Phillips from seventeen different owners. The theater was next to the Franklin Savings Bank directly on the corner and across the street from J. Wieland's Pharmacy, which stood on the northeast corner. Although the theater proper was built on land bounded by 41st Street and Eighth Avenue, the entrance, due to the plot's odd makeup, was on 42nd Street. Later theaters like the Lyric, wanting a 42nd Street facade, would copy the example set by the American architect Charles C. Haight.

French promised that the 1,900-seat Spanish Renaissance-style theater would be "the largest and the handsomest combination theatre in the United States." The *New York Times* said that "the first impression one gets of it is not of great size; its lines are such that every spectator, even those in the upper gallery, is brought in close relation with the stage." The *Times* also reviewed the theater's roof garden where vaudeville acts were presented. The paper reported: "The main garden is 90 feet square, and is brilliantly lighted by arches and trefoils or powerful electric lights. It will accommodate 650 persons, who, in case of rain, can take refuge in two large-roofed apartments, where free air is a feature and shelter is perfect. The stage is large and some say it is the largest among the roof garden stages."

The main auditorium's opening produc-tion was *The Prodigal Daughter,* an import from London. The show was a spectacle with a cast of almost two hundred, along with nine racehorses, which actually ran a steeplechase course, complete with water hazard and hurdles constructed on a moving treadmill. The show also had a full complement of hounds for the hunt. All did not always go well in the difficult scene. George Odell wrote in *Annals of the New York Stage:* "In the race scene, on May 26th, ... the horse, Columbus, fell, in jumping over the hurdles, and rolled upon his rider, Guttenberg Billy. The fiery steed, Rochefort, ridden by Leonard Boyne, attempted to climb over the iron balcony. The panic was completed when Julia Arthur employed the leading lady's privilege of fainting. . . . Thenceforth, so far as I know, the horses behaved according to the script of the play."

The show was a great success and the New York *Dramatic Mirror* exclaimed: "No mid-summer theatrical performances in this city have ever met with the phenomenal success of those at Mr. French's American Theatre." But subsequent offerings were not successful in drawing audiences; the American suffered losses and finally became a vaudeville house, and its name was changed to the American Music Hall. It briefly presented motion pic-tures before turning, in 1929, to burlesque. The theater couldn't weather the Great Depression and was demolished in 1932.

In 1895, in the area known as "thieves lair" by locals, Oscar Hammerstein I built his Olympia theater complex. Electric lights had just been installed in the Long Acre area. The theaters that made up the Olympia complex on Broadway between 44th and 45th Streets were not a success, although they managed to draw attention to the Square as an entertain-ment center.

The area along Broadway from 37th Street and 42nd Street was dubbed "the Rialto." Soon the Longacre theater district would also be called "the Rialto." In the 1950s and 1960s, Sam Zolotow wrote a popular theater column in the *New York Times* called "News of the Rialto."

Almost eighty theaters were constructed in the Times Square area. Many were built by producers and actor/managers who headed their own stock companies. They leased the land from the original owners who were intelligent enough not to let go of their land holdings. More and more producers like David Belasco and Daniel Frohman had their own houses built. Later, just before, and during the 1920s, impresarios like Florenz Ziegfeld and Earl Carroll would build theaters to house their productions.

Most of the successful theaters in the area were owned by the six members of the Theatrical Syndicate, a trust that was happy to force out its competition. The syndicate was put out of business in 1916 and replaced by another equally powerful group—the Shubert Brothers. The Shuberts' power cannot be overestimated.

During the Depression, when breadlines snaked around Duffy Square at Broadway and 47th Street, it was the Shuberts who kept American theater alive. The Shuberts were forced to break up their near monopoly in the 1950s.

The Square's preeminence was solidified in 1904 when the *New York Times* (founded in 1851) tore down the Pabst Hotel and built its new headquarters, the Times Tower. It is telling that the entrance of the Pabst Hotel faced downtown while the new Times Tower faced uptown.

The move by the *New York Times* to the Square led to the City Council's voting to rename Longacre Square to Times Square. In April 1904, the mayor signed the designation.

The Times Tower gained prominence in the square when the Motogram electric zipper sign was wrapped around the building. The Motogram gave the latest news; thousands of New Yorkers, in the years before the widespread use of radio, would gather in the Square to see the latest reports. Even during radio's and, later, television's prominence in timely news reporting, the Times Tower remained the focal point. New Yorkers gathered to see election results, news of the Japanese surrender in World War II (and the resultant V-J Day celebration), and sports finals.

The Square was also used for mass rallies to sell war bonds for publicity stunts, political demonstrations, and for the annual New Year's Eve celebration. Parades, including Macy's annual Thanksgiving Day parade, marched down Broadway through the Square.

On October 27, 1904, the West Side Subway was opened from Fourth Avenue to 42nd Street on the East Side then across the thoroughfare to Broadway and up to 125th Street. Within one year, the Times Square subway stop had been used by over 5,000,000 people. The laying of the new subway lines through the city, the consolidation of many train lines into Grand Central Terminal at 42nd Street and Vanderbilt Avenue in 1878, and the completion of the Third Avenue and Sixth Avenue elevated trains also in that year increased the popularity of burgeoning Times Square.

In 1905, gasoline-driven buses replaced the horse-drawn streetcars. The city saw its first metered taxi cabs in 1907. Unfortunately, many of the theaters were not built to screen out the increased noise from the traffic. Patrons sitting in the last rows of the orchestra at the Republic Theater could not hear Mrs. Patrick Campbell in *Magda*. Press agent A. Toxen Worm had a brainstorm when George Tyler facetiously suggested that the problem could be solved if 42nd Street were covered with tree bark. Worm thought the idea was the ideal publicity stunt and ordered the street so covered.

The construction of Madison Square Garden on 50th Street between Eighth and Ninth Avenues brought many sports enthusiasts to the area. The money to be made in area nightclubs and later speakeasies, not to mention the money laundering through Broadway investments, led to an influx of gangsters.

The opening of such hotels as the Astor, the Metropole at 41st Street between Broadway and Seventh Avenue (the home of George M. Cohan and Enrico Caruso), the Vendome at Broadway and 41st Street, the Claridge, and the Knickerbocker brought tourists and travelers to the area. The docks, only four avenues away, hosted the arrivals and departures of the giant luxury liners making their port in New York. The Times Square hotels were the nearest deluxe accommodations for these travelers and were halfway between the ports and the rail lines. Fancy restaurants like Rector's, Shanley's, Murray's Roman Gardens, and Churchill's served upper class patrons such as Anna Held and Diamond Jim Brady. The years following World War I were boom years for Times Square. Money was plentiful and New York was the richest American city. This wealth led to changes along the Great White Way. The theatrical unions, such as Actors' Equity, gained power and demanded increases in pay. Inflation, spurred by the success of the stock market, raised production costs, and ticket prices reflected the increased costs and increased taxes needed to support the growing metropolis.

The boom era culminated both financially and artistically with the theatrical season of 1927–28, when 257 plays opened in the 71 theaters around Times Square. Shortly after this, however, the industry suffered three major blows, one financial and two artistic. The first was the stock market crash of 1929, which forced many producers and their backers into receivership. Even the powerful Shuberts lost many theaters. The second was the acceptance of sound pictures by the public. Great movie palaces were built along Broadway in the late 1920s. The construction of these massive halls culminated with the greatest of all, the Roxy Theater, under the auspices of S. L. ("Roxy") Rothafel, the man most responsible for the development of the movie palace. The third big effect on the industry was the emergence of radio as a mass-entertainment force.

During the 1930s, many theaters were darkened by the sudden drop off of theatrical ventures. Many of the houses were converted to radio (and later television) studios or burlesque houses. Still more were demolished or left empty. The Federal Theater Project managed to keep some of the theaters lit. The burlesque houses slowly led to the eventual decline of the 42nd Street area. When Mayor LaGuardia outlawed burlesque, the theaters became grind movie houses and attracted an even lower class of clientele. Soon, low entertainments like Ripley's Odditorium and Hubert's Museum and Flea Circus attracted a decidedly less-ritzy crowd to the Great White Way.

World War II brought a new prosperity to the area, but it was a middle-class and lower-class area. Still, the theater remained the center of the nation's entertainment industry. Due to the popularity of its vigor and unique signage, especially that of Douglas Leigh and the Artkraft Strauss Sign Company, Times Square itself became a great attraction.

The 1960s and 1970s saw a worsening of the area and a drop in the number of legitimate shows produced on Broadway. Many of the 42nd Street theaters fell into further disrepair and showed kung-fu or porno films round-the-clock. The opening of the Port Authority Bus Terminal brought runaways and vagrants into the area, and Eighth Avenue became known as one of New York's most undesirable locations. Hustlers of three-card monte and other scams mixed with pickpockets. Peddlers selling fake Gucci bags and imitation Rolex watches crowded the sidewalks. As drugs and prostitution flourished around 42nd Street and Eighth Avenue, numerous plans, all discarded, promised to clean up the area.

Many New York landmarks, including Lindy's Restaurant, the Astor Hotel, the Paramount Theater, and the Roxy Theater were demolished for high-rise office buildings, which increased land values and destroyed the low-rise ambiance of the area. Many of the great spectacular signs were taken down and replaced by simple illuminated billboards.

During the 1980s, there was a resurgence of activity around the area. Zoning changes made it more profitable to build in the area, and more and more skyscrapers were constructed, pushing out still more of the ancillary businesses that served the theater industry. Preservationists waged an unsuccessful battle to save the Helen Hayes and Morosco theaters. This led to an increased determination to save the remaining theaters. In late 1987, most of the remaining theaters enjoyed landmark status (over the objections of their owners) and a major redevelopment of 42nd Street was announced by Mayor Edward Koch's administration, but condemnation of buildings in the area and new construction were stalled by a series of lawsuits. The latest stock market crash, in October 1987, made new construction less attractive. Many of the individuals involved in the redevelopment plan were indicted, and the entire plan came under increased criticism. The Koch administration, astoundingly in favor of redevelopment, insisted on pursuing the plan even after it seemed unwise and unfair to do so.

The future of Times Square as New York's entertainment center is uncertain. First-run films are not given premieres in the Square, and often open simultaneously throughout Manhattan and the suburbs; Broadway shows, with ever-increasing ticket prices and a reliance on blockbuster musicals, are pricing themselves out of existence.

Even blockbuster hits such as *Phantom of the Opera*, considered a massive Broadway show, cannot hold a candle to the spectacles of the past. Because salaries are expensive and scenery can be amortized, the physical productions grow and the casts shrink. The thought of producing a show the size of Cole Porter's *Anything Goes* (11/21/34) with forty-one principals and a chorus of twenty-five (and this during the Depression) is unthinkable today. The recent Lincoln Center revival had a total of thirty-three cast members. Ziegfeld's production of the musical comedy *Show Boat* (12/27/27) had thirty-three principals, thirty-one people in the Jubilee Singers, twelve dancers, and thirty-two ladies and sixteen gentlemen in the chorus—124 cast members in all. A more recent show, *Oklahoma!* (3/31/43), had twenty-

three principals, sixteen singers, and eighteen dancers. *Phantom of the Opera,* currently at the Majestic Theater, has only thirty-five people in its cast, certainly not an extravaganza by traditional standards.

Very few productions originate on Broadway. The Shuberts and their ilk put their money behind tried-and-true productions that have been successfully mounted in London, off-Broadway, or regional theaters and that will appeal to the broadest possible audience.

There is less and less room, given runaway production costs, for independent producers to put work up on Broadway. The impresario with good ideas and not much capital cannot find a foothold in the new Times Square. The early geniuses who helped make the area so unique could not possibly have succeeded in today's world. High rents and new construction are forcing out small stores and businesses and they are being replaced with chain stores and fast-food restaurants.

The increase in large skyscrapers further deprives the area of its shops, restaurants, signage locations, and vital nightlife. New buildings often close at 6 p.m. and leave their surrounding blocks empty. Times Square might soon become a ghost town after dark, much as the Wall Street area becomes deserted after the business day.

When Edward Arlington Robinson, on his way to a Broadway show, wrote "The White Lights, Broadway 1906, " he could not have realized just how prophetic his poem would be:

Here, where the white lights have begun
To seethe the way for something fair,
No prophet knew, from what was done,
That there was triumph in the air.

Let us hope that his words will remain true.

A

AARONS AND FREEDLEY · Today the Shuberts and Nederlanders are the theater owners of note, but prior to the Depression, most producers owned their own theaters. This was a logical outgrowth of the nineteenth-century tradition of the great actor-managers. These actor-managers produced their own shows in which they starred with their stock companies. That tradition faded in the late 1920s as a new generation of producers came on the scene. Other circumstances leading to the end of the actor-managers were the creation of Actors' Equity and the increased costs of producing theater, which precluded keeping large companies on salary throughout the year.

Also, as American playwrights came into their own, their plays often replaced the European and British repertoire preferred by the old school. This change in drama led to a change in acting style, a change that was hastened by the new popularity of the movies.

As the theater district moved to Times Square, producers rushed to build theaters for their own productions. Owning their own theaters allowed producers to save costs and to avoid the control of competitors. Producers Alex Aarons and Vinton Freedley were no exception. The success of *Oh, Kay!* led the two producers to follow in the path of others and build their own theater. The name Alvin was arrived at by combining the first letters of each producer's first names.

Alex A. Aarons was born in Philadelphia in 1891, the son of composer-producer Alfred E. Aarons. Vinton Freedley was born in the same year in the same city.

Among the shows produced by Aarons and Freedley, together and separately were *La-La-Lucille* (1919); *For Goodness Sake* (1922); *Elsie* (1923); *Lady, Be Good!* (1924) with Fred and Adele Astaire; *Tell Me More!* (1925); *Tip-Toes* (1925); *Oh, Kay!* (1926); *Funny Face* (1927); *Here's Howe!* (1928); *Hold Everything!* (1928); *Treasure Girl* (1928); *Spring Is Here* (1929) and *Girl Crazy* (1930).

That show was the last at the Alvin Theater under Aarons and Freedley's management. They lost their theater to the mortgage holders, as did many other theater owners during the Depression.

Aarons and Freedley continued their partnership both at the Alvin and at other Broadway houses after the loss of the Alvin.

Pardon My English (1933) was Aarons' last Broadway show.

After Aarons' retirement in 1933, Freedley continued on his own (Aarons died on March 14, 1943). Freedley produced *Anything Goes!* (1934); *Red, Hot and Blue!* (1936); *Leave It to Me!* (1938); *Cabin in the Sky* (1940); *Let's Face It!* (1941); *Jackpot* (1944); *Memphis Bound!* (1945); and *Great to Be Alive!* (1950). Freedley died in New York on June 5, 1969.

Aarons and Freedley had their greatest successes when presenting shows by inspired talents. They were not the sort of creative producers who could save weak shows though their own talents. But their long list of hits proves that they recognized talent and could put together attractive packages that enabled the artists to work to their best advantage.

The team had seven shows by the Gershwins to their credit. Four of these shows featured libretti by Fred Thompson in collaboration with a series of talents, including Guy Bolton, who was also responsible for four scripts. Five of the shows featured the duo-pianists Phil Ohman and Vic Arden. Freedley alone produced four

Cole Porter shows. Ethel Merman appeared in three of their shows.

The shows Aarons and Freedley produced were not necessarily the most artistic endeavors of the people they worked with, but they were among the most popular.

ABBOTT, GEORGE (1887–1995) · George Abbott, or Mr. Abbott as he was known by his contemporaries, enjoyed what is probably the most creative and certainly the longest career in the American Theater. He was involved with 122 productions as playwright, producer, director, actor or play doctor. Often he held more than one role in the same show.

He was responsible for giving many people their first breaks in the theater. Among those who scored their first successes with George Abbott productions were Leonard Bernstein, Garson Kanin, John Kander and Fred Ebb, Betty Comden and Adolph Green, Jerome Robbins, Frank Loesser, Jean and Walter Kerr, Harold Prince, Richard Bissell, Jerome Weidman, Jerry Bock and Sheldon Harnick, Bob Merrill, as well as hundreds of performers, including Carol Burnett, Desi Arnaz, and Nancy Walker.

George Abbott was born in Forestville, New York, on June 25, 1887. His early jobs included Western Union messenger, cowboy, steel worker, swimming instructor, basketball coach, and salesman.

His first play, *The Head of the Family,* a one-act, was presented by the Harvard Dramatic Club in 1912. He first appeared on Broadway as an actor in *The Misleading Lady* (11/25/13) at the Fulton Theater (see Helen Hayes Theater).

His first writing assignment was in collaboration with James Gleason on *The Fall Guy* (3/10/25), which premiered at the Eltinge Theatre.

Among the important shows written, directed, and/or produced by George Abbott were *Broadway* (1926), which he would direct it again as his last Broadway assignment, opening on his one hundredth birthday, *Chicago* (1926); *Coquette* (1927); *Twentieth Century* (1932); *Three Men on a Horse* (1935); *Jumbo* (1935), the first musical directed by Mr. Abbott; *Boy Meets Girl* (1935) by Kaufman and Hart; *On Your Toes* (1936); *Brother Rat* (1936); *Room Service* (1937); Rodgers and Hart's *The Boys from Syracuse* (1938), *Too Many Girls* (1939) and *Pal Joey* (1940); Martin and Blane's *Best Foot Forward* (1941); *On the Town* (1944); Jule Styne and Sammy Cahn's Phil Silvers starrer *High Button Shoes* (1947); *Where's Charley?* (1948) with Ray Bolger; Irving Berlin's *Call Me Madam* (1950) with Ethel Merman; *A Tree Grows in Brooklyn* (1951); *Wonderful Town* (1953) with Rosalind Russell and Edith Adams; Rodgers and Hammerstein's *Me and Juliet* (1953); Richard Adler and Jerry Ross's *The Pajama Game* (1954) and *Damn Yankees* (1955); *Once Upon a Mattress* (1959); Bock and Harnick's *Fiorello!* (1959) and *Tenderloin* (1960); *Take Her, She's Mine* (1961); Stephen Sondheim and Burt Shevelove's *A Funny Thing Happened on the Way to the Forum* (1962); and Sumner Arthur Long's *Never Too Late* (1962).

Mr. Abbott's career continued through the late sixties, seventies, and eighties, although he had progressively fewer successes. Among his later productions were *Fade Out-Fade In* (1964) with Carol Burnett; Kander and Ebb and Liza Minnelli's Broadway debut in *Flora, the Red Menace* (1965); and *How Now, Dow Jones* (12/7/67; 220 performances).

A major revival of *On Your Toes,* which opened at the Virginia Theater on March 6, 1983, was Mr. Abbott's last Broadway success. A production of *Broadway* opened at the Royale Theater on June 25, 1987, Mr. Abbott's one hundredth birthday. (Unfortunately, it played for only four performances.)

He continued actively pursuing his interests by directing at small theaters and continuing to write for the theater until his death. For exercise he enjoyed his lifelong interests in golf and ballroom dancing. George Abbott died on January 31, 1995.

ACTORS' EQUITY · Actors' Equity is the labor union of all professional actors in the American theater. The organization has jurisdiction over all Broadway, off Broadway and League of Resident Theaters performers. It represents these actors in all negotiations. Actors may join Equity by being cast in an Equity production or by amassing points in smaller regional and summer stock theaters.

The association was founded on December 22, 1912, by 112 actors as the American Federation of Actors, but it took until May 26, 1913, for the constitution and bylaws to be adopted.

Given the sorry state of the theater industry, four out of five Equity members are unemployed. In the Times Square area, Equity members can often be found as waiters and waitresses in theatrical restaurants and handing out flyers at the TKTS Booth (where discounted tickets for that night's performances are sold). Less than 5 percent of the membership earns more than $10,000 annually in the theater.

At the turn-of-the-century, the exploitation of actors was rife throughout the theater industry. Poor working and traveling conditions, as well as exploitative employers, made actors' professional lives difficult and precarious. This lack of basic amenities worked into the hands of unscrupulous producers who capitalized on the bad communications and great distances between them and their employees. The producers were following in the footsteps of the many captains of industry that exploited workers as a basic economic practice.

While not all producers were untrustworthy, the standard theatrical practices often left the actors stranded in cities far from their home base of New York. Often producers put shows into rehearsal without the capitalization necessary to open. Rehearsals (for which the actors were not paid) could last months or until the producer raised the money. Performers were often expected to provide their own costumes and keep them in reasonable shape. These hardships may have made for many amusing anecdotes in future biographies, but being stranded in the middle of nowhere with hostile locals and no money wasn't something the actors looked forward to.

The Pabst Grand Circle Hotel in New York was the scene of the first meeting to create the organization. Francis Wilson was elected as the first president. The original members of the committee were Albert Bruning, Charles D. Coburn, Frank Gillmore, William Harcourt, Milton Sills, and Grant Stewart.

The preamble to the constitution of Actors' Equity states that the organization will do what it can to "advance, promote, foster and benefit the profession. " It spells out the conditions under which an actor may be employed, elaborates on several benefits to the membership and instructs the association to work for improved legislation on behalf of the profession.

The producers didn't take the fledgling organization seriously. Problems were exacerbated by the producers' unwillingness to discuss problems with actors' representatives. Clearly, a strong action was necessary by the organization. Its first important action, the actors' strike of 1919, lasted thirty days and closed thirty-seven plays in eight cities, prevented the opening of sixteen others, and was estimated to cost the industry $3 million, a huge sum at the time.

During the strike, George M. Cohan sided with management. He had come up through the ranks of performers and felt he had good relationships with both actors and producers. His attitude was more sentimental than logical. Marie Dressler, who remembered her days as an $8 dollar a week chorus girl, helped bring the chorus girls into the strike. She became the first president of the Chorus Equity Association, which later merged with Actors' Equity. This strike resulted in Equity being recognized as the official trade union of the acting profession.

In 1960, Broadway was again disrupted by a second strike. Contractual negotiations were undertaken between the association and the League of New York Theaters, the producers' organization. An agreement was reached under which actors received higher rehearsal salaries, higher minimum salaries, provisions for a pension plan and welfare benefits.

In 1961, the two organizations agreed that no member of Equity would be required to work in a theater "where discrimination is practiced against any actor or patron by reason of his race, creed or color."

Equity has a reputation for a wariness and distrust of producers. Its newsletter, *Equity News,* reflects the bureaucracy of the main organization and echoes the attitude of its staff and many of its more radical members. To its credit, Equity has been trying of late to represent the needs of those actors outside of the Broadway arena. But, too often, Equity seems to operate without an understanding of the legitimate problems producers and other theatrical professionals face. Critics accuse Equity of operating with too much rigidity, preferring to close shows and lose jobs rather than bend rules to allow for special exceptions.

Unfortunately, the current state of the theater industry encourages producers to cut corners and save money at the expense of others. Shows are produced by pharmaceutical heiresses, washed up television actors, and purveyors of ladies lingerie. Where once there was one name above a show title, there are now often five or six or more. Equity can hardly be blamed for being confused as to whom exactly is in charge.

It would seem time for all participants, including Actors' Equity, to make concessions in order to control ticket prices and encourage investment. Like all the other theatrical trade unions, Actors' Equity must share part of the blame for the depressed state of current theater.

ADAMS, MAUDE (1872–1953) · Maude Adams was the favorite actress of a generation of theatergoers from the turn of the century until the 1920s. Best known for her interpretations of the characters of James M. Barrie, Adams was perhaps the best-loved actress of her generation.

Born on November 11, 1872, to businessman James Kiskadden and actress Annie Adams, she made her first appearance in her hometown of Salt Lake City in her mother's arms in the show *The Lost Child*. She was only nine months old. When the family moved to San Francisco in 1875, a year after arriving in California, she became known at age seven as "La Petite Maude." On October 17, 1877, when she was seven years old she made her debut in the play *Fritz*. In 1882, having outgrown children's parts, she attended a little over a year of school at the Collegiate Institute in Salt Lake City. It was to be her only formal schooling.

The next year she joined a traveling stock company in the company of her now-widowed mother. They arrived in New York City in 1888 and the young actress made her debut in *The Paymaster*. A series of roles with the E. H. Sothern stock company followed and in 1890 she was taken under the wing of producer Charles Frohman.

Frohman paired her with John Drew in October 1892 in an attempt to make them stars. They first appeared together in the French farce *The Masked Ball*, adapted by Clyde Fitch. Drew and Adams acted together for four years. Among the shows that Drew and Adams appeared in was 1894's *The Bauble Shop*. During that time author James M. Barrie caught her performance and was inspired to adopt his novel *The Little Minister* into a vehicle for her. She opened in the play in 1897, already manager of her own company. Her performance as Barbie in Barrie's play ensured her fame and began the love affair between her and her audiences.

Through her career she became forever associated as the premiere interpreter of Barrie's plays. In addition to *The Little Minister*, she also appeared in *Quality Street* (1901), *What Every Woman Knows* (1908), *The Legend of Lenora* (1914), and *A Kiss for Cinderella* (1916).

But Adams' greatest success was in Barrie's *Peter Pan* (11/6/05). The production was an immense success playing 223 performances—an amazing run for its time. It proved to be so popular that Adams made two return engagements on the Empire's stage as the boy who wouldn't grow up. Her subsequent New York appearances were in 1912 and 1915.

Of course, she also appeared in non-Barrie productions. These included two of Rostand's plays, *L'Aiglon* in 1910 and *Chantecler* (1911).

She was such a success in the latter show, playing a rooster who thought his crowing makes the sun come up, that on one occasion she received twenty-two curtain calls.

In 1918, while touring in *A Kiss for Cinderella*, she was caught in the great influenza epidemic. After becoming deathly ill, she decided to retire from the stage. She did make a few more appearances, notably touring in 1931 32 opposite the great Otis Skinner's Shylock in *The Merchant of Venice*. Her Portia was well reviewed which wasn't always the case with her attempts at Shakespeare. She appeared as Juliet in 1899 but her performance was not a success. She also played Viola in *Twelfth Night* for two performances in 1908 and one performance as Rosalind in *As You Like It* in 1910. She again played in *Twelfth Night* in 1934 as part of a summer stock tour but this time she played Maria.

Later that year, having retired once and for all from the stage, she recreated some of her best-loved roles for radio to great success.

Acting wasn't her only interest; she was an avid lighting designer. She lighted all her tours and she designed the lighting bridge of Frohman's Empire Theatre. Her interest in lighting led to her invention of an incandescent bulb used for color film. However, she didn't patent it and refused to sue when others stole her ideas. From 1921 to 1923 she spent in Schenectady, New York working with General Electric Company engineers.

Her interest in the theater continued although she was retired from performing. In 1937 she founded the drama department at Stephens College in Columbia, Missouri where she remained as a full-time teacher for a decade. Following three more years of part-time teaching she retired for good.

She died at her farm in Tannersville, New York, on July 17, 1953 following a heart attack.

ADELPHI THEATER · See GEORGE ABBOTT THEATER.

AL HIRSCHFELD THEATRE · 302 W. 45th Street. Architect: G. Albert Lansburgh.

Opening as the Martin Beck Theatre: November 11, 1924; *Madame Pompadour*. Vaudeville impresario Martin Beck played out chapter one of his Broadway adventures when he built the Palace Theatre. Forced by the Keith/Albee vaudeville interests, Beck returned to his West Coast-based Orpheum Circuit. When he was forced out of the Orpheum Circuit he returned to New York for the second chapter of his life on Broadway. Beck built the theater bearing his name in 1924 on what many people considered the wrong side of Eighth Avenue. However, the 1,200-seat theater proved immensely popular with audiences and theater people.

The first attraction at the Byzantine-style theater was the operetta *Madame Pompadour*, with music by Leo Fall, a favorite of Viennese audiences. Broadway audiences, however, were growing tired of operetta by the end of the twenties and instead wanted musicals in a more modern vein. *Madame Pompadour* closed after eighty performances.

The famous Clyde Fitch play *Captain Jinks of the Horse Marines* was adapted into a musical called simply *Captain Jinks* (1925). Actress Florence Reed shocked audiences as Mother Goddam in the sensational play *The Shanghai Gesture* (1926). The play was laughed at by the critics, but audiences couldn't wait to see the proceedings. Actor James Gleason, who would later achieve much success as a character actor in Hollywood, wrote a play, *The Shannons of Broadway* (1927), which opened at the Martin Beck. Following this, the Theater Guild took over the stage of the Martin Beck with a series of plays.

The first Guild play at the theater was *Wings Over Europe* (1928) by Robert Nichols and Maurice Browne and directed by the great Rouben Mamoulian. Next, the Guild presented Dudley Digges, Claudette Colbert, Glenn Anders, and Helen Westley in Eugene O'Neill's little-known play, *Dynamo* (1929). O'Neill himself described the play's theme as "the passing of the old idea of a Supreme Being and the failure of Science, all-important in this day, to supplant it with something satisfying to the yearning soul of men permeated with the idea that the creations of Science are miraculous as the creations of the Supreme Being." Miriam Hopkins, Claude Rains, Henry Travers, Helen Westley, and Morris Carnovsky starred in the next Guild presentation, *The Camel Through the Needle's Eye* (1929). The play was a natural for the Guild, which often presented middle-European light comedies.

Lee Strasberg, Luther Adler, Lionel Stander, George Tobias, Gale Sondergaard ,and Franchot Tone starred in *Red Rust* (1929). This was the second Soviet play to play Broadway, and it was just as unsuccessful as the first, *The First Law*. It proved to be an important event nonetheless for it was the first play presented by the Theater Guild Acting Company, which later metamorphosed into the Group Theater.

Philip Barry's drama *Hotel Universe* (1930) followed with Ruth Gordon, Morris Carnovsky, Glenn Anders, and Franchot Tone in the leading roles. *Roar China* (1930) featured a huge cast of mostly Asian actors. The drama concerned the Chinese rebellion and the British response. A model of a British warship filled the immense stage in a particularly stunning effect. The Lee Simonson set was among the most impressive of any in Broadway's history. The first production of the new Group Theater, which evolved from the Theater Guild Acting Company, was *The House of Connelly* (1931) by Paul Green. It was presented at the Martin Beck Theatre under the auspices of the Theater Guild, with Franchot Tone, Art Smith, Stella Adler, Morris Carnovsky, Clifford Odets, and Robert Lewis in the cast.

After moving their successful production of *Elizabeth the Queen* to the Martin Beck, the Lunts chose the theater for the opening of their next play, Robert E. Sherwood's comedy *Reunion in Vienna* (1931). In 1932, another group took over the stage of the Martin Beck Theatre. The Abbey Irish Theater Players presented productions of *Playboy of the Western World, Shadow of a Gunman, The Far-off Hills* and *Juno and the Paycock* at the theater.

Next came Katharine Hepburn's return to Broadway after success in Hollywood. The play was *The Lake* (1933), and the director was one of the most hated geniuses in the history of Broadway, Jed Harris.

Yellow Jack (1934) was Sidney Howard's dramatization of the yellow fever epidemic in Cuba and the search for its cause by Walter Reed. In *Romeo and Juliet* (1935), Katharine Cornell received raves as Juliet, as did Basil Rathbone as Romeo. The production also boasted the enormous talents of Orson Welles, Brian Aherne, John Emery, and Edith Evans. Cornell kept her dressing room at the Martin Beck with a revival of her classic production of *The Barretts of Wimpole Street* (1935). The story of Robert and Elizabeth Barrett Browning also starred Brian Aherne, Brenda Forbes, and Burgess Meredith. Cornell continued her stay after the run of *Barretts* with a production of John van Druten's *Flowers of the Forest* (1935).

Maxwell Anderson's *Winterset* (1935) was written entirely in blank verse. Burgess Meredith, who had appeared in the last two Cornell productions, starred in the drama about Sacco and Vanzetti with Richard Bennett, Eduardo Ciannelli, and Margo. The Guild was the American representative of Shaw, but it was not consulted when the playwright gave permission to Guthrie McClintic, the husband of star Katharine Cornell, to produce and direct *Saint Joan* (1936).

Maxwell Anderson's next play, *High Tor* (1937), won the second Drama Critics Circle Award. The play starred Burgess Meredith, Hume Cronyn, and Peggy Ashcroft. Helen Hayes appeared twice at the Martin Beck in the late thirties. First, she revived her acclaimed performance in *Victoria Regina* (1938). She later appeared in the Ben Hecht and Charles MacArthur courtroom drama *Ladies and Gentlemen* (1939).

The Martin Beck's next success was Lillian Hellman's antifascist drama *A Watch on the Rhine* (1941) with Paul Lukas, Mady Christians, George Coulouris, and Lucile Watson in the leads. The play examines the moral dilemma a man faces when forced to defend his beliefs.

In S. N. Behrman's comedy *The Pirate* (1942), Alfred Lunt played an actor who pretends to be a notorious pirate in order to impress a young innocent played by Lynn Fontanne. Behrman's next play at the Martin Beck was even more successful. *Jacobowsky and the Colonel* (1944), Franz Werfel's comedy, was adapted by Behrman for the talents of Louis Calhern, Annabella, J. Edward Bromberg, Oscar Karlweis, and E. G. Marshall.

After a transfer of the Leonard Bernstein, Betty Comden, and Adolph Green musical *On the Town* from the 44th Street Theatre came an original musical, *St. Louis Woman* (1946). The Harold Arlen and Johnny Mercer musical had a libretto by Arna Bontemps and Countee Cullen. The Arlen and Mercer score was among the greatest for any musical.

Eugene O'Neill's *The Iceman Cometh* (1946) premiered at the Martin Beck with James Barton, E.G. Marshall, Nicholas Joy, and Dudley Digges in the cast. Katharine Cornell again appeared in a production of a Shakespeare play at the Martin Beck in *Antony and Cleopatra* (1947). The great actress returned to the Martin Beck stage in *That Lady* (1949).

Helen Hayes, appeared on the Martin Beck's stage in Joshua Logan's *The Wisteria Trees* (1950), an Americanized version of Chekhov's *The Cherry Orchard*. Tennessee Williams' drama *The Rose Tattoo* (1951) was the theater's next hit. Maureen Stapleton, Eli Wallach, and Don Murray opened in the passionate drama. Another great American dramatist, Arthur Miller, had an important play premiere at the Martin Beck, a thinly disguised indictment of the McCarthy hearings, *The Crucible* (1953).

The Teahouse of the August Moon (1953), by John Patrick, opened with David Wayne, Paul Ford, and John Forsythe. The comedy was an immediate success and became one of the decade's biggest hits. Patrick's play won five Tony Awards, the New York Drama Critics Award, and the Pulitzer Prize.

An all-star revival of George Bernard Shaw's *Major Barbara* (1956) starred Cornelia Otis Skinner, Burgess Meredith, Eli Wallach, and Glynis Johns along with director Charles Laughton. The next offering at the Martin Beck, the operetta satire *Candide* (1956), was

also an all-star production. This time the stars were the creative team including Leonard Bernstein, Dorothy Parker, Lillian Hellman, Richard Wilbur, and Tyrone Guthrie.

Tennessee Williams had a flop at the Martin Beck when *Orpheus Descending* (1957) opened with Maureen Stapleton. Williams' next offering was the next success at the Martin Beck. Geraldine Page, and Paul Newman starred in *Sweet Bird of Youth* (1959). Williams summed up the play's theme (and a thread running through all his works) when he stated: "Desire is rooted in a longing for companionship, a release from the loneliness which haunts every individual."

The sixties began auspiciously for the Martin Beck with the first Broadway musical by the team of Charles Strouse and Lee Adams. They kicked off their long, successful Broadway collaboration with *Bye Bye Birdie* (1960).

Next, the Martin Beck hosted the work of another Broadway newcomer who would become one of the most successful writers of the musical theater. Jerry Herman's *Milk and Honey* (1961), the story of a group of Americans visiting Israel, starred Robert Weede, Molly Picon, Mimi Benzell, and Tommy Rall.

The theater's offerings during the remainder of the sixties showed great promise, but somehow none of the shows caught on with Broadway audiences. These included Edward Albee's adaptation of Carson McCullers' *Ballad of the Sad Cafe* (1963); *I Had a Ball* (1964), a musical with a fun, bright score by Jack Lawrence and Stan Freeman; the Royal Shakespeare Company's importation *The Persecution and Assassination of Marat As Performed by the Inmates of the Asylum of Charenton Under the Direction of the Marquis de Sade* (1965) with Glenda Jackson, Ian Richardson, and Patrick Magee; Edward Albee's Pulitzer Prize-winning drama *A Delicate Balance* (1967) with Jessica Tandy, Hume Cronyn, and Rosemary Murphy; and *Hallelujah, Baby!* (1967) with a superior score by Jule Styne, Betty Comden and Adolph Green.

The Martin Beck estate sold the theater to the Jujamcyns in 1968. And finally, the Martin

Beck housed a hit, *Man of La Mancha*, which moved from off-Broadway on March 19, 1968. Star Richard Kiley was given the show's big song, "The Impossible Dream (The Quest)" with music by Mitch Leigh and lyrics by Joe Darion.

Edward Albee's third production at the Martin Beck, *All Over* (1971), starred Jessica Tandy, Betty Field, Colleen Dewhurst, and George Voskovec. *All Over* was a disappointment in a disappointing decade. The Martin Beck Theatre finally housed a hit show in the seventies with *Dracula* (1977). Frank Langella starred as the Transylvanian vampire count and was proclaimed one of Broadway's brightest stars.

The eighties proved even more depressing for the Martin Beck than the seventies. John Kander and Fred Ebb, the songwriting team responsible for *Cabaret,* saw their musical *The Rink* (1984) open at the Martin Beck. The show had all the ingredients for success: a libretto by Terrence McNally and two starring roles for Liza Minnelli and Chita Rivera.

Into the Woods (1987) was the first success at the Martin Beck in almost a decade. The Stephen Sondheim and James Lapine musical garnered mostly favorable reviews. After *Into the Woods,* the hit musical *Grand Hotel* (1989) opened at the Martin Beck. A hugely successful revival of *Guys and Dolls* (1992) was the next to play the theater. Starring Peter Gallagher, Faith Prince, and Nathan Lane, *Guys and Dolls* inaugurated a new era of revivals on Broadway and at the Martin Beck.

The next revival was an ill-conceived revival of Rodgers and Hammerstein's last show, *The Sound of Music* (1998). It was followed by a more successful revival, *Kiss Me Kate* (1999). The next show at the Beck was the musical *Sweet Smell of Success* (2002), an undeserved failure with a score by Marvin Hamlisch and Craig Carnelia.

On June 21, 2003, the theater was renamed for famed theater artist Al Hirschfeld. Two ill-conceived revivals followed, *Wonderful Town* (2003) with Donna Murphy and *Sweet Charity* (2005). A new musical, *The Wedding Singer* (2006) is the latest tenant of the theater.

ALVIN THEATER · See NEIL SIMON THEATER.

AMBASSADOR THEATRE · 215 W. 49th Street. Architect: Herbert J. Krapp. Opening: February 11, 1921; *The Rose Girl.* The Ambassador was the first of the Shuberts' six theaters built on 48th or 49th Street. They saw the 49th Street block as having the potential of 42nd Street.

The theater was built diagonally across its lot. This allowed greater seating and a closer relationship between the rear wall and the stage. In 1985, the New York City Landmarks Preservation Commission accorded landmark status to the Ambassador's interior, though it refused to so designate the exterior.

The Ambassador's opening production, *The Rose Girl,* was an undistinguished operetta by Anselm Goetzl and William Cary Duncan that played for ninety-nine performances. The story was so bad that Jake Shubert wondered whether it would help to switch Act One with Act Three. Although well located in the district, the Ambassador has never had great success.

Its next production, *Blossom Time* (1921), proved to be its longest running until almost fifty years later. The Sigmund Romberg, Dorothy Donnelly operetta would again play the Ambassador on March 4, 1931, for twenty-nine performances and again starting September 4, 1943, for only forty-seven performances—its last Broadway appearance.

Next came *The Lady in Ermine* (1922) followed by another operetta. *The Dream Girl* (1924) did even worse even though its score was by the great Victor Herbert. This was Herbert's last operetta; in fact, he died prior to the Broadway opening.

The 1930s were bleak for the Ambassador. The Shuberts, like many other producers, had trouble holding on to their theaters. They sold the Ambassador in 1935. The new owners' policy of staging only dramatic works afforded the theater few opportunities for success. The only two productions of this period to achieve any notice were an eight performance run of the Abbey Theater production of *Juno and the*

Paycock, by Sean O'Casey and a small musical revue, *The Straw Hat Revue* (1939). This revue, which grew out of Catskill hotel revues, was most notable for newcomers Imogene Coca, Alfred Drake, and Danny Kaye.

Radio, movies, and television occupied the Ambassador until 1956, when the Shuberts regained control of the theater. But later productions, with one exception, proved no more successful than those mounted in the past. These included Lawrence and Lee's *The Gang's All Here* (1959) and *The Absence of a Cello* (1964).

The theater's greatest success came with Robert Anderson's four one-act comedies, *You Know I Can't Hear You When the Water's Running* in 1967. After that success, the Ambassador resumed its revolving-door policy including the shows *We Bombed in New Haven* by Joseph Heller; the Tom Jones and Harvey Schmidt musical, *Celebration*; a revival of Sandy Wilson's *The Boy Friend* starring Judy Carne; *Paul Sill's Story Theater*; Melvin Van Peebles' *Ain't Supposed to Die a Natural Death*; *The Secret Affairs of Mildred Wilde* by Paul Zindel; and *Scapino* with Jim Dale.

Three one-person shows next played for a time at the Ambassador—Linda Hopkins in *Me and Bessie*; Billy Dee Williams in *I Have a Dream*; and Estelle Parsons in *Miss Margarida's Way.*

A lame musical revue, *Eubie!* (1978) was followed by *Leader of the Pack* (1985), which featured Ellie Greenwich and her songs. Savion Glover's transfer from the Public Theater of *Bring On Da Noise—Bring On Da Funk* (1996) was closely followed by another transfer of the hit revival of *Chicago.*

Broadway historians blame the Ambassador's relatively lackluster career to the extreme width of the theater due to its odd placement on the lot and its relatively bland façade.

AMERICAN AIRLINES THEATRE · 229 W. 42nd Street. Architect: George Keister. Opening: October 2, 1918; *Information Please.* Arch Selwyn and his brother Edgar came to New York from Cincinnati and conquered

Broadway. They acted, produced, acted as agents and landlords. The brothers found the opportunity to purchase a portion of 42nd Street and decided to erect three theaters on the land.

The 1,180-seat theater was designed in a fan shape, making the farthest seat seem close to the stage.

The Selwyn opened with the play *Information Please,* which ran only 46 performances. The first hit for the theater was the Rudolf Friml, Otto Harbach musical *Tumble Inn* (1919). The Selwyn's next booking had the delightful title, *Helen of Troy, New York* (1923). *The Constant Nymph* (1926) was the Selwyn's next attraction.

The Selwyn Brothers sold the theater in 1927. A huge success was George S. Kaufman and Edna Ferber's *The Royal Family* (1927). Noel Coward's revue, *This Year of Grace!* (1928) was followed by Cole Porter's *Wake Up and Dream* (1929) and *Three's a Crowd* (1930), the theater's last success. Eight flops followed, the most notable being the last, *The Great Magoo* (1932) notable solely because it contains the song "It's Only a Paper Moon" by Harold Arlen and E. Y. Harburg.

The Depression forced the American theater into a decline, and the 42nd Street theaters suffered particularly. The Selwyn was not different with eleven failures in a row. Most of the 42nd Street houses were converted to burlesque, but in 1934 the Selwyn became a movie theater. It remained a movie theater until it was decided to make it part of the 42nd Street redevelopment. One respite from the grind film policy was in the 1950–51 season when a one-hour long version of *The Respectful Prostitute* was shoehorned five times a day between film showings.

The Roundabout Theatre Company was given the theater and its name was changed to the American Airlines Theatre. The Roundabout did an excellent and respectful job in renovating the theater. However, as it was being modified, the terra-cotta clad Selwyn Building and lobby fell into an adjacent hole and were destroyed.

AMERICAN THEATER WING · The American Theater Wing is one of the oldest service organizations benefiting the Broadway community. In recent years, it has been closely associated with the Tony Awards, which it administers. The Tony Awards are the most visible of the Wing's projects, which include grants and special entertainments. Critics have condemned the organization as existing merely to serve itself. Supporters claim it renders real service to Broadwayites. The truth is probably somewhere in the middle.

ANCO THEATER · 254 West 42nd Street. Architects: J. M. McElfatrick & Co. Opening: December 5, 1904; *It Happened In Nordland*. The Lew M. Fields Theater was built by Oscar Hammerstein I as his eighth (and final) Broadway house. It was leased by producer Lew Fields who promptly named it in honor of himself. The theater was designed by Hammerstein who invented the first antifire system in any New York theater. A series of pipes led from the rooftop water tank to the stage. This early sprinkler system is still being used in concept by modern theater builders. However the auditorium was ugly and uncomfortable.

The opening production, Victor Herbert and Glen MacDonough's *It Happened in Nordland,* was a hit for the new theater. Hammerstein had a way of losing most of the theaters he built, and he lost this one in 1906. Producer James K. Hackett bought the theater and promptly named it in honor of himself. The theater reopened on August 27, 1906, with *The Little Stranger*. Three of the few successful shows produced at the Hackett were *The Witching Hour* (1907); *Salvation Nell* (1908); and *A Woman's Way* (1909), the latter two starring Mrs. Fiske.

In 1910, Hackett lost the theater to William B. Harris, a leading producer. Harris promptly named the theater in honor of himself. The city widened 42nd Street causing the theater's box office and the balcony entrance to be moved. Since he had to redesign the exterior, Harris hired architects Herts and Tallant to alter the interior. The team removed 14 proscenium boxes and a few rows of seats. Harris reopened a remodeled theater with *Maggie Pepper* (1911). The Harris Theater was seldom successful.

The Selwyn Brothers assumed control of the theater in 1914 and used the house as a secondary theater. They would move productions from their more successful theaters to the Harris where they would complete their runs. New productions included *The Lie* (1914) and *Rolling Stones* (1915).

Producer H. H. Frazee leased the theater and installed his production *Wedding Bells* (1919) and in 1920 he bought the theater and promptly named it after himself. His first production there was *The Woman of Bronze* (1920). Under Frazee's leadership, the theater was the home to *Dulcy* (1921), with Lynn Fontanne in her first starring role.

Producer John Cort was the next to try producing at the theater. He reopened the theater as Wallack's Theater with *Shipwrecked* (1924) as the initial production. *Laff That Off* (1925) was his biggest success at the theater.

The Depression marked the end of the theater's legitimate policy. Beginning in 1930, the theater showed films exclusively. In 1940, it was remodeled and renamed the Anco.

The theater showed movies until it was razed in 1997 as part of the new Times Square redevelopment plan.

ANNE NICHOLS' LITTLE THEATER · See LITTLE THEATRE.

ANTA · See AMERICAN NATIONAL THEATRE AND ACADEMY.

ANTA THEATER · See VIRGINIA THEATER.

ANTOINETTE PERRY AWARD · See TONY AWARD.

APOLLO THEATRE · 234 W. 43rd Street (originally the Bryant Theater with entrance at W. 42nd Street). Opening: As a vaudeville and movie house in 1910; as a legitimate theater with *Jimmie* November 17, 1920. Like other theaters, and like Times Square itself, the

Apollo Theatre has seen its fortunes rise and fall. The house opened as the Bryant Theater in 1910, featuring a combination movie and vaudeville policy. As the 42nd Street corridor established itself as the leading legitimate theater block in New York, the Bryant's location made it more valuable as a venue for musical comedies, which commanded higher-priced tickets.

As a result, the Selwyn Brothers, Arch and Edgar, leading producers of their day, bought the theater renovated it and renamed it the Apollo. They built a common façade with the Times Square Theatre which they also owned. They christened the theater with the musical *Jimmie* (1920). The theater suffered a succession of failures, including Sigmund Romberg's *Love Birds* (1921) and *Daffy Dill* (1922). *Poppy* (1923), starring W. C. Fields, played 346 times at the Apollo, which at that time was the theater's longest run.

The 1920s were a decade of long-running revue series. The Apollo was home for the *George White's Scandals* for most of their history. The first *Scandals* (1924) at the Apollo, the sixth edition, boasted a score by George and Ira Gershwin (their last for the series). It was followed yearly by other annual editions of the popular series. Between editions were the George White productions of *Manhattan Mary* (1927) and *Flying High* (1930).

The Apollo's bad luck with straight plays continued with its next offering, *The House Beautiful* (1931), which is best remembered for inspiring Dorothy Parker's quip," *The House Beautiful* is the play lousy." The last edition of the *Scandals* to play the Apollo was the third from last in the series. It opened on September 14, 1931.

The last legitimate theater success at the Apollo was the musical *Take a Chance* (1932). The last show to play the Apollo was the unsuccessful Bill Robinson revue, *Blackbirds of 1933*. The Depression, which had shuttered so many of the Broadway theaters, finally reached the Apollo. A movie policy was initiated, and a year later, the Minsky Brothers began presenting burlesque shows on its stage.

The burlesque policy remained in effect until Mayor LaGuardia's crackdown, and in 1937 the Apollo became a grind (24-hour) movie house.

Forty years later, the Broadway theater seemed to be undergoing a slight upsurge in business. There was a lack of available theaters, and the owners of the Apollo, the Brandt Organization, decided to enter the legitimate theater field. Over $350,000 was spent to restore the Apollo to its former glory. Improvements both in the auditorium and backstage were completed in time for its first legitimate show under its new policy. The New Apollo reopened with *On Golden Pond* (1979), starring Frances Sternhagen and Tom Aldredge. The show received mildly positive reviews. The theater's renovation received much better notices.

Although the Brandts changed the entrance to the theater from 42nd to 43rd Street, the New Apollo was still considered somewhat off the beaten track. Also, around this time, the number of independent producers operating on Broadway was severely reduced and, as a result, product grew scarce.

An unsuccessful play, *Bent,* had a short run followed by a transfer of Lanford Wilson's *The Fifth of July* (1980) from the Circle Repertory Theater. *The Fifth of July* proved to be the most successful of the house's bookings, although it hardly paid back its costs. The final offering at the New Apollo was *The Guys in the Truck,* a failure in 1983, which starred Elliot Gould.

The theater briefly returned to its former grind policy before being shuttered. In the fall of 1987, the theater was renamed the Academy Theater with a short-lived booking of comic Redd Foxx. The theater underwent another transformation, and in September 1988 the theater's name was changed to the Alcazar de Paris. The theater was remodeled as a dinner revue theater, featuring Parisian inspired cabaret acts. It was a quick failure, and the name reverted to Academy. The last production on its stage was *Legends in Concert,* an impersonator show that opened and closed in May of 1989.

When the New 42nd Street project was

announced, the Brandts offered to make the Apollo a cornerstone of the renovation. But the powers that be decided that what the street needed was another large musical theater barn and took over the Apollo and the Lyric Theatre next door under eminent domain. The two theater s were torn down and replaced by the Ford Center, which incorporated some of the architectural details of the Apollo.

ARLEN, HAROLD (1905–1986) · Harold Arlen, one of America's greatest composers of popular music, is just beginning to receive the respect due him. Equally at home writing for cabaret, motion picture, and stage, Arlen wrote many standards for a diverse group of stars.

He was born Hyman Arluck on February 15, 1905. He first sang in the choir of the synagogue in Buffalo, New York, where his father was a cantor. He was also influenced by early jazz recordings and, when still in his teens, formed his own group, The Snappy Trio. That group soon evolved into The Southbound Shufflers. These bands played local clubs and excursion boats around Buffalo. Then he and his friends formed The Buffalodians, for which Arlen sang and arranged the tunes. The Buffalodians were successful enough to get a small recording contract, and in 1925, Arlen was encouraged to come to New York. After his move, he became a singer, pianist and arranger with various dance bands before landing a job in Arnold Johnson's pit orchestra for the Broadway revue, *George White's Scandals of 1928.*

His unique singing style, influenced by liturgical singing and the techniques of black vocalists, led to jobs in vaudeville. He appeared on the Loew's Vaudeville Circuit and made it to the venerable Palace Theater. Though Arlen would make his greatest mark as a composer, he continued singing, making albums throughout his career. He cut sides with the Red Nichols Orchestra and sang on his own albums for Capitol, Columbia, and Walden Records.

While a rehearsal pianist for the Vincent Youmans show *Great Day,* Arlen was encouraged by songwriter Harry Warren to become a composer. A musical riff Arlen used to call the

performers back from their rehearsal breaks was developed into his first hit, "Get Happy." The success of "Get Happy" led to a job writing the scores for a series of Cotton Club revues with his lyricist, Ted Koehler. In 1933, he and Koehler wrote their greatest hit, "Stormy Weather." His great success at the Cotton Club included such standards as "Kickin' the Gong Around," "Between the Devil and the Deep Blue Sea," "I Love a Parade," "I've Got the World on a String," "Minnie the Moocher's Wedding Day," "Happy As the Day Is Long," "Ill Wind," "As Long As I Live," "Raisin' the Rent" and "You Gave Me Everything but Love." At the Cotton Club, Arlen cemented his relationships with black performers including Cab Calloway, Lena Horne, and Ethel Waters. He continued providing nonstereotypical scores for black performers throughout his career.

The Cotton Club led back to Broadway and songs for musical revues, including *The Nine Fifteen Revue* (1930) ("Get Happy"); *Earl Carroll's Vanities* (1930) ("Hittin' the Bottle"); *Earl Carroll's Vanities of 1932* ("I've Got a Right to Sing the Blues," "Rockin' in Rhythm"); *Americana* (1932) ("Satan's Li'l Lamb"); *George White's Music Hall Varieties* (1932); *Life Begins at 8:40* (1934) ("Fun to Be Fooled," "Let's Take a Walk Around the Block," "You're a Builder Upper"); and *The Show Is On* (1936).

Success in the revue format brought Arlen the opportunity to write for book shows, many of which prominently featured black performers. These shows included *You Said It* (1931) ("Sweet and Hot," "You Said It"); *Hooray for What!* (1937) ("Down with Love," "In the Shade of the New Apple Tree"); *Bloomer Girl* (1944) ("The Eagle and Me," "Right As the Rain"); *St. Louis Woman* (1946) ("Any Place I Hang My Hat Is Home," "Come Rain or Come Shine"); *House of Flowers* (1954) ("I Never Has Seen Snow," "A Sleepin' Bee"); *Jamaica* (1957) ("Ain't It the Truth," "Napoleon"); and *Saratoga* (1959) ("Goose Never Be a Peacock," "Love Held Lightly").

While these shows were rarely commercially successful, the scores Arlen wrote, mainly in collaboration with E. Y. Harburg or Johnny

Mercer, were as rich as any on Broadway. His shows featured such greats as Lena Home, Pearl Bailey, Diahann Carroll, Ricardo Montalban, Celeste Holm, Dooley Wilson, Ed Wynn, Bert Lahr, Ray Bolger, the Nicholas Brothers, Ray Walston, Geoffrey Holder, Josephine Premice, Ossie Davis, and Howard Keel.

Arlen also had a long career in Hollywood writing for such films as *The Wizard of Oz* ("Over the Rainbow," Academy Award, 1939); *At the Circus; Blues in the Night* ("Blues in the Night," "This Time the Dream's on Me"); *Rio Rita; Star Spangled Rhythm* ("Hit the Road to Dreamland," "That Old Black Magic"); *Cabin in the Sky* ("Happiness Is a Thing Called Joe"); *The Sky's the Limit* ("My Shining Hour," "One for My Baby"); *Up in Arms* ("Now I Know"); *Here Come the Waves* ("Ac-cent-tchu-ate the Positive"); *Out of This World* ("Out of This World"); *Casbah* ("For Every Man There's a Woman," "Hooray for Love"); *My Blue Heaven* ("Don't Rock the Boat, Dear"); *The Petty Girl; Down Among the Sheltering Palms; Mr. Imperium* ("Let Me Look at You"); *The Farmer Takes a Wife* ("Today I Love Everybody"); *A Star Is Born* ("The Man That Got Away"); *The Country Girl* ("Dissertation on the State of Bliss"); and *Gay Purr-ee* ("Paris Is a Lonely Town").

Arlen's total output doesn't match that of the greatest Broadway composers like Irving Berlin, Richard Rodgers, or Jule Styne and, except for *Bloomer Girl,* he never had a major hit show. But his work was consistently brilliant. His range of compositions equals that of the most versatile theater composers: Jule Styne, Frank Loesser, and Cy Coleman. But Arlen's music, be it for a Tin Woodman, a runaway slave, a madam, or the most innocent of naives, always reflects Arlen's unique voice. He always wrote with a complete belief in and understanding of the character. He never let the audience know, as so many composers do, that there is a composer behind the character. His point of view was always the point of view of the character and each character's voice is both unique and unmistakably Arlen's.

His work was inherently dramatic; even his revue songs were never simply pop songs. His work has enriched Broadway by attempting to entertain as well as subtly inform audiences about other kinds of people and different ideas and to move them with rich, true emotions.

Harold Arlen died on April 23, 1986.

ASTOR HOTEL · Broadway between 44th and 45th Streets. The Astor Hotel was the most celebrated hotel in Times Square and perhaps the most famous in all New York. The plot of land was originally part of the Medref-Eden Farm. Around 1830, William B. Astor, Lord Astor's grandfather, purchased the property for $34,000 from the bank that foreclosed on the Medref-Eden farm. Most people felt the investment was a bad one for the site was so far uptown. Lord William Waldorf Astor willed the property to his son, Major John Jacob Astor of the British Horse Guards.

Major Astor, an important New York City real estate owner, made a lot of money from the Astor Hotel property. He received half a million dollars per year from the land lease. When the lease was renegotiated in 1928, the new lease increased the amount to $700,000 per annum, a fee the hotel could afford since the hotel's income was $2 million per year.

The eleven-story hotel opened on September 9, 1904. It was an immediate success, and the opening coincided with the burgeoning importance of Longacre Square.

In its more than half century of operation, the Astor had hosted nine presidents and many celebrities. Charles Evans Hughes was staying in Suite 170 when he was running against Woodrow Wilson for the presidency. Hughes went to sleep early, sure that he was to be the next President. When he awoke, he learned that the California vote went to Wilson.

General John D. Pershing stayed at the Astor before setting out for Europe to head the American expeditionary force in World War I. General Douglas MacArthur spent his honeymoon night in Suite 386.

By 1921, rumors were already circulating concerning the fate of the hotel. A number of people were sure the "gray lady of Broadway" would be demolished. Instead, the lease was renewed and the lobby and dining rooms were enlarged. Prohibition took its toll on the Astor's profits, so eleven stores, renting for $80 a square foot, were added to the street level.

Following Prohibition, the Astor was given Hotel Liquor License Number One because of its pristine record during the dry period. In January of 1935, over six thousand people rang in the New Year at the Astor. This was the largest turnout since Prohibition had been repealed.

In 1935, the hotel was completely renovated. On January 6, 1936, Robert K. Christenberry succeeded Colonel Gorman as general manager. Gorman had been with the Astor for twenty-five years. Christenberry sought to upgrade the Astor facilities. By that summer, the rooms were air-conditioned. The Astor became the first fully air-conditioned hotel in the Northeast. By the late 1930s, the Astor had seven public dining rooms: the Astor Roof Garden, the Skywalk Cocktail Lounge, the Bar-Cafe, the Cocktail Terrace, L 'Orangerie, the Hunting Room, and the Astor Grill.

With the situation in Europe becoming more and more uncertain, the Astor introduced on September 21, 1940, chess and checkers in L'Orangerie. "Many hotel guests wish to indulge in some form of 'homey' past-time during their leisure. The innovation will provide 'escape' to many guests whose mental burdens have increased during the current international crises."

On January 7, 1942, with its male staff drafted for service, twenty women were employed to occupy the previously exclusively male job of elevator operators. The management declared: "Employment requirements call for beauty and intelligence."

In June of 1944, Christenberry was named president, treasurer and a director of the hotel. He ordered another renovation of the hotel in 1949. By 1952, the hotel's public rooms were the Columbia Room for dining and dancing; the Astor Roof, also a dining and dancing space; the Bar Cafe; the Hunting Room; the Grand Ballroom, which was the largest in

New York; the North Garden Lounge with its Japanese rock garden; the Coral Room; the Yacht Room; the Rose Room; College Hall; the East Ballroom; and the outdoor, roof-top Skywalk Cafe.

In 1954, rumors of the hotel's imminent demolition were again circulating up and down Broadway. Instead, William Zeckendorf and two partners bought the hotel. Zeckendorf announced, "The principals are as one in their intention to perpetuate the Astor as a great hotel." On September 1, 1954, the deal was closed. Only fourteen days later, on September 15, 1954, the Sheraton Corporation bought the hotel from the new owners.

The Sheraton Corporation changed the hotel's name to the Sheraton-Astor. They, in turn, traded the hotel back to the Zeckendorf concern in December of 1957. When the deal was completed in March of 1958, the name reverted to the Astor.

The Astor's age and the changing hotel trade in New York had dealt a blow to the venerable hotel. In late 1966, Erwin O. Schel, general manager of the hotel, stated that restoration of the hotel was impossible. "Hotels generally are built to last 35 years. Major things need to be done to it. You simply can't expect a 65 year-old lady to be as spry as a 5 year-old. Arteries harden. Age happens. That's true of a building too.

"The jet plane has changed the hotel business more than any other factor. It has shortened the stay. Businessmen from Boston used to come and stay overnight. Now they fly the shuttle in three-quarters of an hour.

"Steamship travelers from Europe would spend two or three nights at a hotel before going home. Now they get off the boat, grab a cab, go to Kennedy Airport and wake up in Kansas City.

"Our guests fly over our heads. A man from Indianapolis has a 2-week vacation. He used to spend it in New York. Now he goes to Bermuda. The Rotary holds a convention in Japan. New York pales after the marvelous adventure in Tokyo.

"The guests used to arrive with six suitcases

and stay a week. Now they stay two days with a permanent-pressed suit and shirts they can wash out. The motels did that to the tourist habit.

"There used to be a Mexican lady, a grande dame who came here twice a year with her relatives, a maid and six trunks. They expected service and they got it. I would go over their suite with white gloves.

"I remember the assistant managers would greet guests while wearing morning dress or tuxedo, depending on the time of day. You would personally escort a guest to his room. Now you have push button elevators."

In 1966, the Astor was finally slated for demolition at the beginning of 1967. The property was sold for $10.5 million. Schel was especially upset over the demolition of the ballroom, which had been remodeled in 1964. "It's a shame to destroy something as beautiful as that. I don't want to be around to see it."

Jimmy Durante, who rented room 472 for over twenty years, felt that Times Square had changed—for the worst. "It just don't look and feel like New York," Durante said. "When I heard about the Astor, I thought it was a shame. My suite looked up Broadway and you could see the names going up and down on the theaters. Today that's all motion picture theaters. It ain't the same any more."

In 1967, the Astor was demolished to make way for the Minskoff Building.

ASTOR THEATRE · 1537 Broadway at 45th Street. Architect: George Keister. Opening: September 21, 1906; *A Midsummer Night's Dream*. Owners Wagenhals and Kemper built the Astor directly on Times Square. The theater was built with a twelve-story office building above it, an unusual arrangement at the time. Annie Russell starred in the premiere attraction, *A Midsummer Night's Dream*.

Prominent tenants of the theater included *A Yankee Tourist* (1907), which featured a young Wallace Beery in the cast; *The Man from Home* (1908) and the also long running *Seven Days* (1909).

Between 1913 and 1920, the theater switched back and forth between holding live theater and motion picture presentations. MGM leased the theater for a first-run showing of its epic *Quo Vadis* in 1913. George M. Cohan opened two of his shows in the theater, *Hello, Broadway* (1914) and *The Cohan Revue of 1916* (1916). Comedian Raymond Hitchcock played the theater in *The Beauty Shop* (1914).

The first Pulitzer Prize play, *Why Marry?* by Jesse Lynch Williams, opened on Christmas Day, 1917. The last performance of this decade, *East Is West* (1918), was a huge success.

During the 1920s, legitimate theater use for the Astor ended. Productions included *Cornered* (1920); Sigmund Romberg's *The Blushing Bride* (1922); and *The Bronx Express* (1922). The final legitimate offering at the Astor was *Dew Drop Inn* (1923).

By 1925, the theater had turned to a permanent motion-picture policy. Top pictures were frequently premiered at the Astor, beginning with the silent film *Quo Vadis*. Among the other films booked at the Astor were Billy Wilder's *One Two Three;* Vincente Minnelli's musical *Meet Me In St. Louis; The Secret Life of Walter Mitty* with Danny Kaye; *Road to Bali* with Bing Crosby, Bob Hope and Dorothy Lamour; *Happy Go Lucky; I Wanted Wings;* Alfred Hitchcock's *Spellbound; The Vikings* with Kirk Douglas; and MGM's remake of the film that began the Astor's motion picture policy, *Quo Vadis*.

The Astor and the Victoria Theater down the block were topped by the fabulous Astor/Victoria sign. This was the largest sign in the world and is best known in recent years as the site of the Budweiser spectacular. The sign was 270 feet long and over 60 feet high. It and the Astor and Victoria theaters were torn down along with the Helen Hayes and Morosco theaters in 1982.

AUGUST WILSON THEATER · 245 W. 52nd Street. Architect: C. Howard Crane. Opening: As Guild Theater, April 13, 1925; *Caesar and Cleopatra*. The Theater Guild, the most important producing entity of the 1920s and 1930s, was using the Garrick Theater to present its shows. The Guild decided it needed its own building to house its productions and provide space for its school, so it commissioned C. Howard Crane, Kenneth Franzheim, and Charles Bettis to design a new theater. Set designers Norman Bel Geddes and Lee Simonson consulted on the project, which resulted in the Guild Theater.

At its opening, the theater was called "Home for All the Arts of the Theater." It existed "for drama, for beauty, for ideas." Strangely, the architects decided to build the theater on the second floor of the "Italianstyle" building with a Spanish-tile roof. Despite the design talents involved, the Guild was judged as less than a success by artists and audiences. Lawrence Langner, the founder of the Theater Guild wrote, "We made the ghastly mistake of providing a theater with all the stage space necessary for a repertory of plays without enough seating capacity to provide the income necessary to support the repertory." The design of the auditorium was also deemed boring by audiences who were used to the European-style interior decorations of most Broadway theaters.

The Theater Guild opened the new house with a production of George Bernard Shaw's *Caesar and Cleopatra,* starring Helen Hayes. President Calvin Coolidge, in Washington, threw a switch that illuminated the theater on opening night. The theater housed some of the finest work on Broadway. The Guild's eighth season began with Alfred Lunt and Lynn Fontanne in George Bernard Shaw's *Arms and the Man* (1925). Ferenc Molnar's *The Glass Slipper* (1965) was the next attraction, but after playing to the Theater Guild's 15,000 subscribers, it closed. During this time, the Theater Guild continued to present works at other theaters, while hits played the Guild.

The Lunts were the Theater Guild's chief acting asset. They appeared together and separately in several productions at the Guild Theater, including *Goat Song* (1926); *At Mrs. Beam's* (1926); *Juarez and Maximilian* (1926); *The Brothers Karamazov* (1927); S. N. Behrman's *The Second Man* (1927); Shaw's *The Doctor's Dilemma* (1927); *Caprice* (1928) and

Behrman's *Meteor* (1929). Lunt was featured in Eugene O'Neill's *Marco Millions* (1928) and Lynn Fontanne starred in *Pygmalion* (1926).

While the Lunts were in rehearsal, other actors were featured on the Guild's stage. Edward G. Robinson was featured in Pirandello's *Right You Are If You Think You Are* (1927). Dudley Digges played Mephistopheles in Goethe's *Faust* (1928). In November 1928, Winifred Lenihan, Helen Westley, Gale Sondergaard and Dudley Digges were in Shaw's *Major Barbara* directed by Philip Moeller. Otto Kruger, Claude Rains, Alice Brady, and Gale Sondergaard opened the twelfth season with *Karl and Anna* (1929). Rouben Mamoulian directed the next production, *The Game of Love and Death* (1929) with Alice Brady, Otto Kruger, and Claude Rains.

Turgenev's *A Month in the Country* (1930) starred Alla Nazimova, Dudley Digges, and Douglas Dumbrille. Katia the maid was played by Hortense Alden, better known as Katharine Hepburn. The twelfth season of the Theater Guild was brought to a close with the third edition of *The Garrick Gaieties* (1930), a musical revue.

Lunt and Fontanne returned to the Guild stage in Maxwell Anderson's *Elizabeth the Queen* (1930). The next production, *Midnight* (1930), was undistinguished except for the inclusion in the cast of Clifford Odets. Franchot Tone, Helen Westley, June Walker, Lee Strasberg, and Woodward (Tex) Ritter were among the cast in *Green Grow the Lilacs* (1931). The play gained notice again when it was adapted for the musical *Oklahoma!* (1943).

Most of the Theater Guild's larger and more ambitious productions were staged at the Martin Beck Theatre. One of its finest productions, however, opened at the Guild Theater on October 26, 1931. This was Eugene O'Neill's *Mourning Becomes Electra.* The five-hour long production starred Alla Nazimova and Alice Brady. Shaw's *Too True to Be Good* (1932) was not a hit. The next play was a dramatization of Pearl Buck's *The Good Earth* (1932). Ina Claire followed next in S. N. Behrman's comedy, *Biography* (1932). Shirley Booth, Leo G. Carroll, Judith Anderson, and Humphrey Bogart appeared in Somerset Maugham's translation of *The Mask and the Face* (1933), which closed the fifteenth season.

The opening of the 1933 season on October 2 marked George M. Cohan's next to last Broadway appearance and Eugene O'Neill's only comedy, *Ah, Wilderness!* Its success meant that the Theater Guild had to mount the rest of the season's productions at other theaters. The 17th season opened with Ruth Gordon and Glenn Anders in *A Sleeping Clergyman* (1934), which was followed by an epic, *Valley Forge* (1934) by Maxwell Anderson.

The next production of note was a revue, *Parade* (1935). Lunt and Fontanne opened with *The Taming of the Shrew* (1935) costarring Bretaigne Windust, Richard Whorf, Le Roi Operti, and Sydney Greenstreet. The thirties ended with highlights including Behrman's *End of Summer* (1936) and Ben Hecht's *To Quito and Back* (1937).

As fine as these productions were, the Theater Guild was losing money because of the relatively small seating capacity of the theater and the scale of the Guild's productions. The Guild also was at the forefront of those producers willing to take chances, so many of the typical Broadway audiences weren't ready for Guild productions. As a result, the Theater Guild found it necessary to lease the theater to other producers. The best of these outside productions was William Saroyan's *The Time of Your Life*, which moved to the Guild in 1940. Since other producers were no more successful than the Theater Guild in paying the bills, the Theater Guild leased the theater as a radio theater in 1943.

It was renamed the WOR Mutual Theater on March 19, 1943. In 1950, the American National Theater and Academy (ANTA) bought the theater and renamed it the ANTA Playhouse. ANTA renovated the theater and opened its first production on November 26, 1950. It was Robinson Jeffers' *The Tower Beyond Tragedy* with Judith Anderson. Next came a hit, Gloria Swanson and Jose Ferrer in a revival of Ben Hecht and Charles MacArthur's *Twentieth Century* (1950).

Revivals at the playhouse included *Desire Under the Elms* (1952) with Karl Malden and *Golden Boy* (1952) with John Garfield and Lee J. Cobb. The next big hit was *Mrs. McThing* (1952) featuring Helen Hayes, Ernest Borgnine, Jules Munshin, and Brandon de Wilde. Helen Hayes was also in the theater's next hit, a revival of *The Skin of Our Teeth* (1955). It also starred Mary Martin, George Abbott, and Don Murray. The Lunts returned in *The Great Sebastians* (1956) by Lindsay and Crouse.

The theater was renamed the American Academy of Dramatic Arts in 1953 and renamed again the ANTA Theater on December 21, 1954, with the opening of *Portrait of a Lady*. A hit that actually stayed in the theater was Paddy Chayefsky's *Middle of the Night* (1956) starring Edward G. Robinson. *Say, Darling* (1958) starred Vivian Blaine, Johnny Desmond and Robert Morse. It was a surprise hit with a score by Jule Styne and Comden and Green. Next came the Pulitzer Prize-winning play, *J. B.* (1958). The Archibald MacLeish drama starred Raymond Massey, Pat Hingle, and Christopher Plummer.

The sixties were good years for the theater. A musical revue based on the writings of James Thurber was aptly named *A Thurber Carnival* (1960). Hugh Wheeler's *Big Fish, Little Fish* (1961) was directed by Sir John Gielgud. Later that year, *A Man for All Seasons* (1961) by Robert Bolt starred Paul Scofield and became the longest run at the theater.

On October 13, 1963, history was made when Robert Noah's play *The Advocate* opened on Broadway and was broadcast on five Westinghouse stations. The company invested $60,000 in the William Hammerstein and Michael Ellis production which was bankrolled for $100,000. Robert Noah's play was taped in a television studio in Mineola, Long Island. Live pickups of the ANTA's audience were broadcast before the opening, during the intermission and after the show.

James Baldwin's *Blues for Mister Charlie* (1964) with Rip Torn, Diana Sands, Pat Hingle, and Rosetta Le Noire was followed by *The Owl and the Pussycat* (1964), a light comedy with Diana Sands and Alan Alda. The last big hit of the sixties was *The Royal Hunt of the Sun* (1965) starring Christopher Plummer and George Rose.

The seventies reflected the decline in Broadway's offerings. Helen Hayes, James Stewart, and Jesse White started the decade off right in a revival of *Harvey* (1970). A revival of *Cat on a Hot Tin Roof* was a hit in 1974 with Elizabeth Ashley, Keir Dullea, Kate Reid, and Fred Gwynne. *Bubbling Brown Sugar* (1976) was a surprise hit. Another was the Goodspeed Opera Company's revival of *Whoopee!* (1979). It starred Charles Repole and ran until Tom Stoppard's *Night and Day* (1979) with Maggie Smith replaced it later that year.

The 1980s saw even less of merit at the theater. *Oh, Brother!* (1981) with a score by Michael Valenti was an undeserved failure. In August of that year, the theater was bought by the Jujamcyn chain. The name was changed to the Virginia Theater, after Virginia M. Binger, owner with her husband James. The theater was renovated again, but still it was not considered a top Broadway house. I was followed by an excellent revival of Rodgers and Hart's *On Your Toes*. *City of Angels* (1989) a musical by Cy Coleman, Larry Gelbart, and David Zippel was another success.

Jelly's Last Jam (1992) was a musicalization of the life of Jelly Roll Morton, self-proclaimed inventor of jazz. The show marked a welcome return to Broadway by Gregory Hines. Savion Glover, the remarkable tap dancer was his co-star.

Smokey Joe's Café (1995) was the next hit at the theater. The show, built around the songs of Lieber and Stoller received lukewarm reviews from the critics but canny marketing to the suburban audiences kept the show running.

On October 16, 2005, the theater was re-named for playwright August Wilson. The new name brought a new hit, *Jersey Boys* (2005), a half concert/half musical version of the story of The Four Seasons. The show, like *Smokey Joe's Café*, is entertaining tourists and should continue for seasons to come.

THE AUTOMAT · 1557 Broadway between 46th and 47th Street. The Automat was one of Times Square's most enduring landmarks for more than fifty years. The coin-operated cafeteria boasted plain, sturdy food in clean, anonymous surroundings. The food was basic and cheap, and a good square meal could be bought for less than one dollar. The patron simply walked up to a wall of glass windowed doors and inserted the price of an item in its accompanying slot. The customer then opened the glass door and voilà—a piece of coconut cream pie or baked beans in a crock.

The Automat was born in Germany shortly before the turn of the century. Joseph V. Horn and Frank Hardart brought the first Automat to 818 Chestnut Street in Philadelphia in 1902. Horn & Hardart streamlined the German equipment for Philadelphia, made it sturdier for America's greater population and gave it some modern touches. The idea—an early form of fast food for a low price—proved popular. The Automat offered a glimpse of the future in which dreams of the industrial revolution had come true. Here was machinery used to help make life easier for humans. It had the virtues of being both easy and anonymous.

The idea was so popular in Philadelphia that plans were made by Horn & Hardart to manufacture new machines and install them in New York. And what better place than the Crossroads of the World, Times Square. That other modern convenience, the subway, had reached the square, theaters were going up on every block and great, luxurious hotels like the Astor and Knickerbocker served the finest clientele. Of course, there were risks. Times Square was also known as the culinary center of New York. Nicknamed "Eatinghouse Square," by local wags, it had such restaurants as Rector's, the Cafe de l'Opera, the Knickerbocker Grill, and Shanley's. How would the Automat do against these great lobster palaces?

To help combine the best of both culinary worlds, the opening of the Automat on July 2, 1912 was a society bash. Director John Murray Anderson and Jenny Wren planned the gala opening as a benefit for charity. The top personalities in society and the theatrical world rubbed elbows, strictly by invitation. Beans in a pot, doughnuts, franks, and other Automat favorites weren't in sight that first night. Sherry's, the restaurant beloved of high society, catered the affair in their grandest style. For a nickel, the hoi polloi would receive a plate of caviar from behind the glass door. From the milk spigots flowed not milk but champagne. Meyer Davis' orchestra serenaded the wealthy who ate, drank, and were generally merry on both levels of the restaurant.

Few of the opening night participants would ever set foot in the Automat again, but the job was done. Word was out, and the Automat had arrived. In fact, it proved so popular that mounted police were posted to keep the crowds away from the huge leaded glass windows. On its first day, the Automat brought in 8,693 nickels.

The Times Square Automat was not only novel, but also beautiful. Its most outstanding feature was a stained-glass window thirty-feet long and two stories high. The designer, Nicola D' Ascenzo also modeled windows for the Cathedral of St. John the Divine. The name "Automat" was emblazoned across the facade surrounded by garlands of fruit and flowers. Inside, the dining room featured marble topped tables on pristine white tiled floors. The central column was decorated with carvings that reached to the ceiling in a twisting pattern of leaves and vines. Beveled glass mirrors set into a mahogany framework topped the Automat machinery.

The success of the Times Square Automat led to an expansion of the chain throughout the New York area. By the 1940s, the Automat had reached its peak of popularity, with nearly fifty outlets in the city serving over 350,000 customers a day. But the original Automat was still the flagship of the chain.

Almost all the food cost a nickel. A hamburger or bacon and eggs were two nickels. Coffee, an Automat staple and considered the best in New York, cost a nickel until 1952, when it was raised to a dime. Immediately, sales dropped off.

The success of the Automat reflects the changes occurring in America at the time. There was the novelty of the great machine serving humanity daily bread. Never mind that the food was all made by people in the central kitchens-first located at 47th Street and later at 50th Street and 11th Avenue—or that it was real live people who refilled the slots.

The lower classes of the city were ready for the Automat, and they could get there easily. When the great eating emporiums flourished, only the upper crust could afford transportation. A carriage ride all the way to Times Square could cost as much as a month's rent to a poor family. But the opening of the subway and the growing popularity of the automobile gave people of all classes easy access to all sections of the city. People who couldn't afford Rector's and who didn't have the time to eat a five-course meal on their lunch hour flocked to the Automat. There was also the new immigrant class. They or the second or third generation were just getting their feet wet in the American experience. A place like the Automat was perfect for their needs. It only cost a couple of nickels, and they didn't have to face anybody. If they were unsure of dress or manners, the Automat ensured invisibility. If they didn't quite have a grasp of the language, that was fine. They didn't have to talk to anyone.

Going to the Automat wasn't like going to a restaurant simply to eat. The neat rows of windows displayed the food like merchandise. Eating at the Automat was like going shopping for lunch. You picked out the product you wanted from many choices and paid for it. This was the era when self-service was just beginning to be accepted in retailing, and the Automat followed the popular trend and translated it into restaurant terms.

The Automat was among the first hangouts for a new generation of actors, composers, lyricists and directors. While Victor Herbert ate at Shanley's, Irving Berlin was eating at the Automat. In fact, Berlin set one number in his revue, *Face the Music,* in the Automat. Cast members Katharine Carrington and J. Harold Murray faced the Depression squarely as they dined at the Automat and sang, "Let's Have Another Cup of Coffee."

Senior Executive Vice President and Secretary of Horn & Hardart, Robert F. Byrnes, first joined the company at the Automat in Times Square in 1925. In 1988, he commented on the changes he witnessed over his fifty years with the company: "It was the depression and people were starting to think about watching their nickels and dimes. But Broadway at that time was a seething mass of people, a class of people. They wanted to see something for nothing. They could walk down Broadway. The street was the show.

"They were getting to eat out for the first time. A different class emerged. These were the people who were offered this inexpensive means of walking in and getting a cup of coffee, nobody says anything to them, and they leave their cup on the table and walk out."

Inevitably people's tastes changed, and the Automat changed too in an attempt to keep up with the times."

At the outset there was no cafeteria. It was all Automat. The initial menu was buns, beans, fish cakes and coffee. There was a special window later, that if you wanted a grill item to order, you'd go to the cashier and buy a token for bacon and eggs and then walk back to a concealed cafeteria and put your token into the slot marked bacon and eggs. They didn't have to face anyone again. As the demand for the short-order items grew, the cafeteria was opened to service. Pies, cakes, sandwiches, and desserts all still came from the windows. There was no refrigeration, although there were heating units in the drums so that hot foods like baked beans in the pot could be served. By 1950, the demands of the customers forced the relationship to become 30 percent Automat and 70 percent cafeteria.

Even with the increased cafeteria service, the management that remained maintained the philosophy that everything would be made in one place. This enabled an absolute uniformity of quality in all stores. Hamburgers were premade, not cooked, and sent out to the grills. All stews and soups were centrally prepared

and then warmed over at the Automat. There were four deliveries from the new commissary, which took up the square block between 49th and 50th Street and 11th and 12th Avenues.

To keep customers coming back, prices were kept low, and the places were kept immaculately clean. But social and economic conditions began to evolve after the Second World War that would kill the Automat.

Along with a saturation of the market came an increase in the price of raw materials and a rise in prices. The modes of transportation changed, the trolleys stopped and the elevated trains came down. As more and more neighborhoods were cleaned up, rents increased. The George Washington Bridge went up, the Lincoln and Holland Tunnels were opened, and the population dispersed. The ethnic mix of the population changed, and many of the new immigrants didn't want to eat out. Their food was different from ours, and they weren't in as big a hurry as their predecessors to assimilate American customs. These new arrivals preferred to stay in their ghettos.

In 1939, air-conditioning was added to the restaurants. With heat in the winter and now air conditioning in the summer, the Automats became almost too comfortable. What the company refers to as "undesirables" hung out at the Automats. Originally, there were tables that sat four people. When the Automat became crowded people shared tables. But with a change in the type of patrons, people were loath to share their space. Robert Byrnes remarked, "There were about 200 tables and you would find 200 customers, one at each table because they didn't want to face each other."

At the same time, the counter restaurant concept came in a la Chock Full of Nuts. There, the customers could come in and not face anyone and still get out in a hurry. Even if the place was crowded, customers still weren't obliged to sit beside or across from anyone.

As its clientele changed and business slackened off, the Automat began to lose money. There was also a change in people's attitudes toward the machinery. At first, the Automat was a symbol of the future. Once the future arrived, the Automat seemed dated. With the war effort, technology changed. Transistors and computers made mechanical devices passé. When prices increased, tokens were substituted for coins. That meant the patron had to first go to a cashier for the token. The lunch counter seemed so much easier.

In the old days, the Automat was viewed as a family restaurant, but as Times Square deteriorated, fewer and fewer families frequented the neighborhood. With the great movie palaces gone and less and less product on Broadway, there was no reason for parents to take their children to the Automat. For the children brought up in the space age, the appeal of the Automat was short-lived.

The actual turning point for the company came at about 1957, when business radically changed for the worst, but the Automat hung on until 1969. By that time, things had gotten so bad that a plan was drafted for the company to go out of business. The plan was implemented through gutting their buildings and renting the space to outside concerns. In 1973, Horn & Hardart bought a mail-order company that became "a phenomenal investment." And then came the new revolution—the fast food hamburger.

The decision was made to convert the Automats to fast food restaurants. The Broadway Automat was changed over to a Burger King when the company acquired the New York Burger King franchise in 1974. They also now operate Arby's in New York and, in 1981, gained control of Bojangles Fried Chicken. The last Automat in New York was at 3rd Avenue and 42nd Street. It was closed without warning on April 8, 1991, thereby avoiding landmark status, in the late 1980s.

In the 1940s, the Automat system was in its heyday. There were between forty-five and fifty Automats in the city and over 350,000 people were fed there every day. Robert Byrnes likes to remember this story: "One day an elderly man died in an Automat and on the same day a woman gave birth in the washroom."

AVON THEATER · See KLAW THEATER.

B

BARRYMORE FAMILY · The Barrymores were the greatest family in American theater history. During their notable careers (which spanned five decades on the stage) their personal lives were as well reported as their distinguished careers. Their exploits were parodied in the George S. Kaufman and Edna Ferber comedy, *The Royal Family*.

Georgiana Drew Barrymore (1856–1893) Georgiana was the daughter of Louise Lane Drew and John Drew. Her mother first appeared on stage at the age of five in a melodrama, Meg Murnock, or the Hag of the Glen. Louisa Lane specialized in playing adult roles even before she reached her teens. After two unsuccessful marriages, Louisa met John Drew, a great Irish comedian. Louisa and John Drew had three children: Louisa, who would not undertake a theatrical career; John Drew Jr., who achieved perfection in drawing room comedies; and Georgiana. Georgiana was trained by some of the greatest actors of her time, among them Edwin Booth and Lawrence Barrett, in addition to her own distinguished family. Actor Otis Skinner called Georgiana "the funniest comedian I've ever seen; she made you hold your stomach laughing, but she was never distressing." Her parents barely saw each other because John Drew was often on the road. In fact, they were only together half the time of their twelve-year marriage. While her father was on the road, her mother became the first woman to run an American theater, the Arch Street Theater in Philadelphia. Georgiana was taken on the road with her father. In 1876, she married

Maurice Barrymore. She died in California on July 2, 1893.

Maurice Barrymore (1839–1905) Maurice Barrymore was born Herbert Arthur Chamberlain Hunter Blyth in India. Instead of following in his family's footsteps in the Indian Civil Service, Herbert left India for England where he became the country's amateur boxing champion before launching an acting career. After two years of touring, he adopted the name Maurice Herbert Blythe and later assumed the surname Barrymore. In 1875, Maurice came to America and made his debut in *Under the Gaslight*. The young matinee idol made his New York debut in *Hamlet* at the Fifth Avenue Theater. Also featured in the cast were Edwin Booth making his New York debut and John Drew. After the run of the play, Drew brought Barrymore home to Philadelphia and introduced him to Georgiana. Their marriage produced three children (Lionel, Ethel, and John), each of whom achieved notable success on the stage. Maurice Barrymore died in Amityville, Long Island, on March 26, 1905.

Lionel Barrymore (1878–1954) Lionel first went on the stage at the age of fifteen during the 1893–94 season in Philadelphia under the aegis of his grandmother, Louisa Lane Drew. He never really enjoyed performing and, following this engagement, retired from the stage for two years. He joined his uncle John Drew's acting company and made his first real success in *The Mummy and the Hummingbird* during the 1902 season, playing an Italian organ grinder. Lionel preferred character parts as if seeking to hide his real personality behind the makeup. He specialized in these parts in plays until 1906 when he again left the stage because of ill health. Whether he was actually ill or only looking for an excuse to quit the theater is uncertain.

He moved to Paris to study painting, with no intention of returning to the theater. Three years later, having achieved little success, he returned to America. In 1909, he appeared in the movies, relieved at not having to face an audience. But even the great director D. W. Griffith couldn't provide Lionel with enough work, so he was forced to return to the stage. He achieved success in *Peter Ibbetson*, *The Jest*, and, in 1918, *The Copperhead* in which he was first acclaimed a great star. A disastrous production of *Macbeth* followed, but he again, achieved fame with *The Claw*.

In 1925, he left for Hollywood where he remained for the rest of his life. Lionel Barrymore died on November 15, 1954.

Ethel Barrymore (1879–1959) Whereas Lionel fancied himself a painter, his sister Ethel would have preferred to be a concert pianist (she practiced for five hours a day as a youngster). But the power of the family was too great, and Ethel was forced into an acting career. Her mother's ill health brought Ethel to California in 1892. But her mother's illness worsened and she died leaving her daughter to make all the funeral arrangements. Upon her arriving in New York, her grandmother informed her that she would have to make her own living. Ethel, then only fourteen years old, made her debut as Julia in *The Rivals* in Montreal on January 25, 1894. The production was brought to New York at the Empire Theater. Also in the cast was the legendary Joseph Jefferson and Ethel's grandmother, Mrs. John Drew. John Drew was appearing with Maude Adams as part of producer Charles Frohman's stock company at the Empire.

Drew arranged for Ethel to appear in basically a walk-on part in *The Bauble Shop*. In addition to her brief appearance, Ethel understudied the role of Lady Kate played by Elsie De Wolfe. When the play went on tour, Ethel was given De Wolfe's part.

Ethel must have made some impression on the theatrical world, for while she was playing in *Rosemary* again with her uncle, famed actor and Frohman star, William Gillette, summoned her to London. He featured her as Miss Kitteredge in his production of *Secret Service* and let her understudy the ingénue part. Laurence Irving, son of Sir Henry Irving implored his father to cast Ethel in *The Bells* which also starred Ellen Terry and in Laurence Irving's play *Peter the Great* also with Henry Irving.

In 1900, she returned to America under Charles Frohman's management. She played a small role in *Catherine*. Frohman hired her for the tour of *His Excellency, the Governor* in 1900.

Clyde Fitch, probably the most popular American playwright of his time, had two shows running on Broadway. He had just finished a third play and wanted it to play alongside his other plays in New York. The play, *Captain Jinks of the Horse Marines*, concerned a Madame Trentoni who is mistaken as an opera star by New York society. Barrymore was given her first starring role in the lead. A two-week limited engagement was arranged at the Garrick Theatre, a huge success at its New York premiere on February 4, 1901.

The run was extended to three months and then to six months. All the while, Ethel Barrymore was enjoying the adulation of New York. Her early vehicles included, *Carrots*, a one-act play, and *A Country Mouse* (1902); *Cousin Kate* (1903) and *Cynthia* (1903); *Sunday* (1904); *A Doll's House* (1905); *Alice Sit-by-the-Fire* (1905); *The Silver Box*; and revivals of *Captain Jinks of the Horse Marines; His Excellency the Governor* and *Cousin Kate* (1906–07); *His Sister* (1907–08); and *Lady Frederick* (1908).

Following the engagement of *Lady Frederick* at the Hudson Theatre, Ethel married Russell Griswold Colt, the son of the president of the United States Rubber Company. After her sojourn for married life and motherhood, she returned in Sir Arthur Wing Pinero's play *Mid-Channel* (1910) followed by *The Shadow* (1915) as a wheelchair-bound woman.

During her rehearsals of *The Shadow*, Ethel had picked up a book of short stories by Edna Ferber titled *Roast Beef Medium*. She was so taken with the character of Emma McChesney that she asked Ferber and George Hobart to write a play for her based on the stories. The result was *Our Mrs. McChesney* (1915). The triumphant success of the play was bittersweet for Ethel because her longtime producer, Charles Frohman, was killed in the bombing of the *Lusitania* earlier that year.

Her next play was also a triumph but it almost didn't make it to opening night. Zoe Akins, a popular playwright of her day wrote a new play titled *Declassee*. It was all set to go into rehearsal when in August of 1919 the actors went on strike. Ethel was instrumental in leading the strike. After it was over she returned to *Declassee*, which opened on October 16, 1919. At the two hundredth performance, she broke the house record of the Empire Theatre.

She continued in a variety of plays throughout the next decade, which was most notable for the production of Somerset Maugham's *The Constant Wife* (1926). She toured in the play and returned to New York to see a theater named after her. The Shuberts opened the Ethel Barrymore Theatre on West 47th Street on December 17, 1928.

She then briefly joined her brothers in Hollywood for *Rasputin and the Empress*. The film was a success although she didn't like acting in films. But she was not truly interested in a stage career, nor did she see herself as a great actress. She would rather have seen her brothers' careers overtake her own and was more interested in baseball and boxing than the theater. As the drama became more and more realistic with the emergence of O'Neill, Ibsen, and their like, Ethel became more disenchanted. She seemed purposely to pick parts that didn't suit her. But the public still adored her, as much for her elegance and bearing offstage as her onstage performances. In 1928, the Shuberts presented her in Martinez Sierra's *The Kingdom of God* in the new Ethel Barrymore Theater. Her great success as Sister Gracia was not repeated until 1940, when she appeared on stage in *The Corn Is Green*. Between Broadway roles, she appeared in motion pictures.

Her last stage appearance was in 1950 at a benefit for the American National Theatre and Academy in *The Twelve-Pound Look*. She died on June 18, 1959.

John Barrymore (1882–1942) John, too, evinced no desire for a stage career. He tried supporting himself as an artist and illustrator and, though somewhat successful, found acting to be the easiest way to make money. As the most handsome and talented of his siblings, John found acting relatively painless, although he became easily bored with long runs and as early as 1914 came on stage drunk.

He made his stage debut on October 31, 1903, at Cleveland's Theater, Chicago, playing Max in *Magda*. He made his New York debut in December of that same year, at the Savoy Theater in *Glad of It*. Later that year, he appeared as a member of William Collier's company in *The Dictator*, which also had a run in London. His sister, Ethel, arranged for him to appear with her in *Sunday* and *Alice Sit-by-the-Fire*. He then rejoined William Collier in Australia in *The Dictator*. In 1906, he again appeared with his sister in *His Excellency the Governor*.

In May 1908, he made his musical comedy debut in the Chicago production of *A Stubborn Cinderella* and then in the Charles Dillingham production of *The Candy Shop*.

He much preferred light comedy in which he could be suave and debonair and exhibit "the great profile." He followed in his father's footsteps as a matinee idol in plays like *The Fortune Hunter* (1909) and Schnitzler's *The Affairs of Anatol* (1910).

By 1916, Barrymore, bored with easy roles, found great success in John Galsworthy's *Justice*; George Du Maurier's *Peter Ibbetson*; Tolstoy's *The Living Corpse,* retitled for Broadway, *Redemption*; *Richard III* (1920); and *Hamlet* (1922).

Following the close of *Hamlet,* Barrymore left for Hollywood. Among his notable films were *A Bill of Divorcement, Grand Hotel, Twentieth Century,* and *Counselor at Law.* He wouldn't return to Broadway until 1940, with a production of *My Dear Children* at the Belasco Theatre. By this time, Barrymore was washed up in films, and the parts that came along were mostly parodies of himself. His role in *My Dear Children* was no exception. Ill health forced the closing of the production after only four months. John Barrymore died on June 29, 1942.

BARRYMORE THEATER · See ETHEL BARRYMORE THEATER.

BEACH · The Beach—the concrete island separating Broadway and Seventh Avenue across the street from the Palace Theatre was the hangout for out-of-work vaudevillians in the teens and twenties. They would gather on the little island and brag about their recent bookings and hefty contracts. Usually these exploits were greatly exaggerated.

The Beach even had its poet—Philip Stack, a clerk in the Brooklyn Edison Company, who wrote poems under the pseudonym Don Wahn. Stack sent his poems to Walter Winchell and let Winchell print them in his column without any charge. These poems soon became an important part of the column. Wahn wrote this paean to the Beach.

They stand nearby the Palace day on day
And talk in low and falsely hopeful tones,

Their snappy clothes, pathetically gay,
Bespeak ability to wheedle loans;
They swap their gags like children
   swapping toys,
And rip their lucky brothers into bits;
Their food and drink is Broadway's
   blatant noise —
Their Bible is Variety or Zit's.
So, lolling there, the weeks go swiftly by,
While faded clippings yellow in their
   hands;
They hum the current hits and watch it
   die —
And, penniless, they quote their rash
   demands.
Ah, you, who stand there seven days in
   seven,
God grant you make the two-a-day in
   heaven.

BELASCO, DAVID (1859–1931) · David Belasco was the total theater man. Belasco was obsessed with the theater and played many different roles—playwright, producer, theater owner, actor, director, and stage manager. He wrote almost seventy plays, some in collaboration and produced 121 productions. He was known for the naturalism of his productions as well as their remarkable electrical effects. However, although there are many anecdotes about Belasco the man, almost nothing is remembered about his work.

He began his career in San Francisco as a callboy and play adapter. He moved up to actor and made his first stage appearance in 1871 at the California Theatre in San Francisco. He later met Dion Boucicault, the greatest author of melodramas. Boucicault taught Belasco the value of theatricality and high emotion, and Belasco began to attempt play writing. He was also influenced by the great actors with whom he performed—Edwin Booth and John McCullough performed with him in 1874.

In 1879, Belasco had his first success as a playwright with *Hearts of Oak,* which was first produced in Chicago. Emboldened by the experience, Belasco moved to New York the following year. He became stage manager of the

Madison Square Theatre and by 1886 a stage manager and producer for Daniel Frohman at the Lyceum Theater.

His plays include *Lord Chumley* (1888) and *Men and Women* (1890), both written with H.C. DeMille; *The Heart of Maryland* (1895); *DuBarry* (1901); *The Darling of the Gods,* with Luther Long (1902); *The Girl of the Golden West* (1905); *Temperamental Journey* (1913); *The Return of Peter Grimm* (1921); and *Salvage* (1925). Most of these were melodramas that were popular for a time and then forgotten; as new playwrights changed the style of theater in Europe and America, melodramas like Belasco's fell by the wayside.

These new masters of the drama—Ibsen, Strindberg, Wilde, Shaw, Zola—brought realism to the stage. Belasco, realizing that tastes were changing, was entranced with the possibilities that these playwrights opened up. Belasco is thought of as the man who introduced realism into the American theater and who, as a producer, perhaps went too far. For Alice Bradley's play *The Governor's Lady* (1912), he reproduced a Child's Restaurant on the stage. And when a boarding house set was required for Eugene Walter's *The Easiest Way* (1909), Belasco actually bought one and had it reconstructed on the stage. This wasn't really art but pure showmanship. Art is in the illusion of reality, but with Belasco there was no illusion.

On his quest for realism on the stage, Belasco did make certain innovations. He pioneered stage lighting, especially at the theater he built—the Stuyvesant, which was renamed the Belasco Theatre. A favorite effect of his was recreating a sunset. He was the first to conceal the footlights in order to make the stage even more realistic. His theater had the latest in stage equipment, which he used to produce the most astounding effects. But these were effects without emotion. The plays he produced were simply more modern versions of the melodramas with which he achieved his first fame.

Belasco wore a priest's collar and robes, although he was not particularly religious. He concentrated on his facade and built his personality for its effect, just as he produced his plays. His ego enabled him to understand the importance of the director in the shaping of the drama. He might not have believed a director was necessary for others, but he could extend his control as producer by directing the actors also. But his direction relied on tricks and facade as did his producing. A favorite ruse was the temper tantrum he would throw to make the actors work harder. After lambasting the cast, he would throw his pocket watch onto the floor and crush it with his foot. This astounding action would galvanize the cast. Belasco never told them that he had a trunk full of dollar pocket watches in his office.

His legacy is in his legend. All that is left of the artist is the Belasco Theatre (the second, his first was built in 1902). Puccini adapted two of his plays into *Madame Butterfly* and *The Girl of the Golden West.* He retired in 1930 and died on May 14, 1931. His ghost was said to show up at every opening night at his theater until that of *Oh! Calcutta!*

BELASCO THEATRE · 111 W. 44th Street. Architect: George Keister. Opening: October 16, 1907; *A Grand Army Man.* The theater today known as the Belasco was called the Stuyvesant Theater when producer, director, playwright David Belasco built it in 1907. The Stuyvesant took the name Belasco in 1910 when the original Belasco Theatre reverted to its original name, the Republic. When it was built, the Belasco was the best-equipped theater of its era. The $750,000 theater boasted a huge elevator stage, areas for scene shops and the most complete lighting setup (designed by Louis Hartman) of any theater. The technical innovations introduced by Belasco made possible all the realistic effects he doted on.

Above the east wing of the theater was Belasco's ten-room duplex apartment which was accessible by private elevator.

Unfortunately, for all the hits the Belasco housed, it was never considered a prime Broadway theater. Lee Shubert said, it was on "the wrong side of the right street." Closer to Sixth Avenue than Times Square, the theater was somewhat off the beaten path.

Ferenc Molnar's *The Devil* was presented at the Belasco with Edwin Stevens and at the Garden Theater with George Arliss. Both productions opened on August 18, 1908, and were immediate hits. This must be the only time a play has opened in two theaters on the same day. *The Devil* was followed by *The Fighting Hope* (1908) and *The Easiest Way* (1909).

Belasco's love of feminine pulchritude and melodrama led to a sort of stock company of Belasco heroines, among them Blanche Bates, Lenore Ulric, Ina Claire, Jeanne Eagles and Katharine Cornell. Plays featuring these actresses included *Polly with a Past* (1917); *Daddies* (1918); *The Son-Daughter* (1919); *Kiki* (1921); *The Harem* (1914); *Lulu Belle* (1926); and *Mima* (1928).

Vincent Youmans' *Hit the Deck* sailed into the Belasco on April 25, 1927. Humphrey Bogart starred in *It's a Wise Child* (1929), and David Belasco's last production, *Tonight or Never* (1930).

After Belasco's death on May 14, 1931, the theater was leased to Katharine Cornell. She appeared in *Lucrece* (1932) and Sidney Howard's *Alien Corn* (1933). The theater was then leased to Mrs. Hazel L. Rice, wife of playwright Elmer Rice of *Street Scene* fame.

The Group Theater inhabited the theater in late 1934 when *Gold Eagle Guy* moved from the Morosco. They presented such notable plays there as Clifford Odets' *Awake and Sing* (1935); *Dead End* (1935); Clifford Odets' *Golden Boy* (1937) and *Rocket to the Moon* (1938); and Irwin Shaw's *The Gentle People* (1939).

The forties began with an appearance by John Barrymore acting a parody of himself in *My Dear Children* (1/31/40). The $50,000 advance sale was one of the largest in Broadway history. It seemed that everyone wanted to catch a glimpse of the Great Profile on his way down the ladder of success.

The 1940s saw productions of *Johnny Belinda* (1940); *Mr. and Mrs. North* (1941); *Trio* (1941), a frank but tasteful treatment of lesbianism that the management of the theater refused to let run more than two months; *Kiss Them for Me* (1945); Arthur Laurents' *Home*

of the Brave (1945); Gertrude Berg as Molly Goldberg in *Me and Molly* (1948); and *The Madwoman of Chaillot* with Martita Hunt and Estelle Winwood (1948).

In 1949, the Belasco became an NBC radio theater, returning to legitimate use on November 5, 1953, with *The Solid Gold Cadillac* followed by George Axelrod's *Will Success Spoil Rock Hunter?* (1955) with Jayne Mansfield in a leading role.

The Pulitzer Prize was awarded to the Belasco's next hit, Tad Mosel's *All the Way Home* (1960). The British invasion of the sixties came to the Belasco in the form of *Inadmissible Evidence* (1965) and Frank Marcus' *The Killing of Sister George* (1966). Al Pacino made his Broadway debut at the Belasco in *Does a Tiger Wear a Necktie?* (1969).

As Broadway's fortunes fell in the late 1960s, so did those of the Belasco. *Oh! Calcutta!* moved to the Belasco from the Eden Theater off-Broadway on February 26, 1971, and caused a sensation with critics and audiences. It also caused a sensation with the ghost of David Belasco who was often seen in his private box on opening nights. After *Oh! Calcutta!*, Belasco's ghost never reappeared. Perhaps he realized that there were to be no more successes at the theater. The Shubert Organization used the theater as a final home for musicals on their last legs like *Ain't Misbehavin'*. It also leased the space to a succession of shows that had little chance for success. These included *The Rocky Horror Show* (which later became a cult movie), *An Almost Perfect Person*, *The Goodbye People* and *Hide and Seek*. These plays quickly came and went. The 1986–87 season was devoted to the works of Shakespeare presented to the city's school children by the New York Shakespeare Festival.

In 1991, Tony Randall's Natonal Actors Theatre began operations at the Belasco. But, with few exceptions, their offerings were failures.

BERLIN, IRVING (1888–1989) · Composer and lyricist Irving Berlin was certainly the most successful and prolific songwriter in

American history. His songs span over fifty years from his first song, "Marie from Sunny Italy" (1907, lyrics only) to his last performed song, "An Old Fashioned Wedding" (1966), written for a revival of *Annie Get Your Gun.*

During the six decades of his career, he was the composer most able to chart America's taste in popular song; and he influenced scores of others in his field.

He was born Israel Baline in Mohilev, Russia, on May 11, 1888. When Berlin was five, his family settled on the Lower East Side of New York. After the death of his father, when he was eight, he left school and by his teens was singing in Bowery saloons and restaurants. Songwriting was just becoming big business, and he began writing lyrics for others' tunes and plugging songs for publishers. His first song, "Marie from Sunny Italy," had music by M. Nicholson. Although he never learned to read music, Berlin was on the way to becoming a professional songwriter. In 1909, he was hired as a staff lyricist by the Ted Snyder Company, and soon Berlin matched his words to his own music. The next year, he performed in vaudeville and then musical comedy in *Up and Down Broadway.* His first big success, "Alexander's Ragtime Band," was published in 1911 and catapulted Berlin to the top of his field.

In 1914, having already had songs interpolated into revues and musicals, he saw his first full Broadway score presented. The show was *Watch Your Step* and presented the song "Play a Simple Melody. " During World War I, Berlin joined the U.S. Army and was inspired to write "Oh, How I Hate To Get Up in the Morning!" The song appeared in an all-soldier revue, *Yip! Yip! Yaphank!* (1918), which also featured another big hit, "Mandy."

The young composer was so successful that he was asked to contribute most of the score to the *Ziegfeld Follies of 1919.* For the annual revue, he wrote the theme song of the *Follies,* "A Pretty Girl Is Like a Melody." Reacting against the extravagance of the *Follies,* Berlin joined with Sam H. Harris and built the Music Box Theater. There, the two partners presented Berlin's *Music Box Revues* (1921, 1922, 1923,

1924), a series of small scale but lush revues that introduced such songs as "Say It with Music;" "Pack Up your Sins and Go to the Devil;" "Learn to Do the Strut;" "An Orange Grove in California;" "What'll I Do;" and "All Alone." The Marx Brothers starred in Berlin's next show, *The Cocoanuts* (1925).

His next smash hit song was contributed to the musical *Betsy* (1926); the song was "Blue Skies." He returned to the *Ziegfeld Follies* in 1927 with a score that included "Shaking the Blues Away." Berlin's next score was for *Face the Music* (1932), which featured the songs "Let's Have Another Cup of Coffee" and "Soft Lights and Sweet Music." *As Thousands Cheer* (1933) followed with a cast that included the great Ethel Waters, who introduced one of the most powerful and dramatic of all theater songs, "Supper Time." Other hits from the score were "Easter Parade;" "Harlem on My Mind;" "Heat Wave;" and "How's Chances?"

Berlin spent the remainder of the 1930s in Hollywood writing, primarily for Fred Astaire and Ginger Rogers, such movie scores as *Top Hat* (RKO, 1935), *Follow the Fleet* (RKO, 1936) and *Carefree* (Fox, 1938). He also contributed scores to two Alice Faye vehicles, *On the Avenue* (Fox, 1937) and *Alexander's Ragtime Band* (Fox, 1938), as well as other films.

Berlin returned to Broadway and the shows *Louisiana Purchase* (1940) ("Fools Fall in Love;" "It's a Lovely Day Tomorrow"); *This Is the Army* (1942); *Annie Get Your Gun* (1946) ("Anything You Can Do;" "Doin' What Comes Natur'lly;" "The Girl That I Marry;" "I Got Lost in His Arms;" "I Got the Sun in the Morning;" "They Say It's Wonderful;" and "There's No Business Like Show Business"); *Miss Liberty* (1949) ("Let's Take an Old Fashioned Walk"); *Call Me Madam* (1950) ("It's a Lovely Day Today" and "You're Just in Love"); and *Mr. President* (1962), Berlin's last score and the least successful of his shows.

Among the many awards he received are the Medal for Merit for *This Is the Army;* the Legion of Honor; a Congressional Gold Medal for "God Bless America," as well as an Academy Award for "White Christmas" (1942).

Irving Berlin contributed more hits than any of his contemporary Broadway composers. His more than 800 songs captured the spirit of the nation unlike that of any other songwriter. He died on September 22, 1989.

BERNARD B. JACOBS THEATRE · 242 W. 45th Street. Architect: Herbert J. Krapp. Opening: January 11, 1927; *Piggy.* The Chanin Brothers built the Royale Theatre in 1927 on what is considered the most important of all Broadway cross streets. Because of its high concentration of theaters, 45th Street is the one street in the Times Square area where foot traffic is thought to affect box office.

The Chanins purchased a large plot of land on Eighth Avenue between 44th and 45th Streets. On the land they built the Golden Theatre, Theatre Masque, Majestic Theatre and the Lincoln Hotel (currently the Milford Plaza Hotel).

The first offering at the 1,058-seat theater was *Piggy* (1927), a musical comedy by Cliff Friend and Lew Brown. *Piggy* never caught on with the public. Producer William B. Friedlander even changed the name of the show to *I Told You So* during the run.

The Royale's next production, *Judy* (1927), made way for a musicalization of *The Importance of Being Ernest,* called *Oh, Ernest!* (1927). The next offering, *Rang-Tang* (1927), starred the popular black performers Aubrey Lyles and Flournoy Miller.

The Madcap (1928) starred Mitzi, Harry Puck, and Arthur Treacher. Though old fashioned, the show caught on and played a respectable run. Following it was the theater's first straight play, the mystery *Sh! The Octopus* (1928).

The first smash hit for the theater was the Mae West vehicle *Diamond Lil* (1928). West had written a script similar to another by Mark Linder. The two joined forces and *Diamond Lil* was born. Half the show was owned by Owney Madden, a gangster best known as proprietor of the Cotton Club. *Diamond Lil* was followed by a failure, the musical *Woof, Woof* (1929).

The Shuberts began management of the Royale in 1930. A big success was the review

Second Little Show (1930). Howard Dietz and Arthur Schwartz wrote the songs. However, the show's hit tune, "Sing Something Simple," was written by Herman Hupfeld.

Mae West returned to the Royale in *The Constant Sinner* (1931). A more subdued play, *When Ladies Meet* (1932), opened at the Royale. Maxwell Anderson's *Both Your Houses* (1933), was an expose of political morality. The play won the Pulitzer Prize.

After a few more inconsequential shows, the theater's name was changed. When producer John Golden lost his John Golden Theater on 54th Street, he leased the Royale, renaming it the Golden Theater. George Abbott directed the first offering, Norman Krasna's *Small Miracle* (1934). It featured Ilka Chase and Myron McCormick. *Rain from Heaven* (1934) by S. N. Behrman opened with Jane Cowl and John Halliday.

During the Depression, the theater's fortunes fell along with Broadway's, and in December 1936, it was taken over by CBS as a radio theater. Golden moved operations to the Masque Theater next door, and he renamed it the John Golden Theater. In 1940, CBS relinquished its lease, and the theater's name reverted to the Royale. After housing a series of plays that moved from other houses, the Royale housed popular comedienne ZaSu Pitts in *Ramshackle Inn* (1944). *School for Brides* (1944), its title a takeoff on Moliere's *School for Wives,* enjoyed a long run. Mae West then returned to the Royale in *Catharine Was Great,* which had originally opened at the Shubert Theater.

Louis Calhern and Dorothy Gish starred in *The Magnificent Yankee* (1946) by Emmet Lavery. Ina Claire appeared at the Royale in *The Fatal Weakness* (1946) by George Kelly.

Moss Hart's *Light Up the Sky* (1948) was an affectionate and sometimes barbed spoof of the Broadway theater in the same style as his and George S. Kaufman's *Once in a Lifetime.* Christopher Fry's London hit, *The Lady's Not for Burning* (1950), opened at the Royale with Richard Burton, John Gielgud, and Pamela Brown.

Leonard Sillman opened the biggest hit in

his series of *New Faces* revues at the Royale on May 16, 1952. The show introduced such future stars as Carol Lawrence, Alice Ghostley, Robert Clary, Eartha Kitt, Paul Lynde, and Ronny Graham. The terrific songs, written by Arthur Siegel and June Carroll, included the standard "Love Is a Simple Thing." *New Faces of 1952* with its 365 performance run was the last successful popular Broadway revue for years. In the early 1950s, audiences could see the same type of show in the comfort of their living rooms through the miracle of television; there was no need to go to Broadway.

Andre Gide's play *The Immoralist* (1954), based on his novel, explored the theme of homosexuality. More popular was Sandy Wilson's affectionate parody of twenties' musicals, *The Boy Friend* (1954). The musical introduced a new star to Broadway, Julie Andrews.

Thornton Wilder's *The Matchmaker* (1955) was a rewrite of his early failure, *The Merchant of Yonkers.*

Another comedy, *The Tunnel of Love* (1957), by Joseph Fields and Peter DeVries starred Tom Ewell. *The Entertainer* (1958) by John Osborne was hailed for its performance by Laurence Olivier. The play also starred Joan Plowright and Brenda de Banzie.

Robert Dhery's revue *La Plume de Ma Tante* (1958) did not have any hit songs or any stars, but audiences were entranced by the Gallic entertainment. Another revue, *From the Second City* (1961), introduced Barbara Harris, Alan Arkin, and Paul Sand to New York.

Bette Davis appeared at the Royale with Patrick O'Neal, Margaret Leighton, and Alan Webb in Tennessee Williams' *The Night of the Iguana* (1961). Williams' play opened to mixed reviews.

Lord Pengo (1962) by S. N. Behrman opened with Charles Boyer, Agnes Moorehead, Brian Bedford, and Henry Daniell. The next hit at the Royale, *The Subject Was Roses* (1964) by Frank D. Gilroy, won the Pulitzer Prize. *The Subject Was Roses* opened with critics hailing Gilroy's tight dialogue and detailed realism, in great contrast to the work of the best-known Broadway dramatists of the day.

One of the biggest hits of the 1960s was the French farce *Cactus Flower* (1965). Lauren Bacall made her Broadway debut in the comedy. The sixties was the last decade in which audiences were willing to be charmed on Broadway. Later audiences wanted to be wowed by Broadway, but in the sixties they were still content to sit back and watch a star go through his or her paces.

A notable booking at the Royale was the musical *Grease,* which moved to the theater from the Broadhurst in 1972 and remained for eight years. By the time *Grease* closed, the set was actually peeling and the cast was less than prime, but it had racked up 3,388 performances, a record at the time.

Who's Life Is It Anyway? (1979) was a British import with Tom Conti. Brian Clark's play was a success on Broadway. Conti played a paralyzed man who wants to gain control of his life by getting the right to die. When Conti left the cast, the producers, faced with the problem of finding a replacement, made the unlikely choice of television star Mary Tyler Moore. Clark adapted the script for a female lead, and Moore received excellent reviews.

Alexander Cohen presented the American version of a British revue, *A Day in Hollywood/A Night in the Ukraine* (1980) at the Royale. The revue was directed and choreographed by Tommy Tune and featured David Garrison, Peggy Hewett, Frank Lazarus, and Priscilla Lopez.

Tim Rice and Andrew Lloyd Webber's third Broadway success, *Joseph and the Amazing Technicolor Dreamcoat* moved from off-Broadway on January 27, 1982. The show was a failure with the critics but a hit with audiences, playing 751 performances.

Andrew Lloyd Webber returned to the Royale with his show *Song and Dance* (1985). The musical featured Bernadette Peters in the first act, a one-woman musical. The second act featured dancer Christopher d' Amboise and a small chorus.

George Abbott directed a revival of his play *Broadway,* written in collaboration with Philip Dunning. The show opened on Abbott's one hundredth birthday, June 25,

1987. Unfortunately, the poorly produced production was not a success, running only four performances.

The Royale was dark for a long period until the New York Shakespeare Festival's production of Caryl Churchill's English play *Serious Money* opened in January 1988. The play was not a success in its transfer from off-Broadway.

On May 3, 1988, theatergoers were treated to the premiere of David Mamet's *Speed-the-Plow*. The comedy, a production of the Lincoln Center Theater Company, featured brilliant performances by Joe Mantegna and Ron Silver. The third cast member, making her Broadway debut, was the rock star Madonna. Unfortunately, her talents proved insufficient to the play's needs.

Judd Hirsch starred in Herb Gardner's play *Conversations with My Father* (1992). A transfer from London, J. B. Priestley's play *An Inspector Calls* (1994) was a complete rethinking of the classic play and a spectacular production. Another English import, Yasmina Reza's three-character play *Art* (1998) was a hit. In the late nineties it seemed as if the theater depended on English imports for its hits. The next hit was from London, too. Michael Frayn's *Copenhagen* (2000) was a dense, political, and scientific play but the drama made a hit on both sides of the Atlantic.

A series of undistinguished revivals followed in quick succession until another revival, *Glengarry Glen Ross* (2005) gave the theater a much needed success. During the run of that show, the theater's name was changed to the Bernard B. Jacobs Theatre, named after one of the directors of the Shubert Organization. At the same time, the Plymouth Theatre was named after Jacobs' associate, Gerald Schoenfeld. Theatergoers were appalled, forgetting that producers had a proud tradition of naming theaters after themselves.

BERNSTEIN, LEONARD (1918– 1990) · Although best known for his work in the classical music field, Leonard Bernstein has had enormous success as a Broadway composer. Born in Lawrence, Massachusetts, on August 25, 1918, Bernstein began his music studies with Helen Coates and Heinrich Gebhard. He was educated at the Boston Latin School and Harvard University. At Harvard, he continued his studies with Walter Piston, Edward Burlingame Hill, and Tillman Merritt. He then attended the Curtis Institute, Philadelphia, under Randall Thompson, Isabelle Vengerova, and Fritz Reiner. Next, he became assistant to Serge Koussevitzky after an apprenticeship. In 1943, he assisted Artur Rodzinski as conductor of the New York Philharmonic. When guest conductor Bruno Walter became ill, Bernstein, in the best show business tradition, took over the baton and became a star.

His first show, *On the Town* (1944), was based on a Jerome Robbins ballet, *Fancy Free*, for which Bernstein had written the music. It was followed by *Wonderful Town* (1953).

His next show, *Candide* (1956), was a failure, but the album, recorded by Goddard Lieberson for Columbia Records, made the show a cult favorite. *West Side Story* (1957) featured the songs "Somewhere," "Maria," "I Feel Pretty," and "Tonight."

Bernstein's heavy conducting and composing schedule prevented him from pursuing a steady career writing for Broadway. His next and last show, *1600 Pennsylvania Avenue* (1976) was a failure with Alan Jay Lerner contributing the libretto and lyrics.

Leonard Bernstein died on October 14, 1990. Though Bernstein did not write as much as some of the other songwriting greats like Kern, Rodgers, or Berlin, the quality of his scores is unsurpassed.

BIJOU THEATRE · 209 W. 45th Street. Architect: Herbert J. Krapp. Opening: April 12, 1917; *The Knife*. The Bijou was built by the Shuberts, but because of its small size, it never achieved much success. In 1918, Tallulah Bankhead made her first Broadway appearance here in *The Squab Farm*.

During the Depression, while other theaters were transformed to movies or radio use, the Bijou was shuttered. There was the occasional film booking during the forties and fifties, such as the American premiere of *The Red Shoes*.

The theater reopened as a legit house in 1957. The first production of Eugene O'Neill's *A Moon for the Misbegotten* reinstated the short-lived legitimate policy. The theater reopened as the D. W. Griffith Theater, a movie theater. Its first presentation, *The Connection*, opened October 3, 1962.

The next year, the theater was sold again and became a Japanese cinema house called the TOHO. The film *Yojimbo* opened there January 22, 1963, as the first attraction.

In 1973, the Bijou again became a legitimate theater under its original name. However because of its small size and the high operating costs of Broadway productions, the theater could be used for only small, intimate shows without stars or big production values. *Mummenschanz*, a mime theater, was the most notable tenant. It played at the Bijou for 1,326 performances. The Bijou ended its spotted history when it was demolished along with the Helen Hayes and Morosco theaters to make way for the Marriott Marquis Hotel.

BILLY ROSE THEATER · See NEDER-LANDER THEATER.

BILLY ROSE'S DIAMOND HORSESHOE· See CENTURY THEATER.

BILLY ROSE MUSIC HALL · See ED SUL-LIVAN THEATER.

BILTMORE THEATER · 261 W. 47th Street. Architect: Herbert J. Krapp. Opening: December 7. 1925; *Easy Come, Easy Go* (moved from the George M. Cohan Theater). The Biltmore Theater has had a spotty history. Despite its prime location, the theater has had few long runs. It was built by the Chanin Brothers, who would eventually build, and lose, six theaters in Times Square. The Biltmore was the second of the Chanins' Broadway theaters. With one thousand seats it was an ideal size to serve plays and musicals equally well. The theater was the first built on the north side of 47th Street.

In its first years, the Biltmore's offerings were, for the most part, unexceptional. They included such moderate hits as *Kongo* (1926), *Loose Ankles* (1926), *The Barker* (1927), and *Jimmie's Women* (1927).

Later in the 1920s, the Biltmore was host to a controversial play, *The Pleasure Man* (10/1/28) by Mae West. The show was closed by the police only two days after its premiere. Among the shocking proceedings on the stage was a party of female impersonators.

A long dry spell hit the Biltmore in the midst of the Depression. It didn't have a hit until January 1, 1934 with the opening of *Big Hearted Herbert,* which played for 154 performances. But the modest success wasn't enough to keep the theater profitable. The Chanins lost the Biltmore as well as their other holdings.

To the rescue came the Federal Theater Project with its *Living Newspapers,* a series of shows that dramatized current events on the stage, *Triple-A Plowed Under* (1936), the first *Living Newspaper* and *Injunction Granted* (1936).

Among the only businesses showing a profit during the Depression were the movie studios. Warner Brothers bought the Biltmore and installed George Abbott as its principal producer. His first production at the Biltmore was the John Monks Jr. and Fred Finklehoffe comedy *Brother Rat* (1936). It was the theater's first big hit.

After two failures, *Brown Sugar* and *All That Glitters,* the theater had a string of hits including *What a Life* (1938) which introduced the character of Henry Aldrich; *My Sister Eileen* (1940); *Kiss and Tell* (1943); and *The Heiress* (1947), a dramatization by Ruth and Augustus Goetz of Henry James' *Washington Square*.

David Merrick's first producing effort, *Clutterbuck,* opened at the Biltmore on December 3, 1949. It played 218 performances, primarily through the aggressive public relations stunts ordered by Merrick.

Beginning in 1952, the theater was leased to CBS. David Cogan purchased the theater in 1958 and booked a series of successful shows including *Take Her, She's Mine* (1961) by Phoebe and Henry Ephron and Neil Simon's *Barefoot in the Park* (1963).

The biggest hit in the Biltmore's history was *Hair* (1968; 1,750 performances) by Galt MacDermot, James Rado, and Gerome Ragni. *Hair* was more than just a rock musical. It was one of the last of the truly influential Broadway musicals. The staging and loose construction of the script as well as the unconventional score influenced both theater professionals and audiences. *Hair* was a phenomenon of its time. A later revival presented at the Biltmore in 1977 was a failure.

On December 10, 1987, the Biltmore suffered a fire of mysterious origins. The stage area and front of house was damaged by the fire, but luckily no structural damage occurred, although the theater's ornate plasterwork was damaged. The police said that vagrants had been using the theater as a drug haven.

On February 16, 1988, the theater was auctioned off. It was sold for $5.35 million to Morris Gluck, a businessman who promised to retain the building's function as a theater. Gluck purchased the building from Sam Pfeiffer who had purchased the building two years before from David Cogan, the owner of the building since 1958.

The Nederlanders, in association with producer Stewart Lane, purchased the Biltmore in 1993.

Biltmore went through several other owners who all defaulted on loans before being able to restore and reopen the theater. Following the lead of the Roundabout Theater's occupancy of the old Selwyn Theatre on 42nd Street (renamed the American Airlines Theatre), the renovated Biltmore is now occupied by the Manhattan Theater Club. The theater reopened with the musical *The Violet Hour* in 2003. *Brooklyn Boy* by Donald Margulies (2005) and *Rabbit Hole* (2006) were other notable productions by Manhattan Theatre Club at the Biltmore.

BOCK AND HARNICK · Songwriters Bock and Harnick were the preeminent musical theater composing team of the 1960s. They showed an almost sweet regard for their characters' humanity and displayed an ability to universalize the problems and dreams of these characters in such shows as *Fiddler on the Roof* and *The Rothschilds*. But their work could also be satirical and sophisticated, especially in their shows *The Apple Tree* and *Fiorello!*

Jerry Bock (1928) Composer Jerry Bock was born in New Haven, Connecticut on November 23, 1928. His early musical comedy successes included the Sammy Davis Jr. vehicle *Mr. Wonderful* (3/22/56), which ran for 383 performances.

Sheldon Harnick (1924) Lyricist Sheldon Harnick was born in Chicago, Illinois, on April 30, 1924. After writing for the Northwestern University Waa-Mu shows, he achieved his first professional success as a contributor to revues including Leonard Sillman's *New Faces of 1952* and Ben Bagley's *Shoestring Revue* (1957).

The team's Broadway shows include *The Body Beautiful* (1958); *Fiorello!* (1959), winner of the coveted Pulitzer Prize for drama; *Tenderloin* (1960); and *She Loves Me* (1963).

Their next Broadway assignment was their masterwork, *Fiddler on the Roof,* one of the greatest musicals ever written. *Fiddler on the Roof* opened on September 22, 1964 with a superior book by Joseph Stein and brilliant direction and choreography by Jerome Robbins. *Fiddler on the Roof* played 3,242 performances, making it, for a while, Broadway's longest-running musical.

The team followed *Fiddler on the Roof* with *The Apple Tree* (1966), consisting of three one-act musicals, based on Mark Twain's "The Diary of Adam and Eve," Jules Feiffer's "Passionella," and Frank R. Stockton's "The Lady or the Tiger." Bock and Harnick's last Broadway musical as a team was *The Rothschilds* (1970).

After the team's breakup, Jerry Bock retired from the musical theater. Sheldon Harnick went on to provide lyrics to Richard Rodgers' music for *Rex* (1976). Unfortunately, that show, Harnick's last Broadway offering, was a failure. His later attempts to mount a Broadway production included musicalizations of the movie

It's a Wonderful Life and Dickens' *A Christmas Carol*. Neither has made it to New York.

BOOTH THEATRE · 222 W. 45th Street. Architect: Henry B. Herts. Opening: October 16. 1913; *The Great Adventure*. The Sam S. Shubert Theatre and the Booth Theatre were designed together as one building. The combination of the Booth and Shubert's shared facade forms Times Square's most famous pedestrian thoroughfare—Shubert Alley. The architectural firm responsible for the design of the theaters was Herts & Tallant, the firm that also designed the Helen Hayes, the Longacre, the New Amsterdam, the Liberty, and the Lyceum theaters.

The Venetian Renaissance building was built by producers Winthrop Ames and Lee Shubert. The two men had built the New Theater on Central Park West, the northernmost location for a Broadway theater. That theater failed, and the impresarios decided to locate their next theater in a more traditional spot off Times Square. When their theater was finally finished in 1913, they named it after noted 19th century actor Edwin Booth.

Because building laws prohibited protruding ornamentation, the theater was decorated with polychromed stucco. The theater's intimacy is due to both its fine design and its small capacity with room for 808 people, including standees.

The first productions to find success at the Booth were *Experience* (1914); *The Bubble* (1915); Clare Kummer's *A Successful Calamity* (1917); *Seventeen* (1918); *The Green Goddess* (1921); *Seventh Heaven* (1922) by Austin Strong; and *Dancing Mothers* (1924) with Helen Hayes as a young flapper. James Cagney was a dancer in two editions of the *Grand Street Follies*. The first premiered in 1928 with Cagney as choreographer; the second premiered a year later.

During the 1930s, hits were scarce at the Booth. The theater's location kept it booked, but the plays did not enjoy long runs. Only when the decade was half over did the theater finally have a hit, George S. Kaufman and Moss Hart's great comedy *You Can't Take It with You* (1936). The zany comedy won the Pulitzer Prize, as did the next great hit at the Booth, William Saroyan's *The Time of Your Life* (1939).

The forties included such hits as *Claudia* (1941); *The Two Mrs. Carrolls* (1944); and Norman Krasna's *John Loves Mary* (1947) starring Nina Foch in her Broadway debut.

Come Back Little Sheba (1950), William Inge's first Broadway play kicked off the fifties with a hit and was followed by *An Evening with Beatrice Lillie* (1952); Gore Vidal's sardonic comedy *Visit to a Small Planet* (1957); Henry Fonda and Anne Bancroft in William Gibson's *Two for the Seesaw* (1958); and Paddy Chayefsky's spiritualistic comedy/drama *The Tenth Man* (1959).

In the 1960s, the hits began with Julie Harris in *A Shot in the Dark* (1961); Murray Schisgal's *Luv* (1964); and Leonard Gershe's *Butterflies Are Free* (1969).

That Championship Season (1972) was written by Jason Miller, who won a Pulitzer Prize for his efforts. The play transferred from the Public Theater to the Booth. The next hit at the Booth was also a transfer from the Public Theater—Ntozake Shange's *For Colored Girls Who Have Considered Suicide When the Rainbow Is Enuf* (1976).

Bernard Pomerance's *The Elephant Man* (1979) continued in the growing trend of plays opening in nonprofit theaters and then transferring to Broadway. The nonprofit arena took the place of the long out-of-town tryout tour. That same year saw a restoration/redesign of the theater's interior by designer Melanie Kahane.

Stephen Sondheim and James Lapine's *Sunday in the Park with George* (1984) won the Pulitzer Prize. It was followed by Herb Gardner's hit play *I'm Not Rappaport* (1985). Shirley Valentine (1989) was a popular hit imported from Britain. A rare musical at the Booth, *Once on This Island* (1990), transferred from Playwrights Horizons. It was followed by a cut-down revival of Frank Loesser's musical *The Most Happy Fella* (1992) which faired poorly.

Following some inconsequential plays, the next hit was *Having Our Say* (1995), the story of the Delaney Sisters. That long run was followed by several failures until *Via Dolorosa* (1999), David Hare's monologue based on his visits to the Middle East. More one-person shows followed David Hare's turn. Barry Humphries appeared in *Dame Edna: The Royal Tour* (1999) which was followed by a revival of Lily Tomlin's *The Search for Signs of Intelligent Life in the Universe* (2000). That was followed by *Bea Arthur on Broadway* (2002), an unsuccessful attempt to mimic the success of Elaine Stritch's autobiographical evening.

Paul Newman appeared as the Stage Manager in a revival of Thornton Wilder's *Our Town* (2002), which was later shown on television. Martin McDonagh's *The Pillowman* (2005) was a stark examination of Eastern European repression. Three monologues formed the basis of Brian Friel's *The Faith Healer* (2006) in a new production.

BRADY, WILLIAM A. (1863–1950) · Producer William A. Brady is perhaps best remembered as a presenter of melodramas with a refined air about them. Plays like *Trilby* and Barrie's *Alice Sit-By-the-Fire* are the best known of his productions. He always mounted his productions with the utmost taste, regardless of the cost, featuring performers under his management such as Helen Hayes, Douglas Fairbanks, Grace George (his second wife), Alice Brady (his daughter), and Helen Gahagan.

Brady began his theatrical career in San Francisco in 1882. Following a move to New York, he leased the original Manhattan Theater starting in 1896 and then built the Playhouse Theater in 1911 for his own productions. The next year, he also became manager of the 48th Street Theatre.

Brady was one of the few producers—Ziegfeld was another—who saw the powers of the new art of motion pictures. Brady owned a film-distribution company, the World Film Corporation, in the late teens. He was president of the National Association of the Motion Picture Industry for five years beginning in 1915. President Woodrow Wilson appointed him chairman of a committee to organize the movie industry in 1917.

Among the plays Brady produced on Broadway were, *The Two Orphans* (1904); *Way Down East* (1903); *Uncle Tom's Cabin* (1901); *Foxy Grandpa* (1902); *The Pit* (1904); *Trilby* (1905); *Runty Pulls the Strings* (1911); *Baby Mine* (1910); *Bought and Paid For* (1911); *The White Feather* (1915); *The Ruined Lady* (1920); *The Skin Game* (1920); *Street Scene* (Pulitzer Prize) (1929); and *A Church Mouse* (1931).

Although Brady produced many of the most successful shows in Broadway history, he was often broke. In fact, in 1922 he admitted being broke 10 times in the preceding 20 years. Brady was broke before and would be broke again, but for all the ups and downs of his career he will be remembered as a smart entrepreneur who was able to adjust to the immense changes in popular culture as the century turned. The range of Brady's productions, from *Way Down East* to *Street Scene* was not that wide but demonstrates an ability to adapt to the changes in popular taste, an ability not shared by some of his contemporaries.

BRICE, FANNY (1891–1951) · Fanny Brice was among the most beloved of all Broadway performers. Her range of characterization was incredible. She could be the broad, physical comedienne telling her Jewish-accented stories of Becky in the ballet and Mrs. Cohen at the beach as well as the lonely, soulful torch singer who introduced "My Man" to America. Later in her career, she added still another facet to her stage personality, the irrepressible hellion, Baby Snooks.

She was born in New York on October 29, 1891, as Fanny Borach and early on saw the stage as the natural outlet for her flamboyant personality. At the age of thirteen, looking for a way to get into Keeney's Theatre in Brooklyn for free, she entered an Amateur Night contest. She sang "When You Know You're Not Forgotten by the Girl You Can't Forget" and won first prize, a five dollar gold piece. Seeing how easy show business was she continued to enter and win amateur contests. During this time she changed her name to Brice. Her mother, estranged from "Pinochle Charlie" Borach, also adopted the name Brice as did her three other children.

Brice almost made it to Broadway when George M. Cohan cast her in a musical. But her inability to dance caused her firing. She took dancing lessons and joined the Traveling Burlesque Company. When the leading lady dropped out of an evening performance, Fanny was summoned in her stead. Unable to play the number straight, Brice turned it into a comic tour de force. It was then she decided to become a comedian.

The next year she was cast by producer Max Speigel for his musical, *College Girls*. She needed a number for her specialty turn and went to the young Irving Berlin who wrote "Sadie Salome" for her to perform with a Yiddish accent.

She soon drew the attention of Florenz Ziegfeld, who starred her in seven editions of his *Follies*—1910, 1911, 1916, 1917, 1920, 1921, 1923. She later appeared in two more *Ziegfeld Follies,* this time presented by the Shuberts—1934, 1936. Her other stage appearances were in *The Honeymoon Express* (1913); *Nobody Home* (1915); *Music Box Revue* (1924); *Fioretta* (1929); and two for her husband producer Billy Rose—*Sweet and Low* (1930), and *Crazy Quilt* (1931). Among the songs she introduced are "My Man;" "Rose of Washington Square;" "Second Hand Rose;" and "I Found a Million Dollar Baby in a Five and Ten Cent Store."

After leaving the theater, she had a successful career on radio, mostly as Baby Snooks. She made a few movies and recordings, but they didn't reflect her importance as a star. Fanny Brice died on May 29, 1951.

Her life provided the material for the Broadway musical *Funny Girl* (1964) which was later transferred to the screen. The sequel, *Funny Lady,* also became a hit movie. Barbra Streisand portrayed Fanny Brice in all three projects.

BRILL BUILDING · 1619 Broadway. Architect: Victor Bork Jr. Completed in 1930.

The Brill Building has long been the home of America's music publishers. The ten-story building at the corner of 49th Street and Broadway was the embodiment of Tin Pan Alley. Until the 1960s and a wave of mergers and corporate takeovers, the Brill Building was the home to most of the large music publishers and the ancillary businesses that help to fuel the phenomena known as the American popular song.

BROADHURST THEATER · 235 W. 44th Street. Architect: Herbert J. Krapp. Opening: September 27, 1917; *Misalliance.* The Broadhurst Theater was built by the Shuberts and playwright/producer George H. Broadhurst as a companion for the Plymouth Theater. They were located next to another two linked theaters, the Booth and the Shubert. The land for all four theaters had been leased from the Astor Estate to the Shuberts. Like the two earlier theaters, the Broadhurst and Plymouth had a pedestrian alley adjacent to their side exits. The alley, now closed off, was parallel to the more famous Shubert Alley.

The 1,155-seat theater has been among the most popular Broadway theaters, housing major hits in almost every decade since its opening. It opened with William Faversham's production of George Bernard Shaw's *Misalliance* (1917).

The Broadhurst was equally suitable for musicals. The first hit musical was the Nora Bayes vehicle, *Ladies First* (1918). Rachel Crothers' *39 East* (1919) starred Alison Skipworth. *Smilin' Through* (1919), later a successful movie, starred Jane Cowl, who coauthored the play with Allan Langdon Martin.

During the 1920s, there were many hits at the theater, including George S. Kaufman and Marc Connelly's *Beggar on Horseback* (1924); Michael Arlen's *The Green Hat* (1925), starring Katharine Cornell as the bride whose husband commits suicide on their wedding night; *Hold Everything* (1928); Jed Harris' production of *Broadway* (1926); and *June Moon* (1929). Beginning in 1929, the Shuberts assumed full control of the theater.

More hits came the theater's way including Ben Hecht and Charles MacArthur's screwball comedy *Twentieth Century* (1932); *The Petrified Forest* (1935) featuring Leslie Howard and Humphrey Bogart; and Helen Hayes in an astounding performance *Victoria Regina* (1935).

The 1940s were marked by a series of now forgotten musicals, including *Boys and Girls Together* (1940) with Bert Lahr, *High Kickers* (1941) with George Jessel and Sophie Tucker; and *Early to Bed* (1943) with an exceptional Fats Waller score. Helen Hayes starred in Anita Loos' comedy *Happy Birthday* (1946), one of the few nonmusicals produced by Rodgers and Hammerstein.

The 1950s were a decade of great successes at the Broadhurst. The revival of Rodgers and Hart's sardonic musical *Pal Joey* (1951) which played longer than the original production; Rosalind Russell as *Auntie Mame* (1956); *The World of Suzie Wong* (1958); and the Pulitzer Prize-winning musical *Fiorello!* (1959).

Successes continued in the 1960s with Tommy Steele in *Half a Sixpence* (1965); Woody Allen's comedy *Play It Again, Sam* (1969); and *Twigs* (1971) by George Furth.

A huge hit (for a while it was the longest running musical in Broadway history) was *Grease*. It originated off-Broadway and moved to the Broadhurst on June 7, 1972. After skipping around to other theaters, it eventually tallied 3,388 performances. Neil Simon's *The Sunshine Boys* (1972) followed. *Godspell,* another long running off-Broadway musical, briefly moved to the Broadhurst. Bob Fosse's *Dancin'* (1973) was another hit at the popular theater. During the 1980s, the theater hosted another smash, Peter Shaffer's *Amadeus* (1980) with Ian McKellen and Tim Curry in the leads.

Following 1983's *The Tap Dance Kid*, came a revival of Arthur Miller's *Death of a Salesman* (1984) with Dustin Hoffman as Willy Loman. The female version of Neil Simon's *The Odd Couple* with Sally Struthers and Rita Moreno occupied the Broadhurst stage in 1985.

The remarkable Trevor Nunn production of the Royal Shakespeare Company's adaptation of Dickens' *Nicholas Nickleby* (1986) starred Roger Rees as the title character and became a true Broadway event, spanning two evenings in the theater.

Neil Simon's Brighton Beach trilogy continued with *Broadway Bound* (1986) which ran for two years. Andrew Lloyd Webber's *Aspects of Love* (1990) was a failure becoming, at the time, the biggest money-loser in Broadway history. This dubious distinction has since been surpassed many times. A number of flops followed until Kander and Ebb's musical, *The Kiss of the Spider Woman* (1992) with Chita Rivera, Brent Carver, and Anthony Crivello in the leads. Stephen Sondheim and George Furth made a rare diversion into straight plays with their fiendishly derived *Getting Away with Murder* (1996). An ill-fated, ill-conceived revival of *Once Upon a Mattress* (1996) starring the ill-suited Sarah Jessica Parker was a quick and deserved failure.

Choreographer Bob Fosse received his own tribute revue with the aptly named *Fosse* (1999), inspired by the success of *Jerome Robbins' Broadway*. Though not as artistically successful, the show did please audiences into the next decade. Sondheim returned to the Broadhurst stage with a revival of *Into the Woods* (2002). The almost-legendary flop musical, *Urban Cowboy* followed in 2003. *Never Gonna Dance*, an Astaire/Rogers-inspired show was also a flop that same year. Billy Crystal's one-person memoir *700 Sundays* was a smash hit in 2004. On the opposite side of the success spectrum was *Lennon* (2005), a mistaken biography of John Lennon that pleased no one. From England came *The History Boys* (2006) for a limited engagement. Following it was the triumphant (?) return to Broadway of *Les Miserables*.

The Broadhurst is one of Broadway's most successful theaters. Although the shows it houses are not always hits, the theater is usually booked and always popular with producers and audiences alike.

BROADWAY THEATRE · 1681 Broadway. Architect: Eugene DeRosa. Opening: As the Colony motion picture theater December 25,

1924. As legitimate theater December 8, 1930; *The New Yorkers*. Vaudeville theater owner B. S. Moss opened Universal's Colony Theater as a premier motion picture house on Christmas Day, 1924 with a showing of the Douglas Fairbanks silent film, *The Thief of Bagdad*.

Five years later, after the introduction of sound pictures, the theater adapted a legitimate policy. Its name was changed to the B. S. Moss' Broadway Theatre with the opening performance of its first show, Cole Porter's *The New Yorkers* (1930). There was a previous Broadway Theatre at Broadway and 41st Street, but that theater was razed in 1929.

The 1,765-seat theater was suited only for large musicals. It was slightly renamed to Earl Carroll's Broadway Theatre with the opening of his *Vanities* (1932). Later that year, the theater began a vaudeville policy, but it too failed. Another unsuccessful musical, *The O'Flynn* (1934) opened at the theater and quickly closed and the theater's name reverted to B. S. Moss' Broadway Theatre on October 12, 1935, when it again showed films. The name was changed yet again to the Cine Roma on February 25, 1937, with the showing of *Lealta Di Donna*. The name was changed for the last time to simply Broadway on November 13, 1940, when Walt Disney's cartoon feature *Fantasia* opened.

Fantasia was not a success for Disney or the theater, and again the Broadway housed live theater. A number of musicals that had opened at other houses moved to the Broadway to finish their runs. The first musical to originate at the theater under the new policy was Irving Berlin's *This Is the Army*, which opened, significantly on July 4, 1942. Also in the '40s, came *Carmen Jones* (1943), *Beggar's Holiday* (1946) with a score by Duke Ellington and John Latouche.

During the 1950s, a series of unsuccessful productions were staged at the Broadway until Sammy Davis Jr. held forth in *Mr. Wonderful* (1956). *Gypsy* (1959; 702 performances) gave Ethel Merman the greatest role of her career singing brilliant Jule Styne and Stephen Sondheim standards.

The 1960s were lean years for Broadway and for the Broadway Theatre. It was treated to an ill-conceived remodeling that removed most of its detailing and character.

Merman returned to the theater in its next genuine hit, the 1966 revival of *Annie Get Your Gun*. The revival moved to the Broadway from Lincoln Center. Next came *The Happy Time* (1968) with a fine John Kander and Fred Ebb score.

Director Harold Prince brought his reinterpretation of the musical, *Candide* (1974) to the Broadway. Another revival, a black version of *Guys and Dolls,* was less successful two years later. The seventies closed with Harold Prince directing Patti LuPone in the Andrew Lloyd Webber and Tim Rice musical *Evita* (1979).

The Broadway had another huge hit with *Les Miserables* (1987) but after it moved to the Imperial Theatre the theater was surrounded by a remarkably soulless thirty-five-story skyscraper designed by Fox & Fowle covered in polished granite, which is cantilevered over the auditorium. Broadwayites commended the developers for sparing the historic theater from destruction.

Cameron Mackintosh, one of the most successful of London's producers followed his production of *Les Miserables* with another smash hit, *Miss Saigon* (1991). That show ran until 1997. It was followed by a series of negligible entertainments until Baz Luhrmann's *La Boheme* (2002). Andrew Lloyd Webber produced *Bombay Dreams* (2004) which was colorful but not a hit. Chat show host Oprah Winfrey was one of the producers of the Broadway musical *The Color Purple* (2005).

BROOKS ATKINSON THEATER · 256
W. 47th Street. Architect: Herbert J. Krapp. Opening: February 15, 1926; *The Night Duel*. The Brooks Atkinson Theater was originally owned by the Chanin Brothers, who named it after actor Richard Mansfield. The Mansfield was the third theater built by the Chanins, but they lost them all in the Depression. The 999-seat house proved perfect for intimate dramas and small revues. In its early years,

when production costs were lower and musicals did not have to occupy huge barn like theaters, some book shows held forth from the Mansfield's stage.

The Mansfield had its first hit with a now forgotten drama, *The Ladder* (1926). Antoinette Perry, for whom the Tony Awards are named, made her second appearance at the Mansfield in this show. Despite negative reviews, millionaire Edgar B. Davis liked the show and poured over $500,000 into it to keep it running.

With *The Ladder,* the theater's only success in its first years, and unprofitable at that, the Chain's booking policy was clearly amiss. Lew Fields took over booking the house and renamed it Lew Fields' Mansfield Theater. He opened his new theater on October 26, 1928, with Rodgers and Hart's *Present Arms* (1928) and followed it with their musical *Chee-Chee* (1928).

Fields next produced and starred in the aptly titled *Hello Daddy!* (1928). He hired his children Herbert and Dorothy to supply the book and lyrics respectively. Jimmy McHugh wrote the music.

The theater was then renamed the Mansfield Theater, and here *Indiscretion,* a failure, opened on March 4, 1929. The theater's next show, *The Green Pastures* (1930), was Marc Connelly's adaptation of Roark Bradford's *Ol' Man Adam an' His Chillun,* a retelling of Old Testament stories. Connelly won the Pulitzer Prize for his efforts.

When the Chanins lost the theater in 1933 the Mansfield went dark. From March to December of 1932, there were no bookings at the theater. The Depression continued to take its toll, and the theater did not house a hit until *Behind Red Lights* (1937), a play about prostitution on the fashionable East Side of Manhattan.

The 1940s saw the theater's fortunes pick up. A revue, *Meet the People* (1940), introduced Nanette Fabray to Broadway audiences. *Anna Lucasta* (1944) arrived direct from the American Negro Theater in Harlem. Actress Ruth Gordon 's autobiographical play, *Years Ago* (1946) starred Bethel Leslie.

After a series of failures, the Mansfield spent the 1950s as a television theater. On September 12, 1960, owner Michael Myerberg, who had bought the theater in 1945, renovated the auditorium and renamed the theater after critic Brooks Atkinson. The opening show was a lively musical revue *Vintage '60.*

The first hit under the theater's new name was also Neil Simon's Broadway debut. *Come Blow Your Horn* opened on February 22, 1961. Its success of *Come Blow Your Horn* proved to be the theater's only long-running hit in the sixties forcing Meyerberg to take the Nederlanders as partners in 1967.

The first hit in the decade was Peter Nichols' brilliant *A Day in the Death of Joe Egg* (1968).

The first hit of the 1970s was Julian Barry's biographical play, *Lenny* (1971). Upon Myerberg's death in 1974, the Nederlanders purchased his share in the theater.

The theater's next success was the two-character comedy *Same Time, Next Year* (1975). There would not be another hit at the Brooks Atkinson until *Noises Off* (1983), Michael Frayn's knockabout farce.

Comedian Jackie Mason in his one-man show, *The World According to Me,* scored a surprise hit in 1986.

The next success at the theater didn't come until 1999 with a production of *The Iceman Cometh* with Kevin Spacey in the leading role. *Jane Eyre* (2000), a musical transfer from Canada was a deserved flop. *Jackie Mason's Laughing Room Only* (2003) continued his yearly forays onto the Great White Way. The most recent success at the theater featured Nathan Lane and Matthew Broderick in a revival of Neil Simon's play *The Odd Couple* (2005).

BROWN, LEW · See DESYLVA, BROWN AND HENDERSON.

BRYANT THEATER · See APOLLO THEATRE.

C

CADILLAC WINTER GARDEN THEATRE
· See WINTER GARDEN THEATRE.

CAPITOL THEATER · 1645 Broadway,
southwest corner of 51st Street. Architect:
Thomas Lamb. Opening: October 24, 1919.
The Capitol Theater was, at the time of its
construction, the largest theater in New York.
The movie palace was another step in the career
of S. L. ("Roxy") Rothafel, the leading manager
of Broadway's motion picture theaters.

Before it became the city's entertainment
hub, Times Square was an area comprised
mostly of shops catering to the carriage industry. As the motorcar gained popularity,
the stables and carriage factories evolved into
filling stations and garages. A livery stable, a
blacksmith shop, and a gas station occupied
the site of the Capitol Theater. The land was
owned by the Jacob Wendell estate, which was
bound by somewhat Puritanical restrictions.
The terms of the lease forbade the manufacture
of corsets or cosmetics.

Builder Messmore Kendell recognized the
importance of the underdeveloped site and
leased it from the Wendell estate. He hired
Thomas Lamb, a great theater architect who
had already designed the Rialto, and Rivoli
theaters. Lamb's favorite architectural style was
that of the Adam brothers. He used that and
the Empire style for the auditorium, which sat
5,300 patrons.

Sherry's Restaurant, formerly on Fifth
Avenue, was the source of three enormous
rock-crystal chandeliers. Artist William Cotton
painted beautiful murals for the auditorium
walls.

Because the theater was built during World
War I, construction materials, especially steel,
were in short supply. Luckily, the city was con-
structing the IRT subway system northward
from Times Square at the time. As the tunnels
were completed, their trusses were sold to Kendall for use in the building of the Capitol.

When completed, the building was hailed
as a masterpiece. Kendall had his own apartment at the top of the six-story building. In the
apartment, Kendall could see the action on the
stage by peering through a secret window. From
Kendall's window above the balcony level the
stage was almost a full city block away.

The stage area was the domain of Major
Edward Bowes, who had an apartment suite
below Kendall's. He was later known for his
Amateur Hour radio show. Bowes was a part
owner of the Cort Theater and had invested
heavily in San Francisco real estate. However,
Bowes had a hard time developing a viable
entertainment policy for the Capitol.

The theater was beset with problems from
the beginning. Just before the opening, the
theater's bricklayers decided to go on strike.
Left with a huge hole in the rear stage wall after
the workers broke off negotiations, Kendall was
forced to undertake drastic action. He called a
meeting of the board and when they were assembled he passed out aprons and trowels. The
board members, realizing their investment was
at stake, pitched in and mended the hole.

The opening was further postponed because
the lobby boasted mahogany paneling. The
New York City Building Department was
concerned that the theater wasn't fireproofed.
They went over the entire building with blow-
torches, torching the mahogany to check the
theater's safety.

The opening night's program consisted of
a live stage show, which preceded the feature

film. The stage show was titled *Demi-Tasse*. In the cast were Paul Frawley and Mae West. Arthur Pryor's band played for the opening night revels. The evening began with an overture by the Capitol Symphony, a short color film, a travelogue, another short subject that starred a pack of talented dogs, a film of director Ned Wayburn rehearsing the evening's show and finally the revue proper.

About the only notable aspect of the revue was a song written by George Gershwin and Irving Caesar. The song was "Swanee," and, surprisingly, it received little attention. Gershwin's other contribution, "Come to the Moon" (written with Ned Wayburn and Lou Paley) also went unnoticed, despite its elaborate setting. By the time the opening film, *His Majesty, the American* with Douglas Fairbanks, hit the screen the battle was lost.

The show received lukewarm to negative reviews. Mae West developed a sudden case of tonsillitis after reviewers carped at her "rude way of singing." Pryor's band was also dismissed.

Although changes were made in the show, they didn't halt the theater's troubles. On October 28, 1919, four days after the grand opening, Prohibition went into effect. And at the beginning of the next week's bill, the ushers went on strike demanding the right to accept tips.

The negative publicity surrounding the Capitol kept audiences away in droves. The operation was losing Kendall thousands of dollars a week, money he could ill afford to lose. Kendall sold the theater to a shady character named F. J. Godsol. Godsol was owner of Goldwyn Pictures. He was also briefly jailed for selling mules to the French during World War I. Unfortunately, the French thought they had bought horses.

Godsol's first problem was what to do with Major Bowes. He decided to make the showman a vice president of Goldwyn Pictures at $25,000 a year. As managing director of the Capitol, Bowes received a similar salary. Bowes' new responsibilities at Goldwyn kept him busy, so he wasn't too upset when Godsol hired S. L. Rothafel to spruce up the theater's operation.

June 4, 1920, was the date set for the reopening of the Capitol. Roxy was busy whipping together a new gala show in the Roxy tradition. When directing the show, Roxy sat in the middle of the auditorium and shouted at the action on stage through a megaphone. The Bell Telephone Corporation's scientists were working on a new idea—the public address system. Roxy, always ready for a new invention, gladly agreed to try their experimental microphones and speaker systems.

The public address system was a huge success, saving Roxy his voice and making it unnecessary for him to run constantly from audience to stage and back. Roxy like the idea so much that he arranged for the entire theater to be wired. Now, when someone wanted to call the performers in their dressing rooms, they simply paged them over the system.

At the same time, radio station WEAF was begun in Manhattan. This early, experimental radio station even boasted sponsors like Macy's and Gimbel's. WEAF wasn't content to simply broadcast from their studio. They began taking their microphones around New York and presenting live remote broadcasts. On November 11, 1922, they broadcast for the first time the Metropolitan Opera's production of *Aida* from the Kingsbridge Armory in the Bronx.

Ironically, Major Bowes was against radio for the same reason that the movies were against pay television in the fifties. He figured that people wouldn't pay for their entertainment in theaters if it was coming into their homes for free. But Roxy saw the possibilities of the new medium and agreed to allow a broadcast from the Capitol.

On November 19, 1922, the Grand Orchestra, led by Erno Rapee, struck up "Ein Heldenleben" by Richard Strauss on the Capitol stage. It was the first time any of Strauss' music had been performed in the United States. Throughout New York and as far as WEAF's powerful signal would reach, audiences listened to the proceedings at the Capitol. Roxy was at a microphone in the wings explaining the stage action and what it meant to be in the Capitol amid all the splendor.

Of course, this made the listeners feel they were missing the action and led them to the Capitol to see for themselves the elaborate stage shows and the motion pictures. The Capitol shows became so successful that it was decided to repeat the program weekly on Sunday evenings. WEAF was also part of a small network, which meant its broadcasts were also carried in Providence, Rhode Island, and Washington, D.C.

Every Sunday, audiences heard Roxy's voice over the airwaves opening his show with the words, "Hello, everybody. This is Roxy speaking." And every show ended with Roxy signing off with the familiar words, "Good night… pleasant dreams… God bless you." Supporting Roxy, was his "gang," which included soprano Florence Mulholland, basso profundo "Daddy" Jim Coombs, and audience favorite Beatrice Belkin. The concertmaster of the Capitol Grand Orchestra was the young Eugene Ormandy.

As time went on, the radio's audience grew. The NBC Blue Network throughout the country carried the Capitol shows starring Roxy. Now the Capitol was the best-known theater in America, and Roxy was equally famous as America's greatest showman.

Bowes wasn't happy with Roxy's success and grew increasingly miserable when people claimed they didn't eve know he was associated with the Capitol. Bowes became more and more intolerant of the situation and antagonistic towards Roxy. The situation was getting worse, and clearly, something had to happen to resolve the problem. The solution came not within the Capitol Building but from without. Roxy was hired to oversee a new theater, one that would be the greatest in the world and would also, incidentally, be named after him.

On July 26, 1925, Major Bowes took over the operation of the Capitol radio show and began his own career on the air. Bowes continued to present the Capitol in classy terms. He created "The Capitol Family" and continued on the NBC Blue Network.

By now, the Capitol was a member of the Loews' chain. The Loews owned a huge chain of theaters and needed shows to fill their stages. The Capitol became the flagship of the Loew's Circuit. Louis K. Sidney, who took a more egalitarian approach to the Capitol's shows, was brought in to head the work. David Mendoza and his associate, Eugene Ormandy, headed the Capitol Grand Orchestra. Walter Roesner and his Capitolians augmented it.

The entire stage area was overhauled including the addition of a lift in the orchestra pit. The Capitol was now well suited to stand up to the new Roxy Theater.

Sidney changed the Capitol's shows further by introducing variety acts. One program in October 1927 featured a 55-member chorus and 40 ballet dancers in a show entitled, *The Spirit of Syncopation.*

The Capitol stage policy lasted longer than that of many of its rivals. Although in 1932 the theater claimed that 100,000 paying customers visited the theater weekly, the Depression finally took its toll and in 1935 an "all the show on the screen" policy was inaugurated.

The Capitol continued as just another movie palace, albeit a spectacular one, into the sixties. With the advent of television (a word banned on the Capitol's stage) and the flight to the suburbs, the Capitol's fortunes dwindled. The land was soon more valuable than the theater. Already, the lobby had been renovated and an escalator ran up the once glorious marble staircase.

The Capitol was razed in the mid-sixties to make way for an office block.

CARROLL, EARL (1893–1948) · Earl Carroll was one of the greatest producers of extravagant musical revues in the first three decades of the century. The others were Florenz Ziegfeld and George White. Carroll's revues stressed the female form and celebrated it with bawdy good humor. His shows were the closest to the burlesque tradition, and, in fact, many of his stars first achieved fame in burlesque. These included Milton Berle, Joe Cook, Sophie Tucker, Jimmy Savo, as well as Ted Healy, Jessie Matthews, W. C. Fields, Jack Benny, Helen Broderick, and Patsy Kelly.

Carroll was a staff writer for a music publisher from 1912 to 1917. He wrote lyrics and music for a succession of Broadway shows, although none of his songs are played today. Among the shows he wrote for are *Pretty Mrs. Smith,* written with Alfred G. Robyn and Henry James (1914); *So Long Letty* (1916); *The Love Mill* (1916); and two editions of the *Earl Carroll Vanities* in 1923 and 1924.

The *Vanities* were the naughtiest of the great revues. Where Ziegfeld would make sure his girls were the best dressed showgirls, Carroll would make sure that girls he hired were the best undressed. The *Vanities* featured forgettable songs and sketches and mostly second-rate stars. The main attraction was always the girls, reflecting the producer's main interest—sex. Not everyone was amused. The *Brooklyn Eagle* wrote that "Carroll's showmanship consisted in selling gutter humor and naked female flesh to morons."

Carroll desired to be a producer and director, not because he felt he could contribute something to the art, but so he could capitalize on his position to meet girls. His affairs made headlines, thereby boosting ticket sales.

If anything rivaled Carroll's obsession with sex, it was his love of aviation. Carroll was a flyer during World War I and was sent on many reconnaissance missions in France. After the war, he established a flying school in China. In 1925, Carroll became the first person to land a plane in Central Park. He received permission for the publicity stunt because he was carrying Santa Claus, who would distribute presents to children waiting in the Sheep Meadow. Joe Cook grudgingly acted as Santa Claus.

Unfortunately the weather was atrocious, with visibility next to zero and sleet beginning to fall. When Carroll attempted to land, he caught a wing of the plane on a tree. Much to the delight of the children the plane went into a ground loop before coming to rest. Carroll and Cook were unhurt but the plane was demolished.

The Depression brought bankruptcy and hard times to Broadway. Carroll was no exception, and he left New York to open the Earl Carroll Restaurant in Hollywood in December 1938. Carroll died in a plane crash on June 17, 1948. When the wreckage was located on Mt. Carmel, Pennsylvania, it was discovered that Carroll, his companion Beryl Wallace, and the crew had died before the plane hit the ground. Carbon dioxide had escaped from the fire extinguishers, killing the passengers.

In an interview with *Family Circle Magazine* entitled "Your Last Day on Earth," Carroll reflected on his life. "It has been my lifework to stage and produce shows built around beautiful girls. To many people this work of mine may seem insignificant; I deal in beauty, it's true. But we are all starved and hungry for beauty; there is too little of it in the world. A hundred years from now I hope the parade of young American girls will still be walking under the sign of my theater... which reads: 'THROUGH THESE PORTALS PASS THE MOST BEAUTIFUL GIRLS IN THE WORLD'."

CASA MANANA · See EARL CARROLL THEATRE.

CASINO DE PARIS · See NEW YORKER THEATER.

CASINO THEATRE · (1) Broadway and 39th Street. Architects: Francis Kimball and Thomas Wisedell. Opening: October 21, 1882; *The Queen's Lace Handkerchief.* The Casino, which stood at the southeast corner of Broadway and 39th Street, was one of the best-loved 19th century houses until it was demolished in 1930. The Moorish-style theater opened on a stormy night with a leaky roof and unfinished auditorium. But it soon recovered from its dismal premiere. Producer Rudolph Aronson presented his light opera company at the theater for its first years. In 1890, he added New York's first roof garden on top of the Casino. Productions in the 1,300-seat auditorium included early operettas and two successful shows, *Nell Gwynn* and *Erminie.*

The theater's most famous show was *Florodora,* which opened November 10, 1900, with a spectacular line of chorus girls. The original

Florodora Sextette was comprised of Daisy Greene, Marjorie Relyea, Vaughn Texsmith, Margaret Walker, Agnes Wayburn, and Marie L. Wilson. The Sextette elevated the chorus girl into star status. The chorus became an attraction in its own right. Florenz Ziegfeld took the concept of the Florodora Sextette and improved on it. The show ran for over five hundred performances, one of the longest runs of the early nineteen hundreds.

Following *Florodora's* run in 1902, the theater was involved in a lawsuit concerning its legal ownership. Lee Shubert bought the theater from the Bixby family, who owned it as an investment. The Bixbys had leased it to the Sire brothers, who in turn leased it to Charles Lederer. The affair started when Lee Shubert bought out Lederer's sublease. Lederer was happy to sell, because he was remiss in paying his rent and was about to be kicked out of the theater anyway. Shubert discovered that all the subleases were up at the same time and avoided the Sires by going to the Bixbys.

A Chinese Honeymoon (1902) was the Shuberts' first big hit in New York and established their reputation. Then came a succession of moderate hits, *The Runaways* (1903); *Winsome Winnie* (1903); *Lady Teazle* (1904); and *The Earl and the Girl* (1905).

The remainder of the century's first decade saw a succession of failures at the Casino. *The Social Whirl, The Blue Moon, The Gay White Way, Nearly a Hero, The Mimic World, Marcelle, Mr. Hamlet of Broadway, Havana,* and *The Girl and the Wizard* were mostly imports of English operettas with some American songs interpolated.

The Shuberts continued to keep the theater occupied with many other modest successes as well as downright flops. *The Mikado,* which had premiered at the Madison Square Roof Garden in 1902, played the Casino three times, in 1910, 1912 and 1913. None of the engagements was successful. *Up and Down Broadway* (1910) contained the hit song "Chinatown, My Chinatown" by Jean Schwartz and William Jerome. *The Blue Paradise* (1913) broke the long succession of failures with its score

by Sigmund Romberg, Edmund Eysler, and Herbert Reynolds. The next hit at the Casino wasn't until 1922 with the production *Sally, Irene and Mary.*

The theater stayed dark for most of its last decade. In 1930, the Depression as well as the constant move uptown of the theater district sealed its fate and the Casino was torn down.

CASINO THEATER · (2) See EARL CARROLL THEATRE.

CENTRAL THEATER · See MOVIELAND.

CENTURY THEATER · (1) 235 W. 46th Street, basement of the Paramount Hotel. Designer: Albert Johnson. Opening: Billy Rose's Diamond Horseshoe 1938. The Century Theater was known as Billy Rose's Diamond Horseshoe for most of its life. Impresario Billy Rose brought his show to the new theater from the Pioneer Palace of the Fort Worth Fair in 1938. Albert Johnson designed the theater with a patriotic color scheme—red, white and blue. The Diamond Horseshoe initially recreated an evening in the Gay Nineties as seen through the eyes of Lillian Russell and Diamond Jim Brady, and Rose cast it with a number of former stars, including operatic star Fritzi Scheff, minstrel Eddie Leonard, the shimmy dancer Gilda Gray, show girl Ann Pennington and a spry seventy-year-old who performed handsprings—Emma Francis. Also appearing were Joe Howard, composer of "I Wonder Who's Kissing Her Now," early talkie star Charles King, and Harry Armstrong, the man who wrote "Sweet Adeline."

There was also a group of leggy chorines featuring the famous six-foot-two Stuttering Sam. The four Rosebud girls joined her and the other beautiful chorus girls. These women, nearly as big around as they were tall, taken together weighed almost 1,200 pounds.

About half way through the show's twelve-year run, Rose hired Nicky Blair as manager. Blair ran other nightclubs in his career, including the Paradise, the House of (Helen) Morgan, and Texas Guinan's club. Blair later opened the Carnival across the street from Madison Square Garden.

When the Diamond Horseshoe finally closed in 1951, the theater became the Mayfair. It was later renamed the Staircase and then again the Mayfair. Finally, it became the Century. Among the shows that played the Century were *On Golden Pond, Lone Star and Private Wars, Are You Now or Have You Ever Been...* and *Banjo Dancing.*

In the mid-1980s, the theater was devoted to the Chaiken CPA Review, a course designed to help students pass the test enabling them to become Certified Public Accountants. On November 17, 1987, the New York City Landmarks Preservation Commission denied landmark status for the theater's interior in a move that puzzled preservationists.

In January 1988, the theater was converted back to its nightclub origins. The one-time owners of Studio 54 announced that they would open the space as New York's newest club but it was not to be and the space remained dark.

CENTURY THEATER · (2) See JOLSON'S 59TH STREET THEATER.

CHANIN'S 46TH STREET THEATER · See 46TH STREET THEATRE.

CHARLES HOPKINS THEATER · 153 W. 49th Street. Architects: Murphy and Dana. Opening: November 10, 1914; *The Marriage of Columbine.* Producer Charles Hopkins built the Punch and Judy Theatre on a small parcel of land directly off Times Square in 1914. Like the Bijou, which followed it three years later, the Punch and Judy was an intimate house built for small-cast, single-set plays with a decidedly experimental bent. The interior was modeled after the Shakespearian era Blackfriars Theatre in London. The theater was unique in one respect when it was time for the show to begin, a medieval style musician would play a trumpet fanfare from the roof of the building.

The house never achieved any great success, mainly because its small size made profits difficult for even the biggest hits. Unfortunately, producers weren't interested in the limited grosses of small theaters and instead opted for medium-sized houses for their productions.

As the Punch and Judy, the theater housed few hits. In 1921, it hosted *March Hares,* a transfer from the Bijou by the Shubert Brothers. The play, a romantic satire, only managed sixty performances between both houses. In 1926, in an attempt to change the theater's luck, Hopkins changed the name to the Charles Hopkins Theater. But the theater fared little better with its new name.

Productions included those on the level of *Devil in the Cheese* (1926), a "fantastic comedy" that starred Fredric March and Bela Lugosi. The next season, Hopkins presented the A. A. Milne play *The Ivory Door* (1927). Henry Hull, Louise Closser Hale, and Donald Meek starred in this medieval fantasy.

Hopkins was building a small following for what *Best Plays* editor Burns Mantle called "Charles Hopkins' funny little theater." Hopkins presented another A. A. Milne play on March 4, 1931. The play was entitled *Success* when first presented in England, but the title belied its fate on Broadway.

The Depression took its toll on all Broadway theaters, and even the Charles Hopkins with its low overhead couldn't escape. Milne, one of Hopkins' favorite writers, was presented again in the theater's last legitimate season. *They Don't Mean Any Harm* opened February 23, 1932, but played for only fifteen performances.

Hopkins' checkbook convinced him that the future of his theater was dim, and so in 1933, unlike many producers who couldn't accept the realities of Broadway in the Depression, Hopkins changed his theater to a movie policy.

In 1935, the theater's name was changed to the World Theater and in the 1960s presented X-rated films. One of its most successful engagements came in 1972 with the film *Deep Throat.* It was then made a member of the Embassy Theater chain, called the Embassy 49th

Street Theatre. It specialized in second run and children's fare. The theater was razed to make way for a new building in June 1987.

CIRCLE IN THE SQUARE THEATER

· 1633 Broadway on 50th Street. Architect: Allen Sayles. Opening: November 15, 1972; *Mourning Becomes Electra*. The Circle in the Square organization moved on November 15, 1972, to this new location in a new office building, which also houses the Gershwin Theater. As New York's premier classic theater group, Circle in the Square brought to Times Square exactly the sort of play that is usually abhorred by legitimate producers.

Under the artistic direction of Theodore Mann and with the expertise of Managing Director Paul Libin, Circle in the Square proved to be an important part of the Broadway theater scene. Its first full season included productions of *Medea* with Irene Papas; Siobhan McKenna in *Here Are Ladies;* a star-studded revival of Chekhov's *Uncle Vanya* with George C. Scott, Lillian Gish, Nicol Williamson, Julie Christie, and Barnard Hughes; Anne Jackson and Eli Wallach in *The Waltz of the Toreadors* and Eugene O'Neill's *The Iceman Cometh,* starring James Earl Jones.

As a not for profit theater, the group could afford to present the kinds of shows that would be impossible to produce under normal circumstances. Other notable productions include Jim Dale's athletic performance in *Scapino* in 1974, George C. Scott's staging of O'Neill's *All God's Chillun Got Wings* in 1975 and, later that season, an exemplary revival of O'Neill's *Ah, Wilderness!,* starring Geraldine Fitzgerald, as well as an incendiary production of *The Glass Menagerie* with Maureen Stapleton and Rip Torn.

In 1976, Richard Chamberlain and Dorothy McGuire starred in Tennessee Williams' *The Night of the Iguana.* The next year's highlight was a revival of Moliere's *Tartuffe* with John Wood, Tammy Grimes, and Mildred Dunnock.

New plays have also premiered at the theater, including *Spokesong* by Stewart Parker and *Loose Ends* by Michael Weller, both in 1979, and *Eminent Domain* by Percy Granger, starring Philip Bosco and Betty Miller. Musicals have been represented only twice and with mixed results. In 1975, Raul Julia starred in Frank Loesser's *Where's Charley?,* and Christopher Chadman and Joan Copeland were featured in a revival of Rodgers and Hart's *Pal Joey* the next year.

Other seasons have included productions of *Once in a Lifetime* with John Lithgow and Treat Williams (1978); *The Man Who Came to Dinner* with Ellis Rabb (1980); *Present Laughter,* starring George C. Scott (1982); *The Caine Mutiny Court Martial* with John Rubinstein, Michael Moriarty and William Atherton (1983); *Heartbreak House,* starring Rex Harrison and Amy Irving (1983); *Arms and the Man* (1985); *You Never Can Tell* with Philip Bosco, Uta Hagen, and Amanda Plummer (1986); and Tina Howe's *Coastal Disturbances* with Timothy Daly and Annette Bening (1987).

The theater is shaped as a long oval with the audience surrounding the stage in bleacher-style seating. The tongue-shaped stage has had its detractors, but for the most part it has worked out surprisingly well. The theater seats 648 patrons, slightly smaller than the smallest commercial houses. Because of its arena setting and steeply raked seating no one in the audience is ever more than ten rows from the stage.

The Circle in the Square's producing arm went bankrupt in the early nineties (it remained an eminent theater school). The theater was subsequently booked by a number of unsuccessful Broadway shows. An off-Broadway production of Stephen Sondheim's *Sweeney Todd* (1989) moved to the Circle in the Square but didn't make much of an impact. Better was an exciting production of an early Tennessee Williams play, *Not about Nightingales* (1999). The revival of the cult musical *The Rocky Horror Show* (2002) was well performed and produced. It was followed by *Metamorphoses* (2002), the unique brainchild of director Mary Zimmerman. William Finn wrote the score to *The 25th Annual Putnam County Spelling Bee* (2005), a transfer from the off-Broadway Second Stage theater company.

COHAN, GEORGE M. (1878–1942)

· George M. Cohan was known as "the man who owned Broadway." This actor, singer, dancer, producer, director, composer, lyricist, and soft touch became the embodiment of the song and dance man, the complete performer. Through the Warner Brothers picture *Yankee Doodle Dandy* (1942), new generations have discovered the legend of George M. Cohan.

Cohan was born on July 3, 1878. But he considered missing the anniversary of the independence of his country by only a few hours a technicality. As far as he was concerned, the Fourth of July was his natal day. He took that close call with fate and made a career out of it. His shows waved the flag harder than anyone else. Cohan wrote the most successful patriotic numbers of all time with the possible exception of Irving Berlin's "God Bless America." The best known of these was "You're a Grand Old Flag." He wrote the supreme war song, "Over There," and even starred as a president of the United States in musical comedy.

Soon after his birth in Providence, Rhode Island, Cohan joined his family's vaudeville team—The Four Cohans. George, father Jerry, mother Helen, and sister Josephine covered the country with their song-and-dance act. At the age of fifteen, George, not exactly a shrinking violet, began contributing skits and songs to the family's act. His ego, aggressive personality and unlimited energy made him continuously test himself and his fellow human beings. Nothing was ever good enough for George. He was a man of the theater, and he was determined to succeed in it as no man had ever succeeded before. As for his family, they would just have to keep up as best they could.

George made good on his first goal, Broadway, with his show *The Governor's Son* (1901), which opened at the Savoy Theater. His next outing, *Running for Office* (1903), also starred the Four Cohans.

Cohan took these failures and learned from

them. Already he was the only Broadway author, composer, and lyricist who worked in the native vernacular and whose shows weren't rehashings of the same formula operettas. Cohan was the only composer whose work was 100 percent American in style and tone. Not for Cohan were the staid drawing-room comedies imported from England. He translated his own brand of speed and exuberance to the stage and broke new ground by planting the seeds of American farce.

Though Cohan offstage was the gregarious, Irish upstart, his stage persona was more genteel and sophisticated. In fact, this character showed Americans that they need not be European to possess class and élan. His stage persona took the best of European sophistication and added to it the totally American qualities of enthusiasm and precocity.

For his next show, *Little Johnny Jones* (1904), Cohan again starred with his parents and wife, Ethel Levey, and he also wrote the book and composed the score. But for this outing, he added another job—director. He also began at the same time his lifelong friendship and collaboration with producer Sam H. Harris. It contained Cohan's first hit songs, "Life's a Funny Proposition After All," "The Yankee Doodle Boy," "I'm Mighty Glad I'm Living That's All" and, perhaps his most famous tune, "Give My Regards to Broadway." After a profitable hiatus on the road, *Little Johnny Jones* returned to Broadway for a run of almost four months.

Cohan's next Broadway venture, *Forty-Five Minutes from Broadway* (1906), contained more Cohan standards, "Mary's a Grand Old Name," "So Long, Mary," and "Forty-Five Minutes from Broadway." One month later, Cohan, his parents, his wife, and Truly Shattuck opened in *George Washington, Jr.* (1906). This show contained his first great patriotic hit, "You're a Grand Old Flag." The original title of the song, "You're a Grand Old Rag," was changed at the urgings of patriotic groups.

Cohan's attempts at playwriting were not quite as successful. His first was titled *Popularity* (1906). The next year, Cohan, never wanting to let a good idea go to waste, rewrote *Running for Office* as *The Honeymooners* (1907). With his next show, *The Talk of New York* (1907), Cohan officially became the co-producer with Sam H. Harris. The hit Cohan songs included "When We Are M-A Double R-I-E-D," "When a Fellow's on the Level with a Girl That's on the Square," and "Under Any Old Flag at All."

Fifty Miles From Boston (1908) contained the great Cohan hit, "Harrigan." Perhaps he was saving his energy for his next show, which only opened two months later. That was *The Yankee Prince* (1908), a title that seemed to describe Cohan himself. In fact, all of Cohan's shows were semi autobiographical in spirit if not fact. *The Yankee Prince's* run wasn't due to the score or its hits (there were none), but rather because for the first time since *Running for Office* in 1903 the Four Cohans were back together again on Broadway. Cohan premiered a third show in 1908, *The American Idea* (1908).

Broadway was discovering the revue at the end of the first decade of the century. *The Cohan and Harris Minstrels* (1909) was among the first revues seen on Broadway. Cohan and Harris next presented a straight play version of Winchell Smith's *The Fortune Hunter* (1909), which starred John Barrymore. This first non-Cohan production presented by the team turned into a great success.

Cohan's next success was again autobiographical in title. *The Man Who Owns Broadway* (1909) opened nearly a year after *The American Idea*. Cohan's next offering was a straight play, *Get-Rich-Quick Wallingford* (1910). Cohan and Harris' next straight offering, *The Aviator* (1910) by James Montgomery, was later adapted into the musical *Going Up* and presented to great success by Cohan and Harris.

A year later, the next Cohan musical opened, *The Little Millionaire* (1911). Cohan, his parents, and Donald Crisp, kept the show running for the longest run of his career. Exactly a month later, he co-produced the musical *The Red Widow* (1911). In between,

Cohan and Harris presented another play by Winchell Smith, *The Only Son* (1911). The star of *The Only Son,* Wallace Eddinger, would have better luck in another Cohan and Harris production, the straight play *Officer 666* (1912) by Augustin MacHugh.

Two months later, Cohan presented and starred in a revival of his 1906 hit *Forty-Five Minutes from Broadway.* Cohan's next Broadway outing was as author of the straight play, *Broadway Jones* (1912), starring Cohan and his parents.

Four more straight plays followed—J. B. Fagan's *Hawthorne of the U.S.A.* (1912) with Douglas Fairbanks in the lead; *Stop Thief* (1912); Edgar Selwyn's *Nearly Married* (1913); and finally Cohan's own *Seven Keys to Baldpate* (1913), which starred Wallace Eddinger.

Cohan and Harris next offered the musical *The Beauty Shop* (1914). Roi Cooper Magrue and Walter Hackett's play *It Pays to Advertise* (1914) ran under Cohan and Harris' auspices. Cohan's next play, *The Miracle Man,* opened thirteen days later.

Hello, Broadway! (1914) was the first show to have an original Cohan score since *The Little Millionaire* more than three years earlier. Fred Ballard's comedy, *Young America* (1915) starred Otto Kruger and Peggy Wood. Cohan collaborated with Max Marcin on *The House of Glass* (1915). Cohan alone wrote *Hit-the-Trail Holliday* (1915), which opened only twelve days later with Fred Niblo headlining.

Cohan again contributed a new score to Broadway, this time for *The Cohan Revue of 1916* (1916). More straight plays followed: *The Intruder* (1916) by Cyril Harcourt; *Captain Kidd, Jr.* (1916) by Rida Johnson Young; *The Willow Tree* (1917), an English import by J. H. Benrimo and Harrison Rhodes; *A Tailor-Made Man* (1917) by Harry James Smith; and another import, *The King* (1917) by G. A. Caillavet, Robert de Flers, and Emmanuel Arene.

Cohan and Harris then presented Louis Hirsch's musical *Going Up* (1917). This was followed by the *Cohan Revue of 1918* (1917). Its author called it "a hit-and-run play batted out by George M. Cohan." The young Irving Berlin contributed half the score to the show. Seven plays followed, the most notable being *Three Faces East* (1918) by Anthony Paul Kelly and Cohan's *A Prince There Was* (1918) in which he starred.

Cohan's next musical was *The Royal Vagabond* (1919). Cohan was responsible for doctoring this European operetta while it was still on the road. He called it a "Cohanized Opera Comique."

During the run of *The Royal Vagabond* came the actors' strike of 1919. Cohan was the most vocal of the managers who fought the actors. He considered the strike a personal affront and refused to join Actors' Equity, the new union, for the remainder of his career. Cohan's immovable stance led to a break with his longtime friend and producing partner, Sam Harris. The strike was symbolic to Cohan of the increasingly less freewheeling atmosphere of Broadway. He grew more and more embittered and longed for the happier days when shows could be mounted with limited budgets and limitless enthusiasm. Cohan viewed the theater as a community, especially since his earliest memories were of trouping with his family. He couldn't understand why a strike was necessary at all—why "the show must go on" wasn't the most important credo to everyone in the theater. Cohan and Harris' last co-production for seventeen years was *The Acquittal* (1920) by Rita Weiman and Cohan.

Cohan was barred from performing since he refused to join Actors' Equity but he continued his producing activities. His play *The Tavern* (1920) is still produced around the country. Following a production of Augustin MacHugh's *The Meanest Man in the World* (1920), Cohan produced and co-directed the musical comedy *Mary* (1920). His next success was a production of *The O'Brien Girl* (1921), a musical. He then produced *So This Is London* (1922) by Arthur Goodrich.

Cohan's next musical, for which he supplied his usual book, music and lyrics, was *Little Nellie Kelly* (1922), which he also produced and directed. Nellie was a name Cohan always liked

since it was his mother's nickname. Cohan's score again contained some popular successes including, "You Remind Me of My Mother" and "Nellie Kelly, I Love You." *Little Nellie Kelly* proved to be Cohan's biggest hit.

Cohan's next musical was *The Rise of Rosie O'Reilly* (1923). His next three productions were of his own plays, *The Song and Dance Man* (1923); *American Born* (1925); and *The Home Towners* (1926). None of these plays ran longer than 96 performances. Cohan's friends and associates banded together to force Actors' Equity to give him special dispensation to appear on Broadway; he appeared in *The Song and Dance Man* and *American Born*.

He then produced Margaret Vernon's play *Yellow* (1926), which starred a young Spencer Tracy, a Cohan discovery. Tracy turned up a year later in Cohan's next production, *The Baby Cyclone* (1927). Cohan himself appeared in his play *The Merry Malones* (1927), and although he produced the show he did not direct it. Four more straight play productions followed, including his own *Whispering Friends* (1928).

The last show for which he would author the book and score was *Billie* (1928). For his last Broadway score, Cohan contributed a big hit, the title song. Nine more straight play productions (including three revivals) followed, but they were all failures. Cohan became increasingly bitter about the Broadway scene and retired over and over again during his last years.

He produced one last show, *Fulton of Oak Falls* (1937), with his old partner Sam Harris. Cohan wrote and starred in the show. The Theater Guild had convinced him to appear in Eugene O'Neill's only comedy, *Ah, Wilderness!* in 1933, and Cohan's last musical appearance on Broadway came in a Sam Harris production, the Rodgers and Hart musical, *I'd Rather Be Right* (1937). In it, Cohan portrayed then-President Franklin Roosevelt. Cohan's last appearance was in the poorly received play, *The Return of the Vagabond* (1940), which Cohan produced, starred in, and wrote.

Cohan died on November 4, 1942, at the age of sixty. At the time of his death, he was working on a new show, *The Musical Comedy Man.*

COHAN AND HARRIS THEATER · See HARRIS THEATER.

COLONY THEATER · See BROADWAY THEATER.

COMDEN AND GREEN · Betty Comden and Adolph Green were the preeminent lyricist team in the history of musical theater. They contributed to the development of the art of the musical both in the theater and on the screen. They were the longest-running writing team in Broadway history, yet because their subjects tended to be comedic rather than dramatic they had not received their due by critics and historians.

They both began their careers as members of The Revuers, a nightclub act, which also included Judy Holliday (then named Judith Tuvim), for which they both wrote and performed. Their early collaborations for The Revuers was a success in the Greenwich Village club the Village Vanguard and less than a success in the more swank environs of the Rainbow Room. They went to Hollywood to star in the movie *Greenwich Village* but were mostly cut from the picture.

Leonard Bernstein, a former co-camper and roommate of Adolph Green, caught their new act at the Blue Angel and convinced them to write the book and lyrics for the new musical adaptation of his ballet, *Fancy Free. On the Town* (1944) was a smash hit and contained such standards as "New York, New York" and "Lucky to Be Me."

Unfortunately their next outing was not as successful. *Billion Dollar Baby* (1945), for which they teamed up with composer Morton Gould, was a failure. And their subsequent outing with composer Saul Chaplin, *Bonanza Bound* (1947), closed in Philadelphia before coming to Broadway. Discouraged by their flops, the team went to Hollywood, where they joined MGM for a series of successful film musicals. They wrote the screenplay for *Good News* (1947), penned lyrics for *Take Me Out to the Ball Game* (1949), adapted their Broadway success *On the Town* to the screen that same year and contributed a screenplay to the last pairing of Fred Astaire and Ginger Rogers—*The Barkleys of Broadway* (1949).

In 1951, the team made another attempt at Broadway and met their next collaborator, Jule Styne. The initial entry in the Styne, Comden and Green canon was *Two on the Aisle* (1951). Following that success, Comden and Green returned to Hollywood to write the screenplay for their best movie and perhaps the greatest movie musical of all time, *Singin' in the Rain* (1952). They followed that with another huge success for MGM, *The Band Wagon* (1953). The film was released after their next Broadway assignment, *Wonderful Town,* opened in 1953. For this tribute to New York City, Comden and Green were reunited with Leonard Bernstein.

They next contributed songs in collaboration with Jule Styne for the legendary Mary Martin version of *Peter Pan* (1954). Their songs, "Never Never Land" and "Distant Melody," among others, perfectly captured the mood of the J. M. Barrie classic. *Peter Pan* was followed by the movie musical, *It's Always Fair Weather* (1955).

In 1956, they teamed up again with their partner from The Revuers, Judy Holliday, and had a smash hit. The show, *Bells Are Ringing* (1956) yielded such gems as "Just in Time" and "The Party's Over." *Say, Darling* (1958), a modest hit with a Jule Styne score, followed. "Dance Only with Me" is the best known of the largely forgotten songs.

While Jule Styne worked on *Gypsy,* Comden and Green returned to Hollywood for the screen adaptation of *Bells Are Ringing.* The threesome reunited for the Phil Silvers, Nancy Walker musical *Do Re Mi* (1960). "Make Someone Happy" was the big hit from that score. *Subways Are for Sleeping* (1961) featured "Comes Once in a Lifetime."

Styne went on to write the smash *Funny Girl* with Bob Merrill, and Comden and Green went to Hollywood again for the all-star comedy *What a Way to Go* (1964). The three saw their next show, *Fade Out-Fade In,* premiere in 1964 with Carol Burnett.

The team would produce what is possibly their best score with Styne for their next show, *Hallelujah, Baby!* (1967).

The pair next collaborated on the Strouse and Adams musical *Applause* (1970), starring Lauren Bacall. In 1978, they collaborated with Cy Coleman for the remarkable *On the Twentieth Century* (1978).

The failure *A Doll's Life* (1982) had music by Larry Grossman. Comden and Green's last Broadway show was a reteaming with Cy Coleman, *The Will Rogers Follies* (1991).

Green called their collaboration "an unconscious give-and-take." Betty Comden called it "mental radar." Whatever it was, it has resulted in some of the most joyfully enthusiastic moments in the musical theater. Their shows, especially if they contributed librettos too, are marked by a smart, urbane innocence perfectly captured in the personality of Judy Holliday. Their characters are plain people, who express their feelings with an exuberance and joie de vivre. Comden and Green's wit, humor, and slightly wry look at the world have resulted in one of the finest catalogs of productions in Broadway history. Their virtuosity was remarkable. They were the perfect collaborators both with each other and with those who have supplied the music for their shows.

Adolph Green died on October 23, 2002.

COMEDY THEATER · 108 W. 41st Street. Architect: D.G. Malcolm. Opening: September 6, 1909; *The Melting Pot.* The Comedy Theater, among the first Shubert theaters in New York, was not especially successful. Among its noteworthy early productions were four in 1910: *Affinity, A Man's World, Three Daughters of Monsieur Dupont* and *The Family.*

The theater became William Collier's Comedy Theater with the opening of *I'll Be Hanged If I Do,* the fifth show to open in 1910. Shows produced during that period included *Bunty Pulls the Strings* (1911) and *Fanny's First Play* (1912). The name was changed back to Comedy with the opening of *Her Own Money* on

September 1, 1913. *Gentlemen from Number 19* (1913) and *Consequences* (1914) were other productions at the Comedy.

As the theater district moved northward into Times Square, the Shuberts gave their less-promising productions to the Comedy, left behind below 42nd Street. In 1916, the Washington Square Players took over the Comedy. As a member of that company Katharine Cornell made her Broadway debut. The following year, Ruth Draper made her debut here.

The Depression hit the theater hard. The Comedy, by now well off the beaten track, was closed from 1931 to 1935. Later in the thirties, boy genius Orson Welles directed and performed at the Comedy as part of the Federal Theater Project. The theater was known as the Mercury, named after Welles' theater company. Welles presented enormously successful productions of *Doctor Faustus* and *Julius Caesar,* which opened on November 11 and 12, 1937. The Mercury Theater productions were controversial. Welles described his *Julius Caesar*: "Our *Julius Caesar* gives a picture of the same kind of hysteria that exists in certain dictator-ruled countries of today. We see the bitter resentment of freeborn men against the imposition of a dictatorship. We see a political assassination, such as that of Huey Long. We see the hope on the part of Brutus for a more democratic government vanish with the rise of a demagogue (Antony) who succeeds the dictator. Our moral, if you will, is that not assassination, but education of the masses, permanently removes dictatorships."

Welles' productions were the great successes in the theater's history. On December 29, 1939, the theater's name and policy changed again. It became the Artef Theater, a Yiddish theater, during the run of the Yiddish drama *Uriel Acosta.* The Yiddish policy continued until the theater was razed in 1942.

CONCERT THEATER · See JOHN GOLDEN THEATER.

CORNELL, KATHARINE (c.1898–1974) · Katharine Cornell, Laurette Taylor,

Helen Hayes, and Lynn Fontanne were the great actresses of their time. Alexander Woollcott dubbed Katharine Cornell "The First Lady of the American Theater." (He disliked her husband, Guthrie McClintic, and titled a *New Yorker* Profile, "The Tyranny of the Tantrum.") At her death, critic Brooks Atkinson wrote in the *New York Times,* "If she had a great reputation it was not because she had manufactured it. It was because—in addition to that personal magnetism—she had the integrity and taste of a lady."

Katharine Cornell was born in Vineyard Haven, Massachusetts, to a family with theatrical interests. Her grandfather and father were in love with the theater. In fact, her grandfather had a small stage in his home where he and his friends put on amateur productions. Her father, a doctor, was doing postgraduate work in German when she was born. Her parents returned to Buffalo and his father gave up medicine to become manager and part owner of the Star Theatre.

There is some mystery about the year of her birth. She once claimed her birthday to be February 16, 1898. When she reached her seventies she moved the year back to 1893. She explained the discrepancy by stating, "When an actress is younger she likes to lower her age, but when she is older she likes to add to her years."

This early background sparked her interest in the theater. While at boarding school at Oaksmere School in Mamaroneck, New York, she produced and acted in the classics. After graduation she stayed on for two years to teach drama. She assumed all jobs in the theater including that of playwright.

Edward Goodman, the director of the Washington Square Players, came to the school to direct one of her plays and invited her to come to New York.

With an inheritance to fall back on, she accepted and in 1916 appeared with the Players in *Bushido.* Her only line was, "My son, my son." She then joined the Jessie Bonstelle Stock Company in Detroit and Buffalo, remaining with the company for three seasons. The company performed a new play every week for ten performances. Jessie Bonstelle recognized the young actress' talents and brought her to London, where the company performed *Little Women.* Cornell played Jo, a leading role.

While still in London, she was noticed by two women who recommended her to actor/producer Allen Pollock. He was casting Clemence Dane's drama *A Bill of Divorcement* and chose the young actress to open in the play on Broadway with himself in a leading role.

Before *A Bill of Divorcement* opened, Cornell made her Broadway debut at the Klaw Theater in Rachel Crothers' *Nice People* (1921). No one took notice except casting director Guthrie McClintic. He wrote in his notebook, "Interesting. Monotonous. Watch." They were married by the following fall.

Producer Charles Dillingham opened *A Bill of Divorcement* (1921) at the George M. Cohan Theatre on a particularly busy week, back in the days when Broadway might see more than one opening on a single night.

Several minor roles followed, until Cornell took on the title role in George Bernard Shaw's *Candida,* which opened at the 48th Street Theatre (1924). *Candida* led to *The Green Hat* (1925), which guaranteed her stardom. She made one of her best-loved appearances as Elizabeth Barrett in Rudolf Besier's *The Barretts of Wimpole Street* (1931) at the Empire Theatre with Brian Aherne. She appeared in her only Chekhov play, *The Three Sisters* (1942), with Judith Anderson and Ruth Gordon at the Ethel Barrymore Theater.

She starred in S. N. Behrman's *No Time for Comedy* opposite Olivier (1939) at the Ethel Barrymore Theater, following the run with a six-month tour. The play was the third presentation by The Playwrights' Company.

By the 1950s, her output began to slow down, and her successes grew less frequent. Her last appearance was in *Dear Liar,* which toured cross-country from October 1959 to March 1960. It opened in New York at the Billy Rose Theater on March 17, 1960. After her husband's death on October 29, 1961, she retired from the stage.

She seldom appeared on radio or television and appeared only in one movie, *Stage Door Canteen.* Her autobiographies, *I Wanted to Be an Actress* (1939) and *Curtain Going Up* (1943) were successful books.

Katharine Cornell died on June 9, 1974.

CORONET THEATER · See EUGENE O'NEILL THEATER.

CORT THEATRE · 148 W. 48th Street. Architect: Edward B. Carey. Opening: December 29, 1912; *Peg O' My Heart.* John Cort, a producer who had done most of his work on the West Coast, built the Cort Theatre. Cort wanted to begin production east of the Mississippi and built the Cort as his East Coast flagship theater. He built the Louis XVI-style theater on the "wrong side" of Broadway. Conventional wisdom had it that those theaters east of Broadway, like the Henry Miller and Lyceum, or west of Eighth Avenue, like the Martin Beck, were too far off the beaten track to draw audiences. However the Cort, east of Broadway between Sixth and Seventh Avenue, was an immediate success and was thought a "lucky" theater.

The theater started its life with a huge hit, J. Hartley Manners' play *Peg O' My Heart.* The show starred Manners' wife Laurette Taylor, considered one of the greatest of all American actresses. The play had a remarkable run at the Cort Theater of 607 performances at a time when even 100 performances indicated a hit. The Cort had another hit with its next presentation, *Under Cover* (1914). With 999 seats the theater was suited to both plays and musicals. Its next hit, Victor Herbert's *The Princess Pat* (1915) contained one hit song, the "Neapolitan Love Song."

The teens saw more hits at the theater including *Flo Flo* (1917) with music by Silvio Hein and *Abraham Lincoln* (1919), John Drinkwater's play, produced at a time when some Americans still remembered the late president and his death.

The 1920s were stellar years for the theater. Hits included the musical *Jim Jam Jems* (1920);

Captain Applejack (1921); George S. Kaufman and Marc Connelly's Hollywood satire *Merton of the Movies* (1922); and Ferenc Molnar's *The Swan* (1923).

The Shuberts took over the lease of the theater in 1927 with John Cort's retirement. Katharine Hepburn made her theatrical debut at the Cort. The play was *These Days* which opened on November 12, 1928, and played eight performances.

The 1930s began with Jed Harris' brilliant production of Chekhov's *Uncle Vanya* (1930). George Abbott provided two hits at the Cort in the late thirties. The first was the hilarious *Boy Meets Girl* (1935) by Sam and Bella Spewack and *Room Service* (1937), written by John P. Murray and Allen Boretz.

During the next decade, the theater was equally successful. *The Male Animal* (1/9/40; 243 performances) by James Thurber and Elliott Nugent; Paul Osborn's *A Bell for Adano* (1944); *Lady Windermere's Fan* (1946) featured Cornelia Otis Skinner and Estelle Winwood; and Grace Kelly's Broadway debut in Strindberg's *The Father* (1949).

Hepburn returned to the Cort in Shakespeare's *As You Like It* (1950) which was followed by drama critic Wolcott Gibbs' *Season in the Sun* (1950); the Pulitzer Prize drama *The Shrike* (1952); another Pulitzer Prize drama, *The Diary of Anne Frank* (1955); and Dore Schary's drama of Franklin Delano Roosevelt, *Sunrise at Campobello* (1958).

The theater's success continued into the sixties. The first offering, Brendan Behan's *The Hostage* (1960) was followed by *Advise and Consent* (1960). At the end of the decade, the theater was converted to television. Merv Griffin presented his talk show here from 1969 to 1974. The Cort reopened to live theater with the musical *The Magic Show* (1974) which played almost two thousand performances.

In recent years, the Cort's luck seems to have run out. As fewer and fewer shows are produced on Broadway, little quality product has been available for the Cort. Notable tenants have been *Ma Rainey's Black Bottom* (1984) by August Wilson, *The Heiress* (1995) with

Cherry Jones, Wendy Wasserstein's *An American Daughter*, John Leguizamo's one-person show, *Freak* (1998), Hal Prince's most recent Broadway show, *Hollywood Arms* (2002), and the charming *A Year in the Life of Frog and Toad* (2003) featuring Frank Vlastnik.

CRAIG THEATER · See GEORGE ABBOTT THEATER.

CRITERION THEATER · See OLYMPIA.

D

DE MILLE, AGNES (1905–1993) · Agnes de Mille was instrumental in raising the art of Broadway choreography to new heights of sophistication and psychology. She was not content simply to have her dancers perform until the music stopped. Rather her ballet-inspired choreography revealed characterization and motivation and was often narrative in form.

She had her greatest success with the composing team of Rodgers and Hammerstein. Their constant attempts to stretch the conventions of musical comedy and operetta allowed de Mille to rise to the occasion time and time again.

Her first and only appearance as a dancer in a Broadway show came with the *Grand Street Follies* (1928). She then went to London to choreograph the Cole Porter musical *Nymph Errant* (1933). The show, starring Gertrude Lawrence, was mildly successful but did not cross the Atlantic. After another London assignment *(Why Not Tonight?)*, she made her Broadway choreographic debut with *Hooray for What!* The show opened on December 1, 1937, with a score by Harold Arlen and E. Y. Harburg.

A jazz version of *A Midsummer Night's Dream* called *Swingin' the Dream* opened on November 29, 1939, with an impressive cast, including Louis Armstrong, Maxine Sullivan, Benny Goodman and his sextet, Bud Freeman's Summa Cum Laude Band, Dorothy Dandridge, Jackie "Moms" Mabley, Butterfly McQueen, and Muriel Rahn. De Mille shared the choreographic assignment with Herbert White.

Her first solo venture on Broadway was for the landmark musical *Oklahoma!* She received ecstatic reviews from the critics.

Miss de Mille's other choreograph works for the stage, with her ballets indicated in quotes: "Venus in Ozone Heights" and "Forty Five Minutes for Lunch" for *One Touch of Venus* (1943); "Civil War Ballet" for *Bloomer Girl* (1944); "Carousel Waltz" for *Carousel* (1945); "The Chase" for *Brigadoon* (1947); *Allegro* (1947), for which she was also director; *Gentlemen Prefer Blondes* (1949); *Out of This World* (1950), for which she was director only; *Paint Your Wagon* (1951); "Pas de Deux" for *The Girl in Pink Tights* (1954); "Huckleberry Island Ballet" and "The Town House Maxixe" for *Goldilocks* (1958); "Dublin Night Ballet" for *Juno* (1959); *Kwamina* (1961); *110 in the Shade* (1963); *Come Summer* (1969), for which she was also director .

Agnes de Mille died on October 6, 1993.

DESYLVA, BROWN, AND HENDERSON · Lyricists B. G. DeSylva and Lew Brown and composer Ray Henderson were among the most popular of Broadway composers in the 1920s and 1930s. Their upbeat numbers seemed to exactly define the bubbly, insouciance of the twenties. Though none of their shows have lasted, they wrote some of the most endearing songs in the American popular song canon.

B. G. DeSylva was born on January 27, 1895, and died on July 11, 1950. He also collaborated with George Gershwin, Victor Herbert, Jerome Kern, Emmerich Kalman, and Lewis Gensler. DeSylva moved into producing toward the end of his involvement in Broadway. He later became a respected executive at Paramount Pictures.

Lew Brown was born on December 10, 1893, and died on February 5, 1958. He also wrote with Harry Akst, Charles Tobias, and Sam Stept.

Ray Henderson was born on December 1, 1896, and died on December 31, 1970. He also collaborated with Ted Koehler, Jack Yellen, and Irving Caesar.

DeSylva, Brown, and Henderson were responsible for the following revues and musicals with their famous songs in quotes: *La La Lucille* (1919), DeSylva alone; *Sally* (1920), DeSylva only, "Whippoorwill" and "Look for the Silver Lining"; *George White's Scandals* (1922), DeSylva only, "I'll Build a Stairway to Paradise"; *Orange Blossoms* (1922), DeSylva only, " A Kiss in the Dark"; *The Yankee Princess* (1922), DeSylva only; *George White's Scandals* (1923), DeSylva only, "The Life of a Rose"; *Sweet Little Devil* (1924), DeSylva alone; *George White's Scandals* (1924), DeSylva only, "Somebody Loves Me"; *Big Boy* (1925), De-Sylva only, "California Here I Come, " "If You Knew Susie," "Keep Smiling at Trouble"; *Tell Me More!* (1925), DeSylva alone, "Kickin' the Clouds Away"; *George White's Scandals* (1925); *Captain Jinks* (1925), DeSylva alone; *George White's Scandals* (1926) "Birth of the Blues," "The Black Bottom," "This Is My Lucky Day"; *Queen High!* (1926), DeSylva only and also as co-librettist, "You Must Have Been a Beautiful Baby"; *Piggy* (1927), Brown only; *Good News!* (1927), "The Best Things in Life Are Free," "Good News, " "Just Imagine, " "Lucky in Love"; *Manhattan Mary* (1927); *George White's Scandals* (1928), "I'm on the Crest of a Wave"; *Hold Everything!* (1928), DeSylva also as co-librettist, "You're the Cream in My Coffee"; *Follow Thru* (1929), DeSylva also as co-librettist, "Button Up Your Overcoat," "Then I'll Have Time for You"; *Flying High* (1930), Brown and DeSylva also co-librettists; *George White's Scandals* (1931), Henderson and Brown only, "Ladies and Gentlemen, That's Love," "Life Is Just a Bowl of Cherries," "That's Why Darkies Were Born," "This Is the Missus," "The Thrill Is Gone"; *Hot-Cha!* (1932), Henderson and Brown only and Henderson as co-librettist; *Take a Chance* (1932), DeSylva only, also as co-librettist, "Eadie Was a Lady" "Rise and Shine"

"You're an Old Smoothie"; *Strike Me Pink* (1933), Brown and Henderson only, and both also as co-librettists, co-producers and co-directors; *Say When* (1934), Henderson only and also as co-producer; *Calling All Stars* (1934), Brown only, also as co-librettist, producer and co-director; *George White's Scandals* (1935), Henderson only; *Yokel Boy* (1939), Brown only, also as librettist, producer and director; *Du Barry Was a Lady* (1939), DeSylva co-librettist and producer only; *Louisiana Purchase* (1940), DeSylva producer only; *Panama Hattie* (1940), DeSylva co-librettist and producer only; *Ziegfeld Follies* (1943), Henderson only.

DIETZ AND SCHWARTZ · The song writing team of Arthur Schwartz and Howard Dietz elevated the art of revue writing to new heights. They collaborated on what is considered the greatest of all revues, The Band Wagon. Their long career spanned thirty years and resulted in the creation of many great standards. Schwartz and Dietz were of the most successful writers of ballads such as "Dancing in the Dark," "I Guess I'll Have to Change My Plans," "You and the Night and the Music" and "Alone Together." Their comedy and upbeat songs were equally well constructed, such as "New Sun in the Sky," "Triplets," and "That's Entertainment."

Howard Dietz (1896–1983) Howard Dietz was born in New York on September 8, 1896. He attended Townsend Harris Hall and Columbia University. While at Columbia, he frequently contributed to Franklin P. Adams' column, "The Conning Tower." His early interest in language landed him a position as a copywriter in the Philip Goodman Company ad agency. He obtained the position by writing a contest-winning advertisement for Fatima Cigarettes.

After his discharge from the Navy, Dietz obtained a job with Samuel Goldwyn, the motion picture producer. The publicity post led to a long career with what eventually became Metro-Goldwyn-Meyer.

Dietz wrote for the stage as a sideline to his publicity work for the movies. It's ironic that he felt his retirement income would come from his MGM pension. In fact, it was his ASCAP royalties that allowed him to live in comfort.

Dietz's first Broadway lyric was for *Poppy* (1923), a W. C. Fields vehicle and the first time Fields played a legitimate role on Broadway. Dietz's lyrics and his contributions to "The Conning Tower" did not go unnoticed. Philip Goodman, who was involved in advertising as well as the theater, suggested to Jerome Kern that he might use Dietz as lyricist on his next show. Kern took Goodman's advice, and the result was *Dear Sir* (1924). This start, though inauspicious, did bring Dietz to the attention of Arthur Schwartz, a lawyer.

Arthur Schwartz (1900–1984) Arthur Schwartz was born in Brooklyn, New York, on November 25, 1900. Like Berlin and others, Schwartz taught himself to play the piano. While at school, Schwartz played piano in neighborhood movie houses. He attended New York University and Columbia University. After graduation, he taught English for the New York public school system. Forsaking the teaching profession, he entered a legal practice in 1924. Four years later, he wrote to Howard Dietz on the advice of publisher Bennett Cerf. Schwartz had already had one of his songs published, "Baltimore M.D., You're the Only Doctor for Me," with lyrics by Eli Dawson.

Schwartz wrote to Dietz that he was the lyricist most like Lorenz Hart in style. This was a high compliment from Schwartz, but Dietz was unimpressed. He responded by suggesting that Schwartz team up with an established lyric writer to gain from the education, as he himself had done with Jerome Kern. Then when they both became famous they could write together.

The musical *Queen High* (1926) provided Schwartz with his first job. Schwartz collaborated on two songs with fellow composer Ralph Rainger and lyricist E. Y. Harburg: "Brother Just Laugh It Off" and

"I'm Afraid of You." Unfortunately, by the time the show opened on Broadway, the Schwartz songs were cut.

George and Ira Gershwin were hard at work on their score for *Oh, Kay!* (1926) when Ira was forced to Mt. Sinai Hospital to have his appendix removed. George chose Dietz to work on the score during Ira's recuperation. Dietz wrote the title song's lyrics, "Heaven on Earth," and the verse to "Clap Yo' Hands."

Dietz's next assignment, *Hoopla,* was probably the first show in history to close out of town after only one act. Dietz's life as a publicist was turning out much more successful than his theater career. Metro-Goldwyn-Mayer had been formed in 1924, and Dietz was made director of advertising and publicity because of his creation of the Leo the Lion trademark and the *Ars Gratia Artis* motto for Goldwyn Pictures.

Jay Gorney and Dietz had better luck with *Merry-Go-Round* (1927), their next collaboration, than they did with *Hoopla.* Henry Souvaine contributed some of the music, with Morrie Ryskind also writing lyrics.

At the end of the 1920s, Tom Weatherly, a producer and Broadway bon vivant, decided to put on a revue called *The Little Show.* Dwight Deere Wiman was brought in to help produce the venture, and Dietz was called in to write the lyrics.

Weatherly asked Dietz whether the name Arthur Schwartz rang any bells. Dietz showed him the correspondence between Schwartz and himself, and Weatherly promptly labeled the coincidence fate. Their first song together was a satire on the movie title songs that were being foisted on the public. The new team's answer to the fad was "Hammacher Schlemmer, I Love You," a paean to the noted New York hardware company.

The Little Show (1929) contained their first great hit and a subsequent standard, "I Guess I'll Have to Change My Plan."

While Dietz was attending to his motion-picture duties, Schwartz collaborated with other lyricists. Less than a month after the opening of *The Little Show* Arthur Schwartz wrote music to Agnes Morgan's lyrics for some of the tunes in *The Grand Street Follies* (1929). Schwartz's next assignment was writing the music for two London musical comedies, *Here Comes the Bride* (1930), and *The Co-Optimist*.

Dietz and Schwartz were reunited for *The Second Little Show* (1930).

After a failed collaboration with composer Arthur Swanstrom on *Princess Charming* (10/13/30), Schwartz reteamed with Dietz for *Three's a Crowd* (1930), the first of the great Dietz and Schwartz Broadway revues. The score contained the great Dietz and Schwartz ballad, "Something to Remember You By."

The Band Wagon (1931) featured Fred and Adele Astaire, Helen Broderick, Frank Morgan, and Tilly Losch. It was the first American revue with real sophistication. The score contained the team's greatest song, "Dancing in the Dark," as well as "New Sun in the Sky," and "I Love Louisa."

Dietz and Schwartz then produced a series of classic reviews and musical comedies including *Flying Colors* (1932) ("Alone Together;" "Louisiana Hayride;" "Fatal Fascination;" "A Shine on Your Shoes"); *Revenge with Music* (1934) ("You and the Night and the Music" and "If There Is Someone Lovelier than You"); *At Home Abroad* (1935) ("Got a Bran' New Suit;" "Hottentot Potentate;" "Love Is a Dancing Thing;" "O What a Wonderful World;" "Thief in the Night"); *Between the Devil* (1937) ("I See Your Face Before Me;" "By Myself;" "Triplets").

Schwartz then collaborated with Dorothy Fields on the Ethel Merman vehicle *Stars in Your Eyes* (1939). Dietz, meanwhile, joined forces with Vernon Duke on *Jackpot* (1944) and *Sadie Thompson* (1944). Schwartz then tried his luck with Ira Gershwin on *Park Avenue* (1946).

In 1945, Dietz and Schwartz joined forces again for the revue *Inside U.S.A.* (1948) ("Blue Grass;" "Haunted Heart;" "Rhode Island Is Famous for You;" "First Prize at the Fair;" "Protect Me"). This show, which was produced at the Century Theater, was the last of the great Broadway revues. Television, the medium in which much of the cast would achieve their fame, was the death knell of the Broadway revue.

In 1950, Dietz made an excursion, rare for a Broadway lyricist, into the world of opera. He provided the English lyrics to the Metropolitan Opera's production of *Die Fledermaus*. He repeated the job for the Metropolitan in 1952 when he wrote the English lyrics for Puccini's *La Boheme*.

For *A Tree Grows in Brooklyn* (1951), Schwartz teamed up again with Dorothy Fields. The fine score included "Make the Man Love Me;" "I'm Like a New Broom;" "Look Who's Dancing;" "Love Is the Reason;" "I'll Buy You a Star;" and "Growing Pains." Their next show was *By the Beautiful Sea* (1954) ("Alone Too Long;" "More Love than Your Love;" "The Sea Song").

The Gay Life (1961), based on Arthur Schnitzler's play *The Affairs of Anatol*, contained two beautiful ballads, "Magic Moment" and "Something You Never Had Before." The team's last Broadway show, *Jennie* (1963; 82 performances), was a vehicle for Mary Martin. Their final score contained another standout ballad, "Before I Kiss the World Goodbye."

Following that disappointment, the team attempted other projects, notably a musical version of *Mrs. Arris Goes to Paris*. But none would reach the stage. Howard Dietz died in New York on July 30, 1983, after a long bout with Parkinson's disease. Arthur Schwartz died on September 4, 1984.

DUKE, VERNON (1903–1969) · Duke was one of Broadway's master songwriters and also a classically trained musician who composed serious works under his real name, Vladimir Dukelsky. He escaped Russia during the Revolution and went to Europe. While there, he composed ballets for Diaghilev's Ballet Russe. Although his training under such greats as Reinhold Gliere and Marian Dombrovsky seemed to promise him a great classical career, Dukelsky achieved his greatest success as a musical theater composer.

He arrived in New York in 1929 after trying his hand at several musicals in London, including *Yvonne* (1926) (dubbed "Yvonne the Terrible" by Noel Coward); *The Yellow Mask* (1928), and *Open Your Eyes* (1930).

In New York, Duke interpolated songs into *The Garrick Gaieties* (1930), before attempting a complete score. His first American score for *Walk a Little Faster* (1932), written with E. Y. Harburg, included Duke's first great hit song, "April in Paris." He then continued his collaboration with Harburg for the *Ziegfeld Follies of 1934* (1934) and another hit, "I Like the Likes of You." He next contributed both music and lyrics to the standard "Autumn in New York" written for the revue *Thumbs Up!* (1934). The next edition of the *Follies* in 1936 saw Duke teamed with Ira Gershwin, and they wrote another standard, "I Can't Get Started."

After *The Show Is On* (1936) came Duke's first musical comedy, the classic *Cabin in the Sky* (1940) with lyrics by John Latouche. The score contained three hits, the title song, "Honey in the Honeycomb" and, perhaps Duke's greatest song, "Taking a Chance on Love," which had lyrics by Latouche and Ted Fetter. Latouche and Harold Adamson teamed with Duke for an Eddie Cantor vehicle, *Banjo Eyes* (1941) ("We're Having a Baby (My Baby and Me)") and was followed by *It Happens on Ice* (1941); *The Lady Comes Across* (1942); *Jackpot* (1944); and *Sadie Thompson* (1944). None were successful. Duke's last Broadway show introduced Bette Davis to the musical theater. *Two's Company* (1952) had lyrics by Sammy Cahn and poet Ogden Nash.

Duke found his next assignment off-Broadway. Impresario and director Ben Bagley brought Duke and Ogden Nash to the Phoenix Theater to contribute a score for Bagley's *The Littlest Revue,* (1956). His last show, *Zenda* (1963), closed in Los Angeles.

Duke's songs are models of cohesive melody and great emotion. They sound very simple and easy to hum, but when studied they reveal their intricacies, and they're difficult to play. Now, through the help of Bagley and singer Bobby Short, Duke's work is reaching a wider audience and his songs are being rediscovered and appreciated by a new generation of music lovers.

E

EARL CARROLL THEATER · Southeast Corner of Seventh Avenue and 50th Street. Architect: George Keister. Opening: February 25, 1922, *Bavu.* The Earl Carroll Theater had two lives in two theaters on the same site. The first Earl Carroll Theater was built by the producer with money supplied by Texas oil baron William Edrington, Carroll's principal backer.

The theater opened with a three-act melodrama, *Bavu,* written and directed by Earl Carroll. The author, director, producer, composer, and lyricist was best known as the producer of the annual revue series, the *Earl Carroll Vanities. Bavu* closed after twenty-five performances. Two more flops, *Just Because* and *Raymond Hitchcock's Pinwheel* followed before the theater's first hit, *The Gingham Girl* (1922). The next hit in the theater was the first edition of the *Earl Carroll Vanities* (1923).

With the advent of the Depression, Carroll's fortunes floundered and he was forced to rent the theater to Radio Pictures for $12,750 a month plus half the taxes. The company was going to use the theater to premiere its film production of *Rio Rita,* originally a show produced by Ziegfeld. As if in reaction to their plans, Carroll leased Ziegfeld's old stomping ground, the New Amsterdam Theater, for his next edition of the *Vanities.*

The old Earl Carroll Theater seated only one thousand people, making it unsuitable for the large productions to which Carroll aspired. When Ziegfeld built his own new theater in 1927, Carroll, unfazed by his financial problems, set about to build a new space of his own.

William R. Edrington, a Texas oil baron, was Carroll's chief backer. They bought the land east of the original theater for a million dollars and leveled the building on that site. The builders retained the office building atop the old theater, but tore out the theater itself.

Carroll spent $4.5 million of Edrington's money on his new theater. Architect William Keister and interior designer Joseph Babolnay created an art deco masterpiece. The new lobby was three times as large as the old one. Remarkably, the new theater's seating capacity was also tripled. There were seats for 1,500 patrons in the orchestra alone. The boxes sat 200 people and the loge and balcony areas seated 1,300.

To utilize the space to its maximum, the 60-by-100-foot space under the balcony was given to lounge areas and balcony space. The theater was the first to be completely cooled backstage, in the auditorium and in the public areas.

The interior of the building was a classic art deco design. Carroll finished off the theater by hanging the now famous sign over the stage door, "Through These Portals Pass The Most Beautiful Girls In The World."

The theater's premiere attraction was the *Earl Carroll's Vanities of 1931* (1931), which opened with the Depression in full swing. There was a staff of eighty-four men in the house. There was no box office, but rather a long table with eight attendants in front of the ticket racks. During intermission, the ushers wheeled a huge chromium-plated tank down the aisles and dispensed free ice water to the audience.

Carroll couldn't make the theater a success. The show was especially lavish and could not recoup its cost on the low ticket prices. It also was expensive to operate the giant theater and maintain its lavish interior. Within six months, Carroll lost the theater. He was sued by the

Seven Fifty-five Corporation for $366,632.90. Carroll also owed $64,952.20 for three months back rent, taxes and interest.

Ziegfeld decided to take it over. He changed its name to the Casino and reopened the space with a revival of his great hit, *Show Boat* (1932). During the run of *Show Boat,* Ziegfeld died and the show closed.

George White, the other of the big three to produce an annual revue series, used the theater for *Melody* (1933), one of the last Broadway operettas. A vaudeville show entitled *Casino Varieties* opened next with, in an attempt to counter the effect of the Depression on the box office, a top ticket price of $1.50. This was the theater's last legitimate show. The theater closed only four years after its opening.

Clifford Fischer, a former agent for the Orpheum Circuit, took up the theater's lease. He took out the seating and put tiers in the balcony and orchestra upon which he installed tables. Fischer, responding to a French wave that was sweeping over New York, called the new theater-restaurant The French Casino. The theater opened on Christmas Day, 1934, featuring a show modeled on the Folies Bergere—ironic, since this, too, was Earl Carroll's inspiration. The revues at the French Casino were very successful. The glamorous theater was perfectly suited to the spectacular shows on the stage.

The French Casino prospered until showman Billy Rose, owner of the Casino de Paris, bought the building. He redecorated the interior in a more Latin manner and extended the stage out from the proscenium. He renamed the space the Casa Manana, featuring a $2.50 price for dinner, dancing, and the show. It opened on January 10, 1938, and closed by the end of the year.

In 1939, the six-story office building fronting Seventh Avenue was razed. The auditorium and stage house still stood, but the interiors were replaced with retail space. A Whelan's Drug Store and then a Woolworth's took the place of the magnificent theater. When the Woolworth's was torn down in 1990 the theater was discovered above the store's false ceilings.

Unfortunately, it was too late to save any of the theater itself.

EARL CARROLL VANITIES · There were three great revue series that graced Broadway in the early years of the century—the *Ziegfeld Follies,* the *George White's Scandals* and the *Earl Carroll Vanities.* Each of the three had its own trademark, the special stamp of its producers. Florenz Ziegfeld relied on star-filled extravaganzas featuring top talents performing material by some of America's greatest composers. George White produced jazzy, fast moving revues with flappers and sheiks and a hint of bawdiness. Earl Carroll, on the other hand, employed few great stars, relied on mostly second-rate material but surpassed his competitors with vulgarity, burlesque inspired humor and ample nudity.

There were eleven editions of the *Vanities* and two *Earl Carroll Sketchbooks.* Among the stars that appeared in the series were Patsy Kelly, Peggy Hopkins Joyce, Joe Cook, W. C. Fields, Milton Berle, Ray Dooley, Jack Benny, Helen Broderick, Lillian Roth, and Jimmy Savo.

Carroll was author of the famous sign that hung over his stage door, "Through These Portals Pass the Most Beautiful Girls in the World." It was a direct challenge to Ziegfeld whose aim was "Glorifying the American Girl."

Vanities were presented in 1923, 1924, 1925, 1927, 1928, 1930, 1931, 1932, and 1940.

Carroll was killed with showgirl Beryl Wallace in a plane accident on June 17, 1947.

ED SULLIVAN THEATER · 1697 Broadway between 53rd and 54th Streets. Architect: Herbert J. Krapp. Opening: November 30, 1927; *The Golden Dawn.* In 1910, Arthur Hammerstein was determined not to ever speak to his father, Oscar Hammerstein I, again. By 1927, eight years after Oscar's death, Arthur was left to run the Hammerstein empire on his own. By then, Oscar II had made a name for himself on Broadway. Arthur decided to build the Hammerstein Theater on Broadway as a tribute to his father, using his profits from the Rudolf Friml/Herbert Stothart operetta *Rose-Marie* to finance the project. Arthur installed a life-size bronze statue of his father in the theater's lobby.

Early successes at the theater include *Golden Dawn* (1927) and *Sweet Adeline* (1929), the latter with a fine score by Jerome Kern and Oscar Hammerstein II that included the songs "Why Was I Born?" and "Don't Ever Leave Me."

Arthur, a heavy investor in the stock market, lost most of his fortune in the crash. He badly needed a hit show. Unfortunately his next production, *Luana* (1930) was not it. By the thirties, the operetta was going out of favor.

With his theater dark and no prospective show in the wings and its neighboring office building almost empty, Arthur was forced to sell. Later that year, after one more producing attempt, he declared bankruptcy. The young producing team of Frank Mandel and Laurence Schwab bought the theater. They joined with Oscar II to present shows in what was renamed the Manhattan Theater.

The first production in the Manhattan was *Free for All* (1931). It was followed by *East Wind* (1931) and *Through the Years* (1931). The theater remained dark until Billy Rose bought it and renamed it the Billy Rose Music Hall. Rose opened it on June 21, 1934, as a theater restaurant. Rose's luck was no better than that of his predecessors. He sold it, and on November 27, 1934, the theater reopened as the Manhattan Music Hall.

The Manhattan Music Hall was also a failure, and on February 14, 1936, the theater was renamed the Manhattan Theater. The Federal Theater Project presented a play by Edwin and Albert Barker—*American Holiday* (1936). The closing of *American Holiday* marked the end of the theater as a live venue. CBS bought the theater and made it a CBS Radio Playhouse in September 1936. When television took over the airwaves, CBS converted the space into a television studio. Its most famous tenant was the "Ed Sullivan Show." In 1967, the theater was renamed, in the emcee's honor, the Ed Sullivan Theater. In the eighties, the theater

was used by the Reeves Communications Company to tape their television production "Kate and Allie."

The "David Letterman Show" now occupies the theater.

ELTINGE THEATER · See EMPIRE THEATER (2)

ELYSEE · See JOHN GOLDEN THEATER.

EMBASSY 49TH STREET THEATER · See CHARLES HOPKINS THEATER.

EMPIRE THEATER · (1) 1430 Broadway at 40th Street. Architect: J. B. McElfatrick. Opening: January 25, 1893; *The Girl I Left Behind Me.* Frank Sanger and Al Hayman built producer Charles Frohman what was to become the most beloved theater in New York history. Frohman hired J. B. McElfatrick as architect of the Empire, the first of seven theaters that the architect designed. The Empire building was five stories tall and achieved many firsts. It was the first theater to have electricity, although it also had a backup gas system in case the electricity went out. The theater was also the first to be built entirely on the first floor. Other theaters, following the example of English predecessors, were built with the balcony at ground level and the orchestra underground. The Empire was probably also the first theater to have an electric sign. It was also the first theater to follow the 1892 building code, which provided greater fire-prevention measures. Finally, the Empire hosted three companies in their initial engagements: those of John Drew, Maude Adams, and owner Charles Frohman.

Frohman's initial attraction, *The Girl I Left Behind,* by David Belasco was an immediate success, as was the new theater. Surprisingly, although reviews of the theater were favorable, when his lease came up for renewal Frohman decided to gut the interior and hire John M. Carrere and Thomas Hastings to redo it. The New Empire Theater opened on October 13,

1903, with John Drew starring in *Captain of Dieppe.*

The first years of the Empire's history saw many classic productions. Among them were Dumas' *Lady of the Camellias* (1895) with Olga Nethersole, Oscar Wilde's *The Importance of Being Ernest* (1895) with Henry Miller, Viola Allen, and William Faversham and *When Knighthood Was in Flower* (5/2/04) with Julia Marlowe and Tyrone Power, Sr.

Among the most famous of all productions at the Empire was the J. M. Barrie classic, *Peter Pan* (1905) starring Maude Adams. By most accounts the greatest of all Pans, Adams returned to the Empire as Peter Pan in special holiday attractions in 1906, 1912, and 1915. Adams had previously appeared at the Empire with leading man Robert Edeson in Barrie's *The Little Minister* (1898). Later, she also appeared at the Empire in another Barrie play, *Quality Street* (1908). Another success at the Empire for Adams was *The Pretty Sister of Jose* (1903). On February 6, 1905, she opened two plays in repertory *'Op O' My Thumb* and a revival of *The Little Minister.* On January 15, 1908, she appeared at the Empire in *The Jesters.*

Other notable productions at the theater in its earliest years were *The Good Hope* (1907) and George Bernard Shaw's *Captain Brassbound's Conversion* (1907) both with Dame Ellen Terry; and Sir Arthur Wing Pinero's *Trelawny of the Wells* (1911) with Ethel Barrymore.

Frohman, one of the greatest producers of his time, died on May 7, 1915, when a German submarine sank the Lusitania. Frohman's brother Daniel, a legend in his own right, was an executive of Paramount Famous Lasky Corporation. The corporation was brought in by Hayman and it took over management of the Empire, but it was both unsuccessful and insensitive to the Empire's artists. In 1920, producer Gilbert Miller took over the management.

J. M. Barrie had other productions at the theater without star Maude Adams. Among them were *Dear Brutus* (1918) with Helen Hayes and William Gillette and *Mary Rose* (1920) with Ruth Chatterton.

Other notable productions of the 1920s were *Blood and Sand* (1921) with Otis Skinner and Cornelia Otis Skinner; *The Dove* (1925) with Judith Anderson; Noel Coward's *Easy Virtue* (1925) with Jane Cowl; *The Captive* (1926) with Helen Menken and Basil Rathbone; *Her Cardboard Lover* (1927) with Jeanne Eagles and Leslie Howard; and P. G. Wodehouse's *Candle-Light* (1929) with Gertrude Lawrence and Leslie Howard.

Maude Adams wasn't the only star associated with the Empire. Katharine Cornell opened in the *Age of Innocence* on November 27, 1928. Her subsequent appearances at the Empire included the classic play *The Barretts of Wimpole Street* (1931), *The Wingless Victory* (1936), and *Candida* (1937).

John Gielgud starred on the Empire Stage in *Hamlet.* The production opened on October 8, 1936, and played 132 performances, the longest-running *Hamlet* in New York history until the 1964 production starring Richard Burton, which played only five more performances.

Gilbert Miller's reign at the Empire drew to a close in 1931. The theater was sold to the 1432 Broadway Corporation. Luckily, they were adept at booking the theater. Their first offering was *The Barretts of Wimpole Street* on February 9, 1931.

During the 1930s, there was the American premiere of Kurt Weill and Bertolt Brecht's *The Threepenny Opera.* The musical opened at the Empire on April 13, 1933. Unfortunately the show wasn't a success and only played twelve performances. Zoe Akin's *The Old Maid* (1935) starred Judith Anderson. The great Ethel Waters played the Empire in Dorothy and DuBose Heyward's *Mamba's Daughters.* The play opened January 3, 1939, and ran 162 performances.

The Empire's most famous tenant was *Life with Father.* Howard Lindsay and Russel Crouse wrote the classic comedy. Mrs. Lindsay, Dorothy Stickney, starred in the play along with her husband. *Life with Father* opened on November 8, 1939, and ran eight years, 3,224 performances, the longest-running play in theater history.

The Empire changed hands again on July 31, 1946, when real estate operator Jacob Freidus purchased it. The new owner was, unfortunately, not interested in theater and saw the Empire for its development possibilities. Then playing at the Empire were Alfred Lunt and Lynn Fontanne in Terrance Rattigan's comedy O *Mistress Mine*. The comedy opened on January 23, 1946, and proved to be the Lunts' longest running hit, eventually playing 451 performances.

Howard Lindsay, Dorothy Stickney and John Drew Deveraux returned to the theater in the Lindsay and Crouse play *Life with Mother*. The comedy opened October 20, 1948, and ran 265 performances.

Two years after he purchased the theater, Freidus sold the property to the Astor family. On October 11, 1952, Viscount Astor II died. The family hurriedly sold their properties to raise capital. A textile firm, M. Lowenstein & Sons, purchased the theater.

Three other hits were to play the Empire. In Carson McCullers great play, *Member of the Wedding* (1950); *I Am a Camera* (1950) and the Empire's last tenant, *The Time of the Cuckoo* by Arthur Laurents, which opened on October 15, 1952. After 263 performances, on May 30, 1953, the play closed. On that date, Shirley Booth led the audience in singing "Auld Lang Syne," and the curtain came down for the last time.

Brooks Atkinson wrote of the Empire: "It had the finest auditorium of any theater in its time, the largest and most hospitable lobby and all the comforts of a cultivated institution. The ticket-taker wore full dress and silk hat. The Empire retained its prestige long after Charles Frohman died. He built so well that the pride and luster of his theater outlived him."

Cornelia Otis Skinner led a benefit for the American National Theater Academy on Sunday, May 24, 1953, at the Empire. The benefit's theme was "Highlights of the Empire." She described the theater as "That beloved gilt-prosceniumed and red-plush theater which really IS theater. It was a lovely and exciting temple."

The Empire was replaced by an office building.

EMPIRE THEATER · (2) 236 W. 42nd Street. Architect: Thomas W. Lamb. Opening: September 11, 1912. Producer A.H. Woods hired Thomas W. Lamb, one of the preeminent motion picture theater architects in the twenties and thirties, to design the Eltinge Theater, named after famed female impersonator Julian Eltinge. Lamb came up with a distinguished beaux-arts design for his theater.

The theater was successful, with a variety of productions; most notably the opening production *Within the Law* (1912) starring Jane Cowl. John Barrymore appeared in *The Yellow Ticket* (1914), and the farce *Fair and Warmer* (1915) was another hit but Woods, like other producers, fell on hard times when the Depression hit. He lost the theater, and in 1931 it became a burlesque house. When Mayor Fiorello LaGuardia cracked down on burlesque in 1943, the theater was converted to a movie policy as the Laff-Movie. In 1954, it became the Empire Theater.

Because the Empire contained only 759 seats, which were spread over two balconies and an orchestra, the 42nd Street Redevelopment Project did not recommended that the Empire be saved. Only the facade would be incorporated into the plan. True to their word, the Empire was destined to serve as the lobby of the AMC Movie complex with the central elevators rising through the proscenium to the backstage area. In order to save the façade and the gutted interior, the theater was put on rollers and moved two hundred feet down 42nd Street. The theater's proscenium and mural were saved in part. Truly a desecration of art.

ETHEL BARRYMORE THEATER · 243–49 W. 47th between Seventh and Eighth Avenue. Architect: Herbert J. Krapp. Opened: December 20, 1928; *The Kingdom of God*. Ethel Barrymore was, in the 1920s, considered one of the top Broadway actresses. The Shuberts admired her artistry and wanted to put her under contract. They offered to build a theater in her name if she would join the Shubert fold. She agreed, and the Shuberts hired Herbert J. Krapp, noted theater architect, to design the building.

On December 20, 1928, the new theater opened with the eponymous star in G. Martinez Sierra's *The Kingdom of God*. The theater was hailed as ideal. It would later also prove to be a popular theater, housing successes in every decade.

The Kingdom of God and the theater's next attraction, *The Love Duel* (1929), were directed by E. M. Blythe. Blythe was in reality Miss Barrymore herself. Several plays were next presented at the theater without Miss Barrymore, among them *Death Takes a Holiday* (1929).

Ethel Barrymore returned to the theater in her next play, *Scarlet Sister Mary* (1930). British author Ivor Novello's drawing room comedy, *The Truth Game* (1930), marked Billie Burke's return to the stage following the death of her husband, Florenz Ziegfeld. The star for whom the theater was named returned in a revival of *The School for Scandal* (1931).

In 1932, Ethel Barrymore severed her relationship with the Shuberts. They retaliated by removing her first name from the marquee of the theater.

The Barrymore was a perfect midsize house for the production of musicals. Its first, Cole Porter's *The Gay Divorce* (1932), opened with Fred Astaire (his first appearance without his sister, Adele). Another sophisticate premiered his work at the Barrymore. Noel Coward's sparkling *Design for Living* (1933) starred Alfred Lunt and Lynn Fontanne and the playwright.

Other successes of the decade include Clare Boothe's comedy drama *The Women* (1936); *Knickerbocker Holiday* (1938) with Walter Huston; and S. N. Behrman's *No Time for Comedy* (1939), starring Katharine Cornell, Laurence Olivier and Margalo Gillmore.

Ethel Barrymore appeared for the last time in the theater in *An International Incident* (1940). Unfortunately it ran a scant 15 performances. Its failure was deserved. But the failure of its next tenant was not. *Pal Joey* (1940), with

a score by Rodgers and Hart, opened with Gene Kelly, Vivienne Segal, and June Havoc starring. More successful were *Best Foot Forward* (1941) and Tennessee Williams' classic *A Streetcar Named Desire* (1947). The Pulitzer Prize winning drama top-lined Jessica Tandy, Kim Hunter, and Karl Maiden and made a star of Marlon Brando whose performance as Stanley Kowalski electrified theatergoers.

During the 1950s, husband and wife Rex Harrison and Lilli Palmer starred in John Van Druten's *Bell, Book and Candle* (1950) and another husband and wife team, Hume Cronyn and Jessica Tandy, starred in the theater's next big hit, *The Fourposter* (1951) by Jan de Hartog.

Other successes during the 1950s include *Tea and Sympathy* (1953), which marked Robert Anderson's Broadway debut as a playwright; *The Desperate Hours* (1955); Enid Bagnold's *The Chalk Garden* (1955); and *New Faces* (1956), which marked the debuts of T. C. Jones, Maggie Smith, Jane Connell, John Reardon, Virginia Martin, and Inga Swenson.

The Barrymore premiered another Pulitzer Prize-winning attraction with Ketti Frings' play *Look Homeward Angel* (1957) and also had a hit with *A Raisin in the Sun* (1959) by Lorraine Hansberry.

Irene Mayer Selznick produced one last show at the Barrymore, *The Complaisant Lover* (1961). Peter Shaffer, had a hit production later in the sixties, *Black Comedy* (1967).

As the number and quality of shows produced on Broadway declined in the seventies and eighties, the theater suffered from a scarcity of first-rate material. The Barrymore had a hit in the Michael Stewart and Cy Coleman musical *I Love My Wife* (1977). The musical, *Baby* (1983), by Richard Maltby Jr. and David Shire was not a success.

Other productions at the theater include David Rabe's *Hurly Burly* (1984); *Lettuce and Lovage* (1990) with Maggie Smith and Margaret Tyzak; Cy Coleman's look at 42nd Street streetwalkers, *The Life*; Zoe Wanamaker as the title character of *Electra* (1998); Judi Dench in *Amy's View* (1999); and the Sondheim revue

Putting It Together (1999). Charles Busch's play *Tale of the Allergist's Wife* (2000) was the last success to play the theater.

The Barrymore has proven itself to be an ideal and highly versatile Broadway theater, suited to musicals, dramas, comedies, revues and even one-man shows. The theater, owned by Shubert Organization, remains an integral part of the Broadway theater scene.

EUGENE O'NEILL THEATER · 230 W. 49th Street.

Architect: Herbert J. Krapp. Opening: November 24, 1925; *Mayflowers*. The Shuberts built this theater as the Forrest, named after the great American actor Edwin Forrest. It was part of the Shuberts plan to build six theaters on 48th and 49th Streets in an attempt to emulate the success of 42nd Street. The brothers arranged for the Forrest Theater to be built along with an accompanying hotel.

The theater's 1,200 seats (later reduced to 1,101) meant that the stage could accommodate both musicals and straight plays. The early years of the Forrest were marked with failure. James Cagney, Mary Boland, and Osgood Perkins starred in *Women Go On Forever* (1927), which was a hit despite critical drubbing.

Another series of failures followed until Edgar Wallace's play *On the Spot* (1930) opened at the then-dubbed Wallace's Forrest Theater. Another bleak period followed, which was relieved by only the modest success of Rachel Crothers' *As Husbands Go* (1933).

After seven more flops, the Shuberts lost control of the Forrest as part of their bankruptcy settlement. Although the Shuberts regained some of their theaters at bargain prices, they decided not to try for control of the Forrest. It was a mistake they would regret. For, only a few months later, the Forrest hosted one of the American theater's greatest successes, *Tobacco Road*. Jack Kirkland's play, based on the Erskine Caldwell novel, opened at the Masque Theater on December 5, 1933. It soon moved to the Forrest where it enjoyed an enormous run, playing from September 1934 to May 1941. The show finally totaled a run of 3,224

performances, making it the second longest-running play in Broadway history.

The Forrest went from feast to famine after *Tobacco Road*, and another four years of failure followed. Finally, in 1945 the theater was sold and redecorated, and on October 25, 1945, it reopened as the Coronet with *Beggars Are Coming to Town*. The Coronet had better luck than the Forrest. Its second offering was Elmer Rice's hit *Dream Girl* (1945).

The theater's success continued with Arthur Miller's Broadway debut, *All My Sons* (1947), *Angel in the Wings* (1947), and *Small Wonder* (1948). A revival of *Diamond Lil* (1949) starred the play's author, Mae West. Another hit revue, *Tickets Please* (1950) also featured Larry Kert, Roger Price, and Dorothy Jarnac.

The theater changed names again with the opening of William Inge's *A Loss of Roses* (1959). It was then dubbed the Eugene O'Neill Theater. The first hit at the O'Neill was *Show Girl* (1961), a revue with Carol Channing. Herb Gardner's comedy *A Thousand Clowns* (1962); Bock and Harnick's under appreciated musical *She Loves Me* (1963) followed.

Neil Simon bought the theater at the end of the sixties and installed a number of his own productions. The first was *Last of the Red Hot Lovers* (1969), followed by *The Prisoner of Second Avenue* (1971); *The Good Doctor* (1973); *God's Favorite* (1974); *California Suite* (1977); *I Ought to Be in Pictures* (1980); *Fools* (1981) and, finally, a revival of the Neil Simon, Cy Coleman and Carolyn Leigh musical *Little Me* (1982).

The Jujamcyn Theaters organization bought the O'Neill from Simon and installed a string of failures.

Finally they struck gold with *Big River* (1985), Roger Miller's tepid musicalization of *Huckleberry Finn*. David Henry Hwang's *M. Butterfly* (1988) was a success as was a musical revue based on the catalog of Louis Jordan, *Five Guys Named Moe* (1992). A revival of *Grease* (1994) caught fire at the O'Neill with a succession of unlikely casting choices. Brian Dennehy appeared in Arthur Miller's *Death of a Salesman* (1999). The fine musical *The Full*

Monty (2000) with music by David Yazbek deserved a much better fate but was overshadowed by the opening of *The Producers* that same season. Antonio Banderas made his musical theater debut in a revival of Maury Yeston's *Nine* (2003). Another revival, of Stephen Sondheim's *Sweeney Todd* (2005) brought Patti LuPone back to Broadway.

F

FEDERAL THEATER PROJECT · The Federal Theater Project was an arm of the Works Progress Administration during the Depression. It provided federal subsidy of the theater in order to increase employment and stimulate the nation's economy. Broadway was hard hit by the Depression. Fewer shows were produced as angels (Broadway investors) found their resources wiped out by the stock market crash. Audiences, too, forsook the theater as an unnecessary luxury. Without product or audience, many theater owners went into receivership, and the map of Broadway was changed forever.

Theaters were demolished, turned into burlesque houses or radio studios or simply left abandoned. Actors, ill suited for other jobs, which didn't exist anyway, had nowhere to turn. Relief Administrator Harry Hopkins realized the needs of artists, including actors. He saw to the establishment of the Federal Music Project, Federal Art Project, and Federal Writers' Project. Mrs. Hallie Flanagan of Vassar College was hired by the government to oversee the fourth such program, dubbed the Federal Theater Project. Altogether, the WPA employed 40,000 artists by the end of 1936.

Of the thousands of performers and stage technicians who found employment were such later luminaries as John Houseman, Orson Welles, Arlene Francis, E. G. Marshall, Arthur Kennedy, Will Geer, and Joseph Cotten. Composers Marc Blitzstein and Virgil Thomson and playwrights Arthur Miller and Dale Wasserman also worked on the experimental project. Future directors John Huston and Nicholas Ray received training on the project. Scenic and costume designers such as Howard Bay and Fred Stover were joined by such lighting designers as George Izenour.

The Project officially began on August 27, 1935, inaugurated by Hopkins as a "free, adult, uncensored" federal theater. Its first production, *Black Empire*, opened at Los Angeles' Mayan Theater on March 26, 1936. The first New York production was *Injunction Granted*, which opened at the Biltmore Theater on July 24, 1936. Other productions by the Broadway contingent of the Project included *Horse Eats Hat* (1936) at the Maxine Elliott's Theatre; *It Can't Happen Here*, which opened at twenty-two theaters around the country on October 27, 1936; *Doctor Faustus* (1937) at the Maxine Elliott's Theatre; *Revolt of the Beavers* (1937); *Processional* (1937) at the Maxine Elliott's Theatre; *S.S. Glencairn* (1937), including *Moon of the Caribbees, In the Zone, Bound East for Cardiff* and *The Long Voyage Home* at the Lafayette Theater; *One-Third of a Nation* (1938) at the Adelphi Theater; *Haiti* (1938) at the Lafayette Theater; *Big Blow* (1938) at the Maxine Elliott's Theatre; *Sing for Your Supper* (1939) at the Adelphi Theater; and *Life and Death of an American* (1939) at the Maxine Elliott's Theatre.

The project wasn't limited to only traditional plays. Flanagan, seeking to build a national theater out of the Federal Theater Project, encouraged all kinds of theater, circuses, marionette and children's shows, vaudeville and variety.

But the Federal Theater, which vowed to be "uncensored," proved to be a problem for conservatives. The shows couldn't help being controversial since they reflected the state of the country and its politics. One of the more objectionable parts of the project was the series of "living newspapers." The experimental theater took subjects from the headlines and created plays around the issues. These shows personalized the facts of the news stories and brought them home to the project's surprisingly mixed audience.

The government canceled the first living-newspaper production, about the Ethiopian war. *Triple A Plowed Under* was the second and dealt with the agriculture problems of the country. Others dealt with problems like housing, cooperatives, health care, labor unions, race relations, industry, movies, natural resources, and public utilities. The newspaper's most famous editions included *Power,* produced at the Ritz Theatre. *Power* was an examination of a power failure and solutions to the problem.

The Project dealt with American issues, sometimes provoking controversy, sometimes not. Historical dramas received their due with five revolving around the character of Abraham Lincoln. Two of these were called *Abraham Lincoln,* one written by John Drinkwater and another by Ralph Kettering. *Mrs. Lincoln* was written by Ramon Romero and Howard Koch scripted *The Lonely Man.*

The most successful drama about Lincoln was *Prologue to Glory* by E. P. Conkle. After almost a year's run in New York, the production moved to the New York World's Fair in Flushing Meadows.

With the government on the lookout for Communists behind every proscenium, the Federal Theater Project was doomed to be censored and, finally, disbanded. The most famous case of censorship involved the production of the Marc Blitzstein musical, *The Cradle Will Rock,* a pro union expose of the steel industry. Orson Welles and John Houseman were the producers of the controversial piece. It was scheduled to open on June 16, 1937. Since the nation was then going through deadly strikes, the subject was especially timely and controversial—so controversial that the government sent a memo to Flanagan ordering that "no openings of new productions shall take place until after the beginning of the coming fiscal year." Actually, *The Cradle Will Rock* was the only opening scheduled.

With the opening canceled, the company was doubly intent on presenting the show. Actor's Equity, always distrustful of the WPA, had ruled that its members could not perform on stage in a Federal Theater Project play. The musicians' union also disliked the Project and forbade its members from playing in the show, despite its pro-union slant.

So on the opening night, Houseman and Welles told the audience assembled outside the theater about their problems and marched the entire group to the little Venice Theater. Marc Blitzstein was seated at his piano, alone on stage. The actors, forbidden to appear on the stage, simply took seats around the audience and stood up to say their lines. The result was tremendously exciting, and *The Cradle Will Rock* is remembered as one of the greatest triumphs of the thirties. It ended up playing 104 performances.

The House Un-American Activities Committee was quick to identify the Federal Theater as one of its targets when it began its inquiries in August 1938. Congressman J. Parnell Thomas (later jailed for defrauding the government) blasted the Project: "It is apparent from the startling evidence received thus far that the Federal Theater Project not only is serving as a branch of the Communistic organization but is also one more link in the vast and unparalleled New Deal propaganda machine."

The Federal Theater Project couldn't survive the storms of controversy. On June 30, 1939, the Project was disbanded.

FIELDS FAMILY · The Fields family spanned almost a century of the American theater and spread their talents over a wide variety of roles. Lew Fields and his sons and daughter (Herbert, Joseph, and Dorothy) concentrated their talents on the musical theater—Lew as a producer, director, and performer, Herbert as a librettist, Joseph as a librettist and playwright, and Dorothy as a librettist and lyricist.

Lew Fields (1867–1941) Lew Fields, the patriarch of the Fields family, is credited with giving the young songwriting team of Rodgers and Hart their first important professional commissions to write Broadway musicals. He also enjoyed a long career as partner of Joseph Weber with whom he presented many popular burlesques on Broadway hits of the time.

Herbert Fields (1897–1958) Herbert Fields enjoyed long collaborations as librettist to many of Broadway's preeminent songwriters. He began his career with Rodgers and Hart and then wrote a number of musical comedies with Cole Porter. He collaborated on eight shows with his sister Dorothy who was also a lyricist.

Dorothy Fields (1904–1974) Dorothy, the baby of the family, overcame much sexism to become one of Broadway's preeminent lyricists. One strength lay in her ability to utilize current slang in her lyrics. Throughout her long career, she remained in the vanguard of the musical theater, always up-to-date and able to change along with popular taste. She was the only member of her family to make a successful transition to film, writing for such great composers as Jerome Kern.

Joseph Fields (1895–1966) Joseph wrote many successful comic plays, usually in collaboration with Jerome Chodorov. He also collaborated with Oscar Hammerstein II and Anita Loos on musicals and plays. He pursued his career apart from his father and siblings. His sweet and somewhat sentimental works are discussed after those of the rest of his illustrious family.

* * * *

The saga of the Fields family started when Lew Fields began his more than fifty years in the American theater as the boyhood partner of Joseph Weber. The team was "Dutch comics" in early musical comedies. They based their characters on stereotypes of New York's Dutch population. Weber and Fields were the most popular comedy team of their time, and the partners billed themselves the Dutch Senators. By 1885, they were able to put together their own company of performers. On March 27,

1896, they took a lease on the Broadway Music Hall at Broadway and 29th Street and soon renamed it the Weber and Fields Music Hall. The team wrote and performed burlesques of other theater productions and presented well-known vaudeville performers. The theater opened with its first burlesque, *The Geezer,* on September 5, 1896. Other popular burlesques were *Pousse Cafe* (1897); *Hurly Burly* (1898); *Whirl-I-Gig* (1899); *Fiddle Dee Dee* (1900); *Hoity Toity* (1901); *Twirly Whirly* (1902); and *Whoop-Dee-Doo* (1903). On May 28, 1904, the team broke up following a performance at the New Amsterdam Theatre. Weber continued his management of the theater on his own under the name Weber's Theater.

On December 5, 1904, along with two partners, Henry Hamlin and Julian Mitchell, Lew Fields opened the Lew Fields Theater on 42nd Street. Marie Cahill was the chief member of Fields' new company, which presented the Victor Herbert and Glen MacDonough musical *It Happened in Nordland.* Oscar Hammerstein I was the owner of the theater who leased the venue to Fields and his partners. Fields' name was taken off the theater in 1906 when it was renamed the Hackett Theater. Fields then leased the Herald Square Theater downtown, beginning operations on August 30, 1906. When Weber lost his theater in 1912, he reteamed with Fields.

They built their own theater on 44th Street and named it the Weber and Fields New Music Hall. The team didn't hold onto the theater's lease for long, for in late 1913 the Shubert Brothers took over the theater's operation. On June 5, 1913, Fields moved his operation to the space above and called it the Lew Fields 44th Street Roof Garden. The Shuberts also owned this roof garden theater. Typically, Fields lost the space by the end of the year. The last theater named for Fields was the Lew Fields Mansfield Theater, which bore his name from April 26, 1928, to March 4, 1929. Today the theater is known as the Brooks Atkinson Theater.

As he got older, Fields turned more and more to producing. Fields hit his stride in the twenties with the production of a series of musicals by Richard Rodgers and Lorenz Hart. Fields produced the shows of which many had a libretto by his son Herbert.

Lew Fields was the librettist and producer of *A Lonely Romeo* (1919). He continued his support of the young team of Rodgers and Hart with *Poor Little Ritz Girl* (1920). Richard Rodgers was just eighteen when the show opened on Broadway.

Fields produced and starred with Delyle Alda in *Blue Eyes* (1921) and *Snapshots of 1921* (1921). He directed *The Greenwich Village Follies* in 1923 and 1924. His production of *The Melody Man* (1924) was not a hit.

Herbert Fields made his Broadway debut choreographing the *Theater Guild* production *The Garrick Gaieties* (1925). Herbert went on to collaborate with Rodgers and Hart on the shows *Dearest Enemy* (1925); *The Girl Friend* (1926); choreographed the second edition of the *Garrick Gaieties* (1926); *Peggy-Ann* (1926).

He went on to write the libretti to *Hit the Deck* (1927) and *A Connecticut Yankee* (1927), both produced by his father. Lew wrote three libretti in 1928 with moderate success. *Present Arms*; *Chee-Chee* and *Hello Daddy!* For the latter, Herbert wrote the libretto, father Lew produced and starred (in his last appearance on Broadway) and Dorothy acted as lyricist to Jimmy McHugh's music. She had previously made a splash with her lyrics to Jimmy McHugh's music for *Blackbirds of 1928* (1928). The team's hit song for the Lew Leslie revue was "I Can't Give You Anything But Love."

Lew Fields' last Broadway show was the *Vanderbilt Revue* (1930). He co-produced and co-directed the proceedings, which boasted a score by a variety of writers, including daughter Dorothy and Jimmy McHugh.

Herbert began his long collaboration with Cole Porter in 1929 with the show *Fifty Million Frenchmen* (1929).

Dorothy had her final Broadway collaboration with Jimmy McHugh in *The International Revue* (1930). They contributed one smash hit, "On the Sunny Side of the Street," to the Lew Leslie production. Dorothy and Jimmy McHugh's final collaboration, *Clowns in Clover*,

closed out of town in 1933. They went out with a bang, for the score contained another standard, "Don't Blame Me."

Herbert wrote many libretti in the 1930s including *The New Yorkers* (1930); *America's Sweetheart* (1931); and *Pardon My English* (1933).

Both Herbert and Dorothy took a long break from Broadway in the late thirties and both returned, with different shows, in 1939. Dorothy made her return to the theater after six years with *Stars in Your Eyes* (1939), starring Ethel Merman with music by Arthur Schwartz and book by J. P. McEvoy. Herbert reteamed with Cole Porter for *Du Barry Was a Lady* (1939); *Panama Hattie* (1940); and, with his sister collaborating on the libretti, for *Let's Face It!* (1941); *Something for the Boys* (1943); and *Mexican Hayride* (1944).

European style operetta, pronounced dead at the end of the twenties, made a surprisingly successful return to the Broadway stage with *Up in Central Park* (1945). Sigmund Romberg wrote the music, and Dorothy returned to lyric writing for the show. She also collaborated with Herbert on the book. "Close as Pages in a Book" became the hit.

Herbert and Dorothy's entertaining but minor efforts for Porter didn't prepare Broadwayites for the genius of their next show, *Annie Get Your Gun* (1946). The Irving Berlin score was his finest, and the book by the Fields siblings was their masterwork. Ethel Merman perfectly adapted the role of sharpshooter Annie Oakley to her talents. *Annie Get Your Gun* proved to be one of the top Broadway musicals of all time.

Surprisingly, the team's next show, *Arms and the Girl* (1950), showed little of the talents they exhibited in *Annie Get Your Gun*. Dorothy wrote lyrics to Morton Gould's music and collaborated with Herbert and director Rouben Mamoulian on the script.

Dorothy collaborated again with composer Arthur Schwartz on two shows, *A Tree Grows in Brooklyn* (1951) ("Make the Man Love Me") and *By the Beautiful Sea* (1954). For the latter Herbert joined Dorothy on the script but the results were weak.

Herbert's last show was *Redhead* (1959). He collaborated again with his sister on the book. Additional librettists were David Shaw and Sidney Sheldon (later to be a major novelist). Albert Hague collaborated with Dorothy on the score but only one song, "Merely Marvelous," was heard after the show closed.

Herbert Fields died on March 24, 1958.

After a seven-year break, Dorothy resumed her career without her brother with *Sweet Charity* (1966). Cy Coleman collaborated with Dorothy on the score. Dorothy's lyrics perfectly matched Coleman's jazzy rhythms, providing exactly the right tone for the alternately romantic, vulgar, and sentimental score. "Hey Big Spender" was the big hit, but the rest of the score was much more sophisticated and entirely more worthy of public acclaim.

Dorothy Fields' last Broadway show, *Seesaw* (1973), was also written in collaboration with Cy Coleman.

Dorothy Fields died on March 28, 1974. Of all the Broadway lyricists, she was most able to keep abreast of her times. She utilized slang and idiomatic phrases without sounding forced or trendy. Her more poetic lyrics never become cloying, and her imagery remains sharp, fresh and hip. It's to her credit that she could collaborate with composers as widely divergent in style as Arthur Schwartz, Jerome Kern (in the movies), and Cy Coleman. In a field largely dominated by men, she held her own and was never forced into a "feminine" viewpoint.

* * * *

Joseph Fields' first Broadway production was *Schoolhouse on the Lot* (1938), written in collaboration with his longtime partner Jerome Chodorov. The two had met while working in Hollywood at Republic Pictures. The team's next collaborations included the hits *My Sister Eileen* (1940) and *Junior Miss* (1941).

Fields went it alone with his next play, *The Doughgirls* (1942). Pearl Harbor had been bombed three weeks after the opening of *Junior Miss,* and wartime comedies became very popular. Fields next directed *The Man Who Had All the Luck* (1944) that flopped at the

Forrest Theater. He teamed up with Ben Sher to write the play *I Gotta Get Out* (1947) that flopped at the Cort Theater.

Fields' two flops were followed by two of his biggest hits, the musicals *Gentlemen Prefer Blondes* and *Wonderful Town.* He wrote both libretti in collaboration with his partner Jerome Chodorov. *Gentlemen Prefer Blondes* (1949) opened with Carol Channing and Yvonne Adair in the leads. *Wonderful Town* (1953) was based on Chodorov and Fields' play *My Sister Eileen.* The score was by Leonard Bernstein and Betty Comden and Adolph Green. Rosalind Russell and Edith Adams starred, and George Abbott directed.

The team's next musical, *The Girl in Pink Tights* (1954) opened with a score by Sigmund Romberg, the same composer who had collaborated with Joseph's brother and sister on *Up in Central Park.* Romberg had died three years before the opening of *The Girl in Pink Tights,* and orchestrator Don Walker put together the songs from Romberg's jottings and unfinished songs. Leo Robin added lyrics.

The team's next play, *Anniversary Waltz* (1954), opened at the Broadhurst Theater. Fields next directed the play *The Desk Set* (1955) at the Broadhurst Theater. Chodorov and Fields were back with *The Ponder Heart* (1956) at the Music Box Theater. Fields collaborated with humorist Peter DeVries on *The Tunnel of Love* (1957) at the Royale Theatre.

Fields tried his hand in collaboration with Hammerstein at supplying a libretto for the Rodgers and Hammerstein musical *The Flower Drum Song* (1958), a lightweight examination of the clash of cultures between the "younger generation" and older Chinese immigrants, at the St. James Theatre. Fields also co-produced the show with the songwriters. Fields co-produced *Blood, Sweat and Stanley Poole* (1961) at the Morosco Theatre.

Joseph Fields died on March 3, 1966. His work was solid and skillful with a rich humanity and sentimental side. He was a witty man whose plays took everyday occurrences and extracted the comedy inherent in the situations in a warm, loving manner.

58TH STREET THEATER · See JOHN GOLDEN THEATER.

51ST STREET THEATER · See MARK HELLINGER THEATER.

54TH STREET THEATER · See GEORGE ABBOTT THEATER.

FILMARTE · See JOHN GOLDEN THEATER.

FINE ARTS THEATER · See JOHN GOLDEN THEATER.

FOLIES BERGERE · See HELEN HAYES THEATER.

FORREST THEATER · See EUGENE O'NEILL THEATER.

48TH STREET THEATRE · 157 W. 48th Street. Architect: William A. Swasey. Opening: August 12, 1912; *Just Like John*. The 48th Street Theatre was built by producer William A. Brady. Though it housed many successes, his theater was not to have an especially notable history. The theater's first successes were *Never Say Die* (1912); *Today* (1913); *The Midnight Girl* (1914); *Just a Woman* (1916) and *The Man Who Stayed at Home* (1918).

The Storm (1919) was a melodrama of the Canadian woods. *Opportunity* (1920) was another hit play at the 48th Street Theatre. Owen Davis wrote the comedy, which featured subsequent Hollywood movie star Nita Naldi.

The theater was renamed the Equity 48th Street Theatre on October 2, 1922, with the opening of *Malvaloca*. A successful revival of Ibsen's *The Wild Duck* (1925) was the theater's next success. The name was changed back to the 48th Street Theatre on June 1, 1925, with the play *Spooks*.

A series of plays with improbable but all too typical plots followed. The comedy *Puppy Love* (1926) starred Spring Byington.

Jean Bart's drama *The Squall* (1926) opened at the 48th Street Theatre with a cast headed by Blanche Yurka, Romney Brent, and Dorothy Stickney. *Unexpected Husband* (1931) starred Josephine Hull. *The Pagan Lady* (1930) was a name few audiences could resist. The drama starred Lenore Ulric as a woman who is tempted by the son of an evangelist.

In the 1930s, the Depression forced the sale of the theater. In 1937, the Labor Stage, an arm of the International Ladies Garment Workers Union, used the space for plays, lectures, and meetings. It was called the Windsor Theater during this period, which began with the production of *Work Is for Horses* (1937). The union's other theater, also called the Labor Stage, was originally the Princess Theater.

On September 1, 1943, the Windsor became the 48th Street Theatre again. Its big hit, the biggest of its entire life, was Mary Chase's classic comedy *Harvey* (1944). Frank Fay starred in the fantastic play as the pixilated Elwood Dowd. Another big hit at the theater that was transferred successfully to Hollywood was *Stalag 17* (1951).

In 1955, a water tower on the roof fell apart, and the theater was flooded. The damage was extensive, and the theater was razed.

44TH STREET THEATRE · 216 West 44th Street. Architect: William A. Swasey. Opening: January 23, 1913; *The Man with Three Wives*. The theater was built as Weber and Fields' Music Hall named after the venerable musical comedy team Joeseph Weber and Lew Fields. Soon after, the Shuberts purchased the property and renamed it the 44th Street Theatre. The basement of the theater was home to the Little Club, a speakeasy. Later, the basement was used as the Stagedoor Canteen. The theater's roof was also utilized for a rooftop theater, which went through many names and managements. The best known was the Nora Bayes. In 1917, the Shuberts built a conventional theater on the roof.

The first musical presented at the theater, *The Girl on the Film* (1913), was a modest success. Like many of its contemporaries, it was based on a European operetta. The operetta *The Midnight Girl* (1914) was another successful

European transplant. Yet another European operetta was *The Lilac Domino* (1914). *Katinka* (1915) was an even bigger success for the theater. Rudolf Friml and Otto Harbach wrote the operetta, now forgotten but at the time an enormous hit.

The Shuberts made a stab at an annual series of revues with their production of the *Shubert Gaieties of 1919*. The producers had one of their greatest hits in another operetta *Blossom Time*. The 44th Street hosted the first revival of *Blossom Time* (1923) (there were eventually seven).

Betty Lee (1924) starred Joe E. Brown, Gloria Foy, and Hal Skelly. The score was by Louis A. Hirsch, Con Conrad, Otto Harbach, and Irving Caesar. An unlikely success was Arthur Hammerstein's operetta *Song of the Flame* (1925), which had a strange grouping of songwriters. There was music written in the operetta style by Herbert Stothart and more modern melodies written by George Gershwin. The lyrics were by Otto Harbach and Oscar Hammerstein II.

An English operetta, *Katja, the Dancer* (1926), was brought to the theater and was a success. *A Night in Spain* (1927) was a popular revue, which bore only a passing resemblance to anything Spanish.

By the end of the 1920s, operettas were going out of favor with audiences. The 44th Street Theatre followed the trends and hosted one of the new jazz-influenced musicals, Bert Kalmar and Harry Ruby's *The 5 O'Clock Girl* (1927), starring Mary Eaton, Pert Kelton, Oscar Shaw, and Danny Dare. The hit song was "Thinking of You."

The most famous tenant of the 44th Street Theatre was another Kalmar and Ruby show, the Marx Brothers classic *Animal Crackers* (1928). Joining Groucho, Harpo, Zeppo, and Chico was Marx regular, Margaret Dumont. The score featured what would become Groucho's theme, "Hooray for Captain Spalding!"

Unfortunately, *Animal Crackers* was just about the only successful presentation at the theater in this period. The next offering, *Broadway Nights* (1929) was a flop. Producer

Billy Rose presented *Billy Rose's Crazy Quilt* (1931) with a terrific score by Harry Warren, Mort Dixon and himself. Despite a big hit song, "I Found a Million Dollar Baby (in a Five and Ten Cent Store)" and the efforts of cast member Fanny Brice, then Mrs. Rose, the show failed.

A Little Racketeer (1932) is notable only because composer Dimitri Tiomkin contributed several melodies. The E. Y. Harburg and Lewis E. Gensler revue *Ballyhoo of 1932* (1932) didn't catch on, despite the talents of Grace and Paul Hartman, Bob Hope, Willie and Eugene Howard, and Lulu McConnell.

The theater housed two shows in 1934, which were appreciated only after they closed. The first was Virgil Thomson and Gertrude Stein's opera *Four Saints in Three Acts* (1934). The second was Noel Coward's musical, *Conversation Piece* (1934). Coward wrote the book, music and lyrics, including the now famous "I'll Follow My Secret Heart." Yvonne Printemps and George Sanders starred.

Marc Connelly's Pulitzer Prize-winning play *Green Pastures* (1935) enjoyed a revival at the 44th Street Theatre. Kurt Weill's antiwar musical *Johnny Johnson* (1936) featured Luther Adler, Morris Carnovsky, Lee J. Cobb, John Garfield, Elia Kazan, Robert Lewis, Sanford Meisner, and Art Smith. The Group Theater production had a book and lyrics by Paul Green. The revue *Crazy with the Heat* (1941), another failure, featured music and lyrics by Dana Suesse. Another revue, *Keep 'Em Laughing* (1942) was also a failure.

The theater hosted a few straight plays. One of these, *Winged Victory* (1943) was produced by the U.S. Army Air Forces. The two-act drama was written by Moss Hart. The show was as large in scale as a musical and, in fact, had original music composed by David Rose.

The 44th Street Theatre's short life ended when the Astor estate, which owned the theater's land, sold the property to the *New York Times*. The newspaper kept the theater in operation for five years before tearing it down in 1945 and building an addition to its printing plant.

49TH STREET THEATRE · 235 W. 49th Street. Architect: Herbert J. Krapp. Opening: December 26, 1921; *Face Value.* The Shuberts built the 49th Street Theatre, but it wasn't one of their more successful houses. An early hit was the revue *Chauve-Souris* (1922). Despite the Russian theme, the show was, typically, ersatz Russian. American composers, including L. Wolfe Gilbert and Abel Baer, wrote a number of tunes in a slightly Russian manner. Hit songs from the show included "Dark Eyes" by A. Salami, "Two Guitars," and the "Volga Boat Song." The show was so popular that it eventually had four revivals and a new edition in 1943. The second revival opened at the 49th Street Theatre on January 14, 1925, and ran sixty-nine performances.

The theater was the home for a number of hit plays with somewhat thin plots including, *Whispering Wires* (1922), a mystery thriller and *Give and Take* (1923), a farce by Aaron Hoffman. *The Judge's Husband* (1926) was another success.

The Shuberts lost the 49th Street Theatre when the Depression hit. The Federal Theater Project leased it for a time. In 1938, it became a movie house, and in the 1940s it was torn down.

46TH STREET THEATRE · See RICHARD RODGERS THEATRE.

FORUM THEATER · See MOVIELAND.

FRAZEE THEATER · See ANCO THEATER.

FREEDLEY, VINTON · See AARONS AND FREEDLEY.

FRENCH CASINO · See EARL CARROLL THEATRE.

FRIML, RUDOLF (1879–1972) · In the early part of the century, the musical theater took two separate paths: (1) the homegrown American musical comedy represented by the works of George M. Cohan, Irving Berlin, and Jerome Kern; and (2) the European operetta represented by Victor Herbert, Sigmund Romberg, and Rudolf Friml. Friml was one of the masters of this now outmoded form. From his operettas came some of the best-loved melodies of the early years of American popular song.

Friml was born in Prague, Bohemia, on December 7, 1879. At the age of eleven, one year after composing a barcarolle, he attended the Prague Conservatory where he studied under the tutelage of Dvorak and Jiranek. He completed the normal six-year course in half the allotted time and soon began touring Europe with violinist Jan Kubelik. He made his first appearance in the United States in 1901. He returned to play solo piano at Carnegie Hall in 1904 and again in 1906 to perform his own work, "Piano Concerto in B-Major" with Walter Damrosch conducting the New York Symphony Society.

When diva Emma Trentini broke relations with Victor Herbert, producer Arthur Hammerstein was forced to find a composer to write a score for his production of *The Firefly* (1912). Trentini was a major star who had just triumphed in Herbert's *Naughty Marietta,* and finding a composer equal to her volatile temperament was not easy. Through music publisher Max Dreyfus, Hammerstein found Friml and commissioned him to write the score with librettist Otto Harbach. The score contained three Friml standards, "Giannina Mia," "Love Is Like a Firefly," and "Sympathy."

The success of *The Firefly* led Hammerstein to sign Friml for additional projects. The first, *High Jinks* (1913), got its title from the name of a perfume which, when sprayed on its target, produced uncontrolled mirth. Back with Hammerstein, Friml and Harbach came up with *Katinka* (1915), starring Adele Rowland. *You're in Love* (1917) starred Marie Flynn as the sleepwalking heroine who made an impressive stroll on a ship's boom hanging over the audience. The play is notable today for giving Oscar Hammerstein II his first Broadway assignment, that of assistant stage manager.

Surprisingly, the next Harbach/Friml partnership resulted in a quick flop, *Kitty Darlin'*

(1917). Maybe Arthur Hammerstein's astute producing was the missing element. In the next Friml show, Hammerstein paired him with Rida Johnson Young, one of the few women lyricists on Broadway. The result, *Sometime* (1918), featured popular comedian Ed Wynn and the sultry Mae West in an early Broadway appearance.

Gloriana (1918), the next Friml offering, opened only twenty-two days after *Sometime.* For *Gloriana,* Friml teamed up with another woman lyricist, Catherine Chilsholm Cushing. Harbach, Hammerstein, and Friml were successful again with *Tumble Inn* (1919), a minor musical. *The Little Whopper* (1919), starred Vivienne Segal and was based on a silent movie, *Miss George Washington, Jr.* Friml's next score came more than two years later. Unfortunately, *June Love* (1921) proved less endearing than its predecessor.

Friml had his songs interpolated into the fifteenth edition of the *Ziegfeld Follies* (1921). The next full score under the Hammerstein banner was *The Blue Kitten* (1922). Friml was again teamed with Harbach who was joined by William Cary Duncan as a co-lyricist. *The Blue Kitten* was followed by the premiere of *Cinders* (1923). The failure of *Cinders* and Friml's sporadic output in the early twenties led many people to believe that he was washed up as a composer, but his next show proved to be his most popular.

Arthur Hammerstein, who still believed in Friml, paired him with his nephew Oscar for *Rose-Marie* (1924). Herbert Stothart also contributed music to the operetta. Mary Ellis played the title role, and operetta favorite Dennis King played her lover. The score yielded three giant hits: "Indian Love Call" remains the best known. The title song shows little of the European influence of earlier Friml melodies, and the "Song of the Mounties" (with music by Friml and Stothart) was the rousing male chorus number necessary in any good operetta. *Rose-Marie* also became the greatest financial success in Broadway history until Rodgers and Hammerstein's *Oklahoma!* in 1943.

Friml's next Broadway show, *The Vagabond King* (1925), proved almost as successful as *Rose-Marie,* with Friml returning to his European roots. The production, with lyrics by Brian Hooker, starred Dennis King and Carolyn Thomson. Friml again supplied an exceptional score with the numbers "Only a Rose," "Song of the Vagabonds," "Some Day," and "Huguette Waltz" achieving the longest-lasting fame.

The White Eagle (1927) was not a success. In his last Broadway success, *The Three Musketeers* (1928), Friml worked in familiar territory, musicalizing a classic European work, Justin Huntley McCarthy's novel, *If I Were King.* Dennis King repeated his prior successes in Friml shows. P .G. Wodehouse and Clifford Grey created the lyrics for the spectacular score. Among the best songs were the tremendously popular "March of the Musketeers," "Ma Belle," "My Sword and I," and "Your Eyes and One Kiss."

During the 1930s, Broadway audiences' tastes were changing. New American songwriters like Rodgers and Hart and DeSylva, Brown, and Henderson were capturing Broadway's fancy. Operetta was seen as more and more passé. Friml's last two shows, *Luana* (1930) and *Music Hath Charms* (1934) were failures.

Because Friml could not change his writing style, his career languished for the remainder of his life. He wrote an occasional song for film adaptations of his stage shows. Friml also concentrated on recordings, featuring him at the piano leading orchestras through his repertoire. In 1956, he worked with lyricist Johnny Burke on new songs for the remake of *The Vagabond King.* This was his last assignment. Rudolf Friml died on November 12, 1972.

FULTON THEATER · See HELEN HAYES THEATER.

G

GAIETY THEATER · 1547 Broadway between 45th and 46th Streets. Architects: Herts and Tallant. Opening: September 4, 1909; *The Fortune Hunter.* Klaw and Erlanger built the Gaiety for George M. Cohan, who shared in its management. The theater was noted for several architectural features. The audience area was built in what was known as the "mushroom" design, which reflected its configuration. The theater was also noted for the absence of pillars holding up the balcony, which in earlier theaters had drastically hampered sightlines. With cantilevered balconies, pillars became unnecessary. Another innovation featured in the new house was the orchestra pit. Prior to this, most orchestras were on the audience level and stages were raised accordingly. This "invisible orchestra" allowed the stage height to be lowered and the sight lines of the first rows to be improved and brought forward.

The first production was Cohan's *The Yankee Prince,* which played a few performances in the theater prior to opening in Washington, D.C., on September 20, 1909. This served as a dress rehearsal for both the new theater and the touring cast of the show.

Surprisingly, although the house was known for its orchestra pit, it seldom housed a musical comedy. The first full production at the theater came with the opening of *The Fortune Hunter* (1909). Other productions in the Gaiety's first decade included *First Lady of the Land* (1911); *Officer 666* (1912); *Stop Thief* (1912); *Nearly Married* (1913); *Erstwhile Susan* (1916); *Turn to the Right!* (1916); and *Sick-A-Bed* (1918).

The huge success of *Turn to the Right!* did not prepare the theater owners for the Gaiety's greatest hit, *Lightnin'* (1918) which ran a then astounding 1,291 performances. The show,

written by Frank Bacon and Winchell Smith, was the story of Lightin' Bill Jones, a landlord whose hotel conveniently straddled the border of Nevada and California. When the constabulary came after him, Lightin' would simply cross the border into another jurisdiction. Frank Bacon also starred in the comedy, which ran for three years. This made *Lightnin'* the longest-running play in Broadway history, a position it held until *Abie's Irish Rose* overtook it in the mid-1920s.

Following *Lightnin',* the Gaiety housed a string of failures: *The Wheel* (1921); a revival of *Alias Jimmy Valentine* (1921); and *Madeleine and the Movies* (1922). The next hit was *Loyalties* (1922) by John Galsworthy, chosen as a best play by Burns Mantle, editor of the *Best Plays* series.

The next play, *If Winter Comes* (1923) was a failure, but the theater's fortunes picked up with a production of Frederick Lonsdale's comedy, *Aren't We All?* (1923).

The Youngest (1924) was followed by *Loggerheads,* which moved to the Gaiety from the Cherry Lane Theater off-Broadway. George Gershwin's modern musical, *Tell Me More!* opened at the Gaiety on April 13, 1925. *These Charming People* (1925) was followed by *By the Way* (1925).

The theater's last year of operation as a legitimate house was 1926. Its last show was the modest hit *Love in a Mist* (1926).

Following the run of *Love in a Mist,* the theater was closed and soon reopened as a motion picture house. In 1932, the theater was converted to a Minsky's burlesque house. In 1943, the name was changed to the Victoria. The first movie to play the Victoria was *The City That Stopped Hitler-Heroic Stalingrad,* which opened on September 4, 1943. The auditorium was remodeled by designer Edward Durell Stone in 1949. Gone was the Louis XV auditorium and in its place a dropped ceiling and walls covered in aluminum mesh. The auditorium was enlarged to 1,050 seats. In 1980, the theater was renamed the Embassy.

The Victoria and its next-door neighbor the Astor Theater had the world's longest sign positioned on their shared roofs. The signage location above the two theaters was used primarily as an advertisement for their current movie attractions. The most spectacular of these was for *The Vikings.* When the theaters ceased to show first-run features, the sign was put to more prosaic uses. The huge Budweiser billboard was perhaps the best known of these.

The Victoria was demolished along with the Astor, Morosco, Bijou, and Helen Hayes theaters on March 22, 1982.

GEORGE ABBOTT THEATER · 152 W. 54th Street. Architect: R. E. Hall & Co. Opening: December 24, 1928; *Potiphar's Wife.* The Craig Theater couldn't have opened at a worse time—just as the Depression was changing the face of Broadway. Producers lost millions in the market as well as their theater holdings. The theater's location north of the theater district proper sealed its fate. From the beginning, the Craig was a disaster.

On November 27, 1934, the original owners, the Houston Properties Corporation, lost the theater, and it was renamed the Adelphi. The first show, *The Lord Blesses the Bishop,* didn't bode well for the success of the new venture when it closed after only seven performances. The theater remained a failure, and it was taken over by the Federal Theater Project.

Under the new management, the theater became successful for the first time. *It Can't Happen Here* was an enormous hit for the theater and the Federal Theater Project. The show was written by Sinclair Lewis and was unique in that it opened on October 27, 1936, in eighteen cities. New York alone had four productions.

Playwright Arthur Arent's *One-Third of a Nation* (1938) was one of the Federal Theater

Project's Living Newspapers. The show was the best known of all the Project's presentations, seen by over two thousand people in New York alone. Ten other cities later presented the show. The theme of *One Third of a Nation* was the problems of the nation's slums. The title of the piece was taken from Franklin Roosevelt's second inaugural address.

The last significant production at the Adelphi by the Federal Theater Project was *Sing for Your Supper* (1939). Its best-known song was "Ballad for Americans" by Earl Robinson and John Latouche.

With the end of the Federal Theater Project, the Adelphi was taken over by the Royal Fraternity of Master Metaphysicians. In December 1940, they changed the name of the theater to the Radiant Center. Three years later, on October 18, 1943, the theater became the Yiddish Art Theater. Its opening production was *The Family Carnovsky.* But the theater wasn't successful as a Yiddish theater either.

On April 20, 1944, the theater became the Adelphi Theater again. The musical *Allah Be Praised!* opened at the Adelphi but only ran twenty performances. When out-of-town producer Alfred Bloomingdale asked play doctor Cy Howard what to do, Howard suggested to Bloomingdale that he "Close the show and keep the store open nights."

Finally, the theater's luck changed with the opening of *On the Town* (1944). The show was directed by George Abbott who gave three talents, Leonard Bernstein, Betty Comden, and Adolph Green, their first Broadway break. The big song was "New York, New York."

Unfortunately, *On the Town* led the way to another series of flops. *Carib Song* (1945) starred the great choreographer and dancer Katharine Dunham. *Nellie Bly* (1946), with a score by Johnny Burke and James Van Heusen, starred William Gaxton, Marilyn Maxwell, and Victor Moore. *Three to Make Ready* (1946) was the third in a series by Morgan Lewis and Nancy Hamilton. *Three to Make Ready* moved to the St. James Theatre to make way for the next tenant, another failure about world travelers, but a spectacular one.

Around the World in Eighty Days (1946) was the brainchild of Orson Welles, who wrote the extravaganza's book and directed the show. In addition, Welles became producer when Michael Todd decamped while the show was in tryouts. Cole Porter wrote music and lyrics to the show, but none of the songs achieved any success.

Kurt Weill saw his musical version of Elmer Rice's play *Street Scene* open at the Adelphi Theater (1947). Anne Jeffreys, Polyna Stoska, Brian Sullivan, Sheila Bond, and Danny Daniels ably rendered the wonderful score, with lyrics by Langston Hughes.

Music in My Heart (1947), a musical with melodies by Tchaikovsky, was not a success. *Look Ma I'm Dancin'* (1948) probably should have been a bigger hit than it was. Hugh Martin wrote the catchy score, and Jerome Lawrence and Robert E. Lee contributed the libretto. George Abbott produced and directed in association with Jerome Robbins. Robbins also choreographed the musical, which starred Nancy Walker, Harold Lang, Tommy Rall, and Alice Pearce. *Hilarities* (1948) was apparently a misnomer for a revue that closed quickly.

The Dumont Television network used the theater for a decade beginning in 1948. It was renamed the 54th Street Theater on October 8, 1958, with the opening of *Drink to Me Only.*

Richard Adler and Jerry Ross' hit *Damn Yankees* transferred to the theater in 1958. Another hit, *Bye Bye Birdie* also transferred to the theater to end its run. Adler without his late partner Jerry Ross, tried his hand at both music and lyrics for *Kwamina* (1961), starring Robert Guillaume and Sally Ann Howes.

Richard Rodgers opened his first show without either Lorenz Hart or Oscar Hammerstein II with *No Strings* (1962). Rodgers provided both music and lyrics. The wonderful score contained such hits as "The Sweetest Sounds" and the title tune.

What Makes Sammy Run? (1964) was a musicalization of the famous novel by Budd Schulberg. Ervin Drake composed the score and wrote the lyrics of the score, which included a soon-to-be popular song "A Room without Windows."

La Grosse Valise (1965) had music by Gerard Calvi and lyrics by Harold Rome. This was the last show to play the theater before it was renamed the George Abbott Theater.

Darling of the Day (1968) was a failure by the usually reliable Jule Styne and E. Y. Harburg though the score is much admired. *Buck White* (1969) was a musical failure, most notable for the Broadway debut of Cassius Clay (Muhammad Ali). The theater's last show did even worse. *Gantry* (1970), with Robert Shaw and Rita Moreno opened and closed in one day.

The George Abbott theater was demolished in 1970 to make way for the New York Hilton.

GEORGE M. COHAN'S THEATRE ·

1482 Broadway at southeast corner of 43rd Street; main entrance on 43rd Street. Architect: George Keister. Opening: February 13, 1911; *Get-Rich-Quick Wallingford.* The George M. Cohan's Theatre was built by the team of George M. Cohan and Sam H. Harris, among the busiest producers of the late teens. They also managed the Harris Theater, the Grand Opera House, the Astor Theatre, the Gaiety Theater, and the Bronx Opera House as well as Cohan's Grand Opera House in Chicago.

Cohan, one of Broadway's biggest egotists, thought of the theater as a tribute to his career. The marble lobby featured exhibits on the history of the Four Cohans. The theater's boxes were topped by murals depicting Cohan's many stage successes.

The first great hit at Cohan's Theatre was *The Little Millionaire* (1911). It featured Cohan as composer, lyricist, librettist, director, co-producer and star. The musical also starred Cohan's parents and Donald Crisp.

In *Broadway Jones* (1912), Cohan played a Broadwayite who finds himself in the sticks. The comedy *Potash and Perlmutter* (1913) was a huge hit. Roi Cooper Megrue and Walter Hackett's play *It Pays to Advertise* (1914) starred Grant Mitchell.

In 1915, Cohan and Harris sold their theater to Joe Leblang. The discount ticket seller, knew his limitations and allowed A.L. Erlanger to manage the theater. *Pom-Pom* (1916) had music by Hugo Felix and book and lyrics by one of Broadway's few women lyricists, Anne Caldwell. Mitzi Hajos had the lead. Later that year, *Seven Chances* (1916) opened to acclaim. Another of the theater's early successes was *Come Out of the Kitchen* (1916).

The Kiss Burglar (1918) was a minor musical by Raymond Hubbell and Glen MacDonough. *Head Over Heels* (1918) was an early musical by Jerome Kern. *A Prince There Was* (1918) had as its author Robert Hilliard, who also starred. Cohan rewrote the play and made it a success.

Elsie Janis and Her Gang opened at the Cohan Theatre (1919), featuring the talented actress Eva Le Gallienne. Charles Dillingham and Florenz Ziegfeld produced the show. *The Genius and the Crowd* (1920), a comedy by John T. McIntyre and Francis Hill, was significant because it was the first show Cohan produced on his own following a split with Harris.

Cohan had a great hit with his melodrama, *The Tavern* (1920). The story of Francois Villon was meant by Cohan to be an affectionate travesty, but opening night critics took it seriously and panned the proceedings. However, Robert Benchley, Dorothy Parker, and Robert E. Sherwood enjoyed the play in the spirit in which it was presented and gave it rave reviews. It was revived five times on Broadway and countless times across the country.

Two Little Girls in Blue (1921) had music was by Vincent Youmans and lyrics by Arthur Francis, better known as Ira Gershwin. One of the theater's biggest successes was Clemence Dane's drama *A Bill of Divorcement* (1921). Katharine Cornell starred. *A Bill of Divorcement* moved on to make way for the opening of Ed Wynn's musical, *The Perfect Fool* (1921). George Gershwin composed two of the numbers in the show. *The Love Child* (1922) starred Janet Beecher and Sidney Blackmer.

In between theatrical engagements, the theater presented silent films. Among the most notable of these were Cecil B. DeMille's *The Ten Commandments* (1923) and MGM's *Ben-Hur* (1925) starring Ramon Novarro.

Adrienne (1923), a musical with a score by popular favorites Albert Von Tilzer and A. Seymour Brown, had as its musical director Max Steiner, who would make a name for himself as one of Hollywood's greatest composers.

Owen Davis' farce *The Haunted House* (1924) starred Wallace Edinger as an author who lives his life in the style of the book he is writing. While writing about a haunted house he scares everyone he is in contact with. Another farce by Davis to play the Cohan was *Easy Come, Easy Go* (1925).

A Frank Craven play, *The 19th Hole* (1927), followed the downward path of a golf addict.

Milton Ager and Jack Yellen wrote the score to *Rain or Shine* (1928). Heywood Broun organized a show to give out-of-work actors some employment. The result, *Shoot the Works* (1931), had as contributors to the score and sketches Peter Arno, Broun himself, Dorothy Parker, Nunnally Johnson, Sig Herzig, E. B. White, Ira Gershwin, Irving Berlin, Leo Robin, Dorothy Fields, Jimmy McHugh, Jay Gorney, E. Y. Harburg, and Vernon Duke. Among the performers the show helped out were Imogene Coca, Jack Hazzard, George Murphy, and Broun.

There You Are (1932) was a short-lived musical that marked an end to the theater's legitimate policy. Along with many other Broadway houses, during the Depression the theater adopted a movie policy. In 1938, with Leblang defaulting on his mortgage, the theater was torn down along with the FitzGerald Building, which shared its facade.

GEORGE WHITE'S SCANDALS · *George White's Scandals* were a long running (1919–1939) annual series of revues produced and sometimes written by George White. The *Scandals* were one of the most important of the revue series, a popular genre in the first part of the century.

What made the *Scandals* noteworthy was

the high quality of their material. They were the first revues to assign complete scores to song-writing teams. Until the *Scandals,* songs were submitted to producers who would pick and choose the best. White also put an emphasis on dance, since he was a former hoofer in the *Ziegfeld Follies* and other Broadway shows.

White came up with the idea for the *Scandals* while he was in the *Follies.* He realized Ziegfeld was immersed in the producing styles of the teens and earlier, and he believed he could improve on the revue format. White was sure he could move the revue into more modern fashion in his own series. His revues were much faster paced than Ziegfeld's, reflecting a new trend in jazzy entertainment.

The first *George White's Scandals* was the 1919 edition. White contributed some sketches and lyrics in addition to starring in the revue. He hired Ann Pennington, a dancer who had also appeared as his partner in the *Follies.* Pennington would become a *Scandals* regular, appearing in five editions. White hired up-and-coming composers Richard Whiting and Herbert Spencer for the tunes. Arthur Jackson and White himself handled lyric chores.

White certainly had a knack for finding other young talents. His next edition featured a score by the young George Gershwin and Arthur Jackson. The 1920 edition introduced a new dance step to Broadway, the scandal walk.

White again co-directed, co-authored, produced and starred in his next *Scandals* (1921). Gershwin and Jackson had a hit with their score, which featured "Drifting Along with the Tide." For the fourth edition (1922), B. G. DeSylva and E. Ray Goetz provided lyrics to Gershwin's tunes. The hit song of this edition was "I'll Build a Stairway to Paradise," with lyrics by DeSylva and Arthur Francis (a pseudonym of Ira Gershwin).

The next *Scandals* (1923), was an undistinguished affair. It was followed by the 1924 edition. The Gershwin and DeSylva score presented one great standard, "Somebody Loves Me," which featured additional lyrics by Ballard Macdonald.

For the 1925 edition George Gershwin, who had abandoned the revue field to concentrate on book musicals, was replaced by the songwriting team of DeSylva, Brown, and Henderson. This was the first uniting of the noted songwriting team, who would provide some of their greatest hits for the *Scandals.*

In the 1926 edition, the song writing team was in top form. The trio presented White with three smash hit songs "The Birth of the Blues," "The Black Bottom," and "Lucky Day." Former *Scandals* contributor George Gershwin returned with an interpolation of his "Rhapsody in Blue." White charged $55 a ticket for seats in the front of the orchestra on opening night. He was right to do so, for the show was a huge success.

Because of the long run of the 1926 edition, there was no 1927 show. The next *Scandals* (1928) didn't have a particularly good score; in fact, one song was titled, "Not As Good As Last Year." For the next edition (1929), George White contributed songs to one of his own shows.

In 1930, White was producer and director of a book show, *Flying High.* He returned to his *Scandals* the next year. The 1931 edition boasted a score by Brown and Henderson, but this time without DeSylva. The duo didn't seem to miss their former collaborator, for the score contained five huge hits—"Ladies and Gentlemen That's Love," "Life Is Just a Bowl of Cherries," "That's Why Darkies Were Born," "This Is the Missus," and "The Thrill Is Gone." The cast, too, was the greatest in *Scandals* history. Ethel Merman, Rudy Vallee, Alice Faye, Ethel Barrymore Colt, Ray Bolger, Everett Marshall, and Willie and Eugene Howard were the stars. However, the country was in the middle of the Depression, and theater was suffering. So despite the excellent cast and material, the show didn't run as long as it might have in better times.

There was no *Scandals* the next year, although White did present a revue, *George White's Music Hall Varieties* (1932). The Depression took its toll, and the next *Scandals* was not produced until 1936. The show opened on

Christmas Day of 1935 at the New Amsterdam Theater, site of most of the *Ziegfeld Follies*. The last *Scandals* was the 1939 edition. The score was mostly by Sammy Fain and Jack Yellen. They supplied the standard, "Are You Havin' Any Fun?," which was introduced by singer Ella Logan. The two other hits were by Yellen and Herb Magidson, "Something I Dreamed Last Night" and "The Mexiconga."

The last *Scandals* was White's last Broadway show. He retired from the stage, leaving behind a wealth of great songs and the satisfaction of knowing that he helped boost the careers of many newcomers. The *Scandals* were certainly the revue series most in step with the times, and it was the vision of George White, their producer, director, writer, composer, choreographer, and star, that created them.

GERALD SCHOENFELD THEATRE · 236 W. 45th Street. Architect: Herbert I. Krapp. Opening: October 10, 1917; *A Successful Calamity*.

The Shuberts had leased land from the Astor Estate for the Shubert and Booth Theatres. The remaining land was split between the Broadhurst and Plymouth Theatres. The brothers, who already owned every other theater on the same side of the street, were happy to extend their domain. They backed producer Arthur Hopkins in his wish to have his own theater. Hopkins was already the owner of the tiny Punch and Judy Theatre and the Plymouth allowed him a more positive cash flow. A theater worthy of the best in contemporary drama, the Plymouth fulfilled Hopkins' high-minded goals. A proponent of serious American drama, he rejected the melodrama and parlor plays that typified the theater's offerings at the turn of the century. Hopkins was a staunch believer of spiritualism, and his kindly demeanor and good taste endeared him to the Broadway community. Hopkins, even after his successful years had past, retained offices in the Plymouth Theater. He died in 1950.

Architect Herbert Krapp designed the Plymouth (on 45th Street) and the Broadhurst (on 44th Street) as a single unit, like their neighbors the Sam S. Shubert and Booth theaters. The shared side walls of the Shubert and Booth theaters together with the back of the old Astor Hotel formed the famous narrow walkway known as Shubert Alley. Similarly the Plymouth and Broadhurst formed an alley parallel to Shubert Alley. At the time, zoning regulations demanded a side alley exit from all theaters. The Broadhurst and Plymouth alley was almost immediately closed off to foot traffic.

The first booking, Clare Kummer's *A Successful Calamity,* had originally opened at the Booth and finished its run at the Plymouth. The first production to originate at the Plymouth was the John Barrymore vehicle *Redemption* (1918).

After a run of Shakespeare's *Hamlet* (1918) with Walter Hampden in the title role, Barrymore returned to the Plymouth's stage in *The Jest* (1919). Barrymore was joined by his brother Lionel in the Sam Benelli drama. Hopkins produced and directed the venture, and Robert Edmond Jones, the premier set designer of his day, repeated the assignment he had carried out for *Redemption*. The three men, Hopkins, Jones and Barrymore, were fast becoming Broadway's most formidable artistic team. After a short hiatus, it reopened at the Plymouth on September 19, 1919, for an additional 179 performances. The play was to be presented at the Plymouth once more, on February 4, 1926, with Basil Sydney under Hopkins' direction. Without the Barrymores, the play failed to incite the audiences' passions, and the revival closed after 78 performances.

Rida Johnson Young, best remembered today as lyricist and librettist for a number of Victor Herbert operettas, saw her melodramatic play *Little Old New York* (1920) open at the Plymouth. Genevieve Tobin starred as the girl who masquerades as a boy to win an inheritance rightfully the property of another lad with whom she falls in love.

Zoe Akins' *Daddy's Gone-A-Hunting* (1921) opened with Marjorie Rambeau in the lead. Hopkins produced and directed the comedy *The Old Soak* (1922) by Don Marquis, with Harry Beresford in the title role and Minnie Dupree as his wife. J. P. McEvoy's play *The*

Potters (1923) was meant to be a realistic look at American family life.

High drama returned to the Plymouth's stage with Laurence Stallings and Maxwell Anderson's *What Price Glory?* (1924). Hopkins produced and directed the harrowing World War I drama, which starred William Boyd (later known as Hopalong Cassidy in movies), Louis Wolheim, and Brian Donlevy.

Philip Barry's first play at the Plymouth, *In a Garden* (1925), starred Laurette Taylor and Louis Calhern, but it failed to catch on. Barry had better luck later. In the aptly titled *Burlesque* (1927) Arthur Hopkins, and George Manker Watters treated audiences to what they thought was a realistic view behind the scenes in a burlesque house. The play starred Barbara Stanwyck and Hal Skelly.

Clark Gable and Zita Johann starred in Sophie Treadwell's reworking of the story of Ruth Snyder, the first woman in America to die in the electric chair, entitled *Machinal* (1928).

Holiday (1928), Philip Barry's sparkling comedy, was produced and directed by Arthur Hopkins and starred Hope Williams and Ben Smith. The play is best remembered for its movie version, starring Katharine Hepburn, who was Hope Williams' Broadway understudy.

Hopkins produced Donald Ogden Stewart's play, *Rebound* (1930), at the Plymouth and cast Hope Williams in the lead. Stewart also wrote a small part for himself in the comedy. The play was a hit.

Elmer Rice's *Counselor-at-Law* (1931), starring Paul Muni, reopened on September 12, 1932, for an additional 104 performances. The following year, Clare Kummer had another hit at the Plymouth with *Her Master's Voice* (1933). It starred Laura Hope Crews and Roland Young.

Tallulah Bankhead explored the dramatic possibilities of *Dark Victory* (1934), the story of a woman's emotional triumph over a brain tumor. Samson Raphaelson wrote *Accent on Youth* (1934), starring Constance Cummings. Robert E. Sherwood adapted *Tovarich* (1936) for stars Marta Abba and John Halliday.

Gertrude Lawrence opened in Rachel Crothers' *Susan and God* (1937). In 1943, the star opened City Center's drama program with the same play at affordable prices. Robert Emmet Sherwood followed *Tovarich* with his Pulitzer Prize-winning play *Abe Lincoln in Illinois* (1938). Raymond Massey as the future president captured the hearts and minds of the audience. The play was the first production of the newly formed Playwrights' Company. Otto Preminger directed himself as a Nazi in Clare Boothe Luce's *Margin for Error* (1939) with Sam Levene co-starring.

Tallulah Bankhead returned in triumph to the Plymouth in Thornton Wilder's *The Skin of Our Teeth* (1942). Elia Kazan directed the Pulitzer Prize-winning drama, which also starred Fredric March, Florence Eldridge, Florence Reed, E. G. Marshall, and Montgomery Clift.

Raymond Scott and Bernard Hanighen contributed the score to an odd bit of orientalia, *Lute Song* (1946), the first musical to play the Plymouth. Mary Martin starred along with Clarence Derwent, Mildred Dunnock, and Yul Brynner.

Noel Coward's *Present Laughter* (1946) starred Clifton Webb. Bankhead made another brief appearance at the Plymouth later in the decade in a considerably lesser play, *The Eagle Has Two Heads* (1947). Critics were of one mind—they hated the play in spite of the fact that at each performance Bankhead fell down a flight of ten steps. The fall received the most praise.

Bankhead was back at the Plymouth in Noel Coward's *Private Lives* (1948) with co-star Donald Cook. The revival played 248 performances, the exact same number of performances as the original production of 1931.

Rodgers and Hammerstein produced Samuel Taylor's *The Happy Time* (1950), with Claude Dauphin, Johnny Stewart, Eva Gabor, and Kurt Kasznar. *Dial 'M' for Murder* (1952), a thriller by Frederic Knott, starred Maurice Evans, Richard Derr, Gusti Huber, and John Williams. Herman Wouk adapted his novel *The Caine Mutiny Court Martial* (1954) for the Plymouth stage. Charles Laughton directed Henry Fonda, Lloyd Nolan, and John Hodiak.

Three for Tonight (1955) opened with Marge and Gower Champion, Hiram Sherman, and Harry Belafonte. Peter Ustinov's comedy *Romanoff and Juliet* (1957) opened at the Plymouth with the playwright starring. The light comedy *The Marriage-Go-Round* by Leslie Stevens (1958) starred Charles Boyer, Claudette Colbert, and Julie Newmar. Elizabeth Seal created a sensation as a whore with a heart of gold, in the musical *Irma La Douce* (1960) by Marguerite Monnot, Julian More, David Heneker, and Monty Norman. The musical's big song was "Our Language of Love."

One of the greatest hits of the sixties was Neil Simon's *The Odd Couple* (1965) starring Art Carney and Walter Matthau. Simon followed that success with *The Star-Spangled Girl* (1966) that starred Anthony Perkins, Richard Benjamin, and Connie Stevens. Simon returned to the Plymouth with a bigger success, *Plaza Suite* (1968), an evening of three one-acts all taking place in the Plaza Hotel. Each starred George C. Scott and Maureen Stapleton. The playwright had less success with his first noncomedy dramatic attempt, *The Gingerbread Lady* (1970). Maureen Stapleton starred as an alcoholic singer down on her luck.

For the next few years, beginning in 1973, British productions dominated the Plymouth Theater. Peter Cook and Dudley Moore opened in their two-man show *Good Evening* (1973) in the vein of their previous success, *Beyond the Fringe. Equus* (1974), by the English playwright Peter Shaffer, starred Anthony Hopkins as the psychiatrist of a boy who has inexplicably blinded several horses. Peter Firth starred as the youth. Britisher Simon Gray's play *Otherwise Engaged* (1977) starred Tom Courteney as a man who could never get a moment's peace. After a two-year stay by the Fats Waller retrospective *Ain't Misbehavin'*, which moved from the Longacre Theater, the theater hosted another English import, *Piaf* (1981). Jane Laportaire starred as French singer Edith Piaf, and her performance won more kudos than the script.

The theater's next booking was a true theatrical event. It was the Royal Shakespeare Company's production of *The Life and Adventures of Nicholas Nickleby* (1981) based on the Charles Dickens novel. Roger Rees played the title role. The play took eight hours to perform; audiences had a choice of either seeing it in one day with a dinner break or coming to the theater on two successive nights. *"Nick Nick"* (as it was affectionately dubbed) played to sold-out audiences for a limited engagement of forty-nine performances.

On January 6, 1983, David Hare's *Plenty* transferred to the Plymouth from the Public Theater where it premiered on October 21, 1982. Kate Nelligan and Edward Herrmann starred in the drama, which played ninety-two performances at the Plymouth in addition to the forty-five performances it had enjoyed at the Public.

The Real Thing (1984) by Tom Stoppard continued the British dominance of the Plymouth's stage. Then Lily Tomlin brought her one-woman show, *The Search for Signs of Intelligent Life in the Universe* (1985) to the Plymouth for a limited engagement. Lanford Wilson's *Burn This* opened on October 14, 1987, with John Malkovich and Joan Allen in the leads. Wendy Wasserstein's first Broadway hit, *The Heidi Chronicles* (1989), was a long running tenant at the Plymouth.

The 1990's were an inauspicious decade for the theater with a series of forgettable flops. Notable, though a failure, was Stephen Sondheim's final Broadway musical to date, *Passion* (1994). The show wasn't your typical tourist-aimed commercial musical and couldn't find an audience after the Sondheim fans saw the production. That couldn't be said for the next musical to play the Plymouth, *Jekyll & Hyde* (1997). Frank Wildhorn's loud musical was aimed squarely at the tourist trade and they loved it. Others did not. Harry Connick Jr. had a quick failure with *Thou Shalt Not* (2001), a pretentious musical directed by Susan Stroman. Boy George wrote a good score for *Taboo* (2003), which suffered from poor direction and producing. In the middle of the run of

Brooklyn, the theater was named after Shubert Organization producer Gerald Schoenfeld. The ceremony took place on May 9, 2005. At the same time the Royale Theatre was named after Schoenfeld's partner, Bernard Jacobs.

GERSHWIN, GEORGE AND IRA · George

George Gershwin (1898–1937) George Gershwin was born in Brooklyn, New York, on September 26, 1898, to a poor family of first generation immigrants. In 1912, his parents purchased a piano so that brother Ira could take lessons. But it was George who showed the natural predilection for music. He amazed his family when he sat down at the new piano and played simple tunes.

In fact, George had begun his "studies" at a neighbor's house where he taught himself the basics of piano playing. He went on to more structured schooling with Charles Hambitzer. Hambitzer in turn urged George to study theory, orchestration, and harmony with Edward Kilenyi.

George had ambitions to become a concert pianist, but his teachers convinced him that such a dream was impractical. Luckily, he had an interest in the burgeoning field of American popular song. Like most of his contemporaries, he idolized Jerome Kern and Irving Berlin, two composers who, with George M. Cohan, were most responsible for bringing an American sensibility to what had been a predominantly European art.

"When You Want 'Em, You Can't Get 'Em (When You Got 'Em, You Don't Want 'Em)" was the title of George's first published song, copyrighted in 1916 with lyrics by Murray Roth. George's first Broadway song, "The Making of a Girl," was written for *The Passing Show of 1916* (1916) in collaboration with Sigmund Romberg with lyrics by Harold Atteridge.

George created his first important song, "Swanee," which was written for the Capitol Theater's revue *Demi-Tasse* (1919) and was later interpolated into the Al Jolson show *Sinbad* (1918) after its opening. "Swanee," written with Irving Caesar, was an enormous hit as a result of its exposure in *Sinbad* and

led to composing offers by Broadway producers.

La, La, Lucille (1919), George's first Broadway show, opened at the Henry Miller Theatre with a libretto by Fred Jackson and lyrics by Arthur J. Jackson and B. G. DeSylva. *Morris Gest's Midnight Whirl* (1919) with lyrics by B. G. DeSylva followed.

George White's Scandals of 1920 was a successful installment of the annual revue. George White had the foresight to hire George Gershwin when the composer was just beginning to make a name for himself. Arthur Jackson contributed the lyrics.

George's next Broadway attempt, *A Dangerous Maid,* closed out of town in Pittsburgh. The show is notable as the first for which Ira Gershwin wrote all the lyrics. Ira was concerned that it would appear he was hired only because he was George's brother, so he assumed the name Arthur Francis, the first names of their brother and sister.

Ira Gershwin (1896–1983) Ira was born on December 6, 1896, on the Lower East Side of New York City. He was always interested in language, having written light verse all through school. Ira saw his work published by Franklin P. Adams in Adams' newspaper column, "The Conning Tower."

The first song with lyrics by Ira and music by George to appear in a Broadway show was "The Real American Folk Song Is a Rag." It was put into *Ladies First* (1918) where it received little notice and wasn't published until years later. The first published song with music by George and lyrics by Ira was "Waiting for the Sun to Come Up," which was written for *The Sweetheart Shop* (1920).

Their next Broadway show was *Two Little Girls in Blue* (1921), which opened at the George M. Cohan Theatre. Vincent Youmans and Paul Lanin also wrote some of the music for the score.

George White's Scandals of 1921 had lyrics by Arthur Jackson and music by George. The only semi-success in the score was "Drifting Along with the Tide." The next year's edition of the *Scandals* contained the Gershwins' first standards as a team. The show opened with lyrics also supplied by B. G. DeSylva and E. Ray Goetz. The biggest hit was "I'll Build a Stairway to Paradise," with lyrics by DeSylva and Ira.

For a while, it seemed that George composed minor scores to minor musicals. These included *Our Nell* (1922) (with interpolated songs by George); *The Rainbow* (1923); the 1923 edition of the *Scandals* (1923); and *Sweet Little Devil* (1924) at the Astor Theatre.

On February 12, 1924, *Rhapsody in Blue* premiered at Aeolian Hall. The first show of the year for George was another edition of the *Scandals*. The show's lyrics were by B. G. DeSylva, who contributed the lyrics to the show's big hit, "Somebody Loves Me," with Ballard Macdonald. The song has remained a standard more than sixty years after the show's premiere.

Primrose (1924) opened at the Winter Garden Theater in London with lyrics by Ira and Desmond Carter. The libretto was written by George Grossmith and Guy Bolton. It was the Gershwin's biggest hit to date and it paved the way to a successful return to America.

The brothers' next show, with Ira writing under his own name, was a huge hit. *Lady, Be Good!* (1924) opened at the Liberty Theatre on 42nd Street, produced by Alex A. Aarons and Vinton Freedley with a book by Guy Bolton and Fred Thompson. *Lady, Be Good!'s* jaunty score contained at least two standards—the title song and "Fascinating Rhythm." *Lady, Be Good!* established the brothers as a successful team, and for the next twenty years they wrote together.

Tell Me More! (1925) wasn't as big a success as *Lady, Be Good!* The lyrics by Ira and B. G. DeSylva accompanied one moderately successful song, "Kickin' the Clouds Away."

Tip-Toes (1925) at the Liberty Theatre was twice as successful. The Gershwin brothers' score contained several hits, including "Looking for a Boy," "That Certain Feeling" and "Sweet and Low Down." George's Concerto in F premiered at Carnegie Hall on December 3, 1925. Seven days later, *Song of the Flame*

opened; George's third Broadway show of the year. *Song of the Flame* was an old-fashioned operetta with music also by Herbert Stothart. Otto Harbach and Oscar Hammerstein II wrote the lyrics.

Reunited with his brother Ira, George wrote some of his best tunes for the Aarons and Freedley musical *Oh, Kay!* (1926) at the Imperial Theatre. "Maybe," "Clap Yo' Hands" and "Do, Do, Do" were all hits, but they were overshadowed by "Someone to Watch Over Me."

The Gershwins' next show, *Strike Up the Band,* closed in Philadelphia in September 1927. That temporary setback was partially compensated by their next smash hit, *Funny Face* (1927), the show that Aarons and Freedley used to open their new Alvin Theater. The theater and the show were an immediate success.

Florenz Ziegfeld commissioned George and Sigmund Romberg to compose the score of *Rosalie* (1929). P. G. Wodehouse and Ira Gershwin supplied the lyrics to the hit show. The most famous of the Gershwin brothers' songs was "How Long Has This Been Going On?"

The Gershwins' next show was equally successful. *That's a Good Girl* (1928), their third show to premiere in London, opened at the London Hippodrome.

For *Treasure Girl* (1928), the brothers were back at the Alvin Theater under the auspices of Aarons and Freedley. Gertrude Lawrence, Clifton Webb, and Mary Hay introduced a fine score, including "I've Got a Crush on You," "I Don't Think I'll Fall in Love Today" and "Feeling I'm Falling."

George's *An American in Paris* premiered at Carnegie Hall on December 13, 1928. Walter Damrosch conducted the Philharmonic Symphony Society of New York.

Ziegfeld used the Gershwins' talents for his production *Show Girl* (1929). Gus Kahn collaborated on the lyrics. As with many shows of the same period, *Show Girl's* run was cut short by the Depression.

Ziegfeld again commissioned a Gershwin score, this time for *Ming Toy.* The Depression hit Ziegfeld hard, and the show was never produced. In the score was a Gershwin song that became an enduring standard "Embraceable You," later used in the hit *Girl Crazy.*

The 1930s began for the Gershwins with a revival of *Strike Up the Band* (1930). The revised version opened at the Times Square Theater. Bobby Clark, Paul McCullough, Blanche Ring, and Dudley Clements starred in the early satire. The score included "Soon," "Strike Up the Band" and "I've Got a Crush on You" (previously in *Treasure Girl*).

The Gershwins' next score accompanied another great success. Aarons and Freedley opened *Girl Crazy* (1930) at their Alvin Theater. The cast included Ginger Rogers, Allen Kearns, William Kent, Willie Howard, and, making her Broadway debut, Ethel Merman. The show's orchestra was equally luminous. Among its members were Benny Goodman, Glenn Miller, Red Nichols, Jimmy Dorsey, Jack Teagarden, and Gene Krupa. The show contained five standards, "Bidin' My Time," "Embraceable You," "I Got Rhythm," "But Not for Me," and "Boy! What Love Has Done to Me."

The Gershwins took a brief sojourn in Hollywood to write the score for *Delicious,* released by Fox Film Corporation on December 3, 1931. Five days later, the Gershwins' *Of Thee I Sing* opened at the Music Box Theater under the leadership of producer Sam Harris. George S. Kaufman, who had written the first book of *Strike Up the Band,* collaborated with Morrie Ryskind, the author of the revised *Strike Up the Band.* The score included three standards, the title song, "Love Is Sweeping the Country" and "Who Cares." *Of Thee I Sing* proved to be an enormous success and won the Pulitzer Prize.

Following the premieres of his *Second Rhapsody* on January 29, 1932, and his *Cuban Overture* on August 16, 1932, George saw *Pardon My English* (1933) open at the Majestic Theater with Aarons and Freedley producing. The score contained several hit songs, "My Cousin in Milwaukee," "The Lorelei" and "Isn't It a Pity."

Let 'Em Eat Cake (1933) was a sequel to *Of Thee I Sing.* The song "Mine" was the big hit from the score. William Gaxton, Victor Moore, and Lois Moran repeated their roles from *Of Thee I Sing.*

While George was working on his monumental opera *Porgy and Bess,* Ira worked on his first collaboration with another composer. The Shuberts presented *Life Begins at 8:40* (1934) at their Winter Garden Theater. The music was written by Harold Arlen and the lyrics by Ira and E. Y. Harburg. The hit songs included "You're a Builder Upper," "Fun to Be Fooled," and "Let's Take a Walk Around the Block."

George Gershwin's last Broadway score and what most people consider his masterpiece was *Porgy and Bess* (1935). The show was presented by the Theater Guild at the Alvin Theater. The lyrics were written by Ira and Du Bose Heyward. Todd Duncan, Anne Brown, John W. Bubbles, and Ruby Elzy starred. The show contained George's richest melodies and most theatrical ballads. "Summertime," "My Man's Gone Now," "I Got Plenty O' Nuthin'," "Bess, You Is My Woman Now," and "It Ain't Necessarily So" are among the greatest songs written for the American musical theater.

Ira again collaborated with another composer, this time Vernon Duke. The show was the *Ziegfeld Follies of 1936* (1936), which was presented by Ziegfeld's widow, Billie Burke, and the Shuberts. It opened at the Winter Garden Theater and starred Fanny Brice, Bob Hope, Eve Arden, Gertrude Niesen, and Josephine Baker. The only hit to emerge from the score was "I Can't Get Started."

George and Ira went to Hollywood to script the songs to three movies. *Shall We Dance* was released by RKO in May, 1937. *A Damsel in Distress* was released in November that same year by RKO. Goldwyn released *The Goldwyn Follies* in February 1938.

While in Hollywood, George began having frequent headaches. At first doctors were unable to find anything wrong. As the illness progressed, it was discovered that he had a brain tumor. After an unsuccessful operation, George Gershwin died in Hollywood on July 11, 1937. He was thirty-eight years old.

The Goldwyn Follies was completed after George's death by Vernon Duke and by Kay Swift, who used George's notes to complete the songs. Ira was devastated by the loss of his brother.

Ira collaborated with Kurt Weill on the score to *Lady in the Dark* (1941), which boasted a book by Moss Hart and opened at the Alvin Theater. The show starred Gertrude Lawrence, Danny Kaye, Victor Mature, and Macdonald Carey.

Ira wrote a score for the movie *The North Star*, released by RKO in October 1943. He was teamed with an unlikely partner, Aaron Copeland. A more lighthearted assignment followed when Ira teamed up with Jerome Kern for the movie *Cover Girl*. It was produced by composer Arthur Schwartz for Columbia, which released it in April 1944.

Kurt Weill was again Ira's collaborator for *The Firebrand of Florence* (1945) based on the life of Benvenuto Cellini. The show was a failure, opening at the Alvin Theater.

Weill and Gershwin went to Hollywood to supply the score to *Where Do We Go From Here?* The movie was released by 20th Century-Fox in May 1945.

Ira returned to New York for his last Broadway show, *Park Avenue* (1946). Arthur Schwartz, producer of *Cover Girl*, was Ira's collaborator. The show was presented by Max Gordon at the Shubert Theatre. The score was a bright spot in an otherwise unsuccessful show.

Ira settled permanently in Hollywood, where he supplied the lyrics to a succession of film musicals. The score for *The Shocking Miss Pilgrim* (20th Century-Fox, 1947) was built around jottings George had left at his death. Ira wrote the *Barkleys of Broadway* (MGM, 1949) with Harry Warren. It would prove to be the last film featuring the team of Fred Astaire and Ginger Rogers.

A minor effort, *Give a Girl a Break*, was an MGM film released in 1953. It had music by Burton Lane. Harold Arlen was the composer of one of Ira's biggest movie hits, *A Star Is Born*. Warner Brothers released the movie starring the Judy Garland and James Mason

in October 1954. Ira's last score was written for the Paramount Pictures *The Country Girl* with music by Harold Arlen. It was released in December 1954. *Kiss Me, Stupid,* a Billy Wilder film, contained three previously unpublished songs by the Gershwin brothers. It was released by United Artists in December 1964.

Ira Gershwin died in Hollywood on August 17, 1983.

GERSHWIN THEATER · 1633 Broadway between 50th and 51st Street. Designer: Ralph Alswang. Opening: November 28, 1972; *Via Galactica.* This theater, originally named the Uris, was the first new Broadway theater built in New York since the Earl Carroll Theater went up in 1931. The 1,900 seat theater was built on the site originally occupied by the Capitol Theater, a huge movie palace that critics thought would have served the same purpose as the Uris with more style. However, the Uris was definitely an afterthought. The first priority was to build a massive office building on the site. This was one of the first giant offices in Times Square and was criticized for ruining the low-rise area. Critics at the time prophesized correctly that the Uris was only one of the first of many skyscrapers that would forever change the special qualities of Times Square.

The Uris opened with a short-lived musical, *Via Galactica,* which had music by Galt MacDermot, composer of *Hair,* and lyrics by Christopher Gore. The show ran for only seven performances.

Cy Coleman and Dorothy Fields wrote the score to *Seesaw* (1973), the next offering at the Uris. *Seesaw,* under Michael Bennett's direction, was not successful. More failures followed in the Uris' early years. A revival of *Desert Song* opened in late 1973 and lasted only fifteen performances, and a stage adaptation of Lerner and Loewe's film *Gigi* played 103 performances.

In 1975, the theater found no legitimate bookings. Instead the Uris presented a series of concerts by pop stars. The next year, with the short-lived exception of *Treemonisha* (1975), a previously unproduced opera by ragtime great, Scott Joplin, the theater hosted more pop concerts and ballet companies. The Houston Grand Opera, which had been responsible for the production of *Treemonisha,* revived *Porgy and Bess* in 1976. It was followed by still more concerts.

Finally, the theater had a success with a revival of Rodgers and Hammerstein's *The King and I* (1977). The musical featured original cast member Yul Brynner and Constance Towers. Angela Lansbury assumed the role of Anna with Michael Kermoyan as the King while Brynner was on vacation.

Lansbury returned in another long running show, *Sweeney Todd* (1979), which was the Uris' next tenant. The musical had a score by Stephen Sondheim and book by Hugh Wheeler. Len Cariou co-starred as the demon barber of Fleet Street. *Sweeney Todd* ran an impressive 557 performances but was not a financial success.

Following some bookings of ballet companies, the Uris hosted Joseph Papp's Public Theater production of Gilbert and Sullivan's *The Pirates of Penzance* (1981). Another musical revival, *My Fair Lady* (1981), opened with Rex Harrison repeating his starring role as Henry Higgins and Nancy Ringham playing Eliza Doolittle. Next came *Annie,* which moved from the Eugene O'Neill Theater to end its 2,377 performance run.

The Houston Grand Opera opened a production of Jerome Kern and Oscar Hammerstein II's musical *Show Boat* (1983). On June 5, 1983, during *Show Boat's* run, the name of the theater was changed to the Gershwin, after composer George Gershwin. Critics felt that the songwriter would have been embarrassed to have such a poor theater named after him. They also pointed out that the Alvin was really the theater that should have been renamed the Gershwin, since the Gershwin brothers both had such great successes there.

A lackluster revival of *Mame* (1983) (Lansbury's third appearance at the theater) quickly closed. The Royal Shakespeare Company presented two fine productions, *Cyrano de Bergerac*

and *Much Ado About Nothing,* in repertory at the Gershwin beginning October 14, 1984. The limited run was extremely successful.

Another classic Hollywood musical, *Singing in the Rain,* opened at the Gershwin in 1985 and was a failure. The theater finally had a moderate success with Andrew Lloyd Webber's musical *Starlight Express* (1987). The greatest success in the theater's history is the current production, Stephen Schwartz's musical *Wicked* (2003).

GILDER, ROSAMOND

GLOBE THEATRE · See LUNT-FONTANNE THEATER.

GOLDEN THEATER · See JOHN GOLDEN THEATER and ROYALE THEATRE.

GREEN, ADOLPH · See COMDEN AND GREEN.

GROUP THEATER · The Group Theater, described by itself as "An organization of actors and directors formed with the ultimate aim of creating a permanent acting company to maintain regular New York seasons," was an outgrowth of the Theater Guild. The group was determined to follow the tenants of method acting espoused by Konstantin Stanislavsky and practiced at the Moscow Art Theater. During its decade-long existence during the 1930s, the Group changed the course of American theater.

The Group originated as the Theater Guild Studio, which tried to present somewhat experimental plays for the masses. Therefore its offerings, while experimental in technique, were easily accessible to mainstream audiences. They began in Brookfield Center, Connecticut, at a summer workshop. Twenty-eight actors took part in the workshop.

The first New York production, *Red Rust* (1929), was presented at the Martin Beck Theatre. Other early productions were Waldo Frank's play *New Year's Eve* and Padraic Colum's *Balloon.*

The breakthrough production was Paul Green's *House of Connelly* (1931), which opened at the Martin Beck Theatre. The Group organization was led by Cheryl Crawford, Harold Clurman and Lee Strasberg. With the success of *House of Connelly*, the Group Theater was officially launched as a separate entity from the Guild.

Toward its goal of forming a permanent company, the Group gathered a strong core of actors, including Luther Adler, Ruth Nelson, Morris Carnovsky, Margaret Becker, Art Smith, Phoebe Brand, Elia Kazan, Lee J. Cobb and Roman Bohnen. The core was augmented by such Hollywood stars as Francis Farmer, Jane Wyatt, and Sylvia Sydney. Conversely, some of the Group's actors went on to earn fame in Hollywood. These included Franchot Tone, J. Edward Bromberg, and John (then Jules) Garfield. Boris Aronson was the preferred set designer.

The Group also had its favorite playwrights. The most frequently produced was Clifford Odets, a onetime actor who decided to pursue play writing when his one-act play *Waiting for Lefty* won an award from *New Theater Magazine* for plays of social significance. Odets' first full-length play, *Awake and Sing* (1935), was produced at the Belasco Theatre. The opening night of *Waiting for Lefty* (based on the 1934 taxi drivers' strike) (1935) at the Civic Repertory Theatre was so powerful, the audience rose to its feet shouting "Strike! Strike!" The play was received so powerfully, the Group found itself presenting it to leftish groups all over the country as well as in London, where it was rapturously received.

Another of Odets' successes was *Till the Day I Die* (1935), which was presented with *Lefty* at the Longacre Theater. Other hits of Odets and the Group were *Paradise Lost* (1935), which opened at the Longacre Theater, *Rocket to the Moon* (1938) and, the most successful of all, *Golden Boy* (1937).

The Group also had success with the work of other modem dramatists. These included Dawn Powell's *Big Night* (1933); Maxwell Anderson's *Night Over Taos* (1932); John Howard Lawson's *Success Story* (1932); Sidney Kingsley's Pulitzer Prize winning drama *Men in White* (1933); Irwin Shaw's *The Gentle People* (1939); and William Saroyan's *My Heart's in the Highlands* (1939).

The groups was an energetic proponent of a socialistic system. All the members were paid equally regardless of whether they were on stage or not and no matter how large their part was. During the 1932–33 season the Group put up its needier actors in a ten-room brownstone on West 57th Street. In 1933, Stella Adler returned from Paris, where she studied with Stanislavsky, to the group's summer workshop in Ellenville, New York. Adler felt that Strasberg had misinterpreted Stanislavsky's Method and a rift was created within the company.

In 1937, the disagreements grew so strong that Crawford and Strasberg quit, their dissatisfaction increased by recent defections to Hollywood by Tone, Garfield, Odets, Clurman, and others. Robert Lewis assumed control of the Group Theatre School for the 1937–38 season. Clurman returned from Hollywood, but although the company was still producing hits, it disbanded in 1941.

In 1947, Robert Lewis, Elia Kazan, and Cheryl Crawford, all members of the Group Theatre, founded the Actors Studio. Lee Strasberg became its artistic director in 1951 and brought with him the Method, an acting style that derived from the performer's life experiences.

Upon Strasberg's death in 1982, his post was held by Ellen Burstyn and Al Pacino. In 1988, Frank Cosaro became the Studio's artistic director.

GUILD THEATER · See AUGUST WILSON THEATER.

H

HACKETT THEATER · See ANCO THEATER.

HAMMERSTEIN, ARTHUR (1872–1955) · Arthur Hammerstein, the least flamboyant of the Hammerstein family, is the least remembered. But of all of Oscar Hammerstein I's sons, it was Arthur who would have the most influence on the American theater.

Arthur was one of the most successful Broadway producers of his time. Most of his productions were operettas, primarily by Rudolf Friml and Otto Harbach. Arthur, unlike such great producers as Florenz Ziegfeld, David Belasco, and George White, did not put his own stamp on productions, but they were marked by an emphasis on strong production values. His settings, lighting and costumes were all exquisitely designed and executed.

He was born on December 21, 1872. His father, Oscar Hammerstein I was Broadway's most important pioneer. Arthur was the second son of the impresario, and it was always assumed that he would enter the family's profession. He began his working life as a building contractor, a job well suited to the needs of his father who was always planning to build a new legitimate theater or opera house. The Victoria Theater on Broadway was the younger Hammerstein's first important job. He supervised the construction to his father's architectural plans. Naturally, the Victoria, like many of Oscar Hammerstein's productions, was ready only at the very last minute on March 2, 1899.

In 1905, Arthur was hired by his father to build the Manhattan Opera House down the street from its rival, the Metropolitan Opera House. He inherited his father's interest in opera, and in 1908 he took his first steps towards becoming a producer. The younger Hammerstein's first major move was to sign the great opera singer, Luisa Tetrazzini. She repeated her triumphant London success with her American debut at the Manhattan Opera House.

Hammerstein's success led to his assisting his father in managing the opera house. He entered into negotiations with financier Otto Kahn, a noted member of the Metropolitan Opera board. The rivalry of the two operations was hurting both institutions. The result of the meetings was that the Hammersteins agreed not to produce opera in New York, Philadelphia, Boston, or Chicago for the decade beginning in 1910. In return, the Metropolitan agreed to pay the Hammersteins over one million dollars.

Later, in 1910, Oscar, looking for new horizons, wanted to go to London. Arthur took a loan on his life insurance to finance his father's trip. When Oscar announced plans to build a new opera house in London, Arthur, fed up with Oscar's money-losing schemes, was so incensed that he vowed never to speak to his father again.

Arthur decided to become a producer himself. His first production, under his father's auspices, was Victor Herbert's newest operetta, *Naughty Marietta* (1910). The show, presented at the New York Theater, drew heavily on the Manhattan Opera House's talents, including soprano Emma Trentini, Orville Harrold, the chorus, most of the orchestra, and the conductor. The show was an immediate success.

Arthur's first solo production and the first of ten collaborations with composer Rudolf Friml was *The Firefly* (1912) with book and lyrics by Otto Harbach. Emma Trentini repeated her great success in *Naughty Marietta* with the new show. The next year, Arthur produced another Friml and Harbach show, *High Jinks* (1913). Surprisingly, although the show was a huge hit, the score contained no standards.

In 1914, three of Oscar's sons died. The loss of Abe, Harry, and Willie was an immense blow to their father and caused Arthur, the surviving brother, to forgo his own productions that year. He took over the Victoria, but it was already suffering from the success of the new Palace Theater, the opening of which was facilitated by Oscar's selling his exclusive right to present vaudeville in Times Square. In 1915, Oscar sold the Victoria as well as the Lexington Opera House and was forced into retirement.

Free to produce on his own again, Arthur presented another Friml and Harbach musical, *Katinka* (1915). He produced two shows in 1917, *You're in Love* and *Furs and Frills*. *You're in Love* boasted a Friml score with book by Edward Clark and Harbach and lyrics by Clark. *Furs and Frills* was Arthur's first failure. It had a score by Clark and Silvio Hein, a minor composer. The show did contain an important song, "Make Yourself at Home." It was his nephew Oscar Hammerstein II's first professional song.

Arthur also produced two shows in 1918. The first, *Sometime*, had music by Friml and lyrics and libretto by the author of *Naughty Marietta*, Rida Johnson Young. The cast, an unusual blend of talents, featured Francine Larrimore, Mae West, and Ed Wynn. The second Arthur Hammerstein production of 1918 was *Somebody's Sweetheart* with music by Anthony Bafunno and libretto and lyrics by Alonzo Price. In 1919, Arthur produced only one show, *Tumble Inn*. It featured a Friml and Harbach score.

Always You (1920) was the first complete score written by Oscar Hammerstein II. *Tickle Me*, the second of Arthur's 1920 shows, had music composed by Herbert Stothart and book and lyrics by Harbach and Oscar Hammerstein II. Frank Mandel also collaborated on the libretto. *Jimmie* was the third show presented by Arthur that year. It had the same authors as *Tickle Me*.

Another Friml and Harbach operetta, *The Blue Kitten* (1922), started the new year for Arthur. William Cary Duncan helped on the libretto and lyrics. *Daffy Dill*, a Stothart, Oscar Hammerstein II and Bolton musical was the second 1922 show.

For Arthur, 1923 was a banner year. The first of his three shows that year, *Wildflower*, was Arthur's first show with Vincent Youmans. Harbach and Hammerstein supplied the libretto and lyrics. Herbert Stothart also contributed to the music. It was followed by Arthur's first and last foray into the revue field, *Hammerstein's Nine O'Clock Revue*. The third 1923 show, *Mary Jane McKane*, was written by Youmans, Stothart, Duncan, and Oscar Hammerstein II.

Arthur's sole 1924 production was also his biggest success *Rose-Marie* (1924). The Friml, Stothart, Harbach and Oscar Hammerstein II show broke box office records and earned Arthur $2,500,000.

George Gershwin's only operetta, *Song of the Flame* (1925), had additional music by Stothart with book and lyrics by Oscar Hammerstein II and Harbach.

Next, Arthur produced *The Wild Rose* (1926), one of the few Friml, Harbach and Oscar Hammerstein II flops. *Golden Dawn* (1927), an Emmerich Kalman, Stothart, Harbach, and Oscar Hammerstein II musical, might have been a greater success but by this time the operetta was losing its vogue. *Golden Dawn* did contain two Broadway firsts—the first topless chorus girl and the Broadway debut of Archie Leach. He would become better known in Hollywood as Cary Grant.

Arthur's production of *Good Boy* (1928) was a collaboration between Oscar Hammerstein II and Harbach and Bert Kalmar and Harry Ruby. One of Arthur's rare forays into musical comedy, *Polly* (1929), was written by Philip Charig and Irving Caesar. *Sweet Adeline* (1929) was Arthur's only production of a Jerome Kern show. Oscar Hammerstein II provided the book and lyrics.

With operettas out of vogue and the Depression hurting Broadway's business, Arthur moved to Hollywood to produce movies. His daughter Elaine had already enjoyed a successful acting career on the screen. But his only production, *The Lottery Bride* (1930), made for United Artists, was a failure. He returned to Broadway.

1930, Arthur's last year of producing included two productions on Broadway that were both failures. A Rudolf Friml and J. Keirn Brennan score was featured at the opening of *Luana*. Arthur's last Broadway show, *Ballyhoo*, had a score by Louis Alter, Harry Ruskin, Leighton K. Brill, and Oscar Hammerstein II. The show starred W. C. Fields.

The failures of his Hollywood foray and his last two Broadway shows forced him into bankruptcy. At the courthouse he was quoted as saying, "When Mayor Walker comes back into the city I will ask him to take the statue of my father and put it in some public place, possibly around Times Square. It is a curious thing that when he was exactly my age, my father went through the same thing. In 1897 he lost under foreclosure the Olympia Theater.... In a couple of years, when conditions improve, I'll be back again, bigger than ever." But unlike his father, Arthur didn't bounce back. His producing days over, Arthur led a quiet retirement. He dabbled in inventions and even collaborated on a number one song on the Hit Parade, "Because of You." The 1950–51 hit was certainly a surprise to the family. He died in Palm Beach, Florida, on October 12, 1955.

HAMMERSTEIN I, OSCAR (1847–1919)

Of all the individuals responsible for the emergence of Times Square as the entertainment center of New York, producer. and developer Oscar Hammerstein I was the most important. As the century turned, Hammerstein changed the face of opera and theater in America. "The Father of Times Square" was also the founder of the greatest theatrical family in the history of the American theater.

The five-foot-four-inch producer was a striking figure as he sauntered down Broadway. He sported a pointed goatee and always carried a cigar. His favorite dress was a Prince Albert coat, striped trousers, and an ever-present hat that he designed himself.

Hammerstein was born in Germany on May 8, 1847. He entered a Berlin music conservatory when he was twelve. Although he worked hard on the violin, he proved only a fair student. However, he did acquire one thing in the conservatory—his love of grand opera. After the death of his mother, his relationship with his father deteriorated. With the army in his future and an unhappy life at home, the fifteen-year-old Hammerstein ran away and arrived in New York City in 1863, penniless and unable to speak the language. He found piecework in a cigar factory at $2 a week. Hammerstein's intelligence allowed him to prosper in the cigar works. He invented many gadgets that he gave to his bosses before he learned of the patent system.

In 1868, Hammerstein married Rose Blau, and they had their first son, Harry, the following year. Harry would, like his siblings, be brought into his father's theatrical business. Hammerstein had a distant relationship with his family. His grandson, Oscar Hammerstein II met his grandfather for the first time when he was seven. He expected his sons to become his coworkers, and they did.

Hammerstein quit his job in 1871 against his wife's wishes. He took their savings and invested it in a friend's scheme to present opera in German. The opening night proved successful, but the undertaking failed when audiences fell off during the run. The entire investment was lost (the first of many bankruptcies) but Hammerstein was unconcerned. He had a marvelous time and was bitten with the theatrical bug. Although he returned to the cigar business, he now had a new goal—to become a producer himself.

Hammerstein's second son, Arthur, was born in 1872. That same year, Hammerstein became an American citizen and patented his first invention—a multiple cigar mold. He received $1,500 from the sale of the patent. The success of his patent sale gave Hammerstein courage. In 1874, he established The *United States Tobacco Journal* with $50. The highly successful journal became a leading voice in the business. Hammerstein followed the lead of other publishers of the day and indulged in a little yellow journalism in order to drum up advertising revenue. The journal is still published today.

That same year, Hammerstein acted as guarantor for the opening of his producing friend's Germania Theater. Hammerstein decided that he could write plays and had five premieres at the theater. He even had his incidental music performed at the Germania. The theater survived somewhat longer than the two men's previous theatrical outing. The Germania closed three and a half years later when it became Tony Pastor's.

Hammerstein's third son, William, was born in 1874; another son, Abraham Lincoln Hammerstein, came along two years later. Their mother Rose died, and Hammerstein's younger sister Anna was brought from Germany to help him raise his four sons.

Two years later, in 1878, Anna left to marry Harry Rosenberg. Their son Walter, Hammerstein's nephew, would also enter the theater business. (He owned the Broadway Theatre and later established a chain of movie theaters under the Walter Reade name.) After Anna's departure, Hammerstein married Malvina Jacobi. They would later have two daughters of their own, Rose and Stella.

Hammerstein still had the urge to embark on a theater career, and in 1882 he backed a play called *The Perjured Peasant*. The star was Heinrich Conried who achieved fame in the role. Hammerstein and Conried would be forever linked as enemies. Their disagreements forced the closing of *The Perjured Peasant*. Later, when Conried became general director of the Metropolitan Opera, the feud intensified.

Meanwhile, Hammerstein was still involved in the cigar business. He founded the New York Leaf Tobacco Dealers Protective Association and the New York Leaf Tobacco Board of Trade. In 1884, he invented a pneumatic cigar-making machine, a device that would make a million dollars. Unfortunately, Hammerstein sold the patent for $6,000.

In addition to opera and tobacco, Hammerstein's interests extended to real estate. In 1888, he took his $6,000 from the pneumatic cigar-making machine and a loan against his interests in the *Tobacco Journal* and built an apartment house, the Kaiser Wilhelm on 7th Avenue between 136th and 137th Street. He would eventually build twenty-four apartment buildings and thirty houses.

As Hammerstein's interest in the Harlem neighborhood increased, he figured that Harlem, then a place of middle-class residences, needed its own opera house. To finance the theater, Hammerstein sold the Tobacco Journal for $50,000. His first theater, the Harlem Opera House, was built at 125th Street between 7th and 8th Avenue. That theater, like all his others, was designed by Hammerstein himself. In what was an amazingly ironic comment on Hammerstein's career, he forgot only one thing in his design-the box office.

The new theater opened in 1889. The theater was a success, but Hammerstein, typically, lost money. Hammerstein could always rely on his inventive genius to pull him out of debt. In 1890, he sold another patent that gave him $65,000.

Hammerstein began his lifelong battle with the Metropolitan Opera when its management denied his request to present their stars in Harlem. So he instead created his own company. Soprano Lilli Lehmann was his star and his main draw. The week-long season was a tremendous success, but Hammerstein lost $50,000.

Despite his mixed success with the Harlem Opera House, Hammerstein decided to build another theater in the neighborhood. The Columbus Theater on 125th Street between Lexington and Fourth Avenue opened in October 1890. This time Hammerstein booked vaudeville and minstrel shows into the theater, which ended its first season with three weeks of opera. The theater was a success and drew a steady audience.

In 1891, Hammerstein mounted the American premiere of Mascagni's *Cavalleria Rusticana*. Although he held the exclusive rights to the opera, another production was mounted by a competitor taking advantage of a loophole in the copyright laws. Hammerstein's production was a tremendous success and emboldened Hammerstein to increase his empire.

The first Manhattan Opera House was constructed by Hammerstein in Herald Square. The theater opened in 1892 with the play *Lena Despard.* Although it was a tremendous bomb, Hammerstein wasn't particularly concerned. The failure merely proved to him that grand opera was the only thing that would succeed in the new house.

He was proven wrong. The opera season was an abject failure. Koster and Bial, successful vaudeville producers, teamed up with Hammerstein to present Koster and Bial's Music Hall in the Manhattan Opera House. It was an immense hit.

Hammerstein hadn't forgotten his foray into writing music for the Germania Theater. He bet $100 that he could write an opera in two days. Hammerstein set to work despite his friends' attempts to distract him. They placed organ grinders outside his window at the Gilsey House round the clock. The result, *The Kohinoor,* was deemed unproduceable, and Hammerstein was refused the $100. So naturally, he mounted the production at Koster and Bial's Music Hall. It lost $10,000 but Hammerstein did get his $100.

In 1895, he made his most important move. He took an option on a piece of land between 44th and 45th Street on the east side of Broadway, and on it he built a complex of four theaters, the largest theater group at the time. Although the Olympia created a sensation, it never proved very profitable. The opening was marred by wet paint and a near riot. But the Olympia firmly established Longacre Square, the original name for Times Square, as the new theater district.

Hammerstein featured French music hall star Yvette Guilbert as his star at the Olympia. She drew a large crowd to the theater, and receipts totaled over $15,000 a week. But in 1896, with his usual penchant for argument, Hammerstein lost Guilbert. He devised an original ballet and put it on in the Olympia. The receipts fell to $4,000 a week. Hammerstein couldn't help but realize his error, and he replaced the ballet with a series of *Living Pictures.* The main attraction of the *Living Pictures* was scantily clad women.

Lillian Russell was drawing crowds into the Harlem theaters, and George Bernard Shaw's *Arms and the Man* premiered uptown. Downtown, the less artistic fare continued. Hammerstein and his sons, now all in the business with their father, were arrested for offending public morals. They were released, and Hammerstein learned the lesson of publicity with the resultant rise in profits at the Olympia.

The success brought on by the publicity didn't last long, however. In 1898, the New York Life Insurance Company foreclosed on the Olympia and it was sold at auction. Hammerstein was legally barred from the premises. He owed over a million dollars by this time.

At this time, Hammerstein met a friend on Broadway and gave him a cigar. "I have lost my theaters, my home and everything else. My fortune consists of two cigars. I will share it with you." The story was more than just a humorous anecdote. Hammerstein was by turns despotic and benevolent and seemed unfazed by the roller coaster quality of his fortunes.

The following year, he recovered enough to build the Victoria Theater at Seventh Avenue and 42nd Street. He raised part of the capital by selling more patents. He announced that he chose the name Victoria because "I have been victorious over mine enemies—those dirty bloodsuckers at New York Life."

Audiences packed the Victoria at its opening, and the theater proved a constant success. Hammerstein not only opened the path to theater development in Times Square but his optimism and ability to recover from blows that would have ended the career of a lesser man proved an inspiration to succeeding generations of Hammersteins and other theater professionals.

Hammerstein himself appeared on the Victoria stage. When Lew Dockstader, the minstrel man, complained about the difficulty in finding qualified talents, Hammerstein nominated himself. The press was duly informed and Hammerstein appeared for one performance making his "Debut Extraordinary."

As the century turned, the impresario built the Republic Theater on a plot next to the Victoria. On the shared roof, he opened the Paradise Garden. The roof garden opened with another of Hammerstein's attempts to write opera, but it was a success nonetheless. The Paradise Garden featured the Swiss Farm with barnyard animals and New York's first singing waiters. In 1901, Hammerstein leased the Republic to producer David Belasco who promptly rechristened it the Belasco Theatre.

Leo Tolstoy's drama *Resurrection* (1902) with Blanche Walsh as the star became a big hit. It ran for almost two years at the Victoria and netted $100,000 for Hammerstein. After the run of *Resurrection,* Hammerstein changed the policy of the Victoria to vaudeville. Willie was installed as manager with his father, operating in an office and apartment off the balcony, close by.

The Victoria's success led Hammerstein to construct a theater on 42nd Street. When comic Lew Fields leased it, he named it, appropriately, the Lew M. Fields Theater. The theater was the first to have a fire-fighting system in which water is carried from a tank on the roof.

When Macy's moved to 34th Street, the Manhattan Opera House was demolished. Hammerstein decided to take on his old rival the Metropolitan Opera. He built what he declared would be the largest theater in the world, choosing once again the Herald Square area, a few blocks from the Metropolitan Opera House. The New Manhattan Opera House opened on December 3, 1906, on 34th Street, west of Eighth Avenue (the theater is now known as the Manhattan Center). Again, the theater opened just in a nick of time. When asked what he was opening with, Hammerstein responded, "With debts." The 3,100 seat theater's opening was a tremendous success.

Artistically and financially, the theater had a successful 1906–07 season—and the Metropolitan suffered its first loss in years. The 1907–08 season began auspiciously with *Tales of Hoffman* and the American premiere of *Thais* with Mary Garden singing the lead. In the next few years, Hammerstein presented many other notable operas. His son Arthur signed Luisa Tetrazzini to appear in *La Traviata, Rigoletto* and *Lucia Di Lammermoor.* The American premiere of Debussy's *Pelleas et Melisande* with Mary Garden in the lead proved triumphant.

With the Manhattan Opera House a raging success, Hammerstein appointed Arthur to oversee the construction of a new 4,100-seat theater in Philadelphia. Though the Manhattan and Victoria theaters were bringing in profits, the Philadelphia theater's construction costs drained the family's coffers. To raise capital, Hammerstein sold the Lew M. Fields Theater for $225,000.

By the end of 1908, the Philadelphia theater opened to great acclaim. Back in New York, Mary Garden opened the Manhattan Opera House in *Le Jongleur De Notre Dame.* She played the boy's role at Hammerstein's insistence and critical huzzahs. Later that year, Richard Strauss' *Salome* was another smash at the 34th Street theater, but the Philadelphia house's fortunes declined.

Part of Hammerstein's reason for opening the Manhattan Opera House was to provide opera for the middle class. He never liked society and hated the snobbish attitude at the Metropolitan. In 1909, he commenced buying land in Brooklyn, Cleveland and elsewhere to build opera houses. A tour of his New York operatic successes to Boston, Pittsburgh and Chicago proved critically popular but financially draining. In 1910, he mounted the premiere of Strauss' *Elektra,* an immense success. That same season, he presented the debut of singer John McCormack.

The Metropolitan-Manhattan feud wasn't doing either theater any good. Hammerstein met with the Metropolitan's leading backer, Otto Kahn, in order to arrange some sort of understanding. The result was that the Metropolitan paid Hammerstein $1,250,000 to forgo all producing of opera in New York,

Chicago, Boston, and Philadelphia for a period of ten years. Hammerstein sorely needed the money and accepted the deal. He sold the Philadelphia theater for $400,000, which paid off the mortgage.

Looking for new worlds to conquer, Hammerstein sailed to London on money given to him by his son Arthur. Arthur took a loan on his life insurance to pay for the sailing. In London, Hammerstein bought property that he announced would soon see the construction of another Hammerstein Opera House.

He kept his promise, and the London Opera House opened on Kingsway in November 1911. The theater appeared at first to be popular, but after seven months he had lost a million dollars. In 1913, Hammerstein's fortunes suffered a major blow when he sold the exclusive rights to present vaudeville in Times Square for $250,000. That ended the Victoria's monopoly on the popular art and opened the doors to competition. From that time, the Victoria, Hammerstein's sure breadwinner, began its decline. But he had other ideas for the $250,000. He used it to open the Lexington Opera House, where he intended to present operas in English. Hammerstein felt that gimmick would get him around his agreement with the Metropolitan. At the Manhattan Opera House he presented comic opera.

The year 1914 proved especially tragic for the impresario. His sons Abe, Harry, and Willie all died. The Metropolitan Opera House sued Hammerstein and won. He was prevented from opening the Lexington theater as an opera house and it switched to a movie policy.

In 1915, with his fortunes diminished, Hammerstein sold the Victoria and Lexington. At the age of sixty, he bought a home in New Jersey and married Emma Swift. His last years were spent in a forced retirement.

On August 1, 1919, the man who, John Philip Sousa said, "has done more for music than any other man in America" died.

HAMMERSTEIN II, OSCAR (1895–1960) · Oscar Hammerstein II, the son of William Hammerstein, the manager of the

Victoria Theater, grandson of the great theater builder and impresario Oscar Hammerstein I, and nephew of noted producer Arthur Hammerstein, was the scion of the greatest theater family of its time. Oscar's career as lyricist and librettist was equaled in length and breadth only by author, director, producer George Abbott and by Oscar's partner Richard Rodgers. Oscar was Broadway's preeminent librettist and lyricist. He was among the first authors to attempt a true integration of songs and script in the new American form of musical comedy.

Hammerstein was born in New York City on July 12, 1895. The young man attended Columbia University (1912–16) and Columbia Law School (1915–17). It was at Columbia that Oscar began writing books and lyrics for his first musicals. In fact, his first collaboration with Richard Rodgers was for Columbia University shows. *Up Stage and Down* (1916) was the show and the first Rodgers and Hammerstein songs were "Weaknesses," "Can It," and "There's Always Room for One More."

A year later Hammerstein found his first song, "Make Yourself at Home," with music by Silvio Hein, interpolated into the Broadway show *Furs and Frills*. His first full score was a collaboration with Herbert Stothart. Their show, *Always You* (1920), opened at the Central Theater. The young lyricist also contributed the libretto for the show.

Hammerstein had greater success with his next show, *Tickle Me* (1921). Herbert Stothart was the composer, and the book was written by Hammerstein in collaboration with Otto Harbach and Frank Mandel.

Hammerstein and Stothart next came up with *Jimmie* (1920). After *Jimmie* came a play, *Pop,* written with Frank Mandel. *Pop* closed in Atlantic City before opening in New York. Another Stothart show, *Daffy Dill* (1922) was yet another flop. Hammerstein had even less success with *Queen O'Hearts* (1922) at the George M. Cohan Theatre. The music was by Lewis Gensler and Dudley Wilkinson, and additional lyrics were written by Sidney Mitchell.

Hammerstein would have his first big hit in collaboration with Stothart and Vincent

Youmans. The show, *Wildflower* (1923), had a book by Hammerstein and Otto Harbach. The hit song, "Bambalina," had music by Youmans.

Hammerstein's *Mary Jane McKane* (1923) with music by Youmans and Stothart opened at the Imperial Theatre. Hammerstein again attempted play writing and again found failure with *Gypsy Jim* (1924), written with Milton Herbert Gropper. The two playwrights' next play, *New Toys* (1924) opened and closed quickly at the Fulton Theater.

Clearly, straight playwriting was not for Hammerstein. He would receive greater acclaim as a librettist and lyricist, and in fact his next show, *Rose-Marie* (1924), proved one of his greatest hits. This time, Rudolf Friml was the composer along with Stothart. Arthur Hammerstein, Oscar's uncle, produced. *Rose-Marie* opened at the Imperial Theatre with Dennis King and Mary Ellis.

Hammerstein started a long collaboration with composer Jerome Kern on the show *Sunny* (1925). Harbach worked with Hammerstein on the book and lyrics.

Stothart and George Gershwin were the composers on the next Harbach and Hammerstein show, *Song of the Flame* (1925). Perhaps the show's Russian setting was not suited to either Gershwin or Hammerstein. Harbach, Hammerstein, and Friml's next outing, *The Wild Rose* (1926) was a failure. Harbach, Hammerstein, and Sigmund Romberg's *Desert Song* (1927) was an enormous and immediate hit. Frank Mandel, colibrettist was also producer with Laurence Schwab. Hammerstein's book received weaker reviews than his and Harbach's lyrics.

Hammerstein's next show, *Golden Dawn* (1927), was a failure, but he followed it up with his first classic musical, the enormously successful *Show Boat* (1927). This legendary musical, with book and lyrics by Hammerstein and music by Jerome Kern, opened at the Ziegfeld Theater. *Show Boat* starred Norma Terris, Edna May Oliver, Tess Gardella, Charles Winninger, Howard Marsh, Jules Bledsoe, and Helen Morgan.

Show Boat was the first show to exhibit Hammerstein's concern with human issues. The show's plot dealt with miscegenation and problems of blacks. The score, including "Bill," "Make Believe," "Can't Help Lovin' Dat Man," "You Are Love," "Why Do I Love You?" and "Ol' Man River" is still considered by many to be the ultimate musical theater work.

Hammerstein's next show, *Good Boy* (1928) with music by Herbert Stothart and Harry Ruby, also had lyrics by Bert Kalmar.

The New Moon (1928), with book and lyrics by Hammerstein and music by Romberg, opened at the Imperial Theatre. The operetta contained at least six great hits, "The Girl on the Prow," "Softly, As In a Morning Sunrise," "Stouthearted Men," "Lover, Come Back to Me," "Wanting You," and "One Kiss."

Hammerstein had another of his flops with *Rainbow* (1928), a collaboration with Vincent Youmans. Hammerstein and Kern's *Sweet Adeline* (1929) was a moderate success at Hammerstein's Manhattan Theater. It featured Helen Morgan who introduced the three hits in the score, "Here Am I," "Why Was I Born?" and "Don't Ever Leave Me."

In 1931, Hammerstein had a string of failures, including *The Gang's All Here* (1931), *Free for All* (1931) and *East Wind* (1931). None played more than twenty-threee performances.

Another Hammerstein collaboration with Kern, *Music in the Air* (1932), opened at the Alvin Theater. "I've Told Ev'ry Little Star," "And Love Was Born," and "The Song Is You" were the hit songs in the score.

Hammerstein had two rare London premieres in 1933 and 1934 at the Theatre Royal Drury Lane. The first, *Ball at the Savoy*, with Paul Abraham contributing the music; the second, *Three Sisters*, was written with Jerome Kern.

When Hammerstein returned to the United States, he completed two projects with Romberg. The first was a film, *The Night Is Young*. The second, the musical *May Wine* (1935), opened at the St. James Theatre. After that show, Hammerstein had more Hollywood assignments. *Give Us This Night* featured music by Erich Wolfgang Korngold. *Swing High, Swing Low* had a screenplay cowritten by Hammerstein and Virginia Van Upp. Kern and Hammerstein wrote the score to the film *High, Wide and Handsome,* which was a hit in 1937.

Gentlemen Unafraid was Hammerstein and Kern's next stage production. It opened in St. Louis on June 3, 1938, and closed there on June 12. Then it was back to Hollywood for *The Lady Objects* with music by Ben Oakland and lyrics by Hammerstein and Milton Drake; *The Great Waltz,* a film with music by Johann Strauss II and *The Story of Vernon and Irene Castle.* This teaming of Fred Astaire and Ginger Rogers had a script by Hammerstein and Dorothy Yost.

Hammerstein's bad luck on the stage continued with his next collaboration with Jerome Kern. *Very Warm for May* (1939) at the Alvin Theater contained a fine score, including "All the Things You Are," "That Lucky Fellow," "In the Heart of the Dark," and "All in Fun." Hammerstein had his only collaboration with Arthur Schwartz in *American Jubilee.* The show premiered at the New York World's Fair of 1940. The Romberg operetta *Sunny River* (1941) continued his string of failures. Hammerstein was generally thought to be washed up. Aware of the talk along Broadway, he needed a hit to revive his career.

Desperate as he felt for renewal, Hammerstein was nonetheless unprepared for the amazing turnaround he was to enjoy as the lyricist and librettist in the team of Rodgers and Hammerstein, the most successful songwriting partnership in the history of musical theater. The Theater Guild approached Hammerstein to collaborate on a new show with Richard Rodgers. Rodgers' longtime partner, Lorenz Hart, was having his own personal problems and the composer was looking for a new collaborator.

The new team's first production changed the course of musical theater and broke most of the commonly held conventions. *Oklahoma!* began a second great chapter in Hammerstein's career.

As a retort to all those who said he was washed up artistically, he took out an ad in *Variety,* which read:

> Holiday Greetings from Oscar
>   Hammerstein 2nd author of
> SUNNY RIVER (6 weeks at the St. James)
> VERY WARM FOR MAY (7 weeks at the
>   Alvin)
> THREE SISTERS (7 weeks at the Drury
>   Lane)
> FREE FOR ALL (3 weeks at the
>   Manhattan)
> "I've Done It Before And I Can Do It
>   Again!"

For his next production, Hammerstein chose to adapt Georges Bizet's opera *Carmen.* The show, *Carmen Jones,* opened at the Broadway Theatre on December 2, 1943, to rave reviews. The all-black show was a success, running 502 performances.

Although the team of Rodgers and Hammerstein had their occasional failures their great successes, *Oklahoma!, Carousel, South Pacific, The King and I* and *The Sound of Music* introduced a unique voice into the American theater. Rodgers' melodies to Hammerstein's lyrics were more expansive and soaring than those written with Hart. Hammerstein's lyrics and libretti were warm and humane and touched on themes of tolerance and understanding.

Oscar Hammerstein died on August 23, 1960. As a tribute, the lights were dimmed on Broadway and taps was played in Times Square.

HAMMERSTEIN'S MANHATTAN THEATRE · See ED SULLIVAN THEATRE.

HAMMERSTEIN'S ROOF GARDEN · See VICTORIA THEATRE (1).

HAMMOND, PERCY · See CRITICS.

HARBACH, OTTO (1873–1963) · In the American theater of the early twentieth century, there were over one hundred musicals premiering each season. Composers, lyricists and book writers working at that time often had the opportunity to work on as many as five to ten shows a season. Otto Harbach was one such prolific librettist and lyricist. Although much of his work in early operetta and musical comedy has not lasted, several of his songs, particularly those written to music by Jerome Kern, have become classics.

Harbach was born Otto Christiansen of Danish immigrant parents in Salt Lake City, Utah, on August 18, 1873. The Christiansens worked on the Hauerbach farm, and their name and their fellow farm workers' names were changed to Hauerbach. After attending Knox College, Otto moved to New York, where he held newspaper jobs from 1902 to 1903. He moved from journalism to advertising for the remainder of the century's first decade.

His first theatrical job brought his first hit song. *Three Twins,* written in 1908 with composer Karl Hoschna, introduced the favorite "Cuddle Up a Little Closer, Lovey Mine." Based on the popularity of the song and the star performance of Bessie McCoy, *Three Twins* ran 288 performances.

Bright Eyes (1910) was the next musical by the Hauerbach and Hoschna team. Their next collaboration proved more successful. *Madame Sherry* (1910) was a triumph at the New Amsterdam Theatre. For this show, Hauerbach contributed both lyrics and book. The show resulted in Hauerbach's second hit song, "Every Little Movement." After Broadway, the show enjoyed a long tour and many revivals as an early mainstay of the touring circuit.

In 1911, the successful team wrote the music for three shows *Dr. De Luxe* (1911), *The Girl of My Dreams* (1911), and *The Fascinating Widow* (1911). None of these shows played more than sixty performances, and no standards were to come from their scores. Hoschna died at the age of thirty-four, only five months after the opening of *The Fascinating Widow,* so Hauerbach was forced to find another partner.

He found an ideal one in Rudolf Friml. Their first show together turned Hauerbach's

fortunes around. *The Firefly* (1912) was all the more remarkable for being Friml's first Broadway score and producer Arthur Hammerstein's first producing venture. The show seemed doomed at the start when Victor Herbert, who had signed to compose the score, dropped out due to an argument with star Emma Trentini. Music publishers Max Dreyfus and Rudolf Schirmer encouraged Hammerstein to give the young Friml a chance. Three of the songs— "Giannina Mia," "Love Is Like a Firefly," and "Sympathy"—attained classic status.

The next year, the Hammerstein, Friml, and Hauerbach team contributed *High Jinks* (1913) to Broadway. The score was a superior operetta work, but perhaps because the big hit was interpolated ("All Aboard For Dixie" by Jack Yellen and George L. Cobb), it was seldom heard after its initial presentation. In 1914, Hauerbach contributed a libretto only to *The Crinoline Girl* (1914). He then Americanized *Suzi* (1914).

Hammerstein, Friml, and Hauerbach teamed up again for *Katinka* (1915). In 1917, the Hauerbach and Friml team contributed two shows, *You're in Love* and *Kitty Darlin'.* Also in 1917, Hauerbach, responding to the mounting antagonism toward Americans with German-sounding names, changed his surname to Harbach.

Harbach, aware of the public's changing tastes in musical theater, tried his hand at the book and lyrics to a real American musical comedy rather than the American operettas as he had been writing. The result, written in collaboration with Louis Hirsch, was *Going Up,* Harbach's third score and libretto of 1917. Although no lasting songs emerged from the score, the effect of a full-sized biplane flying on stage was enough to keep audiences enthralled.

Despite his success in a more modern vein, Harbach rejoined Friml for his next two shows, *Tumble Inn* (1919) and *The Little Whopper* (1919). *Tumble Inn* might have achieved a longer run if it wasn't for the actors' strike of 1919. *The Little Whopper* was Friml's first attempt at a more modern style of composing.

Arthur Hammerstein produced *Tumble Inn* and also Harbach's next show, *Tickle Me* (1920) with a score by Herbert Stothart. *Tickle Me* was Harbach's first collaboration on a libretto with Oscar Hammerstein II, nephew of Arthur. In all, Oscar collaborated with Harbach on ten libretti and/or lyrics. Frank Mandel also collaborated on the book. None of the Hammerstein/Harbach/Stothart songs achieved fame.

Harbach had another successful collaboration with Louis Hirsch in *Mary* (1920). The show was under the direction of George M. Cohan. Its hit song was "The Love Nest."

Harbach worked on a number of shows during the 1920s, including *Jimmie* (1920), *June Love* (1921), *The O'Brien Girl* (1921), *The Blue Kitten* (1922), and *Molly Darling* (1922). None were hits. Harbach's next show, *Wildflower* (1923), proved to be one of his biggest successes. Arthur Hammerstein was the producer, and his nephew Oscar collaborated on book and lyrics with Harbach. Vincent Youmans, one of the greatest composers of the 1920s, wrote most of the score; Herbert Stothart composed the remainder. Several of the songs became quite popular, and a few became minor standards. The best songs were "Bambalina" and the title song.

Jack and Jill (1923) featured a young Clifton Webb. *Kid Boots* (1923) had Harbach contributing the libretto in collaboration with William Anthony McGuire.

The team responsible for the great success of *Wildflower* was reunited for Harbach's next big hit, *Rose-Marie* (1924), with music by Rudolf Friml and Herbert Stothart. Arthur Hammerstein again produced and Oscar Hammerstein collaborated with Harbach on book and lyrics. The score was one of the best of the twenties, with several songs achieving long-lasting fame, including "Indian Love Call," "The Mounties," the title song, "Pretty Things," and "Totem Tom-Tom."

In 1924, Harbach was in the middle of his most productive period. His next show after *Rose-Marie*, *Betty Lee* (1924), had music by Louis Hirsch and Con Conrad and starred Joe E. Brown.

Vincent Youmans was again tapped for a Harbach show, this time with Irving Caesar collaborating on lyrics with Harbach as he had on *Betty Lee*. The show was *No, No, Nanette* (1925). Almost the direct opposite of *Rose-Marie* in tone, *No, No, Nanette* was the quintessential twenties musical with flappers, fast women and bobbed hair. The terrific score contained one of the greatest hits of the twenties, "Tea for Two," with lyrics by Caesar, and "I Want to Be Happy."

Harbach's second 1925 show, *Sunny* (1925), was an even bigger hit than *No, No, Nanette*. It marked Harbach's first collaboration with the great Jerome Kern. Oscar Hammerstein again collaborated on book and lyrics. Marilyn Miller, one of the greatest stars of the twenties, headlined as Sunny.

Her supporting cast included Clifton Webb, Cliff Edwards, Pert Kelton, and Jack Donahue. The score was one of Kern and Harbach's best and contained many standards including "D'Ye Love Me?," "Sunny," and "Who?"

On his next outing, *Song of the Flame* (1925), Harbach collaborated with Oscar Hammerstein II, Herbert Stothart and a young new composer, George Gershwin. Arthur Hammerstein produced. It contributed a hit song, "The Cossack Love Song."

The year 1926 started slowly but ended with a bang for Harbach. His fourth show of the year, after *Kitty's Kisses*, *Criss-Cross* and *The Wild Rose*, *The Desert Song*, was another Hammerstein II and Harbach operetta. Sigmund Romberg supplied the rousing music with Frank Mandel helping on the book. The score included such standards as "The Riff Song" and "One Alone." Amazingly, Harbach had a fifth show open in 1926. *Oh, Please!* had a book by Harbach and Anne Caldwell and music by Vincent Youmans.

Harbach's first show of 1927, *Lucky*, was followed by *Golden Dawn*. In *Golden Dawn*, Stothart, Harbach and the Hammersteins were teamed with composer Emmerich Kalman to little effect.

Harbach's output began to slow as the twenties drew to a close. In 1928, Harbach had only one show, *Good Boy*. Hammerstein produced, and Stothart conducted and composed the score with Harry Ruby. Hammerstein II and Harbach collaborated with Henry Myers on the script, and Bert Kalmar contributed the lyrics.

Two years passed before Harbach's next show, *Nina Rosa* (1930). Harbach contributed the libretto to the Romberg/Caesar score. Broadway's output had fallen off with the advent of the Depression, and Harbach's career suffered accordingly. Royalties assured him a comfortable life, so he wasn't about to work too hard to get projects on.

His next Broadway show was a success with critics and audiences. *The Cat and the Fiddle* (1931) paired Harbach with Jerome Kern. The fine score boasted such standards as "Try to Forget," "She Didn't Say Yes," and "The Night Was Made for Love."

The following year saw Kern and Harbach contributing to one of their greatest successes, *Roberta* (1933). The score was one of Kern and Harbach's finest, featuring "Smoke Gets In Your Eyes," "Don't Ask Me Not to Sing," "I'll Be Hard to Handle" (with lyrics by Bernard Dougall), "Let's Begin," "The Touch of Your Hand," "Yesterdays," and "You're Devastating."

Harbach's last Broadway show, *Forbidden Melody* (1936), featured a score by Sigmund Romberg and was one of the last European-style operettas. The show was a disappointing end to a remarkable career. Harbach was a craftsman whose writing certainly inspired others to do their best work. Harbach died in New York City on January 24, 1963, outliving virtually all of his collaborators.

HARBURG, E. Y. (1898–1981) · E. Y. ("Yip") Harburg was perhaps Broadway's most complex lyricist. At once outspoken, liberal, and uncompromising, Harburg was also sentimental, romantic, and humorous. He was a man of strong moral and political beliefs who felt tolerance for those whose politics differed with his own. He believed in the power of lyrics and used that power to move audiences both emotionally and artistically in shows such as *Finian's Rainbow* and *Bloomer Girl*.

He began as a lyricist while still at New York City's Townsend Harris Hall High School along with schoolmate Ira Gershwin. While at City College, Harburg had his work published in Franklin P. Adams' influential column "The Conning Tower." After graduating, Harburg followed in the footsteps of Gershwin and became a lyricist.

Harburg's first partner was composer Jay Gorney. After contributing songs to a succession of musical revues, the team struck gold with "Brother Can You Spare a Dime," which was practically the official anthem of the Depression. The show was *Americana* (1932). Along the way, Harburg also collaborated with Harold Arlen, Burton Lane, and Vernon Duke. Harburg's wit and social consciousness shone through in all his lyrics.

Three early revues contained hit songs by Harburg. *Walk a Little Faster* (1932) featured Duke and Harburg's classic "April in Paris." People couldn't believe that Harburg had never actually visited Paris but got his inspiration from a travel brochure.

The *Ziegfeld Follies of 1934* (1934) also had a Harburg and Duke score, although it interpolated many songs by other songwriters. The show featured the Harburg/Duke success "What Is There to Say?" *Life Begins at 8:40* (1934) had music by Harold Arlen and Harburg teamed with his old friend Ira Gershwin. The three songwriters came up with such hits as "Let's Take a Walk Around the Block," "You're a Builder Upper," and "Fun to Be Fooled."

Hooray for What! (1937) was Harburg's first book show, written in collaboration with Arlen. Songs included "Down with Love," "Moanin' in the Mornin'," and "In the Shade of the New Apple Tree." The antiwar musical gave Harburg ample opportunity to express his pacifist leanings.

He explored both race relations and woman's rights with the show *Bloomer Girl* (1944). The brilliant musical opened with Celeste Holm, David Brooks, Joan McCracken, and Dooley Wilson singing such Arlen/Harburg hits as "Right As the Rain," "The Eagle and Me," "T'morra' T'morra'," and "Evalina." Harburg was professional enough to make sure that he not only got his points across but also entertained the audience. Harburg also codirected *Bloomer Girl* with William Schorr.

Harburg's greatest success was certainly *Finian's Rainbow* (1947), written in collaboration with Burton Lane. Harburg also contributed the libretto along with Fred Saidy. *Finian's Rainbow* contained one of the theater's finest scores, including such brilliant songs as "How Are Things in Glocca Morra," "Look to the Rainbow," "Old Devil Moon," and "When I'm Not Near the Girl I Love." His associates felt that Harburg, who at times could be magical and mischievous himself, was closely reflected in the character of Og the leprechaun. *Finian's Rainbow* starred an exceptional cast, including David Wayne, Ella Logan, Donald Richards, and Albert Sharpe.

Flahooley (1951) was a rare failure for Harburg. However, the score, with music by Sammy Fain, featured some excellent songs, including "He's Only Wonderful," "The World Is Your Balloon" and "Here's to Your Illusions."

Artistically, *Jamaica* (1957) suffered because it was too often a vehicle for its star, the singer Lena Horne. The terrific score by Arlen and Harburg included such fine songs as "Ain't It the Truth," "I Don't Think I'll End It All Today" and "Napoleon."

Harburg tackled the Lysistrata legend for his Broadway show, *The Happiest Girl in the World* (1961). The music was adapted by Harburg from the works of Jacques Offenbach to which he added lyrics, which perfectly reflected the Harburg view of the world.

Harburg's last Broadway show, *Darling of the Day* (1968), was written with Jule Styne. The show starred Vincent Price and Patricia Routledge. Though the show was a failure, Harburg considered it his *My Fair Lady*. Perhaps not as wonderful as the Lerner and Loewe show, *Darling of the Day* does have an excellent, sadly unappreciated score.

Harburg is also known for his many movie songs, most notably the score for *The Wizard of Oz* .He died on March 5, 1981.

HARNICK, SHELDON · See BOCK AND HARNICK.

HARRIS THEATRE · (1) 226 W. 42nd Street. Architect: Thomas W. Lamb. Opening as a movie theater, May 14, 1914, with *Antony and Cleopatra;* as a legitimate theater. August 19, 1914, with *On Trial.* The Candler family, who had made their money from Coca-Cola, built the Candler Theatre on 42nd Street next to the Candler office building which they had constructed two years earlier. They built the theater as a movie theater but had architect Thomas Lamb design the house so that it could also serve as a fully equipped legitimate theater. The theater proper fronted 41st Street but the entrance was on the well-travelled 42nd Street. Its theatrical policy began with the show *On Trial* (1914).

The producing team of George M. Cohan and Sam Harris along with movie magnate George Kleine took over the theater's operation. Soon thereafter Kleine dropped out at the two partners renamed the Candler Theatre the Cohan and Harris Theatre. They opened their first production, *Object-Matrimony* (1916). After a brief sojourn by *The Intruder* (1916), the theater had a hit with *Captain Kidd, Jr.,* written by operetta librettist Rida Johnson Young.

The theater hosted three offerings in 1917. The first, *The Willow Tree* (1917) by J. H. Benrimo and Harrison Rhodes, had Fay Bainter in the lead. The musical revue, *Hitchy-Koo* (1917), the first in a continuing series, starred comedian Raymond Hitchcock, Irene Bordoni, Leon Errol, Grace LaRue, and Frances White. An even bigger hit was *A Tailor-Made Man* (1917) by Harry James Smith. The play opened with Grant Mitchell achieving stardom in the leading role.

Another long run at the Cohan and Harris Theatre was Anthony Paul Kelly's play *Three Faces East* (1918). Violet Heming and Emmett Corrigan opened in the play.

Cohan himself appeared in *The Royal Vagabond* (1919) at the Cohan and Harris Theatre. The musical was originally written by Anselm Goetzl, William Cary Duncan, and Stephen

Ivor Szinngey. Cohan contributed music to the show. Songs were also written by Harry Tierney and Joseph McCarthy and Irving Berlin.

The Acquittal (1920) marked the end of the Cohan and Harris producing relationship. Following *The Acquittal,* the musical *Honey Girl* (1920) opened at the theater with a score by popular songwriter Albert Von Tilzer and Neville Fleeson.

When the partnership with Cohan dissolved, Harris took over the operation of the theater. He changed the name to the Sam H. Harris Theatre. There had previously been a Harris Theater, but its name was changed to the Frazee in 1920. *Welcome Stranger* (1921) was the first offering under the banner of the Sam H. Harris Theatre.

Six-Cylinder Love (1921), William Anthony McGuire's comedy, starred Donald Meek, June Walker, Ernest Truex, and Hedda Hopper in the days before she became one of the most powerful columnists in Hollywood.

The theater hosted one of its most notable attractions when John Barrymore starred in *Hamlet* (1922). Producer Arthur Hopkins presented the play at the Harris because his own Plymouth Theater was occupied with Don Marquis' comedy, *The Old Soak.* Barrymore's portrayal of Hamlet set a Broadway record for the tragedy until Richard Burton's production played for 137 performances in 1964. On its closing night, over one thousand people were turned away from the box office.

Edna May Oliver, Eva Condon, and Andrew Lawlor starred in Owen Davis' Pulitzer Prize-winning drama *Icebound* (1923). Although Owen Davis had a big success with the drama *Icebound,* he was best known as a writer of farce. His *The Nervous Wreck* (1923) was an immediate hit. The play was later adapted into the musical *Whoopee.*

One Helluva Night lived up to its name. The play opened on June 4, 1924, and closed the same night. *Topsy and Eva* (1924) was a hit musical for the theater. *Alias the Deacon* (1925) was a comedy by John B. Hymer and Le Roy Clemens.

The comedy *Love 'Em and Leave 'Em* (1926)

was written by George Abbott and John V. A. Weaver. *We Americans* (1926) was a drama starring Muni Weisenfreund, better known later as Hollywood star Paul Muni.

In 1926, Harris sold his interests to the Shubert Brothers who booked the theater with film attractions in addition to theater events. The theater wasn't lucky enough to host the hit musical *No, No, Nanette* but it did host *Yes, Yes, Yvette* (1927). The show had lyrics by *Nanette's* lyricist Irving Caesar and starred Jeanette MacDonald and Charles Winninger.

Congai (1928), a play by Harry Hervey and Carleton Hildrith, was staged by Rouben Mamoulian and starred Helen Menken. *Mendel, Inc.* (1929), about an eccentric inventor whose wife has to go to work to support the family, starred Alexander Carr and the sometime vaudeville team of Smith and Dale.

Rhapsody in Black (1931), an all black revue, had an impressive cast, including Ethel Waters, Valaida, and Eloise Uggams. A play, *Sing High, Sing Low* (1931) was a failure. *The Black Tower* (1932) was a disappointment.

The Shuberts, like many of their rivals, lost many of their holdings because of the Depression, and the Harris was no exception. And the Harris became one of the city's grind movie houses. The 994-seat theater was planned to become a twin movie theater under the Times Square Redevelopment Plan. But it was instead demolished.

HARRIS THEATER · (2) See ANCO THEATER.

HART, MOSS · See KAUFMAN AND HART.

HAYES, HELEN (1900–1993) · Playwright Robert Emmett Sherwood once commented that Helen Hayes "seems to regard the theater much as a champion mountain climber regards Everest: it is a challenge to her remarkable determination and courage and skill." Sherwood, writing in the theater magazine, *The Stage,* was referring to Hayes' reluctance to settle for one stage persona. Rather, she insisted on tackling a wide variety of roles. Most of her characters were genteel and seemingly civilized, but they all had an inner strength and maturity. They were marked by a sort of sly, mischievous twinkle in the eye with a promise of sexuality beneath their refined exterior.

"The First Lady of the American Theater" was born in Washington, D.C., on October 10, 1900. She evinced a talent for acting at an early age, first appearing as Prince Charles in the Columbia Players' production of *The Royal Family* in 1905 at the National Theatre. In 1908, when she was eight years old, she appeared in three more productions in her hometown: *Little Lord Fauntleroy, The Prince Chap,* and the lead in *The Prince and the Pauper.*

Her New York debut was in the Victor Herbert musical *Old Dutch* (1909), which premiered at the Herald Square Theater. The Gerry Society did not allow children to sing in Broadway shows, so composer Victor Herbert had Miss Hayes and another actor mime the leading couple's actions as they sang their love duet.

Hayes made many appearances on Broadway, and she scored a great success in the role of Cora Wheeler in Booth Tarkington's comedy *Clarence* (1919) at the Hudson Theatre.

Of Hayes' performances in *Quarantine* (1924), critic Heywood Broun reported that a woman sitting behind him exclaimed "Isn't she just too cute?" no less than twenty-one times. The young actress desperately wanted to present a more grown-up image when she attacked the part of Cleopatra in George Bernard Shaw's *Caesar and Cleopatra* (1925) at the Guild Theater under the auspices of the Theater Guild.

The critics seemed to feel that the actress was more suited to play an ingénue than the Queen of Egypt.

Her crack at maturity would finally come with William A. Brady's revival of James Barrie's *What Every Woman Knows* (1926). Brady had a lease on the little Bijou Theatre and still had four weeks left to use it. He approached Helen Hayes to assay the role best remembered for Maude Adams' striking interpretation. Despite her nervousness at stepping into the shoes of Maude Adams, Hayes took the job and it proved to be a turning point in her career.

Coquette (1927) at the Maxine Elliott Theatre was another success for Helen Hayes. The play marked her emergence as a star of the first order. Her role, written by George Abbott and Ann Preston Bridgers, proved perfect for her talents.

Ferenc Molnar's *The Good Fairy* (1931) marked her return to Broadway after a visit to Hollywood to make several pictures that received mixed reviews. Following her return to Hollywood and a starring role opposite Gary Cooper in *A Farewell to Arms,* Hayes received an Academy Award for *The Sin of Madelon Claudet.*

Her next great success on Broadway was in Maxwell Anderson's *Mary of Scotland.* Anderson had seen the actress in *Mr. Gilhooley* (1930). Though it was a failure (audiences would not accept their favorite little actress as a prostitute), Hayes herself received good notices and Anderson was determined to write her a play. The result was *Mary of Scotland* (1933) in which Hayes played the title role of Mary Queen of Scots. The Theater Guild production opened at the Alvin Theater.

In her next stage appearance, she again portrayed a member of British royalty. *Victoria Regina* (1935), by Laurence Housman, opened at the Broadhurst Theater with Vincent Price costarring. The play spanned Victoria's life from age seventeen to sixty and finally to eighty. To achieve the effect of age, she had costume designer Rex Whistler make specially padded costumes. She was advised by Charles Laughton to fill her cheeks with apple slices, but when the apples proved too tasty, she replaced them with cotton wool. The final effect was not cosmetic but came from inside Hayes. She patterned her speech and carriage after her paternal grandmother. In her last scene, many audience members did not believe it was still Helen Hayes on stage. For her performances as Queen Victoria, she was hailed as the greatest American actress of her generation.

Shakespeare would provide her next Broadway success as Viola in *Twelfth Night* (1940).

Maurice Evans played Malvolio in the production at the St. James Theatre. Hayes had another moderate run in Maxwell Anderson's *Candle in the Wind* (1941) at the Shubert Theater.

In 1909, the young Helen Hayes was forbidden to sing on stage; in 1946, she was finally given the chance. The occasion was *Happy Birthday* (1946), a play by Anita Loos that opened at the Broadhurst Theater under the auspices of producers Richard Rodgers and Oscar Hammerstein II. The team wrote a song for the play, "1 Haven't Got a Worry in the World." Hayes won the Tony Award for best actress—it was the first time the award had been given.

Hayes' first appearance in London's West End came next. The opportunity arose when the great American actress Laurette Taylor died. Before her death, Taylor asked that Helen Hayes be given the opportunity to play Amanda in Tennessee Williams' *Glass Menagerie* if she herself could not. Helen Hayes opened at the Theater Royal, Haymarket, July 28, 1948.

Hayes had considered retirement and the death of her daughter Mary in 1949 convinced her to give up performing. But Joshua Logan enticed her back to the stage with his adaptation of *The Cherry Orchard* entitled *The Wysteria Trees* (1950) at the Martin Beck Theatre.

Mary Chase, the author of *Harvey*, had her play *Mrs. McThing* (1952) optioned by ANTA, the American National Theater and Academy. They convinced Helen Hayes to undertake the title role. Brandon de Wilde was her costar.

In November 1955, the Fulton Theater was renamed the Helen Hayes Theater in her honor. During the run of *Mrs. McThing*, Helen Hayes' mother, Brownie, died. The actress received another blow when, on April 21, 1956, her husband, playwright Charles MacArthur, died.

After an appearance in the movie *Anastasia*, Hayes returned to Broadway in Jean Anouilh's *Time Remembered* (1957) at the Morosco Theatre. Her costars were Susan Strasberg and Richard Burton.

Hayes played her first role in the Helen Hayes Theater in Eugene O'Neill's *A Touch of the Poet* (1958).

In 1966, Hayes joined the repertory company APA Phoenix. Not all her roles were starring ones, but she enjoyed flexing her theatrical muscles and also being away from the pressures of a normal Broadway run. While at APA-Phoenix she appeared in Sheridan's *The School for Scandal*, Pirandello's *Right You Are If You Think You Are, We Comrades Three* and *You Can't Take It With You*. During the next season, she was in George Kelly's *The Show Off* (1967). She also appeared in her husband and Ben Hecht's classic, *The Front Page* at the Ethel Barrymore Theater in October 1969, replacing another actress for six weeks.

After her Oscar winning performance in the movie *Airplane*, Helen Hayes opened opposite James Stewart in Mary Chase's *Harvey* (1970) at the ANTA Theater. *Harvey* was her last Broadway appearance and her next-to-last stage appearance.

She retired from the stage after a 1971 production of O'Neill's *Long Day's Journey Into Night* at Catholic University in Washington, D.C. Critics raved about her performances as Mary Tyrone in the harrowing drama.

Helen Hayes died in Nyack, New York on March 17, 1993.

HELEN HAYES THEATER · (1) 210–14 W. 46th Street. Architects: Herts and Tallant. Opening: April 27, 1911, as theater/restaurant Folies Bergere; as Fulton Theater October 20, 1911, *The Cave Man;* as Helen Hayes Theater November 21, 1955, *Tiger at the Gates*. Producers Henry B. Harris and Jesse Lasky opened a Broadway branch of the Parisian nightclub Folies Bergere on April 27, 1911. The club, which some consider the first American nightclub, was not successful enough to continue as a cabaret. The owners renovated the space into a legitimate theater and called it the Fulton.

The theater was a moderate success from the beginning. *Linger Longer Letty* (1919) was written by Al Goodman, Bernard Grossman, and Anne Nichols. Charlotte Greenwood starred in one of the only musical comedy series to be based on one character. Letty Pepper, played by Greenwood, was a favorite of audiences, especially when she kicked her feet high over her head.

In 1921, A. L. Erlanger took over the theater and hired Joseph Urban to remodel the interior. Urban painted over William DeLeftwich Dodge's murals including "Vaudeville Paying Homage to Les Folies-Bergeres" that topped the proscenium.

Orange Blossoms (1922) was Victor Herbert's last musical comedy produced in his lifetime. Edith Day introduced a great Herbert standard, "A Kiss in the Dark." Despite many plusses, the show received mixed reviews.

The theater's greatest hit and the biggest hit of the twenties, was Anne Nichols' comedy *Abie's Irish Rose* (1922) which played 2,327 performances. The remarkably successful show was to move to other theaters before finally closing.

Nifties of 1923 (1923) was a failure, despite a score by contributors such as Eubie Blake, Noble Sissle, George Gershwin, Irving Caesar, Harry Ruby, Bert Kalmar, and Ira Gershwin. However, Ira Gershwin (writing under his pseudonym Arthur Francis) wrote lyrics to music by Raymond Hubbell, not his brother. Irving Caesar provided the lyrics to the song by George Gershwin. *Sitting Pretty* (1924) was a Jerome Kern, P. G. Wodehouse and Guy Bolton musical in the vein of their Princess Theater shows—small, intimate, American-themed productions.

A drama that would, in another medium, change the history of entertainment opened at the Fulton. The play was *The Jazz Singer* (1925), which was later made into the world's first talking picture by Warner Brothers with stage great Al Jolson in the lead. The original play was written by Samson Raphaelson and starred George Jessel as the cantor's son who wants a life in the theater rather than a life devoted to religion.

Beatrice Lillie appeared in her first American book musical, *Oh, Please!* (1926) at the Fulton. The Vincent Youmans score had lyrics by Otto Harbach and Anne Caldwell.

Hamilton Deane and John Balderston were the playwrights responsible for scaring the wits out of audiences at the Fulton Theater with their play *Dracula* (1927), based on Bram Stoker's novel. The play starred Bela Lugosi, who later replayed the character in many motion pictures.

The first of Leonard Sillman's *New Faces* (1934) revues introduced actors Imogene Coca, Hildegard Halliday, and James Shelton to New York audiences. But by far the greatest new face was that of Henry Fonda.

Another long-running comedy, *Arsenic and Old Lace* (1941), graced the Fulton's stage. The comedy, by Joseph Kesselring with an assist by Howard Lindsay and Russel Crouse, starred Josephine Hull and Jean Adair as two maiden aunts who bury a number of lonely old men in their basement.

Lillian Hellman's play *The Searching Wind* (1944) starred Montgomery Clift and Dudley Diggs. Arnaud D'Usseau and James Gow's play, *Deep Are the Roots* (1945), explored the problems of black veterans returning from World War II.

Lillian Hellman had her second Fulton Theater premiere with *Another Part of the Forest* (1946). Patricia Neal starred in the leading role. William Wister Haines' *Command Decision* (1947) starred James Whitmore, Paul Kelly, and Paul Ford. Anita Loos adapted Collette's story *Gigi* (1951) for the stage and cast Audrey Hepburn, Mel Ferrer, and Marian Seldes in the leads.

The Seven Year Itch (1952), George Axelrod's comedy about the male libido, starred Tom Ewell and Vanessa Brown. It was later made into a very successful movie with Ewell and Marilyn Monroe.

The theater was to undergo one last renovation. A marquee was added to the façade and many of the theater's decorations were removed. Finally, the entire auditorium was painted a pinkish beige.

On November 21, 1955, with the opening of *Tiger at the Gates,* the theater was renamed to honor actress Helen Hayes. Jose Quintero directed Fredric March, Florence Eldridge, and

Jason Robards Jr. in Eugene O'Neill's autobiographical drama *Long Day's Journey Into Night* (1956). The production won the Pulitzer Prize award for drama that year. Another O'Neill play, *A Touch of the Poet* (1958), starred Helen Hayes, Eric Portman, Kim Stanley, and Betty Field.

Jean Kerr's comedy *Mary, Mary* (1961) starred Barbara Bel Geddes and Michael Rennie. Another Jean Kerr play was the Helen Hayes Theater's next tenant. *Poor Richard* (1964). Brian Friel's comedy *Philadelphia Here I Come* (1966) was a hit in the 1965–66 season.

The Prime of Miss Jean Brodie (1968) had Zoe Caldwell in the lead. Jay Presson Allen's play was later successfully transferred to the screen. Alec McCowen also had a tour de force in his portrayal of Frederick Rolfe/Baron Corvo in Peter Luke's play *Hadrian VII* (1969). A light comedy, Bob Randall's *6 Rms Riv Vu* (1972), starred F. Murray Abraham, Jerry Orbach, Jane Alexander, and Jennifer Warren.

The Me Nobody Knows opened at the Helen Hayes Theater after a successful run off-Broadway. It eventually played for 587 performances. The Gary William Friedman and Will Holt revue, based on children's poetry and writing, featured a cast of youngsters, including Irene Cara. *Rodgers and Hart* (1975) was a revue based on the songs of the great composing team, Richard Rodgers and Lorenz Hart.

George S. Kaufman and Edna Ferber's comedy satire of the Barrymores, *The Royal Family* (1975), was mounted as an all-star revival.

The classic O'Neill drama *A Touch of the Poet* (1977) opened for a second time at the Helen Hayes Theater. This production starred Milo O'Shea, Geraldine Fitzgerald, Jason Robards Jr., Kathryn Walker, and George Ede under the direction of Jose Quintero.

Perfectly Frank (1980) was another revue that focused on the career of a major Broadway composer. Frank Loesser was the subject of the show. *The Crucifer of Blood* (1978) was a Sherlock Holmes mystery, starring Paxton Whitehead as the intrepid deducer and Timothy Landfield as his assistant John Watson, M.D. Glenn Close also starred in the mystery.

The Crucifer of Blood was the last semisuccess to play the Helen Hayes Theater.

A long battle to save the Helen Hayes, Morosco, and Bijou theaters and the Astor and Victoria movie theaters was fought in the late seventies. Despite the best efforts of preservationists, architects, theater people and audiences the pro-developer city government and the builders won the battle, and in 1982 the theaters were torn down to make way for the Marriott Marquis Hotel.

HELEN HAYES THEATER · (2) See LITTLE THEATRE.

HENDERSON, RAY · See DESYLVA, BROWN AND HENDERSON.

HENRY MILLER'S THEATRE · 124 W. 43rd Street. Architects: Harry Creighton Ingalls and Paul R. Allen. Opening: April 1, 1918; *The Fountain of Youth*. Henry Miller's Theatre, home of distinguished straight plays, especially those from London, saw its fortunes fall along with Broadway's. The theater was built by English actor/manager Henry Miller and his partners in the real estate firm of William A. White to house Miller's productions. Miller made sure that his architects included a balcony in their designs because he remembered his youth and the years when he had only enough money for the balcony seats. He wanted other young people of small means to be able to enjoy the theater too.

The first production at the theater, *The Fountain of Youth*, was a failure and closed after only 32 performances. The second offering, *A Marriage of Convenience* opened on May 1, 1918, with Billie Burke starring. It played for only fifty-three performances.

Coal restrictions during World War I increased theater business because people left their homes to sit in a warm theater. The first hit to play the theater was *Mis' Nelly of New Orleans* (1919), which played 127 performances.

On May 26, 1919, the theater housed a musical, George Gershwin's *La, La, Lucille!*

Alex Aarons and George B. Seitz produced the show, which was one of the few musicals produced on the Henry Miller stage. The "New Up-to-the-Minute Musical Comedy of Class and Distinction" was Gershwin's first complete score for a Broadway production.

The teens ended with a successful production of *The Famous Mrs. Fair* (1919), which ran 343 performances, well into the twenties. Also in the early twenties were the openings for *Wake Up, Jonathan* (1921); Booth Tarkington's *Intimate Strangers* (1921) with Alfred Lunt and Billie Burke; *The Awful Truth* (1922), starring Ina Claire; and *Romeo and Juliet* (1923) with Jane Cowl and Dennis King.

Helen Hayes starred at the Henry Miller in *Quarantine* (1924) along with Sidney Blackmer.

Noel Coward's *The Vortex* opened on September 16, 1925. It was followed by Ferenc Molnar's *The Play's the Thing* (1926) and George M. Cohan's play *The Baby Cyclone* (1927). The house long run record was set with *Journey's End* (1929), which ran 485 performances.

In 1930, the theater was bought by manager/producer Gilbert Miller. During the thirties, the theater's success continued. Philip Barry's *Tomorrow and Tomorrow* opened on January 13, 1931, and ran 206 performances. Helen Hayes returned to the theater in *The Good Fairy* (1931) by Molnar. It was followed by Sidney Howard's *The Late Christopher Bean* (1932); Eugene O'Neill's *Days without End* (1934); Lawrence Riley's *Personal Appearance* (1934) with Gladys George; Edward Woolf's *Libel* (1935), which marked the emergence of director Otto Preminger as a major talent; and Terrance Rattigan's *French without Tears* (1937).

Next, the theater presented an American classic, Thornton Wilder's *Our Town*. It opened on February 4, 1938, with little advance word. The play received mixed reviews in Boston before coming to New York. In fact, the Boston run was canceled before its scheduled closing. The show was booked into the Henry Miller, but the theater gave it only a limited guarantee, believing the show to be a sure failure. The reviews at its Broadway opening were mixed,

and audiences stayed away. When the play won the Pulitzer Prize, business picked up. By this time, the play had to make room for the Henry Miller's next booking, Clair Boothe's *Kiss the Boys Goodbye* (1938), so it was transferred to the Morosco Theatre, where it concluded its 336 performance run.

The theater's first play of the 1940s was *Ladies in Retirement* (1940). *Harriet* (1943) followed, starring Helen Hayes, as Harriet Beecher Stowe. Julius J. and Philip G. Epstein's comedy *Chicken Every Sunday* (1944) followed the run of *Harriet*. Norman Krasna, a popular writer of light comedies, had a major success with *Dear Ruth* (1944). Moss Hart staged the play, which starred Virginia Gilmore and Lenore Lonergan. June Lockhart, best known as the mother in the television series "Lassie" and the daughter of Gene Lockhart, starred in *For Love or Money* (1947) at Henry Miller's Theatre. F. Hugh Herbert's play ran 263 performances.

The 1950s started with a hit for the theater, T. S. Eliot's *The Cocktail Party* (1950). The play starred Alec Guinness, Irene Worth, and Cathleen Nesbitt. *The Cocktail Party* was the first big British hit to play the theater, which enjoyed a reputation as the American home of English shows.

F. Hugh Herbert had another success at the theater with *The Moon Is Blue* (1951). Barbara Bel Geddes and Barry Nelson starred in the long-running play. Edward Chodorov's hit comedy *Oh, Men! Oh, Women!* opened on December 17, 1953. Another English offering, Graham Greene's *The Living Room*, opened on November 17, 1954, with Barbara Bel Geddes but lasted only twenty-two performances. It was quickly replaced with another import, Agatha Christie's *Witness for the Prosecution* (1954), which did considerably better with its 645 performance run.

The "British invasion" continued on October 10, 1956, with *The Reluctant Debutante* by William Douglas Home. A hilarious production of Feydeau's comedy *Hotel Paradiso* opened at the theater on April 11, 1957. The play starred Bert Lahr and, making her stage debut, Angela Lansbury.

Elmer Rice's last play, *Cue for Passion* (1958) was a failure and closed after thirty-nine performances. Another failure by a great dramatist, Noel Coward's *Look After Lulu,* opened on March 3, 1959. Tammy Grimes starred in the play for thirty-nine performances.

The next hit at the theater was Saul Levitt's courtroom drama, *The Andersonville Trial.* The play opened on December 29, 1959, with George C. Scott and Albert Dekker. Movie star Bette Davis opened on September 14, 1960, in the short-lived production, *The World of Carl Sandburg.* A much bigger hit was Lawrence Roman's *Under the Yum-Yum Tree* (1960), starring Gig Young.

Joseph Stein's play *Enter Laughing* opened on March 13, 1963, with Alan Arkin and Vivian Blaine. A long series of flop plays followed. Lawrence Roman's *P.S. I Love You* (1964) starred Geraldine Page and Lee Patterson and closed after twelve performances. Jerome Lawrence and Robert E. Lee's *Diamond Orchid* (1965), a drama about Eva Peron closed after five performances. Other plays at the theater included *The Promise* with Ian McKellen; Jack Gelber's *The Cuban Thing* with Rip Torn, Jane White, and Raul Julia; Terrance McNally's *Morning, Noon and Night;* and Julius J. Epstein's *But, Seriously* with Richard Dreyfuss and Tom Poston. Epstein's play opened on February 27, 1969, and closed on March 1, 1969, the last production to play the theater until the 1990s.

After Henry Miller's death on April 9, 1926, the theater remained in his family's hands. His son, Gilbert Miller, a noted producer in his own right, oversaw the theater's operation. In 1966, Gilbert Miller's widow sold the theater and it became the Park-Miller Theatre, which showed male porno films. In 1978, the theater became the disco Xenon. Xenon continued until 1984—until the death of disco. The theater then became a dance hall, Shout!!, which featured 1950s rock and roll.

The Roundabout Theatre Company opened an American version of the acclaimed British revival of *Cabaret* (1998) at the theater, which was renamed the Kit Kat Klub. The off-off-Broad-

way hit *Urinetown* (2001) transferred to the theater, again named the Henry Miller's Theatre.

It was torn down, leaving only the façade, in 2005. A sad end to an historic theater.

HERBERT, VICTOR (1859–1924) · The Irish-born composer and conductor Victor Herbert was the most important and prolific of the early composers of musical comedy and operetta. He was a major influence on an entire generation of musicians. His thirty-year career included many triumphs both on stage and off. Among his best-known shows are *Babes in Toyland, The Red Mill, Naughty Marietta, Mlle. Modiste, Sweethearts, Eileen* and *Orange Blossoms.* Herbert was instrumental in the formation of ASCAP.

Herbert was born in Dublin on February 1, 1859. When his father died, his mother remarried and the family moved to Stuttgart. He attended Stuttgart Conservatory and studied with Bernhard Cossman and Max Seifriz. He spent many years as a cellist with German and Austrian symphony orchestras, including five years with the Court Orchestra of Stuttgart.

After immigrating to the United States in October 1886, Herbert became a cello soloist at the Metropolitan Opera House. He also played in the symphony orchestras of Anton Seidl and Theodore Thomas. He soon graduated to conductor, first with the 22nd National Guard Band, and from 1898 to 1904 he conducted the Pittsburgh Symphony. In 1898, he performed his own work, the "Concerto No.2 for Cello and Orchestra, Op. 30," with the New York Philharmonic.

Herbert wrote forty-four complete scores for the stage. In addition, he composed two operas, *Natoma* in 1911 and *Madeleine* in 1913. They were not successful, although their music has won greater appreciation today. Herbert wrote many orchestral works, including "A Suite of Serenades" written for the Paul Whiteman Aeolian Hall concert, at which George Gershwin's "Rhapsody in Blue" also appeared.

Herbert was a portly figure known for his generosity, business sense, appreciation of fine food and drink and love for Ireland. His

1892 work "Irish Rhapsody" contains some of his most heartfelt melodies. He was also a staunch supporter of composer's rights. His suit against Shanley's Restaurant set the stage for the establishment of ASCAP.

In 1894, he was commissioned by The Bostonians to compose the score for the operetta *Prince Ananias*. This group was founded in 1879 as the Boston Ideal Opera Company to present Gilbert and Sullivan operettas.

After its success, the composer collaborated with Harry B. Smith on the great hit, *The Wizard of the Nile*. Herbert would write thirteen scores with Harry B. Smith, who matched Herbert's prolificacy but not his talent. Many critics felt that Herbert never had a collaborator worthy of his talents. Although many of his scores are famous today, their libretti and lyrics are dated or second-rate.

The Wizard of the Nile was followed by a dazzling succession of operettas that featured lush melodies, stirring ballads and delightful character songs. In 1896, Herbert premiered *The Gold Bug* with lyrics by Glen MacDonough. The next year, two shows written with Harry B. Smith premiered—*The Serenade* and *The Idol's Eye*. In 1898, Herbert and Smith presented *The Fortune Teller*. The following year, three Herbert shows made their debut: *Cyrano de Bergerac* (Smith); *The Singing Girl* (Smith) and *The Ameer* (Frederic Rankin and Kirke La Shelle). In 1900, Herbert and Smith's *The Viceroy* opened (1900). The first of his masterpieces opened three years later—*Babes in Toyland* (1903), with book and lyrics by Glen MacDonough, remains a favorite more than 80 years after its opening. The songs "March of the Toys," "Toyland" and "I Can't Do That Sum" are still played in pops concerts and occasional revivals. Herbert followed the triumph of *Babes in Toyland* with *Babette* (1903) written with Harry B. Smith.

MacDonough and Herbert's next show was *It Happened in Nordland* (1904).

Miss Dolly Dollars (1905) with words by Smith, had a number with an enduring title—"A Woman Is Only a Woman but a Good Cigar Is a Smoke." Though Kipling originated the phrase, it entered the language through the popularity of the song.

In the same year were the premieres of *Wonderland* (1905), written with Glen MacDonough, and one of the composer's greatest successes, *Mlle. Modiste* (1905). The latter opened with Fritzi Scheff in the lead. Also in the cast in a chorus role was movie pioneer, Mack Sennett. *Mlle. Modiste* contained two of Herbert's great classics, "Kiss Me Again" and the rousing, "I Want What I Want When I Want It." Henry Blossom supplied the words to that score and to Herbert's next great hit, *The Red Mill*.

The Red Mill (1906) contained four Herbert standards, "When You're Pretty and the World Is Fair;" "Moonbeams;" "Every Day Is Ladies' Day with Me;" and "The Streets of New York." Largely because of its four hit songs, the show is still revived today. Three months after the opening of *The Red Mill*, Herbert and Edgar Smith saw their *Dream City and the Magic Knight* open on Broadway. Herbert's sole 1907 offering, *The Tattooed Man* (1907) was a minor effort by the composer and Harry B. Smith. *Algeria* (1908), written with Glen MacDonough fared little better. *Little Nemo* (1908), based on the comic strip *Little Nemo in Slumberland* by Winsor McKay, was an elaborate fantasy.

The Prima Donna (1908) was written with Henry Blossom. The program of the Fritzi Scheff vehicle carried a brief statement by producer Charles Dillingham—"Made in America."

Old Dutch (1909) was written in collaboration with George V. Hobart. The show is best remembered today for marking the Broadway debut of the girl who played Little Mime—Helen Hayes.

In 1910, another Herbert classic premiered—*Naughty Marietta* (1910). Herbert wrote the show with Rida Johnson Young. Together they came up with what some consider Herbert's finest score. Among the songs were the hits, "Tramp! Tramp! Tramp!;" " 'Neath the Southern Moon;" "Italian Street Song;" "I'm Falling in Love with Someone;" and "Ah! Sweet Mystery of Life."

Herbert followed the triumph of *Naughty Marietta* with the minor effort, *When Sweet Sixteen* (1911), in collaboration with George V. Hobart. The composer next attempted two grand opera productions. They were nowhere near as successful as his operettas.

Herbert returned to the Broadway stage with a Shubert Brothers production, *The Duchess* (1911). The lyrics were by Joseph W. Herbert and Harry B. Smith. Smith worked on Herbert's next show, *The Enchantress* (1911). It was, remarkably, Herbert's third show to open in a little more than a month. The librettist, listed as Fred de Gresac, was actually Mme. Victor Maurel, the wife of a famous French baritone.

The Lady of the Slipper (1912) boasted a star-studded cast that included Vernon Castle, Elsie Janis, Montgomery and Stone, and Peggy Wood. James O'Dea supplied the lyrics. *Sweethearts* (1913) was another of Herbert's shows with a celebrated score. It had lyrics by Robert B. Smith and book by Harry B. Smith and Fred de Gresac. Two songs were standouts, "Sweethearts" and "Every Lover Must Meet His Fate."

The Madcap Duchess (1913) had book and lyrics by Justin Henry McCarthy and David Stevens. *The Only Girl* (1914) was "a musical farcical comedy." It had one somewhat popular song, "When You're Away."

Herbert's *The Debutante* (1914) had Robert B. Smith lyrics. The day after its opening, *Watch Your Step* opened with Irving Berlin's jazzy score and pointed the way to the future of the American musical theater. Henry Blossom penned the book and lyrics for Herbert's next venture, *The Princess Pat* (1915), which was a success. The song that has lasted the longest is the "Neopolitan Love Song," a favorite of sopranos since its introduction.

Herbert's next show featured both the musical theater's past, represented by Herbert, and its future, represented by Berlin. Both composers created the score for the revue, *The Century Girl* (1916). Blossom supplied Herbert's lyrics. The show was the idea of the great producers Charles Dillingham and Florenz Ziegfeld.

With Ziegfeld at the helm, it was inevitable that the show would be a lavish extravaganza. In one scene entitled "The Music Lesson," both Herbert and Berlin were portrayed on stage. Herbert's hit "Kiss Me Again" was played for the scene, and Berlin wrote a counter melody to the tune.

Blossom also collaborated on Herbert's next show, *Eileen* (1917), with the great Herbert song, "Thine Alone." Ziegfeld tapped Herbert's talents for another revue, the legendary *Miss 1917*. The show opened without a chance of making back Ziegfeld's investment. Although it played to sold-out houses the show lost money due to its huge weekly operating expenses. The revue had a few Herbert songs, but the majority of the score was written by Jerome Kern, whose star was rising as fast as that of Irving Berlin. As Kern and Berlin had greater and greater successes, Herbert found his shows increasingly less popular.

Her Regiment (1917) had book and lyrics by William Le Baron. Ziegfeld hired Herbert to compose a few numbers for the *Ziegfeld Follies of 1917* (1917). His next operetta, *The Velvet Lady* (1919), again featured Blossom's words. *Angel Face* (1919), with Robert B. Smith lyrics, introduced an enduring standard, "I Might Be Your Once-in-a-While."

My Golden Girl (1920) had book and lyrics by Frederic Arnold Kummer. It contained one interesting number, "Ragtime Terpsichore," in which Herbert attempted to write in the jazz idiom. However, the show was still basically a romantic operetta. Herbert next composed a few numbers for the *Ziegfeld Follies of 1920*. His next operetta, *The Girl in the Spotlight* (1920), teamed him with Robert B. Smith.

Herbert's fortunes fell even further with his next show, *Oui Madame*. It was his last collaboration with Robert B. Smith and closed out of town in 1920. The composer's output then slowed even further. He contributed to the *Ziegfeld Follies of 1921* and *1922*.

His next to last show, *Orange Blossoms* (1922) had lyrics by B. G. DeSylva and a book by Fred de Gresac. Herbert proved that although his output had slowed he still had much to offer and could still write a superior score. For *Orange Blossoms,* Herbert wrote a beautiful song, "A Kiss in the Dark."

He completed his usual assignment for the *Ziegfeld Follies* and followed it with a concert work, "Suite of Serenades," commissioned by Paul Whiteman for his famous Aeolian Hall concert. The Suite was a major success and reemphasized Herbert's preeminence in American music.

For the composer's final operetta, *The Dream Girl* (1924), Rida Johnson Young supplied the lyrics and collaborated on the book with Harold Atteridge. Sigmund Romberg, another top operetta composer, also composed songs for the score. The Shubert production wasn't quite up to Herbert's usual standard but was a great public success. Herbert's last Broadway assignment was for the 1924 edition of the *Ziegfeld Follies*. He composed three instrumental numbers for the revue. After Herbert's death, Ziegfeld interpolated a medley of Herbert's greatest songs.

As a newspaper gimmick, columnist S. Jay Kaufman published in the *Evening Telegram* an article presenting the winner of an informal poll on who was America's greatest composer. Herbert won handily.

Victor Herbert died on May 26, 1924.

HERMAN, JERRY (1931) · Herman's work defines what most people think of when asked to describe the Broadway musical. His shows are glitzy, upbeat extravaganzas, long on energy and catchy tunes that the audience is sure to hum while leaving the theater.

Herman was born on July 10, 1931, in New York City. He was educated at the University of Miami and Parsons School of Design. His first score was for *I Feel Wonderful* (1954), a college revue that moved to off-Broadway. Herman followed with another revue, *Nightcap* (1958), which enjoyed a four hundred-performance run in the Showplace nightclub, off-Broadway. Another off-Broadway show, *Parade,* followed in January 1960.

The modest success that Herman had thus far enjoyed certainly didn't portend the enormous successes of his Broadway book shows. The first was *Milk and Honey* (1961). Molly Picon, Robert Weede, and Mimi Benzell starred in the show set in Israel. *Milk and Honey* ran for 543 performances, a long run by Broadway standards, yet the young songwriter didn't receive much notice, because most critics attributed the show's success to the large Jewish audience for Broadway musicals.

His next show, *Madame Aphrodite* (1961), played only thirteen performances off-Broadway. Two years later, Herman would have his biggest success when David Merrick hired him to write the score to Michael Stewart's musicalization of Thornton Wilder's *The Matchmaker.* The show was *Hello, Dolly!,* and this time Herman was definitely considered a major talent.

Hello, Dolly! opened on January 16, 1964, with Carol Channing in the lead. It became one of the most successful musicals in Broadway history, achieving 2,844 performances. After it passed the record number of performances held by *My Fair Lady, Hello, Dolly!* was for a time the longest-running show in Broadway history. It was shortly thereafter overtaken by *Fiddler on the Roof,* which opened nine months after *Hello, Dolly!*

Herman's next show proved almost as popular as *Hello, Dolly! Mame* opened on May 24, 1966, with Angela Lansbury portraying Patrick Dennis' zany character. *Mame* contained another first-rate score by Herman. Most popular were the title tune and "It's Today." Other songs that received notice were "If He Walked Into My Life" and "Open a New Window." *Mame* also gave a boost to the careers of Lansbury's costars, Beatrice Arthur and Jane Connell. It played a total of 1,508 performances on Broadway.

Lansbury, Herman and *Mame* librettists Lawrence and Lee teamed up again for *Dear World* (1969), a musical version of Jean Giradoux's *The Madwoman of Chaillot.* The show did not repeat the success of *Mame* and lasted only 132 performances.

Mack and Mabel (1974) followed and, despite having what some fans consider Herman's most mature score as well as the contributions of Bernadette Peters and Robert Preston, the show played only sixty-five performances. Although the failure of the show meant that few people were exposed to the score, two songs, "I Won't Send Roses" and "Time Heals Everything," have achieved minor success. Herman's next show performed slightly worse than even *Mack and Mabel. The Grand Tour* (1979) starred Joel Grey in an unsuccessful musicalization of S. N. Behrman's play *Jacobowsky and the Colonel.*

With three failures in a row, critics proclaimed Jerry Herman's career finished. Skeptics pointed to the success of *Hello, Dolly!* and *Mame* as flukes and suggested that Herman's style wasn't suited to the supposedly more-sophisticated Broadway of the eighties.

But on August 21, 1983, Herman surprised Broadway with *La Cage Aux Folles,* a huge hit in the style of his previous extravaganzas. George Hearn and Gene Barry played homosexual lovers in the adaptation of the French screen hit. The most popular of the songs, "I Am What I Am," even had the rare distinction of hitting the charts in a disco version.

La Cage was a huge hit with all the Broadway pizzazz and slick professionalism associated with Herman's name. Formerly blasé Broadwayites took notice when *La Cage Aux Folles* was nominated for a Tony Award for best musical, competing against Stephen Sondheim's *Sunday in the Park with George.* Throughout his career, Herman attempted ever more serious subjects. With *La Cage,* Herman was able to give audiences the expected razz-ma-tazz and also a profound message. After the triumphant opening of the show, Herman vowed never to write another show for Broadway. Sadly, he has kept his promise.

Herman wrote a television score, *Mrs. Santa Claus* for Angela Lansbury. He also wrote another stage score, *Miss Spectacular* for a casino in Las Vegas. However, the casino was sold and the project was, unfortunately, put on hold.

HILTON THEATRE · 214 W. 42nd Street. When Canadian producer Garth Drabinsky

was looking for a theater to house his Broadway productions, he met with the 42nd Street Redevelopment contingent and was given free reign to knock down the Apollo Theatre and the Lyric Theatre. He also made a deal which forbad any theatrical usage for the Time Square Theatre next door. A press conference was held on the stage of the derelict Apollo Theatre that, along with the Lyric Theatre, had been allowed to fall into disrepair by the 42nd Street Redevelopment committee. He announced plans to knock down both theatere (saving their facades) and building a huge, barn-like auditorium in the place of their more intimate surroundings. He got the Ford Motor Company to pay up to put their name on the new theater. It would be named the Ford Center for the Performing Arts—a name many felt was more suited to a theater in the Midwest. Indeed many other cities, including Chicago, had Ford Centers.

Drabinsky promised to keep much of the Apollo's interior décor in the new theater.

The resulting theater was cheaply constructed and considered just another huge barn-like theater. It has had a spotty history.

The theater opened with the hit *Ragtime* (1998) with a score by Lynn Aherns and Stephen Flaherty. A lavish revival of *42nd Street* (2001) enjoyed a long run only to be replaced by another lavish show, *Chitty Chitty Bang Bang* (2005). It was a failure. Before its opening, the agreement with the Ford Motor Company expired and the theater was renamed. After an agreement with the Hilton Hotels chain was signed, the theater was renamed the Hilton Theatre. A dance musical, *Hot Feet* (2006), then took to the stage but received almost unanimous pans.

HIPPODROME · Sixth Avenue between 43rd and 44th Street. Architect: J. H. Morgan. Opening: April 12, 1905; *A Yankee Circus on Mars.* For most Broadwayites, the Hippodrome is synonymous with spectacle just as the Roxy connotes lavishness. The theater, the largest in the world, certainly lived up to its reputation. It presented the biggest shows ever seen in New York or anywhere else.

The Hippodrome was the brainchild of Elmer S. Dundy and Frederic Thompson, the builders and operators of Coney Island's Luna Park. Their backer, John W. Bates, urged the team to conquer Broadway at his expense. They set to work to build the biggest and most sophisticated theater of its time.

Thompson envisioned a stage big enough to hold six hundred people. It was 110 feet deep and 200 feet wide and was divided into 12 sections. Each section could be raised or lowered by hydraulics. The Hippodrome also had a huge tank that could hold a lake big enough to float boats in or take the spill from a huge waterfall. The water pumps could handle 150,000 gallons of water. Because of the huge machinery required to run these devices, the stage weighed 460,000 pounds.

The roof and balcony of the building used 15,000 tons of steel. The roof itself was constructed from four giant steel trusses, the largest in any American building. The skeleton of the building was covered by 6,000 bricks.

One of the most important elements of the Hippodrome's design was the lighting system. Over 25,000 light bulbs were used to illuminate the theater and stage. Nine thousand of these were used for the stage, and another 5,000 were arranged in a stunning sunburst pattern in the auditorium.

Under the stage was a complete menagerie area where the famous Hippodrome elephants were kept. The theater also had a full complement of offices, costume shops, property houses, and scenery shops. The elaborate scenery itself was changed by a unique system of cranes that would carry the equipment up to the fly area high above the stage.

The Hippodrome and its shows were a publicist's dream. On March 12, 1905, a month before it opened, the theater received its first great publicity coup when Police Commissioner William McAdoo had the building surrounded by one hundred police officers. They were sent because of a complaint by the Sabbath Association that construction workers were putting in long hours on Sunday. Since construction had started in July 1904, almost a year earlier, it seems strange that action was taken only then. Nonetheless, when the next shift of workers showed up, they were stopped by the police. Thompson and Dundy took matters in hand, giving each of the workers a card that invited him into the theater as a sightseer. The police were powerless to stop the men from entering as guests of the management. After they had entered the auditorium, they were instructed to put material over the windows so that the police couldn't see what was happening inside.

The excitement rose as the building neared completion. Thompson and Dundy walked their menagerie to Manhattan all the way from Luna Park. A herd of elephants led the parade followed by camels, 175 horses, and even a team of bloodhounds. They marched, on foot and in vans, over the Brooklyn Bridge, up Broadway and across 42nd Street to the theater.

By opening night, the stage was set for what was certainly the largest opening in theater history, one that had cost $4 million. On April 12, 1905, the theater was ready for opening. The ticket prices ranged from 25 cents for the cheapest seats to $2 for the boxes. The theater seated 5,200 patrons. The *New York Clipper* described the theater as "remarkable for its grandeur and magnitude, a place of magnificent distances."

The opening show was *A Yankee Circus on Mars*. The play was written by George V. Hobart. Jean Schwartz, along with Manuel Klein composed the music. They, along with Harry Williams, contributed the lyrics. The settings were designed by the brilliant Arthur Voegtlin, who created most of the great special effects that helped make the Hippodrome's fame.

The star was one of Broadway's favorite actresses, Bessie McCoy, who made her entrance in a gold chariot driven by two white horses. A thirty-foot airship landed on the stage and disgorged a Martian who asked the Americans to bring a circus to his planet. At one point in the proceedings, the Barlow's Magnificent Hippodrome Elephants appeared behind the steering wheels of autos. The pachyderms drove ten chorus girls around the Hippodrome's huge stage. The show also featured 280 chorus girls. Apart from the Hippodrome elephants, the only other regular star of Hippodrome shows was Marceline the Spanish clown. He appeared in every Hippodrome show for a decade. Marceline became as big an attraction as the Hippodrome itself.

The *Yankee Circus* was only the first part of the opening night program. Next came the *Dance of the Hours,* which featured 150 dancing girls. That piece was in turn followed by *Andersonville, or A Story of Wilson's Raiders.* This spectacular pageant traces the story of a Union officer and a Southern belle. The first scene takes place during a West Point ball. Then we are whisked to the Andersonville prison. Our hero digs a tunnel out of the prison but is spotted by the guards. They chase him to a Southern mansion. Inside, the heroine gives the soldier a horse, and he gallops away with bloodhounds in hot pursuit. The scene then changes to Rocky Ford Bridge over what appeared to the audience to be a real lake. Four hundred and eighty soldiers meet at the bridge and fight to the death. A team of horses pulling a caisson charges across the stage while the soldiers fight on the bridge and in the water. After the battle, the scene changes to the McLean House at Appomattox. The Civil War ends as the hero is united with the heroine.

The reviews all agreed that the Hippodrome show was the greatest seen on any stage. *A Yankee Circus on Mars* played for 120 performances. The run was long by the standards of the day and even more remarkable when one considers the number of patrons that the theater held.

Thompson and Dundy realized that their next offering would have to surpass the premiere attraction. They decided to mount another show with a circus theme. *A Society Circus* (1905) was indeed bigger and better than the previous show. The spectacular presentation lasted four hours. Sydney Rosenfeld wrote the book and Manuel Klein wrote the lyrics. Despite the rave reviews, audiences were strangely unsatisfied with the show. True, it was bigger than *A Yankee Circus on Mars,* but it was not substantially different. With business falling off, Thompson and Dundy were in trouble. They simply couldn't afford to keep the theater open without a sizable audience.

The only producers with enough nerve to take over the Hippodrome were the Shubert brothers. They reopened a fixed-up version of *A Society Circus* on September 2, 1906, and made a popular success of the show. It ended up running 596 performances with a reduced top price of $1.50.

The next show, *Pioneer Days* and *Neptune's Daughter* (1906), amassed an astonishing $91,000 advance at the box office. The first half of the evening's bill was a Wild West story of bad guys, good guys, and Indians. Everyone was fighting each other, and stagecoaches were forever running in and out. The end of the show was a climactic battle between the Indians, the settlers and the cavalry. Over six hundred performers took part in the melee.

The second act, *Neptune's Daughter,* featured a violent storm complete with huge waves and lightning flashes. A ship capsized, and only one passenger survived—a baby. He grew up and prayed to the gods of the sea. Then, as if by magic, Neptune himself, surrounded by mermaids, appeared from the waters of the tank. The audience was thrilled. How could he have risen from the sea? The show began an hour before, surely no one could hold his breath that long. So how did he do it?

During the finale a troupe of mermaids and mermen, accompanied by sea horses, walked down a broad flight of steps that led into the pool. Down they went into the pool never to be seen again. They simply disappeared into the waters.

The audience was astonished at the trick. Word got around the city of the marvelous finale to the Hippodrome show. It swelled the box office to $60,000 a week. Considering the Shuberts needed only one-tenth that amount to break even, the show was a great success.

Next came *The Auto Race* (1907). It also had on the bill *The Battle of Port Arthur* and *Circus Days.*

The next Hippodrome show, *Sporting Days* (1908), was accompanied by *The Land of Birds Ballet* and *Battle of the Skies*. *Sporting Days* featured a depiction of a real baseball game on what was surely the only indoor stage large enough. It also featured a rowing match on the Hippodrome's pool, which stood in for the Hudson River, and a horse race. For *The Land of Birds Ballet,* four hundred dancers enacted beautiful avian delights.

But it was the *Battle of the Skies* that most captured the audience's attention. It portrayed a huge battle over the streets of New York in the far away year of 1950.

A Trip to Japan (1909) was next. Along with the title show was *Inside the Earth* and *The Ballet of Jewels*. The climax of the opening melodrama was a fire atop a tall building. Luckily, the hero was also a tightrope walker. To save his girlfriend, he walked across telephone wires. Another highlight of the first act was the stunt performed by Desperado. He jumped off a high platform through forty feet of air and then hit a giant slide, which deposited him on his feet on the stage floor.

Inside the Earth actually featured an entire tribe of Maori natives who played a tribe of Incas who lived in a cave in New Zealand. The heroine was kidnapped to an island in the center of the Hippodrome's great pool. The island sank with its inhabitants, and the heroine sank beneath the waters. Despite the spectacular effects, the show was not a critical success. However audiences kept it open for 447 performances.

The International Cup (1910) was accompanied by *The Ballet of Niagara* and *The Earthquake*. *The International Cup* had planes landing on the Hippodrome's stage. Its exciting finale featured a shipwreck at sea in a perilous storm. *The Earthquake* took place in a Central American country that contained the fabled Valley of the Moon inhabited by aliens from outer space. Naturally, there was the Earthquake of the title, abetted by the mighty hydraulics beneath the stage. Islands bearing golden moon girls rose from the Hippodrome tank. The reviews were favorable for

the melodrama, ballet and special effects of the Hippodrome shows.

A topic ripe for the Hippodrome treatment was *Around the World* (1911), paired with *The Ballet of the Butterflies* and *The Fairies Glen* and *The Golden Barge*. The show followed its cast from New York State to the Swiss Alps and a race on the slippery peaks and then to a battle with Bedouins on the sands of Egypt. It led to a sandstorm that gave way to the slave markets of Constantinople. A circus was the entertainment at a coronation in India, and then there was a midnight gondola ride in Venice. A runaway bull highlighted the action in Spain, which led, surprisingly, to Hawaii and hula dancers. From Hawaii, the intrepid travelers somehow ended up in Ireland.

Under Many Flags (1912) was the optimistic story of world peace brought about through the invention of a machine of destruction. A man invented a blimp that could travel two hundred miles an hour and carry a payload of explosives. Another man stole the airship and traveled around the world with it to Brittany, Holland, Scotland, Arizona, and Persia. As a result of the flight, the world's leaders signed the Treaty of Universal Peace.

The next Hippodrome extravaganza, *America* (1913) was followed by a nontypical offering on April 9, 1914, Gilbert and Sullivan's *H.M.S. Pinafore,* which ran eighty-nine performances. *Wars of the Worlds* (1914), was somewhat topical, since Europe was involved in the beginnings of World War I.

The Shuberts put in the *Mammoth Midwinter Circus Supreme.* It also featured a film, *The Heart of Maryland,* a cartoon, a medley of Southern songs, and a dancing-waters ballet. The show wasn't successful, and the Shuberts began to get cold feet. They put in a series of films and vaudeville acts that did little to attract audiences. The Shuberts owed $100,000 in back rental, and the sum was mounting daily.

Following the Shuberts' failures came Charles B. Dillingham, an up-to-date producer of the time, who decided to clean up the Hippodrome and, instead of the customary old-fashioned extravagant melodrama, presented a fast-paced Broadway-style revue. The difference was that the Hippodrome would enable Dillingham to give the show a spectacular production.

Dillingham opened *Hip-Hip-Hooray* (1915) in a newly scrubbed Hippodrome. For the show, he hired Broadway composer Raymond Hubbell and John Golden, a noted lyricist and producer. R. H. Burnside wrote the libretto and directed the proceedings. Bandmaster John Philip Sousa composed a new work, "The New York Hippodrome March." Sousa even appeared in the show along with comic Nat Wills and Toto, a clown who replaced Marceline. The show heralded a new successful era at the Hippodrome. Dillingham celebrated the theater's success with a huge parade composed of 1,274 performers.

Dillingham next presented *The Big Show* (1916), a lavish revue that created a number of firsts in Hippodrome history. It was the first Hippodrome show to feature a genuine superstar, dancer Anna Pavlova. It was also the first to contain a smash hit song—"Poor Butterfly." Between editions of the Hippodrome shows and on its dark nights, Dillingham filled the theater with concerts and benefits. These featured such stars as Pavlova, Paul Whiteman's Orchestra, John McCormack, Carmella Ponselle, Al Jolson, DeWolf Hopper, W. C. Fields, Houdini, Weber and Fields, Vernon and Irene Castle, Babe Ruth, George M. Cohan, Gus Edwards, Amelita Galli-Curci, Feodor Chaliapin, Tito Ruffo, Leon Errol, and Mme. Ernestine Shumann-Heink. Vernon Castle made his last stage appearance at a Hippodrome benefit.

With the war raging in Europe, it seemed appropriate for Dillingham to call his next show *Cheer Up* (1917). The finale of the show was a resplendent version of Coney Island in all its gaudy fame. At the end, The Disappearing Diving Girls dove into the Hippodrome tank and disappeared beneath the waters. The number was constructed around the talents of swimmer Annette Kellerman, *w*ho had become a Hippodrome regular after the run of *The Big Show.*

Dillingham's next show was aptly titled *Everything* (1918). This revue had some music and lyrics contributed by Irving Berlin. It starred Houdini, DeWolf Hopper, and Belle Story.

With America now in World War I and Prohibition about to go into effect, Dillingham had the nerve or optimism to title the next Hippodrome show *Happy Days* (1919). The title proved even more ironic when the actors struck the Broadway theaters in the actors' strike of 1919. Dillingham, though sympathetic to the actors, remained a member of The Producing Managers' Association, which opposed Equity. When the Hippodrome's 412 stagehands walked out, Dillingham quit as manager of the Hippodrome. The stagehands went back on the job, and when the strike was settled Dillingham returned to the theater.

With the war over, Dillingham titled his next show *Good Times* (1920). The show featured Abdullah's Arabs, Nanette Flack, The Poodles Hanneford Family of trick horsemen, Joe Jackson, Joseph Parsons, and Belle Story.

Get Together (1921) was heavy on ballet. It featured *The Thunder Bird Ballet* by Vera Fokine, directed by Russian choreographer Michel Fokine. There was also an ice ballet based on *The Red Shoes.*

Get Together was followed by *Better Times* (1922). Most critics and the public felt *Better Times* was the best of all the Hippodrome spectaculars. Unfortunately it was also the last. The show ran for 405 performances, after which Charles Dillingham left the theater. Production costs were rising as the theater struggled to maintain a cast of one thousand people as well as a massive physical plant.

Because the Hippodrome occupied a large chunk of prime property, the site was viewed with interest by a number of real estate developers. The U.S. Realty and Improvement Company owned the theater and its land and tendered offers. But the theater was saved when E. F. Albee decided to take it over and present vaudeville in the huge hall.

Albee took out all the complex stage mechanics and replaced the stage with a small wooden platform. The proscenium was brought in to a more manageable size, and the Hippodrome became just another vaudeville theater. The theater reopened on December 17, 1923, with an undistinguished vaudeville bill.

The Hippodrome presented what might be called high-class vaudeville with movies thrown in for good measure. By 1929, vaudeville was all but dead, and so was the Hippodrome. Morris Gest leased the theater to present *The Passion Play* but it closed after five weeks with a $250,000 loss. In July 1930, the theater was closed tight.

RKO had inherited the theater from Albee. RKO sold it to Frederick Brown, a real estate investor. Brown then sold it to the Fred T. French Operators, Inc. for $7.5 million. The French company announced that they would tear the theater down and construct an 83-story office building on the site.

Unfortunately, the country was in the midst of the Depression and construction was at a standstill. The Hippodrome sat empty until master showman Billy Rose decided to rent the theater to present a new musical, *Jumbo.*

Rose cleaned up the exterior of the theater and renovated the interior to resemble a huge circus arena. The seating area was altered so that it sloped in one continuous line from the far reaches of the balcony to the stage floor. Albert Johnson designed the new interior as well as the production.

Richard Rodgers and Lorenz Hart were assigned the task of writing the score for the mammoth show. Rose hired Ben Hecht and Charles MacArthur to script the proceedings. Rose employed Jimmy Durante, Gloria Grafton, Paul Whiteman and his orchestra, Poodles Hanneford, Donald Novis, and Arthur Sinclair to head the cast. Then he chose 1,200 animals to appear in the circus setting. The show was so big that it needed two directors, John Murray Anderson and George Abbott. They whipped the show into shape amid countless delays.

Jumbo finally opened on November 16, 1933. The critics were unanimous in their praise. *Jumbo* was a huge hit but it cost so

much to run that it was forced to close. The Hippodrome was closed again. In 1939, it was used briefly as a basketball court. Then in September of that year, crews came and knocked down the theater.

Ironically, development plans for the site continued to fall through. Twelve years passed before the site was finally utilized. In 1952, a garage, appropriately named the Hippodrome Garage, and an office building opened.

HOLIDAY THEATER · See MOVIE-LAND.

HOLLYWOOD THEATER · See MARK HELLINGER THEATER.

HUDSON THEATRE · 139 W. 44th Street. Architect: J. B. McElfatrick & Co. Opening: October 19, 1903; *Cousin Kate.* After Oscar Hammerstein I's pioneering efforts in the new theater district growing up around Times Square at the turn of the century, the best regarded theater locations were on 42nd Street. Producer Henry B. Harris chose to build his Hudson Theater on 44th Street following the lead of Daniel Frohman's Lyceum Theater built the year before on 45th Street. Harris hired J. B. McElfatrick to design his theater. But for some unknown reason McElfatrick dropped out of the job and the theater was finished by Israels and Harder. Unfortunately, this rocky beginning proved to be the norm for the theater. The Hudson has had a spotty career ever since its inception.

The 1,006-seat theater, considered one of the more modern of its time, seemed to have a bright future. Harris did present *Cousin Kate* (1903) with Ethel Barrymore in the lead. He also presented Shaw's masterpiece *Man and Superman* (1905).

But Harris lost his life on the *Titanic,* and his widow Rene did not have much luck in producing plays. She presented a few successes including Sean O'Casey's *The Plough and the Stars* (1927). One of the only musical successes at the Hudson was the black show *Hot Chocolates,* which opened June 20, 1929.

It had an above-average score by Fats Waller, Harry Brooks and Andy Razaf. Cab Calloway, and Edith Wilson were featured, and Duke Ellington contributed two tunes.

Like many of the other Broadway houses, the Hudson ceased legitimate use with the Depression. Mrs. Harris lost the playhouse to foreclosure, and the new owners leased it to CBS. It reopened as the CBS Radio Playhouse Number 1 on February 3, 1934.

Three years later the theater returned to its original use with a production of *An Enemy of the People* (1937). The writing team of Howard Lindsay and Russel Crouse bought the theater in 1944. Their play *State of the Union* opened at the Hudson on November 14, 1945 and ran for 765 performances. This enormous run was capped with the play's winning the Pulitzer Prize. On March 23, 1949, Sidney Kingsley's *Detective Story* opened at the Hudson and ran an estimable 581 performances.

This return to live theater lasted just over a decade, until NBC bought it and converted it for television in 1950. Among the television shows presented from the theater were *Broadway Open House* (1950–54) and *The Tonight Show* (1954–59)

In 1960, the theater again became a stage house. Among the few successes were Lillian Hellman's *Toys in the Attic* (1960) and a revival of Ann Corio's *This Was Burlesque* (1970). Mostly the theater remained dark.

In 1968, the theater was renamed the Avon-Hudson with porno films the featured attractions. A succession of uses followed. In 1981, the theater became the Savoy, a disco and concert venue. The New York Landmarks Commission gave landmark status to the theater in 1987. And so, in the 1990s instead of being destroyed as planned, the theater was restored and incorporated into the Hotel Macklowe and used for meetings and conferences.

I

IMPERIAL THEATRE · 249 W. 45th Street. Architect: Herbert J. Krapp. Opening: December 25. 1923; *Mary Jane McKane.* The 1,650-seat Imperial Theatre has proved to be among the most successful of all musical comedy houses. Its ideal location across from the Golden and Royale theaters and down the block from the Music Box and now demolished Morosco and Bijou theaters gave the Shubert brothers, its owners, a prime musical theater.

The Shuberts wanted a replacement for their aging Lyric Theatre. They chose a lot running between 45th and 46th Streets. The land fronting 46th Street was less expensive but 45th Street was a more desirable location. So the thin entrance was erected on the 45th Street side of the lot and the theater proper was built on the cheaper land on 46th Street.

The theater opened on Christmas Day 1923, with *Mary Jane McKane,* a musical with music by Vincent Youmans and Herbert Stothart and book and lyrics by William Cary Duncan and Oscar Hammerstein II. The producer was Oscar's uncle, Arthur Hammerstein.

Rose-Marie (1924) opened with Oscar Hammerstein II again at the Imperial, this time as book and lyric writer in conjunction with Otto Harbach. Herbert Stothart and Rudolf Friml composed the stirring melodies, and Arthur Hammerstein again produced.

A decidedly more modern musical, *Oh, Kay!* (1926), boasted a superior score by George and Ira Gershwin and Howard Dietz and a serviceable book by Guy Bolton and P.G. Wodehouse. *Oh, Kay!'s* exuberant score and superior production by producers Alex A. Aarons and Vinton Freedley were responsible for its success.

Operetta returned to the Imperial with Sigmund Romberg's *The New Moon* (1928). It had lyrics by Oscar Hammerstein II, who also collaborated on the book with Frank Mandel and Laurence Schwab. The three librettists were also credited with the show's direction. Schwab and Mandel also handled producing chores. *The New Moon* was among the last successful operettas mounted on Broadway.

Popular songwriters J. Fred Coots, Arthur Swanstrom and Benny Davis contributed the score to the theater's next hit, *Sons o' Guns* (1929). Though none of the songs achieved great success, the show was a big hit with audiences, despite the stock market crash and the onset of the Depression.

The Depression changed the fortunes of many Broadway producers. Some, like the Chanins, lost all their holdings. The Shuberts also had some setbacks. Some of their theaters were sold to the burgeoning radio industry, and some simply went dark. But the Imperial managed to house a series of highly successful shows.

Ed Wynn was coauthor, producer, and director as well as star of *The Laugh Parade* (1931). Harry Warren, better known for his later Hollywood scores, contributed music with accompanying lyrics by Mort Dixon and Joe Young. The big hit from the score was "You're My Everything."

Broadway's preeminent revue writers, Howard Dietz and Arthur Schwartz had another success with their revue *Flying Colors* (1932). *Flying Colors* had skits by George S. Kaufman, Charles Sherman, Corey Ford, and Howard Dietz. Dietz also directed the show.

The Gershwins returned with *Let 'Em Eat Cake* (1933), a sequel to their satirical musical comedy *Of Thee I Sing.* Kaufman directed the show and wrote the book with Morrie Ryskind. William Gaxton, Victor Moore, and Lois Moran all repeated their roles from its predecessor.

Say When (1934) was also not a hit, although its creators received fame later. The show had music by Ray Henderson and lyrics by Ted Koehler. Bob Hope, Harry Richman, and Prince Michael Romanoff, later of restaurant fame, starred.

One of the greatest of all musical comedy songs, "Begin the Beguine," graced the Imperial tenant *Jubilee* (1935). Moss Hart wrote the book while sailing the seas with composer/lyricist Cole Porter. The show was very funny and sophisticated in its telling of a royal family who is given a few days of freedom to taste the pleasures enjoyed by commoners. The show starred Mary Boland, Melville Cooper, June Knight, and Charles Walters. Also included in the cast was Montgomery Clift. Another hit song, "Just One of Those Things," came from the playful Porter score.

Richard Rodgers and Lorenz Hart's *On Your Toes* (1936) was the Imperial's next musical offering. The songwriters also wrote the book in collaboration with George Abbott. Abbott also collaborated on the direction with Worthington Miner. A major contribution to the show was George Balanchine's choreography, especially for the now classic "Slaughter on Tenth Avenue."

The theater hosted a rare nonmusical production with Leslie Howard's ill-conceived version of *Hamlet*. It ran only thirty-nine performances. The operetta form was almost totally dead, but the Shuberts opened the Franz Lehar operetta *Frederika* (1937) at the Imperial. Despite an excellent cast and production, the public was not interested.

Dietz and Schwartz fared as badly with a book show, *Between the Devil* (1937). Again the elements were all top-notch. Vilma Ebsen, Jack Buchanan, and Evelyn Laye starred, and the score included "I See Your Face Before Me" and "By Myself."

The Imperial finally had another big hit with the return of Cole Porter. He wrote the score

to *Leave It to Me!* (1938), which accompanied the libretto by Bella and Samuel Spewack. The score contained the usual compliment of hit songs, including "Get out of Town," "Most Gentlemen Don't Like Love," and "My Heart Belongs to Daddy." The last song was introduced by a newcomer, Mary Martin.

Rodgers and Hart had another hit at the Imperial with their college musical *Too Many Girls* (1939). The show had a lightweight book by George Marion Jr. As producer and director, George Abbott kept the production moving briskly.

The 1940s were even more popular than the 1930s at the Imperial. In 1940, Irving Berlin's production of *Louisiana Purchase* opened. Morrie Ryskind of *Let 'Em Eat Cake* fame wrote the book to *Louisiana Purchase*. The Berlin score contained such enduring hits as "Fools Fall in Love" and "It's a Lovely Day Tomorrow."

Let's Face It! (1941) was another Cole Porter vehicle to play the Imperial. The librettists were Herbert and Dorothy Fields. The show's wonderful cast included Eve Arden, Nanette Fabray, Benny Baker, Edith Meiser, Vivian Vance, Mary Jane Walsh, Frances and Jack Williams, and newcomer Danny Kaye in his first starring role on Broadway.

Director Max Reinhardt's operetta, *Rosalinda,* moved to the Imperial to complete its 520-performance run. Mary Martin returned to the Imperial in *One Touch of Venus* (1943), the Kurt Weill, Ogden Nash musical. She perfectly personified a mortal's view of Venus. The offbeat book was by the somewhat dyspeptic humorist S J Perelman and poet Nash. The show was directed by Elia Kazan.

After a continuation of the run of *The Ziegfeld Follies* from the Winter Garden Theater came one of the Imperial's greatest successes. Irving Berlin's *Annie Get Your Gun* (1946) which ran 1,147 performances). It top-lined Ethel Merman as Annie Oakley. *Let's Face It*'s librettists Herbert and Dorothy Fields repeated the chore for *Annie Get Your Gun*. The entire show proved to be one of the classics of the American musical theater. Richard Rodgers and Oscar Hammerstein II produced with Joshua Logan directing. The Irving Berlin score was the tunesmith's finest. The hits included "They Say It's Wonderful," "Anything You Can Do," "Doin' What Comes Natur'lly," "I Got the Sun in the Morning," "You Can't Get a Man with a Gun," and the show business anthem "There's No Business Like Show Business."

After a minor effort, *Along Fifth Avenue* (1949), came another offering by Irving Berlin. *Miss Liberty* (1949), the story of the Statue of Liberty, was not as successful as *Annie Get Your Gun,* although the score was delightful.

The Leonard Bernstein version of *Peter Pan* (1950) followed, with Jean Arthur and Boris Karloff. Ethel Merman was tapped by Berlin to star in *Call Me Madam* (1950), a slightly disguised story about Washington socialite Perle Mesta. Howard Lindsay and Russel Crouse wrote the book, and George Abbott directed.

Joshua Logan, director of *Annie Get Your Gun,* also directed the Imperial's next tenant, *Wish You Were Here* (1952) as well as coauthored the libretto and coproduced. Harold Rome's show was not a success at first, but producers Leland Hayward and Logan worked on improving the show after it opened.

John Murray Anderson's Almanac (1953) was one of the last large revues on Broadway. Cole Porter's last Broadway show, *Silk Stockings* (1955), opened at the Imperial with Don Ameche and Hildegarde Neff in the leads. "All of You" was the hit in the score. Frank Loesser's ambitious musical version of *They Knew What They Wanted* was titled *The Most Happy Fella* (1956). Metropolitan Opera star Robert Weede and Jo Sullivan had the leads. The musical epic contained some of the most sweeping melodies heard on any Broadway stage in addition to traditional musical comedy songs, semioperatic arias, and sung narrative.

Audiences loved the David Merrick production *Jamaica* (1957) and its star Lena Horne. But the show was a far cry from what its authors contemplated. Composer Harold Arlen and lyricist E. Y. Harburg contributed a first-rate score.

Harold Rome had another hit at the Imperial with *Destry Rides Again* (1959) starring Andy Griffith and Dolores Gray. Everyone thought a western musical couldn't be a hit on sophisticated Broadway, but Rome and librettist Leonard Gershe proved them wrong with this David Merrick production.

Merrick moved *Gypsy* to the Imperial from the Broadway Theatre with Ethel Merman continuing in the starring role. He then premiered Bob Merrill's musical *Carnival!* (1961) at the Imperial with Anna Maria Alberghetti and Jerry Orbach starring. Gower Champion directed the proceedings, and the hit song was "Love Makes the World Go Round."

Merrick retained his lease on the theater with the next attraction, a transfer of the London success, *Oliver!* (1963). Lionel Bart's musical contained several big hit songs, including "As Long As He Needs Me," "Consider Yourself," and "Where Is Love?"

The Imperial Theatre's greatest success came next—*Fiddler on the Roof* (1963), claimed by some to be the greatest of all musicals. Jerry Bock and Sheldon Harnick provided the score, and Joseph Stein wrote a strong libretto. Zero Mostel had the role of his career as Tevye the milkman. The best-known song was "Sunrise, Sunset." *Fiddler on the Roof* was produced by Harold Prince and directed by Jerome Robbins to whom much of the credit for its success was given.

Cabaret moved to the Imperial from the Broadhurst Theater in 1967. It was followed by another John Kander and Fred Ebb show, *Zorba* (1968). Joseph Stein, author of the book to *Fiddler on the Roof,* wrote the libretto to *Zorba.* Harold Prince produced and directed the show.

Minnie's Boys (1970) was a musicalization of the early career of the Marx Brothers and starred Shelley Winters. Richard Rodgers and Martin Charnin chose as the basis for their musical *Two By Two* (1970), the story of Noah. Danny Kaye starred in the show.

A greater success, although its material was weak was *Pippin* (1972). The show, with score by Stephen Schwartz and book by Roger O.

Hirson, owed its success to the direction and choreography of Bob Fosse.

In the seventies, Broadway saw fewer and fewer musicals mounted because of the high cost of production. The Imperial hosted a revival of O'Neill's *Anna Christie* with Liv Ullmann and Victor Borge's *Comedy with Music*. Neil Simon's comedy hit *Chapter Two* (1977) starred Judd Hirsch, Anita Gillette, Cliff Gorman, and Ann Wedgeworth.

Neil Simon also provided the script to the Imperial's next tenant, the musical *They're Playing Our Song* (1979), a decidedly minor effort with its Marvin Hamlisch and Carole Bayer Sager score.

Another long-running musical occupied the Imperial's stage. *Dreamgirls* (1981) owed much of its success to Michael Bennett's brilliant staging. Henry Krieger provided the music and Tom Eyen the book and lyrics. The show made a star of Jennifer Holliday who scored on the pop music charts (rare for Broadway scores in the seventies and eighties) with "And I Am Telling You I'm Not Going."

After *Dreamgirls* closed on August 11, 1985, the Imperial hosted another long-running hit, *The Mystery of Edwin Drood* (1985) with book, music and lyrics by Rupert Holmes. George Rose, Howard McGillin, Betty Buckley, Patti Cohenour, and Cleo Laine starred in the Joseph Papp production. Shortly before closing, the show officially changed its name to *Drood*. The name change did put it further up the alphabet in the *New York Times*' ABC theatrical listings but did little else.

Les Miserables which transferred to the Imperial from the Broadway Theatre in 1990. It was followed by Hugh Jackman's Broadway debut, playing in the Peter Allen bio-musical, *The Boy from Oz* (2003). Songwriter David Yazbek did his usual superior job on the latest musical to hit the Imperial's stage, *Dirty Rotten Scoundrels* (2005) starred John Lithgow and Norbert Leo Butz.

J

JOHN GOLDEN THEATER · (1) 202 W. 58th Street. Architect: Harrison G. Wiseman. Opening: November 1, 1926; *Two Girls Wanted* (transfer from the Little Theatre). The first John Golden Theater opened at 202 W. 58th Street between Broadway and Seventh Avenue with the play *Two Girls Wanted.* Harrison G. Wiseman was the architect for this theater. The building had a stormy future. On September 17, 1935, the theater's name was changed to the 58th Street Theater with the play *Few Are Chosen.* The name was changed again to the Filmarte on September 20, 1936, with the movie *La Kermess Heroique.* On April 2, 1940, with the movie *The Life of Giuseppe Verdi,* the name was changed again to the Fine Arts Theater. On February 14, 1942, the theater briefly returned to a legitimate policy under the name the Concert Theater with the musical revue *Of V We Sing.* The show starred Betty Garrett and Phil Leeds but only lasted seventy-six performances. The Concert Theater became the Rock Church in 1943. It became a theater again on January 15, 1946, when it was renamed the 58th Street Theater. In April 1946, the theater became an ABC Radio Theater. On January 28, 1948, the movie *Fanny* opened at the theater, now named the Elysee.

The theater was finally taken over by ABC as a television studio.

JOHN GOLDEN THEATER · (2) 252 W. 45th Street. Architect: Herbert J. Krapp. Opening: February 24, 1927; *Puppets of Passion.* Actually, two Broadway houses have been named the John Golden Theater in honor of the noted producer and author.

The Chanin Brothers built the current John Golden Theater as their fifth theater in the Times Square area.

The eight hundred-seat theater's first tenant, *Puppets of Passion,* closed after only twelve performances. In 1927 and 1928, there were other bookings but none proved successful. Finally, the first success at the Theater Masque came with Patrick Hamilton's drama *Rope's End* (1929). The show later became the basis for the Alfred Hitchcock movie *Rope.*

As the Chanins' fortunes declined during the Depression, the theater did not fare well. Productions included the Albert Hackett and Frances Goodrich play *Up Pops the Devil* (1930), starring Sally Bates and Brian Donlevy; the Norman Krasna comedy *Louder, Please!* (1931) directed by George Abbott; the comedy *Goodbye Again* (1932), starring Osgood Perkins; and *Post Road* (1934), which starred Percy Kilbride (later famous as Pa Kettle) and Lucile Watson.

A series of failures followed, and the Chanins lost the Theater Masque along with their other theaters. The first success under the new name, the John Golden Theater, was *Shadow and Substance* (1938) by Paul Vincent Carroll, starring Julie Haydon and Sir Cedric Hardwicke.

A bona fide long running hit, the thriller *Angel Street* (1941) was produced by Shepard Traube and starred Judith Evelyn, Vincent Price, and Leo G. Carroll. The play had begun in London as *Gaslight.* It had been successful there, and a few summer theater productions followed. A production in Hollywood under its original title was moderately received, so when the show opened at the John Golden as *Angel Street* it was understandable that nobody expected it to be a hit. Even the lessees of the theater, the Shubert brothers, had expected the play to be a quick failure. They ordered tickets printed for only the first three performances. Even Traube was not going to put his own money into the show; he had raised money by selling $15,000 shares to fifteen angels. But the reviews were raves, and audiences began telling friends of the surprise hit at the John Golden Theater.

Unfortunately, *Angel Street* was not an omen for things to come. A modest comedy, *The Soldier's Wife* (1944), by Rose Franken played at the John Golden. A few more modest successes and a few failures followed, and in the middle of 1946, the theater was changed to a motion picture policy. It reverted to a legitimate policy on February 29, 1948, with the production of a one-man show featuring Maurice Chevalier. He was the first of a series of performers who presented one-person shows at the theater, including Emlyn Williams, Cornelia Otis Skinner, and Victor Borge. The latter opened his show *Comedy in Music* on October 2, 1953, and played 849 performances at the theater.

An acclaimed production of Samuel Beckett's *Waiting for Godot* (1956) was not a hit, despite raves for Bert Lahr's performance. After this, in the late 1950s and 1960s, the theater housed a series of two-person revues. First came *A Party with Betty Comden and Adolph Green*. Comden and Green were two of Broadway's most cherished lyricists, and they held their audiences in thrall for a thirty-eight-performance run commencing on December 23, 1958, and again for forty-four performances commencing on April 16, 1959. The next two performers to hold forth on the John Golden stage were the English songwriters and humorists Michael Flanders and Donald Swann and their delightful show *At the Drop of a Hat* (1959). Then came *An Evening with Mike Nichols and Elaine May* (1960) followed by a concert by Yves Montand (1961).

The next hit was a small revue from London called *Beyond the Fringe* (1962) with its cast of Peter Cook, Dudley Moore, Jonathan Miller,

and Alan Bennett. In 1964, Victor Borge returned with his show, which had a 192-performance run. Another hit revue, twice as large as *Beyond the Fringe*, was the South African show *Wait a Minim* (1966), which featured the traditional music of South Africa.

After a series of failures came the celebrated American comedy team of Bob Elliot and Ray Goulding with their hilarious show *Bob and Ray the Two and Only* (1970). In 1972, David Rabe's Vietnam-era drama *Sticks and Bones* (1972) came to the John Golden Theater via Joseph Papp's Public Theater with Elizabeth Wilson and Tom Aldredge in the leads.

Lyricist Sammy Cahn's revue *Words and Music* (1974) was followed by a Pulitzer Prize winner, *The Gin Game* (1977), the two-person drama that starred Hume Cronyn and Jessica Tandy. Another success was the English import *A Day in Hollywood, A Night in the Ukraine* (1980) with Priscilla Lopez, Peggy Hewett, Frank Lazarus, and David Garrison. Frank Lazarus and Dick Vosburgh supplied the score, and Tommy Tune provided the imaginative direction and choreography. Composer Jerry Herman even contributed a few songs to beef up the show.

An off-Broadway transfer, Beth Henley's Pulitzer Prize-winning *Crimes of the Heart* (1981) gave way to David Mamet's expose of the real estate industry *Glengarry Glen Ross* (1984). Another Pulitzer Prize winner, Marsha Norman's *'Night Mother* (1984) starred Anne Pitoniak and Kathy Bates. Athol Fugard's powerful play *Blood Knot* (1985) was revived at the theater with Zakes Mokae and Fugard starring.

Falsettos (1992), a mating of William Finn's *March of the Falsettos and Falsettoland* in one evening proved to be a success. It was followed by Terrence McNally's paean to opera and its students, *Master Class* (1995). *Sideman* (1998) explored the world of jazz musicians and Edward Albee's *The Goat or Who Is Sylvia?* (2002) became the most controversial play of the year. *Avenue Q* (2003), a transfer from off-Broadway's tiny Vineyard Theatre was a deserved smash hit with its slightly naughty take on an adult styled *Sesame Street*.

JOLSON, AL (1886–1950) · Al Jolson is considered the greatest performer of all time by those who were lucky enough to see him in action. A little of his dynamic personality comes through in his movie performances, which offer an indication of his prodigious energy. Jolson was defined by his energy and humor. He introduced more hit songs than any other performer, with the possible exception of Bing Crosby. He was a unique link with America's entertainment heritage, for it was Jolson who brought the minstrel tradition into musical comedy, movies, radio and finally television. He was the one performer who embodied the complete range of the American popular arts.

Jolson was born Asa Yoelson in St. Petersburg, Russia, on March 26, 1886. When his family came to the United States, Jolson's father found work as a cantor in a Washington, D.C., synagogue. Jolson left home on several occasions to make a name for himself on the stage only to return beaten. At a Washington, D.C., vaudeville theater, Jolson was in the audience while the singer/comedian Eddie Leonard performed on stage. Jolson sang along with his big voice and Leonard, after his initial shock, was impressed. Leonard teamed with Jolson in an act which repeated their first meeting. Jolson would pretend to be a paying customer who just couldn't help joining in from the balcony.

Jolson appeared as an extra on Broadway in *The Children of the Ghetto* (1899) at the Herald Theater. Jolson joined Lew Dockstader's Minstrels in 1908 while both acts were appearing in Little Rock, Arkansas. Will Oakland, a producer and songwriter, recommended Jolson to Dockstader who hired the young performer. Jolson adopted the blackface makeup, which became a trademark for him when he was part of an early act, Jolson, Palmer and Palmer. To Jolson, the blackface was simply another gimmick for what would otherwise be simply another singing act. Somewhat shy, he also found it easier to portray a character rather than himself. Jolson was never the kind of performer who adopted blackface in order to make fun of blacks. He never assumed the stereotypes most often connected with the blackface comic. Jolson simply used the conceit as a means to make himself stand out from other singers. Later when he was inextricably linked to the character, he used the makeup to signal that a highlight of the performance was coming up. Other blackface performers, like Cantor, kept their Jewish identities and characterizations even when in blackface.

The minstrel tradition was quickly dying. Jolson realized that he would have to move on to other more sophisticated entertainments if his career was to proceed. The Shuberts opened their new Winter Garden Theater with *La Belle Paree* (1911). The show was a typical early mishmash of styles. Its subtitle, *The Cook's Tour through Vaudeville with a Parisian Landscape,* left room for just about anything.

Jolson's second Broadway success was *Vera Violetta* (1911). This time, he was top-billed with the French star Gaby Deslys. Jolson was the smash hit of the show, and he introduced another gimmick in his performances. While singing his numbers "Rum Tum Tiddle" and "That Haunting Melody," Jolson jumped off the stage and continued performing up and down the aisles.

The Whirl of Society (1912) was the third Jolson show at the Winter Garden. It opened with Stella Mayhew and Jose Collins as Jolson's costars. In it, he created the character Gus, one he would play five more times on Broadway and also in the movies.

Under New York's blue laws, performances on Sunday were illegal. But Jolson got around it by performing for show people only without sets, props, or his blackface. These Jolson concerts electrified members of the Broadway community who were otherwise unable to witness Jolson in action because their own shows were running the same nights as his.

The Honeymoon Express (1913), again at the Winter Garden, gave Jolson his first song success. "My Yellow Jacket Girl" isn't remembered today, but at the time it was a big success. Supporting Jolson was Gaby Deslys and Harry Pilcer. Fanny Brice was also in the cast in her third Broadway appearance. Jolson created another sensation by stopping the show midstream and asking the audience, "Would you rather see the rest of the show or just hear me sing?" The answer was self-evident, and for the next few hours Jolson would dismiss the cast and perform an impromptu concert. During the run, Jolson had trouble with an ingrown toenail. While singing "Down Where the Tennessee Flows," he sought to relieve the pressure on his foot by going down on one knee.

Dancing Around (1914) was mostly undistinguished. Jolson's next Broadway appearance was in *Robinson Crusoe, Jr.* (1916). This time, Jolson was given a Sigmund Romberg score, which took more and more of a backseat to Jolson's interpolations as the fun continued. Jolson added several songs that he made into big successes. "Yacka Hula Hickey Dula" was another in the current wave of Hawaiian inspired songs. "Where Did Robinson Crusoe Go with Friday on Saturday Night?" was in the same spirit as "Who Paid the Rent for Mrs. Rip Van Winkle? (When Rip Van Winkle was Away)," which Jolson introduced in *The Honeymoon Express.*

Jolson opened in *Sinbad* (1918), another excuse to do his usual shtick. This time, he put in a ramp from the stage into the audience. Jolson discovered what became three of his most famous songs and interpolated them into the score of *Sinbad:* "Rock-A-Bye Your Baby with a Dixie Melody" was Jolson's favorite song of all time; "Swanee," by George Gershwin and Irving Caesar, was inserted into the show while it was on the road; and perhaps the most famous of all, "My Mammy," was introduced after the show had reopened after a brief vacation for Jolson.

On November 18, 1918, the Armistice was signed, and a huge concert was scheduled for the Metropolitan Opera House for the benefit of the returning soldiers. After Enrico Caruso finished singing "Vesti la Giubba," Jolson ran on the stage before the applause was over for the great tenor. "Folks, you ain't heard nothin' yet," exclaimed Jolson, and so another piece of the Jolson legend fell into place.

For Jolson's next show, *Bombo* (1921), the Shuberts built him a new theater and named it, unsurprisingly, the Jolson Theater. Lou Silvers, *Bombo's* conductor, and B. G. DeSylva wrote "April Showers." DeSylva also wrote "California, Here I Come," another huge hit for Jolson. Gus Kahn contributed "Toot Toot, Tootsie."

Big Boy (1925) had everything going for it. For one thing it costarred Eddie Cantor, who introduced one of his greatest hits, "If You Knew Susie." Jolson introduced more great songs into the score; "California, Here I Come" was reintroduced, as well as "Keep Smiling at Trouble."

Big Boy's run was prematurely halted when Jolson came down with another bout of strep throat. When Jolson left a show, that was it—there was no discussion of replacing him or having an understudy go on. Jolson knew as well as anyone else that you couldn't replace the World's Greatest Performer.

Jolson next appeared as a late addition to the cast of *Artists and Models,* a revue series produced by the Shuberts. He played the show for only four weeks and then took it on the road where it achieved the then highest gross in history, over $60,000.

After the *Artists and Models* tour, Jolson went to Hollywood and made one of the most important pictures in the history of Hollywood, *The jazz Singer.* Contrary to popular legend there had been other talking pictures, but before this none achieved any success. With Jolson, *The Jazz Singer* changed the future of movies forever.

Before *The Jazz Singer's* release, Jolson was hired by the Shuberts for $10,000 a week to star in the road tour of *A Night in Spain. The Jazz Singer* opened on October 7, 1927, and for a while at least Jolson became the property of Hollywood.

By 1931, Jolson's movie career was stalled. His pictures were successes (*The Singing Fool* [1928] was the biggest money-making picture in Hollywood history until *Gone With the Wind* surpassed it), but his roles became more and more alike, and the vehicles were mostly unmemorable. Whereas Jolson on stage could stop the show and just give a concert, he was forced in the movies to stick to the script no matter how bad it was. Besides the films already mentioned, there were the disappointing *Say It with Songs* and the equally clichéd *Mammy* (1930) and *Hallelujah I'm a Bum* (1933) with a Rodgers and Hart score. Later that year, he made a movie of his stage show *Big Boy*, but it wasn't much of a success.

Jolson opened on Broadway in *The Wonder Bar* (1931). Unfortunately, the show wasn't tailored to Jolson's talents, and none of the usual Jolson interpolations caught fire.

Jolson's last appearance on Broadway was in a book show, *Hold On to Your Hats* (1940) with a score by Burton Lane and E. Y. Harburg. Jolson had committed to doing the show because his wife Ruby Keeler was to be given a part. But Keeler departed both the show and the marriage during the Chicago run, and Jolson was left in what to him was an increasingly alien Broadway.

Although Jolson and the show had received rave reviews, he lost interest. Claiming that he couldn't stand the cold of New York's winter, Jolson left the production, and it closed. It was revived briefly in July 1941 in Atlantic City. Once more, Jolson seemed unsatisfied and felt he would lose his voice if he continued.

Jolson's career went into decline, with radio appearances and touring for the USO taking up most of his time. More and more he was considered a nostalgic figure. Then the Columbia picture *The Jolson Story* (1946), starring Larry Parks as Jolson, reawakened interest in the singer. The film was followed by a new recording contract for Decca Records and a continuing radio series for Kraft. Then came *Jolson Sings Again* (1949), another big hit. Television was the new medium, and Jolson approached it warily. A final tour of Korea for the USO left Jolson exhausted and sick, and on October 23, 1950, shortly after his return home from overseas, the World's Greatest Performer died.

JOLSON'S 59TH STREET THE-ATER · 932 7th Avenue between 58th and 59th Street. Architect: Herbert J. Krapp.

Opening: October 6, 1921; *Bombo*. This theater had an especially difficult history. The site was originally the Central Park Gardens which were replaced by the Central Park Riding Academy. The horses left in 1916 and the Shuberts purchased the land.

They built the theater for one of their biggest stars, Al Jolson. He opened his successful musical *Bombo* (1921) there. *Bombo's* score was written by Sigmund Romberg and Harold Atteridge. As usual, the hit songs were written by others and interpolated into the score. Unfortunately, *Bombo* was one of the theater's few successes.

After a series of failures, another huge hit opened, *The Student Prince* (1924). This time, Romberg, along with lyricist/librettist Dorothy Donnelly, came up with a smashing score. "Deep in My Heart, Dear," "Drinking Song," "Golden Days," "Students' Life," and "Serenade" were all big hits at the time. Sixty years after its creation, *The Student Prince* is still much performed.

A couple of moderate successes followed, including a revival of the Shubert's warhorse, *Blossom Time*. Romberg and Donnelly saw the curtain rise on *My Maryland* (1927), another success.

A revolution hit the Broadway theater in 1923 with the arrival of Constantin Stanislavski and his Moscow Art Theatre. The three-month booking introduced such future stars as Maria Ouspenskaya and Akim Tamiroff. Once America got wind of Stanislavski's acting techniques, including the much-misinterpreted Method system, American acting was never the same.

The last three months of 1929 and the early months of 1930 were taken up by some halfhearted revivals of past operettas (*Robin Hood, Sweethearts, The Fortune Teller, The Merry Widow, Babes in Toyland, The Count of Luxembourg, The Serenade* and *Mlle. Modiste*). This series of revivals marked the end of Shubert ownership.

The Depression hit the Shuberts hard, and they were forced to sell the theater. It would never again have a success. The theater, renamed Shakespeare's Theater, reopened with the Sothern and Marlowe's Shakespearean troupe presented *A Midsummer Night's Dream* (1932). Two years later, the theater reopened as the Venice Theater with *Africana* (1934), a three performance new edition of the popular revue that opened originally in 1927.

Maurice Schwartz took over operation of the theater and named it after his theatrical troupe. The Yiddish Art Theater was the new name of the auditorium with the opening of *The Brothers Ashkenazi* (1937). It was again renamed the Jolson Theater with *Comes the Revolution* (1942). Yiddish theater returned, and the theater was renamed the Molly Picon Theater with the opening of *Oy Is Das a Leben* (1942).

The Shuberts returned to the theater which they renovated and renamed the Century Theatre. *Follow the Girls* (1944), a musical with music by Philip Charig and lyrics by Dan Shapiro and Milton Pascal, was surprisingly a success. *Follow the Girls* starred Jackie Gleason, Gertrude Niesen, and Irina Baranova.

The success didn't transfer to other shows. On March 29, 1954, the theater was dubbed NBC Theater with the inside adapted to television. In the fall of 1959, it became the Video Tape Center. The theater was demolished in 1962 and replaced by an apartment building.

K

KAUFMAN AND HART

Moss Hart (1904–1961) Moss Hart, stage-struck as a youth, worked for the producer/director Augustus Pitou, a specialist in plays featuring Irish tenors. Pitou produced Hart's first play, *Beloved Bandit*. It closed out of town. Hart was introduced to Kaufman, who agreed to work on Hart's next idea, *Once in a Lifetime* (1930).

Hart also enjoyed a successful career, mainly in musical theater, apart from his collaboration with Kaufman. Among his successes are an Irving Berlin revue, *Face the Music* (1932); the musical *The Great Waltz* (1934); the musical *Jubilee* (1935); a David Freedman revue, *The Show Is On* (1936); the musical *Lady in the Dark* (for which Hart was also codirector [1941]); *Winged Victory,* for which Hart was also codirector (1943); *Christopher Blake* (1946); *Light Up the Sky* (1948); and *The Climate of Eden* (1952). Hart also directed the musicals *My Fair Lady* (1956) and *Camelot* (1960). He died a year after the opening of *Camelot,* on December 20, 1961.

George S. Kaufman (1899–1961) George S. Kaufman was one of the theater's most versatile participants. He was equally adept at playwriting and directing, but his greatest asset was as a play doctor. Kaufman began a journalistic career at the *Washington Times* in 1912. For nine years, he contributed a humor column. Kaufman's column was also printed in the *New York Evening Mail* from 1914 to 1915: Kaufman moved from Washington to New York where he served on the drama staffs of the *New York Tribune* and the *New York Times*.

There was no better play editor in the theater. He was often called on by producers to fix ailing productions. Kaufman, a shy man, nevertheless had many followers who thrived in his presence, for Kaufman was one of the great humorists. He used his wit constructively, to teach, scold and show his affection. Kaufman's shyness was but one aspect of his insecurity. He always preferred to write with collaborators, and did so in all but two cases.

Prior to his collaboration with Moss Hart, Kaufman enjoyed many successes. Among his most notable plays, with his collaborators noted in parenthesis, were, with Marc Connelly—*Dulcy* (1921); *To the Ladies* (1922); *Merton of the Movies* (1922); the musical *Helen of Troy, New York* (1923) and *Beggar on Horseback* (1924). He also wrote *The Butter and Egg Man* (1925); the musical *The Cocoanuts* (Morrie Ryskind; 1925); *The Royal Family* (Edna Ferber; 1927); the musical *Animal Crackers* (Morrie Ryskind; 1928); *June Moon* (Ring Lardner; 1929); and the musical *Strike Up the Band* (Morrie Ryskind; (1930).

Kaufman's collaborations with Hart include: *Once in a Lifetime* (1930); *Merrily We Roll Along* (1934); *You Can't Take It with You* (1936); the musical *I'd Rather Be Right* (1937); *The Fabulous Invalid* (1938); *The American Way* (1939); *The Man Who Came to Dinner* (1939); *George Washington Slept Here* (1940); and *Dream On, Soldier,* a special production for the American Red Cross (1943).

During and after his collaboration with Hart, Kaufman collaborated on the following plays and musicals: the revue *The Band Wagon* (Howard Dietz, 1931); the Pulitzer Prize-winning musical *Of Thee I Sing* (Morrie Ryskind, 1931); *Dinner at Eight* (Edna Ferber, 1932); the musical *Let 'Em Eat Cake* (Morrie Ryskind,933); *First Lady* (Katharine Dayton,1935); *Stage Door* (Edna Ferber,1936); *The Late George Apley* (John P. Marquand,1944); *The Solid Gold Cadillac* (Howard Teichmann, 1953); and the musical *Silk Stockings* (Leueen MacGrath and Abe Burrows,1955).

Kaufman died six months before Hart, on June 2, 1961.

KERN, JEROME (1885–1945) · Jerome Kern and George M. Cohan were the first composers for the Broadway stage to give the musical an American feeling. Cohan brought vaudeville and music hall influences into the musical. Kern was more in touch with the musical's European roots. He gave the European operetta a real American sound and had a greater impact than Cohan on the transition from operetta to a truly American musical theater.

Kern was born in New York City on January 27, 1885. He attended the New York College of Music, where he studied piano with Alexander Lambert and Paolo Gallico and harmony with Dr. Austin Pierce. Kern was introduced to the great operetta traditions when he went to England and Germany. When he returned to the United States in 1904, Kern found work at T. B. Harms, a leading music publisher. While at Harms, Kern became acquainted with most of the leading artists and producers of early musical comedy.

Kern began interpolating songs into American versions of foreign musicals. As an American, Kern was influenced by the harmonies and rhythms employed by America's classical and popular writers. In 1904, Kern interpolated songs into *Mr. Wix of Wickham,* an English show transplanted to America with Julian Eltinge as the star.

More important to Kern was his next interpolation, "How'd You Like to Spoon with Me?" with lyrics by Edward Laska. The song was included in the show *The Earl and the Girl* (1905). The song became the first hit for Kern, and soon Broadway producers were demanding his talents.

Kern had songs interpolated into many shows that opened during the early 20th century, including *The Catch of the Season* (1905); *The Little Cherub* (1906); *My Lady's Maid* (1906); *The Rich Mr. Hogenheimer* (1906); *The Orchid* (1907); *The Dairymaids* (1907); *Fascinating Flora* (1907); *The Great White Way* (1907); *A Waltz Dream* (1908); *The Girls of Gottenberg* (1908); *Fluffy Ruffles* (1908); *The Dollar Princess* (1909); *The Gay Hussars* (1909); and *The Kiss Waltz* (1911).

Kern finally had his first full score commissioned for *The Red Petticoat* (1912). Paul West supplied the lyrics to the Kern songs. The next year, Kern wrote his second full score for *Oh, I Say!* (1913). Harry B. Smith wrote the lyrics for the show. In 1914 Kern and Smith wrote "You're Here and I'm Here" for *The Laughing Husband,* and Kern saw a great early hit, "They Didn't Believe Me," premiere in *The Girl from Utah* (1914), with a lyric by Herbert Reynolds.

Kern had a banner year in 1915. He had five shows open that year, including one of his most enduring hits, *Very Good Eddie.* The first was *90 in the Shade.* Smith again provided lyrics, and the libretto was written by Guy Bolton, who would become an important player in Kern's career. The second show was *Rosy Rapture,* a J. M. Barrie play produced in London. For *Nobody Home,* Bolton again supplied the book with most of the lyrics by Schuyler Greene. Elsie Janis was the star and lyricist of *Miss Information.*

The final Kern musical of the year was *Very Good Eddie.* Schuyler Greene was the lyricist along with Herbert Reynolds. Guy Bolton and Philip Bartholomae contributed the libretto. Elisabeth Marbury and F. Ray Comstock produced the show, which was an immediate hit.

Nobody's Home and *Very Good Eddie* were the first two of what are now known as the

Princess Theater shows. Elisabeth Marbury was a well-known literary agent of the day. She had the idea that a kind of permanent company devoted to the American musical should be established, similar to several companies that were at that time devoted to American drama. Comstock owned the Princess Theater, which, with only 299 seats, had difficulty finding tenants. Marbury's idea was a perfect long-term solution to his problem.

Kern and Bolton were the first writers hired as the core of the new company. The Princess shows are generally acknowledged as the first of the modern musical comedies. Because of the small size of the theater, they were necessarily intimate shows and broke away from the general operatic tradition. The songs were better integrated into the story than in the old-style shows, and the plots revolved around American characters in American settings. The shows were less overtly romantic than the typical musical comedy, and they were more in tune with current trends and feelings.

Kern's next show, produced in London, was more traditional. *Theodore and Co.* (1916) had lyrics by Adrian Ross and Clifford Grey.

Kern was back in the United States for his next show, *Have a Heart*, the first Kern show to boast lyrics by P. G. Wodehouse and first of five written by him in 1917. Bolton and Wodehouse contributed the book. "And I Am All Alone" was a mild success from the score. Harry B. Smith was the lyricist for *Love O' Mike*.

That same year, *Oh, Boy!*, another Bolton, Wodehouse and Kern production, contained several great songs: "The Land Where the Good Songs Go," cut prior to the opening; "Nesting Time in Flatbush," probably the funniest song in the show; and the enduring classic " 'Till the Clouds Roll By," one of the greatest of all American popular songs.

Leave It to Jane (1917) was the third show by the successful trio. The score was one of the team's most consistent. "Cleopatterer," "The Crickets Are Calling," "The Siren's Song," and the title song all received a measure of success. The songs are enchanting and written with

the humorous innocence that hallmarked the team's work.

Miss 1917 was hailed by reviewers. It played to sold-out houses, and yet it closed prematurely. Produced by Charles B. Dillingham and Florenz Ziegfeld, the show's running costs were greater than the ticket prices could cover.

In 1918, Kern was busy with another five shows on the boards. *Oh, Lady! Lady!!* was the first of the year's Kern, Bolton and Wodehouse shows. None of the songs achieved great fame, but a song that was cut from the show, "Bill," would later become one of the great hits from *Show Boat*. The other 1918 efforts were all rather minor: *Toot-Toot!*, *Rock-a-bye Baby* and *Head Over Heels*.

In 1919, Kern wrote only one musical, *She's a Good Fellow*. It is most noteworthy as the first Kern show for which Anne Caldwell supplied the book and lyrics. Caldwell was one of the only women working in what was then a male-dominated field. Her success led to a slight opening for women in the ranks of composers, lyricists and librettists.

Caldwell worked on a total of nine shows with Jerome Kern. Her second, *The Night Boat*, was the first of three shows written by Kern in 1920. Two of the songs, "Left All Alone Again Blues" and "Whose Baby Are You?," achieved some success. Anne Caldwell also contributed lyrics to Kern's next show, *Hitchy-Koo of 1920*. The annual revue starred popular comedian Raymond Hitchcock.

Kern's last show of 1920 was one of his greatest successes. *Sally* had a book by Guy Bolton and lyrics by Clifford Grey, Anne Caldwell, P. G. Wodehouse and B. G. DeSylva. The star was one of the most beloved performers on the American stage, Marilyn Miller.

The score contained many great Kern melodies, including the title song, "Wild Rose" and "Whip-Poor-Will." The best song, however, was one of Kern's most enduring standards, "Look for the Silver Lining." The DeSylva lyric was perfectly married to Kern's simple melody.

Kern's next show, *Good Morning, Dearie* (1921), also had a long run, in part because of the success of *Sally*. *Good Morning, Dearie* boasted a book and lyrics by Anne Caldwell. "Ka-lu-a," "Blue Danube Blues" and "Good Morning, Dearie" are still remembered by Kern fans.

Fred and Adele Astaire were the stars of Kern's next show, *The Bunch and Judy* (1922), which was followed by *Stepping Stones* (1923). *Sitting Pretty* (1924), at the Fulton Theater, was the last of the Bolton, Wodehouse and Kern shows.

Kern provided his only score in collaboration with Howard Dietz for *Dear Sir* (1924). Like most of his contemporaries, Dietz was in awe of Kern and was amazed that the master had called on him for his musical. *Dear Sir* wasn't a success, but it did give Dietz his start in musical comedy.

Kern's next show, *Sunny* (1925), another great success, reunited the composer with his star of *Sally*, Marilyn Miller. Otto Harbach and Oscar Hammerstein II provided the book and lyrics. *Sunny* contained such big hits as "Who?," "D'ye Love Me?" and the title song.

For *The City Chap* (1925), which opened at the Liberty Theatre, Kern teamed with lyricist Anne Caldwell. For *Criss-Cross* (1926), Caldwell and Kern were together for the last time. Otto Harbach also contributed to the lyrics.

For *Lucky* (1927), Kern's next show, Bert Kalmar and Harry Ruby provided the lyrics and coauthored the libretto with Otto Harbach. At this time, Kern began the most important phase of his career. His last six shows, written with either Oscar Hammerstein II or Otto Harbach, contain some of the greatest songs of the American musical theater. Although some of these shows may not be well remembered today, their songs have endured for over half a century.

Show Boat (1927) is generally considered Kern's masterpiece. *Show Boat* was presented by Florenz Ziegfeld at the Ziegfeld Theater. The cast, Charles Winninger, Howard Marsh, Norma Terris, Helen Morgan, Edna Mae Oliver, and Jules Bledsoe perfectly personified Edna Ferber's fascinating characters.

The score was equally brilliant, containing such standards as "Can't Help Lovin' dat Man," "Life Upon the Wicked Stage," "You Are Love," "Why Do I Love You?" and "Bill." *Show Boat* has been revived numerous times on Broadway and around the world.

Sweet Adeline (1929), at Hammerstein's Theater, was a vehicle written for one of the stars of *Show Boat* and one of the greatest Broadway stars—Helen Morgan. The torch singer was the lead character in the new show. Oscar Hammerstein II repeated his lyric and libretto duties. Two of Morgan's numbers, "Why Was I Born?" and "Don't Ever Leave Me" are among Kern and Hammerstein's most dramatic songs.

Otto Harbach provided the book and lyrics to *The Cat and the Fiddle* (1931) at the Globe Theater. The score was filled with beautiful Kern melodies, and Harbach's lyrics fitted the show's European ambiance perfectly. "The Night Was Made for Love," "She Didn't Say 'Yes'," "Try to Forget" and "One Moment Alone" have all become standards.

Music in the Air (1932) retained *The Cat and the Fiddle's* European feeling. Oscar Hammerstein II provided the book and lyrics for the show. "I've Told Every Little Star" was the best-received song in the score, which also included "There's a Hill Beyond a Hill," "And Love Was Born," and "The Song Is You."

Roberta (1933) is one of Kern's most recognizable titles. The recognition is mostly due to the successful movie version with Fred Astaire and Irene Dunne. The stage version starred Lyda Roberti, Bob Hope, Tamara, Sydney Greenstreet, Fay Templeton, and George Murphy. Otto Harbach supplied the libretto and lyrics. Among the songs featured in the show were "The Touch of Your Hand," "You're Devastating," "Yesterdays," "Let's Begin," "I'll Be Hard to Handle," and the classic "Smoke Gets in Your Eyes."

Kern's last show was *Very Warm for May* (1939) at the Alvin Theater. Oscar Hammerstein II provided the lyrics and libretto. He also codirected the show with Vincente Minnelli. The wonderful score featured "In Other

Words, Seventeen," "All in Fun," "In the Heart of the Dark," "Heaven in My Arms," and the evergreen "All the Things You Are."

Following *Very Warm for May*, Kern composed the classic song "The Last Time I Saw Paris" with Oscar Hammerstein II. He wrote scores to films, including *One Night in the Tropics, Swing Time, You Were Never Lovelier, Can't Help Singing*, and *Cover Girl*. After the successful sojourn in Hollywood, Kern returned to New York to work on a new musical with Dorothy Fields. It was produced by Rodgers and Hammerstein and based on the life of Annie Oakley.

Before work commenced on the show, on November 5, Kern collapsed on Park Avenue and 57th Street. Because he had no identification, Kern was taken to the City Hospital on Welfare Island. Hospital personnel found Kern's membership card in ASCAP. The organization informed Hammerstein, and he arranged for doctors to examine Kern. The composer was diagnosed as having a cerebral hemorrhage. He was moved to Doctors' Hospital on November 7. Kern intermittently regained consciousness, but his condition steadily worsened. On the last day of Kern's life, Hammerstein sat at Kern's bedside and gently sang "I've Told Every Little Star" hoping to rouse him. After finishing the song, Hammerstein looked at his friend and realized that he had died. The date was November 11, 1945.

KIT KAT KLUB · See HENRY MILLER THEATRE.

KLAW THEATER · 251–57 W. 45th Street between Broadway and 8th Avenue. Architect: Eugene De Rosa Opening: March 2, 1921; *Nice People*. The Klaw Theater led an unimpressive existence. On September 18, 1929, it reopened as the Avon Theater with Preston Sturges' comedy *Strictly Dishonorable*. In September 1934, CBS took it over as a radio playhouse. The theater was razed in 1954.

L

LABOR STAGE · See 48TH STREET THEATRE.

LAFF-MOVIE · See ELTINGE THEATRE.

LANE, BURTON (1912–1997) · Composer Burton Lane has not had as many of his shows produced as his contemporaries, but his shows have all contained superior scores. When not writing for Broadway, Lane had a successful career in Hollywood. Each of Lane's Broadway scores, written with such greats as Harold Adamson, E.Y. Harburg, Alan Jay Lerner, and Al Dubin, were full of rich, inventive melodies.

Lane showed an early predilection for music; he took his first piano lessons at age three. He returned to the piano after his parents imposed a six-year break so that he could concentrate on his school studies. Amazingly, Lane was so good that he was given an audience with J. J. Shubert, one of the Shubert brothers, the two most powerful men on Broadway. Lane, only fourteen at the time, was assigned the score for a new Shubert show. The show wasn't produced, because the star was not available, but had it been, Lane would have been the youngest songwriter in Broadway history.

The next year, Lane went to Remick Publishing Company, where he was given a job plugging songs. While at Remick's, Lane was befriended by George Gershwin. He also met lyricist Howard Dietz who was working on the revue *Three's a Crowd* (1930) with his partner Arthur Schwartz. When the show opened, it contained two Dietz and Lane songs, "Out in the Open Air" and "Forget All Your Books."

He next had a song put in *The Third Little Show* (1931) and nine in the 1931 edition of the *Earl Carroll Vanities* with lyrics by Harold Adamson. The *Vanities* score led to Hollywood and his first film score, *Dancing Lady,* in 1933. The movie contained the first hit song of the twenty-one-year-old composer "Everything I Have Is Yours," and also marked the film debut of Fred Astaire.

In 1940, after a series of successful films, Lane wrote the score to *Hold On to Your Hats* (1940). The show marked the return to Broadway from Hollywood of Al Jolson who costarred with Martha Raye. The great Jolson left the show after supposedly catching pneumonia, and the show quickly closed. Lane's score, written with lyricist E. Y. Harburg, contained the hits "The World Is in My Arms" and "There's a Great Day Comin' Manana."

La.ffing Room Only (1944), a vehicle for Olsen and Johnson, was produced by the Shuberts at the Winter Garden Theater. Lane tried his hand at writing his own lyrics for the show, which included one big hit, "Feudin' and Fightin'." The song had lyrics ascribed to Al Dubin but were actually written by Lane and Frank Loesser.

Lane's next score was written with Harburg for one of the best Broadway musicals, *Finian's Rainbow* (1947). The show opened at the 46th Street Theatre with Ella Logan, David Wayne, Donald Richards, and the Lyn Murray Singers. Lane collaborated with E. Y. Harburg on the excellent score, which included "How Are Things in Glocca Morra," "When I'm Not Near the Girl I Love," "If This Isn't Love," "Old Devil Moon," and "Look to the Rainbow."

Almost twenty years passed before the next Broadway score by Burton Lane. *On a Clear Day You Can See Forever* (1965) starred Barbara Harris, John Cullum, and William Daniels. The show proved Lane had not lost his touch.

With lyricist and librettist Alan Jay Lerner, Lane composed a winning score.

Lane and Lerner contributed more fine work to their next show, *Carmelina* (1979). Unfortunately, the show had many troubles and never recovered in time for its opening. The show marked Lane's last Broadway assignment. Although his Broadway output was not extensive, the quality of his work is impressive. His songs have a depth rarely seen on Broadway. They are not just pop songs but true theatrical statements that help define their characters, advance the plots and express true emotions.

Burton Lane died on January 5, 1997.

LERNER AND LOEWE

Alan Jay Lerner (1918–1986) Alan Jay Lerner was born in New York on August 31, 1918. He was the scion of a fortune that his family built through the Lerner Shops chain of women's clothing stores. Lerner was sent to the best schools in England and the United States. It was during this exceptional schooling that Lerner developed his love of the English language. He graduated from Harvard in 1940.

During college, Lerner had lost the sight in one eye during a boxing match. That injury kept him out of World War II and enabled him to pursue his writing career after graduation. He began in radio as a scriptwriter. The career lasted two years, during which time Lerner wrote hundreds of scripts. But during his years at Harvard, Lerner had caught the theater bug. He contributed to a couple of the Hasty Pudding shows, *So Proudly We Hail* and *Fair Enough.* Like Loewe, Lerner was a member of the Lambs Club and had contributed some lyrics to *The Lambs Gambols,* a small revue.

In 1942, producer Henry Duffy was looking for a team of writers to write shows for his theater in Detroit. Duffy approached Loewe, asking to use the score to *Salute to Spring,* a 1937 failure. Earle Crooker had written the lyrics to the score, which Loewe felt could use some improvement. Loewe told Duffy that a new lyricist would have to be found.

A few days later, Loewe came across Lerner playing cards in the club. Loewe approached Lerner, and two days later the two of them found themselves bound for Detroit. The first Lerner and Loewe collaboration, *Life of the Party* (1942), premiered in Detroit with Dorothy Stone, Margaret Dumont, Charlie Ruggles, and Charles Collins starring.

Frederick Loewe (1904–1988) Frederick Loewe was born in Berlin, Germany, to Austrian parents on June 10, 1904. His father Edmund, a leading vocalist, encouraged his son in music, and he became a child prodigy on the piano. The young Loewe studied with Eugene d'Albert and Ferrucio Busoni. At the age of thirteen, he became the youngest soloist to appear with the Berlin Symphony. When only fifteen, he wrote the song "Katrina," which was a huge hit in Europe.

The family emigrated to the United States in 1924, so the elder Loewe could appear in operetta. Unfortunately, Edmund Loewe died shortly after the family arrived in New York. Left virtually penniless, the young Loewe had to make his own way.

Time and popular taste in music worked against the young composer. Operetta was being replaced by a more distinctive American style on the nation's stages and in its clubs. Composers like Rudolf Friml and Sigmund Romberg soon found their European style of composition out of favor, replaced by the syncopations of Irving Berlin, George Gershwin, and Cole Porter.

Loewe found work in Greenwich Village as a piano player. A series of odd jobs followed, including work as a busboy in a cafeteria, a riding instructor in New Hampshire, a boxer in Brooklyn, a cowboy out West, a pianist on a ferry, plying the international waters between Miami and Havana, Cuba, and a piano player in a beer garden in the Yorkville section of Manhattan.

Loewe finally broke into the theater as a rehearsal pianist for one of the last operettas, *Champagne Sec* (1933). The job served to only whet his appetite for a composing career. He joined the Lambs Club in order to meet people working in the theater. The scheme worked beyond his wildest expectations.

While at the Lambs, Loewe became friends with actor Dennis King. King was set to appear with Oscar Shaw in the play *Petticoat Fever* (1935) at the Ritz Theatre. He was taken with a song, "Love Tiptoed Through My Heart," which Loewe wrote in collaboration with Irene Alexander. King decided to interpolate the song into the play. For the first time, a Frederick Loewe song was heard on Broadway.

Loewe had another song interpolated into a revue, *The Illustrators' Show* (1936). The song was "A Waltz Was Born in Vienna," written in collaboration with Earle Crooker. The popularity of the song lasted longer than *The Illustrators' Show.*

Crooker, a script writer and sometime lyricist, collaborated with Loewe on a full-length score to a new musical, *Salute to Spring* (1937) that premiered in St. Louis. The show was a great success but didn't transfer to New York.

Producer Dwight Deere Wiman enjoyed the team's work and commissioned them to compose the songs for his next Broadway show, *Great Lady* (1938). The operetta was produced at the Majestic Theater. In the cast were Norma Terris, of *Show Boat* fame, Irene Bordoni, a saucy French chanteuse, and Helen Ford, star of many Rodgers and Hart shows.

After the failure of *Great Lady,* Loewe resumed his piano playing in restaurants and clubs and continued going to the Lambs Club. But for a time, his Broadway activities stopped. In 1942, while at the Lambs, Loewe was introduced to the young Alan Jay Lerner.

* * * *

Although not the best of friends, the two men got on well enough. Lerner was notoriously unreliable though remarkably talented and Loewe was disliked as an extremely mean person. However, their talents certainly meshed and they decided to team up for another show. The result was *What's Up?* (1943). The directors were Robert H. Gordon and George Balanchine. The show starred Jimmy Savo, Larry Douglas, and Lynn Gardner. Despite the talents on hand, the show wasn't a hit.

For their next project, the team chose *The Day Before Spring* (1945), which opened at the National Theatre. In spite of some favorable reviews and what is regarded as a good score, the show never caught on with audiences.

The Day Before Spring was Lerner and Loewe's last failure together. From then on, each of their shows achieved great success. The first was *Brigadoon* (1941), a story of the power of love and faith, which opened at the Ziegfeld Theater. The score was a lyrical evocation of the Scottish Highlands. "Come to Me, Bend to Me," "The Heather on the Hill" and "Almost Like Being in Love" all became hits. The other songs, more traditional musical comedy numbers, such as "My Mother's Wedding Day," were equally expert.

Lerner next undertook a project with Kurt Weill. *Love Life* (1948) was the result. It opened at the 46th Street Theatre with Nanette Fabray and Ray Middleton. It was produced by Cheryl Crawford and directed by Elia Kazan.

Lerner returned to his partnership with Frederick Loewe for *Paint Your Wagon* (1951). The show was a light-hearted adventure set against the backdrop of the California gold rush. Lerner and Loewe's score was, according to the reviewers, much more entertaining than the book. "They Call the Wind Maria" was a huge hit as was another of the show's ballads, "I Talk to the Trees."

Their next Broadway offering was their biggest success, but it took six years for it to reach the stage. The musicalization of George Bernard Shaw's *Pygmalion* was turned down by most of Broadway's veteran composers and lyricists. E. Y. Harburg, Dietz and Schwartz, Noel Coward, Cole Porter, and Rodgers and Hammerstein all passed on the project. Lerner and Loewe attempted it and worked on the project for two years before giving up.

After the aborted attempt, both Lerner and Loewe split to pursue projects that never reached fruition. In 1954, the two songwriters reunited to tackle the project again. This time, the work seemed to come together more easily and *My Fair Lady* (1956) opened at the Mark Hellinger Theater.

My Fair Lady starred Julie Andrews as Eliza Doolittle and Rex Harrison as her mentor, Henry Higgins. The show was produced by Herman Levin and directed by Moss Hart.

The illustrious score contained many hits. Perhaps the most successful was "I Could Have Danced All Night." But "On the Street Where You Live," "I've Grown Accustomed to Her Face," "Wouldn't It Be Loverly?" and "The Rain in Spain" all became standards. *My Fair Lady's* run was a Broadway record until 1971, when it was overtaken by *Hello, Dolly!*

After the success of *My Fair Lady*, there was tremendous pressure put on Lerner and Loewe. The result was bound to be a disappointment, and *Camelot* (1960) was considered so by most of the critics.

Prior to its opening at the Majestic Theater, *Camelot* had a stormy tryout period; director Moss Hart suffered a heart attack, and Lerner was hospitalized. The songwriters and Hart produced the story of King Arthur and Guinevere. The stars were Richard Burton in his only musical theater appearance, Robert Goulet in his Broadway debut, and Julie Andrews, following her great success in *My Fair Lady*.

Despite mostly unfavorable reviews, the show went on to become one of the most produced Broadway musicals. This is due in large part to the superior score by Lerner and Loewe. "I Wonder What the King Is Doing Tonight," "If Ever I Would Leave You," and "How to Handle a Woman" all won a fair amount of success on records and television. The Kennedy administration was called Camelot after the title and spirit of the show.

The difficulties that accompanied *Camelot's* birth and Loewe's heart problems led to the composer's decision to retire. It was a decision he adhered to with the exception of brief collaborations with Lerner on a movie version of Antoine de Saint-Exupery's *The Little Prince* (1975) and the stage adaptation of *Gigi* for which they won a Tony Award.

Lerner was not ready for retirement and searched for other collaborators. His first choice was Richard Rodgers, who also lost his collaborator, Oscar Hammerstein II, around the same time Lerner and Loewe broke up. The announced project was a musical dealing with extrasensory perception (ESP) and with a proposed title of *I Picked a Daisy*.

But the Rodgers and Lerner collaboration did not occur. The two professionals found they had divergent working styles, and the project was dropped. Lerner took the idea to Burton Lane with whom he had collaborated on the movie *Royal Wedding*.

The working relationship with Lane proved slightly more successful than that of Rodgers and Lerner. The result was *On a Clear Day You Can See Forever* (1965).

Lerner turned to composer Andre Previn for the music of *Coco* (1969), a musicalization of the life of fashion designer Coco Chanel, with Katharine Hepburn in the leading role. *Coco's* score was unappreciated though excellent. Soon after Hepburn left the show, it closed.

Failure was to dog Lerner's heels till the end of his career. *Lolita, My Love* by Lerner and John Barry closed out of town in 1971. *Music! Music!* (1974), a revue that contained no original songs had Lerner's book. Lerner's collaboration with Leonard Bernstein, *1600 Pennsylvania Avenue* (1976), was written to commemorate the American Bicentennial.

Lerner and Lane collaborated again in 1979 to worse results than their first outing, though the score is topnotch. *Carmelina* (1979) was based on the film *Buona Sera, Mrs. Campbell* and starred Georgia Brown, Virginia Martin, Gordon Ramsey, and Cesare Siepe.

Lerner's last Broadway outing was *Dance a Little Closer* (1983), written with Charles

Strouse. The show was based on Robert E. Sherwood's play *Idiot's Delight*. Like Lerner's other work, even this failure contained great lyrics.

Alan Jay Lerner died on June 14, 1986. Frederick Loewe died on February 14, 1988.

During their heyday, the team of Lerner and Loewe produced some of the most enduring of all American musicals. The Lerner and Loewe hallmark was witty, sophisticated, and emotionally complex lyrics married to lively, passionate music that enthralled a generation of theatergoers. Their songs were sometimes sentimental, sometimes satirical, and always professional.

LEW FIELDS' 44TH STREET ROOF GARDEN · 216–30 W. 44th Street between Broadway and Eighth Avenue. Architect: William Albert Swansey. Opening: June 5, 1913; *All Aboard*.

The theater was one of many rooftop theaters built in the days before air-conditioning and stringent fire codes. The auditorium had an erratic career as a number of different ventures.

It was reopened as the Folies Marigny in January 1914. A little over a year later, it was rechristened Castles-in-the-Air. The theater was named for Vernon and Irene Castle and was used for their shows. They opened the theater on June 14, 1915, with a show called *Look Who's Here*.

On December 1, 1917, the date of the opening of the wartime revue *Over the Top,* the theater was renamed the 44th Street Roof Theatre. The theater was renovated and walls and roof were added making the roof theater a traditional house. *Over the Top* had a score in part by Sigmund Romberg. Fred and Adele Astaire, the successors to the Castles as Broadway's top dance team, starred.

Popular comedienne, singer and songwriter Nora Bayes had the theater named after her on December 30, 1918, with her vehicle *Ladies First*. Though Bayes and Seymour Simon wrote most of the score along with A. Baldwin Sloane and Harry B. Smith, the hit songs "The Real American Folk Song Is a Rag" and "Some

Wonderful Sort of Someone" had music by George Gershwin and lyrics by Ira Gershwin and Schuyler Greene, respectively.

The Nora Bayes Theater became simply the Bayes Theater on September 11, 1922, with *East Side West Side*. Yiddish theater was presented beginning with the opening of *The Three Little Business Men* on September 3, 1923. The theater was renamed Thomashefsky's Broadway Theater, after actor Boris Thomashefsky. Nora Bayes again took over on May 12, 1924, with *Two Strangers from Nowhere*. The theater again became the Bayes Theater.

The theater was renamed Giglio's Radio Theater on August 28, 1937, with *La Figlia Brutta*. The theater's name changed for the last time with *Fickle Women* on December 15, 1937. The name was again Nora Bayes Theater.

When the theater below was razed in July 1945 so too was the roof theater. Today, the *New York Times* printing plant occupies the site.

LEW FIELDS' MANSFIELD THEATER · See BROOKS ATKINSON THEATER.

LEW FIELDS' THEATRE · See ANCO THEATER.

LIBERTY THEATRE · 234 W. 42nd Street. Architects: Herts and Tallant. Opening: October 5, 1904; *The Rogers Brothers in Paris*.

Marc Klaw and Abraham Erlanger built the Liberty for the Rogers Brothers, a couple of "Dutch" comics. The comedy team had previously opened the Victoria Theater up the block and was popular enough to assure success to the new theater's premiere, *The Rogers Brothers in Paris*. They would return to the Liberty in *The Rogers Brothers in Ireland* (1905). During its heyday as one of Broadway's most successful musical houses, the Liberty presented some of the best talents on the Great White Way.

George M. Cohan had two productions play the Liberty. The first was *Little Johnny Jones* (1904), which marked Cohan's emergence as the top musical comedy talent of his time.

Cohan wrote, directed, produced, and starred in the show, which also featured his father and mother and his wife Ethel Levey.

Cohan's next hit at the Liberty Was *Little Nellie Kelly* (1922). The score included "You Remind Me of My Mother" and "Nellie Kelly, I Love You." By the twenties, Cohan saw his fame begin to wind down as newer talents entered the scene. One was Jerome Kern.

Kern had several musicals premiere at the Liberty. The first, *Have a Heart* (1917), was a minor show with a Guy Bolton, P.G. Wodehouse libretto and Wodehouse lyrics. Though none of the songs achieved standard status, "You Said Something" had a brief vogue. Kern's next show at the Liberty, *The Night Boat* (1920), isn't well remembered today, but the score he wrote with Anne Caldwell did contain two popular songs, "Whose Baby Are You?" and "Left All Alone Again Blues."

Charles Dillingham's production of *The City Chap* (1925) also had a Kern/Caldwell score, but none of the songs outlasted the show's run.

Two annual revues played the Liberty. The first was *Hitchy-Koo of 1919*. Raymond Hitchcock, a popular comic and monologist, served as master of ceremonies in the annual revue's only stop at the Liberty. The score was by the young Cole Porter and introduced one of his earliest hits, "An Old Fashioned Garden."

George White's Scandals began one of its two yearly editions at the Liberty with the 1919 version. The score by Richard Whiting and Arthur Jackson didn't have any hits, so for the next edition White enlisted George Gershwin to contribute tunes. The *Scandals of 1920* introduced the "Scandal Walk," and the *Scandals of 1921* contained "Drifting Along with the Tide." Gershwin would create better scores in two other productions that opened at the Liberty.

The first is one of Gershwin's greatest hits, *Lady, Be Good!* (1924). The score written with his brother Ira boasted many of the Gershwins' most enduring standards, "Fascinating Rhythm," "The Half of It Dearie Blues," and the title song. Fred and Adele Astaire starred in

the show along with Cliff Edwards and Walter Catlett. The libretto was by Guy Bolton and Fred Thompson. The other Gershwin show to play the Liberty was *Tip Toes* (1925). Alex Aarons and Vinton Freedley repeated their roles as producers, as did the librettists and songwriters of *Lady Be Good!* Again the Gershwins provided an exceptional score, including "Sweet and Low Down," "Looking for a Boy," "These Charming People," and "That Certain Feeling."

Black shows were big successes during the late twenties and early thirties. The last big hit to play the Liberty, *Blackbirds of 1928* (1928) was one of the most successful. It featured a stellar cast, including Adelaide Hall, Mantan Moreland, Aida Ward, Elisabeth Welch, and Bill Robinson. The score by Dorothy Fields and Jimmy McHugh included "Doin' the New Low-Down," "1 Can't Give You Anything But Love," and "Porgy." Three years later, Fields and McHugh again contributed two songs for an all-black show at the Liberty, *Singin' the Blues* (1931), but it was not a hit.

The Liberty was one of the most successful theaters on 42nd Street. In 1932, the theater began a vaudeville policy. The Depression took a further toll, and the theater, like its neighbors, became a grind movie house.

Today the Liberty's auditorium sits vacant behind an unmarked doorway at the exit of the AMC Cinemas on 42nd Street. With its lobby destroyed, the Liberty awaits its fate in the new 42nd Street.

THE LITTLE THEATRE · 238 W. 44th Street. Architects: H. C. Ingalls and F. B. Hoffman Jr. Opening: March 12, 1912; *The Pigeon* Producer/director Winthrop Ames specialized in the mounting of small, intimate plays in the first decades of this century. He had trouble placing these small shows in the average Broadway house, which contained about 800 seats, so Ames built his own theater with only 299 seats. Ames wanted to give the marginally commercial plays he presented a chance, since there was no off-Broadway alternative at the time. As he himself put it, he wished to produce "the clever, the unusual drama that has a chance of becoming a library classic."

Ames had his architects design a neofederal building with such homey amenities as a working fireplace in the lobby. The sparsely adorned auditorium contained no boxes or balcony, just a gently sloping orchestra section. Above the theater proper, Ames had his offices.

The first production at the theater was John Galsworthy's comedy *The Pigeon.* The show was moderately successful with a sixty-four performance run. Arthur Schnitzler's *The Affairs of Anatol* (1912) opened with John Barrymore and Doris Keane in the leads. Barrymore returned to the stage of the Little in George Bernard Shaw's *The Philanderer* (1915).

By this time, Ames realized his plan wasn't working. Even with sell-out business, Ames could barely support a star's salary like Barrymore's. For just as he couldn't lose much money on the small productions, he also couldn't make much if the plays were hits. He announced his intention of refurbishing the house by increasing the number of seats to 1,000 by adding a balcony and enlarging the auditorium. However Ames' plan didn't reach fruition, for the cost of remodeling would have amounted to as much as he was losing in ticket sales. So instead, in 1917, he opted to increase the seating to 450 seats with reconfigured seating and the added balcony.

The first long run at the Little was Rachel Crothers' comedy *A Little Journey* (1918). The next offering, *Please Get Married* (1919) starred Ernest Truex.

In 1920, the theater was renovated by architect Herbert Krapp who again increased the seating capacity as well as improving the acoustics.

The First (1920) was written by actor Frank Craven as was the play *Spite Corner* (1922).

By now Ames' family fortune was being quickly depleted. By 1922, he had lost $504,372 on the operation of the Little, despite its many successes. Luckily, the Booth Theatre, owned by Ames and the Shuberts, offset some, but not all, of the losses.

Guy Bolton, best known for his collaboration with P. G. Wodehouse and Jerome Kern,

had his straight play *Polly Preferred* (1923) produced. Bolton's straight plays were exactly like his musical libretti only without any songs.

Bolton's next offering at the Little, *Chicken Feed* (1923), was produced by John Golden who took the lease on the theater with F. Ray Comstock and L. Lawrence Weber. The play ran to good houses when it was forced to close, because Weber wanted to move his production of *Little Jesse James* to the theater from the Longacre Theater.

John Golden presented another hit play, *Pigs* (1924), at the Little. *Pigs* was written by Anne Morrison and Patterson McNutt and directed by Frank Craven. The play was originally entitled *Johnny Jones, Jr.,* but since George M. Cohan had already written a musical *Little Johnny Jones,* Golden decided another title was in order.

Winchell Smith fell in love with Marc Connelly's comedy *The Wisdom Tooth* and planned to open it at the Little Theatre on February 15, 1926. However, the out-of-town tryouts in Washington, D.C., and Hartford were complete failures. The show, starring Thomas Mitchell, almost closed out of town, but Golden wired Smith. "We have had plenty of successes. Let's have a failure for a change. The Little Theatre needs a tenant. Try it out for a week or two there." Golden congratulated himself later, for *The Wisdom Tooth* proved to be a great success with a 160-performance run, and critics compared Connelly with James M. Barrie.

A bigger hit was *Two Girls Wanted* (1926). Rachel Crothers returned to the Little Theatre as playwright and director of *Let Us Be Gay* (1929). Another hit was Elmer Rice's *The Left Bank* (1931).

By 1931, Ames had left the theater business. His last activity in the theater was the production of his own play *Mr. Samuel* (1930) with Edward G. Robinson. The play marked the end of Ames' theater career. Ames died on November 3, 1937. At his death, his estate was reduced to $77,000.

In February 1935, CBS took over the theater as the CBS Radio Playhouse, but the theater returned to legitimate use on September 28, 1936, with the production of *Pre-Honeymoon,* which moved from the Lyceum Theater. Anne Nichols, best known as the author of *Abie's Irish Rose,* wrote the play, and the theater was renamed Anne Nichols' Little Theater.

The theater's name was changed back to the Little Theatre with the opening of *Edna His Wife* (1937), a one-woman show starring Cornelia Otis Skinner.

The *New York Times* took over operation of the theater in January 1942 and renamed it New York Times Hall. They used the space as a conference hall and permitted an occasional concert. The theater became an ABC television studio in 1959.

The theater returned to legitimate use with the black revue *Tambourines to Glory* (1963) and a reversion of its original name. The show, by Langston Hughes and Jobe Huntley, didn't catch on.

When Frank Gilroy's Pulitzer Prize-winning play *The Subject Was Roses* moved from the Royale Theatre on September 7, 1964, the Little was renamed the Winthrop Ames Theater. In March of 1965, the theater resumed its original name and again became a television studio, this time for the Westinghouse network. Among the television shows that were broadcast from the stage of the theater were the "Merv Griffin Show" and the "David Frost Show." Griffin's show made the theater famous, for at the beginning of every show announcer Arthur Treacher said it was coming from "the Little Theatre off Broadway."

The theater again housed live performances with the opening of *My Sister, My Sister* (1974) by Ray Aranha. Three years later, the theater saw the opening of its greatest hit, Albert Innaurato's comedy *Gemini* (1977). The 1,788 performance run was abetted by a popular television advertisement. The Little was given special status by Actor's Equity and other unions to permit plays to run profitably in its small auditorium.

In 1981, Adcadesign redesigned the theater for its new owners, The Little Theatre Group. The next hit was Harvey Fierstein's three one-act plays, *Torch Song Trilogy* (1983). Fierstein's popular play dealt with gay themes in a sometimes frank way.

Shortly after the opening of *Torch Song Trilogy,* in July 1983, the name of the Little was changed again. It was renamed the Helen Hayes Theater as a tribute to the First Lady of the American Theater. The previous Helen Hayes Theater had been demolished after a particularly bitter fight to save it and the Morosco Theatre. Those citizens who took part in the battle to save the theaters were not appeased by the renaming of the Little Theatre.

The owners of the theater, Martin Markinson and Donald Tick bought the theater from Westinghouse for $800,000 in 1979. They decided to sell it at auction on March 24, 1988. The owners said there would be a $5 million minimum value put on the theater. Rocco Landesman, president of the Jujamcyn Theater chain said he was thinking of purchasing the theater. Apparently the owners forbade the Shuberts or Nederlanders from buying the house. The auction was a failure, and the theater was not sold.

The Nerd (1987) by Larry Shue turned out to be a surprise hit. Two one-act musicals made up *Romance, Romance* (1988). Alfred Uhry's *Last Night of Ballyhoo* (1997) looked at Jews in Atlanta's high society. *Dirty Blonde* (2000) was an examination of Mae West, *Say Goodnight, Gracie* (2002) found Frank Gorshin impersonating George Burns and Tovah Feldshuh acted like Golda Meir in *Golda's Balcony* (2003).

LOESSER, FRANK (1910–1969) · Frank Loesser was the most versatile of all the Broadway composers. He wrote lyrics to his own tunes, and all but one of his Broadway shows were hits (another, *Pleasures and Palaces,* closed out of town). His output on Broadway was small compared with that of his contemporaries, but each of his shows was a unique contribution to the art of the musical theater.

Loesser was born in New York on June 29, 1910. He was educated at Townsend Harris Hall, and he dropped out of City College.

While holding various odd jobs, Loesser began writing song parodies to popular tunes of the day. RKO Radio Pictures hired Loesser as a staff lyricist after he published his first song, "In Love with a Memory of You," with music by William Schuman. None of Loesser's work at RKO reached the screen, and he returned to New York. He later worked at Universal Pictures. As a contract writer for Paramount Pictures, he wrote the lyrics to hundreds of songs, a high percentage of which became standards. Those that didn't become immediate hits still manage to stand the test of time.

When writing for the movies, Loesser was primarily a lyricist. He collaborated with such greats as Burton Lane, Jule Styne, Hoagy Carmichael, Jimmy McHugh, Arthur Schwartz, and Victor Schertzinger. His film titles include *College Swing, Destry Rides Again, Thank Your Lucky Stars, The Perils of Pauline, Let's Dance, Happy-Go-Lucky, Seven Days Leave,* and *Hans Christian Andersen.*

Among his movie songs are "The Moon of Manakoora," "Moments Like This," "Says My Heart," "Small Fry, " "Heart and Soul," "Two Sleepy People," "The Lady's in Love with You," "Hey, Good Looking'," "See What the Boys in the Back Room Will Have," "I Hear Music," "Delores," "I Said No," "I Don't Want to Walk Without You," "Sand in My Shoes," and "Kiss the Boys Goodbye."

Other Loesser greats are "Can't Get Out of This Mood," "What Do You Do in the Infantry," "Murder,

He Says," "Leave Us Face It We're in Love," "Spring Will Be a Little Late This Year," "Rumble, Rumble, Rumble," "Poppa, Don't Preach to Me," ''I Wish I Didn't Love You So," "Tallahassee," "What Are You Doing New Year's Eve?," "That Feathery Feeling," "On a Slow Boat to China," "Baby, It's Cold Outside" (Academy Award, 1949), "No Two People," "Thumbelina," "Inchworm," "Anywhere I Wander," and "A Woman in Love."

Loesser's first Broadway assignment was with a revue, *The Illustrator's Show* (1936). It was not an illustrious debut, but it did land him a contract with Universal Pictures as a staff writer. He then joined Paramount for a long, successful stint.

His next Broadway show was a musicalization of Brandon Thomas' farce, *Charley's Aunt,* entitled *Where's Charley?* (1948) for which he contributed both music and lyrics. It starred Ray Bolger and Allyn Ann McLerie. Many hits emerged from the show, including "Once In Love with Amy," "The New Ashmolean Marching Society and Student Conservatory Band," "My Darling, My Darling," and "Make a Miracle."

Two years later, audiences at the 46th Street Theatre were treated to the definitive Broadway depiction of Times Square when the curtain went up on *Guys and Dolls* (1950). Abe Burrows wrote the libretto with Jo Swerling, the original librettist also credited, and George S. Kaufman directed. The show starred Robert Alda, Vivian Blaine, Sam Levene, Isabel Bigley, Pat Rooney, and Stubby Kaye. It was full of great Loesser tunes, including "If I Were a Bell," "Sit Down You're Rockin' the Boat," "I've Never Been in Love Before," "My Time of Day," " A Bushel and a Peck," "I'll Know," and the hilarious "Adelaide's Lament."

With musicals based on an English farce and the New York underworld behind him, Loesser next tackled the Italian winemaking community of Napa, California, with *The Most Happy Fella* (1956). The show was based on Sidney Howard's drama, *They Knew What They Wanted.* The show was almost entirely sung; in fact some thought it closer to opera than traditional musical comedy. Loesser himself wrote the book so that the songs and story would be truly integrated. Despite the operatic overtones of the score, several of the numbers achieved success on the hit parade. The most popular were "Standing on the Corner," "Joey, Joey, Joey" and "Big D." Other hits were "Warm All Over" and "My Heart Is So Full of You." The score was considered so exceptional that Columbia records issued the entire show on a three record set, a first for a Broadway musical. *The Most Happy Fella* featured opera star Robert Weede, Susan Johnson, Jo Sullivan (later Mrs. Loesser), and Art Lund.

Loesser's next challenge was the quiet, bucolic *Greenwillow* (1960), based on a novel by B. J. Chute. Anthony Perkins made his musical comedy debut in a cast that also included Cecil Kellaway and Pert Kelton. The one big hit from the show was "Never Will I Marry," made popular through a recording by Barbra Streisand.

Loesser's last Broadway show won him the Pulitzer Prize. *How to Succeed in Business Without Really Trying* (1961) was a broad satire of the American workplace. Robert Morse attained stardom through his portrayal of the ruthless worker on his way to the top. Rudy Vallee, Bonnie Scott, Virginia Martin, Charles Nelson Reilly, and Claudette Sutherland all turned in first-rate performances under Abe Burrows' direction. Among the songs, "I Believe in You" achieved standard status, although people unfamiliar with the show hardly realized the love song was sung by the hero to his own reflection.

Loesser's next attempt at Broadway, *Pleasures and Palaces* closed out of town in 1965 despite some favorable reviews.

Loesser affected Broadway in other ways besides his scores. Through his publishing company, Frank Music, he encouraged the careers of many Broadway newcomers. Loesser convinced George Abbott to hire Jerry Ross and Richard Adler to write the score of *The Pajama Game*. He also gave Meredith Willson the encouragement needed to start him on what eventually became *The Music Man*. Loesser later coproduced the show along with Kermit Bloomgarden. Loesser also encouraged composer Moose Charlap and lyricist Norman Gimbel and others.

Loesser died of cancer on July 26, 1969.

LOEWE, FREDERICK · See LERNER AND LOEWE.

LOGAN, JOSHUA (1908–1988) · Joshua Logan was one of Broadway's preeminent directors who also sometimes assumed the role of playwright. His main strengths lay in his vibrant staging of musical comedies, including some of the greatest in the genre. Logan was partially responsible for the success of such landmark musicals as *South Pacific* and *Annie Get Your Gun*. Logan worked with such great songwriters as Richard Rodgers (teamed with both Lorenz Hart and Oscar Hammerstein II), Irving Berlin and Harold Rome.

Logan's first musical assignment was for the Rodgers and Hart show *I Married an Angel* (1938). He went on to direct such musicals as *Knickerbocker Holiday* (1938); *Stars in Your Eyes* (1939); *Two for the Show* (1940); *Higher and Higher* (1940) for which he was also colibrettist; *By Jupiter* (1942); *This Is the Army* (1942); *Annie Get Your Gun* (1946); *South Pacific* (1949) for which he was also colibrettist, choreographer, and coproducer; *Wish You Were Here* (1952) for which he was also colibrettist and coproducer; *Fanny* (1954) for which he was also colibrettist and coproducer; *All American* (1962); *Mr. President* (1962); and *Look to the Lilies* (1970).

Logan also worked on many straight plays, although for the most part they weren't as noteworthy as his musical projects. Among the straight plays he directed are *It's You I Want* (1935); *To See Ourselves* (1935); *Hell Freezes Over* (1935); *On Borrowed Time* (1938); *Mornings at Seven* (1939); *Charley's Aunt* (1940); *Happy Birthday* (1946); *John Loves Mary* (1947); *Mister Roberts* (1948) for which he was also coauthor; *The Wisteria Trees* (1950), which he also adapted and produced; *Picnic* (1953), which he also produced; *Kind Sir* (1953), which he also produced; *Middle of the Night* (1956), which he also produced; *Blue Denim* (1958); *The World of Suzie Wong* (1958); *Tiger Tiger Burning Bright* (1962); and *Ready When You Are C.B.!* (1964).

LONGACRE THEATER · 220 W. 48th Street. Architect: Henry B. Herts. Opening: May I. 1913; *Are You a Crook?* Many Broadway producers made their fortunes in industry or business and with their profits turned to the colorful world of Broadway. One of these was H. H. Frazee, owner of the Boston Red Sox. Frazee hired architect Henry B. Herts to design his Longacre Theater. Herts had recently broken up with his partner Hugh Tallent and was anxious to prove that he could go it alone.

For the Longacre Theater, Herts chose an Italian Renaissance design and employed limestone and terracotta as the building materials. Frazee was delighted with Herts' sophisticated design and made plans to produce musicals in the 1,400 seat auditorium.

Surprisingly, his first offering was a play, *Are You a Crook?* Perhaps he should have stuck to his original notion of presenting only musical comedy, for *Are You a Crook?* closed after twelve performances. His next offering was a musical, *Adele* (1913), by Frenchmen Jean Briquet and Adolf Philipp. The show was a hit with Georgia Caine, William Danforth, Alice Yorke, and Hal Forde in the leads.

John Barrymore was the next star to command the Longacre's stage in a melodrama entitled *Kick In* (1914). It was followed by another success, *A Pair of Sixes* (1914). *The Great Lover* (1915), starring Leo Ditrichstein, spoofed the world of opera. *Nothing But the Truth* (1916) was a comedy whose main character bets he can go an entire day without telling a lie. William Collier starred.

Leave It to Jane (1917), was a musical by Jerome Kern, P. G. Wodehouse, and Guy Bolton, the trio known for their small, intimate musicals with integrated libretti and scores.

Guy Bolton, in collaboration with George Middleton, was also responsible for the next hit at the Longacre, *Adam and Eva* (1919). The William B. Friedlander musical *Pitter Patter* (1920) starred William Kent, Jack Squire, and John Price Jones. Also in the cast was future Hollywood star James Cagney.

The Champion (1921) starred Grant Mitchell. *Little Jessie James* (1923) was a charming musical with a score by Harry Archer and Harlan Thompson. It introduced the hit song "1 Love You." *Moonlight* (1924), also a small musical, boasted a score by Con Conrad and William B. Friedlander. Conrad and Friedlander had another musical presented at the Longacre, *Mercenary Mary* (1925).

George S. Kaufman had a big success with his play *The Butter and Egg Man* (1925). The show starred Gregory Kelly as an out-of-towner who decides to invest $20,000 in a Broadway show. The comedy, one of Kaufman's best, is notable as the only play he wrote without the aide of a collaborator.

Miriam Hopkins had appeared at the Longacre in the musical *Little Jessie James.* She returned to its stage in a decidedly different kind of show, an adaptation of Theodore Dreiser's *An American Tragedy* (1926). The play made almost as much of a splash as the novel originally had. It was among five shows that District Attorney Jacob H. Banton regarded as morally unacceptable. Philip Kearney's drama remained open, despite the government's displeasure. Roger Pryor appeared as a Walter Winchell type of reporter in *Blessed Event* (1932). The title referred to one of Winchell's favorite slang phrases.

The Depression hurt the Broadway theater as less money was available for risky investments. The

Longacre suffered along with many other theaters. A high point of the thirties was the series of productions the Group Theater presented at the Longacre. The first was a double bill of Clifford Odets' two one-act plays, *Waiting for Lefty* and *Till the Day I Die* (1935). *Waiting for Lefty* had been given a single performance at the Civic Repertory Theater on January 5, 1935, and caused an immediate sensation.

The second play, *Till the Day I Die,* told of a German Communist who is tortured by police. His only recourse is to commit suicide. The cast of the two plays included Elia Kazan, Lee J .Cobb, Robert Lewis, Russell Collins, Alexander Kirkland, Roman Bohnen, and Odets himself. *Lefty* continued as a classic of the American theater. After its closing at the Longacre, it toured union halls around the country.

Odets and the Group Theater returned to the Longacre with the show *Paradise Lost* (1935), the story of a mild-mannered businessman and his radical partner. *Paradise Lost* traced what Odets considered the continuing decline of the American middle class.

Another playwright, almost diametrically opposed to Odets in style and substance, also had two plays performed at the Longacre in the thirties. Paul Osborn's *On Borrowed Time* (1938) told of a grandfather who keeps Death at bay up a tree so that he can enjoy a few more moments with his grandson. Joshua Logan directed the cast, which included Peter Holden, Dorothy Stickney and Dudley Digges.

Osborn's other production at the Longacre, *Mornings at Seven* (1939), was a gentle comedy of three sisters and their families. A later revival in 1980 was a hit and ran 564 performances at the Lyceum Theater.

Three's a Family (1943) by Phoebe and Henry Ephron was produced by John Golden. The farce had what critic Burns Mantle called a "confused but possible ending." It was the last play presented at the Longacre until 1953. The theater was used for radio and television productions in the interim.

The Dorothy Parker and Arnaud d'Usseau play *The Ladies of the Corridor* (1953) was the first play after the Longacre returned to a legitimate policy. Jean Anouilh's play *Colombe* was adapted by Louis Kronenberger as *Mademoiselle Colombe* (1954) and starred Julie Harris as Colombe, a young innocent who discovers her own strengths in the backstage world of a Paris theater. The play was Anouilh's seventh successive failure on Broadway.

His next play, *The Lark* (1955), changed his luck. Julie Harris starred as Joan of Arc, Boris Karloff as Cauchon, and Theodore Bikel, Sam Jaffe, Christopher Plummer, and Joseph Wiseman rounded out the cast.

Samuel Taylor's *The Pleasure of His Company* (1958) opened with Cornelia Otis Skinner, Cyril Ritchard, George Peppard, Charlie Ruggles, and Walter Abel. Eugene Ionesco's anticonformist play *Rhinoceros* (1961) opened with Zero Mostel (as the man who becomes the animal), Eli Wallach, Jean Stapleton, Anne Jackso,n and Morris Carnovsky. It was the only Broadway production for the Roumanian-born French playwright. *A Case of Libel* (1963) by Henry Denker opened with Van Heflin, Larry Gates, Mel Dowd, Sidney Blackmer, and Philip

Borneuf in the cast. The play was based on Quentin Reynold's libel suit against Westbrook Pegler as reported by Louis Nizer in his book *My Life in Court.*

Lorraine Hansberry's drama *The Sign in Sidney Brustein's Window* (1964) starred Gabriel Dell, Rita Moreno, and Alice Ghostley. The play later found more appreciative audiences, and it has enjoyed many productions throughout the country. Unfortunately Miss Hansberry died on January 12, 1965, and never witnessed her play's success.

Robert Anderson's *I Never Sang for My Father* (1968) explored the relationship of an estranged father and son, two frightened people who feel they should love each other but who bury their emotions under the protection of selfishness. *I Never Sang for My Father* starred Teresa Wright, Lillian Gish, Hal Holbrook ,and Alan Webb.

Terrence McNally's rollicking comedy set in a homosexual bathhouse, *The Ritz* (1975) starred Jack Weston, Rita Moreno, F. Murray Abraham, Stephen Collins, and Jerry Stiller.

The Fats Waller retrospective *Ain't Misbehavin'* moved from the Manhattan Theater Club to the Longacre on May 9, 1978. It made stars of its cast members Armelia McQueen, Ken Page, Nell Carter, Charlene Woodard and Andre De Shields. *Ain't Misbehavin'* was the best of all the revues that attempted to examine a composer's career. Deaf actress Phyllis Frelich electrified audiences in the Mark Medoff play *Children of a Lesser God* (1980). John Rubinstein costarred in the production, which won a Tony Award and was the Longacre's last success.

LUNT-FONTANNE THEATER · 205 W. 46th Street. Architects: Carriere and Hastings. Opening: January 10, 1910; *The Old Town* In 1909, producer Charles Dillingham hired the high-class architecture firm of Carriere and Hastings to design the Globe Theatre, which later became the Lunt-Fontanne. Carriere and Hastings are best known for their designs for the New York Public Library (1898–1911), the Frick Collection (1913–1914) and the Manhattan Bridge approach (1912–1915).

Dillingham's life-style was as flamboyant as his personality, and he spared little expense in his new theater. He wanted to cater to the carriage trade, and so he made sure that the interior and exterior of the building were lavishly decorated. An additional entrance on West 46th Street, which was designed for patrons who wanted to make grand entrances, supplanted the theater's original entrance on 1555 Broadway. Above the 46th Street doors was a balcony from which audience members could view arrivals.

Inside, the theater proper was decorated in hues of gold, blue and ivory. Above the auditorium was a dome that could be opened to the sky in good weather. Upstairs, the theater contained private apartments for Dillingham and his retinue. The six-story Renaissance revival-style building presented an awesome facade to passersby and theatergoers.

Dillingham was primarily a producer of musicals, and so the early years of the theater were spent, almost exclusively, with musicals and revues. Dillingham's initial offering at the Globe was a Gustave Luders and George Ade musical, *The Old Town*. The main draw of the show was the popular team of Dave Montgomery and Fred Stone. Peggy Wood was also featured. Montgomery and Stone were riding high on the popularity of their last two musicals, *The Wizard of Oz* and Victor Herbert's *The Red Mill*.

Dillingham's next show, *The Slim Princess* (1911), also included popular American humorist George Ade on the creative staff. This time, Ade's original story was the basis for the book. Leslie Stuart and Henry Blossom were responsible for the score. The cast of *The Slim Princess* included popular musical comedy stars Queenie Vassar, Charles King, Elizabeth Brice, and Joseph Cawthorn. But the biggest star in the show, and one of the biggest in the early part of this century, was Elsie Janis.

Producer Charles Frohman's advice to fellow producers was "When in doubt, do Cinderella." Dillingham took Frohman's advice in his next offering at the Globe, *The Lady of the Slipper* (1912). Elsie Janis returned to the Globe's

stage, as did Montgomery and Stone and Peggy Wood. The cast also featured dancer Vernon Castle. The songs were by Victor Herbert, who had contributed uncredited music to *The Slim Princess,* and lyricist James O'Dea.

If the 232-performance run of *The Lady of the Slipper* was remarkable, then the 295-performance run of Dillingham's next production, *Chin-Chin* was almost a miracle. *Chin-Chin* (1914) opened with Dillingham favorites Montgomery and Stone in the leads. The music was by Englishman Ivan Caryll, and lyrics were by Anne Caldwell and James O'Dea. Montgomery and Stone played two slaves of Aladdin's lamp.

Dillingham was smart enough to realize that tastes in popular music were changing and the old-fashioned operettas and comic operas were becoming dated. The producer hired the young Irving Berlin to write the score to the next production at the Globe, *Stop! Look! Listen!* (1915). The show opened with a libretto by the prolific Harry B. Smith.

The Globe's first straight play presentation was *The Harp of Life* (1916). Laurette Taylor starred in the play, which was written by her husband, J. Hartley Manners. *The Harp of Life* marked Taylor's return to New York after a period in England.

In the second year of touring *Chin-Chin,* Dave Montgomery died. Fred Stone went on to appear at the Globe in *Jack O'Lantern* (1917). The musical had music and lyrics by Ivan Caryll and Anne Caldwell. The hit song from the show was an interpolation by Irving Berlin, "I'll Take You Back to Italy."

Dillingham's production *The Canary* (1918) had songs by Ivan Caryll, Irving Berlin, Anne Caldwell, P. G. Wodehouse, Harry Tierney, Harry B. Smith, Benjamin Hapgood Burt, and others. Despite the large number of composers and lyricists, the show was a musical comedy, not a revue. Of course, at the time, there was sometimes little difference between the two forms.

Dillingham's production of *She's a Good Fellow* (1919) boasted a score by Jerome Kern and Anne Caldwell. Joseph Santley (in drag), the Duncan Sisters, Olin Howland, and Ivy Sawyer starred. The show's run was cut short by the actor's strike of 1919, which helped establish Actor's Equity. Along with Irving Berlin and Jerome Kern, George Gershwin was responsible for the new direction of Broadway musicals. Gershwin finally had a show of his produced at the Globe with the second edition of the *George White's Scandals* (1920). Arthur Jackson was Gershwin's collaborator on the score. *Scandals* regulars Ann Pennington, Lou Holtz and Lester Allen, and George White himself, starred in the show. The *Scandals* was the first show presented in the Globe that was not produced by Dillingham.

Dillingham returned to producing at the Globe with *Tip Top* (1920). Ivan Caryll and Anne Caldwell provided the score for the show, which starred Fred Stone, the Duncan Sisters, and Rags Ragland.

George White's chief rival, Florenz Ziegfeld, presented the 1921 version of the *Ziegfeld Follies* (1921) at the Globe. Performers included W. C. Fields, Raymond Hitchcock, Ray Dooley, and Vera Michelena. Fanny Brice was given the two best songs—"My Man" and "Second Hand Rose."

Jerome Kern had another show open at the Globe, *Good Morning, Dearie* (1921). Anne Caldwell wrote the book and lyrics. Among the best songs in the score were the title tune and "Blue Danube Blues." The biggest hit in the show was "Ka-Lu-A."

George White's Scandals returned to the Globe (1922) with music by George Gershwin and lyrics by B. G. De Sylva, E. Ray Goetz and Arthur Francis. Francis was a pseudonym for George's talented brother, Ira. The cast included Lester Allen, Winnie Lightner, George White, and W. C. Fields. Paul Whiteman and his Orchestra also appeared onstage. The most famous of the Gershwin songs was "I'll Build a Stairway to Paradise."

Fred Stone appeared along with his wife Allene and daughter Dorothy in the aptly titled *Stepping Stones* (1923). Jerome Kern and Anne Caldwell wrote the score, which included the beautiful ballad "Once in a Blue Moon."

The *Scandals* returned to the Globe (1923) with Gershwin again supplying the score along with lyricists B.G. DeSylva, E. Ray Goetz, and Ballard Macdonald. None of the songs achieved success.

Ed Wynn was composer, lyricist, librettist, producer and star of *The Grab Bag* (1924). The show proved to be a huge hit with Wynn's highjinks. It was followed by one of the Globe's biggest hits, *No, No, Nanette* (1925). The show's tremendous success was due mostly to the great Vincent Youmans and Irving Caesar score. The hit songs included "Tea for Two" and "I Want to Be Happy." Another factor in the great success of the show was its star Louise Groody. Groody was the first star to receive a salary plus a percentage of the box office receipts. As a result, she was the first musical comedy star to earn over a million dollars.

Ziegfeld produced his revue *No Foolin'* (1926) at the Globe. Ziegfeld planned the show as the 1926 edition of his *Follies,* but because of a breakup with his former partners and owners of the New Amsterdam Theater Marc Klaw and A.L. Erlanger he was refused the right to the *Follies* name. Out of town, the show was titled *Ziegfeld's Palm Beach Nights, Ziegfeld's Palm Beach Girl* and *Ziegfeld's American Revue of 1926.* After its Broadway opening as *No Foolin',* Ziegfeld retitled the show *Ziegfeld's American Revue.*

When the show toured following its Broadway run, Ziegfeld, having settled his argument with Klaw and Erlanger, could at last call the show the *Ziegfeld Follies of 1926.*

Jerome Kern, Otto Harbach, and Anne Caldwell were responsible for the Dillingham production of *Criss Cross* (1926). Fred Stone and his daughter Dorothy appeared in the show.

Vincent Youmans' second production at the Globe, *Oh, Please!* (1926), had a hit song, "I Know that You Know" and a talented cast, including Beatrice Lillie, Charles Winninger, Helen Broderick, and Charles Purcell.

Three Cheers (1928) was to star Fred Stone and his daughter Dorothy, but prior to the opening, Stone, who had taken up flying, crashed the plane he was piloting. His injuries prevented him from appearing in *Three Cheers*. Will Rogers, Stone's closest friend, replaced him in the show.

The last show to play the Globe was the Jerome Kern and Otto Harbach musical *The Cat and the Fiddle* (1931). The brilliantly tuneful score featured such hits as "I Watch the Love Parade," "She Didn't Say Yes," "The Night Was Made for Love" and "Try to Forget." The show starred Odette Myrtil, Georges Metaxa, Bettina Hall, and George Meader.

The stock market crash wiped out Dillingham's savings, and the great producer was forced to sell his beloved theater. Beginning in 1932, the Globe showed motion pictures. Twenty-five years later, in 1957, Roger L. Stevens (City Playhouses Group) and Robert W. Dowling bought the theater and had the interior completely refurbished with design by Roche & Roche. The Broadway entrance was closed, the box office was added to the 46th Street lobby, the second balcony was removed and a mezzanine was added. The refurbished interior was also redecorated with an 18th century motif. The theater was renamed for the greatest of all American acting teams, Alfred Lunt and Lynn Fontanne.

The renamed theater's second opening took place on May 5, 1958, with the stars who gave it their names in the leading roles of Fredrich Duerrenmatt's explosive drama *The Visit*. The unrelenting drama of the play kept many theatergoers away. Sadly, it marked the end of the team's career on Broadway.

The theater's greatest hit, *The Sound of Music* (1959), marked the end of another great team's Broadway career. It would be the last collaboration for Richard Rodgers and Oscar Hammerstein II. The Mary Martin vehicle received decidedly mixed reviews but was an enormously popular hit with the public. Critics cited the operetta's sentimentality as its greatest fault. The score also received mixed notices, although many of the songs, chiefly "Climb Ev'ry Mountain," "Sixteen Going on Seventeen," "My Favorite Things," and the title song became standards.

One of Broadway's funniest musicals, *Little Me* (1962), followed *The Sound of Music* at the Lunt-Fontanne. The Cy Coleman and Carolyn Leigh score was perhaps the wittiest and brashest ever to play on Broadway. It was perfectly complimented by Neil Simon's hilarious libretto. The hit songs from the score were "I've Got Your Number" and "Real Live Girl." The reviews were excellent, but a newspaper strike hurt the musical's business.

Richard Burton opened in William Shakespeare's *Hamlet* on April 9, 1964. His performance was generally hailed, and the production enjoyed a 137-performance run, a record for the play on Broadway.

A series of middling musicals followed *Hamlet*.

Julie Harris was allowed to sing in the James Van Heusen, Sammy Cahn musical *Skyscraper* (1965). "Everybody Has the Right to Be Wrong" was the most popular song in the otherwise undistinguished score. The same songwriting team was responsible for the next attraction at the Lunt-Fontanne, *Walking Happy* (1966). The title tune and Norman Wisdom's performance were the chief draws. Lyricist Carolyn Leigh teamed up with film composer Elmer Bernstein for the David Merrick production *How Now, Dow Jones* (1967). The score contained a bona fide hit, "Step to the Rear." The show's book by Max Shulman was considered the biggest flaw in the show that starred Marlyn Mason, Anthony Roberts, and Brenda Vaccaro.

Hal Linden, Jill Clayburgh, Keene Curtis, and Paul Hecht starred in Jerry Bock and Sheldon Harnick's final musical as a team, *The Rothschilds* (1970).

During the seventies, there were a series of revivals at the Lunt-Fontanne. These included Stephen Sondheim's *A Funny Thing Happened on the Way to the Forum* with Phil Silvers and Larry Blyden; the Richard Adler and Jerry Ross hit *The Pajama Game* with Hal Linden and Barbara McNair; and *Hello, Dolly!* with a return performance by Carol Channing. One nonrevival in the seventies was the Richard Rodgers and Sheldon Harnick musical *Rex*

(1976). The show, a retelling of the life of Henry VIII, starred Nicol Williamson, Penny Fuller, and Barbara Andres.

A big hit for the theater was the Duke Ellington revue *Sophisticated Ladies* (1981) with Gregory Hines, Phyllis Hyman, Judith Jamison, and Hinton Battle. *Sophisticated Ladies* covered the best-known songs in the Ellington canon.

The great Peggy Lee made her Broadway debut in the one-person, autobiographical musical *Peg* (1983). It was not a success. Marvin Hamlisch looked at local beauty pageants in the satirical musical *Smile* (1986). *The Gospel at Colonus* (1988) transferred from the Brooklyn Academy of Music. Unfortunately, its brilliant uniqueness was too esoteric for the Broadway public. David Merrick went out with a whimper with his transfer of the Goodspeed Opera House's all-black production of *Oh, Kay!* (1991). A surprise success at the Lunt-Fontanne was *Catskills on Broadway* (1991) with Dick Capri, Mal Z. Lawrence, Freddie Roman, and Marilyn Michaels sending audiences into paroxysms of laughter. A rare sequel and a huge flop was *The Best Little Whorehouse Goes Public* (1994). Maury Yeston had an unexpected success with *Titanic* (1997). And in 1999, *Beauty and the Beast* transferred from the Palace Theatre for a seemingly endless run.

LUNT AND FONTANNE · The husband and wife team of Alfred Lunt and Lynn Fontanne are considered the greatest acting couple in American history. They enjoyed long careers on the Broadway stage, both together and separately from the first decade of the century until their retirement in 1960. The team was responsible for many of the great hits of the Theater Guild, and they certainly accounted for the Guild's long preeminence.

Alfred Lunt (1893–1977) Alfred Davis Lunt Jr. was born in Milwaukee, Wisconsin, to a family that had deep roots in New England. His early love for the theater launched his stage career before his twentieth birth-day. The year was 1912, and Lunt was in Boston ostensibly to attend the Emerson School of Oratory. He made it to only one session of one class before passing the Castle Square Theater and inquiring about employment. School was forgotten, and Lunt was hired to play small parts at $5 a week. After a month, he worked his way up to the generous salary of $20 a week. Lunt's stage debut was in the play *The Aviator*, which opened on October 7, 1912.

Lunt remained at the Castle Square Theater for three years. In 1914, he joined Margaret Anglin's touring company and remained with the company for two years. He then found work in vaudeville, supporting Lily Langtry. Later that same year, 1916, he rejoined the Anglin company.

Lunt moved to New York and made his Broadway debut at the Harris Theatre in *Romance and Arabella* (1917). Two years later, he met Lynn Fontanne in a Chicago production of *A Young Man's Fancy*.

He returned to New York, and had his first great success in the title role in *Clarence*. Booth Tarkington wrote the play expressly for Lunt. *Clarence* (1919) opened at the Hudson Theatre.

After two years with *Clarence*, Lunt opened in another Tarkington play, *The Intimate Strangers* (1921).

Lynn Fontanne (1887–1983) London-born Lynn Fontanne made her stage debut in J. M. Barrie's *Alice-Sit-By-the-Fire* in 1905. The touring production starred Ellen Terry, the idol of Fontanne. The great actress taught the newcomer posture, interpretation and other skills. Terry gave her pupil a letter of introduction to the successful London producer Arthur Collins, manager of the Theatre Royal, Drury Lane. He cast Fontanne in one of his Christmas pantomimes, *Cinderella*, which began a long tour at the end of 1905. After other touring plays, she made her West End debut in *Billy's Bargain* in June 1910.

Actress Laurette Taylor, who had seen

Fontanne in the London production of Edward Knoblock's *My Lady's Dress* in 1914, prompted Fontanne's move to America. Taylor convinced Fontanne to come to New York to act in *The Harp of Life* (1916), a play by Taylor's husband, J. Hartley Manners. The play opened at the Globe Theatre. Fontanne had already appeared on Broadway in a short lived production of *Mr. Preedy and the Countess* at the Thirty-ninth Street Theatre on November 7, 1910.

The biggest hit of her early career came in Marc Connelly and George S. Kaufman's *Dulcy* (1921) that opened at the Frazee Theater. Dulcy was a modern Mrs. Malaprop. The actress received glowing notices in what many critics felt was her first appearance out of the shadow of Laurette Taylor.

* * * *

Lunt and Fontaine had kept in touch following their first meeting in Chicago. They became more and more involved and finally decided to get married at New York's City Hall on May 26, 1922. The marriage took place with no fanfare. Two strangers were asked to be witnesses and were called upon to front the couple a few dollars for the license fee. This humble ceremony was the beginning of a long and successful collaboration on stage and in marriage.

After their marriage, the couple appeared separately in many productions. Notable was Lunt's first dramatic appearance in Sutton Vane's *Outward Bound* (1924) at the Ritz Theatre.

The couple's first appearance together was in *Sweet Nell of Old Drury,* a production mounted at the 48th Street Theatre (1923). There followed one of their greatest triumphs and the beginning of their long association with the Theater Guild. Ferenc Molnar's play *The Guardsman* was a failure when first produced on Broadway in 1913. But the Guild's offer was too good to refuse, and the acting team opened in *The Guardsman* (1924) at the Garrick Theater. The play was a huge success with Dudley Digges and Helen Westley completing the cast. The team played two jealous actors.

Lunt's character disguises himself as a guardsman and makes love to his unknowing wife. She claims to have known it was he all along.

A revival of George Bernard Shaw's *Arms and the Man* (1925) presented by the Theater Guild at the Guild Theater was the Lunts' next production. They gave many other performances in Guild productions, both as a team and separately, though sometimes the productions and plays were not nearly up to the level of the team's performances.

Among the most highly acclaimed shows of their careers are Eugene O'Neill's nine-act marathon *Strange Interlude* (1928) with Lynn Fontanne alone; Maxwell Anderson's *Elizabeth the Queen* (1930); Robert E. Sherwood's *Reunion in Vienna* (1931); Noel Coward's sophisticated comedy *Design for Living* (1933); *Idiot's Delight* (1936), the Pulitzer Prize winner by Robert E. Sherwood; Jean Giraudoux and S. N. Behrman's *Amphitryon 38* (1937); Robert E. Sherwood's *There Shall Be No Night* (1940) at the Alvin Theater; S. N. Behrman's comedy *The Pirate* (1942); and *The Great Sebastians* (1956) by Howard Lindsay and Russel Crouse.

Frederick Durrenmett's *The Visit* (1958) was their last Broadway assignment and opened as the inaugural production in the newly renamed Lunt-Fontanne Theater. Their last New York appearance was in a return of *The Visit,* which played City Center on March 8, 1960. Lunt served as director for the play *First Love* (1961), which opened at the Morosco Theatre. The team retired from the stage to Alfred's boyhood home of Genesee Depot, Wisconsin. Alfred Lunt died on August 4, 1977. Lynn Fontanne followed him on July 31, 1983.

LYCEUM THEATER · 149 W. 45th Street. Architects: Herts & Tallant. Opening: November 2, 1903; *The Proud Prince*. When producer Daniel Frohman opened his new Lyceum Theater on 45th Street, it was the first of the Times Square theaters north of 42nd Street. Other theaters had opened around Columbus Circle, and there was a healthy theater district in Harlem, but the success of the Lyceum and the other theaters surrounding it firmly established the Times Square area as the hub of legitimate theater. Frohman recognized Times Square's importance as the center of the new theater world. His previous Lyceum Theatre was located downtown on 14th Street.

The theater was considered quite modern for its time. There were no balcony supports to block the audience's view. Also, it contained shop space and dressing rooms in a seven-story building to the rear of the theater proper. The neobaroque interior style and beautiful facade made the Lyceum one of the most attractive Broadway houses. It was the first theater building to receive landmark status and is the oldest continuously operating legitimate theater in New York.

Frohman's private apartments contained a window from which he could view the performances below. This was a common practice in theaters whose managements liked to keep a tight rein on their companies. When Frohman's wife, Margaret Illington, acted on the Lyceum stage her husband would signal her from his window if she was overacting.

The theater has had a distinguished past, starting with its first offering, *The Proud Prince* starring E. H. Sothern, a favorite of Frohman. Soon after, William Gillette starred in J. M. Barrie's *The Admirable Crichton* (1903). The biggest hit of the early years of the Lyceum was *The Lion and the Mouse* (1905) by Charles Klein.

Great women graced the Lyceum stage in a number of mostly forgotten plays. Billie Burke, Ethel Barrymore, Lenore Ulric, and Ina Claire all had great success at the theater. Daniel Frohman's brother, Charles, was responsible for most of the bookings in the early years of the theater. Upon his death in 1915, Daniel teamed with David Belasco with a string of popular successes. These included *The Gold Diggers* (1919) and *Berkeley Square* (1929) by John L. Balderston, starring Leslie Howard and Margalo Gillmore.

Belasco died in 1930 and during the ensuing decade and the Depression, Daniel Frohman's fortunes declined, but the theater still housed a number of interesting shows. Charles Laughton

and Elsa Lanchester starred in *Payment Deferred* (1931). *Sailor, Beware!* was a big hit beginning on September 28, 1933 (500 performances) and Ina Claire, who had previously starred at the Lyceum in *The Gold Diggers* returned to the Lyceum in *Ode to Liberty* (1934).

Having Wonderful Time (1937), Arthur Kober's affectionate view of a summer camp for adults in the Catskills, would later be made into the musical *Wish You Were Here*. J. B. Priestley's delightful farce *When We Are Married* (1939) closed the thirties.

However successful the plays staged at the Lyceum were, Frohman's career was suffering. The theater was faced with destruction. A group of investors, however, led by George S. Kaufman, Moss Hart, and Max Gordon bought the theater and allowed Frohman to live in his apartment for $1 a year. It was natural that the first show of the forties would be Kaufman and Hart's riotous comedy *George Washington Slept Here* (1940), but it didn't prove as successful as their other outings. Moss Hart then staged Jerome Chodorov and Joseph Fields' *Junior Miss* (1941). The same authors provided the theater with its next hit, *The Doughgirls* (1942). Kaufman directed the Arlene Francis vehicle. Kaufman then cowrote with John P. Marquand and directed *The Late George Apley* (1944). At the end of that play's run, the Kaufman/Hart/Gordon group sold the Lyceum. Garson Kanin's *Born Yesterday* (1946) was the Lyceum's next smash hit. It made stars of Judy Holliday and Paul Douglas.

In 1949, the Lyceum became a part of the Shubert empire. The 1950s were also rich years for the Lyceum. Clifford Odets' *The Country Girl* (1950) starred Uta Hagen, Paul Kelly, and Steven Hill. Melvyn Douglas starred in *Glad Tidings* (1951) and followed it with *Time Out for Ginger* (1952), one of the most successful plays in the amateur market, receiving countless productions in summer stock and schools. Jean Kerr and Eleanor Brooke continued the comedy tradition at the Lyceum with *King of Hearts* (1954). Jean Kerr's husband, drama critic Walter Kerr, directed Jackie Cooper and Donald Cook in the hit comedy. Viveca Lindfors portrayed the title role in *Anastasia* (1954), written by Broadway veteran Guy Bolton. Another drama followed, the harrowing *A Hatful of Rain* (1955), starring Ben Gazzara, Shelley Winters, and Harry Guardino. During the second half of the fifties, Walter Pidgeon starred in a production of *The Happiest Millionaire* (1956). The next hit was John Osborne's *Look Back in Anger* (1957) with Kenneth Haigh, Alan Bates, and Mary Ure,

The 1960s began with Shelagh Delaney's *A Taste of Honey* (1960), starring Angela Lansbury. The third hit at the Lyceum, was a British import, a production of Harold Pinter's *The Caretaker* (1961) with Alan Bates, Robert Shaw and Donald Pleasence. Ellis Rabb, artistic director of the APA Phoenix company, took over the theater for the rest of the decade. During this period of 1965–69, such plays as *War and Peace, The Cherry Orchard, The Cocktail Party* and George Kelly's *The Show Off,* starring Helen Hayes, appeared on the Lyceum stage.

The 1970s proved to be lean years for the Lyceum and Broadway in general. The best play of the decade at the Lyceum was Arthur Kopit's brilliant drama *Wings* (1979), starring Constance Cummings.

In 1980, an all-star revival of *Morning's At Seven* (1980) opened at the Lyceum. In the cast were Nancy Marchand, Maureen O'Sullivan, Teresa Wright, Elizabeth Wilson, and David Rounds. Hits since then include Athol Fugard's *'Master Harold' ...and the boys* (1982) and *Whoopi Goldberg* (1984). Harvey Fierstein couldn't match the success of his *Torch Song Trilogy* with his new play *Safe Sex* (1987). Tony Randall's National Actors' Theatre took over the Lyceum stage beginning in 1991. Unfortunately, the company's successes were few. After the company left the theater and soon thereafter folded, the Lyceum hosted Tom Stoppard's *The Invention of Love* (2001), yet another successful revival of Paul Osborn's *Morning's at Seven* (2002), the British import *The Play What I Wrote* (2003), the one-man show *I Am My Own Wife* (2003), and a transfer to Broadway of the gruesome,

pointed, and hysterical *The Lieutenant of Inishmore* (2006).

LYRIC THEATER · (1) See Olympia Theatre.

LYRIC THEATRE · (2) 213 W 42nd Street. Architect: V. Hugo Koehler. Opening: October 12. 1903, *Old Heidelberg.* The Lyric was one of the most beautiful of the 42nd Street theaters. Although the entrance to the Renaissance-style theater was on 42nd Street, the main part of the theater fronted 43rd Street. That side features a beautifully ornamented facade with cartouches inscribed "Music" and "Drama." It was cleaned in 1979 by the Brandts with the expectation of reopening it as a legitimate house. But the financial plight of the theater district ruled out any reversal of the theater's movie policy. And when the Times Square Redevelopment began the Brandts were pushed out.

The Lyric was built by developer Eugene C. Potter to house Reginald DeKoven's American School of Opera. The school failed before the theater was finished and Potter leased the unfinished theater to the Shubert brothers.

Leading man Richard Mansfield opened the house in 1903. DeKoven's troupe didn't last long, and the Shuberts subsequently booked some of the greatest actors and productions of its time. Douglas Fairbanks starred in an adaptation of Charles Norris' *The Pet;* Mrs. Fiske, George Arliss, and Dudley Diggs played in *The New York Idea* (1906); Tyrone Power Sr. appeared in *Julius Caesar* (1914); William Faversham also played the part at the Lyric beginning on November 4, 1912.

Musicals included Rudolf Friml's *The Firefly* (1912) and *High Jinks* (1913). *The Firefly* had lyrics by Otto Harbach and featured the Friml favorite "Giannina Mia."

Following the First World War, the theater alternated between first-run film engagements and theatrical offerings. Fred and Adele Astaire starred in *For Goodness Sake* (1922). Although the score was by Paul Lannin, William Daly and Arthur Jackson, newcomers George and

Ira Gershwin contributed the hits "Someone" and "Tra-La-La."

In 1925, the Oppenheimer Brothers assumed management of the theater. Irving Berlin supplied the score to the madcap musical comedy *The Cocoanuts* (1925). Along with the Marx Brothers, the show featured the Brox Sisters, and the Brothers' constant foil, Margaret Dumont. The show later was made into the Brothers' first motion picture success.

The great showman Florenz brought his musicalization of *The Three Musketeers* into the Lyric on March 13, 1928. Rudolph Friml again delighted audiences with such songs as "Gascony," "March of the Musketeers," "My Sword," "One Kiss," and "Your Eyes." The show was a smash hit and ran 319 performances.

Cole Porter's *Fifty Million Frenchmen* (1929) was the theater's last success, opening at the dawn of the Depression and Prohibition. Among its songs were "You Do Something to Me" and "You've Got That Thing." The last legitimate show to play the Lyric was *Run, Little Chillun!* beginning on March 1, 1933.

The Lyric, like other 42nd Street theaters, became a motion picture house because of the Depression, starting its movie policy in 1933. Luckily, as with most of the 42nd Street theaters, economics did not allow for major renovation. Thus the Lyric survived in almost exactly the same condition as when it opened more than eighty years ago although when widescreen came in, the nine original boxes were removed. Attempts by its owners, the Brandts, to reopen the theater as a legitimate house failed in 1979 as Broadway continued its most recent decline. A huge theater with a double balcony, Lyric seated 1,256 patrons. Because of its size, the Lyric under the Times Square Redevelopment Plan, recommended it be used for legitimate theater productions. The Brandts wanted to reopen the theater as well as their Apollo Theatre next door. However, the 42nd Street Redevelopment organization condemned the Lyric and Apollo and gained control of the spaces. In spite of the excellent shape of the Lyric, the heat was turned off and the theater was allowed to deteriorate.

In 1996, producer Garth Drabinsky of the Livent Corporation came from Canada to New York looking for a theater for his productions. He talked the 42nd Street Redevelopment people into allowing him to destroy the Lyric and Apollo theaters and build a new, inferior theater, the Ford Center, in their place. He did, however, have the foresight to save the exteriors of both theaters. A year later, Drabinsky was out, under the threat of countless lawsuits by the New York Stage Government and his investors.

M

MAJESTIC THEATRE · 245 W. 44th Street. Architect: Herbert J. Krapp. Opening: March 28, 1927; *Rufus LeMaire's Affairs.* With 1,800 seats, the Majestic was the largest legitimate house in Times Square. The Majestic was the last theater commissioned by the Chanin Brothers and was built as the flagship of their theater holdings. Unfortunately, the Chanins lost all their theaters during the Depression.

The Majestic was built on the same large plot of land as the Theatre Masque, Royale Theatre, and the Lincoln Hotel (now the Milford Hotel). The theater's interior design is similar to the Richard Rodgers Theatre with its bleacher-style orchestra. However, the sightlines in the Majestic are much better then that of the earlier theater.

The Majestic, booked by the Shubert brothers did not have an easy time attracting hit shows. The initial attraction, *Rufus LeMaire's Affairs,* closed after only fifty-six performances. Sigmund Romberg, the great operetta composer, premiered *The Love Call* (1927) with lyrics by the prolific Harry B. Smith.

Several successful transfers from other theaters held the Majestic's stage, along with a few original failures. Boxer Jack Dempsey actually starred in a Broadway play aptly titled *The Big Fight* (1928).

The Shuberts gained control of the Majestic and filled it with their productions. *Pleasure Bound* (1929) was a minor revue that didn't cost the producers too much, because most of its cast and creative staff were on the monthly Shubert payroll. They probably used the sets and costumes over again in another of their shows.

A Wonderful Night (1929) was a retelling of *Le Reveillon,* the story that served as the basis for the opera *Die Fledermaus.* The music was taken from Johann Strauss. A young cast member was Archie Leach, who would later achieve fame in Hollywood as Cary Grant.

Impresario Lew Leslie, who had scored a big success with his *Blackbirds of 1928,* thought he had another hit with *The International Revue* (1930). He poured $200,000 into the show and hired the *Blackbirds'* songwriters Jimmy McHugh and Dorothy Fields. They came up with a couple of big hit songs, "Exactly Like You", and "On the Sunny Side of the Street." Leslie hired a wonderful cast including Americans Harry Richman and Jack Pearl, the British star Gertrude Lawrence, and the Spanish dancer Argentinita. But despite their talents the show was one of the first victims of the Depression.

Romberg was back with another operetta, *Nina Rosa* (1930). Otto Harbach wrote the book, and Irving Caesar wrote the lyrics. Stars Ethelind Terry, Guy Robertson, and George Kirk couldn't overcome the audiences' antipathy toward operetta.

After a long, dark period, the Majestic presented what seemed a sure hit. Instead of a dated operetta, the Shuberts booked the modern style musical *Pardon My English* (1933). Alex A. Aarons and Vinton Freedley, two of Broadway's most successful producers, presented George and Ira Gershwin and librettist Herbert Fields' newest creation.

Ray Henderson and Lew Brown tried to buck the Depression with their production *Strike Me Pink* (1933). Henderson and Brown contributed the score as well as coauthored the libretto, coproduced the show with silent partner Waxey Gordon, a notorious gangster, and codirected with Jack McGowan. None of their songs caught on with the public.

Murder at the Vanities (1933) was a backstage musical mystery show produced by Earl Carroll. Carroll set the show during a performance of his *Earl Carroll Vanities,* thus advertising his long-running revue series. The show contained a typical "Carrollian" number called "Virgins Wrapped in Cellophane." Carroll later moved his *Earl Carroll Sketch Book* to the Majestic where it concluded its 207-performance run.

A stellar cast was featured in the musical *Stars in Your Eyes* (1939). Ethel Merman led the cast, which also featured Richard Carlson, Jimmy Durante, Mildred Natwick, and Mary Wickes. Jerome Robbins, Alicia Alonzo, and Nora Kaye were all in the chorus. Arthur Schwartz and Dorothy Fields provided the fine score and Josh Logan directed.

Lew Brown had another show at the Majestic, *Yokel Boy* (1939). Brown collaborated on the lyrics with Charles Tobias, provided the libretto, and produced and directed the proceedings. Sam H. Stept wrote the music and was responsible for the one hit song, "Comes Love." Buddy Ebsen, Judy Canova, Dixie Dunbar, and Phil Silvers starred.

In 1942, Cheryl Crawford revived the Gershwin opera *Porgy and Bess.* Although it was not a success when first produced in 1935, the show scored this time around. In the cast were many of the original cast members, including Todd Duncan, Anne Brown, Ruby Elzy, J. Rosamond Johnson, and Warren Coleman.

Another major revival, Franz Lehar's *The Merry Widow* (1943) starred Jan Kiepura, Marta Eggerth, David Wayne, Melville Cooper, Gene Barry, and Ruth Matteson. Audiences were ready to forget troubles in Europe and lose themselves in the Lehar music.

Richard Rodgers and Oscar Hammerstein II opened what many people consider their greatest achievement, *Carousel* (1945), starring Jan Clayton, John Raitt, Mervyn Vye, and Jean Darling. The Theater Guild production, under the brilliant direction of Rouben Mamoulian, proved to be the Majestic's biggest hit up to that time.

Harold Rome's *Call Me Mister,* an affectionate tribute to wartime America, moved from the National Theatre with Betty Garrett, Maria Karnilova, Jules Munshin, and Lawrence Winters leading the cast. *Call Me Mister* struck a responsive chord and amassed a deserved 734-performance run.

Rodgers and Hammerstein struck out with their next offering, *Allegro* (1947). The show probably wasn't as bad as critics thought, but they and the public expected more after *Carousel.* Lisa Kirk scored big with her rendition of "The Gentleman Is a Dope."

The songwriting team redeemed their reputation with a huge hit, *South Pacific* (1949). Mary Martin, Ezio Pinza, Juanita Hall, William Tabbert, and the supporting company were given the opportunity to introduce such songs as "Dites-moi," "A Cockeyed Optimist," "Happy Talk," "I'm Gonna Wash That Man Right Outa My Hair," "Some Enchanted Evening," "There Is Nothin' Like a Dame," " A Wonderful Guy," and "Younger Than Springtime." Under Joshua Logan's direction, the show was an immense hit, erasing the memory of the less-than-successful *Allegro.*

Rodgers and Hammerstein's next production at the Majestic was another disappointment. *Me and Juliet* (1953) opened with Isabel Bigley, Mark Dawson, Bill Hayes, and Joan McCracken in the leads. The show made money, but critics considered it uninspired. "No Other Love" was the only hit tune in the otherwise second-rate score.

Shirley Booth was the star of *By the Beautiful Sea* (1954), along with Wilbur Evans, Mae Barnes, Cameron Prud'homme, and Libi Staiger. The show's score by Arthur Schwartz and Dorothy Fields didn't set off any fireworks though it was entertaining and tuneful.

An even bigger hit was David Merrick's production of *Fanny* (1954) with wonderful songs by Harold Rome. Ezio Pinza returned to the Majestic in the show, ably supported by Walter Slezak, Florence Henderson and, also returning to the Majestic, William Tabbert. *Fanny* was not immediately a success, but with a boost from some imaginative publicity stunts by Merrick and his press agent Richard Maney, the show became a hit.

Next came Meredith Willson's masterwork, *The Music Man* (1957) with Robert Preston, Barbara Cook, Pert Kelton, Eddie Hodges, and David Burns. *The Music Man* accurately pictured the naive America of 1912. Later shows that attempted to cover the same territory often proved too treacly or condescending to their subjects.

In *Camelot* (1960) Alan Jay Lerner and Frederick Loewe nearly equaled the brilliant score of *My Fair Lady*, and director Moss Hart gave the proceedings his usual polish. Julie Andrews was also a success, as was Richard Burton in his musical comedy debut.

A series of failures followed *Camelot*. These included Judy Holliday's return to Broadway in *Hot Spot* (1963); Mary Martin in the Dietz and Schwartz musical *Jennie* (1963) and Arthur Laurents and Stephen Sondheim's *Anyone Can Whistle* (1964) with Angela Lansbury, Lee Remick, and Harry Guardino.

Sammy Davis Jr. starred in a musical version of the Clifford Odets drama *Golden Boy* (1964). It boasted an impressive score by Charles Strouse and Lee Adams and a mostly successful book by Odets and William Gibson.

A quick failure was a musical version of *The Teahouse of the August Moon* entitled *Lovely Ladies, Kind Gentlemen* (1970). David Merrick's production of Jule Styne and Bob Merrill's musical version of *Some Like It Hot*, called *Sugar* (1972), starred Tony Roberts, Cyril Ritchard, and Robert Morse. Gower Champion directed.

Jerry Herman's musical set in the silent film era, *Mack and Mabel* (1974), starred Bernadette Peters and, returning to the Majestic, Robert Preston. The all black musical version of *The Wizard of Oz* entitled *The Wiz* (1975) was supposed to be a quick flop, but it caught on with audiences and was a tremendous hit.

John Kander and Fred Ebb wrote the Liza Minnelli vehicle, *The Act* (1977). It didn't catch on with audiences or critics. *Ballroom* (1978) was Michael Bennett's first musical following the remarkable success of *A Chorus Line,* but the material was third rate and even Bennett couldn't make *Ballroom* come alive.

It was fitting that Richard Rodgers' last show, a musical version of *I Remember Mama* (1979), opened at the Majestic where he had enjoyed some of his greatest successes. However, *I Remember Mama,* starring Liv Ullmann, was a quick failure.

In 1981, David Merrick's *42nd Street* moved to the Majestic from the Winter Garden Theater, and it remained there until 1987 when it moved across the street to the St. James Theatre.

42nd Street was forced to move so that the Majestic could be made ready for what is its most financially successful show, *The Phantom of the Opera* (1988). The Andrew Lloyd Webber musical was an enormous hit in London and prior to opening on Broadway had almost $20 million in advance sales.

MANHATTAN THEATER · See ED SULLIVAN THEATRE.

MANSFIELD THEATER · See BROOKS ATKINSON THEATER.

MARK HELLINGER THEATER · 237 W. 51st Street. Architect: Thomas Lamb. Opening: Hollywood Theater, April 22, 1930, *Hold Everything* (movie): legitimate theater, December 13, 1934, *Calling All Stars*. The 1,600-seat Mark Hellinger is one of Broadway's most beautiful theaters and the last surviving Times Square movie palace. Thomas Lamb, designer of the theater was one of the greatest theater architects, responsible for such other former Times Square landmarks as the Strand, Rialto, and Rivoli. The spectacular interior was designed by Lamb and Leif Neandross, chief designer of the Rambusch Decorating Studios.

Originally called the Hollywood, the theater was one of the last of the great movie houses built in America. The Depression, which hurt both the movie business and Broadway, brought theater construction to a standstill. In fact, the outer lobby of the Hollywood was built to support a much taller building, but the Depression forced the abandonment of that idea. It wasn't until the mid-1980s that the building, which originally housed the outer lobby, had a building built over it. The Novotel Hotel occupies the site.

The Hollywood, which originally had its entrance on Broadway, began in 1930 as a flagship house for its owners, Warner Brothers. Four years later it housed its first legitimate production, *Calling All Stars*. Lyricist Lew Brown produced the show and contributed lyrics to Harry Akst's tunes. Brown also wrote sketches and codirected the show, which starred Judy Canova, Lou Holtz, Jack Whiting, Martha Raye, Gertrude Niesen, and Phil Baker. *Calling All Stars* lasted only thirty-five performances, and the theater reverted to showing movies.

Two years later, on October 28, 1936, the theater was renamed the 51st Street Theater and for a time the theater's entrance was on 51st Street. The new entrance boasted an art deco design inspired by Frank Lloyd Wright. George Abbott's musical adaptation of *Uncle Tom's Cabin,* entitled *Sweet River,* opened in the renamed house but closed after only five performances.

The theater's name reverted to the Hollywood on August 11, 1937, and beginning with *The Life of Emile Zola,* movies were again presented in the ornate auditorium.

In November 1939, the last of the *George White's Scandals* moved from the Alvin Theater to finish its run here. The theater again became the 51st Street Theater with what everyone thought was a surefire hit—Laurence Olivier's production of Shakespeare's *Romeo and Juliet* (1940). The audience was enthusiastic when the curtain rose, but by the end of the evening it was clear the production was not a success. The show featured Olivier's design and direction as well as a star turn as Romeo. Vivien Leigh as Juliet, Dame May Whitty, Edmond O'Brien, Wesley Addy, Cornel Wilde, and Halliwell Hobbes supported him.

The theater again presented motion pictures under its alternate name, the Hollywood. A new musical, *Banjo Eyes* (1941) starred Eddie Cantor as the title character with Audrey Christie,

June Clyde, Lionel Stander, and Bill Johnson in supporting roles. Jacqueline Susann, who later went on to become a best-selling novelist, also appeared in the cast. The show, a musical version of *Three Men on a Horse,* boasted a score by Vernon Duke and John Latouche. The hit song, "We're Having a Baby, My Baby and Me," had lyrics by Harold Adamson.

The theater again reverted to movies. On August 15, 1947, while the film version of *Life with Father* was filling the seats, it was renamed the Warner Brothers Theater.

The theater's name was changed again when Anthony B. Farrell bought it from Warner Brothers for over $1.5 million. Farrell renamed the theater after Broadway columnist Mark Hellinger, who had died on December 21, 1947. His first production at the theater was *All for Love* (1949), a revue starring Grace and Paul Hartman and Bert Wheeler. It lost half a million dollars.

Farrell booked the theater for a while at the end of 1949 with Gilbert and Sullivan. He then mounted his second show, a musical called *Texas Li'l Darlin'* (1949). The musical starred Kenny Delmar, Mary Hatcher, Danny Scholl, and Loring Smith. The score by Robert Emmett Dolan and Johnny Mercer was minor but fun. Surprisingly, the show was a hit, the first for the theater since its opening almost twenty years before.

The success of *Texas Li'l Darlin'* seemed to reverse the theater's fortunes. Despite the lukewarm reception accorded the Hartmans in *All for Love,* they had a hit with the revue *Tickets, Please!,* which moved from the Coronet Theater. Jack Albertson, Larry Kert, Roger Price, and Dorothy Jarnac appeared with the Hartmans. Another revue, *Bless You All* (1950), had a score by Harold Rome and featured Pearl Bailey, Jules Munshin, Mary McCarty, and Gene Barry.

The theater's next hit, *Two on the Aisle* (1951), headlined Bert Lahr and Dolores Gray. The revue marked the first collaboration between composer Jule Styne and lyricists Betty Comden and Adolph Green. *Two on the Aisle* contained many fine revue songs, including "If

You Hadn't But You Did" and "Give a Little, Get a Little Love."

Hazel Flagg (1953), a new Jule Styne musical, had lyrics by Bob Hilliard and a libretto by Ben Hecht based on his screenplay *Nothing Sacred.* Styne produced the show himself and Helen Gallagher, John Howard, Thomas Mitchell, and Sheree North starred. Jack Whiting made a comeback of sorts as the mayor of New York.

The Girl in Pink Tights (1954), Sigmund Romberg's last Broadway show, was posthumously produced at the Mark Hellinger. It proved a surprisingly successful cap to an amazing career. Don Walker adapted Romberg's melodies and sketches into songs that were set to lyrics by Leo Robin.

The next original musical to play the Mark Hellinger was *Plain and Fancy* (1955), which had an Amish setting. The show opened with Barbara Cook, Nancy Andrews, Shirl Conway, David Daniels, and Richard Derr starring. The Albert Hague and Arnold B. Horwitt score contained a bona fide hit, "Young and Foolish," as well as a host of other good songs.

The next offering at the Mark Hellinger was one of the greatest Broadway shows of all time. *My Fair Lady* (1956) opened with Julie Andrews, Rex Harrison, Robert Coote, Stanley Holloway, John Michael King and Cathleen Nesbitt starring. Alan Jay Lerner provided the witty, sophisticated lyrics and libretto, and Frederick Loewe provided the enchanting music. Moss Hart directed and Herman Levin produced. *My Fair Lady* became the longest-running show in Broadway history, a record it held for over a decade.

After a seven-month stay by Rodgers and Hammerstein's last show, *The Sound of Music,* an Italian musical, *Rugantino* (1964), opened at the Mark Hellinger. One of producer Alexander Cohen's most misbegotten ventures, *Rugantino* played in the original Italian with subtitles. The show was one of the most expensive flops at the time although actually not a bad show.

Jule Styne, Betty Comden and Adolph Green returned to the Mark Hellinger with their gentle satire of Hollywood, *Fade Out-Fade In* (1964). The Carol Burnett vehicle opened to mostly favorable reviews and settled in for a projected long run. But problems between Burnett and the creative staff after opening led to a premature closing.

On a Clear Day You Can See Forever (1965) boasted a superior score by Burton Lane and Alan Jay Lerner. There were also exceptional performances by Barbara Harris and John Cullum. Lerner's libretto, however, didn't work well, and it brought down the proceedings.

Three musicals opened and closed at the Mark Hellinger without much success: *A Joyful Noise* (1966) with John Raitt, Susan Watson, and Karen Morrow and with Michael Bennett's choreography; *Illya Darling* (1967), based on the hit film *Never on Sunday* with the film's star Melina Mercouri and director Jules Dassin; and *I'm Solomon* (1968) with Dick Shawn and Karen Morrow in the leads.

Jerry Herman followed his string of hits— *Milk and Honey, Hello, Dolly!* and *Mame* with a failure, *Dear World* (1969). Based on Jean Giraudoux's play *The Madwoman of Chaillot,* the Alexander Cohen production featured the stars of *Mame,* Angela Lansbury and Jane Connell, as well as Milo O'Shea, Kurt Peterson, and Miguel Godreau.

Alan Jay Lerner had another show open at the Mark Hellinger, *Coco* (1969), based on the life of designer Coco Chanel. Andre Previn provided the music for the under appreciated score. The show's draw was its star, Katharine Hepburn, making her musical comedy debut.

After a horrible attempt to convert the book and movie *Exodus* to a Broadway musical entitled *Ari* (1971) and a visit by *Man of La Mancha,* came a big hit, *Jesus Christ Superstar* (1971). The production, which was Andrew Lloyd Webber and Tim Rice's first Broadway hit, was a rock musical based on the life of Christ. The director of *Hair,* Tom O'Horgan, repeated his somewhat unconventional style of staging with this show. Jeff Fenholt starred as Jesus and future Broadway star Ben Vereen made an impression as Judas.

After a potpourri of offerings, the Hellinger hosted another Alan Jay Lerner show, the much-awaited *1600 Pennsylvania Avenue* (1976), written in collaboration with Leonard Bernstein. The show followed the staffs and families who inhabited the White House in its early years. The Bicentennial tribute was a tremendous flop despite an under-appreciated score.

More failures followed at the Mark Hellinger: a reworking of *Kismet* entitled *Timbuktu!* (1978), starring Eartha Kitt; Alexis Smith in *Platinum* (1978); the Brazilian inspired musical *Sarava* (1979), produced by Eugene V. Wolsk with music by Mitch Leigh; and Clark Gesner's musical comedy *The Utter Glory of Morrisey Hall* (1979) starring Celeste Holm, which closed on opening night.

Finally, another success opened at the theater; the raucous, exuberant salute to burlesque *Sugar Babies* (1979) had movie greats Ann Miller and Mickey Rooney in the leads. Producers Terry Allen Kramer and Harry Rigby and Ralph Allen, the show's conceiver, put together the best of burlesque and made sure that director Rudy Tronto and the entire creative staff presented the hoary old burlesque bits in a classy, imaginative setting.

Doug Henning, a superior magician, had achieved success in his first Broadway musical, *The Magic Show.* He tried to repeat his success with *Merlin* (1983) that costarred Chita Rivera, but he couldn't transform the material into a hit.

Ben Vereen returned to the Mark Hellinger in *Grind* (1985). The show opened with a score by Larry Grossman and Ellen Fitzhugh. Harold Prince directed the proceedings. A musical revue, *Tango Argentino* (1985), followed *Grind.* The show featured seven pairs of tango dancers, four singers and a band.

A series of one-man shows and industrial bookings followed at the Mark Hellinger. Peter Allen's musical *Legs Diamond* was the last legitimate show to play the theater. Following that failure, the theater was leased for five years to the same church that occupied the Nederlander Theater. Over the objections of many in the Broadway community, the theater was sold to the church. Despite repeated attempts to buy the church the theater remains a church.

MARQUIS THEATER · Marriott Marquis Hotel. Broadway between 45th and 46th Street. Architect: John C. Portman. Opening: July 9, 1986. The Marquis Theater was built in the new Marriott Marquis Hotel, one of the most controversial buildings in Times Square history. The hotel took the place of the Morosco Bijou and Helen Hayes theaters and The Astor and Victoria movie theaters. The Broadway community did not think the trade was worth it.

The problems with the 1,600-seat theater are not in the plain, unadorned auditorium design but in the theatergoing experience. The box office is located in an especially cramped little room. Patrons must exit the box office area and go outside again to enter the escalator to the theater proper. The escalator empties to an especially cramped hallway that creates a dangerous situation on the up escalator. The theater has no real lobby of its own; instead, the hotel's common area is used as the theater lobby. This is a problem at intermission when patrons want to use the rest rooms. Since there are none reserved for theater patrons, audience members must use the hotel's rest rooms and make sure they have kept their ticket stubs in order to reenter the auditorium. The down escalator is also so poorly designed that it requires the supervision of a guard. Patrons tend to bunch up at the bottom of the escalator, and so the audience is allowed access to the escalator only in small groups.

Designers and theater technicians lambaste the theater because it contains no freight elevator. All sets must be designed to be able to fit in the small elevators of the hotel. The theater has also proved terribly uncomfortable for its performers. When first opened, the stage area was sometimes so cold that the cast could actually see their breath. The hotel and theater share heating and ventilation systems. The Marriott corporation spent about $500,000 to give the theater its own heating, ventilation, and plumbing systems. The systems were also overhauled because of noxious fumes that were seeping into the backstage areas, causing nausea and dizziness. Among the causes for the fumes was an exterior vent for the sewer system, which was located only thirty feet from the theater's air intake. Ten drains in the floor of the theater were spewing sewage, which had backed up through the system.

The theater's design maddened Broadway professionals who noted no such problems in the Helen Hayes or Morosco theaters. They pointed to the problems as another result of uncaring developers who tear down excellent historic theaters and replace them with un-wieldy auditoriums with poor design.

The theater, run by the Nederlander Organization, opened with a concert by Shirley Bassey and comedian George Kirby. After that dry run its first production, *Me and My Girl,* opened on August 10, 1986. The show was a smash in London and repeated its success in this country with its London star, Robert Lindsay.

After the failure of *Shogun: The Musical* (1990) came a heralded revival of *Gypsy* (1991) starring Tyne Daly. More failures followed including the musicals *Nick and Nora* (1991), *The Goodbye Girl* (1993), and *Victor/Victoria* (1995). The latter marked Julie Andrews' return to the theater. Paul Simon's *The Capeman* (1998) was a noted flop despite a fine score. The 1999 revival of *Annie Get Your Gun* with Bernadette Peters was reviled by critics and audiences though Peters' replacement, Reba McEntire, made a decided splash with the critics. Continuing the Marquis' flop parade was *Thoroughly Modern Millie* (2002), a revival of *La Cage Aux Folles* (2004), and Andrew Lloyd Webber's *The Woman in White* (2005).

Finally, in 2006, the theater appeared to have a hit, the delightful musical comedy *The Drowsy Chaperone.* The production received excellent reviews, especially for its star and coauthor, Bob Martin.

The Marquis' auditorium is successful in most respects, but the inconvenient aspects of the theater's construction and the destruction of the Helen Hayes, Bijou, Astor, Victoria, and Morosco theaters still rankle many concerned theatergoers.

MARTIN, MARY (1913–1990) · Mary Martin and Ethel Merman—the two queens of the American musical theater—reflect two very different styles of singing and acting. Whereas Merman was a brassy siren, Martin portrayed a series of sly, sexy women with a tomboyish enthusiasm and spirit.

Martin was born in Weatherford, Texas on December 1, 1913. There she acquired her well-known accent. Her interest in things theatrical seemed always to be with her. At the age of five, she made her stage debut at a local fireman's ball. She took voice lessons with Helen Fouts Cahoon and sang in recital when she was twelve.

For three months in 1930, she went to Ward Belmont Finishing School in Nashville. When she returned to Weatherford and graduation from high school, she opened a dance academy. But she realized she was too inexperienced to teach and went to Hollywood to attend the Fanchon and Marco School of the Theatre. When she graduated, she returned to Texas and soon there were three branches of the Mary Hagman School of the Dance (she had married Benjamin Jackson Hagman while in Tennessee).

The next summer she went back to the Fanchon and Marco school for more training. She went to Hollywood and dubbed numbers for Margaret Sullavan and Gypsy Rose Lee. Universal hired her to coach Danielle Darrieux in singing and dancing, but the French star had her fired after Martin demonstrated a number for the film crew.

Martin arranged an audition for the Trocadero nightclub during the club's weekly Sunday night talent show. The popular radio comedian Jack Benny was in the audience, and he was bowled over by the singer's interpretation of Arditi's "Il Bacio." Benny took Martin to his table and introduced her to Broadway producer Lawrence Schwab. Schwab invited her to appear in a musical comedy that he was planning. She signed a contract, and in the time before the show was to begin rehearsals, she appeared at the Trocadero.

Schwab meanwhile canceled plans for his musical, but he introduced Martin to playwrights Bella and Samuel Spewack, Cole Porter, Sophie Tucker, Victor Moore, William Gaxton, and producer Vinton Freedley. They were all involved in the production of a new musical entitled *Leave It to Me!* (1938). Martin auditioned and was hired on the spot. She replaced singer June Knight, who had introduced "Begin the Beguine" in Porter's *Jubilee*. Knight's new husband would not let her sing "My Heart Belongs to Daddy," which proved to be the hit song of *Leave It to Me!*, and forced the actress out of the show. Martin took over the role and during the number did a modified striptease and stopped the show. *Leave It to Me!* opened at the Alvin Theater.

After its run concluded, Paramount Pictures signed Martin to a contract. She appeared in such movies as *The Great Victor Herbert, Rhythm on the River, Love Thy Neighbor, Kiss the Boys Goodbye, New York Town,* and *Happy Go Lucky*. The films, and Martin, failed to make much of a splash. Martin still owed six pictures to Paramount, when her contract was terminated.

After leaving Paramount, Martin returned to the stage in the musical *Dancing in the Streets*. The show was written by Vernon Duke, John Cecil Holm, Howard Dietz, and Matt Taylor. It closed in Boston prior to coming to Broadway.

After the disappointment of *Dancing in the Streets* came the joy of a starring role in the Kurt Weill and Ogden Nash musical *One Touch of Venus* (1943). Martin appeared in the title role, a statue of the goddess that comes to life. The script was written by S. J. Perelman with Marlene Dietrich in mind. When Dietrich dropped out, Martin replaced her. Today, Martin has a pure, wholesome image typified by the characters Maria of *The Sound of Music* and Peter Pan but in the forties she was always considered a star with a lot of sex appeal. Her comely figure and sensuous soprano voice helped make her a convincing Venus. She was given three exemplary songs,

"That's Him," "I'm a Stranger Here Myself," and "Speak Low."

Martin's next Broadway show was the musical *Lute Song* (1946) by Bernard Hanighen and Raymond Scott. The only song in the score to achieve much fame was "Mountain High, Valley Low." After a sojourn in London at the Theatre Royal, Drury Lane in Noel Coward's *Pacific 1860,* Martin toured the United States in Irving Berlin's *Annie Get Your Gun.*

Oscar Hammerstein II had seen Martin in *One Touch of Venus* and swore that he would write a show for her. He made good on his promise when he, Richard Rodgers and Joshua Logan wrote *South Pacific*. The show, in which Martin gave her most mature, serious performance, is considered the high point in her career. Rodgers and Hammerstein provided her with great songs, including "A Cockeyed Optimist," "I'm Gonna Wash that Man Right Outa My Hair," "A Wonderful Guy," and "Honey Bun." *South Pacific* (1949) opened at the Majestic Theater with a record $500,000 advance sale. After two years, Mary Martin left the Broadway company to take the show to London.

Martin's next Broadway assignment was Norman Krasna's play *Kind Sir* (1953), staged by Joshua Logan with Charles Boyer costarring. The cast also included Margalo Gillmore and Dorothy Stickney.

Kind Sir was followed by Martin's favorite role, the title character of *Peter Pan* (1954). Producer Edwin Lester hired Martin to portray the eternally youthful character in a new musical version of the J. M. Barrie classic written by two songwriting teams—Moose Charlap and Carolyn Leigh and composer Jule Styne and lyricists Betty Comden and Adolph Green. *Peter Pan* moved to Los Angeles and finally to Broadway's Winter Garden Theater. The New York engagement was planned as a dress rehearsal for a live television broadcast. Cyril Ritchard played Captain Hook and Sondra Lee played Tiger Lily. The show became a television perennial on NBC.

Martin then toured Europe in the classic comedy, *The Skin of Our Teeth* by Thornton Wilder. She brought the show to the United

States and appeared in Washington, D.C., New York, Chicago, and finally a television production. The New York premiere took place at the ANTA Theater on August 17, 1955, and played a limited run of twenty-two performances.

The Skin of Our Teeth was followed by national tours of *South Pacific* and *Annie Get Your Gun* and a one-woman show, *Music with Mary Martin.* She next appeared on Broadway in Rodgers and Hammerstein's last show as a team, *The Sound of Music* (1959). Martin opened at the Lunt-Fontanne Theater along with Theodore Bikel, Brian Davies, Kurt Kasznar, Marion Marlowe, Patricia Neway, and Lauri Peters.

Next came one of the actress' few failures, *Jennie* (1963). The musical, based on the early career of actress Laurette Taylor, had a score by Arthur Schwartz and Howard Dietz, but it never jelled, and fights among the creative staff brought on a quick demise.

In 1965 the actress played Dolly Gallagher Levi in Jerry Herman's *Hello, Dolly!* for the troops in Vietnam following a run in Tokyo. The production was then taken to Okinawa and Korea before closing. After a break, it reopened on December 2, 1965, at the Theatre Royal, Drury Lane in London.

Mary Martin opened in the Tom Jones and Harvey Schmidt musical, *I Do! I Do!* (1966). Gower Champion directed the proceedings, based on Jan de Hartog's play, *The Fourposter.* Martin's costar, and the only other performer in the show, was Robert Preston.

After *I Do! I Do!* it was widely assumed that Mary Martin would retire. Instead, she returned to the stage twice more, although the occasions were less than felicitous. *Do You Turn Somersaults?* (1978), costarring Anthony Quayle and *Legends* (1986) with Carol Channing, closed out of town.

MARTIN BECK THEATRE · See the Al Hirschfeld Theatre.

MAXINE ELLIOTT'S THEATRE · 109 W. 39th Street between Broadway and Sixth Avenue. Architect: Ben Marshall. Opening: December 30. 1908; *The Chaperon.* Actress Maxine Elliott selected Ben Marshall, an architect from Marshall and Fox of Chicago, to design a showplace theater. Marshall designed what was the most expensive theater at that time. They modeled the façade after Le Petit Trianon in Versailles. The stage house was clad in custom-molded white brick whose pattern created a lattice effect.

Elliott, a supreme beauty, was dubbed "Venus de Milo with arms." Her only drawback was her lack of great talent. However, her theater, rumored to have been built by an admiring financier, outshone its competition. The theater was among the first to have running water and carpeting. Backstage, the five tiers of dressing rooms boasted full-length mirrors, outside windows and private toilets. On the left side of the backstage was the star's dressing room, a three-room suite. Elliott's husband, Nat Goodwin, was a popular actor. He didn't seem to mind it when Lee Shubert bankrolled the theater's construction.

The theater began inauspiciously. After a string of failures, *The Passing of the Third Floor Back* (1909) by Jerome K. Jerome opened. The next success was *The Gamblers* (1910) by Charles Klein, known for his Hippodrome extravaganzas and his play *A Milk White Flag.* Jane Cowl had the lead. Edward Sheldon's play *Romance* (1913) starred Doris Keane. Part of its fame was due to Sheldon's plot, which concerned a preacher who was attracted to a loose woman. Audiences were relieved that the parson retained his composure throughout. Only nine years later, with the opening of *Rain,* audiences would be entranced by a minister who loses the battle for his virtue.

Musicals also occasionally occupied the Maxine Elliott's stage. Cole Porter's first attempt at Broadway, *See America First* (1916), was unappreciated. In the cast was future movie star Clifton Webb, then a popular musical comedy performer.

Spanish Love (1920) by Avery Hopwood and Mary Roberts Rinehart was the first hit of the twenties. It set the stage for the theater's biggest hit, Jeanne Eagels in *Rain* (1922).

Noel Coward's *Hay Fever* (1925), about an infuriating but fascinating family led by a grand actress, was later constantly revived throughout the world, but it was a failure at its Broadway debut. Another English playwright, Somerset Maugham, saw a near classic premiere at the theater, *The Constant Wife* (1926).

Helen Hayes had a great success (later repeated in the movies) with *Coquette* (1927). The Group Theater featured Lew Ayres in *Success Story* (1932) at the Maxine Elliott's.

The last two successes at the theater were Lillian Hellman's *The Children's Hour* (1934) and the drama *Separate Rooms* (1940). In 1936 the Shuberts leased the theater to the Federal Theatre Workshop.

In 1941, the Mutual Radio Network took over the theater for WOR. In 1944, CBS brought its radio operations to the theater. CBS then transformed the theater into a television studio where the first few years of the Ed Sullivan show, *The Toast of the Town* was presented.

In 1959, the theater was torn down to make room for a skyscraper.

MAYFAIR THEATER · See CENTURY THEATER.

MERMAN, ETHEL (1909–1984) · Ethel Merman and Mary Martin are considered the two greatest actresses in the history of the American musical theater. Merman was the more boisterous of the two women. Whereas Martin was a sexy tomboy, Merman was an up front, no nonsense dame.

Merman was the favorite of such songwriters as Cole Porter, Irving Berlin, and George and Ira Gershwin. Her trademark voice was known for its strength and clarity.

She appeared in many of the greatest shows in musical comedy history, chief among them *Gypsy* and *Annie Get Your Gun*. She introduced such standards as "It's Delovely," "I Got Rhythm," "I Get a Kick Out of You," "Everything's Coming Up Roses," "There's No Business Like Show Business," "Life Is Just a Bowl Cherries."

She claimed she was born in 1912. Musical theater historian Stanley Green puts her birth at January 16, 1909. Biographer Bob Thomas claims she was born a year earlier. Whenever, she was born Ethel Zimmerman in Queens, New York, and was discovered by talent agent Lou Irwin when she performed in a club called Little Russia on 57th Street. Irwin arranged for her to be signed by Warner Brothers, which in 1929 was trying to conquer the new sound pictures. Warner Brothers signed her at $200 per week but couldn't quite figure out what to do with her. Her contract was not renewed after its six-month period.

Producer Vinton Freedley heard Merman sing during an engagement at the Brooklyn Paramount. He arranged for Merman to meet composer George Gershwin at the composer's apartment at 33 Riverside Drive. George was joined with his brother Ira. Merman sang "Little White Lies" and "Exactly Like You" and impressed the two songwriters. They in turn performed two of the songs they had written for their new show, *Girl Crazy*.

Freedley and his partner Alex Aarons were producing *Girl Crazy* (1930) at their Alvin Theater. They offered Merman a contract at $375 per week. While she rehearsed *Girl Crazy* she was booked by Irwin into the Palace Theater.

The critics' enthusiasm over her Palace engagement prepared them for Merman's musical comedy debut. *Girl Crazy* opened with Willie Howard, Ginger Rogers, and a band including Glenn Miller, Jack Teagarden, Benny Goodman, Gene Krupa, Red Nichols, and Jimmy Dorsey. Merman was introduced singing "Sam and Delilah." In her next spot she nailed her stardom with a performance of "I Got Rhythm."

After *Girl Crazy* closed, Merman was booked into several clubs and a return to the Palace. George White was trying out his latest edition of his *Scandals* in Atlantic City. He wired Merman to come and join the faltering show, and she agreed. White paid Aarons and Freedley $25,000 for Merman's services, since they had an option on her next show. The amount was well spent. Merman's talents inspired songwriters Lew Brown and Ray Henderson to come up with one of their most enduring standards, "Life Is Just a Bowl of Cherries." The *Scandals* opened at the Apollo Theatre on 42nd Street on September 14, 1931. Merman also sang a duet, "My Song," with Rudy Vallee, and another effective solo, "Ladies and Gentlemen, That's Love."

After more club appearances and another run at the Palace, Merman went into a new musical, *Humpty Dumpty*. Nacio Herb Brown, Richard Whiting ,and B. G. DeSylva were the composers. *Humpty Dumpty* was in trouble on the road, and the show closed in Pittsburgh. The show was reworked and opened on Broadway as *Take a Chance* (1932). Merman was given the hit tune "Eadie Was a Lady," "I Got Religion," Vincent Youman's "Rise and Shine" and a big hit, "You're an Old Smoothie," in a duet with Jack Haley.

Merman's next success also started out with a shaky out-of-town tryout. Cole Porter's *Anything Goes* originally had a book about a group of shipwrecked passengers. However, the real-life burning of the *Morro Castle* with 134 lives lost made the P. G. Wodehouse and Guy Bolton libretto impossible to produce. Producer Vinton Freedley approached Howard Lindsay and Russel Crouse to rewrite the libretto and keep the passengers safely on board their ship.

Anything Goes (1934) was produced in the days before Xerox machines. Performers received only their "sides," just the scenes they were in. The script was painstakingly typed with carbon copies. With changes in the script arriving daily, Merman's experience as a secretary came in handy. She copied down the changes in shorthand and typed up the corrections for herself and her fellow actors.

The opening night at the Alvin Theater was a smash success. Porter had provided a brilliant score with many standards, including "I Get a Kick Out of You," "All Through the Night," "Blow, Gabriel, Blow," "You're the Top," and the title tune. The role of Reno Sweeney gave Merman her first opportunity to create a classic musical comedy character.

Merman spent another unsatisfying stint in Hollywood. She returned to Broadway to appear in *Red, Hot and Blue!* (1936), another hit show with a score by Porter. Merman, Jimmy Durante, and Bob Hope sang such terrific Porter numbers as "Down in the Depths," "Ridin' High," and "It's Delovely."

Arthur Schwartz and Dorothy Fields gave Merman her next Broadway assignment *Stars in Your Eyes* (1939. Jimmy Durante, Mary Wickes, Richard Carlson, Tamara Toumanova, and Mildred Natwick joined Merman.

Du Barry Was a Lady (1939) was the singer's next Broadway outing. Cole Porter supplied the lively score, and La Merm, as she was dubbed, was ably supported by costars Bert Lahr and the young Betty Grable. B. G. DeSylva produced and collaborated on the libretto with Herbert Fields, and the fine and funny Porter score boasted at least one standard, "Friendship."

DeSylva convinced Merman and Porter to reteam for *Panama Hattie* (1940), her first solo starring role. *Panama Hattie* opened at the 46th Street Theatre with Betty Hutton, Oscar ("Rags") Ragland, Joan Carroll and Arthur Treacher in supporting roles.

Porter was also the songwriter on Merman's next show, *Something for the Boys* (1943). Herbert and Dorothy Fields wrote the script, which at one point was titled *Jenny Get Your Gun*. The producer of *Something for the Boys* was the extraordinary showman, Michael Todd.

Annie Get Your Gun (1946), produced by Rodgers and Hammerstein, opened with an exceptional score by Irving Berlin. The show was an immediate smash hit. Berlin gave Merman a cornucopia of great songs. She introduced no less than five standards in *Annie Get Your Gun*: "They Say It's Wonderful," "I Got the Sun in the Morning," "Doin' What Comes Natur'lly," "There's No Business Like Show Business," and "You Can't Get a Man with a Gun."

Berlin was also responsible for the score of her next show, *Call Me Madam* (1950). Lindsay and Crouse wrote the script, which was based loosely on the career of hostess Perle Mesta. *Call Me Madam* presented Merman as still more of a lady, in fact ambassador to the mythical country of Lichtenburg. The show cost $225,000 to produce. The entire amount was covered by RCA, which bought the rights to the original-cast album. *Call Me Madam* was in trouble while out of town, and changes were added daily until Merman announced, as she did before every show, that it was frozen. From then on, nothing could be changed. When she announced "Call me Miss Birdseye" (an allusion to the show being frozen like Birdseye foods), the authors and director knew that no amount of cajoling could change her mind.

Lindsay and Crouse also wrote the script to her next Broadway show, *Happy Hunting* (1956). The show was not a happy experience for any of the creative staff. Though the score by newcomers Harold Karr and Matt Dubey did contain one hit, "Mutual Admiration Society," there was little else of interest, and Lindsay and Crouse's book was creaky.

Merman's last Broadway appearance in an original musical was also her greatest triumph. *Gypsy* (1959), with a score by Stephen Sondheim and Jule Styne and libretto by Arthur Laurents, was the musical story of Gypsy Rose Lee and her sister June Havoc's adventures in vaudeville and burlesque and starred Merman as the ultimate stage mother, Rose. Styne and Sondheim provided Merman with great songs: "Everything's Comin' Up Roses," "Small World," "Together, Wherever We Go," and "You'll Never Get Away from Me." But the greatest of all and the triumphant apex of Merman's career in musical theater was "Rose's Turn."

In 1966, at the age of fifty-eight, Merman returned to New York to appear as Annie Oakley in a revival of *Annie Get Your Gun* for the Music Theatre of Lincoln Center. Merman's last Broadway appearance came in Jerry Herman's *Hello, Dolly!* The show was originally written for Merman who vowed after *Gypsy* that she would never appear in another original musical on Broadway. She was the last in a long string of Dolly's when she assumed the part in March 1970. Russell Nype, who appeared with Merman in *Call Me Madam* on Broadway and in 1966, 1968, and 1969 in small theaters across

the country, costarred in *Dolly*. On December 27, 1970 the curtain fell for the last time on *Hello, Dolly!* And on the Broadway career of Ethel Merman.

Ethel Merman died on February 15, 1984.

MERRICK, DAVID (1911–2000) · Peter Ustinov called him the greatest producer of the twentieth century. Others have called him the "abominable showman." But whether they love him or hate him, all agree that David Merrick was the most fabulous showman of our time, and maybe of all time. No other producer, not Florenz Ziegfeld nor the Shubert brothers, has matched his percentage of hits or his flair for publicity.

Merrick maintained an aura of mystery about his beginnings. He told a press-agent friend that he was born in 1946, the year he began his Broadway career. A decade later, he claimed he was born on November 4, 1954, the day his first big hit, Harold Rome's musical *Fanny*, opened. We do know that he was born in St. Louis, the son of Celia and Samuel Margoulis. They divorced when he was ten. He graduated with a law degree from St. Louis University, whereupon he made his way to New York. His arrival in 1940 was greeted with little fanfare, and for a while Merrick was unsure of how to proceed with his theatrical plans.

He looked up producer Herman Shumlin, who was then raising money for *The Male Animal*. Merrick invested $5,000, and the success of the play returned to Merrick $20,000 and a place on Shumlin's staff.

Merrick learned about the theater by working as Shumlin's assistant and later as a stage manager of Broadway shows on the road. He waited until it was the right time to break out on his own.

His love-hate relationship with the press began with *Clutterbuck* (1949). The play received less-than-enthusiastic reviews from the critics, so Merrick conceived of a series of stunts to draw public attention to the show.

Merrick's pet project was a musicalization of the Marcel Pagnol trilogy, *Marius, Fanny,* and *Cesar.* He amassed a preproduction fund from one of Herman Shumlin's assistants, and he even threw in a little money of his own. At this time, he didn't own the rights nor had he a script or score or anything but the will to make it happen.

Fanny's (1954) opening might have meant the beginning of his life to Merrick, but the critics were less than inspired. Their reviews were apathetic, and there wasn't a line at the box office window the next morning. But Merrick didn't take his defeat lying down. Just as with *Clutterbuck,* Merrick took his fight to the media.

He allowed scenes from *Fanny* to appear on "The Ed Sullivan Show." He took out the first full-page theatrical ads in the *New York Times* and the *Tribune.* He took out ads in foreign papers, hoping that tourists would see *Fanny* when they came to this country. If they came by ocean liner, they saw ads for *Fanny.* If they came via another city by train, they saw a giant billboard in Penn Station. When they alighted, they were reminded of the show again when they hailed a taxi. He put ads in over forty American cities. When *Fanny* finally closed, the ledger books showed a handsome profit of almost a million dollars.

Merrick often had highly publicized fights with his stars. During the run of *Carnival!* (1961), Anna Maria Alberghetti had a long-running feud with Merrick. After exiting the stage at one performance, her body mike was left on while she went to the ladies' room. It was shortly after this "accident" that Alberghetti came down with a mysterious malady that prevented her from performing unless her weekly check was increased. Merrick refused to be blackmailed and instead sent Alberghetti a lovely bouquet of plastic flowers. He then fired his star and built an enormous publicity campaign around her understudy, Anita Gillette. Merrick went so far as to invite the critics to Gillette's opening night. When the show was ready to tour, Anna Maria Alberghetti's sister Carla got the part.

But all these stories pale beside the saga of *42nd Street.* Merrick's hit best illustrates his luck, charm, and savvy. Based on Warner Brothers' classic 1932 musical, *42nd Street* (1980), the show was planned as the most opulent musical on any stage. Merrick chose as director Gower Champion, the man who delivered Merrick's greatest hit *Hello, Dolly! Dolly's* book writer, Michael Stewart, was brought on the project with newcomer Mark Bramble. The score was the same as that used for the movie, with other Harry Warren/Al Dubin hits added.

While on the road at the John F. Kennedy Center in Washington, D.C., the show was clearly in trouble. It ran about an hour too long. The costumes were late to arrive at the opening night performance and when they did finally show up they were judged unbelievably ugly. Merrick's backers balked at putting more money into what was clearly a bomb. Merrick had been away from theater production during a five-year sojourn in Hollywood and the talk along the Rialto was that the master had lost his touch. To top it all off, director/choreographer Champion came down with what was reported as a bad case of the flu.

Unable to raise more money through his investors, Merrick came up with an unheard of plan; he bought each investor out, saving the investors from certainly losing everything when the show finally reached New York. Merrick then proceeded to whip the show into shape. He threw out all the costumes and ordered a completely new set. By the time the show reached the Winter Garden Theater, it had been totally renovated. The book was reduced to "lead ins and crossovers" according to the program. Champion had been in and out of hospitals and hadn't been seen near the theater for several days.

At the end of the opening-night performance in New York, the audience gave the production a standing ovation. The critics had been asked to stay in their seats following the show, and the local television news teams were asked to send video crews and correspondents. Immediately after the curtain call, Merrick strode on stage amidst thunderous applause. He quieted the audience and announced the death that afternoon of Gower Champion. The resulting publicity catapulted *42nd Street* into legendary status.

The momentum that *42nd Street* gained on opening night, plus later publicity and good word-of-mouth kept the show running for over three thousand performances. *Variety* carried a headline reading, "David Merrick Hits a B'way Homer. 42nd Street Owner Grosses 500G Per Week." This $500,000 was pure profit for Merrick.

Merrick was later in the news when he suffered a near-fatal stroke. While he was in the hospital, Merrick's current wife and his former wife were locked in a battle over the management of his estate. In a two-week whirlwind of legal wrangling and its resultant publicity, Merrick divorced his then-current wife and remarried his previous wife. He appeared in court to prove himself competent to manage his own affairs, and to cap it all off, he escaped the hospital in a wheelchair, racing down First Avenue before being caught.

From his first productions through his triumphal return to Broadway, Merrick infuriated, amused, and astounded his public for almost fifty years. The David Merrick story is rich with fact and fiction, and it's anyone's guess as to where to draw the line. Whatever Merrick touched became news; each of his productions had its own story, which is also a reflection of the change in the theater since World War II.

A partial list of Merrick productions includes *The Willow and I* (1942); *Bright Boy* (1944); *Fanny* (1954); *The Matchmaker* (1955); *Look Back in Anger* (1957); *Romanoff and Juliet* (1957); *Jamaica* (1957); *The Entertainer* (1958); *The World of Suzie Wong* (1958); *Epitaph for George Dillon* (1958); *Maria Golovin* (1958); *La Plume de Ma Tante* (1958); *Destry Rides Again* (1959); *Gypsy* (1959); and *Take Me Along* (1959).

In the sixties, Merrick produced *The Good Soup* (1960); *Vintage '60* (1960); *Irma La Douce* (1960); *A Taste of Honey* (1960); *Becket* (1960); *Do Re Mi* (1960); *Carnival!* (1961); *Ross* (1961); *Subways Are for Sleeping* (1961); *I Can Get It for You Wholesale* (1962); *Stop the*

World I Want to Get Off (1962); *Tchin-Tchin* (1962); *Oliver!* (1963); *Rattle of a Simple Man* (1963); *Luther* (1963); *110 in the Shade* (1963); *Arturo Ui* (1963); *One Flew Over the Cuckoo's Nest* (1963); *The Milk Train Doesn't Stop Here Anymore* (1964); *Hello, Dolly!* (1964); *Foxy* (1964); *Oh, What a Lovely War* (1964); *A Severed Head* (1964); *I Was Dancing* (1964); *The Roar of the Greasepaint The Smell of the Crowd* (1965); *Cactus Flower* (1965); *We Have Always Lived in the Castle* (1966); *Don't Drink the Water* (1966); *I Do! I Do!* (1966); *The Astrakhan Coat* (1967); *Rosencrantz and Guildenstern Are Dead* (1967); *How Now, Dow Jones* (1967); *The Happy Time* (1968); *Promises, Promises* (1968); *Forty Carats* (1968) and *Play It Again, Sam* (1969).

In the seventies, Merrick's productions include *Child's Play* (1970); *The Philanthropist* (1971); *Vivat! Vivat! Regina!* (1972); *Moonchildren* (1972); *Sugar* (1972); *Mack and Mabel* (1974); *The Misanthrope* (1975); and *Very Good Eddie* (1975); *42nd Street* (1980) ran for 3,486 performances.

David Merrick died on April 25, 2000.

MILLER, ARTHUR (1915–2005) · Arthur Miller, the author of such American classics as *Death of a Salesman, A View from the Bridge, All My Sons,* and *The Price,* is one of America's greatest playwrights. His serious and searching dramas probe the themes of human crises of identity and responsibility in relationships. Miller also explores the problems that arise when a person does not acknowledge change or current circumstances. Miller believes his plays are lessons for life.

Miller began his playwriting career in the early forties as the author of radio plays. His first Broadway show, *The Man Who Had All the Luck* (1944), opened at the Forrest Theater and played only four performances but certainly presaged his great talents. *All My Sons* (1947), his first Broadway hit, was soon followed by what many consider his masterpiece, *Death of a Salesman* (1949). The play, staged by Elia Kazan, starred Lee J. Cobb, and Mildred Dunnock. It won the Pulitzer Prize.

Miller's next Broadway outing was an adaptation of Ibsen's *An Enemy of the People* (1950). It was in part a reaction to the wave of McCarthyism that was just beginning to break over the country. Next came another reaction to McCarthy's witch-hunt. The subject, the Salem witch trials of 1692, seemed perfectly analogous to the American political situation in the early fifties. *The Crucible* (1953), though it played only 197 performances, has received countless revivals over the years. The solid cast included E. G. Marshall, Walter Hampden, Arthur Kennedy, Jean Adair, Madeleine Sherwood, Philip Coolidge, Beatrice Straight, and Joseph Sweeney.

Miller changed his tack with his next plays, an evening of two one-acts, *A View from the Bridge* and *A Memory of Two Mondays* (1955). They were sympathetic portrayals of two middle-class Americans. *After the Fall* (1964) was inspired by Miller's marriage to Marilyn Monroe. It was a much better play than initial reaction to it indicates. Critics and audiences could not separate the drama from their feelings about Monroe. That same year, his drama that was set against the horrors of Nazi Germany, *Incident at Vichy* (1964), opened at Lincoln Center. In *Incident at Vichy*, a Jewish psychiatrist tells Prince Von Berg that he must learn to confront his collusion with the Nazis with his own humanity, a major theme in Miller's plays.

In his next Broadway production, *The Price* (1968), Miller portrays two brothers who are joined by their lack of appreciation of each other's differences. Estranged for years, the brothers know only how to be capitalists, without love or heart to make them human. He followed it with other plays: *The Reason Why* and *Fame* (1970); *The Creation of the World and Other Business* (1972); *Up from Paradise* (1974); *The Archbishop's Ceiling* (1976); *The American Clock* (1984); and *Danger: Memory!* (1987).

Despite his lack of success on Broadway at the end of his career, Miller remained a major voice in the American theater. Although solidly rooted in the sensibilities of the forties and fifties, his plays have continued to speak to the common person's universal problems. Miller always believed in the importance of the theater in society. In 1951, he wrote that, "The stage is the place for ideas, for philosophies, for the most intense discussion of man's fate."

Arthur Miller died on February 10, 2005.

MINSKOFF THEATRE · 1515 Broadway between 44th and 45th Streets. Architects: Kahn and Jacobs. Opening: March 13, 1973; *Irene*. The Minskoff Theatre was built in the Minskoff Building on the site of the Astor Hotel. Although it contains many technical innovations, the auditorium is uncomfortable, and with 1,600 seats it is far too large for optimum viewing. The theater has no ornamentation and is considered one of the coldest looking of the new theaters.

Though the walk to the auditorium is well designed, the theater is not. The balcony overhangs too far from the front of the stage and the uppermost seats are also too distant. The orchestra area has what is called continental seating—no center aisles, only two aisles on either side of the seats. Row T, for example, is fifty-two seats wide. Patrons who have tickets in the center of the row must cross over the feet of twenty-five people to get to their seats. On a matinee day, when many audience members have shopping bags, this can be extremely difficult. In its favor, however, the Minskoff was the first New York theater to be fully accessible to handicapped patrons.

The Minskoff has not attracted many successes. Its many critics think that the audience's distance from the stage and the coldness of the theater's design may account for its lack of hits. Architecture, sight lines and acoustics all play their part in an audience's enjoyment of a show. While the theater can make a lot of money at capacity, most shows do not play to full houses. The Minskoff's shows might do better in a more intimate house where a full audience might equal half or three-quarters of the Minskoff's capacity.

The first show to play the theater, *Irene* (1973), seemed to promise a bright future for the new theater. A revival of a successful

1919 musical that originally premiered at the Vanderbilt Theater, it starred Debbie Reynolds, Patsy Kelly, Monte Markham, and George S. Irving.

A series of concerts, ballets, and flop musicals followed *Irene's* opening. *Rockabye Hamlet* (1976) was directed by the usually reliable Gower Champion. But he made a mistake with *Rockabye Hamlet*, a rock version of the Shakespeare classic.

The next original shows to play the Minskoff were *Angel* (1978), a musicalization of Ketti Frings' play, *Look Homeward Angel* that in turn was based on Thomas Wolfe's novel; *King of Hearts* (1978), based on the French film and *Got Tu Go Disco* (1979).

A revival of *West Side Story* (1980) did not pay back its investors. Another revival, *Can-Can* (1981), closed after only five performances. For one year, the theater hosted Joseph Papp's version of Gilbert and Sullivan's *The Pirates of Penzance*, which moved from the Uris Theatre, another huge, modem auditorium.

The theater's failures continued unabated. Charles Strouse and Alan Jay Lerner fell under the theater's curse with their musicalization of Robert Emmett Sherwood's *Idiot's Delight,* which they titled *Dance a Little Closer* (1983). *Marilyn: An American Fable* (1983) was a musical version of the life of Marilyn Monroe that suffered an especially long preview period and became a legendary failure. Following a revival of *Sweet Charity* with Debby Allen, *Teddy and Alice* (1987), a musical starring Len Cariou, was a huge flop. A terrific revue, *Black and Blue,* (1989) was a deserved and rare hit for the theater. More failures followed including Andrew Lloyd Webber's *Sunset Boulevard* (1994), *The Scarlet Pimpernel* (1997), *Saturday Night Fever* (1999), *The Adventures of Tom Sawyer* (2001), and *Dance of the Vampires* (2002). Finally, in 2004, the theater hosted a hit (though undeserved), a revival of *Fiddler on the Roof* starring Alfred Molina. It was followed by a transfer of the Disney production of *The Lion King*.

MOLLY PICON THEATER · See OLSON'S 59TH STREET THEATER.

MOROSCO THEATRE · 217 W. 45th Street. Architect: Herbert J. Krapp. Opening: February 5, 1917; *Canary Cottage.* The Shubert brothers built the Morosco and named it in honor of Oliver Morosco, a West Coast producer who had helped the Shubert's break Erlanger's Theatrical Trust. The Morosco enjoyed a long history of distinguished productions, including *Death of a Salesman* and *Cat on a Hot Tin Roof,* until it was destroyed to make way for the Marriott Marquis Hotel and the Marquis Theater.

Oliver Morosco's management of the theater only lasted seven years, his leaving the result of a particularly confrontational divorce. His first production in his new 1,009-seat theater was *Canary Cottage.* Earl Carroll, famous for his *Vanities,* wrote the music and lyrics and coauthored the libretto with Elmer Harris. He also produced and directed the proceedings.

Following *Canary Cottage,* the theater got onto more serious affairs. Eugene O'Neill's *Beyond the Horizon* (1920) and *The Bat* (1920) by Mary Roberts Rhinehart were early successes. The Pulitzer Prize-winning drama *Craig's Wife* (1925) was written by George Kelly, best known as the author of *The Show-Off.*

Novelist Somerset Maugham's play *The Letter* (1927) next opened at the Morosco. The *Warrior's Husband* (1932) is today best remembered as the first good look theatergoers had at the talents of Katharine Hepburn.

Alexander Woollcott tried his hand at playwriting in collaboration with George S. Kaufman. The result was *The Dark Tower* (1933). Wollcott's fellow journalists slammed the play. Woollcott took the reviews personally and was hugely depressed when the play closed. Tallulah Bankhead and Walter Pidgeon starred in *Something Gay* (1935). Bankhead herself reviewed the play. She said *Something Gay* was "as misleading a title as ever was hung on two hours of plot and dialogue." *Call It a Day* (1936) starred Gladys Cooper, Frances Williams, and Glenn Anders. The Theater Guild produced the Dodie Smith comedy. George M. Cohan was reunited for a brief time with his former producing partner Sam Harris for

Fulton of Oak Falls (1937). Cohan extensively revised radio comedian Parker Fennelly's play for himself. Cohan's acting received glorious reviews, but the critics were less tolerant of his old-fashioned writing.

Noel Coward's delightfully wry comedy *Blithe Spirit* (1941) entranced audiences with the performances of Mildred Natwick, Peggy Wood, Leonora Corbett, and Clifton Webb. One of the biggest hits in the Morosco's history was *The Voice of the Turtle* (1943). The John van Druten comedy starred Margaret Sullavan, Elliott Nugent, and Audrey Christie. Coward wrote *Blithe Spirit* in five days. Van Druten wrote his even bigger hit in three weeks.

The City Playhouses corporation bought the Morosco from the Shuberts in 1943. Arthur Miller's greatest success, and another Pulitzer Prize-winner for the Morosco, was *Death of a Salesman* (1949). Lee J. Cobb created a masterful performance as washed-up salesman Willy Loman and was ably supported by Mildred Dunnock as his long-suffering wife and Arthur Kennedy as his disillusioned, alienated son.

Another great American writer, Tennessee Williams, won a Pulitzer Prize for a play presented at the Morosco—*Cat on a Hot Tin Roof* (1955), the theatrically vibrant drama that starred Burl Ives, Mildred Dunnock, Ben Gazzara, and Barbara Bel Geddes. Elia Kazan staged the proceedings brilliantly. Ives' character of Big Daddy is one of Williams' greatest creations. Helen Hayes, Richard Burton, Susan Strasberg Glenn Anders, and Sig Arno starred in Jean Anouilh's *Time Remembered* (1957). Vernon Duke composed the incidental music for the play.

For the Morosco, the sixties was a decade of comedies, including *Generation* by William Goodhart (1965), starring Henry Fonda, and David Merrick's production of Woody Allen's *Don't Drink the Water* (1966) with Lou Jacobi, Kay Medford, Anita Gillette, Tony Roberts, and Dick Libertini.

In 1968, the theater was sold to a consortium of investors represented by the Bankers Trust Company. Arthur Miller's *The Price* (1968) proved to be an exception from the comedy roster of the sixties. It starred Pat Hingle, Kate Reid, Harold Gary, and Arthur Kennedy. *The Price* surprised and shocked audiences who were used to Broadway comedies that were more rooted in television than theater and big empty musicals with catchy title songs and little else.

Forty Carats (1968), another David Merrick production, returned comedy to the stage of the Morosco. Jay Allen adapted a French play by Pierre Barillet and Jean-Pierre Gredy. Julie Harris starred along with Marco St. John, Polly Rowles, Murray Hamilton, Glenda Farrell, and Nancy Marchand. Julie Harris returned to the Morosco in Paul Zindel's drama *And Miss Reardon Drinks a Little* (1971). The play also starred Nancy Marchand, Virginia Payne, Estelle Parsons, and Rae Allen.

Alan Bates came from London with *Butley* (1972), a play by Simon Gray. An acclaimed revival of Eugene O'Neill's *A Moon for the Misbegotten* (1973) opened at the Morosco with Jason Robards, Colleen Dewhurst, and Ed Flanders starring.

The Shadow Box (1977) was a no-nonsense drama about terminally ill patients and their families. The show boasted steady performances by Laurence Luckinbill, Mandy Patinkin, Josef Sommer, Simon Oakland, Patricia Elliott and, particularly, Geraldine Fitzgerald. *The Shadow Box* won the Pulitzer Prize.

The Theater Guild presented William Gibson's play *Golda* (1977) with Anne Bancroft in an acclaimed performance as Israeli political leader Golda Meir. A year later, Hugh Leonard's play *Da* (1978) starred Barnard Hughes, Brian Murray, and Mia Dillon. Leonard's sequel to *Da, A Life* (1980), also opened at the Morosco. It was not a success. Barnard Hughes did not appear in the play; his wife, Helen Stenborg, did. Also appearing in *A Life* was Roy Dotrice and Pat Hingle.

The Morosco was locked in a battle for survival along with the Helen Hayes and Bijou theaters. Playwright Arthur Miller wrote to James Watt, the Secretary of the Interior, to condemn the plan to destroy the theater. Miller's letter stated in part: "...I think it is the best theater in New York. The relationship of the auditorium to the stage is very nearly perfect; the height of the stage is optimum and the sight lines are superb. Perhaps most vital of all, the acoustical qualities are remarkable for their trueness. All of which is probably unique in a theater that is by no means small."

The Morosco and the people of New York lost, and in 1982, the theater was demolished.

MUSIC BOX THEATER · 239 W. 45th Street. Architect: C. Howard Crane. Opening: September 22, 1921; *Music Box Revue*. Producer Sam Harris, late of the team of Cohan and Harris, built the Music Box Theater with partner Irving Berlin at the start of the 1920s.

The Adamesque exterior was modeled after Philadelphia's Chestnut Street Theatre. The intimate interior, designed by Crane and William Baumgarten in ivory and green proved ideal for plays and small musicals.

Harris and Berlin planned a series of revues for the theater. The big draws of the Music Box Revues were the scores by Irving Berlin and an almost European stylishness and refinement.

The first edition of the *Music Box Revue* (1921) had a cast that included Sam Bernard (who said of the new theater: "It stinks of class"), the Brox Sisters, Florence Moore, Joseph Santley, Ivy Sawyer, Ethelind Terry, and Berlin himself. As planned, it was the score that received the most acclaim. Chief among the songs was "Say It with Music," one of Berlin's most enduring hits.

The second edition (1922) of the series opened with much the same creative team; Berlin writing the music and lyrics, Sam Harris producing and Hassard Short directing. This time, the cast included John Steel, William Gaxton, Charlotte Greenwood, the Fairbanks Twins, and Clark and McCullough. The songs included "Pack Up Your Sins and Go to the Devil."

The third edition (1923) proved only a little less successful than its predecessors. The cast featured a return by the Brox Sisters,

Joseph Santley, Ivy Sawyer, John Steel, and Florence Moore. Newcomers included Grace Moore, Frank Tinney, Phil Baker, and Robert Benchley. Berlin provided his usual hit score, including "What'll I Do?," "Learn to Do the Strut," "The Waltz of Long Ago" and "An Orange Grove in California."

The fourth edition (19924), the last in the series, starred Grace Moore, the Brox Sisters and the comedy team of Clark and McCullough, alongside newcomers Claire Luce, Carl Randall, Oscar Shaw ,and Tamara. The biggest star, however, was Fanny Brice, borrowed from her home in the *Ziegfeld Follies*. Berlin's big hit from the score was "All Alone." Each edition of the series had done slightly worse than the previous edition.

The first straight play to be presented in the theater was *Cradle Snatchers* (1925), a comedy by Russell Medcraft and Norma Mitchell. Another somewhat racy theme was treated in *Chicago* (1926) in which Roxie Hart shoots her lover and with the help of a lawyer who is more theatrical director than barrister gets off without a conviction for the crime. The Maurine Watkins satirical comedy starred Francine Larrimore, Charles Bickford, Edward Ellis, Dorothy Stickney, and Juliette Crosby.

Philip Barry's comedy *Paris Bound* (1927) was an aptly titled show for the Music Box, since the theater's next offering was Cole Porter's musical *Paris* (1928). *Paris* was a Roaring Twenties show whose content was summed up by the title of one of its songs, "Let's Misbehave." "Let's Misbehave" was cut out of town and replaced by the hit song of the show, the equally suggestive "Let's Do It." The star of the evening was the delightful French import Irene Bordoni.

Howard Dietz and Arthur Schwartz made history with *The Little Show* (1929). The songwriting team was warming up for their biggest triumph, *The Band Wagon*. *The Little Show* was one of the first intimate revues that proved to audiences that all the Ziegfeldian trappings were not necessary for the enjoyment of a revue.

The thirties began with *Topaze*. The next

offering was one of the great hits of the decade, George S. Kaufman and Moss Hart's *Once in a Lifetime* (1930). The comedy marked their first collaboration. The cast included Hugh O'Connell, Jean Dixon, Grant Mills, Spring Byington (as a Louella Parsons character), Charles Halton, and George S. Kaufman himself as Lawrence Vail, a playwright whose sanity is ruined by Hollywood.

The Third Little Show (1931), the last edition, opened at the Music Box with Edward Arnold, Constance Carpenter, Carl Randall, and Ernest Truex supporting the zany comedy of Beatrice Lillie. Herman Hupfeld's "When Yuba Plays the Rhumba on His Tuba" was the only original song to achieve any success. Noel Coward's "Mad Dogs and Englishmen" was introduced to American audiences in this show.

George S. Kaufman enjoyed two more hits at the Music Box in rapid succession. The first was the George and Ira Gershwin satirical musical *Of Thee I Sing* (1931). Kaufman wrote the book with Morrie Ryskind. It starred William Gaxton, June O'Dea, Louis Moran, future politician George Murphy, and Victor Moore. The musical was a tremendous success, breaking the house record for the Music Box. Further proof of the show's excellence came when Kaufman, Ryskind and Ira Gershwin were awarded the Pulitzer Prize. The award was not made to George Gershwin, because the Pulitzer Prize went only to writers of words and he had written the music. Despite this obvious gaffe, the authors appreciated the Pulitzer. After all, it was the first time the Pulitzer Prize was awarded to a musical. Before it closed, the show moved to the 46th Street Theater to make way for the next attraction at the Music Box—Kaufman and Edna Ferber's *Dinner at Eight* (1932).

Musical theater returned to the Music Box with the Irving Berlin and Moss Hart revue *As Thousands Cheer* (1933). Harris, who presented most of the plays in his theater, produced the proceedings, and Hassard Short directed. Berlin's score contained one of his biggest hits, "Easter Parade." Ethel Waters let loose with "Harlem on My Mind" and "Heat Wave."

Kaufman returned with his collaborator Moss Hart and their unconventional play *Merrily We Roll Along* (1934). The play told its story in a reverse chronology. Audiences were not so much confused by the strange construction, but they certainly did not care for any of the cynical, disillusioned characters.

Kaufman's next assignment at the Music Box was as play doctor for the Samuel and Bella Spewack drama *Spring Song* (1934) produced by Max Gordon. Unfortunately, Kaufman couldn't save the show.

Kaufman was one of Harris' favorite playwrights, and he returned to the Music Box with *First Lady* (1935), written in collaboration with Katharine Dayton.

Kaufman was also responsible for the next play at the Music Box, *Stage Door* (1936). He collaborated with Edna Ferber on the story of the performers at the Foot-Lights Club.

Kaufman directed John Steinbeck's *Of Mice and Men* (1937), the theater's next hit. The drama opened with Wallace Ford and Broderick Crawford in the leads. Kaufman worked on the script as an editor and technician. The dialogue was all by Steinbeck, who had written the original novel with the intent of turning the property into a play or film.

Kaufman and Hart's satirical musical *I'd Rather Be Right* moved from the Alvin Theater to finish its run at the Music Box. The team then turned to producing with the revue *Sing Out the News* (1938). Harold Rome wrote the music and lyrics and collaborated on the sketches with Charles Friedman, who directed the show. The cast included June Allyson, Mary Jane Walsh, Rex Ingram, Joey Faye, and Will Geer.

Noel Coward's revue *Set to Music* (1939) featured Beatrice Lillie singing such Coward songs as "I Went to a Marvelous Party" and "Mad About the Boy."

Kaufman and Hart were back at the theater with *The Man Who Came to Dinner* (1939) starring Monty Woolley as Sheridan Whiteside, a character based on Alexander Woollcott. The play was an immediate hit and made Woollcott an even bigger celebrity in the public's eyes.

When Sam Harris died in 1941, his share of the theater went to Berlin who later sold half ownership to the Shubert Brothers.

Michael Todd's production of *Star and Garter* (1942) opened at the Music Box with Gypsy Rose Lee, Bobby Clark, Pat Harrington, and Professor Lamberti. Critics were not kind to the show, which had more in common with burlesque than musical comedy, but audiences loved being able to see burlesque in the safe environs of Broadway.

I Remember Mama (1944) was one of the best-loved comedies of the forties. The play, written and directed by John Van Druten, starred Mady Christians, Oscar Homolka, Frances Heflin and, making his Broadway debut, Marlon Brando. The first-time Broadway producers were the renowned songwriting team Richard Rodgers and Oscar Hammerstein II.

Tennessee Williams' *Summer and Smoke* (1948) was not a success. One problem was that audiences had seen *A Streetcar Named Desire* the previous year and expected more of the same. Williams actually wrote *Summer and Smoke* before *Streetcar* and after *The Glass Menagerie,* to which it is very similar in tone.

Kurt Weill's *Lost in the Stars* (1949) was written with Maxwell Anderson. The Playwrights' Company produced the musical that was based on Alan Paton's novel *Cry, the Beloved Country,* which dealt with race relations in South Africa. Weill and Anderson's dramatic score was well served by Inez Matthews, Julian Mayfield, Herbert Coleman, and, the original Porgy, Todd Duncan.

William Inge had three plays open in the Music Box in quick succession. The first, *Picnic* (1953), starred Ralph Meeker and Janice Rule under Joshua Logan's sensitive direction. *Picnic* didn't please all the critics but they did agree that Inge had the makings of a major American playwright.

The critics were unanimous in acclaiming Inge's next play, *Bus Stop* (1955). They praised Inge for tempering his themes of loneliness and the longing for dreams to come true. *Bus Stop* starred Kim Stanley, Albert Salmi, Elaine Stritch, Anthony Ross, Lou Polan, and Phyl-

lis Love. Harold Clurman directed brilliantly, helping Inge make the conflicts more human and sometimes even funny.

Inge's third play was *The Dark at the Top of the Stairs* (1957). Through the story of a boy's suicide, Inge explored the unbreakable links that bind a family and the search for true freedom and tolerance. Pat Hingle and Teresa Wright starred, and Elia Kazan directed.

Claire Bloom and Rod Steiger were featured in the hit play *Rashomon* (1959) at the Music Box, and at the end of that year Peter Shaffer's first play, *Five Finger Exercise* (1959), opened at the theater with Jessica Tandy and Brian Bedford. Shaffer was hailed because of his excellent use of language as well as his incisive understanding of class, society, and sexual tensions.

Following Henry Denker's play about Sigmund Freud, *A Far Country* (1961), with Kim Stanley and Steven Hill, came S. J. Perleman's comedy, *The Beauty Part* (1962). It opened to excellent reviews, but due in part to the newspaper strike of 1962–63, it closed a failure. There were seventeen people in the cast playing forty to fifty parts.

The comedy *Any Wednesday* (1964) opened with Don Porter, Sandy Dennis, Gene Hackman, and Rosemary Murphy. The show, Muriel Resnik's first play, suffered a particularly grueling tryout period before its opening.

Harold Pinter's disturbing drama *The Homecoming* (1967) opened direct from the Royal Shakespeare Company. The play concerns a university teacher's wife who decides to become a prostitute and move in with her in-laws. Some critics viewed the play as an indictment of the drawing-room comedy. Others felt that the play had no viewpoint.

Following Terrence Frisby's *There's a Girl in My Soup* (1967) with Gig Young came Anthony Shaffer's *Sleuth* (1970). The two-character mystery thriller opened with Anthony Quayle and Keith Baxter.

The British invasion continued with Alan Ayckbourn's *Absurd Person Singular* (1974) produced by the Theater Guild and the John F. Kennedy Center. Another English import, *Comedians* (1976) by Trevor Griffiths was followed by another show developed in England. *Side By Side By Sondheim* (1977), a retrospective of Stephen Sondheim's works, starred the original English cast: Ned Sherrin, David Kernan, Millicent Martin, and Julia McKenzie.

Playwright Ira Levin brought another thriller to the Music Box with *Deathtrap* (1978). The play starred John Wood and actress Marian Seldes. She stayed with the show throughout its 1,793 performance run.

John Pielmeier's *Agnes of God* (1982) was another hit at the theater. Geraldine Page and Amanda Plummer starred in the mystery/drama. The remainder of the 1980's was marked with failures until the 1987 premiere of Christopher Hampton's *Les Liasons Dangereuses*. After numerous flops came another hit, *A Few Good Men* (1989) which was mounted as a sort of try-out for the film version of Aaron Sorkin's play.

The 1990's saw no rise in the theater's fortunes. The decade's flops included the musicals *Blood Brothers* (1993), *Swinging on a Star* (1995), and *State Fair* (1996). The new century dawned with Neil Simon's *The Dinner Party* (2000) and a rare success for the theater, *Fortune's Fool* (2002) with Alan Bates and Frank Langella. But failure reared its ugly head with the ugly musical *Amour* (2002). Barry Humphries returned to Broadway in *Dame Edna: Back with a Vengence* (2004), a deserved success that kept audiences in hilarity thoughout its limited run. *In My Life* (2005) was Joe Brooks' self-written, self-produced, and self conscious musical flop that became a laughingstock on the Great White Way.

The Music Box is among Broadway's more felicitous houses but in recent decades failure has been the norm.

N

NATIONAL THEATRE · See NEDER-
LANDER THEATRE.

NEDERLANDER THEATRE · 208 W.
41st Street. Architect: William N. Smith.
Opening: September 1, 1921; *Swords*. The
theater, built on the sight of an indoor tennis
court by Walter C. Jordan, a theatrical agent,
opened as the National in 1921. It reputedly
cost $950,000 to build and contained 1,200
seats. Though Jordan owned the theater, the
Shubert Brothers booked the theater. Its first
production, *Swords,* was also the first play by
Sidney Howard.

The National presented a series of fine plays
with great stars. One of the biggest successes was
John Willard's *The Cat and the Canary* (1922).
Actor/producer Walter Hampden brought
a production of *Cyrano de Bergerac* (1923)
there and returned to the National in *Hamlet,*
which moved from the Hampden Theater.
Chester Morris and Spencer Tracy appeared
in *Yellow,* (1926); magician Harry Houdini
brought his magic show, *Houdini Lives* to the
theater in 1926. More great stars appeared on
the National's stage in the twenties: Fredric
March in *The Half-Caste* (1926) and Ann
Harding in *The Trial of Mary Dugan* (1927).

In 1927, the Shuberts bought the building
and solidified their control. The 1930s and
the Depression, although disastrous for most
theaters, proved no problem to the National.
Great stars continued to grace its stage: Eug-
enie Leontovich, Henry Hull, and Sam Jaffe
in Vicki Baum's *Grand Hotel* (1930); Pauline
Lord, Ruth Gordon, and Raymond Massey
in *Ethan Frome* (1936); and *Tonight at* 8:30
(1936) by Noel Coward, starring the author
and Gertrude Lawrence.

The Mercury Theater under the direction of
Orson Welles presented *Julius Caesar* at the National on November 11, 1937, and followed it
with Thomas Dekker's *The Shoemaker's Holiday*
(1938). Tallulah Bankhead gave her greatest
performance in Lillian Hellman's *The Little
Foxes* (1939). Ethel Barrymore took stage in
Emlyn Williams' *The Corn Is Green* (1940).

The forties were also good years for the
National. Some of the highlights of this decade
were Maurice Evans and Judith Anderson in
Shakespeare's *Macbeth* (1941). Lerner and
Loewe's first musical, *What's Up?* (1943) was
a quick failure. Eva Le Gallienne and Joseph
Schildkraut appeared in Chekhov's *The Cherry
Orchard* (1944). Lerner and Loewe returned
with *The Day Before Spring* (1945), a moder-
ate success.

Harold Rome's musical revue *Call Me Mister*
(1946) with Betty Garrett introduced the songs
"South America, Take It Away," "The Face on
the Dime," and "The Red Ball Express." Judith
Anderson returned, this time with John Giel-
gud, in *Medea* (1947). A musical revue, *Lend
An Ear* (1948) by Charles Gaynor, followed.
John Garfield appeared with Nancy Kelly in
The Big Knife (1949). The forties came to a
close with George Bernard Shaw's *Caesar and
Cleopatra* (1949) with Sir Cedric Hardwicke,
Arthur Treacher, and Lilli Palmer.

The quality of the offerings stayed high
through the 1950s. Katharine Cornell, Grace
George, and Brian Aherne were featured in a
revival of *The Constant Wife* (1951) and Margaret Sullavan and Joseph Cotten followed
in *Sabrina Fair* (1953). The next major production at the National was *Inherit the Wind*
(1955). This huge hit, a retelling of the Scopes
Monkey Trial, starred Paul Muni, Ed Begley,

and Tony Randall. Arlene Francis, Walter Matthau, and Joseph Cotten appeared in *Once More with Feeling* (1958). Harry Kurnitz's light comedy was the National's last success under its original name.

In 1959 the Shuberts were forced to divest themselves of some of their theaters. Seizing the opportunity, showman Billy Rose bought the National and reopened it as the Billy Rose Theater on October 18, 1959, with Shaw's *Heartbreak House*. Katharine Cornell made her last Broadway appearance in Jerome Kilty's *Dear Liar* (1960) with Brian Aherne. Edward Albee's *Who's Afraid of Virginia Woolf?* (1962) grabbed audiences with an intensity rarely seen on Broadway. George Grizzard, Arthur Hill, Uta Hagen, and Melinda Dillon starred in the drama.

As production on Broadway slowed, the theater had increasing spells when it was dark. Edward Albee's *Tiny Alice* was a failure of 1964.

Tammy Grimes and Brian Bedford appeared in a notable revival of Noel Coward's *Private Lives* at the end of the sixties. The Royal Shakespeare Company came to the Billy Rose in 1971 with Peter Brook's outrageous production of *A Midsummer Night's Dream*.

Harold Pinter's *Old Times* (1971) examined a marriage and relationships by having a husband deal simultaneously with his wife and another woman who is actually his wife at a younger age. Another English playwright, Tom Stoppard, had his play *Jumpers* presented in 1974, but it didn't translate well on the American stage and closed after forty-eight performances.

The English influence continued when James and Joseph Nederlander and the British team of Cooney-Marsh bought the theater. In 1979, the name was changed to The Trafalgar and, after a refurbishment, opened with Brian Clark's *Whose Life Is It Anyway?* (1979), starring Tom Conti. Mary Tyler Moore took over the lead role—and won an honorary Tony Award. It was followed with Harold Pinter's drama, *Betrayal* (1980). Pinter kept up his experiments with dramatic form and constructed his play

so that the first scenes took place in the most recent time frame. Each succeeding scene went further back in time. *Betrayal* was like one long flashback.

In late 1980, the theater, renamed again, became the Nederlander. Lena Horne appeared in a one-woman show in 1981. Since then a string of failures have been presented on its stage: *84 Charing Cross Road;* a musical version of James Baldwin's *Amen Corner;* Peter Ustinov's *Beethoven's Tenth;* a musical based on Kenneth Grahame's children's book *The Wind in the Willows;* a musical version of *Raggedy Ann;* and Frank Langella in *Sherlock's Last Case* have all seen short runs at the theater.

Following the run of *Sherlock's Last Case* at the end of 1987, the Nederlanders rented the theater to a church group for services. The church moved to the larger Mark Hellinger Theater in 1989. *Rent* (1996) by Jonathan Larson transferred from Off-Broadway and still occupies the Nederlander at press time.

NEIL SIMON THEATER · 250 W. 52nd Street. Architect: Herbert J. Krapp. Opening: November 20. 1927; *Funny Face*. The early history of the Neil Simon Theater is also the history of the producing team of Alex A. Aarons and Vinton Freedley. Like other producers, Aarons and Freedley wanted their own theater. They convinced real estate mogul Alexander Pincus to build it in 1927 and chose the name Alvin by combining the first letters of their first names. The Adamesque theater is best known for the many successful musicals that enjoyed long runs on its stage. This tradition began with the first production, *Funny Face*.

Funny Face (1927) boasted a score by George and Ira Gershwin and a libretto by Paul Gerard Smith and Fred Thompson. The show starred Fred and Adele Astaire, Victor Moore and Allen Kearns. The score included such standards as "Funny Face," "'S Wonderful," and "My One and Only."

Next, a number of short-running musicals played the Alvin: *Here's Howe!* (1928); *Treasure Girl* (1928), a Gershwin show starring Gertrude Lawrence (with an exceptional score, including "Feeling I'm Falling," "I Don't Think I'll Fall in Love Today," "I've Got a Crush on You," "Oh, So Nice," and "Where's the Boy, Here's the Girl"); and *Spring Is Here* (1929) by Rodgers and Hart.

The Gershwins were back with a major hit, *Girl Crazy* (1930). Ethel Merman, making her Broadway debut, costarred with Willie Howard and, in her second Broadway appearance, Ginger Rogers. The score included "Bidin' My Time," "But Not for Me," "Embraceable You," "I Got Rhythm," "Sam and Delilah," and "Treat Me Rough." In the orchestra were Benny Goodman, Glenn Miller, Red Nichols, Jimmy Dorsey, Jack Teagarden, and Gene Krupa.

After *Girl Crazy,* the theater's ownership reverted to the firm that built it. The new owners booked the Alvin's first straight play, Maxwell Anderson's *Mary of Scotland* (1933) with Helen Hayes as the tragic queen Mary Stuart.

Following his partner's death in 1933, Vinton Freedley returned to the Alvin to produce *Anything Goes* (1934). Cole Porter wrote the score, and Ethel Merman, Victor Moore, William Gaxton, and Vivian Vance sang such hits as "All Through the Night," "I Get a Kick Out of You," "You're the Top," and the title song.

For *Red, Hot and Blue!* (1936), Porter, Merman, and Freedley were reunited with other *Anything Goes* alumni Russel Crouse, Howard Lindsay, and Vivian Vance. Merman was aided and abetted by Bob Hope and Jimmy Durante. The big hit song was "It's Delovely."

The Alvin next hosted Rodgers and Hart's *I'd Rather Be Right* (1937). George M. Cohan made his next to last Broadway appearance as the then-current President, Franklin D. Roosevelt. The libretto by George S. Kaufman and Moss Hart allowed for some gentle ribbing of the current administration as well as room for a good score, which featured "Have You Met Miss Jones?"

Rodgers and Hart returned with *The Boys from Syracuse* (1938) based on Shakespeare's *A Comedy of Errors.* The musical featured such great songs as "Falling in Love with Love," "This Can't Be Love," and "Sing for Your Supper." George Abbott produced, directed and

supplied the book. The musical showcased choreography by George Balanchine.

Another straight play next occupied the Alvin's stage. Alfred Lunt and Lynn Fontanne starred in Robert E. Sherwood's *There Shall Be No Night* (1940). After its New York run, the show was taken on tour and returned September 9 for an additional sixty-six performances before a second tour was undertaken. The play, which featured the young Montgomery Clift, won for Sherwood his third Pulitzer Prize. Altogether, the Lunts played over 1,600 performances, including a run in London, cut short when their theater was bombed during the Blitz.

The following occupant of the Alvin was among the first shows to explore psychiatry, *Lady in the Dark* (1941). The musical starred Gertrude Lawrence, returning to the Alvin in a better vehicle than her previous offering, *Treasure Girl.* Kurt Weill and Ira Gershwin supplied the score to a libretto by Moss Hart.

Musical comedy continued at the Alvin with Cole Porter providing Ethel Merman with another starring vehicle, *Something for the Boys* (1943). This undistinguished show enjoyed a long run, which was surprising because no hit songs came from the Michael Todd production. *Jackpot* (1944), a Vernon Duke and Howard Dietz show, returned Freedley to the Alvin.

In 1946 the Alvin was sold to producer Herman Bernstein.

The Alvin was the home to distinguished performances: Ingrid Bergman in Maxwell Anderson's *Joan of Lorraine* (1946); Maurice Evans in George Bernard Shaw's *Man and Superman* (1947); Henry Fonda and David Wayne in Joshua Logan and Thomas Heggen's wartime comedy *Mister Roberts* (1948); and Claude Rains in Sidney Kingsley's *Darkness at Noon* (1951).

Musical comedy returned to the Alvin with *A Tree Grows in Brooklyn* (1951), starring Shirley Booth. Novelist Betty Smith cowrote the libretto with George Abbott, who also served as director and producer. Arthur Schwartz and Dorothy Fields wrote a beautiful score.

Henry Fonda returned to the Alvin in *Point of No Return* (1951) and Mary Martin appeared in the comedy *Kind Sir* (1953) with Charles Boyer.

Melodies by Harold Arlen next filled the Alvin in *House of Flowers* (1954). Truman Capote was the unlikely author of the book and coauthor of the lyrics with Arlen. Pearl Bailey and Juanita Hall starred in the show, but the best songs, "A Sleepin' Bee" and "I Never Has Seen Snow," went to newcomer Diahann Carroll.

Andy Griffith made his Broadway debut in *No Time for Sergeants* (1955) by Ira Levin. Lucille Ball made her Broadway debut in *Wildcat* (1960). Cy Coleman and Carolyn Leigh provided the score, and N. Richard Nash wrote the book. Stephen Sondheim's first score for which he provided both music and lyrics, *A Funny Thing Happened on the Way to the Forum* (1962), starred Zero Mostel and Jack Gilford. *High Spirits* (1964), top-lined Beatrice Lillie and Tammy Grimes and was based on director Noel Coward's play *Blithe Spirit*. The musical had a fine libretto and excellent score by Hugh Martin and Timothy Gray.

Liza Minnelli was the next major star to make her Broadway debut at the Alvin. The vehicle was the John Kander and Fred Ebb musical, *Flora, the Red Menace* (1965). George Abbott coauthored the script with Robert Russell and also directed the Harold Prince production.

Rosencrantz and Guildenstern Are Dead (1967) was hailed by the London newspaper *The Observer* as "the most brilliant debut of the sixties." Though it didn't prove as successful as expected, the David Merrick production certainly proved a remarkable introduction to the remarkable talents of English playwright Tom Stoppard.

James Earl Jones, and Jane Alexander brought Howard Sackler's epic drama, *The Great White Hope* (1968), to the Alvin. The dramatic retelling of the life of prizefighter Jack Johnson won the Pulitzer Prize. The play was originally produced by the Washington, D.C., Arena Stage and was the first important sign that America's resident theaters would play an ever-increasing role in the development of new American plays.

Company (1970), the Stephen Sondheim musical, was next at the Alvin. Sondheim and librettist George Furth's examination of marriage was an important link between musicals of the past and the new style of musical in which the libretto moved in an often nonchronological fashion.

Shenandoah's (1975) long run was based largely on the success of its television advertisement. The Gary Geld and Peter Udell score didn't have any popular songs, and the show itself received mostly lukewarm reviews.

The next musical at the Alvin became one of the most popular in the theater's history. *Annie* (1977), with music by Charles Strouse and lyrics by Martin Charnin, was based on the comic strip "Little Orphan Annie." The show introduced a new standard, the song "Tomorrow." *Annie* moved from the Alvin, making room for another huge success.

The first play of a trilogy by Neil Simon, *Brighton Beach Memoirs* (1983), moved to make room for the second in the trilogy, *Biloxi Blues*. Again, Matthew Broderick starred. On June 29, 1983, the Alvin was renamed the Neil Simon by its new owners, the Nederlanders.

The theater community raised a small cry over the Alvin's renaming. It seemed unfair that the Alvin, a historic name and the scene of most of the Gershwins' greatest successes, should be renamed the Neil Simon, while the Uris Theatre should be rechristened the Gershwin. But the great sign that spelled out A-L-V-I-N (and had been altered to read A-N-N-I-E while that show was in residence) was changed to S-I-M-O-N.

A legendary flop, *Into the Light* (1986) briefly occupied the Simon's stage. Another great musical failure, *Senator Joe* (1989), a retelling of the career of Senator Joseph McCarthy, closed in previews. Neil Simon returned to the Simon with *Jake's Women* (1992) but by then his talents seemed to have waned and he could only supply failures to the Broadway stage. 1994's *The Rise and Fall of Little Voice* was a transfer from London where it was a moderate hit. Unfortunately, it did not repeat its success in New York. A lavish revival of *The King and I* (1996) starred Donna Murphy as Anna and proved to be a success.

However, the 2000 revival of *The Music Man* was a failure both artistically and commercially. Two years later, *Hairspray* opened and finally the Neil Simon had a smash hit. The show, with score by Scott Wittman and Marc Shaiman and book by Thomas Meehan and Mark O'Donnell, is still going strong at press time.

NEW AMSTERDAM THEATRE · 214 W. 42nd Street. Architects: Herts & Tallant. Opening: November 2, 1903; *A Midsummer Night's Dream.* The renovation of the New Amsterdam was the exceptionally dramatic catalyst in the 42nd Street Redevelopment Project.

Klaw and Erlanger built their new theater as the flagship of their Theatrical Syndicate. They spent $1.5 million and for their money got a legitimate theater, a ten-story office building and a rooftop theater.

The auditorium, designed in the then rare style of art nouveau, was described in the *Dramatic Mirror* as "beyond question the most gorgeous playhouse in New York." The architects used three motifs throughout the building: the history of New Amsterdam from Hendrik Hudson to 1903, the history of theater and the typical art nouveau floral and fauna motifs. Murals and friezes depict scenes from Shakespeare's *Macbeth,* Homer's *Odyssey* and the operas of Wagner. Busts of Shakespeare and Homer look down from on high above the vaulted ceilings. The theater's color scheme was basically green with mauve accents. No primary colors were used in the design.

At the time, the New Amsterdam was the largest theater in New York, with seats for 1,800 patrons. It was among the first nonskyscrapers to use structural steel in its construction. The steel had to perform a unique task. The steelwork had to support the huge cantilevered balconies as well as the entire weight of the rooftop theater. The seventy-ton main girder over the ceiling was the largest piece of steel in any building at the time, measuring ninety feet in length and fourteen feet in height. The huge amount of structural steel was lifted into place from the office tower platform that was constructed first.

The balconies did not have the common pillars blocking the audience's view. Instead, they were cantilevered into the theater's structure. These were the largest cantilevered balconies in the world when they were built. The orchestra was designed to be quickly changed into a ballroom; however, the conversion never took place.

The stage was one of the largest in the city, measuring one hundred feet wide and fifty-two feet deep. The stage floor was divided into four forty-two feet by seven feet hydraulic platforms. These giant elevators could be raised, lowered, or inclined independently from each other.

Under Klaw and Erlanger's direction, the New Amsterdam presented many of the great hits of the early twentieth century. An early musical comedy success, *Whoop-De-Doo* (1903), had Weber and Fields, starring and producing and marking the end of their long partnership. They would change their mind years later and reteam briefly.

On June 6, 1904, the producers opened the Arial Gardens, a different kind of rooftop theater. Most were summer gardens that used a small platform for a stage. But the New Amsterdam boasted a complete miniature theater on its roof. Though it could be used year-round, it was used only during the summer months. The Gardens boasted double-hung windows that could be opened to let in the summer breezes. Its auditorium was nowhere near as successful as its sister theater (see below). The rooftop theater had a raked orchestra and small stage. But the balcony was U-shaped—a throwback to the pre-cantilevered past. Side seating in the balcony actually faced the opposite wall. Behind the stage of the Arial Gardens was an open-air Dutch Garden with refreshments and café tables, perfectly in keeping with the typical roof garden of the period.

The first show, *A Little Bit of Everything,* was a variety program, a style that was favored throughout the Arial Gardens' history. While the main auditorium presented its schedule of shows, the rooftop theater had its own schedule. It replaced variety with a series of musicals and operettas but still closed for the winter months.

New Yorkers saw their first production of Goldsmith's *She Stoops to Conquer* (1905) at the New Amsterdam. The comedy starred Eleanor Robson. Another great American actor, Richard Mansfield, played a limited engagement at the New Amsterdam each season.

The music of George M. Cohan filled the theater when *Forty-Five Minutes from Broadway* (1906) opened. Cohan's *The Governor's Son* was revived upstairs on June 4, 1906 with the Cohan family starring. *The Honeymooners* (1907), which opened at the Aerial Gardens, was a revision of Cohan's musical *Running for Office.*

A smash hit for the New Amsterdam and one of the most influential shows of the early twentieth century was Franz Lehar's operetta *The Merry Widow* (1907). Its first American production opened at the New Amsterdam with Ethel Jackson portraying the widow. The play was influenced by both musical comedy and women's fashions. *The Merry Widow* hat became a quick-selling item. *The Merry Widow* moved upstairs to the Aerial Gardens for the summer of 1908. It finally closed after returning to the main auditorium.

European-style operetta continued on the New Amsterdam stage with *The Silver Star* (1909) by Robin Hood Bowers and Harry B. Smith. A new melodrama, *Madame X* (1910), is now a sort of camp classic. It concerned a lawyer who prosecutes his mother. Of course, in the melodrama, he doesn't know who the lady is. Despite the critics' scoffing, the show enjoyed a Broadway revival and three film versions. There was also a burlesque of the popular hit produced at the Victoria Theater's roof garden.

A European operetta, *Madame Sherry* (1910), opened at the New Amsterdam with a popular Karl Hoschna score. Another European-influenced show that also became a smash hit at the New Amsterdam was Ivan Caryll's *The Pink Lady* (1911). It made a star of Hazel Dawn.

A huge hit in the 1800s, Reginald DeKoven and Harry B. Smith's operetta *Robin Hood* (1912), did not have a long run in its revival at the New Amsterdam. However, during the revival it did mark over 6,000 performances since its first presentation. Another perennial favorite, *The Count of Luxembourg* (1912) featured a score by Franz Lehar, the composer of *The Merry Widow.*

Oh! Oh! Delphine (1912) brought Ivan Caryll's tunes back to the New Amsterdam. Caryll followed this success with another, *The Little Cafe* (1913).

The next tenant of the New Amsterdam changed its history for almost two decades, and the producer became the most successful in Broadway history. On June 16, 1913, Florenz Ziegfeld moved his *Ziegfeld Follies* to the New Amsterdam from the Moulin Rouge. From that year until he moved to the new Ziegfeld Theater in 1927, Ziegfeld presented an annual revue at the New Amsterdam (he missed only one year, 1926, because of a legal problem over the name *Follies*). Ziegfeld brought some of the greatest stars of Broadway to the New Amsterdam. Leon Errol, Bert Williams, Fanny Brice, Will Rogers, Lillian Lorraine, W. C. Fields, Marion Davies, Carl Randall, Elizabeth Brice, Ann Pennington, Ina Claire, Mae Murray, Eddie Cantor, Joe Frisco, Marilyn Miller, John Steel, Van and Schenck, Bert and Betty Wheeler, Brooke Johns, Lupino Lane, Vivienne Segal, George Olsen, Ethel Shutta, and Paul Whiteman were just some of the stars appearing in the *Follies*.

During the reign of the *Ziegfeld Follies* at the New Amsterdam, the theater housed other productions between *Follies* editions including the Victor Herbert and Robert B. Smith classic, *Sweethearts* (1913), Herman Finck and C. M. S. McClelland's *Around the Map* (1915), *The Girl Behind the Gun* (1918) with music by Ivan Caryll, and *The Velvet Lady* (1919) with a score by Victor Herbert and Henry Blossom.

Ziegfeld not only produced the annual edition of the *Follies,* but he also presented many successful musical comedies and a series of revues on the New Amsterdam's roof. In 1915, he hired John Eberson to redesign the theater with a U-shaped balcony and a 22,000-square-foot dance floor. With its opening attraction, *Ziegfeld Midnight Frolic* on March 29, 1915, the producer renamed the roof theater the Ziegfeld Danse de Follies.

Ziegfeld's musical presentations downstairs continued with *Sally* (1920). Marilyn Miller, Walter Catlett, and Ziegfeld favorite Leon Errol starred in the Jerome Kern, P. G. Wodehouse, Clifford Grey, and Guy Bolton show. The hit songs included the title song and two with lyrics by B. G. DeSylva. The first was "Whip-Poor-Will" and the other "Look for the Silver Lining," one of the greatest of all American popular songs.

Ziegfeld and his sometime-coproducer Charles Dillingham refurbished the New Amsterdam's roof, renamed the Dresden and opened a show called *Cinders* (1923). *Cinders* had a score by Rudolf Friml. On September 12, 1923, the roof garden was named the Frolic Theater with a foreign theater troupe's production of *Teatro dei Piccoli.*

Marilyn Miller and Jerome Kern were involved in another hit musical at the New Amsterdam, *Sunny* (1925). This time, Oscar Hammerstein II and Otto Harbach supplied the book. The cast also included Cliff Edwards, Pert Kelton, Jack Donahue, and Clifton Webb. One of the five choreographers was Fred Astaire.

After the short-lived run of the Rodgers and Hart musical *Betsy* (1926) the New Amsterdam hosted an all-star production of *Trelawney of the Wells.*

For one week, the Frolic Theater hosted a play called *He Loved the Ladies* (1927). The show's Thursday matinee played for no patrons. Not one audience member was present when the curtain rose. Statisticians disagree whether the play can claim to have run six performances or seven, and whether a performance counts as a performance if there is no one there to see it.

Musical comedy triumphed again at the New Amsterdam with Ziegfeld's production of *Rosalie* (1928) boasting a score by George and Ira Gershwin. Sigmund Romberg and P. G . Wodehouse contributed an equal number of songs, but they took a back seat to the Gershwin offerings.

Ziegfeld's next offering at the New Amsterdam was the Walter Donaldson and Gus Kahn hit, *Whoopee* (1928). Ruth Etting, George Olsen's Orchestra, Tamara Geva, and Ethel Shutta, joined Eddie Cantor. The better-than-average score yielded such musical comedy gems as "Love Me or Leave Me," "Makin' Whoopee," and "I'm Bringing a Red, Red Rose." The show that followed was the fifth production of William Gillette's American classic *Sherlock Holmes* (1929); it played only briefly at the New Amsterdam.

The New Amsterdam's survival at the beginning of the Depression was a testament to its good reputation with producers and audiences. The beginning of the thirties saw only a slight falling off in the number or quality of shows premiering at the theater. However, the rooftop Frolics Theater did not fare so well.

Bookings fell off throughout Times Square and only the theaters with the most advantageous location could keep lit. As 1930 turned to 1931, *Variety* reported that thirty-one theaters were dark in what was usually a busy holiday season. A theater on a roof, without a proper marquee, wasn't attractive to those producers still operating. Erlanger announced that the Frolics would undergo another transformation. The proscenium arch was filled in with a movable wall of glass. The sound proofed wall allowed the theater to operate as a legitimate theater, a radio studio, and a feature film studio. Erlanger even predicted that the theater would be used for television. In 1930, the theater became NBC Times Square Studio. Erlanger died on March 7, 1930. But his theater continued to prosper for a time.

Earl Carroll's Vanities of 1930 featured Jack Benny, Patsy Kelly, Jimmy Savo, and Herb Williams. Hit songs were mainly by Harold Arlen and Ted Koehler and included "Contagious

Rhythm," "Hittin' the Bottle," and "The March of Time." *Vanities* was followed by probably the greatest revue in musical comedy history, *The Band Wagon* (1931). Max Gordon produced the new revue, which boasted performances by Fred and Adele Astaire, Helen Broderick, Tilly Losch, and Frank Morgan.

The next New Amsterdam attraction was the Irving Berlin and Moss Hart revue *Face the Music* (1932). This sometimes humorous, sometimes trenchant musical revue starred Mary Boland, J. Harold Murray, and Andrew Tombes.

Following the close of *Face the Music,* the theater had its first shaky season. The 1932–33 season found no musical presentation premiering. Producers simply didn't have enough money to launch a large number of new operettas or musical comedies. *Murder at the Vanities* (1933) was the next hit to play the New Amsterdam. The Earl Carroll production gave audiences both a murder mystery and a full musical revue. One production number, "Virgins Wrapped in Cellophane," gives a clue to the reason for the show's long run.

Roberta (1933), with a score by Jerome Kern and Otto Harbach, starred George Murphy, Lyda Roberti, Bob Hope, Sydney Greenstreet, Tamara, and Fay Templeton, marking her fiftieth anniversary in the theater.

Dietz and Schwartz returned to the New Amsterdam with their new show *Revenge with Music* (1934). The show was the only legitimate theater production on 42nd Street. The rest of the theaters had converted to sub-run motion pictures, were presenting burlesque or were closed.

Having hosted many editions of the *Ziegfeld Follies* and the 1930 *Earl Carroll's Vanities,* the New Amsterdam seemed a natural for *George White's Scandals* (1935). The *Scandals* were short on material and stars but long on beautiful seminude chorines. This last edition of the *Scandals* featured hit songs including "Are You Havin' Any Fun?," "The Mexiconga," and "Something I Dreamed Last Night."

On May 7, 1936, the Dry Dock Savings Institution foreclosed on the New Amsterdam Theatre. There was $1.6 million due in interest and taxes. Max Cohen, a theater owner who also owned the Harris and Wallack's theaters put up $500,000 to purchase the New Amsterdam. By then, all the owners of the theater—Erlanger, Ziegfeld, and Dillingham—were dead. Cohen was forbidden to present burlesque in the theater.

The New Amsterdam reopened on July 3, 1937, with a showing of the movie *A Midsummer Night's Dream,* the film version of the first play to occupy the New Amsterdam's stage.

On September 12, 1937, the rooftop theater was renamed the WOR-Mutual Radio Theater and served as home for the show "Tim and Irene's Fun in Swingtime."

Sigmund Romberg found his popularity decreasing when *Forbidden Melody* (1936) opened at the theater. The run reflected the change in taste along Broadway. European operettas were no longer in vogue. New composers like the Gershwins and Rodgers and Hart would inherit the mantle of popularity from such European stalwarts as Herbert, Friml, and Romberg.

A production of *Othello* (1937) was to be the last live attraction at the New Amsterdam for almost fifty years. It featured Walter Huston in the title role.

The rooftop theater returned to legitimate use as the New Amsterdam Roof with the production of *The Petrified Forest* (1943). On September 15, 1951, the theater became the NBC Times Square Television Theater.

Downstairs a motion-picture policy took effect in 1937 and remained in effect until the New Amsterdam was shuttered in the early 1980s. At that time, the new owners, the Nederlanders, proposed to renovate the theater and open Jerry Herman's musical *La Cage Aux Folles.* Renovations took longer than expected and suddenly the Broadway theater scene was less healthy, so *La Cage* opened at the far more attractive Palace Theater in the heart of the theater district.

Other shows were announced for the theater and then withdrawn. Plans to move the lobby to 41st Street across from the Nederlander were scrapped, and subsequently major problems were discovered with the main supporting beam.

The film *Vanya on 42nd Street* gives an excellent tour of the decrepit theater.

Then a miracle occurred. The Disney Corporation took over the New Amsterdam and gave it a first-rate renovation, restoring the theater beautifully. Disney did the right thing and the New Amsterdam today is Broadway's most beautiful theater. The Joseph Urban interior is a marvel and the technical upgrades (with the exception of a light grid hung over the top of the proscenium) are unobtrusive. On May 18, 1997, the New Amsterdam was reborn for new generations. After a shakedown with a few performances of an oratorio titled *King David*, Disney gave the theater an immense hit, *The Lion King* (1997). That show moved to the Minskoff Theatre in 2006 to make room for Disney's theatrical version of *Mary Poppins*.

NEW APOLLO THEATER · See APOLLO THEATRE.

NEW YORK THEATRE · See Olympia.

NEW YORKER THEATER · 254 W. 54th Street. Architect: Eugene DeRosa. Opening: as an opera house, November 7, 1927, *La Boheme*; as a legitimate theater, May 12, 1930, *The Vikings*. Opera impresario Fortune Gallo had his Gallo Theater built to house the San Carlo Opera Company. The house was not a success, and Gallo sold his building. The new owners named the theater the New Yorker Theater with their production of *The Vikings*. The Depression hurt the theater, and it was also unsuccessful.

The theater was redesigned as one of the first theater restaurants in New York, the Casino de Paree, on December 13, 1933. The club was originally called Billy Rose's Casino de Paree but the bantam producer Billy Rose soon sold out his interest.

The man who ran the Casino was Lew Brown, best known as a member of the songwriting team DeSylva, Brown, and Henderson. But Brown wasn't the owner; that distinction went to Tommy Lucchese. Lucchese, like most gangsters, was paranoid. He wouldn't accept a cigar from anyone. Instead, he'd jump in a cab and go to a cigar store where he was not known. Lucchese's caution paid off. He was never arrested and lived a quiet life until he died of cancer in 1967.

Like many mob-operated clubs, the Casino de Paree was successful, but it couldn't survive the effects of the Depression. On January 16, 1936, the theater was renamed the Palladium. The Palladium was short-lived, and in 1937 the Federal Theater Project leased it and renamed it the Federal Music Theater.

The theater's name was changed again, to the New Yorker Theater, and returned to legitimate theater productions on March 21, 1939, with *The Swing Mikado*. In 1943, CBS turned the theater into the CBS Radio Playhouse Number 4.

During the 1970s, the building achieved perhaps its greatest success as the disco Studio 54.

It became a legitimate theater again in 1998 with the Roundabout Theatre taking over the lease. Its revival of *Cabaret*, which moved from the Kit Kat Klub, closed finally in 2004, making way for the Roundabout's revival of Stephen Sondheim's *Assassins* (2004). The show, unfortunately, was not a success financially. Another Sondheim revival, and another commercial failure for the Roundabout followed. *Pacific Overtures* (2004). After poorly received revivals of *A Streetcar Named Desire* (2005) and *A Touch of the Poet* (2005) the theater hosted another failure, *The Threepenny Opera* (2006) with Alan Cumming making his return to the Studio 54 stage.

NEW YORK TIMES HALL · See LITTLE THEATRE.

O

OLYMPIA · 1514–26 Broadway between 44th and 45th Street. Architect: J. B. McElfatrick & Company.

Music Hall opening production December 17, 1895, with Yvette Guilbert; reopened as the New York Theater, April 24, 1899, with The Man in the Moon. Opening as the Moulin Rouge in 1912. Reopened as Wonderland in January of 1913. Renamed the New York Theatre in 1913. Opened as Loew's New York in 1915.

Lyric opening production November 25, 1895, with *Excelsior, Jr.*; reopened as the Criterion Theater, August 29, 1899, with *The Girl from Maxim's;* reopened again as the Vitagraph Theater, February 7, 1914, as a movie theater; reopened again as the Criterion Theater, September 11, 1916, with *Paganini.* Both demolished in 1935.

The Olympia complex established Times Square as the city's theater district and served as a cornerstone for development of the whole area. Earlier in the nineteenth century, the theater district moved from lower Manhattan to the Herald Square area. Oscar Hammerstein I began the move northward to Times Square (then Longacre Square) in 1895 with the Olympia Theater. Hammerstein realized the potential of the area, already used as a transfer point between streetcar routes. He purchased the entire block of the east side of Broadway between 44th and 45th Streets and decided to build a huge complex called the Olympia. Hammerstein crowed, "My theatre will make a place for itself because I will give the public what they have never had before."

In January 1895, the ground was broken. When completed, the complex contained a restaurant, a promenade or central lobby, a bowling alley, billiard rooms, a Turkish bath, a smoking room, an Oriental café, three theaters seating over six thousand people, and a roof garden—an idea imported from Europe. One admission allowed patrons to explore any of the theater's attractions. The Music Hall had a Broadway frontage of seventy-five feet. It was separated from the concert hall by a ten-foot wide alley. Then came another ten-foot wide alley and the theater.

The Music Hall, situated on the 45th Street side had prices of 75 cents to $1.50 for reserved seats. It had eleven tiers of boxes. Hammerstein boasted that it held more boxes than any other theater—124 in all. The theater resembled a European opera house with its huge proscenium crowned by the goddess Fame crowning Poetry and Prose.

The opening of the complex was planned for November 18, but delays pushed the opening back to November 25. Hammerstein claimed that he had lost $3,000 by postponing the opening. The *Times* accused him of overselling the house to make up the difference.

Opening night proved to be an ill omen. The crowds began to arrive in the afternoon, long before the doors were opened. The heavens then opened, and cold rains beat down on the thousands of ticket holders who began to push and shove to get under the marquee. The *Times* reported that the crowd, "with the strength of a dozen catapults, banged at the doors of the new castle of pleasure and sent them flying open. ...puffed sleeves wilted and crimpled hair became hoydenish in the crush and the rain; toes were trampled and patent leathers and trousers were splashed, dresses were torn, and still the crowd pushed on. "The staff was unable to control the throng.

Hammerstein had oversold the theater by almost 4,000 seats. The police called for reinforcements to try to shut the theater doors. At 10 o'clock over 5,000 patrons, as the *Times* put it, "slid through the mud and slush of Longacre back into the ranks of Cosmopolis." A band played until 1 a.m. in the Concert Hall to try to appease the disgruntled crowd.

Hammerstein had private rooms for his guests, but unfortunately the paint was still wet and several of the elite found their clothes marked with the wall covering. The next day, Hammerstein's troubles continued. A steam pipe burst in the cellar, and two workers were killed and others badly scalded.

Yvette Guilbert was to have opened the Music Hall, but she was unavailable until mid-December, and a series of vaudeville acts filled in for her. The Lyric presented Edward E. Rice's *Excelsior Jr.,* starring Fay Templeton. "The Cornerstone of Times Square," as the Olympia was christened, never overcame the disaster of opening night.

ROOFTOP THEATRE

On November 2, 1895 the roof garden hosted a "Bal Champetre" in which the Florenz aerobatic troupe astounded patrons with their triple pirouettes. The roof garden was later renovated and renamed the Jardin de Paris. The first *Ziegfeld Follies* was presented there in 1907 and subsequent editions were also produced there through 1911. The 1912 edition moved to the larger New York Theatre which was renamed the Moulin Rouge.

MUSIC HALL

Yvette Guilbert played the Music Hall on December 17, 1895 and, by January 27 of the next year had become a star. Later that year, Collbri's Midgets, the Aerial Ballet and Grand Opera in Tableaux were presented. The Cherry Sisters, often referred to as the worst act in vaudeville history, appeared on November 28 lasting through the enmity of audiences to December 14.

Among the more notable offerings was Fay Templeton appearing in E. E. Rice's burlesque of *Excelsior Jr.* (1895). Also in the cast were Charles A. Bigelow, Richard Carle, Harry Hearle, Marie Cahill, and Kitty Connor. It marked Templeton's first Broadway appearance in five years.

Little Egypt, a great star of the World's Columbian Exposition in Chicago opened at the Music Hall on January 4, 1897. However, there were more than one act calling itself Little Egypt and which one this was is impossible to determine. Burlesque came to the theater's stage on March 7 with the *Mrs. Radley Bradley Ball*, a satire of the Bradley Martin Ball, a society sensation which was plastered in headlines across the front pages of newspapers.

Another renowned appearance was Anna Held in the musical comedy *La Poupee* (1897). This was her second season in America and her first speaking role. However, an argument with Hammerstein a week into the run led to her exiting the cast. She was replaced by Louise Hepner on October 30. Also in the cast was vaudeville great Trixie Friganza.

In 1897, the president of New York Life wrote Hammerstein a note apprising him that the mortgage would be foreclosed and that a bank employee would run the theater. Hammerstein responded, "I am in receipt of your letter, which is now before me, and in a few minutes will be behind me."

The next year, Hammerstein found himself bankrupted by the Olympia. Previously, he had turned down an offer to rent the two corners of the building as a drug store and haberdashery. The proposed rental was $6,000 annually, but Hammerstein was too proud or optimistic to accept it. New York Life sold the building at auction to producers Henry and M. L. Sire for $967,400. They in turn sold it to Klaw and Erlanger, heads of the Theatrical Syndicate, for almost twice that amount (in 1920, a department store offered $6 million).

The Music Hall was gutted by Klaw and Erlanger who hired architects Herts & Tallant to renovate the interior in the style of a Broadway theater. Gone were all but twelve of the boxes and only two balconies were retained. Klaw and Erlanger renamed the Music Hall the New York Theater and changed the entrance to 44th Street, permanently severing its ties to the Olympia complex.

George Lederer became manager; musical comedy was the order of the day at the New York Theater with occasional forays into vaudeville and burlesque.

NEW YORK THEATRE

The first attraction to play the New York was *The Man in the Moon* with music by Ludwig Englander, Reginald de Koven, and Gustave Kerker. Starring at the April 24, 1899 opening were Christie MacDonald, Sam Bernard, and Marie Dressler. January of 1900 saw the opening of *Broadway to Tokio* with Fay Templeton, Otis Harlan, and Josie Sadler. In August came *Quo Vadis* with Richard Buehler, Alice Fischer, and Joseph Haworth. In October, the smash hit show, *Florodora* moved from the Casino Theatre to finish its run. Hagenback's Trained Animals cavorted on the stage in October and Marie Cahill opened at the theater in Julian Edwards' *Sally in Our Alley* in November.

Julian Edwards' *When Johnny Comes Marching Home* enjoyed a long run beginning in March 16, 1902 with George Backus in the lead.

Composer A. Baldwin Sloane dominated the New York's stage with a series of shows: *Broadway to Tokio* (1900) a spectacular musical with music by Sloane and Reginald De Koven; the musical comedy *A Million Dollars* (1900); Sloane's burlesque of *Nell Gwynn* titled *Nell Go In* (1900); *The Giddy Throng* (1900) a burlesque revue with May Yohe and including the mini-musical *After Office Hours*; and finally *The King's Carnival* (1901) another burlesque by Sloane and Sydney Rosenfeld.

After Sloane's reign at the New York Theatre the first show to open was *The Chaperons* (1902) which featured musical comedy favorite Eva Tanguay and her rendition of "My Sambo" which would remain a favorite in her repertoire. On June 30 of that year, the production

would move upstairs to the New York's rooftop theater which was then named the Cherry Blossom Grove.

It was followed by *King Highball* (1902), which starred Marie Dressler.

One of the most significant musicals of the decade opened at the New York Theater on February 18, 1903. *In Dahomey* was one of the first musical comedy written by black men to play Broadway. Poet Paul Laurence Dunbar contributed the lyrics with music by Will Marion Cook and libretto by J. A. Shipp. Dunbar and Cook had previously written *Clorindy or the Origin of the Cakewalk* in 1898, the same year as Bob Cole and Billy Johnson produced the first black musical comedy, *A Trip to Coontown*. *In Dahomey's* cast featured a who's who of black performers including Bert Williams and his partner George W. Walker, Ada Overton Walker, Lottie Williams, and Shipp himself. The show was so successful, it was presented in London, where a royal command performance was given.

In September or that year, Henry Woodruff and Annie Irish appeared in the ever-popular spectacular *Ben-Hur*. May brough Bertha Galland in Paul Kester's dramatization of Charles Major's novel, *Dorothy Vernon of Haddon Hall*.

The 1904 season was not an especially auspicious one however many stars appeared on the New York's stage including Chauncey Olcott in *Terence*; Richard Carle in *The Tenderfoot*; Eddie Leonard, Elfie Fay and Abbie Mitchell in *The Southerners*; *The Maid and the Mummy* with May Boley and Annie Yeamans; Harry Bulger, Ida Mulle, and Emma Carus in *Woodland*; and on the day after Christmas, C. T. Dazey's *Home Folks* with William S. Hart, Thomas A. Wise, and Julie Herne.

That same season saw the opening of a beloved American play *The Old Homestead*. A particular favorite of the nineteenth century, *The Old Homestead* was written by Denman Thompson and George W. Ryer. The play opened at the New York Theatre on September 12, 1904 and ran for sixty-one performances. Thompson played the lead of Joshua

Whitcomb in all the various incarnations until his death April 14, 1911.

One of the highlights of the 1905 season was George M. Cohan's *Little Johnny Jones* starring the author along with Donald Brian, William Seymour, and Truly Shattuck. Cohan would have four of his musicals play the New York. Other shows that season were *A Pair of Pinks* with Ward and Vokes; *The Shepherd King* with Wright Lorimer and May Buckley; May Irwin in *Mrs. Black is Back*; and the twelfth engagement of *The Prince of Pilsen* to play on Broadway.

Anne Crawford Flexner dramatized one of America's favorite novels, *Mrs. Wiggs of the Cabbage Patch,* which opened at the New York on September 17, 1906 with Madge Carr Cook, Edith Taliaferro, and Myrtle Tannehill in it. That season also saw Cohan's *45 Minutes from Broadway* with Fay Templeton, Donald Brian, and Victor Moore that November. Edwin Milton Royle's smash hit, *The Squaw Man* (1907), starring William Faversham and Julie Opp. That August saw the return of vaudeville to the New York stage.

January 28, 1908 saw a return of legitimate theater with the opening of *The Soul Kiss* starring Cecil Lean and Adeline Genee. It was followed by Richard Carle in *Mary's Lamb* which was a great hit of its day, running until August 29 of that year. Another big hit followed, *Miss Innocence* with Anna Held, Charles A. Bigelow, and Emma Janvier.

George M. Cohan's *The Man Who Owns Broadway* played for 128 performances at the New York beginning on October 11, 1909 with Raymond Hitchcock and Flora Zabelle in the leads. The house wouldn't have another hit until almost a year later when Victor Herbert's classic *Naughty Marietta* (1910) opened with book and lyrics by Rida Johnson Young. Edward Martindell, Emma Trentini, and Orville Harrold starred. The theater's next show boasted an all-star cast including Richard Carle, Jeanne Eagels, Helen Broderick, Ina Claire, Natalie Alt, and Edna Wallace Hopper. Unfortunately, *Jumping Jupiter*, opening in March of 1911, was not a success. That fall, Victor Herbert

had a modest success at the theater with *The Enchantress* featuring Kitty Gordon and Ralph Riggs. It ran for nine weeks.

On April 11, 1912, the New York's name was changed to Moulin Rouge with the opening of *A Winsome Widow* based on the smash hit play, *A Trip to Chinatown.* Raymond Hubbell provided the music. The great Florenz Ziegfeld produced with a stellar cast including Charles King, Leon Errol, Kathleen Clifford, Emmy Wehlen, Frank Tinney, the Dolly Sisters, and Mae West. Its twenty-one-week run was followed by another Ziegfeld show, *The Ziegfeld Follies of 1912.* Raymond Hubbel again provided some songs for a cast including Leon Errol, Harry Watson Jr., Bernard Granville, Bert Williams, Josie Sadler, and Lillian Lorraine. It ran for eleven weeks.

One of Broadway's favorite playwrights of the time, Owen Davis saw his play *Big Jim Garrity* play three weeks commencing October, 1914 with John Mason and Janet Dunbar in the leads. On November 16 of that year, *The Traffic* by Rachael Marshall and Oliver D. Bailey played for one week. It was the final show at the theater before Loew's took over the theater on January 15, 1915.

Management of the Music Hall was acquired by William Morris in 1913. Two years later, Marcus Loew took over the Morris organization and the theater was given over to a movie/vaudeville policy. When Loew took over the New York Theatre, he changed the name to Loew's New York and it became the flagship of the Loew's chain. It retained that role until the 1922 opening of Loew's State Theatre.

LYRIC THEATRE

The Lyric Theatre opened in September 1897 with Chester Bailey Fernane's play *The Cat and the Cherub* featuring Holbrook Blinn, Richard Ganthony, and Grace Sheridan.

The Lyric soon became the Criterion named after a famous London music hall in Piccadilly Circus. Under Charles Frohman's direction, the Criterion offered comic opera, musical comedy, variety and straight plays.

Among his many successes there were *The Girl from Maxim's* (1899) by George Feydeau and starring Josephine Hall and Paul McAllister; *Barbara Frietchie* (1899) by playwright Clyde Fitch and starring Julia Marlowe in her first non-repertory appearance and a revival of David Belasco's *Zaza* (1900) starring Leslie Carter in which Ruth St. Denis also appeared in a minor role. *The Gay Lord Quex* (1900) by Arthur Wing Pinero was another hit for the theater.

The Pride of Jennico (1900) marked the New York debut of George W. Barbier. The show returned to the Criterion later that season, opening on September 3 and playing for an additional thirty-two performances.

One of the most famous plays of the decade, Paul Kester's *When Knighthood Was in Flower,* opened on January 14, 1901 with Julia Marlowe in the lead. Her performance was judged as one of the top two in the Criterion's history. Marlowe had previously appeared in *Barbara Frietchie* at the Criterion and two years after *When Knighthood Was in Flower* would appear in *The Cavalier*. She would play a total of forty-three weeks at the Criterion, a record for any performer.

It was followed at the Criterion by the debut of William Faversham as a star in *A Royal Rival* (1901). The play was adapted by Gerald Du Maurier from *Don Caesar de Bazan*, which premiered in New York at the Olympic Theatre on December 9, 1844. During the run on *A Royal Rival*, on December 9, no less than three adaptations were presented in New York a version by George Henry Trader presented by the Henry V. Donnelly Stock Company at the Murray Hill Theatre for a one week engagement and another version titled *Don Caesar's Return* starring James K. Hackett which premiered on September 3.

David Belasco returned to the Criterion, for the second of his three productions at the theater, with another great hit, *Du Barry* (1901) with the author also producing and directing. Mrs. Leslie Carter, returning from a triumphant stand in London in *Zaza*, starred along with Walter Belasco. The roles of the DuBarry and Zaza were so important to Mrs. Carter's career that for the seventeen years ending in 1907, she appeared altogether in only six roles.

Pinero returned with *Iris* (1902) a five act drama directed by Dion Boucicault. Francis Hodgson Burnett's *The Little Princess* (1903) best remembered for the Shirley Temple film adaptation, was one of the first productions mounted on Broadway specifically for children. The play was performed on matinees only, Sunday through Friday. It later moved to the Savoy Theatre again only playing matinees. It finally concluded its run at the Madison Square Theatre.

James M. Barrie's *Alice Sit-by-the-Fire* and *Pantaloon* (1905) with Ethel and John Barrymore was a legendary production. Johnson Briscoe, theatrical agent and former casting director for Winthrop Ames, recalled, "Ethel Barrymore startled all her admirers by playing the mother of two grown up children ... while still in her mid-twenties. It was one of her greatest successes." John Barrymore played Stephen Rollo in that play, one of his four appearances at the Criterion.

On August 17, 1908, Isadore Duncan made her first appearance as a solo star at the Criterion. *Samson*, a play by Henri Bernstein opened at the theater on October 19 and ran for a more than respectable 152 performances. Making her New York debut was future star Constance Collier. William Gillette and Pauline Frederick also appeared in the cast.

Belasco produced the last of his three plays at the Criterion with Roland Burnham Molineux's play *The Man Inside* (1913). The *New York Times* prematurely reported the death of legit at the Criterion with Belasco's production.

The Criterion lease was acquired by the Vitagraph Company for $50,000 a year in 1914 and was renamed the Vitagraph Theater. This marked the first time a Broadway legitimate theater featuring a full evening of cinema. But movies failed to catch on and the Vitagraph name reverted to the Criterion under the management of matinee idol James K.

Hackett. His reign lasted from 1915 to 1919. Hammerstein, Frohman, and Hackett were responsible, singly, for almost all the Criterion's legitimate stage career.

Young Wisdom (1914) featured Mabel and Edith Taliaferro. Mabel had previously appeared at the Criterion as a child actress. *The Melody of Youth* (1916) featured Eva Le Gallienne in the leading role. *On the Hiring Line* (1919) was an unexceptional production except it marked the last stage appearance of Josephine Hall who appeared at the Criterion twenty years earlier in *The Girl from Maxim's*.

When Hackett's management term ended in 1919 it also marked the end of the Criterion as a legitimate house. In 1920, and until the Paramount Theatre was built, the Criterion was operated by Parmount-Famous-Lasky. Among the films presented at the Criterion were *The Golem, The Covered Wagon, Humoresque,* and *The Ten Commandments*.

John Golden, producer, playwright, and press agent wrote that the Criterion was no more successful than its predecessors. The entire complex was razed in 1935. A new building went up in its place housing a nightclub and dance hall named the International Casino.

Oscar Hammerstein's Olympia complex was a remarkably forward-looking achievement. As what would now be dubbed a performing arts center, the Olympia spurred the development of Times Square, hosted top stars of vaudeville, musical theater and straight plays, saw the introduction of the Ziegfeld Follies, and became an early lynchpin in the emerging Loew's chain of movie theaters.

O'NEILL, EUGENE · (1888–1953) Eugene O'Neill is considered by many theater historians to be the father of twentieth-century American theater. O'Neill pioneered American realism, taking the theater away from the melodramatic and farcical theater that Europe bequeathed to America at the turn of the century. O'Neill was among the earliest playwrights to work in experimental techniques and non-naturalistic styles. He delved into the psyches of his characters as few other playwrights had

before him. Though some of his plays may seem overwritten and dated now, O'Neill set the groundwork for a native theater in the new century. Without his leadership, there might not have been a Group Theater or Tennessee Williams or Arthur Miller. O'Neill, ever the tragedian, won four Pulitzer Prizes and the Nobel Prize for literature.

O'Neill was born on October 16, 1888, to Irish Catholic parents, James O'Neill and Ella Quinlan, at Barrett House, on the northeast side of 43rd Street just off Broadway. Later, Barrett House was converted into part of the Cadillac Hotel around the corner from Rector's Restaurant. O'Neill's father, a matinee idol best remembered for his performance in the play *Monte Cristo,* rivaled Edwin Booth for acting honors.

Eugene O'Neill's home life was especially difficult. He wrestled with his upbringing throughout his life. His parents were able to express affection only by tormenting each other, reconciling their love only through alcohol and narcotics. O'Neill worked autobiographical themes into many of his plays including, most importantly, *Long Day's Journey Into Night* (completed in 1941) and also *All God's Chillun Got Wings* (1923). In these plays he barely disguised the names of members of his family.

O'Neill spent much of the early teens on a variety of vessels sailing the world. He assisted his father on two theatrical tours and thereby learned the intricacies of the theater. Ill health forced him into a sanitarium in 1912 after a stint as a reporter in New London, Connecticut.

In 1915, O'Neill joined a group of young writers who were disenchanted with Broadway and had the youthful optimism to believe they could change the status quo. The group met on Cape Cod at a glorified shack, which they dubbed the Provincetown Playhouse, under the direction of George Cram Cook. The next year, emboldened by their efforts, they set up shop on MacDougal Street in Greenwich Village in a new Provincetown Playhouse.

The year 1917 was important for O'Neill. His talents came to the attention of the Washington Square Players, who later evolved into the Theater Guild. The Players leased the Bandbox Theater on West 57th Street. There they presented O'Neill's one-act play *In the Zone* (1917) to critical applause. The Provincetown Players presented O'Neill's *The Long Voyage Home* (1917) to more acclaim. O'Neill was slowly getting a name for himself in the theater community and beyond.

Beyond the Horizon (1920), the playwright's first important full-length play and first Broadway production, was produced at the Morosco Theatre. The drama was presented during matinees only. When the Morosco's regular tenant, *For the Defense,* closed, *Beyond the Horizon* began a full Broadway schedule.

Beyond the Horizon was a naturalistic play with no melodramatic overtones. Its characters propelled the plot, not theatrical contrivance. O'Neill was criticized for over-writing and for taking a literary rather than theatrical approach to structure, but most critics agreed that *Beyond the Horizon* was a major step forward towards a new American theater. The play received the first of O'Neill's four Pulitzer Prizes for drama.

O'Neill's career flourished as he called on his past for a seemingly infinite number of variations. He would draw on his experiences; mix them with a story in the oral tradition and experimental techniques.

Immediately following *Beyond the Horizon,* O'Neill undertook a number of tasks all at once. He had plays on and off Broadway, some with out-of-town tryouts and others commissioned or waiting to be produced. He was a prolific playwright able to juggle many projects at once, so it seems odd that he quit Broadway in the late thirties to write a cycle of plays, the production of which waited until all were finished.

The Emperor Jones (1920) played at the Provincetown Playhouse. Set to the rhythms of tom-toms beaten at exactly the rate of the human heartbeat, *The Emperor Jones* was highly experimental. The play, which was basically a long monologue, also experimented with the use of ghosts appearing on stage as manifestations of the central character's imagination.

The Pulitzer Prize-winning *Anna Christie* (1921) was O'Neill's next success. The play was a rewrite of *Chris Christopherson,* a drama starring Katharine Cornell that folded in Atlantic City. Arthur Hopkins, one of the most adventurous of Broadway producers, produced Anna Christie. The drama, which opened at the Vanderbilt Theater, was an immediate success. Pauline Lord, in the title role, received glowing reviews, as did her leading man, George Marion, and the sets of Robert Edmund Jones.

The play won for O'Neill his second Pulitzer Prize.

Expressionism, explored in *The Emperor Jones,* was again utilized for dramatic impact in *The Hairy Ape* (1922). Louis Wolheim played the loutish Yank, juxtaposed by O'Neill with the upper class brat Mildred. The play received decidedly mixed reviews, with the negative outweighing the positive.

All God's Chillun Got Wings ostensibly explored the travails of miscegenation. It actually had many of the overtones of O'Neill's youth. The main characters were named Jim and Ella, after O'Neill's parents. Later in a *Long Day's Journey Into Night,* O'Neill would name the mother Mary. His mother's actual name was Mary; she changed it to Ellen and later to Ella.

The opening night of *All God's Chillun Got Wings* (1924) ran into problems before the curtain rose. The first scene, almost a prologue, featured several children. Unfortunately the Children's Society of New York refused to issue the Provincetown Playhouse a license allowing the children to perform. The objection was actually a thinly disguised attempt by racists in the government to keep the play from opening. Ku Klux Klan members had already sent threatening letters to the leads, Paul Robeson and Mary Blair as well as director James Light and O'Neill. A bomb threat was phoned in, threatening the theater with destruction if the play proceeded.

James Light addressed the defiant audience at the opening, asking them whether the play should proceed or not. After receiving a strong yes from the audience, Light proceeded to read the brief prologue since the children were legally unable to appear. The rest of the evening continued without incident. Unfortunately, the play was not a success in the critics' eyes.

Desire Under the Elms (1924) was another presentation of the Provincetown Playhouse at the Greenwich Village Theater. Robert Edmund Jones designed the production and also directed the fine cast. Walter Huston, not yet established as a Broadway performer, starred along with Mary Morris. The play was not a success with the critics, who seemed to feel the dramatic construction was clichéd and shopworn.

O'Neill along with Kenneth Magowan and Robert Edmund Jones presented *The Great God Brown* (1926). O'Neill utilized masks to point up the differences between the characters' true personalities and emotions and how others perceive them. The lead characters let down their masks only when unafraid to bare their innermost souls. After the opening, the critics ran to their typewriters to applaud the play. *The Great God Brown* moved from the Greenwich Village Theater to the Garrick Theater and finally the Klaw Theater.

Marco Millions (1928) was the first O'Neill play to open on Broadway in four years. The previous Broadway production, *Welded* (1924), was not a success. O'Neill's other plays had previewed at the Greenwich Village Theater and many had subsequently moved uptown. The Theatre Guild produced *Marco Millions*. The play opened at the Guild Theater and received mixed to positive notices.

The Guild quickly followed with the opening of *Strange Interlude* (1928). As produced at the John Golden Theater, *Strange Interlude* was an especially provocative play. The drama actually contained three complete three-act plays. The play was referred to by star Lynn Fontanne as a "six day bisexual race." O'Neill put many asides into the dialogue. Director Philip Moeller solved the problem by having the rest of the action freeze while the aside was given.

Strange Interlude was O'Neill's greatest success to date and won for him a third Pulitzer Prize.

O'Neill based his next major work, *Mourning Becomes Electra* (1931), on the *Oresteia* of Aeschylus. Again, New England was chosen as the background for the tragedy. Alice Brady and Nazimova starred in what was actually three plays—*Homecoming, The Hunted,* and *The Haunted.* The play opened under the auspices of the Theater Guild at the Guild Theater. The show ran seven hours with the customary break for dinner. Again, O'Neill garnered great reviews. *Mourning Becomes Electra* was considered by many to be O'Neill's greatest achievement.

O'Neill's next success, a major departure in his usual oeuvre, was *Ah Wilderness!* (1933) an affectionate comedy set in the New England of O'Neill's boyhood. George M. Cohan starred in the sentimental play. Critics were astounded that O'Neill would write such a light, bright comedy. Brooks Atkinson admitted, "As a writer of comedy Mr. O'Neill has a capacity for tenderness that most of us never suspected."

O'Neill had one more play premiere on Broadway, *Days Without End* (1934), before devoting himself to writing a series of plays that he vowed would not be performed until all were finished. He took a break from the play cycle to write *The Iceman Cometh* (1946), which premiered at the Martin Beck Theatre.

During the period that he worked on the cycle, he also completed *Long Day's Journey into Night, Hughie,* and his last completed play, *A Moon for the Misbegotten.* The latter, now considered a great play, was not well received when it opened at the tiny Bijou Theatre (1957).

O'Neill finished drafts of eight of the plays in the cycle, none of which were performed before his death on November 27, 1953. The only play of the cycle to be completed was *A Touch of the Poet.* The remainder were torn up and burned by O'Neill and his wife Carlotta. With his health declining, O'Neill feared that he would die before the plays could be finished and he was determined that no one else should work on them after his death. Only a rough, uncut draft of *More Stately Mansions* survived.

Director Jose Quintero and producers Theodore Mann and Leigh Connell presented *The Iceman Cometh* at the Circle in the Square Theater off-Broadway. Quintero later directed an acclaimed production of *Long Day's Journey* (1956) on Broadway. The production opened at the Helen Hayes Theater. The production starred Fredric March, Florence Eldridge, Jason Robards Jr., and Bradford Dillman. O'Neill was awarded, posthumously, a fourth Pulitzer Prize.

O'Neill brought the American theater into the twentieth century. He allowed it to mature until it could stand on its own against any of the European dramatists. O'Neill, Shakespeare, and Shaw are the most performed playwrights throughout the world. His dramas continue to mesmerize audiences with their stark theatricality and raw emotions.

O'NEILL THEATER · See EUGENE O'NEILL THEATER.

P

PALACE THEATRE   1564 Broadway between 46th and 47th Street. Architects: Kirchoff and Rose. Opening: Vaudeville, March 24, 1913; legitimate theater. January 29, 1966, *Sweet Charity.* Perhaps the best known of all American theaters is the Palace. The Palace was to vaudevillians what Carnegie Hall was to classical musicians: a sign that the performer had reached the height of his or her art.

West Coast vaudeville impresario Martin Beck, head of the Orpheum Circuit, who wanted to conquer the East Coast, built the Palace. Standing in Beck's way was the team of B .F. Keith and E. F. Albee. They controlled the East Coast vaudeville circuit. Albee decreed that any act that played the new theater would be banned from the Keith-Albee circuit. Beck didn't underestimate his competition and gave 75 percent ownership to K&E. However, Beck retained control of the theater's bookings.

The opening program was a matinee on March 24, 1913. The "first-class" vaudeville program was not considered a success by the trade paper *Variety.* The headline reporting the event was "Palace $2 Vaudeville a Joke: Double-Crossing Boomerang."

The Palace appeared to be headed for certain failure, but appearances were deceiving. The theater that would later be referred to as "the home plate of show business" by vaudevillian Pat Rooney Sr. finally made a splash on May 5, 1913. The occasion was an appearance by the almost seventy-year-old Sarah Bernhardt. The tragedian appeared on the Palace stage with her partner Lou Tellegen. Business improved and the Palace was on its way to becoming the Mecca for vaudeville.

The theater changed its bills every Monday at a matinee performance attended by agents, producers, critics and fellow actors. The typical Palace bill consisted of nine acts. The Monday matinee performance was the most important of the week and could make or break a career. It was also considered the toughest audience of the week, and if an act failed to go over it often didn't make it to the evening show.

Most of the Monday afternoon regulars had subscriptions to the theater. In fact, 75 percent of the Palace's business was subscription sales. Business remained good throughout most of the 1920s until new forms of entertainment began to take hold. As radio became more and more popular, many Palace performers gave up the live stage for the microphone. The arrival of talking pictures also dealt a blow to vaudeville and the Palace. A *Variety* article summed up the Palace's declining fortunes when the paper reported on "a line in front of the Palace Monday matinee—on its way to the Roxy." The stock market crash and the Depression finished off vaudeville.

There were some successful acts at the theater after the crash, but they were few and far between. Mostly, the theater resorted to gimmicks to draw patrons. The first idea was to present celebrities who were not true vaudevillians. It had worked with Sarah Bernhardt when the theater was first starting out, so show business wisdom suggested a repeat performance. Nightclub artists like Paul Whiteman who appeared with his band at the Palais Royal were welcomed at the Palace where they were once banned. As talkies gained hold of the public's imagination, washed-up silent-screen stars made personal appearances.

The theater had a strict nine-act vaudeville bill playing two shows a day. But with the theater's fortunes falling, a third daily performance was added in 1929. In the next few years, a fourth and fifth performance was added.

The old vaudeville spirit revived briefly when Kate Smith set a record in August 1931, with her *Swanee Revue* and an eleven-week run. Musical theater stars William Gaxton, Lyda Roberti, and Lou Holtz remained at the Palace for eight weeks. But these successes were exceptional bright spots. When on March 11, 1930, E. F. Albee died, it seemed to mark the end of vaudeville forever and the end of an era at the Palace. On July 9, 1932, the last week of straight vaudeville bill was begun at the Palace.

Thereafter, the Palace added movies to its vaudeville offerings.

Over the next few months, the vaudeville portion of the show faded and the last two-a-day vaudeville show with a movie accompaniment began on November 12, 1932. The once great theater succumbed to the movies on November 17, 1932, with the first film to play the Palace without an accompanying vaudeville show. The movie was the Samuel Goldwyn production of *The Kid from Spain,* starring Eddie Cantor. Only ten days later, a major competitor opened its doors for the first time—Radio City Music Hall.

A straight movie policy continued for a few months at the Palace, but it didn't draw audiences. The major studios had their own flagship theaters in Times Square, including the Warner Brothers, the Loew's State, and the Paramount. So the Palace was forced to scramble for product. Most of the top movies went to the major houses.

From January 7 through February 4, 1933, the Palace reinstated its vaudeville and movie schedule, but by February 11, 1933, the vaudeville was out again. The picture that opened on that day was *The Bitter Tea of General Yen*—on a second run after playing Radio City Music Hall.

On April 29, 1933, vaudeville was brought back and played in a continuous stage show/ movie format, much like the Radio City Music Hall shows of later years. The continuous grind show meant the Palace could only book lesser

acts willing to undergo the torturous regime. That policy also didn't work out, and it ended in the week beginning September 30, 1935.

For the next fourteen years, the Palace stuck to a movie only policy. The vaudeville booking office had long since moved from the sixth floor of the Palace office building to the building housing Radio City Music Hall. Yet ex-vaudevillians without much hope of ever working again still hung out on the Beach across from the Palace.

The theater itself was renovated in August 1941. On May 19, 1949, vaudeville acts once more accompanied movies on stage. The idea originated with Sol Schwartz, the president and general manager of RKO Theaters. Schwartz's idea caught on with the public who oohed and aahed over the theater's $60,000 renovation.

The theater limped along into the fifties with an occasional good week, but as the decade progressed television became an increasingly greater threat to the theater's existence. On October 4, 1951, the theater closed for two weeks for sprucing up to make ready for its next incarnation.

The next turning point in the Palace fortunes came on October 16, 1951, with an appearance by Judy Garland. By this time, Garland's career in pictures was almost finished. She needed the Palace and the Palace needed her. She appeared on a two-a-day policy with such veteran vaudevillians as Smith and Dale whose act "Dr. Kronkite" was the inspiration for the Neil Simon play *The Sunshine Boys.* Garland was booked for a four-week run and stayed for nineteen weeks. She finished on February 4, 1952, with what everyone conceded was a triumphant engagement. More straight vaudeville followed until April 12, 1952, and an appearance by Betty Hutton, which proved almost as popular as Garland's.

Ironically, it was Hutton who replaced Garland in the film version of Irving Berlin's stage hit *Annie Get Your Gun.*

Hutton ran four weeks, and then it was back to Schwartz's eight-act vaudeville policy. The next great event at the Palace took place on January 18, 1953, with an engagement by

Danny Kaye. He played fourteen weeks, a total of 135 performances before 243,250 patrons.

A few more imaginative bookings broke the vaudeville monotony in the fifties. Betty Hutton returned with newcomer Dick Shawn who was "discovered" and became a star. Phil Spitalny and his All Girl Orchestra held the Palace stage for a week in the summer of 1955, and in November the Grand Ole Opry took over the Palace stage.

On November 26, 1956, Judy Garland returned to a triumphant reception at the Palace. This time, comic Alan King was "discovered" at the Palace. Garland concluded another record-breaking run on January 8, 1957, after fifteen weeks at a $7.50 top ticket price.

Jerry Lewis convulsed Palace audiences beginning January 8, 1957, and proved he could make it without his one-time partner Dean Martin. Lewis' four-week run had an advance sale of $90,000, and that was with a top ticket price of only $6.00. During that show, television singer Edie Gorme was "discovered."

Liberace was the next superstar to appear in the Palace with an acclaimed act. However, although he had been booked for four weeks beginning on April 20, 1957, he did poor business and closed after only two weeks.

On August 13, 1957, the Palace again gave up its vaudeville policy. Blockbusters were hard to come by, and in the weeks between their appearances, the theater did not do well. If Liberace could not pack them in, then who could? The only exception to the theater's all-movie policy was a tremendously successful appearance by Harry Belafonte beginning on December 15, 1957. He was booked for eight weeks and stayed for a little over three months, playing to sold-out houses.

On August 19, 1965, the theater was sold to producer James Nederlander. Nederlander restored the theater under the supervision of Ralph Alswang, and in August 1965, the last movie to play the Palace—*Harlow*—premiered.

Nederlander began a new era at the Palace—legitimate theater. The first show, *Sweet Charity* opened on January 29, 1966, with an exceptional score by Cy Coleman and Dorothy Fields. Neil Simon was responsible for the libretto, and Bob Fosse directed. Gwen Verdon perfectly captured the title character. The score contained several standout numbers including "Baby Dream Your Dream," "Where Am I Going?" and "I'm a Brass Band." But the big hit was "Big Spender."

Judy Garland made another appearance at the Palace starting July 31, 1967, in her show *At Home at the Palace.* She appeared with her children Joey and Lorna Luft, comedian Jackie Vernon and vaudeville veteran John Bubbles. She played twenty-four performances. Eddie Fisher and Buddy Hackett opened at the Palace on August 28, 1967, and remained for forty-two performances.

The next musical at the Palace, *Henry, Sweet Henry* (1967), was based on the movie *The World of Henry Orient.* Despite the talents of songwriter Bob Merrill, author Nunnally Johnson, and cast members Don Ameche, Carol Bruce, Alice Playten, Neva Small, and Robin Wilson, the show was a failure.

Though George M. Cohan never played the Palace, the musical *George M!* (1968), starring Joel Grey as the irrepressible Broadway star, opened there. Joe Layton staged the musical with gusto. Supporting Grey were Bernadette Peters, Danny Carroll, Jerry Dodge, Betty Ann Grove, Harvey Evans, and Jill O'Hara.

The next hit to play the Palace was the Charles Strouse and Lee Adams musical *Applause* (1970). Based on *All About Eve, Applause* starred Lauren Bacall, an unlikely musical comedy star. Betty Comden and Adolph Green wrote the script and choreographer Ron Field directed. Bonnie Franklin was hailed as a new Broadway star because of her rendition of the catchy title song. However, Miss Franklin subsequently left Broadway for television and never looked back.

Cyrano (1973) was an especially dismal musicalization of Edmond Rostand's classic *Cyrano de Bergerac. Gentlemen Prefer Blondes,* in which Carol Channing made her first great success, was reworked into the musical *Lorelei* (1974) featuring Carol Channing. Joel Grey returned to the Palace in one of Jerry Herman's few flop shows, *The Grand Tour* (1979).

Lauren Bacall returned in what seemed to be a sure success, *Woman of the Year* (1981) with a fair score by John Kander and Fred Ebb. Despite its long run, *Woman of the Year* never paid back its investors. As a result, the Securities and Exchange Commission revised its rules for investments in Broadway shows. *Woman of the Year,* a forgettable musical, is now chiefly remembered as one of the shows that scared investors away from Broadway.

Jerry Herman recovered from the failure of *The Grand Tour* and presented the Palace his smash hit musical, *La Cage Aux Folles* (1983). Harvey Fierstein wrote the libretto, based on a hugely popular French movie. George Hearn and Gene Barry starred.

La Cage might have run longer, but plans were announced to build a new forty-story office building with 364,000 square feet of office space around the theater, retaining the theater itself. It was considered too expensive to move the show. The architecture firm of Fox & Fowle redesigned the theater as well as the new Embassy Suites Hotel that replaced the old Palace office building. Today, the Palace is barely recognizable from the street having been entirely subsumed by the hotel.

Still, the Palace hosted hit shows. *The Will Rogers Follies* (1991) starred Keith Carradine. The show, which won the Tony Award for best musical, was written by Cy Coleman, Betty Comden and Adolph Green. Disney's stage adaptation of its cartoon hit *Beauty and the Beast* (1994) played the Palace before moving to the Lunt Fontanne Theatre.

Disney's *Aida* (2000), with music by Elton John, was a critical failure but a commercial success at the Palace. An Elvis Presley juke box musical, *All Shook Up* (2005), was a brief tenant and was followed by Elton John's vampire musical, *Lestat* in 2006.

PARAMOUNT THEATER · 1501 Broadway between West 43rd and West 44th Street. Architects: C. W. & George Rapp, constructed 1925–27. Opening: November 19, 1926;

Cavalcade of Motion Pictures. The Times Square Paramount Theater was perhaps the best-loved theater on Times Square. Thousands remember lining up at the theater to hear their favorite band and vocalist. Before adopting a big-band policy, the theater mounted the usual movie palace stage shows, similar to those that later became famous at the Roxy and other giant theaters. The Paramount is the one that remains in most people's minds as the ultimate Times Square theater.

It was built by the Famous Players-Lasky Corporation, the money behind Paramount Pictures, which constructed the Paramount Building above to house their New York headquarters.

The opening program, staged by Broadway director, John Murray Anderson, was a typical, if overblown example of movie-palace offerings. The show was titled a *Cavalcade of Motion Pictures.* After some specialty numbers and the usual speeches, the program began. The show featured a newsreel and some vaudeville type specialties followed by the program proper. After the program came a Paramount Picture—*God Gave Me Twenty Cents,* starring Lois Moran.

Among the notables present at opening night, was a man with his white-haired wife on his arm. As the couple took their seats in a special box, the entire audience rose and gave him a standing ovation. The man was unaware of the applause for he was deaf. He was Thomas Alva Edison, the inventor of the motion picture.

Ticket prices ranged from 40 cents to 99 cents. The theater opened at 10:45 a.m. and closed a little over twelve hours later. Patrons entered the beautiful ticket lobby and then the low-ceilinged Hall of Nations, which opened into the enormous Grand Hall. The Grand Hall lobby was much larger and more ornate than the lobby of the Paris Opera House upon which it had been inspired.

The theater itself sat 3,664 people. The auditorium was criticized at the time but today is viewed in a kindlier light. The only trouble with the theater was the relatively narrow width of the proscenium arch. Later theaters featured huge stages suitable for spectacular presentations and widescreen movies. Most shows staged at the Paramount extended a thrust stage into the auditorium over the orchestra pit. When the big band policy went into effect, the bands played in front of the proscenium. When Vista Vision wide screen films were shown, the sides of the arch were demolished.

The theater presented musical revues, featuring stars of the day like Fred Astaire, Beatrice Lillie, and Ethel Merman, and cut-down versions of Broadway shows. There was a permanent staff, including ballet master Boris Petroff, costume designer Charles LeMaire, and conductor of the Paramount Grand Symphony, Nathaniel Finston. Producing directors, in addition to John Murray Anderson, were R. H. Burnside, a Shubert contract director, Jack Partington, and Frank Cambria. At the Wurlitzer twin organs (called "our masterpiece" by Fanny Wurlitzer, chairman of the board of the Wurlitzer Company) were Mr. and Mrs. Jesse Crawford.

By 1934, in the middle of the Depression, the stage shows were discontinued. Only the organ concerts remained. Then someone got the idea to present big bands and singers. The most famous appearance was that of Frank Sinatra when he sang with the Tommy Dorsey Orchestra and attained the height of his popularity.

The bobby soxers ruled the theater. But after the big band era came television and the beginning of the end for the Paramount. Entertainers preferred to host their own television shows for more money, bigger audiences and less work. They required inflated fees to appear at the Paramount and other theaters.

In the sixties, with the advent of rock and roll, the theater catered to a younger crowd. When school was not in session, the Paramount would draw the younger set in record numbers. But during the day and during the summer when New Yorkers were out-of-town, the theater died.

The Paramount finally closed on August 14, 1965.

The great marquee was taken down, and the theater was gutted. Offices were put in the huge space.

PARADISE GARDENS · See VICTORIA THEATRE (1).

PLYMOUTH THEATER · See Gerald Schoenfeld Theatre.

PORTER, COLE (1892–1964) · Of all the composers and lyricists on Broadway, Cole Porter was the most urbane and sophisticated and, at times, the silliest. Porter was certainly a celebrated wit and bon vivant both at home and in Europe. His wealth and social contacts made him the spokesperson and satirist of the upper classes. Whether down in the depths on the ninetieth floor or beginning the beguine, Porter was an important voice in the musical theater.

Of course, he also spoke to the average person, as witnessed by the hundreds of popular songs to his credit. In his heyday, during the Depression, he fueled the dreams and fantasies of a generation. They could escape to exotic locales with the upper crust in the comfort of a balcony seat.

Porter's facility with rhythms and rhymes masked the hard work he put into the shows. This facility was all the more remarkable when juxtaposed with Porter's own personal torments.

Born in Peru, Indiana, on June 9, 1891, he showed an early talent for music and composed his first published song, "The Bobolink Waltz," at the age of ten.

Porter set out to become a lawyer. Towards that end he enrolled in Worcester Academy and then Yale at the direction of his grandfather. But Porter proved more interested in his extracurricular songwriting than in his studies. While at Yale, he wrote two of that school's more enduring standards, "Bingo Eli Yale" and the "Yale Bullfrog Song." After leaving Yale for the Harvard Law School, his dean suggested that the School of Music might suit his temperament better. So Porter switched majors and began to write musical comedies.

His first break came when he met Elisabeth Marbury, the woman who produced many of Jerome Kern's early hits. Their show entitled *See America First* (1916) was written in collaboration with T. Lawrason Riggs. "I've a Shooting Box in Scotland" became a minor hit.

After the failure of *See America First*, Porter abandoned the stage for three years. He didn't need to work, and so he spent the time touring the world as well as spending a brief sojourn with the French Foreign Legion. While on board a ship bound for the United States, Porter met Broadway producer and comedian Raymond Hitchcock. Hitchcock hired Porter to compose the score to the third edition of a short-lived revue series, *Hitchy-Koo*.

Hitchy-Koo (1919), at the Liberty Theatre, was more successful than his last outing. Porter's score yielded his first full-scale hit, "Old Fashioned Garden." Comedian Joe Cook, making his Broadway debut, introduced the song.

Even early on in his career, Porter explored themes familiar to him from his monied and leisured situation. The lyrics of "I've a Shooting Box in Scotland" were a litany of residences around the world owned by the singer. *Hitchy-Koo of 1919* contained "In My Cozy Little Corner of the Ritz" and "I Introduced," the latter a list of all the greats introduced to each other in one social outing or another.

In 1923, Porter was left over a million dollars by his grandfather, which allowed him more time to travel the world. He returned to the Broadway theater with his score for the *Greenwich Village Follies of 1924* (1924). The show introduced "I'm In Love Again," a moderate hit at the time.

Paris (1928) starred the French performer Irene Bordoni, known for her saucy smile and insinuating air. Porter provided her with what became one of his best-known songs, "Let's Do It."

The reception to Porter's music was tremendous. He realized that celebrity could not only be fun but could also distinguish him from all the other bored millionaires in his circle of friends. Indeed, his popularity extended to his social strata, and he was in great demand for parties and soirees.

Porter's *Fifty Million Frenchmen* (1929) opened at the Lyric Theater. The show was the second one produced by Bordoni's husband, E. Ray Goetz. The book writer was Herbert Fields who later wrote libretti for six other Porter shows. "You Do Something to Me" was the hit of the show, which starred Helen Broderick, Genevieve Tobin, and William Gaxton. The show was a big success in spite of the stock market crash, providing Porter with even more fame.

Several of Porter's songs were interpolated into an English import, *Wake Up and Dream!* (1929). The principal Porter contribution was "What Is This Thing Called Love?"

Porter's work gained new depth with each succeeding score. His melodies were uniquely his own and not based on cliched musical forms currently in vogue. His lyrics, too, showed added layers of emotion. He never relied on the moon-June-croon rhymes of his contemporaries, nor did he resort to straightforward and unimaginative contrivances.

The New Yorkers (1930) opened at the Broadway Theatre. E. Ray Goetz was Porter's producer for the third time. Herbert Fields contributed the book, and Monty Woolley directed his second Porter offering. The score contained several of Porter's best work including "Where Have You Been?," "Let's Fly Away," and "Take Me Back to Manhattan."

The song that became the biggest success and caused the biggest sensation was "Love for Sale." It proved too much even for some audiences to see the beautiful Katharyn Crawford playing a prostitute on the stage. So the character was given to Elisabeth Welch, brought on especially to sing the song. Because Welch was black, audiences seemed better able to accept her rendition of the song. The number's backdrop pictured a city street. The sign Park Avenue was simply changed to Lenox Avenue, and the show went on.

Gay Divorce (1932), at the Ethel Barrymore Theater, starred Fred Astaire in his first solo outing away from his sister Adele, as well as Claire

Luce, Luella Gear, and Betty Starbuck. *Gay Divorce* featured what is considered by many to be Porter's finest song, "Night and Day."

Anything Goes (1934) starred Porter's favorite musical comedy performer, Ethel Merman. Supporting her were William Gaxton, Victor Moore, Vivian Vance (later to achieve greater fame as Ethel Mertz in "I Love Lucy"), and Bettina Hall. The score was among Porter's best, with no less than four gems. "All Through the Night," "I Get a Kick Out of You," "You're the Top," and the title song have all become recognized as classic examples of American popular song.

Porter's next offering, *Jubilee* (1935) contained a score almost the equal to that of *Anything Goes*. "Begin the Beguine" and "Just One of Those Things" were the standouts.

Porter had hit his stride and next provided the score for a zany musical comedy, *Red, Hot and Blue!* (1936), at the Alvin Theater. The title referred to the fact that the heroine had an identifying mark on her posterior caused by her sitting on a waffle iron. The lady in question was Ethel Merman, who was ably abetted by Jimmy Durante and Bob Hope. The score again showed Porter at the top of his class with such great songs as "It's De-lovely," "Ridin' High," and the title song.

While on vacation in the summer of 1937, Porter suffered a horrible riding accident. His horse threw him and fell on his legs, crushing them and causing extensive damage to his nervous system. Porter spent the remainder of his life in constant pain. Even after thirty-one operations, he never fully recovered. In 1958, his right leg was amputated. His friends doubted that he would ever write again and blamed his later failures on his great pain. But Porter bounced back creatively from this tragedy.

You Never Know (1938), Porter's first Broadway assignment after the accident, opened at the Winter Garden Theater. "At Long Last Love" was the most notable song in an otherwise inconsequential score.

Mary Martin got the Porter treatment along with William Gaxton, Victor Moore, and Sophie Tucker in *Leave It to Me!* (1938). Martin introduced "My Heart Belongs to Daddy," which made her a star.

Ethel Merman and Bert Lahr were back in *Du Barry Was a Lady* (1939). Betty Grable, Charles Walters, and Benny Baker helped round out the cast in the Porter hit. Herbert Fields and B. G. DeSylva wrote the book, which told the story of a lowly washroom attendant who dreams he is the King of France. "Friendship" was the archetypal Porter list song, a genre he elevated to an art form.

Merman also appeared in the next Porter musical, *Panama Hattie* (1940), little remembered today. Arthur Treacher, Rags Ragland, James Dunn, and Betty Hutton also appeared in the production.

Let's Face It! (1941) was his second show of the forties. Danny Kaye made the biggest effect with his tongue-twisting songs "Farming" and "Let's Not Talk About Love."

Something for the Boys (1943), at the Alvin Theater, marked Porter's last score written for Ethel Merman. Bill Johnson, Paula Laurence, and Betty Garrett were also in the wartime musical.

Mexican Hayride (1944) was another hit show for Porter; the show had a less than top-notch score, though "I Love You" became a big hit. Bobby Clark and June Havoc starred. This show, like Porter's last four shows, played over four hundred performances, yet none of the scores for these shows achieved the success of Porter's musicals of the thirties.

His next score was for producer Billy Rose's revue *The Seven Lively Arts* (1944). The cast was superlative: Beatrice Lillie, Bert Lahr, Benny Goodman, Alicia Markova, and Dolores Gray headlined. The revue introduced one hit, "Ev'rytime We Say Goodbye," one of Porter's greatest ballads.

Porter's next show, the monumental *Around the World in Eighty Days* (1946) was written for the enormous talents of Orson Welles, who produced, directed, and contributed the book. The young genius also starred in the show, which proved to be an expensive failure. Porter's contributions contained nothing of much interest to his fans.

Word on the Rialto was that Porter was washed up. Although he began the forties with long runs, he had few big hit tunes. Porter seemed to have lost touch with the changing scene on Broadway. After the war, high society and sophistication were decidedly out of fashion. However, at his lowest ebb, Porter came up with his greatest success.

Samuel and Bella Spewack (librettists of *Leave It to Me!)* wrote a modern adaptation of William Shakespeare's *The Taming of the Shrew,* a work totally different from the kinds of shows Porter had been writing. Porter and the Spewacks managed to produce a masterpiece, *Kiss Me, Kate* (1948). It was a show in the best tradition of what came to be known as the Rodgers and Hammerstein styled musical. The songs were not the usual star turns that Porter was so adept at writing. Instead, the songs in *Kiss Me, Kate* defined characters, advanced the plot, and provided an excellent opportunity for Porter to exhibit his characteristically ingenious wordplay. The show opened with Alfred Drake, Patricia Morison, Harold Lang, and Lisa Kirk heading the cast. The score is among Porter's best with "Another Openin', Another Show," "Wunderbar," and "So in Love" receiving the greatest airplay. But the rest of the score was as good as, and sometimes better than, the hit-paraded songs. Porter had proved that reports of the death of his career were premature.

Kiss Me, Kate's producers Saint Subber and Lemuel Ayers commissioned Porter's next show, *Out of this World* (1950). Surprisingly, "From This Moment On," the song that became the best known of the score, was dropped from the show during its out-of-town tryout. The remaining songs as sung by Charlotte Greenwood, William Eythe, Priscilla Gillette, and William Redfield were almost of the caliber of those for *Kiss Me, Kate.*

Porter's next to last show, *Can-Can* (1953), was a much bigger hit. The Parisian locale was better suited to Porter's sensibilities, and the score yielded several hits: "I Love Paris," "C'est Magnifique," and "Can-Can." Lilo, Peter Cookson, and Hans Conreid were the advertised stars, but by the end of the opening

night at the Shubert Theater, another star was born, Gwen Verdon. The production proved to be Porter's second longest run.

His last show, *Silk Stockings* (1955) was based on the film *Ninotchka.* Hildegarde Neff had the Greta Garbo part with support from Don Ameche and Gretchen Wyler. "All of You" was the hit song of the show, which was later made into a movie musical starring Fred Astaire and Cyd Charisse. The musical proved a successful end to Porter's Broadway career.

Porter wrote two scores for the movies, *High Society* and *Les Girls,* as well as an original television musical, *Aladdin.* He died on October 15, 1964.

PRINCE, HAROLD (1928–) · Harold Prince is currently Broadways most successful producer and director. In the wake of a string of failures in the 1970s, Broadway wags announced his career dead. But with his direction of *Phantom of the Opera,* the most successful musical in Broadway history, he has once again risen to the top of his profession.

Prince began as a stage manager for George Abbott. He then became a boy wonder through his partnership with the more experienced producer Robert Griffith. Prince set out on his own when Griffith died in 1961.

Perhaps he is best noted for a series of astonishing musicals he produced and sometimes directed in collaboration with songwriter Stephen Sondheim. Prince is one of the most influential people in the evolution of the American musical. He has an ability to control pacing and structure and a great eye for theatricality and stage pictures.

Prince's record of success is almost unequaled in the history of American theater. His shows as a producer or coproducer include *The Pajama Game* (1954); *Damn Yankees* (1955); *New Girl in Town* (1957); *West Side Story* (1957); *Fiorello!* (1959); *Tenderloin* (1960); *A Family Affair* (1962) as director only; *A Funny Thing Happened on the Way to the Forum* (1962); *She Loves Me* (1963) also as director; *Fiddler on the Roof* (1964); *Baker Street* (1965) as director only; *Flora, the Red Menace* (1965); *It's a*

Bird, It's a Plane, It's Superman (1966), also as director; *Cabaret* (1966), also as director; *Zorba* (1968), also as director; *Company* (1970), also as director; *Follies* (1971), also as codirector; *A Little Night Music* (1973), also as director; *Candide* (1973), also as director; *Love for Love* (play) (1974); *Pacific Overtures* (1976), also as director; *Rex* (1976), as codirector only; *On the Twentieth Century* (1978), as director only; *Sweeney Todd* (1979), as director only; *Evita* (1979), as director only; *Merrily We Roll Along* (1981), also as director; *A Doll's Life* (1982), as director only; *End of the World* (play) (1984), as director only; *Grind* (1985), as director only; and *Phantom of the Opera* (1988).

PRINCESS THEATER · 104 W. 39th Street. Architect: William A. Swasey. Opening: March 14. 1913; one-act plays: *The Switchboard; Fear; Fancy Free; Any Night;* and *A Tragedy of the Future.* The Princess Theater, long a failure as a legitimate house, played an important role in the history of the American musical. In the teens, the Princess served as the home of the first great intimate musicals. They were written by Jerome Kern, Guy Bolton, and P. G. Wodehouse. Later the theater served as the home for the long-running revue *Pins and Needles.*

The Princess, designed by William A. Swasey, was built as a small auditorium by the Shubert brothers, William A. Brady, and Arch Selwyn. The site for the 299-seat theater was chosen for its proximity to the Metropolitan Opera. Unlike other theaters uptown, the Princess had a simple design. There were fourteen rows of seats in the orchestra section and four boxes.

After several false starts, Holbrook Blinn was named director and F. Ray Comstock the manager of Broadway's newest venue. The theater was to feature the works of new playwrights. Four one-act plays were presented at its opening. The opening bill proved to be unpopular, and Brady and Selwyn gave Comstock their shares in the theater.

Comstock decided that a new policy was necessary and asked a leading agent, Elisabeth Marbury, for her help. She represented many of the best-known playwrights, and her business sense was legendary. She was the first agent to get her playwrights a percentage of the gross receipts of their productions instead of a flat fee. Marbury also helped the career of America's leading dance team, Vernon and Irene Castle.

Marbury suggested small, intimate musicals for the Princess' stage. Comstock agreed, but it was decided that the leading Broadway composers wouldn't be interested, given the small size of the house. Marbury approached the young Jerome Kern, who in turn suggested librettist Guy Bolton. Comstock meanwhile booked a production of a decade-old English musical, *Mr. Popple of Ippleton.* The show was entitled *Nobody Home* for its American debut.

Nobody's Home (1915) had some new Jerome Kern numbers interpolated into the original Paul Rubens score. Before the show closed, it was decided to move the production to the Maxine Elliott's Theater nearby. The Princess' small seating capacity simply didn't allow for a big enough profit.

Kern wrote the score for the second Princess Theater show, *Very Good Eddie* (1915). Philip Bartholomae and Guy Bolton contributed the book. Herbert Reynolds and Schuyler Greene wrote the lyrics to Kern's tunes. *Very Good Eddie* led the way to a succession of successful, intimate musicals at the Princess. The following Princess show, *Go to It* (1916) was an adaptation of Charles Hoyt's 1894 hit, *A Milk White Flag.*

The Princess' next show, *Oh, Boy!* (1917), represented another step forward in the gradual evolution of a truly American musical distinct from the European operetta tradition. The Kern, Bolton, and Wodehouse musical was an immediate success. The trio continued their advancement of the musical theater form with the fifth Princess Theater show and their last collaboration, *Oh, Lady! Lady!* (1918) with Vivienne Segal.

For *Oh, My Dear!* (1918), Wodehouse and Bolton collaborated with a new composer,

Louis A. Hirsch. The last of the Princess Theater musicals was the Richard Whiting and Raymond B. Egan musical *Toot Sweet* (1919).

In 1928, the name of the theater was changed for the first time. Beginning with the opening of *Sun-Up* (1928), the theater was called the Lucille La Verne Theater.

The theater was renamed the Princess with *He Walked in Her Sleep* (1929). The old name lasted only a few months. On October 16, 1929, with the opening of the play *Lolly*, the Princess became the Assembly Theater.

The Depression took a toll on Broadway theaters, and the Assembly was no exception. In 1933, the theater became a movie house, the Reo. The International Ladies Garment Workers Union bought the building and used it as a union hall. They presented a show in their theater, which they called the Labor Stage.

The result was Harold Rome's surprise success, *Pins and Needles* (1937). The topical revue starred members of the Union, many of whom were making their performing debuts. *Pins and Needles* became a smash hit and played several editions at the Labor Stage. Until *Hellzapoppin, Pins and Needles* was the longest-running Broadway musical. It played the Labor Stage for most of its 1,108 performance run, leaving for the Windsor Theater in June 1939.

The theater changed again in 1944 when it became the Theater Workshop. On October 31, 1947, the movie *Lucia de Lammermoor* opened in the theater, which was renamed the Cinema Dante. On April 22, 1948, the movie *Not Guilty* opened. This time, the theater was called the Little Met. Its name was changed one last time on April 16, 1952, with the opening of the movie *La Forza Del Destino*. The theater's last name was Cinema Verdi.

In June 1955, the theater, which had figured so strongly in the history of the musical, was razed to make room for an office building.

PUNCH AND JUDY THEATRE · See CHARLES HOPKINS THEATER.

R

RADIANT CENTER · See GEORGE ABBOTT THEATER.

REPUBLIC THEATER · 207 W. 42nd Street. Architect: J. B. McElfatrick & Co. Opening. September 27, 1900; *Sag Harbor.* After building the Victoria Theater on the corner of 42nd Street and Seventh Avenue, Oscar Hammerstein I built the Republic next door on 42nd Street. The Republic thus became the first theater built on 42nd Street. The Republic and Victoria share the same roof and on it Hammerstein built the Paradise Garden.

The first production at the theater was James A. Herne's *Sag Harbor.* Herne appeared in the show as well accompanied by his two daughters, Crystal and Julie, and a young Lionel Barrymore. December 31, 1901, saw an early theatrical favorite, Viola Allen, open in the play *In the Palace of the King.* In February of 1902 Henrietta Crossman played the Republic in two shows, *As You Like It* and *Mistress Nell.*

Hammerstein wasn't interested in operating his new theater and leased it in 1902 to David Belasco, who immediately rechristened the house the Belasco. The producer gutted the theater and hired architects Bigelow, Wallis and Cotton and interior designers Rudolph Allen and William Linde to redesign the interior. With their $125,000 budget, they removed the musician's gallery atop the thirty-five-foot wide proscenium arch as well as all of McElfatrick's stenciling, brocaded walls, decoration on the balcony fronts, and any unnecessary cherubs and their ilk.

Belasco, long known for the excellence and innovation of his electrical effects outfitted his theater with the latest in electrical technology. The first rheostats on Broadway were among the innovations. A further twenty feet under the stage was excavated to make room for a vast labyrinth of machinery underneath the stage to allow for grand scenic effects. During the excavation, workers accidentally struck an underground spring which flooded the theater. Belasco also added a handsome iron and glass marquee outside spelling out his name on frosted glass panels.

Belasco's first production at what was definitely the most technically advanced theater in the world was a transfer from the Criterion Theatre of his own play, *Du Barry,* which premiered September 29, 1902, starring Mrs. Leslie Carter. The great actress exclaimed, "The stage and the auditorium are so related that one is on confidential terms with the audience." Critic Alan Dale of the *New York American* wrote that the theater was "by all odds the most beautiful theatre playhouse in the city, bar none."

Other hits at the Belasco were *The Music Master* starring David Warfield, and *The Girl of the Golden West,* later the basis for the Puccini opera.

In 1910, Oscar Hammerstein I turned over control of the theater to his son Arthur. But Belasco was unwilling to let his lease lapse. Oscar took him to court and Belasco was forced to vacate the theater. He then built the current Belasco Theatre. Hammerstein brought in A. H. Woods as producer. Woods changed the name of the theater back to Republic on September 11, 1910, during the production of *Bobby Burnit,* which opened August 22, 1910. That same year the city widened 42nd Street and the theater lost its marquee and staircase.

The Republic was host to a variety of presentations for the next decade. Attractions included the New York premiere of *Peter Ib-betson* in 1917, the transfer of *Abie's Irish Rose* from the Fulton Theater, and *Common Clay*, 1915.

Like most of the 42nd Street theaters, the Republic ceased to stage legitimate productions during the Depression. The Republic became a Minsky's burlesque house in 1931, but after LaGuardia's crackdown on burlesque it was renamed the Victory Theater with a movie policy on May 9, 1942. It continued as such until 1995 when it was renovated at a cost of $11 million and turned into a non-profit theater devoted to presenting an amazing variety of children's entertainments. The 769 seat theatre (with its exterior staircase restored) is one of the success stories of the Times Square redevelopment.

RIALTO THEATER · Northwest corner of 42nd Street and Broadway. Architect: Thomas Lamb. Opening: April 21. 1916. The Rialto was built on land occupied by Oscar Hammerstein I's Victoria Theater. Like its sister theater the Rivoli, the Rialto was built by Crawford Livingston and Felix Kahn, owners of the Mutual Film Company. This "Temple of the Motion Picture-Shrine of Music and the Allied Arts" was designed by Thomas Lamb, one of the greatest architects of motion-picture theaters.

Lamb designed the interior of the theater in his favorite style, that of the Adam brothers. The Rialto, which opened in 1916, was probably the first theater built expressly to show motion pictures. This was the dawn of feature pictures. The Rialto had no stage area. The screen was mounted directly on the back wall of the theater.

On either side of the screen were two platforms on which soloists performed between shorts and while reels were changed. The same policy was later used by S. L. ("Roxy") Rothafel in Livingston and Kuhn's Rivoli Theater. In the orchestra pit, Hugo Reisenfeld conducted the symphony orchestra that accompanied the silent films.

Lighting dimmers were just coming into use

and Roxy and Lamb installed a series of lights throughout the auditorium that could be faded from one color to the next. The Rialto's "color harmonies" were widely imitated and can be seen today at Radio City Music Hall.

The Broadway facade was marked by a huge sign in a pinwheel shape with sparks that seemed to shoot out and spell the word *R-I-A-L-T-O*. Above the sign, an American eagle beat its electric wings. Atop the eagle, also designed in lights, was the Stars and Stripes.

Livingston and Kuhn were smart enough to hire "Roxy" Rothafel to manage their new theater for $200 a week. Roxy was the genius behind the operation of the Strand Theater, one of the first motion-picture palaces.

The theater's opening was delayed, in part because of meddling by Hammerstein. He made sure he would have an office in the new Rialto Theater. Hammerstein's impish nature took over, and he plotted his revenge on Livingston and Kahn. First, he refused to leave the Victoria, even as it was being demolished. Then he decided to move into the new Rialto on the date specified on his lease. Naturally, the space wasn't ready yet.

The Rialto opened on April 21, 1916. The opening night was a glorious affair with Mary Pickford, Adolph Zukor, and Marcus Loew present. Also at the opening was R. A. Rolfe, Roxy's replacement at the Strand. Everyone was curious to see how Roxy could top his achievements at the Strand.

The Rialto was so successful that its owners decided to lease the site of the Palmer-Singer Garage and built the Rivoli Theater. After taking control of both the Rivoli and the Rialto, Roxy moved on to the Capitol Theater.

The Rialto fell on hard times with Roxy gone and the Mutual Film Corporation unable to make the transition to sound. The Depression hit Broadway hard. The Rialto was sold and razed. In its place was built another Rialto Theater.

The new Rialto had an uneventful life. In 1980, the theater was refurbished, and a legitimate theater policy was attempted. Among the theater's shows (all failures) were *Musical Chairs*

(1980) and *A Reel American Hero* (closed in previews). After this brief period (the shows played less than a month combined time), a movie policy was renewed. The entrance reverted to 42nd Street, and kung-fu movies again became the norm. In May 1987, the theater was in the process of being twinned, having been bought by the Cineplex Odeon chain. After serving briefly as a television studio, the theater was razed and replaced by the new Reuters skyscraper.

RICHARD RODGERS THEATER · 226 W. 46th Street. Architect: Herbert J. Krapp. Opening: December 24, 1924; *Greenwich Village Follies*. Chanin's 46th Street Theatre was one of the six Broadway theaters built by the Chanin brothers, Irwin and Henry, prominent New York developers. They commissioned theater architect Herbert J. Krapp to build the theater and he came up with a unique idea. Instead of dividing the theater into orchestra and balcony, he raked the seats bleacher-style to the upper back wall. Unfortunately, patrons sitting in the rear of the orchestra find their sightlines blocked by the overhang of the balcony.

The Shubert brothers leased the house from the Chanins and booked the theater. Most of the early shows to play the 46th Street had opened at other theaters and were moved here to end their runs. The opening presentation, *The Greenwich Village Follies of 1924*, was no exception. It had run previously at the Shubert and Winter Garden theaters and closed soon after arriving.

The theater had its first big hit with the college musical, *Good News* (1927). DeSylva, Brown and Henderson contributed an enthusiastic score to the show. The hit songs included "The Best Things in Life Are Free," "Just Imagine," "The Varsity Drag," "Lucky in Love," and the exhilarating title song.

Zelma O'Neal starred in *Good News* as well as the theater's next hit, *Follow Thru* (1929). DeSylva, Brown, and Henderson again provided a superior score, including "Button Up Your Overcoat." In addition to Zelma O'Neal, the cast included Jack Haley and Eleanor Powell.

Top Speed (1929) opened with Ginger Rogers making her Broadway debut. Billy Rose presented a revue, *Sweet and Low* (1930). Hit songs included "Cheerful Little Earful" with music by Harry Warren and lyrics by Ira Gershwin and Billy Rose. An even bigger hit was "Would You Like to Take a Walk," with music by Warren and lyrics by Mort Dixon and Rose.

In 1931, the Shuberts gained ownership of the theater from the Chanins in a deal that included the Shuberts giving control of the land under their Century Theatre to the Chanins.

Harold Arlen and Jack Yellen wrote the score to *You Said It* (1931). Benny Baker, Lyda Roberti, and Lou Holtz starred in the musical.

The Depression hit Broadway hard, and the Chanins lost their theaters. Though their name was dropped from the marquee, the 46th Street Theatre continued as one of Broadway's most successful.

Howard Lindsay had a hit comedy at the theater with *She Loves Me Not* (1933). Burgess Meredith, John Beal, and Polly Walters starred in the backstage/college thriller/comedy. *The Farmer Takes a Wife* (1934) was Henry Fonda's entry to Hollywood. He and Margaret Hamilton appeared in both the film version and the Broadway production.

One of the biggest hits in Broadway history, *Hellzapoppin* (1938), opened at the 46th Street Theatre to mostly negative reviews. However, audiences loved it. They were convinced to attend by columnist Walter Winchell, who used his vast power to plug the show whenever possible. Ole Olsen and Chic Johnson were responsible for the craziness on stage (and sometimes in the audience and lobby) that ranged from cheap burlesque jokes to cheaper vaudeville acts.

Cole Porter returned to the 46th Street Theatre (*Anything Goes* moved there from the Alvin Theater) with a zany show, *Du Barry Was a Lady* (1939), which starred Bert Lahr and Ethel Merman.

Merman and Porter were back at the 46th Street with *Panama Hattie* (1940). Also in the cast were Arthur Treacher, Pat Harrington Sr., Oscar ("Rags") Ragland, Joan Carroll, and Betty Hutton.

After the successful run of the eerie play *Dark of the Moon* (1945) came a revival of Victor Herbert's operetta *The Red Mill.* Then another classic musical, *Finian's Rainbow* (1947), opened at the 46th Street. Burton Lane and E. Y. Harburg wrote the brilliant score and Harburg and Fred Saidy contributed the alternately fantastic and trenchant book. The delightful cast included David Wayne, Ella Logan, and Albert Sharpe.

The next three shows at the 46th Street received mixed reviews. The first, *Love Life* (1948), was a under appreciated gem by Alan Jay Lerner and Kurt Weill. Elia Kazan directed the cast, which included Nanette Fabray, Ray Middleton, and Lyle Bettger. Producer Cheryl Crawford presented *Love Life* and also the 46th Street's next offering, Marc Blitzstein's opera *Regina* (1949). Based on Lillian Hellman's *The Little Foxes, Regina* starred Priscilla Gillette, Brenda Lewis, Russell Nype, Jane Pickens, and William Warfield. Nanette Fabray returned in *Arms and the Girl* (1950), with a score by Morton Gould and Dorothy Fields.

The 1950s continued the theater's good fortune with one of Broadway's greatest hits, Frank Loesser's masterpiece *Guys and Dolls* (1950). The musical boasted a superior book by Jo Swerling and Abe Burrows. George S. Kaufman directed the exceptional cast, which included Vivian Blaine, Robert Alda, Isabel Bigley, Stubby Kaye, and Sam Levene.

Audrey Hepburn starred in *Ondine* (1954) with Mel Ferrer. Maxwell Anderson's *The Bad Seed* (1954) was another hit at the 46th Street. Patty McCormack played the murderous child, and Nancy Kelly played her mother.

Gwen Verdon began a long run at the 46th Street in three different musicals. The first was the Jerry Ross and Richard Adler hit *Damn Yankees* (1955). George Abbott directed. Hit songs included "Heart" and "Whatever Lola Wants." Bob Fosse was the brilliant choreographer.

Gwen Verdon kept her dressing room and opened in Bob Merrill's *New Girl in Town*

(1957). The show was also written and directed by George Abbott and choreographed by Bob Fosse. The musical version of Eugene O'Neill's *Anna Christie* contained two wonderful songs, "Look at 'Er" and "It's Good to Be Alive."

Verdon stayed at the theater for *Redhead* (1959). Albert Hague and Dorothy Fields provided the score, including two hits, "Look Who's in Love" and "Merely Marvelous." For *Redhead,* Bob Fosse not only choreographed but also directed.

Bock and Harnick wrote the score to *Tenderloin* (1960). Jerome Weidman and George Abbott's book was about a priest's attempt to clean up Manhattan's notorious Tenderloin district. The cast included Maurice Evans, Ron Husmann, Rex Everhart, Eileen Rodgers, and the ubiquitous Eddie Phillips.

Frank Loesser returned to the 46th Street Theatre with a Pulitzer Prize-winning musical, *How to Succeed in Business Without Really Trying* (1961). The satire made a star of Robert Morse, who costarred with Rudy Vallee, Claudette Sutherland, Charles Nelson Reilly, Virginia Martin, Bonnie Scott, and Ruth Kobart.

Next came Richard Rodgers and Stephen Sondheim's *Do I Hear a Waltz?* (1965). Arthur Laurents based the libretto on his own play, *The Time of the Cuckoo.* Mary Martin and Robert Preston were the sole cast members of the enchanting *I Do! I Do!* (1966), a musical version of Jan de Hartog's *The Fourposter.* Tom Jones and Harvey Schmidt wrote the score.

The theater's next hit had an unlikely subject for a musical. *1776* (1969) traced the founding of the United States. Sherman Edwards' score and Peter Stone's libretto made the proceedings dramatic. In 1971, a revival of the tremendously successful *No No Nanette* opened. Ruby Keeler, Helen Gallagher, Susan Watson, Jack Gilford, and Bobby Van starred. The hit even brought Busby Berkeley back to Broadway.

Raisin (1973) was a musical version of Lorraine Hansberry's *A Raisin in the Sun.* The theater was again host to Gwen Verdon and Bob Fosse with the John Kander and Fred Ebb musical *Chicago* (1975). It costarred Chita Rivera and Jerry Orbach.

The next show, *The Best Little Whorehouse in Texas* (1978), broke the theater's long-run record. Carol Hall provided music and lyrics, and Larry L. King and Peter Masterson wrote the libretto. The show was a popular hit due in part to Tommy Tune and Peter Masterson's energetic direction.

In 1981, the Shuberts sold the 46th Street Theatre to the Nederlanders.

Another offbeat subject, Federico Fellini's *8-1/2*, a movie about an artistically blocked film director, was the basis for a hit musical at the 46th Street. *Nine* (1982) was another success for director Tommy Tune. *Fences* (1987), by August Wilson, starred James Earl Jones and was awarded the Pulitzer Prize.

Neil Simon had two hits in the theater. The first, *Lost in Yonkers* (1991). It was followed by *Laughter on the 23rd Floor* (1993) a recreation of the madcap atmosphere of writing for comedian Sid Caesar in the early days of television.

On April 26, 1990, the theater was renamed in honor of composer Richard Rodgers.

Kander and Ebb had two shows back to back at the theater. The first was the revival of *Chicago* (1996) which moved to make way for the original musical, *Steel Pier* (1997). Unfortunately, the show, Kander and Ebb's last as a team, was not a success. Another flop followed, the musical *Side Show* (1997). Two more musical failures followed, *Footloose* (1998) and *Seussical* (2000). The latter, though a failure on Broadway, has become a smash hit on the amateur market due to the popularity of Dr. Seuss. Neil Simon had another late career failure with *45 Seconds from Broadway* (2001). Choreographer Twyla Tharp took tunes from Billy Joel and fashioned a big hit, *Movin' Out* (2002). Though it did have singing by an onstage pianist and a plot, the show was really a dance concert not a musical.

At press time *Tarzan* (2006) occupies the Richard Rodgers stage, the latest offering by Disney Theatricals.

RITZ THEATRE · See WALTER KERR THEATER.

ROCK CHURCH · See JOHN GOLDEN THEATER.

RODGERS, RICHARD · See RODGERS AND HAMMERSTEIN and RODGERS AND HART.

RODGERS AND HAMMERSTEIN · Richard Rodgers and Oscar Hammerstein II are considered to be the masters of the American musical comedy. Their formula for musical theater consisted of well-integrated songs and book, with songs that reflect the characters' personalities both in words and music. This formula or pattern for show construction and writing has been emulated since the years of their first big hit, *Oklahoma!*

The success of *Oklahoma!* came at a crucial point in both their careers and at a crucial point in the history of the Theater Guild, its producer. Rodgers had already enjoyed a successful career with his longtime partner, Lorenz Hart. The team of Rodgers and Hart were known for their sophisticated, witty contributions to a series of mostly playful, lighthearted shows. When Hart's personal problems stood in the way of further collaboration, Rodgers was forced to seek another partner. He turned to Oscar Hammerstein II, the scion of a great theatrical family.

Hammerstein at the time had his own problems. His last productions were failures, and it was whispered along Broadway that he was washed up as a creative artist. He had already enjoyed a distinguished career with such offerings as *Show Boat, Rose-Marie,* and *The Desert Song* to his credit. Hammerstein was looking for a new partner, one who would challenge him to new artistic heights.

The Theater Guild was also suffering. Their recent productions had proven unsuccessful at the box office, and the producing organization was close to bankruptcy. Theresa Helburn, codirector of the Guild, had recalled an earlier Guild-produced play, *Green Grow the Lilacs,* and thought that it might work as the basis for a successful musical.

The Guild approached Rodgers, who in turn

approached Hammerstein. Rodgers had previously helped the Guild when his early musical *The Garrick Gaieties*, written with Hart, proved to be a great success. The revue had put the early Guild on a firm financial footing.

In transforming *Green Grow the Lilacs* into *Oklahoma!*, Rodgers and Hammerstein took many liberties with the musical comedy tradition. There was no opening chorus sung by a bevy of leggy chorines. Instead, the show opened with a lone figure singing "Oh, What a Beautiful Morning." Furthermore the villain, Jud, was a truly menacing figure, not just a two-dimensional moustache twirler. Another change was that Jud is killed at the end, an uncommon occurrence in musical comedy.

Oklahoma! (1943) was somewhat unique in that it dealt with three-dimensional characters in an American locale. Most musicals at the time still featured the operetta conventions of exaggerated lovers in exotic, foreign locales. *Oklahoma!* boasted a dream ballet choreographed by the great Agnes de Mille. This was the first important musical comedy ballet that actually advanced the plot and wasn't simply an excuse for dancing, though George Balanchine's *Slaughter on Tenth Avenue*, choreographed for Rodgers and Hart's *On Your Toes*, was an early attempt at integration between dance and plot.

The show opened at the St. James Theatre. The production starred a host of unknowns who would, as a result of the success of *Oklahoma!*, become famous. Alfred Drake, Joan Roberts, Betty Garde, Howard da Silva, Celeste Holm, and Lee Dixon were the leads.

Oklahoma! played for five years and nine weeks in New York. That was enough to make it the long-run musical record holder until July 11, 1961, when *Hello, Dolly!* passed it. Questions as to whether Rodgers and Hammerstein could repeat their success were answered when *Carousel* (1945) opened at the Majestic Theater.

The Theater Guild repeated its role as producer. Again, Rodgers and Hammerstein broke new ground. Their lead character, Billy Bigelow, a bully and crook, is killed and reappears as a spirit. The show was also unique in that it dealt with serious subjects that the average musical comedy, meant mainly to entertain, rarely attempted.

The cast was another talented group of unknowns. John Raitt and Jan Clayton were the two star-crossed lovers Billy Bigelow and Julie Jordan. They were given some of the songwriters' greatest songs. "If I Loved You," "Soliloquy," and "What's the Use of Wond'rin'" are all among the finest songs in musical theater. Other hits in the score were "June Is Bustin' Out All Over" and "You'll Never Walk Alone." *Carousel* ran until May 24, 1947.

After a stint in Hollywood, where they wrote the movie musical *State Fair,* the team's next Broadway musical was *Allegro* (1947). It was not nearly so successful as their previous works when it opened at the Majestic Theater. Many of Rodgers and Hammerstein's previous collaborators repeated their chores with *Allegro*. The Theater Guild produced, Agnes de Mille choreographed and moved into the director's seat. Robert Russell Bennett, the noted Broadway orchestrator, also repeated his role.

With *Allegro,* the team attempted to break more musical theater conventions. One idea was to have the musical comedy chorus act as a Greek chorus, but this and other ideas simply didn't work. *Allegro* closed on July 10, 1948. It did contain a minor hit, "The Gentleman Is a Dope."

The team redeemed themselves with *South Pacific* (1949), an immensely successful show. It opened at the Majestic Theater with Mary Martin, opera great Ezio Pinza, Juanita Hall, William Tabbert, and Betta St. John. Joshua Logan coauthored the book with Hammerstein and directed the production.

The score contained more songs destined to become standards. "Dites-moi," "A Cockeyed Optimist," "There Is Nothin' Like a Dame," "Bali Ha'i," "I'm Gonna Wash That Man Right Outa My Hair," "Some Enchanted Evening," "Younger Than Springtime," and "This Nearly Was Mine" made up one of the greatest scores written for any musical. *South Pacific* ran until January 16, 1954.

Their next hit, *The King and I* (1951), opened at the St. James Theatre. Gertrude Lawrence, Yul Brynner, Doretta Morrow, Dorothy Sarnoff, and Larry Douglas starred. The score was up to Rodgers and Hammerstein's high standards. "I Whistle a Happy Tune," "Hello, Young Lovers," "Getting to Know You," "I Have Dreamed," and "Shall We Dance?" were the standouts.

The show followed in the Rodgers and Hammerstein tradition of breaking new ground. Throughout the show, the two leads, Anna and the King, have an adversarial relationship. At the end, they have a grudging respect for each other. Before they have a chance to enter into a typically cliched musical comedy romance, the King dies. *The King and I* played 1,246 performances.

Me and Juliet (1953), at the Majestic Theater, was a second failure for Rodgers and Hammerstein. The story was about two backstage romances. Isabel Bigley, Bill Hayes, Ray Walston, George S. Irving, Joan McCracken, Buzz Miller, and Mark Dawson starred in the cast. "No Other Love," based on a theme Rodgers wrote for the television documentary *Victory at Sea*, was the hit song in the show.

The critics didn't consider the show a failure, although all agreed it wasn't up to the team's usual standard.

Pipe Dream (1955), a musicalization of John Steinbeck's novel *Sweet Thursday*, was the next show on the Rodgers and Hammerstein schedule. It opened at the Shubert Theater. William Johnson, Mike Kellin, Judy Tyler, and Helen Traubel were featured in the cast. Again the critics were disappointed. The audiences were also disappointed, and the show closed after only 246 performances.

Cinderella was the team's next musical, written for television. It played on March 31, 1957, on CBS. Julie Andrews and Jon Cypher were the stars.

Gene Kelly was the director of Rodgers and Hammerstein's next outing, *Flower Drum Song* (1958). It opened at the St. James Theatre. *Flower Drum Song* was the story of the Chinese population of San Francisco and conflicts between the immigrant population and native-born Chinese. It starred Juanita Hall, Ed Kenney, Keye Luke, Larry Blyden, Jack Soo, Miyoshi Umeki, and Pat Suzuki.

The score received modest praise. "I Enjoy Being a Girl" was the one hit. "Love Look Away," and "Sunday" were also singled out by some reviewers. They noted that while the score wasn't top-quality Rodgers and Hammerstein, it was still better than most Broadway offerings.

Rodgers and Hammerstein's sentimentality reached its zenith with *The Sound of Music* (1959), their last show. Based on the early career of the Trapp Family Singers, the show opened at the Lunt-Fontanne Theater. The cast included Mary Martin, Theodore Bikel, Patricia Neway, Nan McFarland, Kurt Kasznar, Marion Marlowe, Lauri Peters, and Brian Davies. The score was in the tradition of the great Rodgers and Hammerstein's shows and yielded the hits "My Favorite Things," "The Sound of Music," "Sixteen Going on Seventeen," "Do Re-Mi," and "Climb Every Mountain."

The film version, released by Twentieth Century-Fox on March 2, 1965, was an even greater success. It became one of the top grossing pictures of all time.

Oscar Hammerstein II died on August 23, 1960, leaving Richard Rodgers without a partner. Rodgers went on to write a succession of musicals with various partners, to varying success.

For his first outing after Hammerstein's death, he contributed the lyrics himself. The show was *No Strings* (1962) at the 54th Street Theater. Diahann Carroll and Richard Kiley had the leads in the romantic musical. Rodgers again broke new ground with the new show. The book makes no comment on the racial differences in the leads. The score yielded a great hit, "The Sweetest Sounds." Rodgers' surprisingly adept lyrics had more in common with Hart's work than Hammerstein's.

The job of writing both music and lyrics was tough, and Rodgers decided to join up with a new partner for his next show, *Do I Hear a Waltz?* Arthur Laurents adapted his play *The Time of the Cuckoo* as the source for the libretto. For his new partner, Rodgers chose Hammerstein's protege, Stephen Sondheim.

The two didn't see eye to eye, and their collaboration was stormy. It did, however, result in a good score. *Do I Hear a Waltz?* (1965), starring Elizabeth Allen and Sergio Franchi, opened at the 46th Street Theatre.

Rodgers next show fared slightly better. *Two By Two* (1970) found him teamed with Martin Charnin. The show, a retelling of the story of Noah, opened at the Imperial Theatre. It starred Danny Kaye in a return to Broadway after an almost twenty-five year absence. The show was not one of Rodgers' best, and the score was largely undistinguished. Critics were especially disappointed in the libretto by Peter Stone and the lyrics by Charnin.

Sheldon Harnick was Rodgers' next choice for a collaborator. *Rex* (1976), at the Lunt-Fontanne Theater, was based on an unlikely subject for Rodgers, the court of King Henry VIII. It was not a success.

Rodgers' last show, though slightly more successful, was still a failure. *I Remember Mama* (1979) opened at the Majestic Theater, His lyricists were Martin Charnin and Raymond Jessel. The musical was based on the straight play version of Kathryn Forbes' story, *Mama's Bank Account,* the same play that Rodgers and Hammerstein had produced earlier in their careers.

Liv Ullmann was the unlikely choice to play Mama but received mostly good notices. Reviews for the show, however, were mostly devastating.

Richard Rodgers died on December 30, 1979.

RODGERS AND HART · Richard Rodgers and Lorenz Hart were the premier collaborators in the early years of the American musical theater. In fact, they were the first team in which the lyricist received equal billing with the composer. Artistically, Rodgers and Hart were the perfect songwriting team. (Later Rodgers and Hammerstein would be equally famous as a team.) Their fame was enduring and well-deserved. Their music and lyrics were superbly integrated in a sophisticated whole. Although their personal relationship was somewhat stormy, their songs never reflected the problems they were having.

Lorenz Hart (1895–1943) Lorenz Hart was born in New York City on May 2, 1895. His parents, Max and Frieda Hart, were immigrants who instilled in their son a love of language and literature. He attended his first play when he was seven and was permanently hooked on the theater.

Richard Rodgers (1902–1979) Richard Rodgers was born in New York City on June 28, 1902. This is where Rodgers and his parents, William and Mamie, lived and where his father practiced medicine. Rodgers showed an early gift for music. He could play the piano when only four years old.

Like most aspiring songwriters of his generation, the young Rodgers hoped for a career in musical comedy. At that time, composing for the Broadway theater was considered the top of the art form. There were no movies or radio, and most popular songs were introduced first on the Broadway stage. Like many of his contemporaries, Rodgers sought to realize his aspirations by writing scores for amateur shows.

Rodgers' first song, for which he supplied the music and lyrics, was "Campfire Days" written while at Camp Wigwam in Maine. His first copyrighted song was "Auto Show Girl" with lyrics by David Dyrenforth. It was registered on June 30, 1917. His first complete score was written for the show *One Minute Please* (1917). It was presented by the Akron Club of which his brother Mortimer was a member. Rodgers wrote the music and lyrics to the show as well as the next Akron Club presentation. *Up Stage and Down* (1919), also a success, resulted in Rodgers' father paying for five of the songs to be published.

* * * *

A friend, Philip Leavitt, introduced Rodgers to the young Lorenz Hart. Leavitt was pleased with the way the two boys got along. He convinced Lew Fields to listen to their songs, and the producer decided to interpolate a Rodgers and Hart number in his Broadway show *A Lonely Romeo* (1919). The song, "Any Old Place with You," was added after the show's opening. Fields was impressed with the team's effort. After several more amateur shows, Fields decided to interpolate some of the team's songs into his next show, *Poor Little Ritz Girl*. In addition Fields announced that he would allow the team to write the remainder of the score, their first Broadway musical.

Poor Little Ritz Girl (1920) opened at the Central Theater. By that time, Fields had gotten cold feet and had cut eight of the Rodgers and Hart tunes. He hired Sigmund Romberg and Alex Gerber to supply additional tunes.

Rodgers and Hart soon found themselves back writing for amateur shows. Herbert Richard Lorenz contributed the script and two songs to *The Melody Man* (1924), a play produced by Lew Fields. Herbert Richard Lorenz was, of course, a nom de plume for Herbert Fields, Richard Rodgers, and Lorenz Hart.

Rodgers and Hart received their big break in 1925. The show was a revue, *The Garrick Gaieties* (1925). It was produced as a two performance special fundraiser. The Theater Guild, which was building a new theater on Broadway, had run short of money and needed the benefit to buy curtains and draperies for the new house. The show was also seen as a way for the Guild to showcase its lesser-known members such as Stanley Holloway, Libby Holman, Romney Brent, and Lee Strasberg. The show proved a great success for the Guild and the cast, and Rodgers and Hart were finally established as a top-rate songwriting team.

For the show, they contributed one of best their tunes, "Manhattan." Still one of the most recognizable of Rodgers and Hart's hits, the song has continued as a standard in the jazz repertoire.

The next Rodgers and Hart project was the first in a long line of Broadway musicals with book by Herbert Fields. *Dearest Enemy* (1925) opened at the Knickerbocker Theater and was an immediate success. "Here In My Arms" was the biggest hit of the show's delightful score.

Billy Rose commissioned the team to write a revue called *The Fifth Avenue Follies*. It opened at the Fifth Avenue Club in January 1926. The trio was back on Broadway with *The Girl Friend* (1926), which opened at the Vanderbilt Theater. Lew Fields, having passed on *Dearest Enemy*, saw the error of his ways and produced the new show. The title tune became a hit at the time as did "The Blue Room," which has enjoyed a somewhat longer life.

Next, Rodgers and Hart were asked to contribute songs to the second edition of the *Garrick Gaieties* (1926) at the Garrick Theater. "Mountain Greenery" was the hit song. They next went to London, contributing the score to *Lido Lady* (1926), which opened at the Gaiety Theater. None of the songs achieved much success.

The team was reunited with librettist Herbert Fields for *Peggy-Ann* (1926). The score was delightful with "A Tree in the Park" and "Where's That Rainbow?" worthy of additional attention. The show was a hit, playing almost ten times as long as Rodgers and Hart's next show, *Betsy* (1926), a failure produced by Florenz Ziegfeld.

The team escaped to London where they contributed a score to another revue, *One Dam Thing After Another* (1927). The hit song was "My Heart Stood Still," which had its American debut in their next outing (with Herbert Fields), *A Connecticut Yankee*.

A Connecticut Yankee opened at the Vanderbilt Theater (1927). The top-notch score contained hits like "My Heart Stood Still," "Thou Swell" and "I Feel at Home with You."

Without Herbert Fields, the songwriters seemed to have difficulty. *She's My Baby* (1928) had a book by Guy Bolton, Bert Kalmar, and Harry Ruby. It opened at the Globe Theatre. Herbert Fields rejoined the team for *Present Arms* (1928). *Chee-Chee* (1928), their next show, was even more of a failure. In fact, it had the shortest run of any Rodgers and Hart show. *Spring Is Here* (1929) was much more traditional and inspired the songwriters to write one of their best tunes, "With a Song in My Heart." They followed it up with two middling productions, *Heads Up!* (1929) and *Simple Simon* (1930), which opened at the Ziegfeld Theater "Ten Cents a Dance" was featured in *Simple Simon*. London called again for *Ever Green* (1930) with Jessie Matthews and Joyce Barbour starring. The hit song was "Dancing on the Ceiling."

Herbert Fields was brought back into the fold for *America's Sweetheart* (1931). It opened at the Broadhurst Theater with Harriette Lake (better known today as Ann Sothern) and Jack Whiting. They introduced the hit song from the show, "I've Got Five Dollars."

Like many of their Broadway contemporaries, Rodgers and Hart were wooed to Hollywood in the early thirties. They completed a series of films (some great, some bad) but they found New York more to their liking and soon returned. Their movies were *The Hot Heiress* (1931); *Love Me Tonight* (1932); *The Phantom President* (1932); *Hallelujah, I'm a Bum* (1933); *Hollywood Party* (1934); and *Mississippi* (1935).

They returned to New York with *Jumbo* (1935), certainly their biggest show and one of the largest shows ever seen in New York. Producer Billy Rose rented Manhattan's enormous theater, the Hippodrome, for the extravaganza that employed an entire circus. Ben Hecht and Charles MacArthur wrote what book managed to be seen amid the clowns, tumblers and animals. The show was so big that both John Murray Anderson and George Abbott shared directorial chores.

Despite rave reviews and a score that featured such Rodgers and Hart perennials as "The Most Beautiful Girl in the World," "My Romance," and "Little Girl Blue," the show was a failure. It managed to run seven months but it cost an astounding $340,000, and the weekly operating cost precluded any profit.

After *Jumbo,* Rodgers and Hart entered their most productive and successful decade. It began with the opening of *On Your Toes* (1936) at the Imperial Theatre. It starred Ray Bolger, Doris Carson, Tamara Geva, Luella Gear, and

Monty Woolley. The score featured such great songs as "There's a Small Hotel," "Glad to Be Unhappy," and the title song. There was an added bonus in the two ballets, "La Princesse Zenobia" and the classic "Slaughter on Tenth Avenue." Both were choreographed by the legendary George Balanchine.

Following a largely unsuccessful return to Hollywood with the film *Dancing Pirate* (1936), Rodgers and Hart presented Broadway with one of their most exuberant hits, *Babes in Arms* (1937) at the Shubert Theater. The songs were top-drawer Rodgers and Hart, and almost every song in the score became a standard. They included "Where or When," "I Wish I Were in Love Again," "My Funny Valentine," "Johnny One Note," and "The Lady Is a Tramp."

George S. Kaufman and Moss Hart contributed one of Rodgers and Hart's most unusual books. The show was *I'd Rather Be Right* (1937), about Peggy and Phil who want to marry but can't afford to until Phil receives a promised raise. Unfortunately, Phil won't receive his raise until the federal budget is balanced. The hapless couple run into President Roosevelt in Central Park. This was the first time that a living president was depicted in a musical comedy.

For the role, they chose George M. Cohan. He was certainly one of the most patriotic Americans and one who could give a mature, serious performance even when dancing and singing.

Peggy and Phil got the best song in the show, "Have You Met Miss Jones?" Cohan did have several good numbers including "I'd Rather Be Right," and "Off the Record." The show is best known today for a scene from it that was included in the James Cagney movie *Yankee Doodle Dandy.*

For their next show, *I Married an Angel* (1938), Rodgers and Hart again supplied the book and George Balanchine choreographed his third Rodgers and Hart show. *I Married an Angel* had a wonderful score, most important of which was "Spring Is Here."

One of the team's greatest successes followed. *The Boys from Syracuse* (1938), at the

Alvin Theater, was based on Shakespeare's *The Comedy of Errors*. George Abbott contributed the book as well as producing and directing the show. The songwriters were obviously inspired by the material, for they wrote a terrific score. "Falling in Love with Love" and "This Can't Be Love" were the big hits, and the remainder of the songs were just as well crafted. The show starred Eddie Albert, Teddy Hart (Larry's brother), Burl Ives, Ronald Graham, Jimmy Savo, Wynn Murray, Muriel Angelus, and Marcy Westcott. *Too Many Girls* (1939) opened at the Imperial Theater. It is noteworthy today as the Broadway debut of Desi Arnaz. The score was sometimes inspired, though it was not as good as their best work. There was however one stand out song, "I Didn't Know What Time It Was."

Higher and Higher (1940), their next Broadway show, was a disappointment at the Shubert Theater. A standard did emerge, the wistful "It Never Entered My Mind." *Pal Joey* (1940) was not the typical musical comedy. For one thing, the lead character, the unscrupulous Joey, was a tough character for forties audiences to accept. He was a scoundrel—talented and attractive but a scoundrel. The score was among the team's most sophisticated and adult. In fact, "Bewitched Bothered and Bewildered" had to have its lyrics softened before radio stations would play it.

The show was not the sort one would expect to open on Christmas Day. The reviews were mixed. The critics wanted to like the show since it was clear superior talents were at work. However, most of them couldn't get past the unsentimental aspects of the show and its cynicism. Gene Kelly as Joey, Vivienne Segal, and Leila Ernst received good notices, but the general public was simply not ready for an adult musical comedy.

They Met in Argentina (RKO 1941) was released prior to the opening of the team's last Broadway show, *By Jupiter* (1942), for which they supplied the book, music and lyrics. The show opened at the Shubert Theater. It might have been their greatest success but for the fact that Ray Bolger, the star, quit to entertain

troops overseas. It achieved the longest run of any Rodgers and Hart show until the revival of *Pal Joey*.

Unfortunately, it was the last full-scale collaboration between Rodgers and Hart. Rodgers was a finely disciplined man used to working regular hours with great determination and single-mindedness. Larry Hart was exactly the opposite. Whereas Rodgers knew exactly where he stood in the world, Hart was insecure and unstable, becoming increasingly more difficult as the partnership progressed. Often, he would disappear for days, forcing Rodgers to halt production or even write lyrics himself. Hart's insecurities led to more missed deadlines and more drinking. Rodgers reached the end of his patience during *By Jupiter* and began quietly to inquire about other partnerships.

Theresa Helburn of the Theater Guild wanted Rodgers to adapt the play *Green Grow the Lilacs* into a musical comedy. Rodgers reluctantly approached Hart, who realized he was not up to the role either mentally or physically. Rodgers then turned to his old friend and sometime collaborator from the early days at Columbia University, Oscar Hammerstein. The result was *Oklahoma!* (1943). Hart was present at the opening of the milestone musical and congratulated Rodgers on his success. But the show must have been a further blow to Hart's already damaged self-esteem.

The last project that the two worked on together was the 1943 revival of *A Connecticut Yankee*. Hart had collaborated with Rodgers on a new song for the show, "To Keep My Love Alive." Following the opening night performance on November 17, Hart disappeared. He remained missing for two days until he was found unconscious in a hotel room. He was taken to Doctor's Hospital, where it was determined he had pneumonia. On November 22, 1943, Lorenz Hart died.

ROMBERG, SIGMUND (1887–1951) ·
Sigmund Romberg was Broadway's most prolific composer, having had more than sixty musical productions produced in his forty-year career. Although Romberg was proficient in

most musical theater styles, he achieved his greatest fame as a composer of operettas. His most enduring shows are still being performed. *Blossom Time, The New Moon, The Desert Song,* and *The Student Prince* are all favorites of light opera companies and summer theaters.

He was born on July 29, 1887, in Nagy Kaniza, Hungary. Romberg came to the United States in 1909 where he held a variety of jobs, from work in a pencil factory for $7 a week to pianist in restaurants. While at Bustanoby's restaurant, he met Edward Marks, a prominent music publisher. Marks encouraged the young man to pursue composing and soon Romberg had his first published song, "Some Smoke (Leg of Mutton)."

The job at Bustanoby's also introduced Romberg to J. J. Shubert of the great Shubert brothers' theater empire. The Shuberts needed shows to fill their theaters, including the huge Winter Garden Theater, home of the annual revues, the *Passing Shows.* Romberg was hired to write the score for *The Whirl of the World* (1914). Songs were freely interpolated into the shows. The Shuberts felt that if the scores needed any popular hits, they could easily be bought. Publishers were all too happy to provide songs to the revue series just to be able to print on their sheet music, "as sung by _____ in the Winter Garden show ___." Romberg obliged them by cranking out a series of good if not exceptional songs.

His next assignments for the Shuberts were a series of mostly forgettable revues and musicals with lyrics by Harold Atteridge. The *Passing Show of 1914* (1914) and *Dancing Around* (1914) were followed by *Maid in America* (1915); *Hands Up* (1915) with lyrics by E. Ray Goetz; *The Blue Paradise* (1915) with lyrics by Herbert Reynolds; and *A World of Pleasure* (1915). These shows were all relatively successful, and most made money for the Shuberts. *The Blue Paradise* contained Romberg's first hit song, "Auf Wiedersehen."

Romberg had six shows open in 1916. The first was a vehicle for the great Al Jolson, *Robinson Crusoe, Jr.* It was followed by the *Passing Show of 1916*; *The Girl from Brazil* with Mat-

thew Woodward lyrics; *The Show of Wonders*; *Follow Me* with lyrics by Robert B. Smith; and *Her Soldier Boy* with book and lyrics by Rida Johnson Young. Naturally, with so many shows to churn out, Romberg needed help. On most of these shows Romberg collaborated with other composers.

It was surprising that Romberg could produce anything of quality considering his output. Yet he did manage to create many successful hits. For *Maytime* (1917), Romberg collaborated with Rida Johnson Young, a lyricist and librettist who also wrote hit shows with Victor Herbert (*Naughty Marietta*) and Rudolf Friml (*Sometime*). She gave Romberg his first long-lasting hit and one of his greatest songs, "Will You Remember (Sweetheart)." Another of *Maytime's* hit songs was "Road to Paradise."

Following his work on the *Passing Show of 1919*, Romberg left the Shubert fold. He decided to go out on his own as a composer and to produce his own shows in association with producer Max Wilner. Their two efforts, *The Magic Melody* (1919) with Clare Kummer's lyrics and *Love Birds* (1921) with Ballard Macdonald, were both failures. Romberg also wrote the music to *Poor Little Ritz Girl* (1920) with Alex Gerber. Richard Rodgers and Lorenz Hart had already written a complete score for the show while it was out-of-town prior to Broadway. But producer Lew Fields threw out most of their score and added songs by Romberg. Despite the interpolations, the show was a failure.

With three unsuccessful shows to his credit, Romberg found it difficult to get more writing assignments, so he returned to the Shubert fold. The Shuberts had Romberg on a salary, so no matter how successful the shows were, Romberg received the same amount of money. Also, because he was a contract employee in the years before ASCAP was established, Romberg did not own his own songs. The Shuberts received all the rights and royalties from them. Occasionally, Romberg would play the piano for rehearsals as well as conduct the orchestra during previews, all to supplement his salary.

The producers sought to placate Romberg by assigning him what eventually became *Blossom Time* (1921). Romberg collaborated with Dorothy Donnelly on the adaptation of *Das Drei Maedelhaus,* a European operetta. The music was based on melodies by Franz Shubert and H. Berte. "Song of Love" was the only hit song to emerge from the score. The Shuberts sent out many national companies for years afterward and the piece became as good as money in the bank. By February 1924, the show had earned the Shuberts an amazing $700,000.

After *Blossom Time,* it was back to the same old grind for Romberg. *Bombo* (1921) was next, another Jolson starrer. Following *Bombo* came *The Blushing Bride* (1922) written with Cyrus Wood and then *The Rose of Stamboul* (1922); *Springtime of Youth* (1922) with Harry B. Smith; and *The Dancing Girl* (1923). Another edition of *The Passing Show* (1923) followed.

In 1924, Romberg had a banner year. He fulfilled his usual assignments for the Shuberts and others with *Innocent Eyes*; *Marjorie*; the *Passing Show of 1924*, the last in the series; *Artists and Models*, the second edition of a new Shubert revue series with lyrics by Sam Coslow and Clifford Grey; and his first show for producer Florenz Ziegfeld, *Annie Dear*, again with Grey.

Romberg's next hit was the biggest of his career. *The Student Prince* (1924) was written in collaboration with Dorothy Donnelly. Its hit songs included "Golden Days," "Deep in My Heart," "The Drinking Song," and "To the Inn We're Marching." The show turned out to be the longest running of all the Romberg operettas.

The success of *The Student Prince* firmly established Romberg as a top composer who could handle a full score with skill. His next show, *Louis the 14th* (1925) was a Ziegfeld production. It was written by Romberg and Arthur Wimperis. The show starred Leon Errol and Ethel Shutta. His second show of the season was *Princess Flavia*.

With his output slowing, his successes grew.

The Desert Song (1926), his next operetta, was another great hit. The lyrics were by Otto Harbach and Oscar Hammerstein II. Harbach, Hammerstein and Frank Mandel wrote the libretto. The superior score included the hits "Ho! (The Riff Song)," "French Military Marching Song," "Romance," "The Desert Song," "One Flower Grows Alone in Your Garden," and "One Alone."

In 1927, a good year for the musical theater, Romberg contributed music to four productions. *Cherry Blossoms* was first with book and lyrics by Harry B. Smith. The failure led to his second production, *My Maryland*. Dorothy Donnelly was the author of book and lyrics of the hit show. The hit song of the show was "This Land Is My Land." Donnelly also collaborated on the third Romberg production in 1927, *My Princess*. It, however, didn't repeat the success of the last show. *The Love Call*, written with Harry B. Smith, did little better.

The composer tried his hand at a show in a more contemporary vein with *Rosalie* (1928). Romberg and P. G. Wodehouse wrote half the score. George and Ira Gershwin contributed the other half of the Ziegfeld production. Romberg's second production in 1928 was even more successful. *The New Moon*, another operetta, had book by Oscar Hammerstein II, Frank Mandel, and Laurence Schwab. Hammerstein and Romberg came up with another fine score. The hits include "The Girl on the Prow," "Lover, Come Back to Me," "Marianne," "One Kiss," "Softly, As in a Morning Sunrise," "Stouthearted Men (Liberty Song)," and "Wanting You." *Nina Rosa* (1930) was Romberg's next show. It had lyrics by Irving Caesar and libretto by Otto Harbach.

The next year found Romberg collaborating again with Hammerstein. The result was *East Wind* (1931), a failure. After a year off, Romberg came up with *Melody* (1933), another show with Irving Caesar. Hammerstein took his next turn with Romberg, and the result was *May Wine* (1935). Laurence Schwab produced the show, which was a minor success. *Forbidden Melody* (1936) had lyrics and book by Harbach.

The operetta form was practically dead on Broadway. During the thirties, Romberg occupied himself with assignments in Hollywood. In the forties, Romberg toured the country with an orchestra that featured his music. Five years passed between *Forbidden Melody* and his next Broadway opening, *Sunny River* (1941). The Romberg and Hammerstein show was one of the first to deal with psychoanalysis, opening the same year as *Lady in the Dark*. It was also notable in that it dispensed with a chorus line, but it was still clearly an operetta.

Apparently, other producers agreed with Gordon that the operetta was still a valid theatrical form. In 1945, Romberg was teamed up with a decidedly modern lyricist, Dorothy Fields, for *Up in Central Park* (1945). The Michael Todd production's surprise success was probably due as much to the renewed interest in American subjects in musicals aroused by the success of *Oklahoma!* as to the piece itself. What was more surprising was the success of the score. The hit, "Close As Pages in a Book," was among Romberg's best compositions.

Although *Up in Central Park* was a hit, it was assumed that its success was unique. While some other lesser operettas were produced, on the whole Broadway ignored the style. Romberg's next to last Broadway show was the last he would live to see. *My Romance* (1948), written with Rowland Leigh, was, appropriately, produced by the Shubert brothers.

On November 10, 1951, Sigmund Romberg died in New York City. But there would be one more Romberg show on Broadway, *The Girl in Pink Tights* (1954). Leo Robin provided the lyrics to the songs that were worked up by orchestrator, Don Walker. The show contained Romberg's last hit song, "Lost in Loveliness."

Romberg's melodies continue to grace theaters all over the world. His shows are even occasionally revived on Broadway and at the New York City Opera. His most successful shows will be performed as long as musical theater is performed.

ROME, HAROLD (1908–1993) · Harold Rome's output might not match that of his contemporaries in quantity, but the quality and success of his shows puts him near the top of the list of Broadway songwriters.

Like other successful songwriters, Rome studied to be a lawyer. He graduated from Yale in 1929, the year of the stock market crash. He worked for a law office and asked for lunch money. The firm refused him, and Rome quit. He began accompanying ballet classes and decided to become a songwriter.

His first show, *Pins and Needles,* was his most successful and somewhat of a miraculous success story. The International Ladies Garment Workers Union (ILGWU) owned a small theater called the Labor Stage. In fact, it was originally the Princess Theater where Jerome Kern, Guy Bolton, and P. G. Wodehouse first presented their landmark Princess Theater shows.

But the ILGWU had other uses for the tiny stage, holding their elections and meetings in the theater. Then union leader Louis Schaffer conceived the notion of producing an amateur show featuring members of the union. The show was intended as both an outlet for talent within the union and an entertaining way to present his union's views. Schaffer hired the young Harold Rome to compose the score and play the piano.

The show was scheduled to be performed for a limited run. As it was, the rehearsals took over a year and a half since they could only be held on the performers' days off or after work. After a long gestation, *Pins and Needles* (1937) opened.

Rome's song titles illustrate the lighthearted approach the show took to its serious themes—"Sing Me a Song of Social Significance," "It's Better with a Union Man," "One Big Union for Two," "The Red Mikado," and "Doin' the Reactionary."

Once the show settled into its 1,108 performance run, additional material was constantly added. Many more contributors were brought in to the production team, and the show evolved as it continued its remarkable run. *Pins and Needles* had become the longest running musical in Broadway history at the time of its closing.

Rome's next project was another satirical revue, this time on a grander scale than *Pins and Needles*. *Sing Out the News* (1938) opened at the Music Box Theater. Rome's score included one popular hit, "Franklin D. Roosevelt Jones," and another topical hit, "My Heart is Unemployed." Despite the libretto by Rome and Charles Friedman and the producing talents of Max Gordon, George S. Kaufman and Moss Hart, the show was not a success.

Rome continued in a topical vein with his next show, written while he was in the Army. *Call Me Mister* (1946) featured ex-servicemen in the cast in much the same manner as Irving Berlin's *This Is the Army*. *Call Me Mister* starred Betty Garrett, Lawrence Winters, Maria Karnilova, Jules Munshin, and Danny Scholl. The score again contained a topical hit, "The Red Ball Express." and a popular hit, "South America Take It Away." Like *Sing Out the News*, *Call Me Mister* made Roosevelt the subject of a song. This time, the song, "The Face on the Dime," was more reverent.

Rome's high regard and affection for the middle class were again expressed in his next show, the lighthearted *Wish You Were Here* (1952), which opened at the Imperial Theatre. Arthur Kober and Joshua Logan wrote the story of a group of New Yorkers enjoying a brief vacation in an adult camp in the Catskill Mountains. Rome's fresh and youthful score included one major hit, the title song, "Wish You Were Here."

The reviews for the show weren't very positive, but in an unusual move, the creative staff stayed on the project after the opening, strengthening the book. One gimmick working for the show was the swimming pool constructed in the center of the stage. The swimming pool proved to be a great attraction. The show steadily built an audience through word of mouth, and several critics returned to the theater to review the new changes in the show. The hard work paid off and *Wish You Were Here* enjoyed a long run.

Fanny (1954) was the brainchild of producer David Merrick. Ezio Pinza followed his spectacular musical comedy debut in *South Pacific* with *Fanny*. Florence Henderson, who had a small part in *Wish You Were Here,* played the title character. Rome's score for *Fanny* was one of his most haunting, The score yielded another hit, the title song, "Fanny."

Merrick bought the stage rights for the Universal picture *Destry Rides Again* (1959) and hired Rome to write the score. Andy Griffith and Dolores Gray headed the cast. New York's garment district was the setting for Rome's next Broadway musical, *I Can Get It for You Wholesale* (1962). It is perhaps best remembered as the Broadway debut of Barbra Streisand in a supporting part.

Rome's final Broadway production was the play with music, *The Zulu and the Zayda* (1965). Louis Gossett, and Menasha Skulnik played the lead roles, which combined two of Rome's favorite subjects. The Zayda, an old Jewish man, was a natural character for Rome to write about. The Zulu was equally familiar to Rome since he had collected African art since 1939. (Eventually he brought together one of the most important collections in the world.) Rome was also intrigued with African music and wove a rich score combining the best of Jewish and African music. Despite its rather unusual subject matter, *The Zulu and the Zayda* deserved a better fate. Its title was confusing to many theatergoers who couldn't tell exactly what the show was about.

Rome's next subject was again quite unlikely. He originally wrote a musical version of *Gone with the Wind* for a 1970 production in Japan. The show was reworked following its Japanese success and opened in 1972 in London. It finally made it to the United States in 1973, but never reached Broadway.

Rome did not have another show produced on Broadway. In his last years, he concentrated on his collection of African art and his painting. Broadway was poorer for the absence of one of its most versatile and creative songwriters.

Harold Rome died on October 26, 1993.

ROYALE THEATRE · See BERNARD B. JACOBS THEATRE

S

ST. JAMES THEATRE · 246 W. 44th

Street. Architect: Warren and Wetmore—F. Richard Anderson. Opening: September 26, 1927; *The Merry Malones*. In 1929, Abraham Erlanger, head of the monopolistic Theatrical Syndicate and among the most hated men in show business, built the Erlanger's Theatre as the flagship of his nationwide chain. He chose 44th Street as a statement against his rivals, the Shuberts, who had several theaters on 44th Street.

Erlanger spent over $1.5 million on the 1,600-seat theater whose architects had Grand Central Station to their credit. With 1,600 seats to fill, Erlanger planned to present large-scale musicals.

Erlanger, not really a producer but a booker of shows through his United Booking Office, chose George M. Cohan's musical *The Merry Malones* as the first show for the new theater. The musical starred Cohan and, he composed the score, wrote the lyrics and libretto, and produced the proceedings. The next hit at Erlanger's was the last musical that Cohan wrote—*Billie* (1928). The show, although written only one year after *The Merry Malones*, seemed dated.

Fine and Dandy (1930) boasted a good score by one of Broadway's only female composers, Kay Swift, and her husband Paul James and included two hits, the title tune and "Can This Be Love."

Erlanger's empire began to crumble during the Depression and he lost the theater. The Astor estate, owner of the land on which the Erlanger stood, took over the theater's operations and put Lodewick Vroom in as manager.

On December 7, 1932, the theater's name was changed to the St. James after a famous London theater. The first attraction under the new name was the revue *Walk a Little Faster*. Beatrice Lillie, Penny Singleton (Blondie in the movies), and comedy team Bobby Clark and Paul McCullough appeared in the revue. The show's fine score was written by composer Vernon Duke and lyricist E. Y. Harburg. The smash hit from the show was "April in Paris."

After short seasons of Gilbert and Sullivan and the Ballet Russe de Monte Carlo, Clark and McCullough returned to the St. James. The show was *Thumbs Up!* (1934), with a score by a variety of songwriters. Again, Vernon Duke came up with a hit, along the same lines as "April in Paris." The song was "Autumn in New York," and Duke also supplied the lyrics. The show's other hit was James F. Hanley's "Zing Went the Strings of My Heart."

Operetta made a rare return to the New York stage with Sigmund Romberg and Oscar Hammerstein I's *May Wine* (1935). Reviews were mixed, although all the critics found something nice to say.

John Gielgud's production of *Hamlet* moved to the St. James from the historic Empire Theater where it concluded its 132-performance run. Shakespeare held the St. James' stage with the Margaret Webster production of *Richard II* (1937), starring Maurice Evans. Evans essayed *Hamlet* (1938) in another Margaret Webster directed production. The play opened with Mady Christians, Katherine Locke, and Alexander Scourby completing the leads. The production was the first complete and uncut version of *Hamlet* to play in the United States. Evans continued his dominance of the St. James stage with Shakespeare's *Henry IV Part I* (1939). The play received excellent reviews. Margaret Webster again directed, Edmund

O'Brien starred in the title role and Mady Christians appeared as Lady Percy.

While Evans and company toured, the last edition of the *Earl Carroll Vanities* (1940) opened at the St. James. The show was a decided failure, supposedly marking the introduction of microphones to the Broadway stage.

Shakespeare returned with Maurice Evans in the Theater Guild and Gilbert Miller production of *Twelfth Night* (1940). Margaret Webster directed a distinguished cast, including Evans, Wesley Addy, Helen Hayes, June Walker, and Sophie Stewart.

Richard Wright adapted his novel *Native Son* (1941) with the help of Paul Green. Orson Welles and John Houseman produced the venture. Welles insisted that among the stage props be a boy's sled upon which was written the word "Rosebud."

The Shubert brothers, took over the St. James late in 1941 and presented as their first productions there, a repertory offering of the Boston Comic Opera Company and the Jooss Ballet Dance Theater. The offerings included revivals of *H.M.S. Pinafore*; *The Mikado*; *The Green Table*; *The Big City*; *Pirates o f Penzance*; *Iolanthe*; *Trial By Jury*; and finally, *The Gondoliers*.

The Theater Guild presented the premiere of Philip Barry's play *Without Love* (1942), which featured Katharine Hepburn, Elliott Nugent, and Audrey Christie. Its departure opened the way for the theater's most important production—*Oklahoma!* (1943). The Rodgers and Hammerstein musical, considered the apex of the art form at its opening, saved the Theater Guild, which had little luck with recent offerings. *Oklahoma!* became the model to which almost every musical aimed.

Frank Loesser, the brilliant composer and lyricist, adapted Brandon Thomas' *Charley's Aunt* into the musical comedy *Where's Charley?* (1948). George Abbott, a champion of new talents, wrote the libretto and directed Loesser's first Broadway show. *Where's Charley?* opened with Broadway and Hollywood star Ray Bolger. Loesser gave him the evening's big hit song,

"Once in Love with Amy," with which Bolger would forever be linked.

Richard Rodgers and Oscar Hammerstein returned to the St. James with their musical, *The King and I* (1951). Gertrude Lawrence starred as Anna, and the King was played by Yul Brynner. Doretta Morrow, previously in *Where's Charley?*, Dorothy Sarnoff; Larry Douglas, and Johnny Stewart were featured.

George Abbott continued his introduction of new talents to Broadway with the musical comedy, *The Pajama Game* (1954). Abbott coauthored the libretto with Broadway newcomer Richard Bissell. The charming, enthusiastic score was written by Richard Adler and Jerry Ross, marking their first collaboration on a book show. The show also marked the choreographic debut of Bob Fosse, one of the Broadway musical's most unique talents. The score contained two smash hits: "Hey There," which leading man John Raitt sang as a duet with himself (he accomplished this feat by singing the song into a dictaphone), and the tango "Hernando's Hideaway." Janis Paige, Reta Shaw, Eddie Foy Jr., Carol Haney, Shirley MacLaine, and Peter Gennaro were also featured in the fine cast.

Johnny Mercer, one of Hollywood's best lyricists, collaborated with Gene de Paul on the score of the St. James' next show, *Li'l Abner* (1956), based on the comic strip by Al Capp. Edith Adams and Peter Palmer starred as Daisy Mae and Abner, Stubby Kaye as Marryin' Sam, and Howard St. John as General Bullmoose. The score was one of the funniest and most high-spirited in Broadway history.

The Shuberts were forced by the federal government to divest themselves of many of their Broadway holdings, and the St. James was included in the judgment. The Jujamcyn Organization bought the theater's lease as well as those of several other former Shubert properties.

The new owners of the building, Scarborough House, Inc., hired designer Frederick Fox to completely redo the theater. The interior was reduced to a shell, and the public areas were completely redesigned.

The theater reopened on December 1, 1958, with a hit show, Rodgers and Hammerstein's *The Flower Drum Song*. Hollywood star Gene Kelly directed the proceedings with Hammerstein and Joseph Fields contributing the libretto.

Carol Burnett and her star-making musical, *Once Upon a Mattress,* moved from off-Broadway to the St. James as a big hit. The score was written by lyricist Marshall Barer and Richard Rodgers' daughter, Mary Rodgers. Laurence Olivier and Anthony Quinn opened in Jean Anouilh's drama *Becket* (1960) at the St. James before being made into a hit motion picture.

Composer Jule Styne and lyricists Betty Comden and Adolph Green provided the scores for two of the next shows at the St. James. The first was a Phil Silvers and Nancy Walker vehicle, *Do Re Mi* (1960). The score was excellent and wide in scope. "Make Someone Happy" was the popular hit, but the rest of the score was more adventurous and much underrated. Sydney Chaplin (Charlie's son), Carol Lawrence, Phyllis Newman, and Orson Bean starred in Styne, Comden and Green's second show at the St. James-David Merrick's production of *Subways Are for Sleeping* (1961). The fine score had its expected hit, "Comes Once in a Lifetime."

Irving Berlin, perhaps the greatest songwriter in American history, left Broadway with a lackluster show, *Mr. President* (1962). Robert Ryan and Nanette Fabray tried to enliven the proceedings, but the show was clearly in trouble.

Hello, Dolly! (1964) was the next show to open at the St. James, and it proved to be an astounding hit. Carol Channing's miraculous performance and Jerry Herman's stirring score propelled the show forward in the best Broadway style.

After a forty-year absence, Shakespeare returned to the St. James. *Two Gentlemen of Verona* (1971) set Shakespeare's words to music by Galt MacDermot with lyrics by playwright John Guare. The musical starred Raul Julia, Clifton Davis, Jonelle Allen, Diana Davila, and John Bottoms.

A string of failures, including a twentieth anniversary revival of *My Fair Lady,* ran at the St. James in the mid-1970s. Comden and Green broke the jinx with *On the Twentieth Century* (1978). Cy Coleman provided a complex score for this musical. The show joined Stephen Sondheim's *Follies* and *Company* as the best musicals of the seventies. All three shows were directed by Harold Prince. Many theater historians consider *On the Twentieth Century* to be the last great American musical comedy.

Barnum (1980), starring Jim Dale, enjoyed a two-year run with Cy Coleman and Michael Stewart's rousing score. More failures followed *Barnum*. Finally *My One and Only* (1983) opened at the theater. Tommy Tune and Twiggy starred in the new musical that used songs by George and Ira Gershwin. The whole affair was charming, stylish and fun.

A musical version of *The Secret Garden* (1991) played the St. James with Mandy Patinkin as the star. A revival of Stephen Sondheim's *A Funny Thing Happened on the Way to the Forum* (1996) opened at the St. James and kept audiences in stitches. Nathan Lane starred and he would make a triumphant return to the St. James in its next smash production.

Mel Brooks and Thomas Meehan began the millennium with a bang with their adaptation of Brooks' classic film comedy, *The Producers* (2001). The show became almost legendary from its first performance becoming the hottest ticket on Broadway. The exceptional cast included Nathan Lane, Matthew Broderick, Brad Oscar, Gary Beach, Cady Huffman, and Roger Bart.

SAM H. HARRIS THEATER · See HARRIS THEATER.

SAM S. SHUBERT THEATRE · 225 W. 44th Street. Architect: Henry B. Herts. Opening: c. September 29, 1913; Forbes-Robertson Repertory. When Sam Shubert died on May 12, 1905, as a result of injuries suffered in a train crash, his devoted brother Lee vowed to build a theater in his honor in every city in the country. Each of the Sam Shubert theaters would have a picture of Sam hanging in its lobby.

Lee fulfilled at least part of his vow when the Sam S. Shubert Theatre opened in New York with the Forbes-Robertson Repertory Company. There is some disagreement about the actual date of the opening. Louis Botto's *In This Theater,* lists the opening as October 2, 1913. George Freedley's *Biographical Encyclopedia and Who's Who of the American Theater* lists the opening as September 29, 1913. Jerry Stagg's *The Brothers Shubert* lists the opening as October 28, 1913. In the appendix of all Shubert productions, Stagg lists the opening as September 3, 1913. Whatever the opening date, the theater was a great success.

After their production of *A Thousand Years Ago* (1914), the Shuberts opened their first musical at the theater, *The Belle of Bond Street* (1914), based on the English musical *The Girl from Kay's.* Franz Lehar's *Alone At Last* (1915) was the theater's first big hit. The show starred Jose Collins and John Charles Thomas. A bigger hit was Jerome Kern's *Love O' Mike* (1917) with lyrics by Harry B. Smith. Clifton Webb and Peggy Wood starred.

Maytime (1917) had music by Sigmund Romberg and book and lyrics by Rida Johnson Young. The show starred William Norris, Peggy Wood, and Charles Purcell. For the first and last time in Broadway history, a second company of a hit musical was presented at the same time as the original. The second company played across the street from the Shubert at the 44th Street Theatre. *Maytime* contained one of Romberg and Young's most enduring songs, "Will You Remember," known better as "Sweetheart.'

Sometime (1918), a Rudolf Friml and Rida Johnson Young musical, was produced by Arthur Hammerstein with the somewhat unlikely team of Mae West and Ed Wynn, and dramatic actress Francine Larrimore.

Good Morning, Judge (1919) was a British musical by Lionel Monckton and Howard Talbot. The show was Americanized and two songs by George Gershwin and Irving Caesar were added. Romberg and Frederic Arnold Kummer

wrote *The Magic Melody* (1919), which starred Charles Purcell and Flavia Arcaro.

The Shubert hosted a number of revues in the 1920s. *The Greenwich Village Follies* (1921), the first edition of the show on Broadway, was staged by John Murray Anderson. This third edition starred Ted Lewis, Irene Franklin, and Peggy Hope. The next edition opened on September 12, 1922, with Savoy and Brennan, John Hazzard, and Carl Randall. Two years later, after a sojourn at the Winter Garden Theater, the *Greenwich Village Follies* returned to the Shubert, opening on September 16, 1924. This time, the score was written by Cole Porter. None of the songs became standards. The 1924 edition ran 131 performances. The final edition to play the Shubert Theatre opened on March 15, 1926, and played 180 performances. The show was a revision of the previous year's edition, which had played the Winter Garden.

Artists and Models (1923) was a Shubert produced revue series. There were five more editions of the series on Broadway, though none appeared at the Shubert. *Vogues of 1924* (1924) starred Fred Allen, May Boley, Odette Myrtil, Jimmy Savo, and J. Harold Murray.

A musical, *The Magnolia Lady* (1924), was not a success. The Shuberts presented *Gay Paree* (1925) at the Shubert with Chic Sale, Jack Haley, and Winnie Lightner. The Shuberts were firm believers in the power of operettas. They insisted on producing them long after the form had gone out of favor. But when *Countess Maritza* (1926) opened, theatergoers found they could still enjoy the old-fashioned musical entertainments. Emmerich Kallman and Harry B. Smith supplied the score, which featured the hit song "Play Gypsies."

Another musical, *A Night in Venice* (1929), starred Ted Healy and not one but two troupes of dancing girls The Allan K. Foster Girls and The Chester Hale Girls. Ranks of women dancing in unison were a staple of twenties and thirties musicals. The choreographer of *A Night in Venice* later took the idea of a corps of synchronized dancers and translated his steps to Hollywood. He was Busby Berkeley.

Everybody's Welcome (1931) starred Ann Pennington, Oscar Shaw, Ann Sothern (then named Harriette Lake), Frances Williams, and the band of Tommy and Jimmy Dorsey. Sammy Fain and Irving Kahal were responsible for most of the score, but again an interpolated song proved to be the classic. "As Time Goes By," composed by Herman Hupfeld, first appeared in the musical.

Another revue, the last of three in a series, was *Americana* (1932). The show contained a song that became the unofficial anthem of the Depression—"Brother Can You Spare a Dime?" composed by Jay Gorney with lyrics by E. Y. Harburg. The score contained some other songs that later achieved some renown. These included "Satan's Li'l Lamb" by Harold Arlen, Harburg and Johnny Mercer; "Woud'ja for a Big Red Apple?" by Henry Souvaine and Mercer; and "Five Minutes of Spring" by Gorney and Harburg.

Suddenly, a spate of straight plays opened at the Shubert. First was Sidney Howard's *Dodsworth* (1934). Next came Robert E. Sherwood's antiwar drama *Idiot's Delight* (1936). The play won the Pulitzer Prize for drama. It reopened at the Shubert on August 31, 1936. Dudley Digges, Margo, Henry Hull, and Leo G. Carroll opened in Maxwell Anderson's *The Masque of Kings* (1937), a failure.

Musical comedy, and a lighter air, returned to the Shubert with Richard Rodgers and Lorenz Hart's smash hit musical, *Babes in Arms* (1937). Audiences heard for the first time such classic songs as "I Wish I Were in Love Again," "Where or When," "The Lady Is a Tramp," "My Funny Valentine," and "Johnny One Note."

S. N. Behrman's *Amphitryon 38* (1937), based on French playwright Jean Giraudoux's original, starred the Lunts. The next offering at the Shubert *I Married an Angel* (1938) boasted a score up to Rodgers and Hart's excellent standards, although only "I'll Tell the Man in the Street" and "Spring Is Here" achieved any renown.

The Theater Guild had a huge hit with Philip Barry's *The Philadelphia Story* (1939). Katharine Hepburn enjoyed her greatest stage success in the comedy of manners. *The Philadelphia Story* opened at the Shubert and saved the Theater Guild, which was then $60,000 in debt.

Rodgers and Hart returned to the Shubert with *Higher and Higher* (1940). The elements for success all seemed to be in place however, the show, an *Upstairs Downstairs* type of comedy, was a failure.

The Shuberts' next offering, *Hold On To Your Hats* (1940), was also a failure but for different reasons. It opened with Al Jolson making a Broadway comeback, ably assisted by the hilarious Martha Raye. The score, by Burton Lane, and E. Y. Harburg, contained the hit "There's a Great Day Coming Manana."

But Jolson was unhappy. He was constrained by the libretto and frequently threw it away completely to the delight of audiences and the chagrin of his fellow cast members. Jolson was also undergoing a messy divorce from Ruby Keeler, who had walked out of both the show and Jolson's life in Chicago to be replaced by Eunice Healy. To top it all off he caught pneumonia. Without its star, *Hold On to Your Hats* had to close.

Two notable revivals next occupied the Shubert's stage. Katharine Cornell, Raymond Massey, Bramwell Fletcher, and Clarence Derwent appeared in George Bernard Shaw's *The Doctor's Dilemma* (1941). Richard Brinsley Sheridan's eighteenth century comedy *The Rivals* (1942) starred Mary Boland, Helen Ford, Bobby Clark, and Walter Hampden.

Rodgers and Hart's *By Jupiter* (1942), their last full score, opened with Ray Bolger, Ronald Graham, Benay Venuta, and Vera-Ellen. The musical, sadly, contains one of the team's most neglected scores. Ray Bolger left the show to join the armed services and the show closed. Mae West returned to Broadway in the Mike Todd and Shubert brothers coproduction of the actress' play *Catherine Was Great* (1944).

Harold Arlen and E. Y. Harburg enjoyed one of their greatest successes with *Bloomer Girl* (1944), a delightful musical comedy with serious overtones. *Bloomer Girl* made powerful statements about human rights in a most entertaining way. The Arlen and Harburg score contained one standard: "Right As the Rain."

A revival of Victor Herbert's operetta *Sweethearts* (1947) was a surprise hit with Marjorie Gateson and Bobby Clark. *Anne of the Thousand Days* (1948) by Maxwell Anderson was a drama of Anne Bolyn and Henry VIII. It starred Joyce Redman and Rex Harrison. The Lunts returned with playwright S. N. Behrman's *I Know My Love* (1949). The production was an adaptation of Marcel Achard's *Aupres de Ma Blonde.*

Lerner and Loewe wrote *Paint Your Wagon* (1951), a story set against the California gold rush. There were two hits in the score: "I Talk to the Trees" and "They Call the Wind Maria." James Barton, Tony Bavaar, and Olga San Juan starred.

Katharine Hepburn returned to Broadway and the Shubert's stage in George Bernard Shaw's *The Millionairess* (1952) with Cyril Ritchard. Rex Harrison returned in. *The Love of Four Colonels* (1953) by Peter Ustinov. His costar was his wife Lilli Palmer.

Rodgers and Hammerstein slipped with *Pipe Dream* (1955), their musicalization of John Steinbeck's novel *Sweet Thursday.* The show opened with Mike Kellin, Helen Traubel, Louise Troy, Judy Tyler, and William Johnson.

The Shubert's next show, the Theater Guild musical *Bells Are Ringing* (1956), was a happy hit with its lead Judy Holliday. Jule Styne, Betty Comden, and Adolph Green concocted a delightful show with an alternately poignant and funny score. The hit songs included "Just in Time" and "The Party's Over."

Bob Merrill wrote the music and lyrics to the musicalization of Eugene O'Neill's *Ah, Wilderness!,* titled *Take Me Along* (1959). David Merrick presented Jackie Gleason, Robert Morse, Eileen Herlie, Walter Pidgeon, and Una Merkel. *Take Me Along* had a small hit with its title song, though "Staying Young" was the best song in the score.

Harold Rome's last full-scale Broadway musical was *I Can Get It for You Wholesale* (1962). The David Merrick production made history when on opening night a star was born. Her name was Barbra Streisand, and although she only had a small role as Miss Marmelstein, a secretary, she stopped the show.

Anthony Newley starred in David Merrick's production *Stop the World-I Want to Get Off* (1962), which he also wrote with Leslie Bricusse. The score contained the standards "Gonna Build a Mountain," "What Kind of Fool Am I," and "Once in a Lifetime." Newley and his costar Anna Quayle handled the superior score well.

Meredith Willson, author of *The Music Man,* fared less well with his musicalization of *Miracle on 34th Street,* which he entitled *Here's Love* (1963). The show opened with Craig Stevens and Janis Paige in the leads. *The Apple Tree* (1966) was the name of Jerry Bock and Sheldon Harnick's evening of three one-act musicals. Jerome Coopersmith and the songwriters wrote the libretti based on Mark Twain's *The Diary of Adam and Eve,* Frank Stockton's *The Lady or the Tiger* and Jules Feiffer's *Passionella.* The evening was wittily directed by Mike Nichols and brilliantly performed by Barbara Harris, Larry Blyden, and Alan Alda.

Golden Rainbow (1968) was ostensibly a musicalization of Arnold Schulman's play *A Hole in the Head.* But the critics announced it was more like a glorified nightclub show put on by its stars Steve Lawrence and Edie Gorme. Walter Marks wrote a good score with a smash hit song: "I've Got to Be Me."

Neil Simon's musical *Promises, Promises* (1968) boasted a score by Broadway newcomers Burt Bacharach and Hal David brilliantly orchestrated by Jonathan Tunick. David Merrick's production proved to be one of the greatest successes of the 1960s. Jerry Orbach, Jill O'Hara, Ken Howard, and Marian Mercer led the cast. *Promises, Promises* contained a big hit song: "I'll Never Fall in Love Again."

Tunick again supplied excellent orchestrations to a very different score that consisted only of waltzes. The show was Stephen Sondheim's *A Little Night Music* (1973) with one of the musical theater's greatest songs, "Send in the Clowns." Hugh Wheeler based his libretto on Ingmar Bergman's film *Smiles of a Summer*

Night. Harold Prince's adroit producing and directing and the fine performances by Glynis Johns, Len Cariou, Laurence Guittard, Patricia Elliott, and Hermione Gingold equaled one of the show's greatest assets, Boris Aronson's brilliant settings.

Two plays occupied the Shubert's stage in 1975. Edward Albee's *Seascape* (1975) opened with Deborah Kerr, Barry Nelson, and Frank Langella. It won the Pulitzer Prize a year after it closed. The second play of the year was a revival of Somerset Maugham's *The Constant Wife* with Ingrid Bergman.

The next tenant at the Shubert Theatre made Broadway history, eventually becoming the longest-running show ever. The show was *A Chorus Line,* a transfer from Joseph Papp's Public Theater. *A Chorus Line* moved to Broadway on July 25, 1975, with a cast that included Carole Bishop, Priscilla Lopez, Robert LuPone, Donna McKechnie, Thommie Walsh, and Sammy Williams.

Its score by Marvin Hamlisch and Edward Kleban contained but one hit song, "What I Did for Love." The book was by James Kirkwood and Nicholas Dante. The Pulitzer Prize-winning show's tremendous success was laid at the feet of director/choreographer Michael Bennett, a true genius. Unfortunately, *A Chorus Line* has outlived two of its creators, Bennett and Kleban. It closed on April 28, 1990, after 6,137 performances.

Crazy for You (1992) was the theater's next success. Using a George and Ira Gershwin score, *Crazy for You* was a crude adaptation of the Gershwin's *Girl Crazy.* Yet the performances, choreography, staging, and design made it a huge hit. It was followed by the musical *Big* (1996), an unfortunate failure by some of the same team from *Crazy for You.*

At press time, the theater has another smash hit on its hands, *Monty Python's Spamalot* (2005), a manic, madcap musicalization of the Monty Python film, *The Search for the Holy Grail.*

SCHWARTZ, ARTHUR · See DIETZ AND SCHWARTZ.

SELWYN THEATRE · See AMERICAN AIRLINES THEATRE.

SHAKESPEARE'S THEATER · See JOLSON'S 59TH STREET THEATER.

SHUBERT BROTHERS · Lee (1873–1953), Sam S. (1876–1905), and J .J. (1878–1963). The Shuberts were the most prolific of all producers, concentrating on productions aimed at the widest possible audience. They were ruthless moguls who at one time owned thirty-one theaters in New York and sixty-three others across the United States, and they were at least part owners of five theaters in London. From their first production, *Brixton Burglary* presented at the Herald Square Theater on May 20, 1901, through the last production under the brothers' control, *The Starcross Story,* presented at the Royale Theatre on January 13, 1954, they presented over 520 productions on Broadway. They also were responsible for countless touring shows and even some London productions. It was estimated that fully one-fourth of the productions presented on Broadway were Shubert productions, and these shows accounted for two-thirds of the total ticket sales for Broadway. After the brothers' deaths, the Shubert Organization was formed, and it continues today.

The Shubert Brothers, specifically J. J. (Jake) and Lee, were known for their lack of humor and their secretiveness. They would firmly deny rumors about productions and then turn around and make the announcement when they were ready. The two brothers were also noted for their frugality and their abhorrence of refunding ticket money no matter what the circumstances. Once, when the scenery and costumes of a Shubert production were lost in a blizzard, J. J. explained to the audience that the show would go on and made a disaster into a triumph. He managed to avoid refunds in the bargain.

J. J. was in charge of the musical productions, including the negotiations with composers, musical directors and choreographers, the operation of the Winter Garden Theater, the regional theater holdings, theater upkeep and construction, and personnel matters. Lee was in charge of booking the Shuberts' vast holdings, the New York theaters except for the Winter Garden, real estate transactions, straight-play productions and the company's finances. His office was conveniently located next to the vault.

David Szemanski, the patriarch of the Shubert family, fled Lithuania for England and finally Syracuse, New York. He sent for his wife Catharine and their six children in 1882. Sam was the first introduced into the world of the theater. He and his brother Levi (Lee) sold papers outside the Wieting Theatre. One fateful day, Sam was invited to come in out of the cold by John Kerr, manager of the theater. Sam took a seat in the rear, and his life was forever changed. When David Belasco brought his production of *May Blossom* to the theater in 1885, he hired Sam to play a small part. Sam undertook a series of increasingly important jobs in Syracuse theaters, ending up with a post as treasurer of the Wieting Theatre.

In 1894, Sam decided to go into producing. He bought the touring rights to Charles Hoyt's *A Texas Steer*. Sam's brothers Lee and Jake joined him in the venture. The success of the abbreviated tour of the Northeast was followed by another tour of a play by Hoyt. The success of the second tour led Sam to risk another step forward in his career. He bought the Bastable Theatre and set himself up as manager. Soon thereafter, a group of speculators agreed to build the Baker Theatre for Sam to manage. Sam was contacted by Abraham Erlanger, head of the Theatrical Syndicate, which was trying to gain a monopoly on all the important American theaters. The Syndicate or Trust, operated by Hayman and Frohman, Nixon and Zimmerman, and Klaw and Erlanger, controlled the plays, and if a theater owner wanted to be able to book plays he had to deal with the Syndicate or lose the show to a rival theater. Once Erlanger gained control of all the important theaters in a region, he took up to 50 percent of each theater's profits. But soon Erlanger lost interest in the little fiefdom the Shuberts had

set up. However, the Shuberts had learned from the Erlanger method of operation.

The brothers purchased more theaters, including the Grand Opera House in Syracuse, thus giving them control of all Syracuse theaters, and then they branched out into nearby Utica. Sam was now ready for the big move. He took a lease on the Herald Square Theater in New York City from its owner Charles Evans. The brothers were warned that the Herald Square on the east side of 35th Street was a surefire failure. They ignored the warnings and contracted with the celebrated actor Richard Mansfield to present his productions at the Herald Square Theater.

The Shuberts brought Erlanger into the operation of the Herald Square to assure product and to be able to get a closer look at the despot's methods. At the same time, the Shuberts bought the rights to tour one of the biggest hits of the 1890s, *The Belle of New York*. This time, the Shuberts acquired rights for the entire country, not just the Northeast.

The first attraction at the Herald Square Theater was a western play, *Arizona* (1900). But it was presented by Kirke La Shelle, not the Shuberts. The supposedly jinxed Herald Square Theater was now a success, but the Shuberts had to wait out two more successful productions after *Arizona* before they became Broadway producers.

Sam was gaining experience as a producer by presenting special matinee productions of new plays at the Herald Square. But the first two were abject failures, slammed by the press and scorned by the public. Sam decided that the lesson here was that he should never present a play by an unknown author (one of the plays was by George Bernard Shaw but he was unknown at the time). Sam learned his lesson well and taught his brothers. They would never again take a chance with a new playwright.

Finally, on May 20, 1901, with *The Brixton Burglary*, Sam Shubert had his name above the title as producer at the Herald Square. The Shuberts continued their acquisition of new theaters, both in the provinces and in New York. With the Herald Square booked with other people's productions, Sam found a new outlet for his producing efforts. He bought the Casino Theatre on 39th Street.

The Shuberts opened their first bona fide smash hit, *A Chinese Honeymoon* (1902) at the Casino Theatre. The show, presented in association with producers Nixon and Zimmerman, solidified the Shuberts' prestige in the minds of the theater community. The success gave the Shuberts enough cash to acquire their first piece of New York property—a plot of land across from the Casino on West 39th Street.

Erlanger, concerned about the burgeoning Shubert empire, tried to force the brothers out of business. The leading theatrical paper of the day, the *Morning Telegraph,* was a mouthpiece for the Syndicate. It promptly began a campaign of rumor and invective against the Shubert family. Lee retaliated in the only way he knew how, financially. He pulled all advertisements for Shubert shows and thus began a lifelong battle with the press.

Channing Pollock, in addition to acting as press agent for the Shuberts, also screened plays for the brothers. In his role of play screener, he was given a copy of Richard Walton Tully's *Rose of the Rancho.* When Tully brought the play to Pollock for his consideration, he added the caveat that the two previous producers who were asked to read the play, Kirke La Shelle and Fred Hamlin, died before they were able to pass judgment. Pollock was not a superstitious man and so gave the matter no thought. When, a few months later Tully asked for his script Pollock found it missing. It finally turned up in the bag that Sam Shubert was carrying on his fatal train ride.

This tragedy struck while the Shuberts were still battling with Erlanger over control of the American theater. A night train to Pittsburgh carrying Sam and two members of his staff collided with a parked work train. On May 11, 1905, Sam died. The blow almost made Lee give up the business, and he went so far as to meet with Erlanger with the intent of selling out the Shubert holdings to the Syndicate. The meeting collapsed, and Lee was even more resolved to keep the business. Sam's will caused an irreparable rift in the surviving brothers' relationship. Sam gave all his holdings to brother Lee. Jake was not mentioned at all in the document.

Lee effectively took control and embarked on a massive expansion. Producers Harrison Fiske and David Belasco signed agreements with the Shuberts, and Lee invited other producers to join in the fight against Erlanger. Then he announced the signing of Sarah Bernhardt, the greatest actress of her day. Other producers rallied around Lee, determined to join the "trust busters." Actually, the Shuberts were building their own monopoly, but at the time they were still the underdogs.

In July 1917, the Shuberts achieved their greatest triumph. They purchased the estate of George Cox, the largest theater holder in the United States. By buying Cox's holdings for an eight-figure fee, they put the final pieces in place for a Shubert empire. Now the Shuberts could guarantee producers the pick of American cities for their tours. Forty of the greatest producers in the country booked their shows into Shubert houses, bypassing the Syndicate.

Of course, the Shuberts continued to build and buy more theaters, but their immediate problem was in supplying their chain with product. The brothers made sure that they put out a practically endless stream of shows. Those that were profitable were kept on Broadway long enough to establish a name and then were sent on the road.

In 1918, the Shuberts presented fifteen shows on Broadway. While the straight plays were most often flops, the musicals, especially the operettas, were hits. The Shubert factory operated in much the same way as the motion-picture industry at the height of the studio system. Among the Shubert contractees were composer Sigmund Romberg, who wrote thirty-four scores for the brothers, lyricist/librettist Harold Atteridge, director J. C. Huffman, set designer Watson Barratt, choreographer Allan K. Foster, and jack of all trades Melville Ellis. Performers under contract to the Shuberts included Al Jolson, who appeared in eleven Shubert productions, and Willie and Eugene Howard. Since the Shuberts owned the largest collection of costumes, sets and equipment in the country, they often asked their writers to compose shows around the current stock.

There seemed to be no stopping the Shuberts' dominance of the American theater scene. But in 1920, they began implementing one of their first unsuccessful policies. Lee announced that they would enter the vaudeville field. Almost immediately, the policy was a failure.

By 1924, the Shubert empire consisted of eighty-six theaters in New York, Boston, Philadelphia, and Chicago. Thirty of these theaters were in New York City. They owned an additional twenty-seven in other cities. They also controlled the booking of 750 other theaters. During some weeks, they earned $1 million from box office receipts.

The Shuberts kept their juggernaut rolling, despite the fact that the relationship between the brothers was constantly deteriorating. Each liked the success that the other's productions brought to the firm, but each also was jealous of the other. By 1927, their relationship had soured to the point that Lee kept his offices in the Shubert Theatre, and Jake moved across the street to the new Sardi Building (owned by the brothers).

The Depression hit the entertainment industry hard, and the Shuberts lost $1 million in its first year. As the Depression deepened, Broadway suffered. Audiences would not be wooed by lower ticket prices; they were becoming more and more choosy. The days when patrons would decide to go to the theater without having a particular show in mind were over. Attendance and profits were declining at a prodigious rate. The Shuberts, never known for the artistry of their productions, were in trouble. The company lost $3 million in 1930 and 1931. At the end of 1931, the Shuberts went into receivership. The Irving Trust Company and Lee Shubert were named coreceivers.

The Shuberts were hit with a number of lawsuits, and their stockholders insisted that the books be reviewed. During the 1932–33 season only five plays were produced by the company. On January 1, 1933, a judge announced that the assets of the Shubert Theatre Corporation would be sold at auction. The auction took place on April 7, 1933. Since the theater business was failing, there were not too many interested bidders. In fact, there was only one, Lee Shubert. He bought the assets of the Shuberts for $400,000 under the name Select Theatres Incorporated. After all the bookkeeping was over with bond holders repaid, it turned out that Lee had bought his own company for $100,000. He was certainly rich enough to retire, but he knew only the theater business. He had no close friendships or relationships, and his work was his life.

The Shuberts weathered the duration of the Depression by booking their theaters for nothing in return for a piece of the box office. Thus, they "produced" shows without investing a dime. They figured rightly that every producer was undergoing bad times and would need the brothers' help. This way, the producers wouldn't have to raise the money for theater rentals, and the Shuberts would have attractions in their houses that just might turn a profit.

Jake's son John was brought into the Shubert fold and began producing shows for the brothers. He picked up where his father had left off, with operettas and musical revues. Jake was nursing wounds he suffered when Lee wouldn't let him have anything to do with the *Ziegfeld Follies,* which the Shuberts produced. Jake prided himself on his revues, and his *Passing Show* series had rivaled Ziegfeld's. But Lee held all the aces, and in 1934, he even booked the *Follies,* the first since Ziegfeld's death, at Jake's Winter Garden Theater. The show was a hit, and that rankled Jake even more. Then, too, his own son had joined the enemy's side. He left for an extended trip to Europe.

Over 60 percent of the plays on Broadway during the worst of the Depression were either produced by the Shuberts or involved Shubert houses, for which the Shuberts received a part of the proceeds. By 1937, it seemed the worst was over. Lee had put over $5 million of his own money into the Shubert Organization to keep it alive, and, therefore, he was largely responsible for keeping the Broadway theater alive. Jake spent most of the Depression in Europe. He produced his first show in years, *Frederika,* in 1937. The operetta closed after only ninety-four performances.

In 1939, Lee began buying more theaters, many of which were theaters that the Shuberts had lost due to the bankruptcy. Although the Depression was almost over, the Shuberts did not increase their producing. They didn't have to. They managed to own pieces in 75 percent of the shows playing on Broadway. They either put up the additional capital needed by a rival producer or leased their seventeen Broadway theaters in exchange for a piece of the box office. Even if they didn't have any money in a show, they still owned 90 percent of the Broadway theaters, so, in effect, they were Broadway.

In 1948, the Shuberts started the Sam S. Shubert Foundation with $500,000. It was planned that eventually all the Shubert assets would go to the foundation. The establishment of the foundation was the beginning of a plan devised by Lee and J. J. to take care of the organization when they retired. The brothers consolidated their empire through the second largest real estate transaction in contemporary New York history (the first was Rockefeller Center). On November 10, 1948, the Shuberts purchased the Booth, Shubert, Broadhurst, and Plymouth theaters, and the Shubert Alley property. The deal cost almost $4 million. The transaction gave them the entire square block between Broadway and Eighth Avenue and 44th and 45th Street, except for the plots on which the Astor and Manhattan hotels stood. The federal government dealt the Shuberts a serious blow when Chairman of the House Judiciary Committee, Emanuel Celler, began a probe of the Shubert operations, charging that the brothers held an unfair monopoly on American theater.

Celler also attacked the Shuberts' house-seat policy. Every show had a certain number of the prime seats set aside for the Shuberts' use. The brothers took these tickets and sold them through speculators and ticket brokers for a huge markup. They didn't claim the profit on their taxes, only the actual price of the tickets. The press discovered, for example, that the Shuberts had held back tickets for the first nineteen rows of the Philadelphia production of *Annie Get Your Gun* in 1946. If each of the tickets cost a top price of $6.60, they would be worth $46,200. But the Shuberts planned to sell them to illegitimate brokers who would scalp the tickets for as much as $75 each. This would bring the Shuberts $525,000. They had only to pay the amusement tax on the actual cost of the tickets—$46,200. Thus, they netted a tax-free profit of $478,800. The Shuberts instructed their box offices to play other games with ticket sales. If the brothers had another producer's show booked into one of their theaters and they wanted the theater for one of their own productions, they could legally kick out the competition's show only if the box-office receipts fell below a certain level. The Shuberts made sure the show didn't reach its minimum by instructing their box-office personnel to simply tell all potential ticket buyers that the show was sold out. They then effectively sold no tickets.

The converse applied when the Shuberts had a show that was not doing good business but that they wanted to appear to be a success. They simply took their own money and bought out all the remaining tickets. True, there were no bodies in the seats, but the tickets were sold.

Publicity from the *Annie Get Your Gun* affair spurred the government's interest in Shubert practices. The attorney general of the United States held his own investigation in addition to Representative Celler's. Independent producers who were unable to get bookings in cities where the Shuberts owned a monopoly of theaters brought suit against the brothers.

The attorney general laid out his allegations against the Shuberts:

The defendants for many years have been, and are now engaged in a combination and conspiracy in restraint of interstate trade in producing, booking, and presentation of legitimate attractions.

They compel producers to book their legitimate attractions through defendants.

They exclude others from booking legitimate attractions.

They prevent competition in presentation of legitimate attractions.

They combine their power to maintain and strengthen their domination in these fields.

The government began to gather witnesses to speak against the Shuberts. Naturally the majority of the actors, producers, directors, etc. chose to remain anonymous, afraid of the all-powerful Shuberts. Lee Shubert was incensed at what he thought was cowardice and at the government's attacks. He reasoned that without the Shuberts the country's road business would collapse since there were barely enough shows produced to keep the Shubert-owned theaters open. Of course, he was right. Without the Shuberts, there would be a vacuum with no others to fill it. In regard to the anonymous complainants, Lee wanted to know where they were when the Shuberts were keeping the American theater alive almost single-handedly during the Depression.

The government was unmoved. It demanded that the Shuberts get out of either the booking business or the theater-ownership business. The brothers were also told to unload a sufficient number of theaters so that whatever competition there was could be given a chance. Lee responded by buying a half interest in Earl Carroll's theater in Hollywood.

Lee decided to fight the government in the courts and have the matter settled once and for all. While waiting for the government to put its case together, Lee kept up normal activities, even proposing a television series called *Shubert Alley*. Then on December 21, 1953, he suffered a series of strokes. He rallied for a while but died on Christmas day. The last show to be produced by the Shubert brothers was *The Starcross Story* which opened and closed on January 13, 1954.

Jake, always the Shubert in the background, would now have to assume control of the empire and fight the battles with the government. Jake had lawyer William Klein on his side. Klein had been with the brothers since 1901 and had brought about and defended thousands of suits. The government faced a temporary setback when a federal district court ruled that the Shuberts were exempt from antitrust laws. The government appealed to the Supreme Court.

Meanwhile, Jake was feuding with Lee's family over control of the empire. He systematically fired every staff member who owed any allegiance to Lee and replaced them with his own handpicked successors. His son John had come over to Jake's side before Lee's death.

As it was, Lee had always seen to the daily operation of the vast empire; Jake was a producer, not an administrator, and he knew nothing of the Shubert holdings. Not only was he in the dark as to the company's operation, but also he didn't have the necessary education to administer the vast company. Unable to grasp the big picture, Jake concentrated on the more trivial aspects of the organization. On February 16, 1958, the government ordered the Shubert organization to sell twelve of its theaters in six cities in two years and stop entirely their booking business.

As Jake slipped into senility, his son John took over the reins of the Shubert Organization, but John was able to produce only one play, *Jules, Jake and Uncle Joe*, and that opened and closed on January 28, 1961. On November 17, 1962, John died of a heart attack.

Jake died on December 26, 1963, at the age of 86. The Shubert empire continued with Lawrence Shubert Jr. in charge, but the organization no longer produced shows. It merely managed theaters and the vast real estate holdings, and little by little the organization lost its connection to the theater.

One of the lawyers involved in defending the Shuberts against the government's antitrust suit was Gerald Schoenfeld. He brought his friend Bernard Jacobs into the business, and soon they took over operation of the Shubert

Organization. Schoenfeld became the chairman, and Jacobs the president.

Extremely savvy attorneys, they brought the Shubert Organization back to life. They began producing and reestablished the organization's dominance of the American theater. The two men, known collectively as The Shuberts even though they were not part of the family, used their great power to bring some of the greatest hits of the London stage to New York. These included the blockbusters *Cats* and *The Phantom of the Opera*. The two men also professed an interest in art and have at times put the Shubert resources behind chancier plays by some of the top playwrights writing in English, including Tom Stoppard, Simon Gray, Harold Pinter, and David Mamet. Of course, the Shuberts did not originate any of these playwrights' productions; they were either London imports or tried out in American regional theaters. The so-called Shuberts, like the brothers who preceded them, loathed taking chances with unproven talents.

The Shubert Organization is a subsidiary of the nonprofit Shubert Foundation, and that gives it certain tax advantages that its competition resents. The Shubert Organization, being the dominant power in American theater, receives its due share of complaints. Some are well-founded, some are just sour grapes. They control seventeen theaters in New York and either own or operate others in Boston, Washington, Philadelphia, Chicago, and Los Angeles. Many of the Shubert—owned theaters outside New York have been demolished and replaced with office buildings. Some view the Shuberts as real estate operators, not really producers.

Many of the smaller Shubert houses like the Belasco in New York sit dark for long periods. Instead of booking the theaters, or making them available to local groups, the Shuberts would rather let them sit empty. They do not like to take chances. Also, by letting the theaters sit, they prove their point that the buildings are unprofitable and local governments should allow them to be destroyed.

Critics also point out that it is the Shuberts who always lead the way with higher ticket prices. True, costs have risen dramatically and the Shuberts are, some critics say, responsible for that too. After all, since their conservative producing style, booking only proven hits, guarantees they'll make money, they can afford to pay stagehands and musicians more. At the same time their competitors, who take greater chances and don't have the financial resources of the Shubert Organization behind them, can ill afford the high guarantees and inflated salaries.

To the Shuberts' credit, they have generally kept up their theater holdings admirably, although with a certain lack of taste in choice of color scheme. They also revolutionized box-office procedures through computerization and the acceptance of credit card sales. Also to their credit are the many charitable activities they support through free leases on their theaters for special events and donations to worthy causes through the Shubert Foundation. However, even now, almost one hundred years since its founding, the Shubert empire is still creating controversy.

SHUBERT THEATER · See SAM S. SHUBERT THEATRE.

SIMON, NEIL (1927) · Neil Simon is the most successful American playwright of the twentieth century. Simon's output even surpasses that of Tennessee Williams, one of the most prolific modern playwrights. Simon's dramatic language is not as poetic as Williams', nor is he as politically motivated as Arthur Miller or as psychologically provoking as Eugene O'Neill. Simon's style relies mainly on jokes and humorous situations. However, Simon does have his serious side, and more recently his plays have become increasingly emotional in content.

Simon has managed to improve his artistry while achieving popular acclaim in almost every play he has written. Some critics have ascribed Simon's success not to any special talent but to his choice of white, middleclass characters —an exact mirror of the average Broadway audience. His detractors distrust his facility in eliciting laughs, and the funnier his plays are the more he sinks in their estimation.

A chronological list of Simon's plays reveals better than anything else his maturation and continued growth. His early comedies are the closest to sitcoms, and his later works have real, honest, uncontrived emotional punch.

Simon began his career as a television writer. He contributed material for the *Phil Silvers Show* (*You'll Never Get Rich*) as well as the *Tallulah Bankhead Show*, the *Sid Caesar Show,* and the *Garry Moore Show*. These programs, mostly running in the late fifties, enabled Simon to build his comic muscle. He had earlier provided sketches for shows presented at a popular summer camp, Tamiment.

Simon's first Broadway work was written in collaboration with his brother Danny, considered one of the great comic technicians in the business. The Simon brothers wrote some sketches for the musical revue, *Catch a Star!* (1955). They also contributed material to Leonard Sillman's *New Faces of 1956*.

Neil Simon had his first Broadway success with *Come Blow Your Horn* (1961), the slightly autobiographical story of two brothers learning to grow up.

Simon's next project was a libretto for the Cy Coleman and Carolyn Leigh musical *Little Me* (1962). Simon's hilarious script was based on the well-known novel by Patrick Dennis. The show, which starred Sid Caesar, Nancy Andrews, Virginia Martin, and Swen Swenson, deserved a much longer run—it remains the funniest musical produced in recent times. Simon's many innovations were overlooked because the show was not "serious."

Simon's next play was *Barefoot in the Park* (1963), one of the most successful productions of the sixties. *Barefoot in the Park* seemed to take up where the earlier play left off. The new piece examined a young couple's first days of marriage. Robert Redford costarred with Elizabeth Ashley.

The Odd Couple (1965) is one of Simon's best known plays, mainly because of the popularity of the hit television series based on it. The original play opened at the Plymouth Theater

with Art Carney and Walter Matthau as Felix Unger and Oscar Madison.

A musical, *Sweet Charity* (1966), came next. Simon based his book on an earlier draft by director/choreographer Bob Fosse. *Sweet Charity* boasted a jazzy score by Cy Coleman and Dorothy Fields.

The Star-Spangled Girl (1966) was one of Simon's few failures. The play opened with Anthony Perkins, Richard Benjamin, and Connie Stevens making up the cast. At the time of its opening, Simon was the first playwright to have four shows running simultaneously on Broadway.

Plaza Suite (1968) consisted of three one act plays, all of which take place in the same suite in the Plaza Hotel. The show opened at the Plymouth Theater (which seemed to house only Neil Simon shows) with George C. Scott and Maureen Stapleton in the leads.

The Burt Bacharach and Hal David musical *Promises, Promises* (1968) opened with Jerry Orbach and Jill O'Hara in the leads. The hip musicalization of Billy Wilder's film, *The Apartment,* gave librettist Simon ample opportunity to examine the mating habits of the white-collar worker.

In *The Last of the Red Hot Lovers* (1969), Simon again experimented with the one-act form. The play opened at the Eugene O'Neill Theater with James Coco, Linda Lavin, Marcia Rodd, and Doris Roberts. Coco's character, Barney Cashman, was seen in three acts trying to overcome the sexual and emotional frustration of his middle age by conquering three women.

The Gingerbread Lady (1970) was only the second failure of Simon's decade-long career. Maureen Stapleton starred as an alcoholic singer. Audiences did not want a Neil Simon who examined loneliness. It was named one of the ten best plays of the year by the *Best Plays* series.

In *The Prisoner of Second Avenue* (1971), Simon was somewhat lighter in mood but still trying to expand his range. The play opened with Peter Falk and Lee Grant. Falk's character finds his life collapsing around him. The play ended on a decidedly downbeat note, but Simon sweetened the message with humor.

The Sunshine Boys (1972) was considered a geriatric *Odd Couple.* It actually told of two vaudevillians, played by Jack Albertson and Sam Levene, who after eleven years of feuding try to reconcile their differences.

The Good Doctor (1973) was Simon's third failure. He adapted several stories of Chekhov and added his own twists but the play failed to find an audience. *God's Favorite* (1974) opened at the Eugene O'Neill Theater with Vincent Gardenia and Maria Karnilova. The play was a contemporary retelling of the story of Job.

With *California Suite* (1977), Simon began to reverse his downward spiral. The West Coast variation of *Plaza Suite* starred Jack Weston, Tammy Grimes, Barbara Barrie, and George Grizzard in the four one-act plays.

Chapter Two (1977) opened at the Imperial Theater with Judd Hirsch, Cliff Gorman, Anita Gillette and Ann Wedgeworth as the cast. The four-character comedy explored the attempts of a recent widower (as Simon was) to reconnect with his own emotions and those of a new woman in his life. By the end of the play, it's clear the couple will get married, and in fact Simon also remarried in real life. *Chapter Two's* run broke Simon's string of failures—for a while. Critics observed that when the author had personal problems, his plays suffered too.

They're Playing Our Song (1979), though a big hit was a lackluster musical and didn't represent Simon or his collaborators, Marvin Hamlisch and Carole Bayer Sager, at their best. *I Ought to Be in Pictures* (1980) opened at Simon's own Eugene O'Neill Theater with Ron Liebman, Dinah Manoff, and Joyce Van Patten. The play was the story of a Hollywood screenwriter who is visited by the estranged daughter he hasn't seen in sixteen years.

Fools (1981) starred John Rubenstein and was also a failure. It was followed by an unsuccessful revival of *Little Me,* which premiered the following year.

Simon again hit his stride with an autobiographical trilogy beginning with *Brighton*

Beach Memoirs (1983). Matthew Broderick made an impressive Broadway debut as Eugene Jerome (the Simon character), winning a Tony Award in the bargain. Joyce Van Patten, Elizabeth Franz, and Zeljko Ivanek costarred. By the time the play closed, its sequel, *Biloxi Blues* (1985), had opened. Matthew Broderick was again the star. *Biloxi Blues* was the story of Eugene's induction into the Army and exposure to a different world.

In the third play of the trilogy, *Broadway Bound* (1986), Eugene is back in Brighton Beach and breaking into radio. *Broadway Bound* featured Jonathan Silverman as Eugene, Linda Lavin as his mother, and Phyllis Newman as his aunt.

Simon's next show, *Rumors* (1988), received less than raves. The play was a throwback to his early farces and played a little more than a year. Then it was back to Simon's trilogy, and the last play, *Lost in Yonkers* (1991). Simon was again inspired by his youth and the play was a success, Simon's last for Broadway.

Still, he persevered with a succession of plays, all failures, including *Jake's Women* (1992), the musical *The Goodbye Girl* (1993), *Laughter on the 23rd Floor* (1993) which was a look back at his years in early television writing for Sid Caesar, *Proposals* (1997), 2000's *The Dinner Party*, and his final Broadway play to date, *45 Seconds from Broadway* (2001).

SMITH, HARRY B. (1860–1936) · Though Harry B. Smith was the most prolific of all Broadway lyricist/librettists, his work is practically unknown today. Smith had no special style or flair for lyric writing. Although he obviously had talent, perhaps his greatest asset was his speed and satisfactory work.

He was author of 123 musicals produced in a forty-five-year career. Including adaptations and straight plays, Smith, by his own count, claimed authorship to more than three hundred shows. Smith's greatest musical successes—*Robin Hood, The Spring Maid, Sweethearts, Watch Your Step, Countess Maritza, The Girl from Utah* and the *Rich Mr. Hoggenheimer*—were written in collaboration with such composers as Ludwig Englander, Reginald De Koven, Victor Herbert, John Philip Sousa, Robert Hood Bowers, Gus Edwards, Jerome Kern, Franz Lehar, Leo Fall, Ivan Caryll, A. Baldwin Sloane, Sigmund Romberg, and Emmerich Kalman.

Smith also estimated that he contributed lyrics to over three thousand songs. His greatest success as a lyricist came with the songs "The Sheik of Araby" (from *Make It Snappy*), "Gypsy Love Song" (from *The Serenade*), and "Yours Is My Heart Alone" (from *Yours Is My Heart*). Smith's brother, Robert B. Smith, was also a successful librettist.

Harry Bache Smith was born in Buffalo, New York, on December 28, 1860. He attempted to become an operatic performer but, meeting with little interest or enthusiasm, he found a job on the *Chicago Daily News* as music critic. Smith began to write humorous verse and stories for a variety of magazines and newspapers.

His verses gained the attention of a major star, Fay Templeton. She commissioned Smith to write the libretto for her production of *Rosita, or Cupid and Cupidity.* George Schleiffarth composed the music for the operetta, which opened in Chicago in 1883. The success of that show led to another commission for *Amaryllis, or Mammon and Gammon,* with music by H. H. Thiele. That show was mounted in Milwaukee in 1884 and was also a success.

Fay Templeton next convinced Smith to abandon journalism and to move to Boston to write full time for the musical theater. She introduced the writer to Colonel John C. McCaull, a leading Bostonian producer. He, in turn, brought Smith together with composer Reginald De Koven. They collaborated on *The Bugun* (1887). Two years later came the team's next show, *Don Quixote,* produced by the Bostonians, a very successful producing organization.

Smith and De Koven's greatest success, one of the biggest hits of the turn of the century, was *Robin Hood* (1891). The success of that show, written in only three weeks, convinced Smith to become a full-time writer for the

theater. He moved to New York and began his career in earnest. *Robin Hood* was the first truly successful American operetta. Smith received royalties on it for over twenty-five years before wisely deciding to sell out his interests for a substantial sum.

In 1895, after five more collaborations with De Koven as well as two other shows, Smith teamed up with Victor Herbert. Herbert had composed a poorly received operetta produced by the Bostonians called *Prince Ananias.* The show's failure didn't deter Smith from approaching Herbert and suggesting they collaborate. Smith added new lyrics to the Herbert score as well as a new libretto. The result was *The Wizard of the Nile* (1895), which opened at the Casino Theatre.

In 1899, Smith had eight shows produced, including *Papa's Wife,* which starred Anna Held. *Papa's Wife* was thought by many to be the precursor to the intimate shows that later developed into the modern musical comedy. In 1911, Smith contributed nine shows to Broadway.

His prolific career continued, although little of his work has lasted his lifetime. His later Broadway shows and their composers included *The Girl from Utah* (Jerome Kern, 1914); *90 in the Shade* (Jerome Kern, 1915); *Sybil* (Victor Jacobi, 1916); *Caroline* (Edward Kunneke and Alfred Goodman, 1923); *Princess Flavia* (Sigmund Romberg, 1925); *Countess Maritza* (Emmerich Kalman, 1926); *The Circus Princess* (Emmerich Kalman, 1927); and *The Red Robe* (Jean Gilbert, 1928).

His last Broadway musical was the 1932 *Marching By.* By then, the operetta was going out of favor and Smith's output slowed to only one or two shows a season. By the time of his death on January 2, 1936, Smith was overshadowed by such modern lyricists as Ira Gershwin, Howard Dietz, and E. Y. Harburg. But he certainly had been hugely popular at the height of his career. Carl Van Vechten flattered Smith when he dubbed the lyricist "the Sarah Bernhardt of librettists." Smith was unable to keep pace with the changing styles of the American musical theater in which romanticism was replaced with sophistication.

SONDHEIM, STEPHEN (1930–) · Stephen Sondheim is considered the leading composer/lyricist of the modern musical theater. Sondheim's shows, usually with Harold Prince as producer and director, have expanded the art of the musical as have those of few of his contemporaries. Sondheim's style is unmistakably his own. The hallmarks of his work are intricate rhythms and melodies composed without concern about Tin Pan Alley. These tunes exist solely for the exigencies of the plot and characters. Sondheim's lyrics are laced with witty, intellectual rhymes, and an abundance of ideas. This high level of intelligence sometimes puts off his critics who find his work coldly intellectual and somewhat emotionally uninvolving. The offbeat subjects of many of his shows and his lack of widely popular songs has sometimes kept Sondheim from achieving widespread fame among the middle-class theatergoers.

Sondheim was born on March 22, 1930. An early friend was James Hammerstein, son of Oscar Hammerstein II. Oscar became the fifteen-year-old Sondheim's mentor. While at Williams College, Sondheim wrote musicals and prepared for a professional career on Broadway.

His first effort, *Saturday Night*, was optioned by producer Lemuel Ayers. Unfortunately, Ayers died before the production could be mounted and it was not to be produced for almost fifty years. Among the Broadway professionals who had heard Sondheim's work was librettist Arthur Laurents. He was working on a new musical with Leonard Bernstein. Laurents introduced Sondheim to Bernstein who was suitably impressed with the twenty-five-year-old's work. Sondheim was hired to provide the lyrics for *West Side Story* (1957).

Among the Sondheim/Bernstein songs were "Tonight," "Maria," "America," "I Feel Pretty," and "Something's Coming." The show starred Larry Kert and Carol Lawrence as Tony and Maria and Chita Rivera, Art Smith, Mickey Calin, Harvey Evans, and Grover Dale in supporting roles.

Sondheim's goal was to contribute both music and lyrics for his next Broadway show. But friends convinced him that working on *Gypsy* would afford him the opportunity to work with an established Broadway composer, Jule Styne and to give him experience writing for a star, Ethel Merman. *Gypsy* (1959) was a musicalization of the memoirs of Gypsy Rose Lee. Arthur Laurents again contributed the libretto. The excellent Sondheim/Styne songs included the standards "Everything's Coming Up Roses," "Together," "Let Me Entertain You," and "Small World." Ethel Merman was ably assisted by Jack Klugman, Sandra Church, Paul Walker, Maria Karnilova, and Jacqueline Mayro.

Although Sondheim's initial Broadway works were successes, he was still determined also to supply the music for his next show. The opportunity came when Burt Shevelove approached him with the idea of musicalizing the comedies of the Roman playwright Plautus. The result was *A Funny Thing Happened on the Way to the Forum* (1962) with a libretto also by Larry Gelbart. Zero Mostel played Pseudolus, a Roman slave with aspirations for freedom.

The success of *A Funny Thing Happened on the Way to the Forum* led to Sondheim's next show, a failure. Arthur Laurents contributed the original idea for *Anyone Can Whistle* (1964). Angela Lansbury, Lee Remick, and Harry Guardino made their Broadway musical debuts in the show.

The failure of *Anyone Can Whistle* led to Sondheim's teaming with Richard Rodgers on *Do I Hear a Waltz* (1965). The show was a musical version of Arthur Laurents' play *Time of the Cuckoo*. Elizabeth Allen and Sergio Franchi starred. Sondheim and Rodgers had a stormy relationship but contributed a good score.

Playwright George Furth approached Harold Prince about producing a script he had written. Prince suggested the material might be more successful as a musical, and Sondheim was brought in to complete the production team. The resulting show, *Company* (1970), opened at the Alvin Theater. Prince also directed the show, which starred Dean Jones, Barbara Barrie, Donna McKechnie, and Elaine Stritch. *Company*, a ruthless examination of marriage set against an aggressively urban setting, was an immediate success.

Sondheim was by then firmly established as a superior and innovative talent. His next project was *Follies* (1971), one of the greatest of all musicals. Harold Prince codirected and produced the show, which had a book by James Goldman. Michael Bennett codirected with Prince and supplied the choreography. *Follies* boasted an impressive physical production. The set was designed by Boris Aronson, the costumes by Florence Klotz, and the lighting by Tharon Musser. The show was about a reunion of a group of former Follies performers. The action took place on two levels, the party itself and among the ghosts of the past who haunted the celebrants' present. The brilliant staging perfectly joined the two worlds. The show, however, was more than an examination of the characters' past and present lives. It succeeded in presenting a psychological examination of their feelings and thoughts. The final sequence took place in Loveland, which was actually a physical realization of the characters' problems. Their psyches were illustrated as acts in a performance of the Ziegfeld Follies.

The show starred Dorothy Collins, Alexis Smith, John McMartin, Gene Nelson, and Yvonne DeCarlo. It opened at the Winter Garden Theater. Audiences, unaccustomed to actually thinking during a musical comedy, sometimes found the show confusing and disorienting but for many the evening was stimulating and moving.

The glamour and immensity of *Follies* led to the more intimate *A Little Night Music* (1973), an elegant rendering of Ingmar Bergman's romantic film *Smiles of a Summer Night.* Hugh Wheeler supplied his first libretto for a Sondheim show with Prince in his usual dual role as producer and director. The show opened at the Sam S. Shubert Theatre with Glynis Johns, Len Cariou, Hermione Gingold, and Patricia Elliott. *A Little Night Music* contained a rich and varied score all in three-quarter time. Surprisingly, one of the songs, "Send in the Clowns," attained popular status.

For his next show, Sondheim was drawn to an unlikely subject, the opening of relations between Japan and the United States in the nineteenth century. *Pacific Overtures* (1975) opened at the Winter Garden Theater. A play by John Weidman was the source, which Weidman and Hugh Wheeler adapted. Prince again produced and directed the production, which featured an all-Japanese cast. The show, which used elements of the Kabuki theater to tell the story, attempted to show great events through the examination of the lives of a few common people.

The next Prince/Sondheim collaboration was the thriller, *Sweeney Todd* (1979). The story was set against England's industrial revolution. Sweeney Todd, the lead character, was a barber who returned home from jail to seek vengeance on those who had ruined his life. His act of vengeance soon turned into full-fledged insanity and Sweeney Todd found an accomplice in Mrs. Lovett, a baker of meat pies. As Mr. Todd dispatched friend and foe, Mrs. Lovett obligingly incorporated their corpses into her baked goods. This grand guignol production opened at the Uris Theatre. Audiences were delighted to be scared out of their wits. Angela Lansbury and Len Cariou starred as the partners in crime.

Furth, of *Company* fame, supplied the book for *Merrily We Roll Along* (1981), an adaptation of the Kaufman and Hart play. The show was told in reverse order. The cast was composed entirely of teenagers and performers in their early twenties. This was a limitation that, when coupled with a misguided design and badly written book, added up to failure. Sondheim's score was typically brilliant. The show opened at the Alvin Theater.

Sondheim might have been discouraged by the failure of *Merrily We Roll Along,* but he was not about to pander to popular taste or let his work sink to the lowest common denominator. His next undertaking, *Sunday in the Park with George* (1984) proved to be one of his most experimental outings. James Lapine contributed the book and direction to the show, which used painter Georges Seurat as a springboard to the examination of what it means to be an artist. The first act of the musical concerned Seurat's life and took place while he is painting his masterpiece, *A Sunday Afternoon on the Island of La Grande Jatte.* The second act took place one hundred years later with the story of Seurat's great-grandson, a modern artist. The show starred Bernadette Peters and Mandy Patinkin. It won the Pulitzer Prize for drama.

For his next excursion, Sondheim again chose an unlikely subject. *Into the Woods* tells the story of three fairy tales, "Little Red Riding Hood," "The Baker and His Wife," and "Jack and the Beanstalk" and what happens after "they lived happily ever after." James Lapine supplied the book as well as the direction. *Into the Woods* (1987) opened at the Martin Beck Theatre. It boasted a score sung by a superior cast, including Bernadette Peters, Joanna Gleason, Chip Zien, Kim Crosby, Tom Aldredge, Ben Wright, Barbara Bryne, Daniele Ferland, and Robert Westenberg.

Sondheim's last original musical for Broadway was *Passion* (1994), an examination of obsessive love. The remarkable score was Sondheim's most dense and thus never achieved the fame that was its due.

Stephen Sondheim has proven himself to be the greatest of the composer/lyricists in the Broadway tradition. The fact that he has seen fit to expand those traditions and not simply work within their confines is both his chief asset and, perhaps, one of his faults. His shows have mostly contained brilliant scores that have a somewhat limited appeal to the average Broadway audience. However, each of his shows has proven, sometimes in retrospect, to be an important part of the history of the American musical theater.

STAIRCASE THEATER · See CENTURY THEATER (1).

STROUSE AND ADAMS · Charles Strouse was one of the leading musical comedy composers throughout the 1960s and 1970s. During his most successful period, he collaborated with lyricist Lee Adams. They supplied a string of lighthearted scores to entertaining musicals. Strouse's music contains catchy themes with a dramatic flair. Adams lyrics seem simple, yet they perfectly complement the theatricality of Strouse's tunes.

Charles Strouse was born on June 7, 1928, in New York City. His interest in music began in his early teens. Later he studied at the Eastman School of Music and under Aaron Copland and Nadia Boulanger.

Lee Adams was born in Mansfield, Ohio, on August 14, 1924. Adams had a lifelong fascination with words and worked as a staff member of *Pageant* Magazine and as editor of *This Week* Magazine.

The two met in 1949 and began writing songs at Green Mansions summer camp. Their revue songs were transferred from the camp setting to off-Broadway and a series of shows for Ben Bagley. *The Shoestring Revue* (1955), *The Littlest Revue* (1956). and *Shoestring '57* (1956) gave the team more time to hone their skills.

They were ready to attempt a full-fledged musical comedy by the late 1950s. Their first effort, *Bye Bye Birdie* (1960) was a true sleeper and an immediate smash. The show, a satire on the newly emergent rock industry, starred Dick Van Dyke and Chita Rivera with Paul Lynde, Susan Watson, and Kay Medford in supporting roles. Dick Gautier played a thinly veiled parody of Elvis Presley in the show. The score contained the team's greatest success, the jaunty "Put on a Happy Face." Their first Broadway show was also the first full musical directed by Gower Champion and the first for which Michael Stewart supplied a libretto.

For their second project, the team turned once again to a satire. Mel Brooks provided the libretto for *All American* (1962). Despite the talents of Ray Bolger and Eileen Herlie and Joshua Logan's direction, the show was a failure. The score, which was almost as good as that of *Bye Bye Birdie*, did contain one standard, "Once Upon a Time."

The next show for which they supplied a

score was a departure from their usual light satire. *Golden Boy* (1964) was a powerful drama by Clifford Odets. It wasn't an obvious choice for musical, but producer Hillard Elkins convinced the team to take it on. Certainly, the score was excellent, combining Broadway razzmatazz with the serious subject matter. Another remarkable aspect of the production was the casting of Sammy Davis Jr. as the prizefighter. Odets had died while writing the libretto and William Gibson took over the task. The show proved controversial with the casting of a black lead against a white woman. People actually shot bullets into the marquee of the Winter Garden Theatre.

For their next project, the team attempted *It's a Bird ...It's a Plane. ..It's Superman* (1966). The show was a pop-art depiction of the famous comic book character. The play was a tongue-in-cheek attempt to bring to the stage what Batman would later bring to television. The show enjoyed a superior score and production under the direction of Harold Prince. Jack Cassidy, Linda Lavin, Patricia Marand, and Bob Holiday starred.

After the failure of *It's a Bird...It's a Plane...It's Superman* came the success of *Applause* (1970). The show was an adaptation of the movie *All About Eve*. In the lead was a newcomer to musical comedy, Lauren Bacall. Betty Comden and Adolph Green supplied the libretto. Although none of the creative contributions were particularly outstanding, the show was their longest run as a team.

Next, Charles Strouse wrote the book and lyrics to his own music for an off-Broadway show, *Six* (1971), which opened to negative reviews, although it boasted excellent choreography by Denny Martin Flinn. The following year, the team had a failure with *I and Albert,* a musical about Queen Victoria that was staged in London.

Seven years after *Applause,* Charles Strouse opened a new Broadway musical, his second based on a comic strip character. The show was *Annie* (1977) with lyrics by Martin Charnin. Andrea McArdle played the title character, assisted by Sandy Faison, Dorothy Loudon,

Reid Shelton, and Raymond Thorne. The song "Tomorrow" became an anthem of prepubescent girls everywhere. The show was directed by Charnin and had a libretto by Thomas Meehan. *Annie* became the most popular musical of its decade.

Strouse and Adams reunited for *A Broadway Musical* but with little result. The show opened and closed on December 21, 1978. William F. Brown supplied the book and Gower Champion the direction. That failure led to Strouse undertaking another London assignment. *Flowers for Algernon* was based on the movie *Charley* and for its American opening was retitled *Charlie and Algernon* (1980).

Strouse and Adams' last Broadway collaboration was a sequel to their first show, *Bye Bye Birdie*. Its name was *Bring Back Birdie* (1981), and again Michael Stewart contributed the book and Chita Rivera starred. She was assisted by Donald O'Connor.

Strouse wrote a children's opera, *Nightingale* in 1982, contributing book, music and lyrics. His next Broadway outing was *Dance a Little Closer,* for which he teamed with Alan Jay Lerner. Lerner also contributed the libretto and direction to *Dance a Little Closer,* an updating of Robert Sherwood's *Idiot's Delight*. The show, which opened on May 11, 1983, at the Minskoff Theatre, unfortunately fared as badly as his last Broadway show, closing after only one performance. Despite the show's poor record, the score is considered a good one.

Strouse's next Broadway score contained some of his best tunes. Unfortunately, the other elements of *Rags* (1986) were not as well written. *Rags* had a book by Joseph Stein and lyrics by Stephen Schwartz. It starred opera diva Teresa Stratas and featured Larry Kert, Terence Mann, Marcia Lewis, Dick Latessa, and Lonny Price.

The fractious backstage atmosphere of *Nick & Nora* (1991) did nothing for the goings on on stage. The show, Strouse's last Broadway musical, was not a success. However, again, Strouse wrote some fine melodies and lyricist Richard Maltby, Jr. managed to fit a few with some above average lyrics.

Meanwhile, Lee Adams made one attempt at Broadway without Strouse. He and composer Mitch Leigh wrote *Ain't Broadway Grand* (1993) but the bio-musical of Mike Todd's life was a flop.

Strouse has reteamed with longtime partner Lee Adams on a variety of projects including adaptations of *An American Tragedy* and *Marty*. He has also written a score to *The Night They Raided Minsky's* with Susan Birkenhead but so far none have reached the stage. Most recently, Strouse wrote the music, book, and lyrics to a new musical, *You Never Know* which was well-received in its out-of-town tryout in Providence, Rhode Island.

At the high points of his career, Charles Strouse has shown a rare ability to time the subjects of his projects to popular taste. *Annie* and *Bye Bye Birdie* both profited by their perfect convergence with what the public was looking for in a Broadway musical.

All of Strouse's shows, and especially those written with Lee Adams, show an exuberance and emotional fullness. The early shows, even when wedded to ungainly books or weak productions, maintained a high level of technique and professionalism.

STUYVESANT THEATER · See BELASCO THEATRE.

STYNE, JULE (1905–1994) · Jule Styne was by any accounting among the most successful of all Broadway composers. His prodigious output is unequaled by his Broadway contemporaries. Many considered Styne the ultimate composer when it comes to writing to suit the talents of stars. He tailored *Gentlemen Prefer Blondes* for Carol Channing; *Gypsy* for Ethel Merman; *Funny Girl* for Barbra Streisand; *Bells Are Ringing* for Judy Holliday. Although these shows remain indelibly associated with their stars, they also exist as perfect examples of cohesive, well-integrated scores that serve their theatrical needs as fully as they serve the needs of their performers. It is this versatility and superb artistry that led many to consider Styne our greatest living composer.

He was born Julius Kerwin Stein in London, December 31, 1905. Styne's family emigrated to the United States in 1913 and settled in Chicago. By the time the youngster was a teenager, Chicago was becoming more and more of an influence in the development of jazz and popular song. The early jazz groups known as the Chicagoans did not escape the notice of the young prodigy. Despite a solid classical background (he made his debut at the age of nine as a solo pianist with the Chicago Symphony), Styne felt more and more drawn to the music of the backroom bars and nightclubs.

A scholarship to the Chicago College of Music enabled Styne to perfect his technique and to study composition, theory and harmony. He formed his own dance band for which he played the piano and contributed arrangements. He joined some of the smaller bands then touring the country, most notably that of Art Jarrett. Styne's early days in Chicago were an important influence in his career.

Styne moved to New York where he earned his living as a vocal coach and then accompanist for Harry Richman, a top Broadway and nightclub performer. Styne received an offer from 20th Century-Fox asking him to come to Hollywood to coach Alice Faye, Tony Martin, Shirley Temple, and other Fox stars.

Styne previously had a big hit with his first song, "Sunday," written in 1927, and it didn't take the studio long to move Styne into the composers stable. Styne moved from Fox to Republic and then to Paramount and Columbia. Among the movies for which he contributed music were: *Anchors Aweigh; Tonight and Every Night; Tars and Spars; The Kid from Brooklyn; It Happened in Brooklyn; Romance on the High Seas; Two Guys from Texas; It's a Great Feeling; The West Point Story; Two Tickets to Broadway; My Sister Eileen;* and *Meet Me After the Show.*

Styne's principal collaborators during his Hollywood years were Frank Loesser and Sammy Cahn. They collaborated with Styne on such songs as "I Don't Want to Walk Without You, Baby," "I've Heard that Song Before," "I Said No," "Victory Polka," "I'll Walk Alone,"

"Anywhere," "It's a Great Feeling," "Saturday Night Is the Loneliest Night in the Week," "Poor Little Rhode Island," "The Charm of You," "I Fall in Love Too Easily," "What Makes the Sunset," "It's Been a Long, Long, Time," "Let It Snow, Let It Snow, Let It Snow," "The Things We Did Last Summer," "Five Minutes More," "Time After Time," "Three Coins in the Fountain" (Academy Award, 1954), and "It's Magic."

After success in Hollywood, Cahn and Styne attempted to write a Broadway musical. The result, *Glad to See You* (1944), was planned as a vehicle for Phil Silvers. His unavailability and other problems forced the show to close out of town. However, a standard did emerge from the score, "Guess I'll Hang My Tears Out to Dry."

The team had much better luck with their next attempt, *High Button Shoes* (1947). This time, they got their man, Phil Silvers, and he and Nanette Fabray opened the show at the Century Theater. The Styne/Cahn score contributed at least one song to the hit parade, the polka "Poppa Won't You Dance with Me." Other standouts were "Can't You Just See Yourself?" and "I Still Get Jealous."

Two years later, Styne again opened a show on Broadway, this time with Leo Robin as lyricist. It was just as big a success as *High Button Shoes*. The show was *Gentlemen Prefer Blondes* (1949), an adaptation of Anita Loos' popular novel. It was noteworthy for several reasons, the most important being the debut of Carol Channing as Lorelei Lee. Styne and Robin provided Channing with the first song that would become her trademark, "Diamonds Are a Girl's Best Friend." The show also featured hits like "Bye Bye Baby," "A Little Girl from Little Rock," and "You Say You Care."

Styne's next show wasn't as successful, but it was important as the first meeting between Styne and his longtime collaborators, Betty Comden and Adolph Green. *Two on the Aisle* (1951) was Styne's only Broadway revue and was written to fit the talents of Bert Lahr and Dolores Gray.

Styne's third collaborator in as many shows

was Bob Hilliard with whom he worked on *Hazel Flagg* (1953), a musicalization of Ben Hecht's movie *Nothing Sacred.* The show was a disappointment despite a fine performance by Helen Gallagher. "Every Street's a Boulevard (in Old New York)" achieved some fame.

Director/choreographer Jerome Robbins was out of town working on a musical version of *Peter Pan,* starring Mary Martin. The show was having trouble, and the writing team of Jule Styne and Comden and Green was called in to bolster the Moose Charlap/Carolyn Leigh score. The principal Styne/Comden and Green songs were "Never Never Land," "Distant Melody" and "Captain Hook's Waltz." *Peter Pan* (1954) played at the Winter Garden Theater before becoming a perennial favorite on NBC with Martin and Cyril Ritchard having the time of their lives in the J. M. Barrie fantasy.

Next, Styne, Comden and Green collaborated on *Bells Are Ringing* (1956), written as a vehicle for Judy Holliday. Comden and Green had cut their theatrical teeth performing with Holliday as members of *The Revuers,* an early musical comedy act that played Greenwich Village clubs. For the new show, the songwriters gave their star two great hits, "The Party's Over" and "Just In Time."

Say, Darling (1958), the trio's next Broadway offering was a play about a musical. The source was a thinly disguised novel by Richard Bissel that told of his experiences working as colibrettist on *The Pajama Game.* The show starred Vivian Blaine, David Wayne, Johnny Desmond, and brash Robert Morse as a spoof on Harold Prince. The show unfortunately never achieved its due. The problem was that the show was more of a play with songs than a full-fledged musical. Audiences were disappointed not to find the typical musical comedy trappings. The one hit from the score was "Dance Only with Me."

Styne then collaborated with Stephen Sondheim on what some consider the greatest musical of all time, *Gypsy* (1959). Arthur Laurents wrote the libretto. Rose was the ultimate stage mother and to play her the producers,

David Merrick and Leland Hayward, chose the ultimate musical comedy star, Ethel Merman. Jerome Robbins was the director and choreographer. Styne and Sondheim perfectly tailored their bravura score to the talents of Merman and also served the dramatic needs of the script. The brassy, challenging score contained several hit songs, "Let Me Entertain You," "Some People," "Together," and "Everything's Coming Up Roses." All the elements of the production fused in Ethel Merman's last number, the thrilling "Rose's Turn," a high point in the actress' career and in the history of musical theater.

Styne next moved on to another collaboration with Comden and Green, *Do Re Mi* (1960). Styne again fashioned a score for Phil Silvers. His costar in this was Nancy Walker with John Reardon, David Burns, and Nancy Dussault rounding out the leads. *Do Re Mi* was the story of the mob's control of the jukebox industry and Phil Silvers' quest for a quick buck. The show's run was based mainly on the comic inventiveness of the stars and the hit song, "Make Someone Happy."

Subways Are For Sleeping (1961) was the threesome's next offering. Sydney Chaplin, Carol Lawrence, Orson Bean, and Phyllis Newman starred. The score was well received with "Comes Once in a Lifetime" achieving the most notice. The show is best remembered for a series of publicity stunts engineered by producer David Merrick.

Styne's next production was his biggest hit. *Funny Girl* (1964), starring Barbra Streisand opened at the Winter Garden Theater. Bob Merrill provided the lyrics to Styne's music. Garson Kanin and Jerome Robbins whipped the show into shape after a particularly stormy tryout. By opening night, it was clear that Broadway had a major hit and a major star on its hands. Regrettably, *Funny Girl* was Streisand's last Broadway appearance. The story of Fanny Brice had the same show business ambiance that had inspired *Gypsy*. The score provided another star with a Styne signature tune. Streisand introduced "People," and the song became hers alone. Other numbers in the score also received airplay. Among them

are "Don't Rain on My Parade" and "Who Are You Now?"

Styne's next show also featured another young star, Carol Burnett. *Fade Out-Fade In* (1964) didn't achieve the fame of *Funny Girl*. None of the Styne/Comden and Green songs clicked with the hit parade, and Burnett's problems with the show forced it to close, reopen, then close for good.

Hallelujah, Baby! (1967) reteamed Styne with his *Gypsy* librettist, Arthur Laurents. The score, with lyrics by Comden and Green, was exceptional, but the book, purporting to follow the progress made by blacks in this century, proved unwieldy. The show won the Tony Award as Best Musical after it had closed. Leslie Uggams, Robert Hooks, and Allen Case starred.

Darling of the Day (1968) was another show with a fine Styne score that achieved little success. This time, the lyrics were by master lyricist E. Y. Harburg. Although the show wasn't a success, the score was wonderfully witty and tuneful and deserves rediscovery.

Styne teamed up with his old partner Sammy Cahn for *Look to the Lilies* (1970). The adaptation of *Lilies of the Field*, wasn't very strong despite the best efforts of the star, Shirley Booth. That failure was followed by *Prettybelle*, which starred Angela Lansbury and closed out of town.

Bob Merrill, who provided Styne with such strong lyrics for *Funny Girl* and not so strong ones for *Prettybelle*, was unable to repeat his popular success with the musical adaptation of the Billy Wilder movie *Some Like It Hot* retitled *Sugar* (1972). Cyril Ritchard and Robert Morse made their second appearances in Styne musicals along with costars Tony Roberts and Elaine Joyce. The show's long run was due more to the work of producer David Merrick rather than the worthiness of the material.

One Night Stand, proved not even equal to its title, closing on October 25, 1980, after eight previews. Herb Gardner provided the lyrics.

With Broadway's fitful success with musical productions in the 1980s and 1990s, Styne was relegated to the wings. His attempt at musicalizing *Treasure Island* with lyricist Susan Birkenhead got no farther than Edmonton, Canada.

Jule Styne's final score also had lyrics by Susan Birkenhead. However, *The Red Shoes* was in trouble from the first preview. Styne's frequent collaborator, Bob Merrill, was brought in to work on new songs. Merrill chose to work under the pseudonym Paul Stryker. That name was chosen because when Styne was a staff writer at Republic Pictures the executives wanted Styne to change his name to Paul Stryker. Despite some wonderful songs and good performances, *The Red Shoes* couldn't overcome a weak book, bad direction, and poor producing.

Jule Styne died on September 20, 1994.

T

THEATER GUILD · The Theater Guild, the oldest producing organization in America, has been producing Broadway shows since its inception in 1919. Although it has been fairly inactive in recent years, its amazingly long history has been marked by incredible highs and incredible lows. All producing organizations of note have presented great plays and all have produced flops, but the Theater Guild has had many close calls when its existence depended on the success or failure of a single production.

The Guild's often shaky finances were the result of an ambitious producing schedule and its choice of plays that did not conform to the public's expectations. Many of the playwrights whom the Guild championed are ranked with the greatest dramatists of our time, including such luminaries as Maxwell Anderson, Robert Emmett Sherwood, S. N. Behrman, Philip Barry, William Saroyan, and Sidney Howard. These American dramatists were joined by many great English and European talents, chief among them George Bernard Shaw. The Guild produced eighteen of Shaw's plays. The other playwright represented by the Guild through most of his career was Eugene O'Neill, considered by many to be the greatest American playwright.

The Guild branched into operating subscription programs for many theaters and also produced movies. The organization also operated the Theater Guild Abroad program, which sent Americans to European theaters. The Guild's activity slowed in the sixties and by the eighties it was practically moribund. However, the Guild has been pronounced dead before only to emerge triumphant time and time again.

Helen Westley, Lawrence Langner, and Philip Moeller formed a new organization described as "a little theater grown up, and should be governed entirely by a Board of Managers, to which its director should be responsible. It should be a professional theater, employ professional actors and produce only long plays, 'which should be great plays.'"

The first board members of the new Theater Guild included Westley, Langner, and Moeller as well as Josephine A. Meyer, Lee Simonson, Edna Kenton, Helen Freeman, and Rollo Peters. Theresa Helburn, though not a member of the board, was named Play Representative. Peters and Freeman left within the first year.

The Guild's roller-coaster financial status began with its first productions. Financier Otto Kahn helped the Guild mount its first production. Kahn, the owner of the Garrick, liked the Guild and allowed them to lease the theater rent free. Langner himself put $1,610 into the new organization. An additional $474 dollars had been raised by selling subscriptions. With $1,000 more from various sources, the Guild was ready to begin production. When the first play opened, the Guild had exactly $19.50 to its credit.

The Guild's first offering was a commedia dell' arte drama by Jacinto Benavente, which John Garrett Underhill translated and titled *The Bonds of Interest* (1919). The show opened at the Garrick Theater on West 35th Street. It was a quick failure with a loss of $500 per week. One reason for the play's run past opening night was the Guild's 150 subscribers. These optimistic theatergoers had paid for a two-play series and so the Guild looked for another play to present.

The second Guild presentation at the Garrick was St. John Ervine's play *John Ferguson* (1919). This time the Guild hit pay dirt. Augustin Duncan, the brother of dancer Isadora Duncan, starred in the melodrama and also directed. The success of *John Ferguson* was due to circumstances other than its questionable dramatic merits. When the actors' strike of 1919 hit Broadway, the newly formed Actors' Equity closed down all Broadway productions. The Guild was spared because of its unique democratic structuring. Therefore, theatergoers who longed to see theater were faced with only two alternatives—*John Ferguson* or nothing.

Its success and popularity was almost embarrassing to the Guild since it was not a "great play." The Guild was certainly not prepared for its success. A business manager was hastily hired. He was future Hollywood director Walter Wanger. The Guild decided to move the play to the larger Fulton Theater, later named the Helen Hayes Theater.

The play's success led to a dramatic increase in the Guild's subscribers—five hundred avid theatergoers signed up for the second season, which began with a series of failures. St. John Ervine was called on to save the Guild. His play *Jane Clegg* (1920), starring Margaret Wycherly, was well received by audiences and critics.

The next season found the Guild's subscription base increased to 1,300 patrons. For its first production of its third season, it presented the American premiere of George Bernard Shaw's *Heartbreak House* (1920). Albert Perry had the leading role at the Garrick Theater where lines formed to see the three and-a-half hour play. The production was important as the first directed for the Guild by Dudley Digges, a mainstay of the Guild from then on.

The third season proved very popular. A. A. Milne's *Mr. Pim Passes By* (1921) starred Laura Hope Crews. Ferenc Molnar's *Liliom* (1921) proved to be an even bigger success. *Liliom* starred Eva Le Gallienne, Dudley Digges, Helen Westley, and Edgar Stehli. *Liliom* later served the Guild well as the basis for Rodgers and Hammerstein's *Carousel*.

Highlights of the next season included

Leonid Andreyev's *He Who Gets Slapped* (1922) and George Bernard Shaw's *Back to Methuselah* (1922). The Shaw play was subtitled a *Gospel of Creative Evolution*. It almost took as long as evolution itself. The Guild broke the play into sections and presented it over three separate evenings in repertory over three weeks. Four directors were called on to stage the massive undertaking. Dennis King, Margaret Wycherly, Walter Abel, and A. P. Kaye starred, each playing a variety of roles. The Guild endeared itself to Shaw by this bold production. When contract negotiations were announced Shaw responded, "A contract is unnecessary. It isn't likely that any other lunatics will want to produce it." Shaw was correct, and even fewer people wanted to see it.

The Guild was broke at the beginning of its fifth season, but it did have six thousand subscribers. Karel Capek's *R.U.R.* (1922) opened the season at the Garrick, was hailed as one of the decade's best plays on October 9, 1922, and introduced the world to the word "robot." Elmer Rice's expressionistic drama *The Adding Machine* (1923) was another highlight of the season.

During the next season, the Guild produced Shaw's *Saint Joan* (1923). The play, like many of Shaw's, was long, and the Guild implored the playwright to let them make cuts because suburbanites could not get to their trains by the time the play was over. Shaw responded, "The old, old story. Begin at eight, or run later trains."

History was made again with the opening of the seventh season. Molnar's play *Where Ignorance Is Bliss* was retitled *The Guardsman* (1924), and the comedy marked the beginning of Alfred Lunt and Lynn Fontanne's long and prosperous association with the Guild. The production also marked the first success of designer Jo Mielziner.

With *The Guardsman*, the Guild hit its stride and entered into its most productive period. It next presented Sidney Howard's *They Knew What They Wanted* (1924) with Pauline Lord, Richard Bennett, and Glenn Anders. *They Knew What They Wanted* won the Pulitzer Prize.

The success of the Guild's productions was hampered by the Garrick's small capacity and off-the-beaten-track location. The theater district had moved from Herald Square to Times Square, and the Guild was determined to move with it. They commissioned C. Howard Crane to design a new theater that would be named the Guild. On April 13, 1925, President Coolidge pressed a button from the White House, which inaugurated the new theater.

The theater's first production was Shaw's *Caesar and Cleopatra* with Helen Hayes and Lionel Atwill. The production received mixed notices. A special fundraising event was planned for a Sunday night at the Garrick Theater. The show, a musical revue, was titled *The Garrick Gaieties*. The evening of May 17, 1925, was the date set for the opening. The show was so successful that it was presented on several occasions until a full run was inaugurated on June 8, 1925. Songs for the *Garrick Gaieties* were provided by a virtually unknown Richard Rodgers and Lorenz Hart. They wrote a delightfully witty score, which included one standard, "Manhattan."

The Guild was now firmly ensconced on Broadway, although its finances were, as usual, in a precarious state due to the expense of running its own theater. Another drain on the Guild's coffers was the permanent repertory theater it launched in New York in 1926. The public did not jump on the repertory bandwagon, and two years later the repertory idea was dropped.

Among the Guild's most successful productions of its middle years were Du Bose and Dorothy Heyward's *Porgy* (1927); Eugene O'Neill's *Marco Millions* (1928) and *Strange Interlude* (1928); Shaw's *Major Barbara* (1928) with Helen Westley, Gale Sondergaard, Dudley Digges, and Winifred Lenihan; and Philip Moeller's adaptation of Sil-Vara's *Caprice* (1928) with Lunt and Fontanne.

By the end of the 1920s, discord began to arise in the Guild's ranks. It seemed, throughout its history, that success bred failure. Perhaps the Guild needed to be lean and hungry to work well. The Guild's artistic success from 1926 to 1928 led to infighting among the Board.

There were other upheavals as well. Some of the Guild's most prominent playwrights left and formed The Playwrights' Company. Some of the Guild's best actors left and created the Group Theater. Even the Lunts eventually left the Guild, though they later returned to act in several productions.

Despite the fighting and upheavals, there were still many successes for the Guild in the late twenties and early thirties, including S. N. Behrman's *Meteor* (1929); Shaw's *The Apple Cart* (1930) with Tom Powers, Claude Rains, Morris Carnovsky, Helen Westley, and Violet Kemble Cooper; Glenn Anders, Ruth Gordon, Morris Carnovsky, and Franchot Tone in Philip Barry's *Hotel Universe* (1930); and Maxwell Anderson's *Elizabeth the Queen* (1930) with Lunt and Fontanne.

The Group Theater presented Paul Green's *The House of Connelly* (1931) under the Guild's auspices at the Martin Beck Theatre. O'Neill's *Mourning Becomes Electra* (1931) starred Alla Nazimova and Alice Brady. Hits of the thirties also included Robert Emmett Sherwood's *Reunion in Vienna* (1931) with the Lunts; Ina Claire in S. N. Behrman's *Biography* (1932); Eugene O'Neill's comedy *Ah, Wilderness!* (1933) with veteran Broadway player George M. Cohan, Elisha Cook Jr., Gene Lockhart, and Marjorie Marquis; and Helen Hayes, Philip Merivale, and Helen Menken in Maxwell Anderson's *Mary of Scotland* (1933).

After an acclaimed production of Shakespeare's *The Taming of the Shrew* (1935) with Alfred Lunt and Lynn Fontanne came one of the Guild's most ambitious offerings, *Porgy and Bess* (1935). George Gershwin composed the music for the black folk opera. His brother Ira and Du Bose Heyward wrote the lyrics. Heyward's libretto was directed by Rouben Mamoulian. The opening at the Alvin Theater met with mixed reviews. Critics differed on whether the show was an opera or a musical. Instead of concentrating on the play, the critics engaged in a war of semantics, trying to neatly pigeonhole the proceedings. The failure was a major disappointment to the Guild, which had been having its usual financial difficulties.

Tyrone Guthrie's production of Dody Smith's comedy *Call It a Day* (1936) starred Gladys Cooper and Philip Merivale. S. N. Behrman's *End of Summer* (1936), starring Ina Claire and Osgood Perkins, was also a success. *Idiot's Delight* (1936), one of the Guild's greatest successes, opened at the Sam S. Shubert Theatre. Robert Emmett Sherwood's play starred the Lunts, Sydney Greenstreet, director Bretaigne Windust, George Meader, and Richard Whorf. *Idiot's Delight's* success made three hits in a row for the Guild, but the luck was not to continue.

Behrman's *Amphitryon 38* (1937) opened with the Lunts, Richard Whorf and Sydney Greenstreet. The play's run was an oasis in a desert of failures. One such failure was the American premiere of Anton Chekhov's *The Sea Gull* (1938), translated by Stark Young. The limited engagement featured excellent sets by Robert Edmond Jones.

Between the success of *Amphitryon 38* and its next hit, Philip Barry's *The Philadelphia Story,* the Guild mounted nine productions, all failures. In 1936, the Guild's debits totaled $60,000. However, *The Philadelphia Story* (1939) revived the Guild. The play opened at the Shubert with Shirley Booth, Vera Allen. Lenore Lonergan, Katharine Hepburn, Van Heflin, and Joseph Cotten. The play saved the Guild from bankruptcy. Gene Kelly, William Bendix, Celeste Holm, Will Lee, Julie Haydon, and Edward Andrews were featured in William Saroyan's *The Time of Your Life* (1939). Also, Eddie Dowling appeared in the play and coproduced with the Guild and codirected with Saroyan.

The Lunts appeared with Alan Reed, Estelle Winwood, Juanita Hall, James O'Neill, and Muriel Rahn in Behrman's *The Pirate* (1942), which was presented in association with The Playwrights' Company. The Guild was at another low when Richard Rodgers again stepped in to replenish the Guild's coffers. The event was one of the milestones of the American theater—Rodgers and Hammerstein's *Oklahoma!* (1943). The musical ran for five years in addition to touring companies and foreign productions. The Guild then had a plentiful cash flow, but surprisingly its output fell. It did not even have the *succes d'estime,* which it had enjoyed in the twenties and thirties. There were other hits, but the huge success of *Oklahoma!* seemed to take the starch out of Theresa Helburn and Lawrence Langner's artistic manifesto.

A production of *Othello* (1943) with Paul Robeson, Jose Ferrer, and Uta Hagen opened to generally favorable reviews. Its run seemed to indicate that for the Guild nothing had changed. But success seemed mostly out of the producers' reach. The failures were forgettable, without the raw energy and political fervor of past flops. Blame was laid at the feet of Langner and Helburn, who were described by one director as "gifted amateurs." They were accused of paying too much attention to the small concerns of the organization without being able to grasp the big picture or make educated decisions. A former staff member said they were incapable of delegating responsibility.

The Guild Theater was becoming a burden since the Guild did not have enough productions to keep it occupied, and the theater didn't have enough seats to attract other producers. In 1944, the Guild sold the theater.

The Guild's next success came with Rodgers and Hammerstein's *Carousel* (1945) at the Majestic Theater. *Oklahoma!* was based on a previous Guild presentation, Lynn Riggs' *Green Grow the Lilacs* (1931). *Carousel* was also based on a play that the Guild had originally presented, *Liliom.* The success of *Carousel* and the failure of most other Guild offerings led the Guild's supporters to ask, Where was the commitment to drama? Why weren't more chances being taken?

The Guild branched out into radio and began broadcasting its show "The Theater Guild of the Air" in 1945. Though the producing organization presented more successful dramas on the stage, these became less and less frequent. Eugene O'Neill's *The Iceman Cometh* (1946) premiered at the Martin Beck Theatre. By this time Armina Marshall (Mrs. Lawrence Langner) had joined Langner and Helburn in running the Guild. The other board members had long since left in disgust.

Later hits for the Guild included William Inge's *Come Back Little Sheba* (1950) with Shirley Booth at the Booth Theatre; *The Lady's Not for Burning* (1950) by Christopher Fry at the Royale Theatre; and *Picnic* (1953) at the Music Box Theater.

During the 1950s the Guild, without much theater activity to keep itself busy, turned to television. In 1953, the "Theater Guild of the Air" transferred to television. Its name was changed to honor its sponsor, United States Steel. The "United States Steel Hour" ran until 1963. The show was among the best of the anthology series to introduce new American writers. The fifties also saw the Guild branch out into motion pictures. Among the notable movies produced by the Guild were *The Pawnbroker*, *Judgment at Nuremberg*, and *A Child Is Waiting*.

Though the 1950s and 1960s were slow decades for the Guild, the organization did mount a few notable productions. Jule Styne, Betty Comden and Adolph Green wrote the Judy Holliday musical *Bells Are Ringing* (1956). Dore Schary's *Sunrise at Campobello* (1958) with Ralph Bellamy opened at the Cort Theatre. Peter Shaffer's *The Royal Hunt of the Sun* (1965) opened at the ANTA Theater (the former Guild Theater) with George Rose, Christopher Plummer, John Vernon, and David Carradine. Harold Pinter's *The Homecoming* (1967) opened at the Music Box Theater and Allan Ayckbourn's *Absurd Person Singular* was also a success.

Since then the Guild has concentrated on managing a subscription series in other cities and the occasional theater cruise. Its producing days are over.

THEATER MASQUE · See JOHN GOLDEN THEATER.

TIMES SQUARE THEATER · 219 W. 42nd Street. Architect: Eugene DeRosa and Pereira. Opening: September 30, 1920; *The Mirage*. The Times Square Theater had a short but noteworthy life as a legitimate theater. Built by Arch and Edgar Selwyn, the Times Square became the third of their three Broadway theaters, the others being the Selwyn and the Apollo. The Times Square boasted a 1,200-seat auditorium designed in the Adam style. The auditorium was decorated in silver, black, and a green that almost became gray. The black velvet stage curtain separated the audience from the large, forty-foot-wide stage.

The theater's facade was shared with the Apollo Theatre next door. The two theaters each had separate marquees. The theater, similar in layout to the Music Box Theater, opened with a hit, *The Mirage*. Edgar Selwyn was the author and Florence Reed starred.

The theater's next offering was the musical comedy *The Right Girl* (1921) written by Percy Wenrich, and Raymond W. Peck and starring Tom Lewis and Robert Woolsey. The revue, *The Broadway Whirl* (1921) soon followed. Blanche Ring, Richard Carle, and Charles Winninger starred.

Three plays followed in quick succession: *The Demi Virgin* (1921); *Honors Are Even* (1921) and *Love Dreams*, a "melody drama" by Anne Nichols, the author of *Abie's Irish Rose*.

The great American actress Katharine Cornell opened in *A Bill of Divorcement* (1921) at the Times Square. The play was one of the actress' earliest successes. *The Charlatan* (1922) followed. Tallulah Bankhead appeared at the Times Square Theater in *The Exciters* (1922).

The next play at the Times Square was Channing Pollock's *The Fool* (1922). The next hit to play the Times Square was *Andre Charlot's Revue of 1924* (1924). On opening night, American audiences were introduced to three great British talents: Gertrude Lawrence, Jack Buchanan, and Beatrice Lillie. *Charlot's Revue* also featured a hit song, "Limehouse Blues," by Philip Braham and Douglas Furber. Theatergoers used to a four-hour Ziegfeld extravaganza were surprised at the revue's fast clip and modern theatricality.

Jerome Kern and Howard Dietz provided the score for *Dear Sir* (1924), the next show to originate at the Times Square. Florenz

Ziegfeld mounted *Annie Dear* (1924) at the Times Square as a vehicle for his wife Billie Burke. Sigmund Romberg, Clare Kummer, and Clifford Grey contributed the score. A third musical, *Kosher Kitty Kelly* (1925) was an ill-disguised rip-off of *Abie's Irish Rose*. Channing Pollock's anti-war play, *The Enemy* (1925), like *The Fool*, garnered mostly negative reviews but was enjoyed by the public.

The Selwyns partnership broke up in 1925 and following the closing of *The Enemy*, there was an ominous portent. The Times Square was used to show motion pictures. The policy didn't last long; on May 31, 1926, the play *Love 'Em and Leave 'Em* moved from the Apollo Theater to the Times Square.

The next hit to play the Times Square was Anita Loos' *Gentlemen Prefer Blondes* (1926), the story of gold digger Lorelei Lee and her friend Dorothy.

While Warner Brothers was premiering its talking picture *The Jazz Singer* to the world, the Times Square was hosting the silent film *Sunrise* by F. W. Murnau. The classic played practically the entire 1927–28 season.

The next season was taken up with Ben Hecht and Charles MacArthur's smash hit play, *The Front Page* (1928). The comedy of the rough-and-tumble world of Chicago newspapers became one of the most enduring plays of the decade.

The Depression heralded a slowdown in the number of productions presented on Broadway. The Times Square was home to the pacifist musical *Strike Up the Band* (1930) with a score by George and Ira Gershwin and a satirical libretto by Morrie Ryskind and George S. Kaufman.

The Times Square hosted six productions during the 1930–31 season. The last of these, Noel Coward's *Private Lives* (1931), was the only success. Coward, Gertrude Lawrence, Laurence Olivier, Jill Esmond, and Therese Quadri comprised the cast.

The 1931–32 season was a complete washout for the Times Square. None of the four plays that managed to open lasted longer than a month. The next season, the last for

legitimate production at the theater, was barely better. It started with the Bella and Samuel Spewack comedy *Clear All Wires* (1932), starring Thomas Mitchell. It was followed by *Foolscap* (1933).

The last play to open at the Times Square was *Forsaking All Others* (1933), a Tallulah Bankhead starrer with Thomas Mitchell directing. The drawing room comedy had the misfortune to open on the day that the federal government closed all the banks. As usual, the actress received glowing notices, although the play did not.

The Times Square Theater was then leased to the Brandts, owners or leasees of most of the 42nd Street theaters. The Brandts began a movie policy for the theater and so it remained. When the renovation of 42nd Street began the Brandts were stripped of their theaters (in spite of the fact that they agreed to renovate them all and begin a legitimate theater policy). Since then the Times Square has stood empty. When Garth Drabinsky gained control of the Lyric and Apollo Theatres, demolishing them and creating the Ford Center for the Performing Arts, he got the 42nd Street Redevelopment people to agree to exclude a theater use for the Times Square. It remains unused at press time.

TIMES TOWER · W. 42nd Street and Seventh Avenue. Architects: Cyrus L.W. Eidlitz and Andrew C. McKenzie, 1904; remodeled by Smith, Smith, Haines, Lundbert & Wheeler, 1966. The Times Tower is the most significant building on Times Square and the focal point of the southern end of the square. It is the scene of the annual New Year's Eve celebration. The building is a symbol of the changes the square has undergone and perhaps a guide to its future.

In what was then called Longacre Square, a quiet crossroads mainly housing carriage factories, the *New York Times* chose to build its new headquarters. The *Herald* had previously chosen a similar site on what became Herald Square, then the center of New York. Adolph Ochs, owner of the *New York Times*, wished for the same visibility. After considering a downtown site at Broadway and Barclay Street, where the Woolworth Building now stands, he realized the uptown flow of the city would make Longacre Square preeminent.

The building, completed in 1904, was the second tallest structure in the city. The triangular site, formed by the convergence of Broadway and Seventh Avenue, led to comparisons with The Flatiron Building on Broadway, Fifth Avenue and 23rd Street. However the Flatiron Building, considered New York's first skyscraper, addressed its location with more success. The Times Tower, though called "The second Flatiron Building," was a rectangular building on a triangular piece of land.

The new skyscraper, inspired by Giotto's campanile, was built on the site of the Pabst Hotel. The hotel and previous buildings occupying the site had faced south towards the city proper. But Ochs and his architects realized that the growing city would surround the tower, and so they pointed its front uptown.

The completion of the Italian-Rennaisance style tower on December 31, 1904, was celebrated with a fireworks display, the forerunner to the annual New Year's Eve celebrations.

The 375-foot-tall tower dwarfed its neighbors, none of which rose more than six stories in height. It also extended down fifty-five feet below the street under the new IRT Subway for which Ochs had lobbied. At one time, the building could be entered directly from the subway, a novel idea at the time.

As the area around the tower grew, so did the newspaper. By 1913, it had grown too large for its building and constructed a new headquarters down the block on 43rd Street. However, the *Times* retained an office for classified-ad placement in the tower.

As news of elections and sports results came into the paper, makeshift banners were hung outside the building. This increased the public's perception of the paper as an important news source. The impromptu celebrations following such announcements made the square a gathering place for important events. In 1928, on the eve of the presidential elections, the Motogram

moving sign was inaugurated. The Motogram's lights wrapped around the building, spelling out the news. Perhaps the most important news flashed by the sign was the announcement of the Japanese surrender marking the end to World War II. The V-J Day celebration was the most impressive demonstration surrounding the tower.

The Times retained ownership of the building until 1961. The newspaper sold the building to Douglas Leigh, the designer of many of Times Square's most fabulous "spectaculars." Leigh sold the building to the Allied Chemical company, and the outside was stripped of its terra-cotta facade. It reopened in 1966, featuring a continuous marble skin. The stark exterior on street level encouraged gatherings by undesirable characters. As the area declined, the Times Tower, now dubbed the Allied Chemical Tower, turned a blind eye on its surroundings.

In 1974, Allied Chemical sold the building to real estate magnate Alex Parker. He already had leased twenty-three floors from Allied Chemical before buying the building for a little over $6 million. Parker decided to call the building Expo America but soon simply called the building One Times Square.

Parker sold the building to Lawrence Linksman and his TSNY Realty Company for over $12 million in 1981. The new ownership is marked by the appearance in 1982 of the Spectacolor Sign. In July 1984, the building was again sold. A partnership bought the building for $16.5 million million dollars and then, one year later, sold it for $20 million.

TONY AWARDS · The Tony Awards, or more properly, the Antoinette Perry Awards, are Broadway's equivalent to the Oscars, Emmys, and Grammys. Like any such awards, the Tonys have their share of detractors, and these naysayers have a point—the system and its choices aren't perfect. Despite the carping and the competition from many other annual theater awards, the Tonys are the most important of Broadway's awards and have been since their inception in 1947.

Antoinette Perry was a producer, director, actress, and active member of the American Theater Wing. The Wing is the sponsor of the awards named for the lady who gave herself selflessly to its activities. She was Chairperson and Secretary of the Wing during its most active period, that of World War II.

Perry began her theatrical career at the age of eighteen in 1906. Her first appearance was in the David Warfield vehicle, *Music Master.* The next year, she starred in David Belasco's production of *A Grand Army Man.* In 1909, she retired from acting to raise her family.

In 1922, Antoinette Perry returned to the theater following her husband's death. She acted and later directed many plays. Among her best-known directorial efforts were Preston Sturges' *Strictly Dishonorable* (1929) and Mary Chase's Pulitzer Prize winning comedy, *Harvey* (1944).

After her death on June 28, 1946, Jacob Wilk talked to producer John Golden about establishing a memorial in her name. Golden approached the American Theater Wing, which took up the motion. Brock Pemberton was made chairperson of a committee formed to explore the possibilities of the memorial. They decided to honor her with an annual series of awards. A panel of theater professionals was entrusted with selecting the first recipients of the newly erected honor. The first members of that committee were Vera Allen, Brooks Atkinson, Louise Beck, Kermit Bloomgarden, Clayton Collyer, Jane Cowl, Helen Hayes, George Heller, Rudy Karnolt, Burns Mantle, Gilbert Miller, Warren P. Munsell, Solly Pernick, James E. Sauter, and Oliver Sayler.

On Easter Sunday, April 6, 1947, the first Tony Awards were handed out. Mickey Rooney, Herb Shriner, Ethel Waters, and David Wayne entertained in the Grand Ballroom of the Waldorf Astoria. During the initial years of the Tony Awards, the winners were announced without any mention of the competition. In the first years, the award went to "distinguished" performers, designers, directors, etc. Later they went to the "best" in each category.

The earliest recipients of the Tony Award were Jose Ferrer and Fredric March for dramatic actor; Ingrid Bergman and Helen Hayes for dramatic actress; Patricia Neal for supporting actress (Dramatic), and David Wayne for supporting actor (Musical). Technical awards went to David Ffolkes for his costumes for *Henry VIII* and Lucinda Ballard won in the same category for her work on *Happy Birthday, Another Part of the Forest, Street Scene, John Loves Mary,* and *The Chocolate Soldier.* Elia Kazan won for his work as director of *All My Sons,* and the talents of choreographers Michael Kidd and Agnes de Mille were also noted. Special awards went to Dora Chamberlain, Mr. and Mrs. Ira Katzenberg, Jules Leventhal, Burns Mantle, P. A. MacDonald, Arthur Miller, Vincent Sardi Sr., and Kurt Weill. That was the extent of the first year's honorees.

In later years, other award categories came and went. Stage technicians was a category in 1948 and from 1950 through 1964. At one time, there was an award for conductors. Producers had their own category once, now they share the award for best play or musical. Music and lyrics received separate awards for a few years in the late sixties and early seventies.

The first winners of the Tony Awards received a scroll documenting their honor. In addition, the men were presented with a cigarette case and the women a compact. The United Scenic Artists held a contest for a new design. The winner was Herman Rosse. His design was a medallion featuring the masks of comedy and tragedy on one side and a portrait of Antoinette Perry on the other. The new award was first issued in 1949. The Tony nominations, four in each category, were announced for the first time in 1956, and usually only one winner was announced in each category.

The Tony Awards have always had media exposure. The first ceremonies, held in hotel ballrooms, were broadcast locally on WOR radio and carried on the Mutual Radio Network. In 1956, the awards were televised locally for the first time. Channel 5, a member of the old DuMont network, broadcast the awards. In 1967, the Tony Awards were broadcast nationally for the first time. Alexander Cohen, a Broadway producer, was in charge of the television broadcast.

The Tony television broadcast has always been considered the most entertaining and sophisticated of the many show-business award shows. However, in recent years, the ceremony has received a fair share of criticism. Critics charged the show with poor writing, inclusion of television stars as hosts rather than Broadway personalities, and a second-rate variety show feel to the proceedings. In 1987, the television ceremony was broadcast for the first time without producer Alexander Cohen at the helm. The 1988 Tony Award broadcast received the lowest ratings in its history.

Many have claimed that the Tonys have sold out to the needs of television and just become a poorly produced advertisement for current Broadway hits. Numbers on the awards are not even presented live. Rather they are pretaped. In the 1988 awards, not only was the *The Phantom of the Opera* segment pretaped, but the actors were lipsyncing to a sound track.

The Tony procedures have also come under attack on occasion. An Eligibility Committee decides on possible nominees. In recent years, some leading performers have been nominated in the supporting category. This was arranged sometimes so that they would have less fierce competition.

The Eligibility Committee sends its list to the Nominating Committee, which decides on the actual nominations. Unfortunately, this committee is made up of members who are removed from the Broadway scene. Because the Theater Wing doesn't want the committee to be accused of favoritism, the Nominating Committee is composed of members who are academicians, ex-critics, theater curators, and ex-theater professionals. Because many of these committee members live outside the New York area, and because some shows play only a limited number of performances, the rules read, "each eligible production and performer shall have been seen by as many members as possible." Since some shows are never seen by any members of the committee or by few, the nominations are skewed towards the long-run hits.

Because of the current scarcity of quality musicals and the general decline in the number of productions, some categories have less than qualified nominees simply to make up the required four nominations in each category. On occasion, the committee has decided to limit the nominations to three or even two in each category.

The voters are made up of selected members of Actors' Equity Association, The Dramatists Guild, the Society of Stage Directors and Choreographers, and the United Scene Artists. Members of the press on the first or second night press lists and producers who are members of the New York Theater and Producers, Inc. and the Board of Directors of the American Theater Wing are also allowed to vote. Press agents are not allowed to vote. The Wing feels they would not be able to overcome their urge to vote only for shows on which they have worked.

The voters must certify that they have seen all performances in each category. This is, of course, impossible. Obviously all 560 or so voters can't have seen all the nominated shows, especially those that closed after only one performance.

There have been a few major gaffs. One such "mistake" occurred in 1972 when Stephen Sondheim and James Goldman's musical *Follies* won seven Tony Awards, including those for Actress, Director, Score, Scenic Designer, Costume Designer, Choreographer, and Lighting Designer. Nonetheless, *Two Gentlemen of Verona,* winner of the book award, carried off the award for Best Musical. Mistakes have been made in at least two instances when the wrong performer was nominated because the committee mistook the actor for another who should have been the actual nominee.

The Tony Award can mean life or death to a marginally successful play. Winning a Tony Award is a powerful publicity tool and can result in thousands of dollars in additional revenues. The Tonys have also had an impact on the theater season proper. It's no surprise that a majority of productions open in the spring at the end of the season so they'll be fresh in Tony voters' minds. In fact, the week before the nomination cutoff date sees a flurry of activity. Some shows have postponed their opening nights until after the Tony cutoff date so they would not look bad by receiving no nominations.

The Tony Award may not be perfect, but it is recognized as the leading theatrical award, and its impact on the theater is enormous.

TRAFALGAR THEATER · See NEDER-LANDER THEATER.

U, V

URIS THEATRE · See GERSHWIN THEATER.

VENICE THEATER · See JOLSON'S 59TH STREET THEATER.

VENITIAN TERRACE GARDEN · See VICTORIA THEATRE (1).

VICTORIA THEATER · See GAIETY THEATER.

VICTORY THEATRE · See REPUBLIC THEATRE.

VIRGINIA THEATRE · See AUGUST WILSON THEATRE.

VITAGRAPH THEATER · See OLYMPIA THEATER.

W

WALLACK'S THEATER · See ANCO THEATER.

WALTER KERR THEATER · 223 W. 48th
Street. Architect: Herbert J. Krapp. Opening as the Ritz Theater: March 21, 1921; *Mary Stuart*. The Shubert brothers built the Ritz in only sixty-six days as a sister theater to the Ambassador. The brothers leased their theater to producer William B. Harris or the Theatrical Syndicate.

The opening production at the Ritz was John Drinkwater's *Mary Stuart* (1921). The first hit was *Bluebeard's Eighth Wife* (1921) with Ina Claire and Edmund Breeze. Claire played a woman whom an American buys as his wife. *In Love with Love* (1923) starred Lynn Fontanne. Sutton Vane's imaginative play *Outward Bound* (1924) starred Fontanne's future partner, Alfred Lunt. The drama opened with Leslie Howard and Margalo Gillmore also in the cast.

The first musical production at the theater was *Hassard Short's Ritz Revue* (1924). Short was one of the revue format's greatest directors. He later directed such classics as *The Band Wagon* and Irving Berlin's *As Thousands Cheer*. The revue opened with Charlotte Greenwood, Raymond Hitchcock, and Madeleine Fairbanks.

Ina Claire, Lynn Fontanne, and Margalo Gillmore were only the first of a string of great actresses to play the Ritz Theatre. Others included Claudette Colbert in *The Kiss in a Taxi* (1925), Helen Hayes in *Young Blood* (1925), Grace George in *The Legend of Lenora* (1927), Alice Brady in *The Thief* (1927), Miriam Hopkins in *Excess Baggage* (1927), Janet Beecher in *Courage* (1928), and Bette Davis in *Broken Dishes* (1929).

The theater's lack of hits resulted in the Shubert Brothers' taking over the booking of their theater in the late 1920s. They didn't fare much better than William B. Harris. The thirties featured other great performers. Mildred Natwick appeared in *The Wind and the Rain* (1934). Dennis King starred with Leo G. Carroll in *Petticoat Fever* (1935).

When the Depression changed the face of Broadway, the Ritz found bookings hard to come by. The Federal Theater Project took over the stage on February 16, 1938, with the world premiere of T. S. Eliot's *Murder in the Cathedral*. The drama of Thomas Becket proved to be a huge success, and its six-week run played to over 39,000 people.

The Project's *Living Newspaper* series dramatized issues from the front pages of the nation's newspapers. *Power* (1937) advocated public ownership and control of utilities. The play was also presented by other Project companies in Seattle, Chicago, San Francisco, and Portland, Oregon.

Pinocchio (1938) was one of the most popular of all the Federal Theater offerings. The play was developed and directed by Yasha Frank.

The Federal Theater was disbanded on June 30, 1939. With the Federal Theater Project out of the picture, the Ritz went dark. At various times, all three broadcast networks used the theater. CBS used the Ritz as a radio studio. Alexander Woollcott broadcast his "Town Crier" radio show from its stage.

The Ritz returned to legitimate theater when Leonard Sillman presented his *New Faces of 1943* (1942). The show starred such new faces as Alice Pearce and John Lund as well as producer and director Sillman.

Tobacco Road moved to the theater for a brief

period. Then in 1943, NBC took control for their radio operations. Later, ABC used the theater for radio and television.

On January 12, 1971, the theater reopened for legitimate productions with a rock musical called *Soon*. The show was not and it closed after three performances. Viveca Lindfors and Rip Torn played in a short-lived revival of Strindberg's *Dance of Death* later that season.

In 1971, the theater was closed for renovation and it reopened on March 7, 1972, with Gwen Verdon in *Children! Children!* The play opened and closed at the same performance. The theater was again dark until Maureen O'Sullivan opened in *No Sex Please, We're British* (1973). The play, which was a huge hit in England, playing over a decade, closed quickly in New York.

The theater closed again, and for a while was called the Robert F. Kennedy Theater with plans to make it a national children's theater. But the Kennedy family sued to have the name changed, and the project folded for lack of funds. The theater was thereafter used to store posters. During that time, the roof began leaking, causing major interior damage. The Jujamcyn chain bought the theater from the city and spent $1.5 million dollars on restoration. The interior was redesigned by Karen Rosen and The Roger Morgan Studios to approximate its original splendor. The first production at the restored Ritz was *The Flying Karamazov Brothers* (1983), a juggling act.

Producer Morton Gottlieb reached a unique deal with Actor's Equity, allowing the Ritz to present plays that might not otherwise have much chance for success. The theater's capacity was reduced by roping off sections of seats. One of the plays presented under this policy was David Wiltse's *Doubles* (1985). A British revue called *Jerome Kern Goes to Hollywood* (1986) had as its only asset a charming performance by the great Elisabeth Welch.

Magicians Penn and Teller (1987) worked their magic on the Ritz's stage in the theater's last hit. The limited engagement was extended and the theater finally had a success.

In late 1989, the Ritz was completely renovated. It reopened with August Wilson's *The Piano Lesson* (1990). The theater was renamed the Walter Kerr Theatre in 1990.

Recent successes have included August Wilson's *Two Trains Running* (1992) and *Seven Guitars* (1996). Two plays with gay themes, Tony Kushner's *Angels in America* (1993) and Terence McNally's *Love! Valour! Compassion!* (1996) were successes at the theater. Two Irish-themed plays followed back to back: Martin McDonagh's *The Beauty Queen of Leenane* (1998) and Conor McPherson's *The Weir* (1999). Both were deserved successes.

The new century opened with a big hit for the theater, the Manhattan Theatre Club's production of David Auburn's *Proof*. The company had another hit follow, *Take Me Out* (2003) in which playwright Richard Greenberg explored homosexuality in major league sports. August Wilson returned to the theater for the last time with *Gem of the Ocean* in 2004. It was followed by another big hit from Manhattan Theatre Club, John Patrick Shanley's *Doubt* (2005).

WARNER BROTHERS THEATER · See MARK HELLINGER THEATER.

WEBER AND FIELDS MUSIC HALL · See 44TH STREET THEATRE.

WEILL, KURT (1900–1950) · Composer Kurt Weill was born in Dessau, Germany, on March 2, 1900. His early career was primarily associated with Bertolt Brecht. Their most famous collaboration was *Die Dreigroschenoper (The Threepenny Opera)*. Another of their works, *Mahagonny*, has also endured through many productions throughout the world.

When Hitler began to come into power, Weill emigrated to the United States. He brought with him his belief in the power of the musical theater, a power never fully realized in the United States. Weill felt, correctly, that he could entertain audiences and still tackle major themes and ideas.

Because of his work with Brecht, Weill had a high regard for authors, especially poets. A hallmark of his career is the collaborations he enjoyed with many great authors whose work in the musical theater was otherwise negligible.

Weill's first Broadway production was an unsuccessful mounting of *The Threepenny Opera* (1933). The translation was by Gifford Cochran and Jerrold Krimsky. Broadway audiences weren't ready for the serious musical theater that *The Threepenny Opera* typified. In 1935, Weill had a production of *A Kingdom for a Cow* in London with Desmond Carter's lyrics. It was Weill's second failure.

He returned to the United States and wrote the music for the antiwar musical, *Johnny Johnson* (1936). Playwright Paul Green contributed the book and lyrics to the show. The Group Theater produced the piece. But the United States wasn't ready for *Johnny Johnson's* cautionary messages.

Weill achieved somewhat more fame with a more successful production, *Knickerbocker Holiday* (1938) at the Ethel Barrymore Theater. The show, the story of Peter Stuyvesant in early Manhattan, also had political overtones, but they were put across in a more palatable manner.

Walter Huston, Richard Kollmar, Ray Middleton, Robert Rounseville, and Jeanne Madden headed the cast. Huston made an especially strong impression in the leading role. He was lucky enough to have Weill's first popular standard to sing, "September Song."

On this show, Weill again chose a prominent playwright as his collaborator. Maxwell Anderson wrote the book and lyrics.

Lady in the Dark (1941), at the Alvin Theater, was Weill's first Broadway success. Weill's collaborator was Broadway veteran Ira Gershwin. The show fit Weill's requirement of an adult theme. This time it was psychoanalysis. Gertrude Lawrence played the lead, a magazine editor who simply couldn't make up her mind. The Weill and Gershwin score was among the best written for any musical. "My Ship" and "The Saga of Jenny" received the most notice.

Weill's next big production was *One Touch of Venus* (1943). Poet Ogden Nash supplied the lyrics to Weill's music. Nash and satirist S. J. Perelman wrote the book. Elia Kazan directed with Cheryl Crawford and John Wildberg producing. The story of a statue that comes to life was written for Marlene Dietrich and played by Mary Martin. The Weill and Nash score yielded many gems. "Foolish Heart" and "Speak Low" were the popular hits. Other songs in the score were equally good. "That's Him," "West Wind," and "The Trouble with Women" all had their partisans.

Weill and Gershwin reteamed for the unsuccessful *The Firebrand of Florence* (1945). The show starred Melville Cooper, Earl Wrightson and Weill's wife, Lotte Lenya.

Weill again enlisted an unusual collaborator for his next production, *Street Scene* (1947). Elmer Rice adapted his classic play for the musical. "Moon-Faced, Starry-Eyed" achieved some success, but for the most part this exceptional score remains largely unknown. It certainly wasn't well appreciated at the time.

Weill tried another experiment, this time with Alan Jay Lerner. *Love Life* (1948) followed a marriage against the background of changing history. Nanette Fabray and Ray Middleton starred as the hapless couple. They and the rest of the cast were afforded some fine songs, including "Here I'll Stay."

Weill's last Broadway show was one of his most impassioned. *Lost in the Stars* (1949) featured lyrics by Weill's past collaborator, Maxwell Anderson. It was based on Alan Paton's novel of black citizens in South Africa. The tragic story was well captured through Weill and Anderson's powerful and dramatic score. Todd Duncan, the original Porgy in Gershwin's *Porgy and Bess,* Herbert Coleman, Inez Matthews, and Julian Mayfield headed the excellent cast. *Lost in the Stars* has won high regard as the years have passed.

Kurt Weill's final project was a musicalization of *Huckleberry Finn* written with Maxwell Anderson. Unfortunately, Weill died before the project could be finished.

Weill's most successful production occurred four years after his death. It was an off-Broadway revival of *The Threepenny Opera*. Lotte

Lenya starred in the remounting of one of Weill's earliest successes. The opening at the Theater De Lys took place on September 10, 1954. It played for ninety-four performances. The Marc Blitzstein translation reopened on September 30, 1955. This time, it ran for 2,611 performances. Other cast members were Charlotte Rae, Scott Merrill, Martin Wolfson, Jo Sullivan, Gerald Price, and Beatrice Arthur. The hit parade success of "Mack the Knife" accounted for much of the success of the show.

Weill's early death at age fifty on April 3, 1950, was a blow to the Broadway community. His scores stand equal to those of Broadway's finest composers. Weill's themes pointed up the possibilities for the American musical theater—possibilities that still have not been fully realized.

WHITE, GEORGE (1890–1968) · George White was an actor, dancer, producer, director, choreographer, composer, lyricist, and librettist. He was the force behind the *Ziegfeld Follies'* biggest rival, *George White's Scandals*. As producer of the *Scandals,* White nurtured many young talents. These included George Gershwin, DeSylva, Brown, and Henderson, and Alice Faye.

White was born in Toronto, Canada, in 1890. He learned to dance while standing on Third Avenue in New York after hawking newspapers. His first stage appearance was at the age of twelve. When he was about sixteen, he teamed up with Ben Ryan, and together they toured vaudeville in a dancing act. A scout for producer Charles Dillingham spotted White and introduced him to Dillingham, who promptly hired White for his next show.

He made his New York debut at the Globe Theatre in *The Echo* on August 17, 1910. He next appeared at the Winter Garden Theater in *The Pleasure Seekers* (1913). This led to his joining the cast of *The Midnight Girl* at the 44th Street Theatre in the middle of its run. By then, he was starting to make his reputation and was hired by Florenz Ziegfeld for the 1915 edition of his *Follies.*

After the *Follies,* White was hired by Ziegfeld for the Jerome Kern and P. G. Wodehouse revue *Miss 1917.* The show was a financial failure, although it played to standing room only houses.

White became convinced that he could outdo Ziegfeld by producing his own revues. He raised the money and opened the first *George White's Scandals* on June 2, 1919. The show featured a score by Richard Whiting and Herbert Spencer, composers, and Arthur Jackson and White himself as lyricists. This was the first instance of a team creating the entire score for a revue. Up till then, revue producers would receive entries from a variety of songwriters and pick the songs that they liked from the samples submitted. White also performed in the show as well as choreographing it.

Also appearing in the first *Scandals* was White's former dance partner from the *Follies,* Ann Pennington. She became the first in a series of regulars who starred in succeeding *Scandals*—eventually appearing in five of the annual revues. Other performers who were part of the informal company were Willie and Eugene Howard (six editions), Florence Williams (four occasions), and Lou Holtz and Winnie Lightner (each appeared three times).

Apart from the regulars, White brought in many top stars from the stage and radio. These performers included Ethel Merman, Rudy Vallee (twice), Alice Faye, Everett Marshall, Charles King, Paul Whiteman and his orchestra, Dolores Costello (twice), Ray Bolger, Ethel Barrymore Colt, Cliff Edwards, Bert Lahr, Ben Blue, Harry Richman (twice), Ella Logan, and Ann Miller.

White's shows were fast and snappy with a youthful exuberance. This was due in large part to the songs that were written for the series. George Gershwin contributed five scores for the series. The lyrics for the Gershwin tunes were written by Arthur Jackson, Ira Gershwin, Ballard Macdonald, and B. G. DeSylva.

DeSylva also contributed to three other *Scandals* with his partners Lew Brown and Ray Henderson. Henderson and Brown contributed one more score to the series but without DeSylva.

Although best known for the *Scandals,* White also produced book musicals. The first was *Runnin' Wild* (1923). This was an all-black musical, featuring Elisabeth Welch, Adelaide Hall, Flournoy Miller, and Aubrey Lyles. The show was typical of the works produced by White. It was fast paced and up-to-the-minute. In fact, it was in *Runnin' Wild* that audiences first heard and saw the Charleston. The Charleston swept through the nation and became the hottest dance craze of the twenties.

White's next non-*Scandals* show was *Manhattan Mary* (1927). The score was composed by *Scandals* regulars, DeSylva, Brown, and Henderson. White coauthored the book with William K. Wells, in addition to producing, directing and starring in the show. Ed Wynn, Harland Dixon, and Ona Munson were also in the cast as were *Scandals* regulars Lou Holtz and Paul Frawley. White played himself.

Flying High (1930), also by DeSylva, Brown, and Henderson, featured Kate Smith, Bert Lahr, and Oscar Shaw. By 1932, the country was deep into the Depression, and money was hard to come by both for the populace and producers. Instead of mounting an expensive *Scandals,* White presented *George White's Music Hall Varieties* (1932), a simpler version of the same formula. Eleanor Powell, Harry Richman, and Bert Lahr headlined, but the show wasn't a success. The songs were written by a variety of songwriting teams, including Harold Arlen and Irving Caesar, Cliff Friend and Herb Magidson, and Carmen Lombardo. But the hit of the show, and a future standard, was Herman Hupfeld's "Let's Turn Out the Lights and Go to Bed."

The next year, White presented his last non-*Scandals* Broadway show, *Melody* (1933). He produced and directed the show, which was a distinct change from his usual offerings. It was written by Sigmund Romberg, mostly noted for his operettas, and Irving Caesar. The show proved to be a failure, despite the talents of Gypsy Rose Lee, Everett Marshall, and Ina Ray Hutton.

Following his last *Scandals* in 1939, White toured with a tab edition called *George White's Scandals Cavalcade.* White brought the show in to Loew's State movie theater in June 1941. In addition to his stage chores, White ran several nightclubs. The first was the Gay White Way where he presented and directed a revue, *Midnight Scandals* in 1941. He also produced and directed an original nightclub revue, *Nice to See You* at the Versailles in April 1953. White's final nightclub show was presented in Jack Silverman's International Theater Restaurant. The show *George White's Scandals* opened on October 9, 1963.

The *Scandals* were also filmed by Hollywood several times. Fox presented *George White's Scandals* in 1934 and *George White's 1935 Scandals* the following year. White wrote, produced, directed and appeared in the two films. *George White's Scandals* was an RKO picture that debuted in 1945. He also appeared as himself in the Warner Brothers picture *Rhapsody in Blue,* also in 1945.

White died in Hollywood on October 11, 1968. He certainly helped define the twenties through his shows, which featured such revolutionary dance crazes as the Charleston and the Black Bottom. In addition to helping the careers of many artists, he also brought Broadway's glamour to millions of people through movies and nightclub entertainments.

WILLIAMS, TENNESSEE (1911– 1983) · Williams was born in Columbus, Mississippi, on March 26, 1911. His mother, much like Blanche in his masterwork *A Streetcar Named Desire,* adhered to largely irrelevant mores and a somewhat unreal idea of then current social convention. Williams' father called his son "Miss Nancy" and relentlessly expressed his disgust for the youngster. The family moved to St. Louis when Williams was eight. After college, Williams finally found the strength to escape his family, but no matter how far he fled, the memories and scars of those years stayed with him.

The Glass Menagerie (1945), at the Playhouse Theater, was his first Broadway success. A previous play, *Battle of Angels,* was closed by its producers, the Theater Guild, in Boston.

The Guild actually apologized to audiences for presenting an obscene play.

Williams' next work was perhaps his greatest achievement. *A Streetcar Named Desire* (1947) opened at the Barrymore Theater. The drama was a milestone in the American theater, firmly demonstrating that Williams was a major playwright. It starred Jessica Tandy as Blanche DuBois, Karl Malden as Mitch, and Kim Hunter as Stella. It also introduced a new star to Broadway, Marlon Brando as Stanley Kowalski.

Williams' next play, *Summer and Smoke* (1948) was unsuccessful at the time, perhaps because it paled in comparison with *Streetcar*. The play opened at the Music Box Theater. It has since been reevaluated and enjoys many revivals. *Cat on a Hot Tin Roof* (1955) opened at the Morosco Theatre.

Sweet Bird of Youth (1959), at the Martin Beck Theatre, featured powerful performances by Geraldine Page and Paul Newman. *Period of Adjustment* (1960), Williams' attempt to write a somewhat traditional sex comedy, opened at the Helen Hayes Theater.

Night of the Iguana (1961), produced at the Royale Theatre, was perhaps Williams' most eccentric play. It was widely parodied at the time. In *Night of the Iguana*, Williams again explored the theme of the human desire to attain peace. The sexuality and violence of Williams' earlier works are still present but tempered and relegated to the sidelines. In a way, it is Williams' most optimistic work. The cast, led by Margaret Leighton, Bette Davis, and Alan Webb, was superb.

Williams did not have another success on Broadway. His later plays all showed a marked change in his abilities. Although his dialogue sometimes remained as trenchant and poetic, his plays became muddled in style and insubstantial at their core. Still, Williams continued writing until his death and, in the end, almost seemed like a character in one of his own plays.

WINDSOR THEATER · See 48TH STREET THEATRE.

WINTER GARDEN THEATER · 1634 Broadway between 50th and 51st Street. Architect: William A. Swasey. Opening: March 20, 1911; *Bow Sing and La Belle Paree.* The Winter Garden Theater was built by the Shuberts on the site of William K. Vanderbilt's American Horse Exchange (1885). In fact, when flop shows were presented on its stage, the critics would say they could still smell the stables. The Shuberts leased the space from Vanderbilt and named their theater after an English theater, and the new theater "devoted to novel, international, spectacular and musical entertainments" was designed to resemble an English garden. An earlier Winter Garden Theater stood on lower Broadway near Bond Street during the mid-19th century. The corner of 50th Street and Broadway featured a triplex nightclub which went under several names including Palais de Danse, Montmartre and Singapore.

The theater itself, built for musical presentations, opened with *La Belle Paree,* a show that included a "one-act Chinese fantasy opera" called *Bow Sing.* The Shuberts tried to pack too much into the evening. By the time Al Jolson, making his Broadway debut, took the stage, the show had already run for three and a half hours. Jolson was not yet well-known and when he sang "Paris Is a Paradise for Coons" in blackface, the audience was unimpressed.

The Revue of Revues (1911) with Gaby Deslys, Harry Jolson (Al's brother), and Ernest Hare opened next. *Vera Violetta* (1911) again featured Al Jolson who starred along with Gaby Deslys, Ernest Hare, Stella Mayhew, and Annette Kellerman. Mae West had a small part in the production but almost stole the show from Deslys.

The Shuberts then inaugurated a series of Sunday evening concerts in the theater, taking advantage of its dark night. The concert series was a great success, since there was little other entertainment in New York on Sundays. The biggest star of the series was Jolson.

Jolson, Stella Mayhew and Gaby Deslys returned to the Winter Garden in *The Whirl of Society* (1912). The show also featured another future rival of the Shuberts—George White, who later mounted the *Scandals,* one of the top yearly revue series. *The Whirl of Society* is best remembered today as the first show that featured a runway down the center of the auditorium.

When Jolson was on the road, the Shuberts had to come up with an attraction for the Winter Garden. The theater was the personal responsibility of J. J. (Jake) Shubert. He controlled all the Shuberts' musical productions. His brother Lee controlled the plays and the empire's finances. J. J. was mad at Florenz Ziegfeld, whom he considered an arch rival. So he decided to outdo Ziegfeld, whose *Follies* were such a success. J. J. settled on an annual revue series, *The Passing Show,* so titled because the Shuberts planned them to run on Broadway for a short time and then tour the country.

The first *Passing Show* (1912) included songs by Louis A. Hirsch and Harold Atteridge, both Shubert contract employees. Songs were also contributed by Irving Berlin and by Earl Carroll, whose *Vanities* later rivaled the Shuberts' revues and Ziegfeld's famous *Follies.* The *Passing Show* starred Adelaide and Hughes, Trixie Friganza, Charlotte Greenwood, Eugene and Willie Howard, and Anna Wheaton.

Paris and all things French were big draws on Broadway in the early years of the century. After all, the French had the raciest of cultures and nude show girls were guaranteed to increase ticket sales. So naturally the Shuberts' next offering at the Winter Garden was titled *Broadway to Paris* (1912). The show had little to do with anything French but composers Max Hoffman and Anatole Friedland came up with some suitably French sounding numbers.

The Honeymoon Express (1913) featured Fanny Brice, Gaby Deslys, Yancsi Dolly (of the Dolly Sisters), as well as Al Jolson. As usual, the show was overly long on opening night. So Jolson simply broke character, came down to the front of the stage, and asked the audience whether they would prefer to see the remainder of the show or sit back and hear an impromptu concert by Jolson. The question was hypothetical.

The Passing Show of 1913 was typically undistinguished, but it did contain one hit song, "You Made Me Love You" by James V. Monaco and Joseph McCarthy. *The Pleasure Seekers* (1913) was produced by Lew Fields and Marcus Loew of the Loew's chain of movie theaters. Next came *The Whirl of the World* (1914), which introduced Broadway to one of its greatest composers, Sigmund Romberg. Romberg became a Shubert contract employee and was forced to churn out shows on demand. Writing under such circumstances did not inspire Romberg, and few of his contract shows for the Shuberts contained successful songs.

The Passing Show of 1914 also had a score by Romberg and lyricist Harold Atteridge. The show was no better than any of the Shubert offerings. However, it did mark the Broadway debut of Marilyn Miller, a delightful dancer, who became a particular favorite with Broadway audiences. Lee Shubert discovered Miller, but he wasn't told that she was only fifteen years old.

Dancing Around (1924) starred Al Jolson, Georgia O'Ramey, and Harland Dixon. Jolson again conquered Broadway despite lackluster material. The Sigmund Romberg, Harry Carroll, and Harold Atteridge score failed to yield a single hit.

The *Passing Show* series continued with the 1915 edition. It opened with Marilyn Miller, starring along with Willie and Eugene Howard, John Charles Thomas, and John Boles. This edition also introduced dances new to Broadway—the hula and pan Pacific drag. The next year's edition opened on June 22, 1916, with Florence Moore and Ed Wynn. It ran 140 performances. The *Passing Show of 1917* was the most successful edition yet.

Jolson returned in *Sinbad* (1918). The musical opened with a score by Sigmund Romberg and Harold Atteridge. As usual the best songs were interpolated. These included some of Jolson's greatest hits, "My Mammy" by Walter Donaldson, Sam Lewis, and Joe Young; "Rock-A-Bye Your Baby with a Dixie Melody" by Jean Schwartz, Joe Young, and Sam Lewis; and "Swanee" by George Gershwin and Irving

Caesar. In *Sinbad,* Jolson introduced one of his best-loved characters, Gus.

The Passing Show of 1918 featured the dance team of Fred and Adele Astaire. This was the Astaires' second Broadway appearance. The next attraction at the Winter Garden was *Monte Cristo, Jr.* (1919), a big hit. The show starred Jack Squire, Adelaide and Hughes, and Tom Lewis.

The Passing Show of 1919 topped all the previous editions. The show featured James Barton, Dick and George Raft, Blanche Ring, Charles Winninger, Reginald Denny, and Walter Woolf. It was followed by *Cinderella on Broadway* (1920) with George Price, Al Sexton, Shirley Royce, and Flo Burt starring.

The title *Broadway Brevities of 1920* indicated its creators were hoping the show would develop into an annual revue, but that didn't happen. Eddie Cantor, Bert Williams, and George LeMaire starred.

There was no *Passing Show of 1920;* the 1921 edition, which opened at the end of 1920, starred Marie Dressler and J. Harold Murray. One of the songs was titled "Beautiful Girls Are Like Opium."

The Whirl of New York (1921) opened with J. Harold Murray, Mlle. Adelaide and Smith and Dale. *Make It Snappy* (1922) opened with Eddie Cantor, Georgie Hale, J. Harold Murray, and Tot Qualters in the leads. "The Sheik of Araby" by Ted Snyder, Harry B. Smith, and Francis Wheeler was the big hit. Cantor satirized Jolson with the tune "My Yiddish Mammy."

In 1922, noted theater architect Herbert J. Krapp was hired to modernize the Shubert. The old auditorium was never popular, considered cold and with bad acoustics. Krapp lowered the ceiling, eliminating the exposed beams (outlined in bare bulbs) and decreased the width of the proscenium. Krapp also eliminated the famous Winter Garden runway filling in with an extra one hundred seats.

The *Passing Show of 1922* starred Fred Allen, George Hassell, Ethel Shutta, and Willie and Eugene Howard. This edition of the *Passing Show* cost the Shuberts $36,000, a lot for a show at the time but not near what Ziegfeld spent on his *Follies.* The sets and costumes were mainly from other Shubert productions.

The Dancing Girl (1923) was noteworthy in that the Romberg, Atteridge, and Irving Caesar score was supplemented by songs by George Gershwin and Cole Porter. However their contribution was no better than Romberg's uninspired melodies. *The Dancing Girl* was followed by the *Passing Show of 1923*, which opened with George Jessel leading the cast.

The *Greenwich Village Follies* (1923) (another revue series) was followed by *Innocent Eyes* (1924). It starred Cecil Lean and Cleo Mayfield along with Mistinguett and Frances Williams. The last of the long-running series was *The Passing Show of 1924*. Romberg, Jean Schwartz, and Atteridge supplied the score. Direction was by J. C. Huffman, and sets were by Watson Barrett—all Shubert contractees.

The *Passing Shows* were over and the Winter Garden's next show, *Big Boy* (1925) marked the last time Jolson appeared at the theater. He interpolated such hits as "California, Here I Come," "If You Knew Susie," and "Keep Smiling at Trouble." But Jolson developed an acute case of laryngitis during the run and had to leave the show.

In addition to the *Passing Shows,* the Shuberts ran a revue series called *Artists and Models.* The 1925 edition boasted the number "The Rotisserie." It featured the chorus girls spinning on a giant spit. The scene was a big hit.

The Clifford Grey and Maurie Rubens musical *The Great Temptations* (1926) was notable only in its casting of Jack Benny, fresh from vaudeville. In 1925, the Shuberts presented a show called *Gay Paree.* They used the title again the following year. The second *Gay Paree* was followed by the operetta, *The Circus Princess* (1927).

Artist and Models of 1927 opened with Ted Lewis, Jack Pearl, Jack Squire, and Gladys Wheaton. One hit song from the score, "Here Am I-Broken Hearted," was by B. G. DeSylva, Ray Henderson, and Lew Brown.

The revue series *Greenwich Village Follies* returned to the theater on April 19, 1926, for its last edition. When it closed after 158 performances it also marked the end of an era at the Winter Garden for after this legitimate booking Warner Brothers leased the theater and converted it into a talkie movie theater. The first movie to play the Winter Garden was *The Singing Fool,* starring, who else but Al Jolson. It remained a motion-picture house until 1933.

The Winter Garden resumed a legitimate policy with the opening of *Hold Your Horses* (1933). Orchestrator Robert Russell Bennett, best known for his work on Rodgers and Hammerstein musicals, tried his hand as a Broadway composer. Owen Murphy and Robert A. Simon provided the lyrics.

Jake Shubert believed he would have the last laugh, albeit posthumously, with his archrival Florenz Ziegfeld. Shubert bought the *Ziegfeld Follies* title from Ziegfeld's widow Billie Burke. The Shubert-produced *Ziegfeld Follies of 1934* had a score by Vernon Duke and E. Y. Harburg. They contributed at least two standards—"I Like the Likes of You" and "What Is There to Say?" The fine cast included Eve Arden, Everett Marshall, Ziegfeld alumnus Fanny Brice, Buddy and Vilma Ebsen, *Passing Show* favorites Willie and Eugene Howard, Robert Cummings, and Jane Froman.

Life Begins at 8:40 (1934) was the clever title of the next Winter Garden tenant. Harold Arlen, E. Y. Harburg and Ira Gershwin contributed a fine score that included such hits as "Fun to Be Fooled," "Let's Take a Walk Around the Block," and "You're a Builder Upper."

Earl Carroll rented the Winter Garden to present *Earl Carroll's Sketch Book.* The show opened on June 4, 1935 with Ken Murray and Sunnie O'Dea starring. Another revue, *At Home Abroad,* more sophisticated than *Earl Carroll's Sketch Book,* opened at the Winter Garden on September 19, 1935 with a fine score by Arthur Schwartz and Howard Dietz. Their songs, "O What a Wonderful World," "Love Is a Dancing Thing," and "Get Yourself a Geisha" were well handled by the talented cast including Beatrice Lillie, Reginald Gardner, Ethel Waters, Eleanor Powell, and Eddie Foy Jr.

Vincente Minnelli designed the sets for the Winter Garden's next offering, the *Ziegfeld*

Follies of 1936. John Murray Anderson, responsible for the previous *Follies* and the *Greenwich Village Follies,* directed. Vernon Duke repeated his past *Follies* assignment, but this time the lyricist was Ira Gershwin. They came up with a great song, "I Can't Get Started." It was sung by Bob Hope and Eve Arden in the production. The show also starred Bobby Clark, Josephine Baker, Fanny Brice as Baby Snooks, Gypsy Rose Lee, the Nicholas Brothers, Jane Pickens, and Gertrude Neisen—a stupendous cast.

Minnelli returned to his directorial chores with *The Show Is On* (1936). He also designed the sets and costumes for the all-star revue. *The Show Is On* brought Bert Lahr, Beatrice Lillie, and Reginald Gardiner back to the stage of the Winter Garden.

E. Y. Harburg, never one to shrink from airing his political and moral beliefs on stage, wrote lyrics with Harold Arlen for the antiwar musical *Hooray for What!* (1937) Harburg chose Howard Lindsay and Russel Crouse to script his story with Lindsay also directing.

You Never Know (1938) was a Cole Porter failure that contained one hit song, "At Long Last Love." Porter had a good excuse for the show's uninspired score. While working on the show he was critically injured in a horseback-riding accident. Porter's legs were crushed by the horse and he never fully recovered from the accident. The story, perhaps apocryphal, was that Porter worked on the lyrics to "At Long Last Love" while waiting for help.

Olsen and Johnson's phenomenally successful revue *Hellzapoppin'* had moved to the Winter Garden from the 46th Street Theatre, where it eventually completed its 1,404-performance run. The Shuberts quickly capitalized on Ole Olsen and Chic Johnson's great popularity by creating the show *Sons O' Fun* (1941) for them. The musical comedy opened with Joe Besser, Ella Logan, and Carmen Miranda completing the cast.

A last Shubert-produced *Ziegfeld Follies* (1943) opened at the Winter Garden the day after the opening of *Oklahoma!.* It ran longer than any other edition of the show. Contributing were the talents of songwriters

Ray Henderson and Jack Yellen and cast members Milton Berle, Eric Blore, Ilona Massey, Arthur Treacher, and the puppetry of Bil and Cora Baird. Berle was the first performer in *Follies* history to be advertised above the title.

Cole Porter returned to the Winter Garden with *Mexican Hayride* (1944). The Mike Todd production opened with a book by Herbert and Dorothy Fields. Bobby Clark, Wilbur Evans, June Havoc, and George Givot starred. Porter's score wasn't one of his best, but it did have one hit song, "I Love You."

Olsen and Johnson returned to the Winter Garden in *Laffing Room Only* (1944). The revue had music and lyrics by Burton Lane. Olsen and Johnson were joined on the stage by Betty Garrett and Fred Waring's Glee Club. *Marinka* (1945) was an attempt to bring operetta back to Broadway. The Emmerich Kalman music failed to catch on with audiences.

Following *Marinka,* the Winter Garden abandoned legitimate production and returned to showing movies. Three years later, a new musical comedy, *As the Girls Go* (1948), opened at the theater. Michael Todd was the producer, Bobby Clark was the star, and Jimmy McHugh and Harold Adamson wrote the score. Todd presented his *Michael Todd's Peep Show* (1950) at the Winter Garden. By the time *Top Banana* (1951) opened at the Winter Garden, television had taken hold of the nation's imagination. *Top Banana,* a satire on television with a jaunty score by Johnny Mercer, was reputedly a takeoff on Milton Berle's early adventures in the new medium. Phil Silvers, Jack Albertson, Rose Marie, and Judy Lynn starred.

The theater's next hit was a major one. *Wonderful Town* (1953) reunited Leonard Bernstein with Betty Comden and Adolph Green, and they came up with what can only be described as a brilliant score. Joseph Fields and Jerome Chodorov based their libretto on their play *My Sister Eileen.* Rosalind Russell made her musical comedy debut with Edith Adams as her sister Eileen. Director George Abbott kept the show moving, and the entire proceedings were hailed by critics. On March 1, 1957, the final edition of the *Ziegfeld Follies* opened at the Winter Garden Theater. Beatrice Lillie, Billy DeWolfe, Carol Lawrence, Harold Lang, and Jane Morgan starred.

Leonard Bernstein collaborated with Stephen Sondheim (in his first Broadway assignment) on the score for *West Side Story* (1957). Robert E. Griffith and Harold Prince produced, Arthur Laurents wrote the libretto, which was loosely based on Shakespeare's Romeo and Juliet updated to contemporary New York. Jerome Robbins directed and choreographed with his usual genius. The show starred Larry Kert and Carol Lawrence (late of the *Ziegfeld Follies of 1957*) as the star-crossed lovers Tony and Maria. The cast also featured Chita Rivera (who became a star due to her fiery performance as Anita), future Broadway lyricist Martin Charnin and Marilyn Cooper.

Meredith Willson tried to repeat his success of *The Music Man* with his next musical, *The Unsinkable Molly Brown* (1960). Tammy Grimes and Harve Presnell starred. Robbins also had a hand in the Winter Garden's next smash hit, *Funny Girl* (1964). Barbra Streisand played Winter Garden star Fanny Brice with Danny Meehan, Kay Medford, Sydney Chaplin, and Jean Stapleton in supporting roles. Jule Styne and Bob Merrill wrote a great score, full of theatrically exciting melodies and rhythms.

A strong central performance and a catchy, heartfelt score was also responsible for the success of the Winter Garden's next hit, *Mame* (1966). The Jerry Herman show had an enjoyable libretto by playwrights Jerome Lawrence and Robert E. Lee, as well as an excellent performance by Angela Lansbury as the title character. Beatrice Arthur, Sab Shimono, Jane Connell, Jerry Lanning, and Frankie Michaels made up the supporting cast. *Mame* was a smash hit at a time when the general consensus was that Broadway was dead.

A brilliant musical, the greatest production to play the Great White Way in decades, was Stephen Sondheim and James Goldman's *Follies* (1971). Sondheim's score was in part a pastiche of the accomplishments of his predecessors in the musical theater, and it also contained sharp, scathing, original numbers. Goldman's libretto broke open the traditional confines of the musical comedy. Through codirectors Harold Prince and Michael Bennett's genius, the show kept the past and present in constant juxtaposition. Boris Aronson's set design, Florence Klotz's costumes, and Tharon Musser's lighting added up to make the most spectacular physical production Broadway had seen since the days of the original *Ziegfeld Follies*.

The *Follies* cast, Dorothy Collins, Alexis Smith, Gene Nelson, John McMartin, Ethel Shutta, Yvonne De Carlo, Kurt Peterson, Marti Rolph, Virginia Sandifur, Harvey Evans, and Mary McCarty brought a resonance to the show that no other musical has come close to capturing. The New York Shakespeare Festival produced the next hit at the Winter Garden, William Shakespeare's *Much Ado About Nothing* (1972). Critics hailed Kathleen Widdoes' and Sam Waterston's performances as well as A. J. Antoon's direction.

Angela Lansbury returned to the Winter Garden in *Gypsy* (1974) with its masterful score by Jule Styne and Stephen Sondheim. The revival was originally mounted in London.

The theater again resounded with the music of Stephen Sondheim when his *Pacific Overtures* (1976) opened. The rather unconventional basis of *Pacific Overtures* was Commodore Perry's forays into feudal Japan. The show explored the different perceptions of life by the two cultures and the unavoidable changes in Japanese traditions.

A revival of *Fiddler on the Roof* with its original star Zero Mostel played the Winter Garden for 167 performances in 1976. Unfortunately, Mostel, a mercurial actor with an amazing range, could not contain himself and constantly mugged his way through the show.

A concert performance by Beatles look-alikes, *Beatlemania*, began previews at the Winter Garden on May 26, 1977. The producers, knowing that the Broadway critics would slaughter the show, refused to hold an official opening night. The expected bad reviews appeared anyway. But *Beatlemania*'s audiences didn't care what the *New York Times* thought. The younger set from New Jersey and Long Island jammed the theater and kept *Beatlemania* running.

A historic opening night occurred at David Merrick's production *42nd Street* (1980). After the curtain rang down on what most critics called a stunning success, Merrick took center stage. He announced to the assemblage that the show's director and choreographer, Gower Champion, had died that afternoon. The Broadway community was stunned; Champion was considered a fine talent and the fact that he died on the eve of what would be his greatest triumph was especially painful.

After *42nd Street* moved to the Majestic Theater, the Shuberts closed the Winter Garden for renovation. It reopened with the blockbuster musical *Cats* (1982). *Cats,* the brainchild of Andrew Lloyd Webber and director Trevor Nunn, received mixed reviews. But the musicalization of T. S. Eliot's children's poetry was presold because of its great success in London. There was a hit song, "Memory," which many people felt owed much to Puccini. Broadwayites were astonished when Eliot, who had been dead for years and who would never have dreamed that his simple poems would become the basis for an overblown spectacle, won the Tony Award for best lyrics. Through the courtesy of Japanese tourists *Cats* went on to run 7,485 performances to become the longest running musical in Broadway history.

When *Cats* finally closed the Winter Garden was renovated and refurbished to make way for the opening of *Mamma Mia* (2001), a smash hit in London based on the songs of the rock group Abba. In May of 2002, the theater's name was changed to the Cadillac Winter Garden Theatre. Like the former Ford Center for the Performing Arts and the American Airlines Theatre, theater owners raised capital by selling the names of their theaters in the great tradition of sports stadiums.

WINTHROP AMES THEATER · See LITTLE THEATER.

WORLD THEATER · See CHARLES HOPKINS THEATER.

Y

YIDDISH ART THEATER · See GEORGE ABBOTT THEATER. See JOLSON'S 59TH STREET THEATER.

YOUMANS, VINCENT (1898–1946) · Vincent Youmans was the quintessential twenties composer. His shows dominated the decade. The closest competitor was George Gershwin, who was born one day before Youmans. Jerome Kern also provided scores to many fine shows in the twenties, including the greatest of his career, *Show Boat*. But Youmans imbued his music with a drive and rhythm that seems to define the decade, its spirit, its speed, and its humor. Zelda Fitzgerald even gave a nod to Youmans in her novel *Save Me the Waltz*.

His hits, all of which occurred in the twenties, included *No, No, Nanette, Hit the Deck*, and *Wildflower*. Though these shows were wonderfully popular, Youmans' career as a whole was not as impressive as some of his contemporaries for two reasons. First, with only ninety-three published songs to his credit, he wasn't that prolific. Gershwin sometimes was represented by four shows in a single season. Youmans only had two shows in a single year on two occasions. Second, he was hampered by a constant battle with tuberculosis and alcoholism.

The composer was born on September 27, 1898, in New York City. He began writing songs while at the Great Lakes Training Station. The camp shows gave Youmans enough of a taste for show business, so that after his discharge, he was committed to a composing career.

Like many of his contemporaries, Youmans broke into the business as a song plugger for Remick's music publishers, his second choice, having been turned down by Max Dreyfus of T. B. Harms publishing. Remick's published Youmans' first popular song, "The Country Cousin," written with lyricist Al Bryan. Youmans landed his first theater job as a rehearsal pianist for producer Alex Aarons' show, *Oui Madame*. Victor Herbert was the composer. Later, composer Harold Arlen got his start in the theater as a rehearsal pianist for Youmans' *Great Day!* Youmans had his first song written for the stage interpolated into a Charlotte Greenwood vehicle, *Linger Longer Letty*. The song was "Maid-To-Order Maid" but it was only in for one performance while the show played Stamford, Connecticut. Youmans next had two songs interpolated into the show *Piccadilly to Broadway* in Atlantic City. The show closed out of town.

Youmans decided to see Dreyfus again and ask for a job. The music publisher was a sort of father figure for his employees and he took pains to give them every opportunity to develop their talents. Dreyfus hired Youmans as a song plugger. Alex Aarons paired Youmans with composer Paul Lannin (fated to be Youmans' lifelong friend and drinking buddy) and brought in George Gershwin's brother Ira to supply the lyrics. At that time, Ira was writing under the name Arthur Francis. The resulting show was *Two Little Girls in Blue* (1921), starring the Fairbanks sisters, Madeline and Marion. The show marked the Broadway debuts of both Youmans and Ira Gershwin. The show was a hit, which made Max Dreyfus happy, for the songs "Who's Who with You," "Dolly," and "Oh, Me! Oh, My" were all successful.

Though Youmans had passed his first test, he was not happy. He was unable to get another Broadway assignment and found himself again behind the piano working rehearsals of Victor Herbert's *Orange Blossoms*. Youmans' drinking increased, despite the fact that his second show, *Wildflower* (1923), proved to be a great success and solidified his place in the musical theater. Arthur Hammerstein produced *Wildflower*, which had book and lyrics by Oscar Hammerstein II and Otto Harbach. Herbert Stothart also composed music for some of the songs. The show opened with Edith Day, Olin Howland, and Charles Judels leading the cast.

Mary Jane McKane (1923) opened at the Imperial Theatre. Mary Hay starred in the show along with Stanley Ridges and Eva Clark. Youmans collaborated with lyricists William Cary Duncan and Oscar Hammerstein II. Herbert Stothart also composed some songs for this show.

Youmans composed his first score without a cocomposer for *Lollipop* (1924). He was teamed with Zelda Sears, one of the few women lyricists writing for Broadway. Youmans now had three shows running on Broadway simultaneously, for *Wildflower* and *Mary Jane McKane* were still running. *Lollipop* was another hit for Youmans. However, the show didn't contain any hit songs and didn't break any new ground. It certainly didn't prepare Broadway for his next triumph.

Youmans' next assignment, *No, No, Nanette* (1925), proved to be an even bigger hit, although it did not run as long as *Wildflower*. *No, No, Nanette* was produced and directed by H. H. Frazee, past owner of the Boston Red Sox. Frazee worked out a precedent-setting deal with his star, Louise Groody, who played the title character. She was the first star in Broadway history to receive a percentage of the box office in addition to a salary.

No, No, Nanette provided Youmans with a modern setting and his talents exploded. He seemed made to compose up-to-the-minute tunes that perfectly captured the syncopation and drive of the era. Irving Caesar's fine lyrics perfectly complemented Youmans' music. The show contained one of the greatest hit songs of the twenties—"Tea for Two." The other smash hit from the score was "I Want to Be Happy,"

a title that seemed to express the mood of the entire country in the giddy years before the Depression.

No, No, Nanette toured successfully and enjoyed a long life in both professional and amateur theaters for years to come. *Nanette* might have run longer on Broadway, but prior to its New York engagement, Frazee ran the show for a year in Chicago, set up three national companies and even sent a company to Europe.

A Night Out was the name of Youmans' next show, written at the behest of producer Alex Aarons. Irving Caesar and Clifford Grey collaborated on the lyrics. The show opened in Philadelphia and closed before coming to New York. *No, No, Nanette* actually opened after *A Night Out* because its pre-Broadway tour went on for so long.

Youmans paired up with lyricist Anne Caldwell for *Oh, Please!* (1926). Caldwell wrote the libretto with Otto Harbach. The show was produced by Charles Dillingham, a gentleman producer. The cast was excellent, featuring Beatrice Lillie, Helen Broderick, Charles Purcell, and Charles Winninger.

Youmans was unhappy with the way his shows were produced, so he produced *Hit the Deck* (1927) himself in collaboration with veteran producer Lew Fields. Leo Robin, and Clifford Grey provided the lyrics and Herbert Fields wrote the libretto. *Hit the Deck* contained two smash hit songs, "Hallelujah" and "Sometimes I'm Happy." Louise Groody, the star of *Nanette*, was also the star here, along with Stella Mayhew and Charles King.

Though Youmans continued his producing career after the success of *Hit the Deck*, he only provided the score for his next show, *Rainbow* (1928). It reunited Youmans with Oscar Hammerstein II, who directed and collaborated on the libretto with Laurence Stallings.

Youmans bounced back to form but a poor libretto, and history, would doom his next show, *Great Day!* (1929). He was so sure of his producing talents that he bought the Cosmopolitan Theatre, long considered a jinxed house. Billy Rose and Edward Eliscu wrote the lyrics for what was one of Youmans' best scores. It contained four big hits, "Happy Because I'm in Love," "More Than You Know," "Without a Song," and the title tune. But despite the great score, the show was a mess. It suffered a particularly painful out-of-town tryout, leading Broadway wags to dub it *Great Delay*. A week after the show opened, the stock market crashed, and Youmans, producer as well as composer, was forced to close the show.

With *Great Day* a failure, Youmans was left with an empty theater. The Depression hurt Broadway terribly, and there were no producers looking for theaters. So Youmans put a play, *Damn Your Honor* (1929), into the house. The play opened to dreadful reviews. Youmans was unable to raise money for any further productions at the theater.

Youmans then fled New York for the more hospitable clime of Hollywood. He saw several of his stage musicals adapted for the screen and wrote an original movie musical, *What a Widow!* It was a flop, and Youmans returned to New York.

Smiles (1930) was a Florenz Ziegfeld production at the Ziegfeld Theater. Youmans had borrowed money from Ziegfeld to bring *Great Day* into New York, and in return he promised to supply a score for Ziegfeld. The result, *Smiles,* had lyrics by Clifford Grey and Harold Adamson. The cast was fine with Fred and Adele Astaire, Larry Adler, Virginia Bruce, Marilyn Miller, Bob Hope, and Eddie Foy Jr., but the show was a failure. Youmans and Ziegfeld fought incessantly and Ziegfeld went so far as to get a court injunction barring Youmans from the out-of-town theater. The hit from *Smiles* was the standard "Time on My Hands" with lyrics by Adamson and Mack Gordon.

Youmans' career was clearly on the skids. His work wasn't bad, but personal problems prevented him from realizing his potential. Youmans had determined that his failures were due to bad management. He produced *Through*

the Years (1931), his next Broadway offering. The show was another huge failure. Again, Youmans handed in a fine score, with lyrics by Edward Heyman. "Drums in My Heart" and the title song received the most notice, but the show didn't work.

Youmans' last Broadway show was "Take a Chance" (1932). Youmans was asked to come in to bolster the score by Richard Whiting, Nacio Herb Brown, and B. G. DeSylva. The show had a good cast, including Ethel Merman, Jack Haley, June Knight, Mitzi Mayfair, and Sid Silvers. *Take a Chance* closed Youmans' Broadway career with a hit.

The composer's last assignment was for the movie *Flying Down to Rio*. Youmans tried to come to an agreement with RKO for more movies. While negotiations slowly proceeded, Youmans discovered he had tuberculosis. Though his health improved, his relationship with RKO did not. He gave up on movies and decided to tackle classical composing as Gershwin had done. Youmans' health wavered as he moved from location to location trying vainly to settle down. He was nearly broke, all the harder on him because he was used to living well. He was unemployable on Broadway, and Hollywood rejected his demands.

Youmans continued his classical lessons and occupied his last years readying a revue that would feature Latin rhythms. The show was titled *Vincent Youmans' Revue,* although there were no songs by Youmans. There was a little ballet and a few Cuban numbers by Ernesto Lecuona. Leonide Massine choreographed the ballet, and Eugene van Grona staged the Cuban numbers. The show was terribly disjointed and closed in Baltimore shortly after its January 27, 1944, opening.

The composer suffered personal disappointments, and another stab at Hollywood proved fruitless. Doctors thought Youmans could still be cured of the tuberculosis, but the patient seemed unwilling to fight. Vincent Youmans died on April 5, 1946.

Z

ZIEGFELD, FLORENZ (1867–1932) · Just as S. L. ("Roxy") Rothafel's name signifies, the apex of motion picture showmanship, Florenz Ziegfeld's name forever stands as a symbol of lavish showmanship in the musical theater. He was a man of superlatives for whom the show was everything. The most renowned producer of his time, he was not a good businessman, for he was often broke and preferred to plow the fortunes he made into the highly speculative world of theatrical producing. Ziegfeld's organization and methods (though not his financial practices) were the precursors to the famous Hollywood studio star system of the thirties and forties.

His monument, the *Ziegfeld Follies* revue series, has become a legend while his competitors' shows the Shubert's *Passing Shows, Earl Carroll's Vanities* and *George White's Scandals* are practically forgotten.

Ziegfeld also produced many book musicals. These included some of the greatest hits of the twenties: *Sally, Kid Boots, Rio Rita, The Three Musketeers, Whoopee,* and his masterwork, *Show Boat.* Ziegfeld gave these musicals and others the sumptuous physical production that was his hallmark.

Ziegfeld's accomplishments go beyond his astuteness as a manager. He made many of the biggest stars of Broadway, paid them stars' salaries and surrounded them with a publicity machine that kept their careers in the ascendancy. He was instrumental in introducing the American public to such stars as Anna Held, Fanny Brice, Eddie Cantor, W. C. Fields, Will Rogers, and Bert Williams.

He was equally influential in his championing of such songwriters as Irving Berlin, George Gershwin, Victor Herbert (late in his career), Rodgers and Hart, Sigmund Romberg, and Rudolf Friml. Ziegfeld's unerring sense of design led to a long collaboration with architect/scenic designer Joseph Urban.

Ziegfeld himself became his greatest creation. He had the reputation of being a flamboyant showman, Casanova, artist, magician, dictator, and arbiter of popular taste. Ziegfeld represented the Broadway mogul to hundreds who sought to emulate him without success. One sign of his genius and celebrity is the fact that his personal traits and practices have become stereotypes themselves.

Ziegfeld was born on March 21, 1867, the son of Florenz Ziegfeld Sr., President of the Chicago Musical College. The Chicago World's Fair of 1893 gave the young Ziegfeld his first taste of show business. The youngster's father was in charge of supplying classical bands for the fair. His son worked with him, although the two seldom saw eye to eye. Ziegfeld junior was more drawn to the flamboyant.

Ziegfeld brought a strongman, Sandow the Great, to Chicago and the fair. Sandow became a huge hit when Ziegfeld, with an unerring sense of publicity, invited the doyennes of Chicago society. The ladies were overwhelmed by the strongman, and soon all society lined up to feel the mighty Sandow's muscles.

In 1895, after visiting Paris, Berlin, and Monte Carlo with Sandow, Ziegfeld ran out of money and became stranded in London. It was the first time he was broke, but it wasn't the last.

Charles Evans, late of the comedy team Evans and Hoey, brought the broke Ziegfeld to a music hall. There Ziegfeld discovered Anna Held, a French chanteuse with an hourglass figure and sparkling eyes. Ziegfeld wooed Held and came away with a contract. Ziegfeld cabled Diamond Jim Brady for sufficient funds for the entourage to sail to New York.

Ziegfeld was an astute enough publicist to realize that it would be a mistake for Anna Held to burst on the Broadway scene. Instead, he opened his production, *A Parlor Match* (1896), with Evans and Hoey featured and Held relegated to a small singing part during the entr'acte. Audiences were captivated by the beauty and felt they had discovered a star.

A year after *The Parlor Match* opened, Held and Ziegfeld were married. For the next few years Ziegfeld concentrated on Held's career. By the end of 1906, he was simultaneously broke and on the eve of his greatest triumph.

Held is credited with coming up with the idea for the *Follies.* She suggested that Ziegfeld could outdo the famed Paris *Folies Bergere* if he gathered together his own bevy of beauties. A popular newspaper column, "Follies of the Day," supplied the title for the revue series. Held suggested that Ziegfeld call the show "Follies of the Year" but the superstitious Ziegfeld wanted a title with thirteen letters—hence *Follies of 1907.*

The *Follies* was announced at the bottom of an advertisement for the Jardin de Paris atop the New York Theater on Broadway and 44th Street. The ad stated "Very soon the Ziegfeld Revue Follies of 1907." It was the first time that the French spelling of revue was used in this country.

Klaw and Erlanger footed the entire bill for the *Follies*—$16,800. The show opened on July 9, 1907, and received mostly rave reviews, though critics could still be shocked at the fifty Anna Held Girls who actually showed their bloomers.

After the *Follies of 1907,* the series became a tradition for the next twenty-five years. Ziegfeld advertised his *Follies* as "An American Institution" and stated their goal as "Glorifying the American Girl." The twentieth and last *Follies* under Ziegfeld's auspices opened on July 1, 1931. The Shuberts and Ziegfeld's widow Billie Burke presented two more *Follies* in 1934 and 1936. The Shuberts alone presented a *Follies*

in 1956. It was ironic that the Shuberts ended up presenting the *Follies* since the Shuberts and Ziegfeld were mortal enemies.

Ziegfeld presented other revues tied into the *Follies.* On the roof of the New Amsterdam Theatre, he presented a series of *Ziegfeld Midnight Frolics.* Material would be tried out in the *Midnight Frolics* before being introduced on the large stage below. The *Midnight Frolics* featured some of the stars appearing in the *Follies* downstairs. The Roof Garden above the New Amsterdam was part cabaret and part supper club. There was a $5 cover charge that usually narrowed the audience down to members of the Four Hundred.

Ziegfeld contributed more to the theater than just the *Follies.* In 1908, in addition to the annual *Follies* edition, Ziegfeld presented two shows: *The Soul Kiss* and *Miss Innocence.* *The Soul Kiss* (1908) starred Adeline Genee, Cecil Lean, and Florence Holbrook and was followed by *Miss Innocence* (1908).

In 1912, Ziegfeld produced two forgettable shows. The first was *Over the River* (1912), a musical with music and lyrics by John Golden in which coproducer Charles Dillingham introduced ballroom dancing to the legitimate stage.

A Winsome Widow (1912), based on Charles Hoyt's *A Trip to Chinatown,* opened at the Moulin Rouge (formerly the Jardin de Paris) and contained one smash hit song, "Be My Little Baby Bumble Bee, " which was originally in the *Follies of 1911.*

In 1913, Ziegfeld and Held were divorced. She continued to appear under Ziegfeld's auspices in vaudeville. On New Year's Eve, 1914, Ziegfeld, attending a ball at the Hotel Astor, ran into actress Billie Burke. They were married on April 11, 1914, after a matinee of Burke's show, *Jerry.* Anna Held died on August 12, 1918.

The next non-*Follies* show presented by Ziegfeld was *The Century Girl* (1916). Irving Berlin composed the music and lyrics with some instrumental pieces composed by Victor Herbert. The following year, *Miss 1917,* one of the most expensive productions of its time, opened with a score by Jerome Kern and P. G. Wodehouse. George Gershwin was the rehearsal pianist for the show. Even with sold-out houses, the show could not recoup its cost. Ziegfeld and Dillingham were forced to close it despite its smash hit status.

Ziegfeld's next musical comedy production, *Sally* (1920), was a happier experience. Kern and Wodehouse collaborated on the score along with colyricist Clifford Grey. The score contained several hits, including "Whip-Poor-Will" and "Look for the Silver Lining." Both songs featured lyrics by B. G. DeSylva. Marilyn Miller starred in the production along with Walter Catlett and Leon Errol.

Eddie Cantor, who got his start with Ziegfeld, was given his first book show, *Kid Boots* (1923). Cantor, band leader George Olsen, Harland Dixon, and Mary Eaton introduced a score by Harry Tierney and Joseph McCarthy. *Kid Boots* had a $16 top ticket price at its opening. Although it was a smash hit, Ziegfeld couldn't stop trying to improve the show. He spent $20,000 on new costumes for the first act finale. It was no surprise to Eddie Cantor when he received the following telegram from Ziegfeld on Christmas Day: "Merry Christmas to you and yours. May we remain together as long as both of us remain in show business, although profits on *Kid Boots* have been far less than *Sally*."

The Sigmund Romberg, Clare Kummer, Clifford Grey show, *Annie Dear* (1924), opened as a vehicle for Billie Burke. Romberg wrote his second book show for Ziegfeld, *Louie the 14th* (1925), with Englishman Arthur Wimperis. Ziegfeld favorite Leon Errol costarred with Ethel Shutta in the show.

In 1926, Ziegfeld was quarreling with Erlanger over the name *Follies*. He was forced to title his 1926 edition of the *Follies, No Foolin'*. Later that year, the producer opened *Betsy* (1926) by Richard Rodgers and Lorenz Hart.

In 1927, Ziegfeld produced two of his biggest successes. *Rio Rita* (1927) opened with a score by Harry Tierney and Joseph McCarthy. *Rio Rita* had a top ticket price of $5.50, which was high for the time.

Ziegfeld's greatest contribution to musical theater history came on December 27, 1927, the opening night of *Show Boat*. The Jerome Kern, Oscar Hammerstein II musical contained what some consider the best musical theater score ever written. Ziegfeld mounted a brilliant production. He did not just produce a spectacle of the eye and ear but used his unerring taste to make *Show Boat* a spectacle of the heart and mind. The musical starred Norma Terris, Helen Morgan, Jules Bledsoe, Edna May Oliver, Charles Winninger, Howard Marsh, and Eva Puck. The musical, considered quite daring for its time, is still performed in major productions on Broadway and around the world.

Rosalie (1928) continued Ziegfeld's amazing output. Where others might produce a single show each year, Ziegfeld produced two or three. *Rosalie* had a score by George and Ira Gershwin and Sigmund Romberg and P. G. Wodehouse. The Gershwins accounted for the show's hit "How Long Has This Been Going On." Marilyn Miller was the star, ably supported by Frank Morgan, Jack Donahue, and Gladys Glad.

The Three Musketeers was Ziegfeld's second production in 1928. Rudolf Friml, P. G. Wodehouse, and Clifford Grey supplied the hit score which contained such great songs as "Ma Belle," "March of the Musketeers," "One Kiss," and "Gascony." The show was Friml's last great achievement. Operettas were on the decline as popular taste shifted to the more modern rhythms of Gershwin, Rodgers, and Berlin.

Whoopee (1928), another big hit for Ziegfeld, was written as a vehicle for former *Follies* headliner Eddie Cantor. The show has a surprisingly strong book and score, although it was written to suit Cantor's varied talents. The hit songs by Walter Donaldson and Gus Kahn included the title tune, "My Baby Just Cares for Me," "I'm Bringing a Red, Red Rose," and the classic torch song, "Love Me or Leave Me." Ruth Etting, Ethel Shutta, Frances Upton, and Jack Shaw starred.

The Gershwins and Gus Kahn contributed the score to *Show Girl* (1929), which included the song "Liza (All the Clouds'll Roll Away)." Jimmy Durante, featured in the show with his partners Eddie Jackson and Lou Clayton, wrote his own numbers. *Show Girl* also featured Ruby Keeler, Duke Ellington and his orchestra, Eddie Foy Jr., Harriet Hoctor, and Nick Lucas.

A definite departure for Ziegfeld was his coproduction with Arch Selwyn of Noel Coward's *Bittersweet* (1929). The English operetta boasted such hits as "I'll See You Again" and "If Love Were All." The stock market crash on October 29 of that year wiped Ziegfeld out. Though he produced more shows, he never regained his fortune.

Rodgers and Hart provided a fantasy for Ed Wynn in *Simple Simon* (1930). The show's showstopper was Ruth Etting's performance of the Rodgers and Hart classic, "Ten Cents a Dance."

Smiles (1930) also contained a smash hit tune "Time on My Hands" by Vincent Youmans, Harold Adamson, and Mack Gordon. Walter Donaldson's "You're Driving Me Crazy" was added after the Marilyn Miller starrer opened. Fred and Adele Astaire costarred along with Larry Adler, Bob Hope, Eddie Foy Jr., and Virginia Bruce.

In 1932, Ziegfeld presented a revival of his greatest hit, *Show Boat.* His last Broadway musical, *Hot-Cha!* (1932), opened with a score by Ray Henderson and Lew Brown. They also contributed the libretto along with columnist Mark Hellinger. Eleanor Powell, Buddy Rogers, Bert Lahr, June Knight, and Gypsy Rose Lee starred. Ziegfeld financed the production with the assistance of gangsters like Dutch Schultz.

Ziegfeld had other accomplishments to his credit besides shows. He hosted a weekly radio series and produced a color movie of *Whoopee* with Samuel Goldwyn. He was also responsible for erecting the magnificent Ziegfeld Theater with a stunning design by Joseph Urban.

Ziegfeld's health, hurt by the pressures of business and avoiding creditors, quickly deteriorated in the thirties. Bill collectors took Ziegfeld's office furniture in lieu of payment. Ziegfeld was stricken with pleurisy, and although he rallied for a time (he sent $6,000 worth of telegrams from the hospital), he died on July 22, 1932.

ZIEGFELD DANSE DE FOLLIES See New Amsterdam Theatre.

ZIEGFELD FOLLIES · The *Ziegfeld Follies* was the first great revue series in the American theater and the series that defined class and entertainment when it ran during the first decades of the twentieth century and for decades afterwards. Florenz Ziegfeld, the genius behind the *Follies,* saw to it that the series exhibited the best talents available in the American musical theater. Ziegfeld hired the top stars, created even more, hired great designers to create sumptuous costumes and lavish settings, commissioned the top songwriting talents from Tin Pan Alley, and wove the whole proceedings together with girls, hundreds of beautiful girls.

The *Follies* show girls were quite celebrated. It was the great couturier Lady Duff-Gordon (Lucile) who introduced Ziegfeld to the concept of the show girl. They were not the chorus. They did not sing, did not dance. They existed simply to be beautiful.

The showman's favorite words were glorification, femininity, and pulchritude. All three applied to his show girls. Where other producers paid their girls $30 a week, Ziegfeld paid his girls $125. The women were never presented in the nude, and Ziegfeld insisted that they be treated with respect. Sex was the byword of Ziegfeld's rivals Earl Carroll, George White, and the Shuberts, but Ziegfeld stressed sensuality, admiring women simply for their statuesque beauty.

Ziegfeld had his favorite performers, most of whom he discovered. Fanny Brice, comedian Bert Williams, Ann Pennington, W. C. Fields, Will Rogers, Leon Errol, Ray Dooley, Lillian Lorraine, Nora Bayes, Eddie Cantor, and Van and Schenck all appeared in multiple editions of the *Follies.*

The *Follies* also boasted a long relationship with its production staff. Many of the *Follies* cost as much as $200,000 to produce. A huge part of the budget was taken up with sets and costumes. Though Ziegfeld was extravagant with money, he had the good taste and design sense to make sure every dime was visible on the stage. Ziegfeld would get his inspiration for *Follies* numbers from the day's headlines, pictures in magazines, postcards and idle comments. He would jot down his ideas and then tell his staff to put together a scene around a specific design element.

Joseph Urban, a noted architect, designed many of the great drops and set pieces for the *Follies*. Ben Ali Haggin designed the scenes called tableaux vivants or living pictures for the *Follies* from 1917 to 1925. The tableaux were artfully posed groupings of seminude show girls draped in fine fabrics. Ziegfeld's costumers included such noted couturiers as Lady Duff-Gordon, Cora McGeachy, and Alice O'Neil. Gene Buck wrote lyrics for many of the shows and is generally credited with fulfilling Ziegfeld's visions on stage. Ned Wayburn, a noted choreographer, staged the dances as well as directing most of the proceedings. The contribution of Albert Cheney Johnston should not be overlooked. The great photographer was the official portraitist for all the *Follies* girls. Since only a limited number of people could see the *Follies* in anyone year, Johnston's photos were the only glimpse many people had of the magical Ziegfeld touch.

Ziegfeld didn't put as much stock in the songs. He was happy as long as the shows were sumptuous and the girls beautiful. However, many great songs were introduced in the *Follies,* either written specifically for Ziegfeld or as popular songs interpolated into the shows. These included "My Man," "By the Light of the Silvery Moon," "Be My Little Baby Bumble Bee," "Row, Row, Row," "Hello, Frisco, Hello," "A Pretty Girl Is Like a Melody," "Second Hand Rose," and "Shaking the Blues Away."

Favorite songwriters of Ziegfeld were Irving Berlin (the first to write an entire *Follies* score by himself), Victor Herbert, Dave Stamper and Gene Buck, Louis A. Hirsch, and Raymond Hubbell. Sketches were contributed by Harry B. Smith, George V. Hobart, Rennold Wolf, and Channing Pollock.

The *Follies* did not begin on a prestigious note. Credit for originating the idea for the *Follies* goes to Ziegfeld's wife, Anna Held, who suggested Ziegfeld model a revue on the French *Folies Bergere*. Librettist/lyricist Harry B. Smith suggested the showman name his show after an old newspaper column of Smith's, "Follies of the Day." But Ziegfeld, who was superstitious, wanted the name of the show to contain thirteen letters. He settled on *Follies of 1907.* The first *Follies* took place at a rooftop theater, the Jardin de Paris, on July 9, 1907. The revue (Ziegfeld was the first to use the French spelling of review), starred Emma Carus, Grace La Rue, and Lillian Lee. The first *Follies* was an immediate hit, following a move to the Liberty Theatre, and became the first Broadway show to run through the hot summer months.

The show's success led Ziegfeld to announce a new edition of the *Follies,* and thereafter the revue became an annual event on Broadway. Ziegfeld's partner in the *Follies* was Abraham Erlanger, one of the most hated producers in theater history. Erlanger owned and operated a string of theaters across the country that was practically a monopoly. If the producer of a show or act wanted to play an Erlanger house, the producer would be forced to join Erlanger's Syndicate. Erlanger tried to dictate to Ziegfeld the content of the *Follies,* but Ziegfeld would have none of it.

In 1911, Ziegfeld joined his name to the *Follies* for the first time. In 1913, after six editions, Ziegfeld finally had enough faith in the series to move it to a large legitimate theater, the New Amsterdam. The *Follies* remained at the New Amsterdam (with one exception) until the last edition under Ziegfeld in 1931. That last Ziegfeld show opened at the new Ziegfeld Theater.

In all, there were twenty-one *Follies* presented by Ziegfeld and some of them had more than one edition. By the time Ziegfeld died in 1932, the *Follies* truly lived up to their reputation as "A National Institution Glorifying the American Girl."

After the showman's death, Ziegfeld's rivals, the Shuberts, bought the right to produce their own edition of the *Follies* from Ziegfeld's widow, Billie Burke, for $1,000. Ziegfeld's estate received 3 percent of the gross. The Shuberts presented three *Follies*, in 1934, 1936, and 1943. There was one revue using the *Follies* name in 1957.

But no *Follies* following the master's death could truly lay claim to the title *Follies*. For one thing, no post-Ziegfeld follies were as lavish because other producers, particularly the Shuberts, were fiscally more responsible and placed a higher priority on making money than on sumptuous productions. Ziegfeld himself, though notoriously heedless of the bottom line, never lost money on a *Follies*, and they often realized a profit after Broadway while touring. Ziegfeld made sure that the annual series that bore his name reflected the pride he had in himself. Hollywood, television and the literary world all used the example of the *Follies* to portray the glamour, romance and extravagance of Broadway when in fact few other shows exhibited these qualities in such quantity. Today the *Follies* and Ziegfeld are still considered the epitome of Broadway's art.

ZIEGFELD THEATER · Northwest corner of Sixth Avenue and 54th Street. Architects: Joseph Urban and Thomas A. Lamb. Opening: February 2. 1927; *Rio Rita*.

Until the mid-1920s, Sixth Avenue was a street of three-story brownstones under a permanent shadow of the elevated train. When the Sixth Avenue el was torn down in 1927, the real estate market, driven by a bearish Wall Street, boomed. Speculators abounded and parcels of the thoroughfare were acquired quickly in the new land rush.

Producer Florenz Ziegfeld had long considered the New Amsterdam Theatre his home base. But this magnificent 42nd Street theater was owned by Abe Erlanger, a man of quick temper with as ruthless a business sense as Ziegfeld himself. So Ziegfeld was not averse to a move.

The owner of the property at Sixth Avenue

and 54th Street was none other than media mogul William Randolph Hearst. The newspaper giant owned several large plots of land surrounding the future site of the Ziegfeld Theater and, in fact, had just constructed the Warwick Hotel on an adjacent block. Hearst recognized that a theater across the street from the Warwick would drive up the value of his as yet undeveloped plots. When plans to dismantle the el were announced, Hearst and his partner Arthur Brisbane approached Ziegfeld.

The producer hired one of the premiere movie palace architects, Thomas A. Lamb, to design their new theater. Lamb's traditional neo-Georgian design just didn't make the dramatic statement that the great showman wanted. So, he turned to his brilliant scenic designer Joseph Urban (who practiced architecture in his native Vienna) to design the theater of his dreams.

Ziegfeld's daughter Patricia cemented the cornerstone that contained a program from Ziegfeld's musical *Sally*, photos of the Ziegfeld family, a program from the original *Follies of 1907*, and a brick from an ancient Greek theater.

The cornerstone was laid with appropriate Ziegfeldian fanfare on December 9, 1926, at 2:47 p.m.. Over eight hundred people, including stars of past and future Ziegfeld productions, watched while a huge audience followed the proceedings on the radio.

The new theater was opened on February 2, 1927, with *Rio Rita*, an operetta boasting a score by Harry Tierney and Joseph McCarthy. The top ticket price for the new show was $5.50. The production transferred to the Lyric Theatre to make room for Ziegfeld's last masterpiece.

Show Boat (1927) opened next at the theater. The Jerome Kern and Oscar Hammerstein II adaptation of Edna Ferber's novel became one of the seminal works of the American musical theater. Hammerstein's treatment of serious social issues and the superior score made *Show Boat* an almost legendary musical. The cast included Norma Terris, Tess Gardella, Edna May Oliver, Charles Winninger, Eva

Puck, Sammy White, Helen Morgan, Howard Marsh, and Jules Bledsoe.

George and Ira Gershwin's musical *Show Girl* (1929) followed. The production might have run longer but for the stock market crash on October 29, 1929. Ziegfeld was practically wiped out by the crash; his landlord ,William Randolph Hearst, was also badly shaken.

Noel Coward's London import, *Bittersweet* (1929) was followed by a Ziegfeld production, *Simple Simon* (1930) starring Ed Wynn and Ruth Etting. The Rodgers and Hart score contained the hit "Ten Cents a Dance."

Ziegfeld's last *Follies* opened at his theater on July 21, 1931. The score was by Mack Gordon and Harry Revel. The next Ziegfeld production at his theater, *Hot-Cha!* (1932), boasted a score by Ray Henderson and Lew Brown. Ziegfeld was forced to raise the capital for the production from mobster, Dutch Schultz. Despite the talents of Bert Lahr, Gypsy Rose Lee, Lupe Velez, and Eleanor Powell, the show was a failure.

Ziegfeld died on July 22, 1932, and management of the theater reverted to the Hearst Company. After the dismal run of *Hot-Cha!*, the theater was converted to motion-picture presentations. Loew's Theatrical Enterprises took over the management for Hearst.

Movies were doing slightly better than theater during the Depression, and the Loew's chain eyed the site. Hearst was having his own financial problems and was forced to sell off vast sections of his financial empire. Obviously, the theater was high on the list of expendable properties. Just before Hearst signed over the deed to the movie chain, in stepped showman extraordinaire Billy Rose.

Rose had long admired the beautiful theater and especially coveted the huge private apartment that Urban had included. Rose saw himself as equal or more than equal to Ziegfeld, so it seemed logical that as Ziegfeld's natural successor he should also possess the late showman's prize asset.

Rose acquired the theater for only $630,000 in 1944. Ziegfeld's spectaculars were marked by his own great taste. Rose may have equaled

Ziegfeld in his vision, but his taste was more vulgar and more populist than his predecessor's. Rose did, however, appreciate the beauty of the theater and hired Gretl Urban, daughter of the late architect, to restore the Ziegfeld to its former glory. To Rose's credit, he always kept the theater in top condition.

Rose reestablished the legitimate policy and presented his production of *The Seven Lively Arts* (1944). Cole Porter contributed the score which featured "Ev'rytime We Say Goodbye" as its hit. The show starred Beatrice Lillie, Bert Lahr, Benny Goodman, Helen Gallagher, and Dolores Gray.

Following a short-lived show, *Concert Varieties* (1945) came one of the theater's biggest successes, a revival of *The Red Mill* (1945), which ran almost twice as long as the original 1906 production. This unexpected success was followed with a revival of *Show Boat* (1946).

These two smash-hit revivals led to another classic musical attraction, *Brigadoon* (1947). The Lerner and Loewe score contained an overabundance of marvelous songs, including "Come to Me, Bend to Me," "Almost Like Being in Love," and "The Heather on the Hill."

The theater's next big success came with the hit show *Gentlemen Prefer Blondes* (1949). Carol Channing and Yvonne Adair starred as Anita Loos' classic gold diggers. The Jule Styne and Leo Robin musical comedy included Carol Channing's signature song "Diamonds Are a Girl's Best Friend."

Laurence Olivier and Vivian Leigh played the Ziegfeld in a revival of *Caesar and Cleopatra* (1951) by George Bernard Shaw. The drama was followed by a revival of the Gershwin's *Of Thee I Sing* on May 5, 1952.

The next hit for the theater was another revival by the Gershwins. *Porgy and Bess* enjoyed a 305 performance run commencing March 10, 1953. This made way for another huge success, *Kismet* (1953) with songs based on melodies by Barodin. The Wright and Forrest score included such standards as "Baubles, Bangles and Beads" and "Stranger in Paradise." Alfred Drake and Joan Diener starred in the Arabian fantasy.

Following *Kismet,* the theater was rented by NBC beginning in 1955. Television occupied its stage until 1963, when live entertainment was again featured. Jack Benny and Danny Kaye presented solo appearances in that year.

A flop musical, *Foxy* (1964) with Bert Lahr, briefly played the theater and was replaced by another Wright and Forrest show, *Anya* (1965). But Anya was not to follow the success of *Kismet,* the team's previous offering.

With *Anya's* closing also came the closing of the Ziegfeld Theater. Billy Rose had passed away and his estate sold the theater for $17 million. The *World Journal Tribune* of Sunday March 19, 1967, carried the following story:

A STONE FOR THE ZIEGFELD The Ziegfeld Theater, or what is left of it, is due for one last show next month. There will be ceremonies when the demolition crew gets down to the corner stone. Patricia Ziegfeld, daughter of the late illustrious impresario, will fly in from Los Angeles. She is now Mrs. William Stephenson, married to a California architect. The memorabilia in the corner stone will be presented to the Smithsonian Institute.

Incidentally, the two enormous reclining figures above the Ziegfeld entrance have already been claimed by souvenir hunters. One entire figure, weighing a ton, will go to the East Hampton estate of theater angel, Evan Frankel, The head of the second statue is earmarked for the Sutton Place Terrace of Zachary Fisher who is building a new skyscraper on the site.

Preservationists tried to save the theater to no avail. Burlington House, a generic office building was constructed on the site. Loew's corporation built a new movie theater immediately to the west and named it the Ziegfeld. Showcases with memorabilia from Ziegfeld's career were set in the lower lobby.

Note to parents, carers and teachers

Read it yourself is a series of modern stories, favourite characters and traditional tales written in a simple way for children who are learning to read. The books can be read independently or as part of a guided reading session.

Each book is carefully structured to include many high-frequency words vital for first reading. The sentences on each page are supported closely by pictures to help with understanding, and to offer lively details to talk about.

The books are graded into four levels that progressively introduce wider vocabulary and longer stories as a reader's ability and confidence grows.

Ideas for use

- Ask how your child would like to approach reading at this stage. Would he prefer to hear you read the story first, or would he like to read the story to you and see how he gets on?

- Help him to sound out any words he does not know.

- Developing readers can be concentrating so hard on the words that they sometimes don't fully grasp the meaning of what they're reading. Answering the puzzle questions on pages 46 and 47 will help with understanding.

For more information and advice on Read it yourself and book banding, visit **www.ladybird.com/readityourself**

Book
Ban
8

Level 3 is ideal for children who are developing reading confidence and stamina, and who are eager to read longer stories with a wider vocabulary.

Special features:

Detailed pictures for added interest and discussion

Wider vocabulary, reinforced through repetition

Hansel and Gretel lived with their father and stepmother in a little house near a wood. Their father was a woodcutter, and he was very poor. They were all very hungry.

6

7

Longer sentences

Simple story structure

One day Hansel and Gretel's father said, "We have no money left. There is no more food for us to eat."

8

9

Educational Consultant: Geraldine Taylor
Book Banding Consultant: Kate Ruttle

A catalogue record for this book is available from the British Library

Published by Ladybird Books Ltd
80 Strand, London, WC2R 0RL
A Penguin Company

001

ISBN: 978-0-72327-319-6

Printed in China

Hansel
and Gretel

Illustrated by Marina Le Ray

Hansel and Gretel lived with
their father and stepmother
in a little house near a wood.
Their father was a woodcutter
and he was very poor. They
were all very hungry.

One day, Hansel and Gretel's father said, "We have no money left. There is no more food for us to eat."

"Then Hansel and Gretel cannot live here," said their stepmother. "We must leave them in the middle of the wood."

"No," said their father.

But their stepmother said, "We must."

Hansel and Gretel were listening at the door.

"I have a plan," said Hansel, and he went out to get some pebbles.

The next day they all
went into the wood.

Hansel dropped pebbles
on the path.

"Wait here," said their father. "We are going to collect wood."

Hansel and Gretel waited all day. Then they followed the pebbles back home.

The woodcutter was glad to see Hansel and Gretel, but their stepmother was angry.

"There is not enough food for us all," she said. "We must take Hansel and Gretel deeper into the wood."

"No!" said their father, "we can't do that."

"We must," said their stepmother. "This time they must not find their way home."

21

Hansel's stepmother locked the door so that Hansel couldn't get out. He couldn't collect pebbles.

The next day they all went deep into the wood. This time, Hansel dropped breadcrumbs on the path.

"Wait here," said their father. "We are going to collect wood."

Hansel and Gretel waited all day. Then they looked for the breadcrumbs on the path.

But the birds had eaten all the breadcrumbs.

Hansel and Gretel went deeper into the wood. They walked for a long time.

In the middle of the wood, they found a house made of sweets and cakes.

In the house lived a witch.
The witch planned to eat
Hansel and Gretel.

She locked Hansel in a cage
and gave him lots of food.

"Soon he will be fat enough to eat," said the witch. "Then I will cook him in my fire."

"Where is the fire?" said Gretel.

"Here," said the witch.
And she opened the oven door.

"I can't see the fire," said Gretel.

The witch opened the
oven door a little wider.

"I still can't see it,"
said Gretel.

37

The witch opened the oven
door as wide as she could.

Gretel pushed her in
and locked the door.

Gretel let Hansel out of
the cage.

"Look at all this money,"
said Gretel. "We can take this
home and buy food with it."

After a long walk, Hansel and
Gretel found their way home.

Their father was very glad
to see them.

"Your stepmother has gone,"
he said.

So Hansel and Gretel and their father all lived happily ever after in their little house near the wood.

How much do you remember about the
story of Hansel and Gretel?
Answer these questions and find out!

- Who do Hansel and Gretel live
  with at the beginning?

- What does Hansel and Gretel's
  stepmother want to do
  with them?

- Can you remember the two
  different things Hansel drops
  on the path?

- What is the
  witch's house
  made of?

- How does
  Gretel get rid
  of the witch?

Look at the different story sentences and match them to the people who said them.

"Soon he will be fat enough to eat."

"Wait here. We are going to collect wood."

"We must leave them in the middle of the wood."

"I can't see the fire."

"I have a plan."

Read it yourself with Ladybird

Tick the books you've read!

For more confident readers who can read simple stories with help.

Level 3

YOU won't like this present as much as I DO!
☐

The Elves and the Shoemaker
☐

Hansel and Gretel
☑

Harry and the Bucketful of Dinosaurs
☐

Jack and the Beanstalk
☐

Furi on Music Island
☐

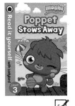
Poppet Stows Away
☑

Rapunzel
☐

The Red Knight
☐

Longer stories for more independent, fluent readers.

Level 4

I am Inventing an Invention
☐

Harry and the Dinosaurs United
☐

Heidi
☐

Katsuma and the Art Thief
☐

Luvli and the Glump-a-tron
☐

The Pied Piper of Hamelin
☐

Sam and the Robots
☐

Snow White and the Seven Dwarfs
☐

The Wizard of Oz
☐